"To repeat: this tidal book, reachi
withdrawing to show what is left beh.

— **NEAL ASCHERSON, AUTHOR OF BLACK SEA**

"An extraordinary, haunting book... a phenomenal achievement."

— **GILLIAN DARLEY, AUTHOR OF EXCELLENT ESSEX**

"Wright is a saboteur of genres and his books encompass multiple worlds. I stand in awe of what he has accomplished here".

— **MIKE DAVIS, AUTHOR OF SET THE NIGHT ON FIRE**

"A huge achievement: a comprehensive portrait of a place and a person, and the best book about Brexit that's yet been written."

— **JON DAY, WHITE REVIEW BOOKS OF THE YEAR**

"A masterful modernist history, and Patrick Wright's most important book, bringing Europe to England by showing it has always been here, at a moment when too many want to believe something else."

— **DAVID EDGERTON, AUTHOR OF THE RISE AND FALL OF THE BRITISH NATION**

"An astonishing chronicle of the great German author Uwe Johnson."

— **HELEN MACDONALD, AUTHOR OF VESPER FLIGHTS**

"Wright is not a biographer or a journalist but a sort of spirit-ethnographer, patient and attentive to change and complexity."

— **BEN RATLIFF, 4COLUMNS**

"Patrick Wright has picked over the landfill of a very specific Estuary culture to devastating effect."

— **IAIN SINCLAIR, AUTHOR OF DOWNRIVER**

THE SEA VIEW HAS ME AGAIN

THE SEA VIEW HAS ME AGAIN:

UWE JOHNSON IN SHEERNESS

PATRICK WRIGHT

WITH TRANSLATIONS FROM THE GERMAN

BY DAMION SEARLS

Published by Repeater Books
An imprint of Watkins Media Ltd
Unit 11 Shepperton House
89-93 Shepperton Road
London
N1 3DF
United Kingdom
www.repeaterbooks.com
A Repeater Books paperback 2021
1
Distributed in the United States by Random House, Inc., New York.

Cover design: Johnny Bull
ISBN: 9781913462581
Ebook ISBN: 9781912248759

Printed and bound in the United Kingdom by TJ Books Ltd

There must be room for more things than go onto a television screen.

—Uwe Johnson, "Conversation on the Novel...", 1973

CONTENTS

FREESTANDING TEXTS AND EXTRACTS FROM UWE JOHNSON'S ISLAND STORIES

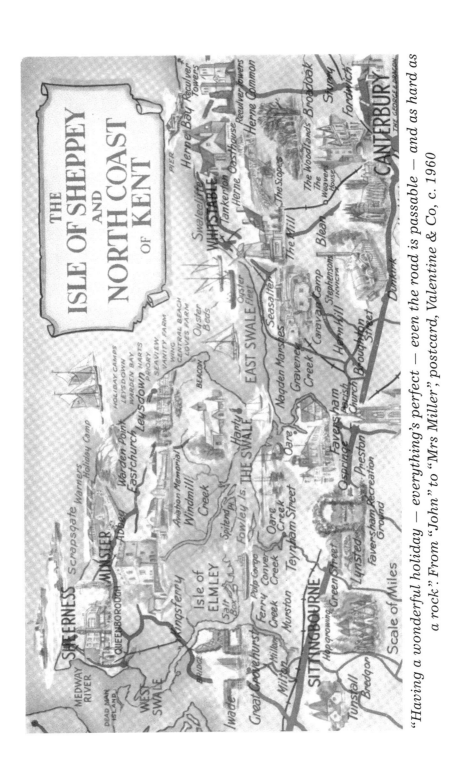

"Having a wonderful holiday — everything's perfect — even the road is passable — and as hard as a rock." From "John" to "Mrs Miller", postcard, Valentine & Co, c. 1960

PREFACE

A sign provided by the council identifies two noteworthy graves in the Isle of Sheppey's main cemetery. The first, at plot 83 FF, marks the last resting place of Mr Frederick Peake, who somehow managed to survive the Charge of the Light Brigade while serving with the 13th Light Dragoons during the Crimean War. Unlike so many who followed their Harrovian commander, Major General James Robert Brudenell, the 7th Earl of Cardigan, into the misdirected charge of 25 October 1854, Sergeant Peake emerged from "the Valley of Death" with no worse than a shattered arm, a pension and a job, both light and enduring, in the stores at the Admiralty dockyard at Sheerness. He was buried to the sound of rifle volleys and the "Last Post" on 27 December 1906, a local hero who had lived quietly across the fields from here, at 37 Alma Road in the part of Sheerness known as Marine Town.

To find the second stone, which nobody has ever tried to elevate with flags or bugles, the visitor who has entered the cemetery by its eastern entrance on Halfway Road must walk past the tiny Jewish graveyard on the right, and press on through many regularly spaced rows of Victorian and early-twentieth-century monuments. Although some of the older graves have sunk erratically into the ground, this municipal amenity lacks the Gothick atmosphere of the churchyard at which the German Romantic poet Jean Paul launched the idea of the Death of God into European consciousness towards the end of the "Age of Enlightenment". Paul's "Speech of the Dead Christ" (1796) is recounted by a dreamer who, having fallen asleep in the evening sunshine, is woken by a tolling bell to find himself in a darkened churchyard where the new atheist vision is coming horribly true. The night sky is filled with a vile grey mist. Avalanches are crashing down nearby and an earthquake sends mortifying tremors through the ground. The dreamer looks on as the graves open to release the dead, who clamber out of their coffins as so many abysmal wraiths and enter the teetering church in which the risen Christ confirms his discovery: "I went through the Worlds. I mounted into the Suns, and flew with the Galaxies through the wastes of Heaven; but there is no God! ... And when I looked up to the immeasurable world for the Divine *Eye*, it glared on me with an empty, black, bottomless *Eye-socket*".[1]

Over the course of his forty-nine years, the fiercely secular German writer whose ashes were put into the earth at plot 54 XD on 10 July 1984, found more in life to worry about than the catastrophic question that Jean Paul, a believer, derived from his dream: "if each soul is its own father and creator, why cannot it be its own destroyer too?" Uwe Johnson's stone lies a few yards inside the cemetery's tree-lined brick wall, beside fields that slope gently down towards Sheerness. Many of the more recent stones nearby are inscribed with loving messages and euphemisms about "falling asleep". Some are also adorned with tributes from the bereaved: flowers, teddy bears and miniature footballs; favourite mugs, plastic angels and − this being February − a painted Santa Claus among the cement mementos, some of which appear to have been acquired (and why not?) from Andre Whelan's concrete garden ornaments factory at the old Bethel Chapel in Blue Town, just outside the Sheerness dockyard wall. Johnson's stone − a large rectangular slab of granite laid flat in the ground − sits bare and silent amongst all this. It gives away less even than the formally restrained Portland stone monuments placed nearby by the Imperial War Graves Commission to mark British servicemen killed in the Second World War.

Johnson's memorial bears only a chiselled name: UWE JOHNSON. No dates, no words of sorrow or description, neither epitaph nor tribute, no gesture towards the Enlightenment values that powered this novelist's extraordinary writing nor to any kind of personal distinction or significance. Though it might seem to embody the judgement of another initially East German writer who described Johnson himself as a man of stone, a "statue of lost cultures"[2] like the inscrutable stone monoliths on Easter Island, this is also the memorial of a man who wanted, by the end of his short life, to disappear into letters. It offers nothing to the visitor who may be wondering why this great German author, whose perpetually reimagined homeland was in Mecklenburg and Western Pomerania on the East German Baltic and whose last and most important novel is set in New York City, ever came to be living in an obscure town beside the Thames Estuary on Kent's northern shore. Nor does it offer any clue as to why Johnson's admirers in Germany may shrink from the thought of the low-lying and marshy island on which their author chose to beach himself, his wife and their young daughter towards the end of 1974: a place more desolate, it has repeatedly been alleged, than anything encountered by Robinson Crusoe among the cannibals of the South Pacific. On the Isle of Sheppey itself, meanwhile, information about Johnson's Kentish decade has been scarce. The council struggled even to locate his grave when, in 2005, a party from the John Brinckman Gymnasium in the no-longer East German town of Güstrow in Mecklenburg announced their intention of turning up to look for traces of their school's illustrious former student.

Johnson had demanded the barest of funerals in his will — "I REQUEST that there shall be no music speeches flowers or any religious or other service whatsoever".[3] Though obediently mute and unyielding by comparison with its neighbours, his stone does nevertheless sometimes catch the visitor by surprise. Under dry conditions it can appear inert and dull, its well-cut lettering largely buried under dust. On winter days that are both windless and wet, the perfectly levelled stone gathers a film of rainwater, which in turn captures the branches of the alders overhead and pulls them down to float as black reflections in a sea of extravagant pink. It's an unexpected transformation — and a secret Kentish tribute to Johnson's own description, written on the Isle of Sheppey, of looking down at the street one wet and stormy day on New York's Upper West Side: "Now it's quiet, the asphalt mirror of Riverside Drive shows us the treetops in their close friendship with the sky".[4]

Perhaps that arresting burst of colour, which can be bright enough to subdue the Christmas ribbons on adjacent graves, may be allowed to stand as an appropriate introduction to this famously reserved writer who nevertheless kept an eye open for utopian moments in which the promise of everyday experience might be revealed. It also reminds us that Johnson, who carried some of the heaviest burdens and responsibilities of the twentieth century through his work, nevertheless once described himself as an "unacknowledged humorist".[5] His neighbour in Sheerness, the artist Martin Aynscomb-Harris, was among those who didn't always get the German writer's jokes. In the end, however, he did provide a local reporter with some English words that might now be remembered before that mute stone: "He was a kind man often misunderstood because of his abrupt manner. He had no time for idle conversation or banalities. He sparred with words. He was a verbal heavyweight — an intellectual whose politics were very much to the left".[6] If we are still reaching for more, we might add a line by another short-lived German-language writer with a gift for imagining impossible islands. In a late work entitled "Bohemia Lies by the Sea", the Austrian poet Ingeborg Bachmann (1926-1973) writes, "I want nothing more for myself. I want to go under".[7]

In German literary circles, where the merest mention of "Sheerness" can still raise a shudder, Johnson is counted among the "casualties" of his generation — a defiantly independent writer who, like his friend Ingeborg Bachmann, appears to have laid waste to his own life.[8] If there was nothing more here than a story of personal disaster brought down on a household whose surviving members have since asserted their right to privacy, there would be no case for going further. That, however, is not the situation.

By the time of his early death, Uwe Johnson had lived in Sheerness for more than nine years. He had moved there primarily to get away from West Berlin, and to find a place where he could complete the keenly awaited fourth and final volume of a novel entitled *Anniversaries: From a Year in the Life of Gesine Cresspahl (Jahrestage: Aus dem Leben von Gesine Cresspahl)*, which is rightly counted among the truly major works of modern European literature. Once on the island, however, he also developed a guarded interest in the life of those around him — so much so that, by February 1979, he would announce to a seminar in Frankfurt that he "had an eye"[9] towards writing a series of stories set in the county of Kent. No such volume was ever completed, although a book entitled *Island Stories* (*Inselgeschichten*) was assembled by the first director of the Uwe Johnson Society in Frankfurt and published under Johnson's name in 1995. Eberhard Fahlke's posthumous anthology of stories, essays and extracts from letters to friends such as Hannah Arendt and Christa Wolf gives a vivid sense of what Johnson liked, or found interesting as well as exasperating, about the economically challenged English town that sat on a remote and muddy island and bravely insisted, even in the depths of winter, on wearing the optimistic name of "Sheerness-on-Sea". Though vivid and revealing, these fragmentary "Island Stories" — some of which are included here in English versions prepared by the American translator Damion Searls — exhaust neither their material nor the perspectives they employ.

Rather than simply trying to tell "the story" of Johnson's English years, I have written this book with broader aims in mind. I have set out to establish who Johnson was and to suggest why both his writing and his characteristic approach to reality should matter to English-speaking readers now. I have also used his reports and despatches to guide my own exploration of the Isle of Sheppey as the gouged, disdained but by no means just distressed English "backwater" in which Johnson once claimed — and this surely wasn't *only* one of his unacknowledged jokes — to have discovered a "moral utopia".[10]

We will never know how or to what extent the Isle of Sheppey might have emerged as a twentieth-century microcosm — "an island that is all the world" in the phrase of the Anglo-Scottish poet Douglas Oliver — had Johnson completed the book of Kentish stories he hinted at in Frankfurt. He did, though, write enough before his early death to demonstrate his appreciation of the island as a vantage point with highly revealing views of England as it was in the Seventies and early Eighties: a crisis-ridden time in which the post-war settlement with its promises of a new British society was collapsing into economic and political turmoil combined with a "deindustrialisation" that turned Sheppey into an early incubator of the landfill world in which we find ourselves today.

Trying to understand a literary work by reading it back into its physical, political or historical "context" can easily lead to pointless reduction. But what if, like Johnson's imagined book of island stories, the work remains hypothetical? Obviously, it can't be jumped into existence with the help of existing drafts or fragments, even those as suggestive as Eberhard Fahlke assembled from Johnson's letters and articles in the Nineties. Yet something else becomes possible if, rather than trying to guess the missing stories into existence, we pick up some of the cues in Johnson's existing work — be they specific observations in letters and articles or more general characteristics such as his interest in place and memory or the close attention he paid to newspapers — and follow them out into the world he thought of engaging more fully. As someone who lived and worked in north Kent in the early Seventies, I have followed Johnson back to the area in the belief that the often derided Isle of Sheppey — here approached as a fragment of just-about-floating England less than forty miles downriver from the gleaming and internationalised citadel that is the City of London — remains among the revealing places where, as Johnson himself came to understand, horizons are wide and all sorts of historical questions bearing on our own time remain open, even though there are no National Trust properties anywhere near the place to do the same. The Isle of Sheppey was a backwater, to be sure. For Johnson, however, its landscape was also a theatre of resemblances, alive with the memory of other claimed backwaters he had known and written about: Staten Island in New York, for example, or the large-skied Baltic scenes of his own childhood and youth in Germany.

So this book explores three coinciding interests. The first is Johnson himself, the brilliant, afflicted East German writer whose truth-seeking novels reveal their commitment to Enlightenment values in their broad social sympathy as well as in their irony, judgement and investigatory procedures. The second is the Kentish Isle of Sheppey with its no-longer naval or steel-making capital town of Sheerness, a part of England where the actuality both of Johnson's world and our own has not been entirely smoothed over by consumerist prosperity, glozing politicians or, for that matter, by the corrosive mockery of mainlanders who continue to treat the place and its people as a great joke. The third is the Seventies, a crisis-ridden decade whose ongoing consequences may now remind us of Hesiod's legend of Pandora's Box. Having watched the powers released at that time transforming reality so vigorously through subsequent decades, I have taken the story of "Uwe Johnson in Sheerness" as the occasion for an investigation that comes at the East German writer from the English side and explores the island (itself offshore from a country that German newspapers have, since the Brexit referendum of 2016, enjoyed calling "the island") on which he chose to spend his last decade in the knowledge of things that have happened since. Johnson once insisted that the novel should be seen as a form of "reconnaissance"[11] and I hope this book, which has been researched, remembered and written during years in which the English air has resounded with appeals to "the world we have lost", reads in a similar spirit. Thanks to Johnson and the sometimes truly sunny Isle of Sheppey, which was, like much of Kent, strongly in favour of leaving the European Union, it's been a time of encounter, reassessment and reflection, and not just of trying to hold out for one dead certainty or the other as the ruins of post-war British modernity are washed away around us.

Call it England or call it Sheppey, the island looks tiny on conventional maps: little more than a mudbank about eight miles across at its broadest point, and eleven in length. Those, however, are not the only dimensions that matter. In the course of writing this book I have learned to sympathise with the man from Gillingham, eight or so miles further up the River Medway, who decided — a full six years before the referendum — to buy himself a small motorboat via the internet and put to sea with the aim of navigating his way around Great Britain. The man in question was no match for Jonathan Raban, who achieved that feat as the sailing author of *Coasting* in 1982. After studying a road atlas, he concluded that he only had to keep the land on his right-hand side in order to end the first stretch of his journey at Southampton. Having proceeded on this assumption for a day and a half, he ran out of fuel and found himself stuck in the mud near some tidal marshes. The lifeboat that came to rescue this slow voyager from his predicament guided him to the quayside at Queenborough where an officer of the coastguard service briskly informed him that he had all the time been circling the Isle of Sheppey: "He had no idea of the magnitude of the journey he was undertaking".[12] Since this unidentified Englishman — he was, as I recall, rudely dismissed as a "dopey sailor" by the island's newspaper — insisted on resuming his journey once refuelled, we may assume that he too had by then seen enough to know not just that small can be large, but also that life isn't necessarily at its richest when it is predictable or easy.

August 2020

More information about the investigation can be found, together with photographs and "filmlets" by Shona Illingworth, at patrickwright.net

PART I.

THE WRITER WHO BECAME A REEF

- *Gesine, do you think I should go to college?*
- *If you want to learn how to see all the sides and corners of things, and how they fit together with other things, or even just how to look at a thought and arrange all its interconnections simultaneously in your head. If you want to train your mind until it takes over everything you think and remember and want to forget. If you want to become more sensitive to pain. If you plan to work with your head.*
- *And if all you'd ever learned in life was how to milk cows or boil potatoes for pigs?*
- *Then lying would be just as bad, and guilt, and responsibility to other people. But your memory would be less sharp — life would be easier, I think.*

> — Gesine Cresspahl talking with
> her daughter Marie
> in *Anniversaries* IV, p. 1,609.

1. READING UWE JOHNSON IN KENT, 1970–3

I first encountered the writings of Uwe Johnson on a hillside where Britain's post-war social democracy was still laying claim to the future. It happened at the University of Kent at Canterbury, then still emerging from its building site as one of the seven new universities urged on Harold MacMillan's Conservative government by the Robbins Committee in 1963. Arriving as a new student in the autumn of 1970, I found a collection of not exactly "plate glass" buildings planted among new bus stops and saplings to the north of the city. They had been designed and put up in a tearing hurry under the direction of two battling men. The first was the Vice Chancellor, Geoffrey Templeman, who had been appointed to bring in an "instant university"[1] on time and, as he quickly became convinced, without mortgaging the project to any dreamer's utopian master plan. The second was the well-known architect and planner Sir William Holford. Having initially imagined the new university as a Siena-like "city on a hill", Holford had withdrawn in bruised frustration a few weeks after the first students arrived in October 1965.

Built on a windswept slope overlooking one of England's great historical views, the first two colleges, Eliot and Rutherford, were identical labyrinths that nevertheless preserved a striking remnant of Holford's cancelled vision. The plan for each may have been derived from a castle-like dormitory designed by the American architect Louis Kahn for Bryn Mawr College in Pennsylvania. Both, however, were placed so that the huge windows of their dining halls framed the sight of Canterbury Cathedral dominating the city below. The view was then coaxed back through the building, ensuring that glimpses of the fragmented cathedral beckoned even from the entrance causeway on the far side of the college. There was nothing at the University of Kent to match the work of Giancarlo De Carlo, the Milanese architect who had inspired architects all over the world with his Collegio del Colle (1962–6), a brilliantly integrated brutalist cluster of student residences on a hillside just outside the Italian city of Urbino. Even so, however, those view-catching windows have justifiably been described as "one of the outstanding architectural experiences offered by any modern university".[2] They also hinted at the university's divided attitude towards history and tradition — a salute, as the college chaplain never doubted, but also, as I was more inclined to hope, a valedictory wave from an institution with a very different future to find. Planted as they were in the so-called "Garden of England", those windows surely gave every student who looked through them in the dying light of the late Sixties a chance to be tempted by the thought of the modernist, tower-building and brutally anti-conservationist Labour Minister of Housing in Edward Hyams's Kentish novel *The Last Poor Man*: "The thing so many people in this country are still clinging to is dead. Oh it makes a handsome corpse, gentlemen ... in parts".[3]

Eliot College, University of Kent at Canterbury, 1966.

The curriculum had been shaped in a similar spirit. People studying English Literature at Oxford or Cambridge may still have been squeezing the long march from *Beowulf* to Virginia Woolf into their fraudulently short eight-week terms, but we flimsy futurists were invited onto a more ambitious path. Created in the knowledge that the realities of our time did not come packaged in nineteenth-century boxes, the Humanities faculty at Kent was dedicated to a wider frame: "Britain and the Contemporary World", as the core foundation course was named (and it was definitely a "course" rather than a "module" of the sort preferred in present-day university jargon). Before arriving, students were asked to read Thomas Mann's novel *The Magic Mountain*, set at another not always improving institution on a hillside: not a building site aspiring to the condition of a new kind of university this time, but a TB sanatorium on a mountain at Davos in the opening years of the twentieth century, where afflicted young people conversed about the challenges and possibilities of an age that we, looking back through two world wars and one welfare state, were invited to survey and understand as the precursor of our own.

In an early lecture, the epigraph "only connect" was lifted from the title page of E.M. Forster's novel *Howard's End* and commended as an injunction that might guide us through fields unintended by Forster himself.[4] Film, history and modern languages were to the fore. We read African and Caribbean as well as English and American literature, and also the "new novel" pioneered by the French authors Marguerite Duras and Alain Robbe-Grillet. Those of us who smoked could learn to do so with greater philosophical pretence under the guidance of Italo Svevo's Triestean masterpiece *Confessions of Zeno*. Lancashire's Louisiana blues man, Champion Jack Dupree ("I'm English now... I love this place"), did what he could to lower the tone with filthy "single *Entendre*" stories during his performance as a "barrel-house professor" in the Junior Common Room, but our introduction to post-war German literature was provided, if I remember correctly, by a young lecturer named Martin Kane. He brought us up against three novels published in 1959, causing that year to be hailed as the "annus mirabilis" in which German literature began to regain its place on the world stage. All three probed the experience of a nation that had swept the world into war, perpetrated mass murder and then emerged from the fire and fury of righteous defeat as two roughly divided states. All three also raised a more general question about the novel and the possibility, or otherwise, of coming to terms with the vast scale of Nazi devastation through a story of individual characters. Günter Grass's *The Tin Drum* and Heinrich Böll's *Billiards at Half Past Nine* were both written by writers with some adult experience of the Nazi years and the Second World War. The novel that caught my attention, however, was called *Speculations about Jakob*.[5] It was the work of a younger and, at the time of publication, quite unknown author, the twenty-five-year-old Uwe Johnson, who had only moved to West Berlin from the German Democratic Republic a few weeks before *Speculations* was published.

It was a tantalising book to read in Britain at that time, when politically diverse voices could already be heard denouncing British entry to the European Common Market as a humiliating surrender to the old and, as we were expected to understand, incurably power-mad German enemy. Issued during the year in which Bertolt Brecht wrote his poem "The Solution", with its mocking suggestion that the time had surely come for the government of the GDR "to dissolve the people / And elect another", *Speculations* was both brilliant and perplexing, as earlier British readers had already discovered. What were they to make of a novel from behind the "Iron Curtain" written in several voices by a man whose debts to the southern American author William Faulkner were both obvious and unexpected? Reviewing Johnson's novel for the *New Statesman*, D.J. Enright (a poet and "mendicant professor", who had studied under F.R. Leavis at Downing College, Cambridge) muttered grumpily that "obscurity" appeared to have become "the hallmark of quality" among those adjudicating literary prizes. He faulted the novel for being "not political, except in being anti-political" and suggested, with an unmistakeable sneer, that "a profitable working motto for new novelists would be: 'Make it Hard'".[6] He also expressed sarcastic relief at the publisher's blurb — always a desperate resort for a reviewer — with its "assurance that the fog in which he wanders is 'the very climate of life under communism' and not the product of his own stupidity". The alternative hypothesis, which I am confident was commended to us at the University of Kent, was that the "difficulty" of the novel did indeed stem not from literary narcissism or incompetence, but from the fractured and guilt-ridden post-war reality that Johnson set out to engage as it conditioned lives in both Germanies. Far from being "anti-political", Johnson was using the novel to pioneer a new form of political writing. Far from setting out to strike positions or sell the party line — or to pretend, like so many works of officially sanctioned "socialist realism", that the promised future was already arriving — he was using fiction to explore, in a manner that could be coldly analytical as well as sympathetic, the ways in which people lived under the constrained circumstances of their time. Far from seeking to impress his readers with formalistic displays of virtuosity, he was inviting them, as citizens of a self-created republic of letters, to participate in an experimental attempt to understand and, as far as may be possible, search out the truth of their post-war situation.

Johnson would give his own account — a credo of sorts — of the challenge facing the German writers of his generation in his preface to *Das Neue Fenster* (*The New Window*), a book of "selections from Contemporary German Literature" he prepared for his American publisher, Helen Wolff of Harcourt, Brace & World, while living in New York City in 1967. The book was intended to introduce American high-school students to a selection of works by a generation of German writers, from East as well as West, who had begun to publish after 1945. Starting with "bare inventories of bare remains"[7] — his examples include Günter Eich's "Inventory", a poem written in the voice of a prisoner-of-war going through his very few belongings — these younger authors had been obliged, as Johnson explained, "to lay the groundwork for a new tradition.

While they stood apart from those writers whose publications had lent a façade of culture to the Nazi regime, they were also separated from the pre-Nazi tradition, which writers in exile had been able to continue. For a decade they had been isolated from international developments in literature, and they were left with a language damaged by twelve years of misuse and dissimulation. They had in common the task of expressing the experiences of dictatorship, genocide, war, and reconstruction in a language that had to be checked and cleaned, so to speak, before it could be employed in the formation of a new realism".[8] This responsibility, as Johnson knew well, had earlier been recognised by Paul Celan, the German-speaking Jewish Romanian poet who in 1958 had famously insisted that, if it were to "come to light again", the German language must "pass through its own answerless, pass through frightful muting, pass through the thousand darknesses of deathbringing speech".[9]

The reviewer D.J. Enright may not have recognised it in Johnson's novel, but this was a necessary challenge for readers as well as writers, and it was further complicated by the fact that the Germany in which Nazism had so recently triumphed had since been divided into two states faced off against one another in accordance with polarised ideologies. Johnson may have seemed to enjoy "difficulty", but he was lucidity itself when compared with other writers he would come across in the West, who embraced "opacity" in the same cause. Celan, for whom a poem was "a making toward something",[10] was among those Johnson encountered at meetings of the writers' association known as Group 47. So too were the expatriated Austrian poet Ingeborg Bachmann, and also Ilse Aichinger, the Austrian author of *Bad Words*, who was married to Günther Eich and would, as it happens, arrive at her own version of Kent when passing through Dover, where "the correlation between walking bent over, walking upright, and walking away is always perfectly clear".[11]

Situated primarily in the GDR, the events in *Speculations about Jakob* are extended over a few months in the autumn of 1956. It was a year of dramatic and fateful occurrences in which the temperature of the Cold War oscillated fiercely. In February, the Soviet leader Nikita Khrushchev delivered his "secret speech" condemning the cult of Stalin at the end of the Twentieth Congress of the Soviet Communist Party. In November, the reformist hopes that Khrushchev had fired in the Eastern bloc were themselves killed off by the Soviet suppression of the Hungarian revolution: an event that coincided with the Suez crisis in the west. The novel, which mostly takes place in the grey northern light of the Baltic province of Mecklenburg, is shaped in relation to these events. It opens with the death of a train despatcher named Jakob Abs. Having recently come back from visiting his mother in a refugee camp in West Germany, which he has not liked at all, Abs has been hit by a shunting train while walking, one foggy November morning, across a very familiar railway line that had just been used to transport Soviet troops into Hungary. The novel then unfolds as a series of interleaved "speculations" about Abs and the events leading up to his unexplained death.

Attentive readers might register the fleeting appearances of a semi-omniscient narrator, but most of the story is distributed between three primary characters who recount events leading up to the death from different and largely unreconciled perspectives: a young woman named Gesine Cresspahl, who had grown up in the fictional Mecklenburg town of Jerichow, latterly unparented and living with Jakob Abs as her adopted brother, and then resettled in the West where she is employed as a translator for NATO; a senior Stasi officer known as Herr Rohlfs, who is interested in using Jakob Abs to recruit Gesine Cresspahl as a spy when she comes East through the "dreaded, dreadful strangeness"[12] of the border on a visit; and a reform-minded intellectual, a philologist named Jonas Blach, who has taught Gesine English at university and is shown teetering on the brink of fleeing West before he finally decides to stay in the GDR (where he is promptly arrested by Herr Rohlfs). The result is an exacting novel which never fully concludes any of its "speculations" about Abs and the circumstances of his unexpected death. It also leaves the reader little choice but to contribute another set of "speculations" about what exactly is going on, who is speaking and in what order.

Re-reading this book now, I wonder what, beyond puzzlement, a British reader might have made of it in 1971. The GDR may nowadays be sufficiently long-gone to re-emerge sporadically in billows of pinkish *Ostalgie*, but it was unmistakably real in the early Seventies, and I would like to think we were impressed by the determination with which Johnson used the novel to pursue a critical understanding that was not captive to either of the warring ideologies governing the divided Germany. Now as then, I admire *Speculations about Jakob* for insisting on a question that might be aimed at governments on both sides of the Cold War division: "What do you do with facts you don't like?"[13] I am also impressed to find that, while consistently refusing the polarised positions of its time, *Speculations about Jakob* does not claim for its author a stance of moral superiority. Though watchful and exactly observed, this is not the book of an all-seeing man of culture holding forth from a lofty peak "above the battle",[14] to use the phrase with which the Swiss novelist Romain Rolland urged writers across Europe to resist calls for nationalist loyalty in the early weeks of the First World War. Johnson may certainly have been an "artist" but, as the critic Reinhard Baumgart pointed out when introducing him as he was awarded the Georg Büchner Prize in 1971, he disliked the trappings of that particular office, preferring to consider himself a storyteller engaged in "a form of truth finding".[15]

"Nobody is made of opinions",[16] so Johnson's character Gesine Cresspahl informs the secret policeman Herr Rohlfs, in one of the novel's many indications that the possibility of a transformed human society was not exhausted by the woeful inadequacies of the East German state after Walter Ulbricht came to power in 1950. The novel does not mock or condemn Abs's decision to return to the GDR from the West, where he has seen Nazi attitudes persisting more or less unchecked and where his suggestion that a chimney sweep should be valued for being "part of society"[17] has been taken for a joke. The novel is both realistic and unillusioned in its exploration of the various ways in which people may adjust and come to terms with life in the GDR, but it also searches for indications of different potentialities. The restlessness that would shape Johnson's life as well as his narratives may be connected to this search for a political reality, in which it might be possible to live with personal integrity — a "moral Switzerland" as later novels will identify this impossible goal in the disappointed yearnings of Johnson's primary character Gesine Cresspahl.

By the early Seventies, we "hopelessly decadent British"[18] were at the beginning of a time in which avant-garde theories of "transgression" would seem to sweep the board in literary studies, but Johnson's was not that kind of writing. *Speculations about Jakob* was formally innovative and could hardly be confused with "socialist realism" of the sort espoused by Stalinist ideologues in Eastern Europe. It was, however, fundamentally interested in testing real situations and in exploring, with the appraising eye that is so characteristic of Johnson, the ways in which people on both sides of Germany's post-war division might hold on to a sense of reality even while confronting or apparently consenting to the ideologies ruling everyday life.

I remember, too, being impressed by the novel's politically nuanced articulation of place and landscape. Johnson makes his way past the anti-"Blood and Soil" scarecrows planted in every forest and meadow in those post-war years to evoke Mecklenburg,

Hardstones in the tower of the thirteenth-century church of St Bartholomew, Recknitz.

which he had himself explored vigorously by water, bicycle and foot, as "the homeland of recollections".[19] The novel surveys the deeply stratified historical geography of this province as it appears on the annotated map on which a schoolteacher of an earlier age has traced how the terrain was gouged and scraped into its present shape by glaciers, which had covered the land with boulders and "hardstones" that have been breaking backs and ploughs ever since the area was settled, first in prehistoric times and later by Romans, Slavs and Germans.

The historical depth of this flat and watery landscape, said to "glow from afar" for those prepared to concede its existence outside ideological or instrumental perspectives, matters little to Herr Rohlfs, the schoolteacher's son. He is the agent of a fiercely curtailed official imagination in which castles and their tree-dressed parks are understood not as "petrified history" but as "memorials to exploitation". There would be no room for wonder, attachment or pastoral consolation in his post-war regime: "Whoever is not for us is against us, and unjust with regard to progress. Who is for us: will be the question; and not: how do you like the night with the dark villages between the curves of the soil under the huge cloudy sky".[20]

Johnson may have anticipated the charge of "nostalgia" here, of showing too much interest in a landscape that had so recently been conscripted into the Nazi imagery of racial belonging. A yearning for a lost and re-imagined Baltic world does indeed haunt his work from the earliest days, and yet he also uses this remembered landscape to confront and reinscribe the outrages of recent history. In *Speculations about Jakob,* Gesine Cresspahl remembers wondering when she heard news of the concentration camps as a thirteen-year-old girl in the little inland town of Jerichow in 1945: "How does it fit with the wet rustling beech leaves under our feet, with the swaying circling of fir tops overhead against the gray night sky... What had it to do with Jerichow that was lying at our feet as we emerged from the thicket on the top of the hill and halted, Jakob and I standing silently side by side: a sombre lump in the hollow, its church tower pointing and a light on in my father's house".[21]

I doubt that we really felt the weight of that distant child's question in Kent, where not always retiring farmers would soon be grubbing up orchards that had once lain under the Battle of Britain, happy to take the compensation offered under the European Economic Community's Common Agricultural Policy. Neither did we have any inkling of the ways in which Johnson's lost and forbidden Mecklenburg articulated a sense of "utopia" close to that imagined by Ernst Bloch, the Marxist philosopher of "hope", some of whose lectures Johnson had attended while studying at the University of Leipzig from 1954–6: "utopia" not as a totalitarian blueprint, nor as the weekend destination it is said have become in the pre-COVID age of Airbnb, but as the often fleeting promise of "a place and a state in which no one has yet been".[22]

I wonder whether we would have been more or less able to grasp Uwe Johnson's direction had we attended to the arguments being developed by Roger Taylor, a young English philosopher who was already at work on a book called *Art, an Enemy of the People*.[23] Writing in *Radical Philosophy* in 1973, Taylor had invited us to consider what people living two hundred years hence might choose if asked to identify the art of our time. Would they select the high Modernist works of Picasso, Moore, Britten and Eliot, or would they actually decide that "twentieth-century century art" consisted of "cranes, gasometers, power stations, farm machinery, cars (not forgetting motor-bikes), bubble-gum machines, petrol pumps, Stevie Wonder, Elvis, Vera Lynn, Ivor Novello, Harold Robbins, Agatha Christie, Leslie Charteris and here perhaps it makes sense to say, etc".[24] Persuaded that the established idea of "art" was actually an exclusive eighteenth-century construct inextricably connected to the rise of capitalism and its new elite,[25] Taylor called for a radically different expression of creativity that might begin with the experience of working people. His examples included an American rancher encountered more than a decade previously by the Polish émigré sociologist Alicja Iwánska, who was then researching what she had assumed to be an entirely "art"-free community named "Good Fortune" in the western reaches of America's Washington State. The man who removed Iwánska's professional blinkers did so by taking her to a barn where he put on a mask and set to work with his welding machine: "'Look at these sparks' he would say. 'Isn't this like in Hollywood? ... and this is me who is doing it all ... sparks like fireworks, like stars, like aeroplanes ... I feel really like God creating the world.'"[26]

Taylor was tempted by Iwánska's conviction that a broader, less professional or "art"-based understanding of creativity was required of anyone who recognized that "Utopian thinking" was "particularly important for the functioning of highly complex modern nations".[27] In later writing, he would go on to associate working-class creativity with "virtual" forms of escape and self-defence: the various means of disappearance and "getting out of it" employed by members of the "unnoticed" majority.[28] Although Taylor taught at the (also new) University of Sussex outside Brighton, he was, by 1973, already sending postcards from the Isle of Sheppey.

2. ON THE MOVE BUT NOBODY'S REFUGEE

The German Empire. c. 1910. Postcard by l'Amidon Remy.

Uwe Johnson had lived through an extreme twentieth-century history by the time he emerged from childhood. Born in 1934 in the Pomeranian town of Kammin, where his agriculturalist father Erich worked as supervisor of a dairy, he spent his first ten years in Anklam, moving in 1944 to an SS-run boarding school (a "German Homeland School" intended to raise a future Nazi elite) in Koscian, a town in a conquered region that had been granted to Poland after the First World War but was then being violently re-Germanised as "Kosten" under a Gauleiter, Arthur Greiser, determined to establish the model Nazi province of "Warthegau".[1] Johnson spent less than a year in this dreadful place, where the "final solution" had been pioneered in 1940 (psychiatric patients are said to have been gassed by SS commandos in a van with the words "Kaiser's Coffee Company" written on its side).[2] In January 1945, the school was closed as the Red Army advanced from the east. The older boys were ordered to join the town's defenders, but those in the first year, including the ten-year-old Johnson, were allowed to flee west.

In some versions of this story, the children were taken to the town square, and told to join the chaotic retreat as best they could. Johnson remembered the circumstances rather differently in conversation with the Swiss writer Max Frisch. In this account, he describes feeling that he couldn't leave before returning a book to the school library (the book was one of Karl May's stories about the North American "Indians", favoured by the Nazis who encouraged Germans to consider themselves an aboriginal people). Having missed the transport as a result of this characteristic punctiliousness (he got to the library to discover the staff had already fled), Johnson took to the road alone "in uniform, with no papers, possibly suspected of being a deserter".[3] Having survived the rout (Frisch describes him speaking of "streams of refugees, hunger, winter, the infantrymen on the retreat; a child's experience that everyone only seeks to help themselves"), he managed to rejoin his family at Anklam before fleeing west into Mecklenburg. This had been a famously backward and peripheral province ever since the decline of the Hanseatic League in the fifteenth century. It is said that the nineteenth-century Prussian chancellor, Otto von Bismarck, "was fond of thinking that when the world was coming to an end, one could always go to Mecklenburg, as it will end fifty years later there".[4] Johnson arrived in time to see the land, which occupying British forces soon ceded to the USSR, being expropriated and brutally purged of its nobility (no regrets from Johnson there: the "Junkers" of Mecklenburg and Pomerania were notorious for having kept the peasantry in abject serfdom for centuries), and incorporated into the "Soviet Occupation Zone" that would itself be re-established as the German Democratic Republic in 1949.

The Johnsons were put up by Erich's sister and brother-in-law in Recknitz, a tiny estate village thirteen kilometres north-east of a small inland town named Güstrow. A few weeks after they moved into a room in the smithy here, Erich Johnson disappeared. He had gone back to Anklam in the

The Old Forge, Recknitz.

hope of taking care of some of the family's affairs there, but never returned. Johnson would later tell Max Frisch that, having been reported as a Nazi by neighbours ("Because he had slightly better furniture than the rest of the petty bourgeois"), he was arrested and incarcerated without further investigation in an internment camp at Fünfeichen (he would be declared dead in 1948). Uwe, his younger sister Elke and their mother Erna lived on without him.

In Recknitz, Johnson, who had started life in the household of a father he later described as "a steward of lordly estates",[5] attended the village school as a refugee, and quickly discovered that "a child can be rented out for three weeks' work on someone else's fields in exchange for a hundred kilos of wheat". He was there in the terrible months that followed the war. In her last novel *City of Angels*, Johnson's friend and correspondent Christa Wolf, who had made her own flight from the east in 1945, would recall how Mecklenburg was then plagued by roaming gangs of Soviet soldiers — "raping and marauding through the countryside, the torn uniforms, the sorry state of their weapons, the peasant carts that had brought them to the centre of Europe".[6] Aggravated by hunger and typhus, among other diseases, these difficulties were also greatly increased after the Yalta and Potsdam treaties, at which Churchill and Stalin famously divided Europe with the

Augraben ditch, Recknitz.

help of a sheet of paper and a blue pencil. Many millions of ethnic Germans were expelled from lands allocated to Russia, Poland and Czechoslovakia, and arrived in East Germany to find the cities closed to them. As Victor Klemperer wrote on 17 August 1945, "they beg their way [and] are to be crammed into overcrowded Mecklenburg".[7] They turn up in Johnson's novels too — hindered by their low status as "refugees" even years later.

The scale of the disaster that unfolded during Johnson's year in Recknitz is suggested by the memorial recently mounted on a great boulder in St Bartholomew's churchyard: it names ninety "victims of War and Tyranny", the great majority of whom died in the immediate aftermath of the Second World War. Johnson would leave a more shocking (and also arrestingly beautiful) image of the refugees who succumbed to starvation and disease. Writing more than twenty years later, he describes a harvest cart full of corpses arriving in his fictional town of Jerichow — a scene said to be derived from things he'd glimpsed as a boy in Recknitz (where refugees are reported to have been accommodated at the nearby mansion of Rossewitz). One evening, Johnson's central character (he preferred the phrase "invented person"[8] for its suggested sense of independent reality), the child Gesine Cresspahl, goes out for a walk that takes her past the mortuary chapel:

When she glanced to the right she saw both of the chapel's double doors standing open, with something that looked like a shoe on the ground right outside them. She tried to tell herself that someone must have just slipped and fallen there, but she knew that now she wanted to see the bodies.

Maybe the living had brought lanterns in the night. The dead weren't piled on one another the way they'd been in the cart. They sat in the little mortuary hall as if alive, their backs leaned against the walls, most of them with their eyes open. Their dresses, pants, and heavy jackets had been left on, out of fear of infection, or else put back on — they were a bit crooked on their bodies, too high on the neck, too high over the knee. Some were touching one another, holding their neighbor seated, otherwise they might slip. There were two together in the northwest corner, as if they'd sat down next to each other on their own. It was a young man, who seemed to Gesine twenty-two years old, with black hair and long muttonchop sideburns, in a neat black suit with shirt and tie — a city man whose shoes had come off somewhere. His head was turned to the side, as if he were looking at the wall. Then, though she was right up next to him, a girl lay half slumped down — a blonde with her hair up, all freckly — and she had slid halfway into the young man's lap, and her posture was so peaceful, his hand on her shoulder seemed a little embarrassed, and not there voluntarily. They looked posed.[9]

Nowadays, the staff at John-Brinckman-Oberschule, in the nearby town of Güstrow, will gladly show visitors a reconstructed version of the small upstairs classroom in which an old desk is still reserved for Mecklenburg's celebrated writer in the back row. Johnson, who moved with his mother and younger sister from Recknitz to Güstrow in the summer of 1946, might just about have managed a smile had he lived to look out of that room at the portrait stele of himself that, since 2007, has stood in the square below. In his first months at the school, he had suffered the disadvantage of being categorised "bourgeois", which in his case, so Johnson would explain at Darmstadt in 1977, meant "the son of a civil servant from an abolished Department of Agriculture".[10] The situation improved once his mother, Erna, whose petit-bourgeois and

John Brinkmann School, Güstrow.

incipiently pro-Nazi attitudes had caused Johnson to recoil, converted him into "the son of a worker" by getting herself a job as a conductor on the railway. Johnson shared his hopes for the possibilities of socialism promised by the emerging GDR with other members of a youth discussion group run by Gerhard Bosinski, a preacher at the cathedral-like Lutheran church across the square from the school who also confirmed Johnson in 1949. Eight members of this circle, which became connected to a movement of similar congregations elsewhere in the GDR collectively known as *Junge Gemeinde*, would be lined up at a show trial in September 1950 and jailed for distributing leaflets brought from the West demanding freedom of expression, pluralism and other

Wieland Förster, portrait stele of Uwe Johnson (2006), Güstrow.

basic rights. They were further condemned by their more or less frogmarched teachers, who assembled to approve of the draconian sentences. Johnson's lesser, although perhaps no less defining, troubles came to a head while he was reading German language and literature at the University of Rostock. He was barred from continuing after his second year, having spoken out in defence of *Junge Gemeinde*, of which he himself was not a member, and insisted that the proscription and harassment of Christian students, encouraged by

Old street in Güstrow with view of the cathedral, postcard, sent 1973.

the official Free German Youth organisation under the young Erich Honecker's leadership in 1953, was unconstitutional as well as wrong.

Between 1954 and 1956, Johnson continued his studies at the University of Leipzig, where he went to work under Hans Mayer, an anti-fascist and independent-minded Marxist literary scholar who had chosen to move from the West to the future GDR when invited to take up a chair at the University of Leipzig in 1948. During Johnson's time at Leipzig, Mayer, whose parents had been murdered at Auschwitz, disputed the Stalinist claim that the literature of the GDR had emerged from the working class insisting, against the apparatchiks of socialist realism, that the literary climate of the new state would only be improved by "a comprehensive confrontation and engagement with modern art and literature".[11] It was here that Johnson, whose work would embody this engagement, also attended lectures by Ernst Bloch, the philosopher of "heritage" and "concrete utopias", who had returned to the GDR from America in 1949 but would be condemned as a "counter-revolutionary" in the clampdown following the Soviet suppression of the Hungarian revolution of 1956 and forced to retire from his post as Professor of Philosophy in 1957. As a student in this increasingly beleaguered crucible of independent Marxist thought, Johnson read György Lukács, Walter Benjamin, Theodor Adorno and Bertolt Brecht, and also modern novels by Sartre and Joyce. Above all, however, he was moved by the novels of William Faulkner, a writer of the American south whose sense of the "burdened past"[12] — an inheritance tainted by slavery, fear of "miscegenation", the idea of white supremacy and the associated "rhetoric of blood"[13] — was keenly studied by various post-war German writers struggling to come to terms with the Nazi past. Above all, it was *The Sound and the Fury* — another famously "difficult" novel with multiple narrators — that would become a decisive influence on Johnson's writing.[14]

Though not among the members of the Leipzig circle who would be sentenced to long jail sentences at show trials in 1956, Johnson, whose mother and sister had by this time moved to the West, was still impeded by the ruling ideology's watchdogs. Barred from continuing towards a PhD after graduating, he remained unable to find employment — a situation he would interpret, so he later told the academicians at Darmstadt, as an "invitation to leave, which would then have justified the label of 'traitor'". He stayed in the GDR for a further three years after his studies at Leipzig, writing and living on freelance literary work and the generosity of friends, including Hans Mayer, who provided him with money and "anonymous writing jobs".[15] He worked as a reader for publishers, prepared index cards for a German dictionary at ten pfennigs a go and produced, for a private publishing firm, a German translation of Herman Melville's *Israel Potter: His Fifty Years of Exile*, a novel about an alleged hero of the American revolution who ends up living much of his life undercover in England, which may also have provided Johnson with his first glimpse of the Thames Estuary.[16] He tried but failed to secure publication of his first novel, *Ingrid Babendererde,* started when he was still nineteen years old and rewritten in 1956 over an unofficial summer vacation at Ahrenshoop, a village in Fischland on the Baltic (the GDR cultural authorities had maintained Ahrenshoop's longstanding tradition as an artists' retreat: it was used by many, including Bertolt Brecht, who came to this place, which had recently been "pure Nazi territory",[17] in the first years of the GDR). The hostility with which state publishers in the GDR rejected *Ingrid Babendererde* — one reader allegedly suggested that this evidently capable writer stood in need of "brainwashing" — hardly seems surprising since the novel, which would remain unpublished until after Johnson's death, tells the story of a high school class, closely derived from his own at Güstrow, graduating during the fierce ideological crackdown of 1953. Johnson, who may well have preferred to continue his battle for truth and a critical independence of thought within the GDR, moved to West Berlin in 1959, a few weeks before Suhrkamp Verlag, the publishing house run in Frankfurt am Main by Peter Suhrkamp and his younger assistant Siegfried Unseld, brought out *Speculations about Jakob.*

Presented at the Frankfurt Book Fair, this novel launched Johnson as a literary prodigy. It was positively received in West Germany, and by no means only by readers keen to construe it as an anti-communist work and to patronise Johnson as a young writer who could be expected to flourish once he had properly aligned himself with the cause of freedom as it was understood by anti-communist ideologues in the West. Within months, this hitherto unknown author had been awarded West Berlin's prestigious Fontane Prize, and he was soon invited to join meetings of the influential association of writers and literary tribunal known as Group 47. In 1961 he embarked on his first lecture tour through the USA before returning to Berlin in time for publication of *The Third Book about Achim.* In 1962, the year in which he was awarded the prestigious International Publishers Prize, Johnson followed Heinrich Böll into a year-long residency at the Villa Massimo in Rome, having been granted a stipend under a German Academy scheme run by the Cultural Ministry of the Federal Republic of Germany. A collection entitled *Karsch and other Prose* appeared in 1964, and the following year saw publication both of Johnson's third novel, *Two Views,* about an almost accidental couple who found themselves divided by the sudden building of the Berlin Wall, and also of his edition of Bertolt Brecht's uncompleted *Me-Ti: Book of Changes,* commissioned by Suhrkamp in collaboration with the Brecht Archives in East Berlin.

By 1963, when *Speculations about Jakob* made its first appearance in English, the publishers at Grove Press in New York could confidently blurb Johnson as "the greatest of the post-war innovators whose work has radically altered the literary landscape of our time". Photographs from this period show an impressive — and not always forbidding — young man, often clad in black leather jacket and cap. His pipe has developed a curved flourish and his spectacles, which had been wholly utilitarian wire-framed things in photographs from "the time you couldn't buy any better ones",[18] have become round and stylish. With his cropped head, Johnson had the look of a fearless, intellectually engaged writer who conformed to no government's mould. A decidedly starry figure who was sometimes likened to Bertolt Brecht, he was known for arguing back fiercely against any suggestion that he had come West as a "refugee" who might be relied upon to denounce and condemn everything about "the Germany that chose the road to socialism".[19]

Uwe Johnson, Berlin, c. 1970.

Johnson had indeed felt obliged to leave the GDR but only, so he would inform *Le Monde* in 1971, "for reasons of hygiene".[20] The decision had been his own, and was made not for partisan political reasons but, as he had earlier explained to the *New York Times*, in defence of his own creative independence and freedom: "If I had stayed and kept quiet I would have been given work".[21] He had conceived of *Speculations about Jakob* as a "literary work", but it was inevitable, once Suhrkamp had accepted the novel for publication in the West, that the authorities in the GDR would interpret it as an attack. He had initially planned to issue the novel under the pseudonym Joachim Catt,[22] but the Stasi surely had the means to penetrate any such disguise. Left with no choice but to "move house", as he sometimes put it, Johnson had boarded a north-south train on the S-Bahn, stepped off at a station in West Berlin and, as he also told the *New York Times*, "got permission to stay in West Berlin without being a refugee... If you become a refugee there are loans, credits and working places available. I insisted on fending for myself so as not to have to say thank you".

Years later, in October 1979, Johnson would explain his objection to being seen as a "refugee" in West Germany for British listeners of BBC Radio 3. The ascription was factually wrong, given that he had actually gone West reluctantly and as a "last resort".[23] However, he did not reject it in order to distinguish himself, as some hostile observers had suggested, from the crowd picking up a new ideology along with other handouts as they passed through the Marienfelde refugee camp in West Berlin. His main objection was that the false label "leads to misunderstanding of my novels ... For instance, my first book has persons living in both parts of Germany. This was something new in German literature and another unknown quality was that living in East Germany was shown to be quite possible and even likeable". Far from repudiating everything about the GDR, Johnson would declare that his years there had given him an "irreplaceable method of interrogation and experimentation". Had he spent the same period in the West, so he joked for *Le Monde,* he would never have known that Marxism was not yet fashionable. He had, of course, "never believed the claims of socialist realism, let alone revolutionary romanticism", judging both guilty of a "shortcutting of reality that consists of denying everything that is bad or unbearable in present facts". On the contrary, "It is reality as I see it that interests me" and the task of literature as it worked between East and West was to serve as an intermediary between people by sending them the information they are eager to learn about each other. This may seem "a modest role", he admitted, but we were no longer living in an epoch in which a writer might stand as referee over a game while also knowing exactly what was going on in the minds of the players. It was possible though, "that if a crowd of writers, everywhere, tell what they are seeing on their side, we might still hope to arrive eventually at a clear picture of a decade".

3. THE BORDER: THE DISTANCE: THE DIFFERENCE

In Canterbury, we had access to Johnson's first three published novels thanks to American translations, some of them reissued by Jonathan Cape and Penguin. Those of us who did set out to read them may well have done so with assumptions that would only have brought another shake to their author's monolithic head. From the early Sixties, he had been widely known as "the poet of the divided Germany",[1] but this again, as he would tell the BBC in 1979, was something "I didn't want to be at all. I just wanted to be a novelist who tries to tell a story".[2] It was a point he'd made many times before: "I have never considered myself a specialist in the division of Germany", he informed *Le Monde* in 1971, going on to reiterate his interest in "the realities of the moment".[3]

Johnson may indeed have been an explorer of experience rather than a pedlar of political ideologies, yet how were we to avoid repeating the question that he himself posed in *The Third Book about Achim*: "What led him to compare two countries: that there was a border between them?"[4] It is hard not to answer that question in the positive after reading the second sentence of that novel, which seems to project his puzzled reader into the reunified Germany of the twenty-first century: "it discourages me", Johnson writes, "to have to add that in the Germany of the Fifties there existed a territorial frontier". He then identifies the reality he sought to explore through invented characters and events, as "the border: the distance: the difference".[5]

At first, that border stands more or less open: so lightly marked, indeed, that people on a train leaving the GDR have to search the "mildewed meadows" outside for proof that they really have passed into the West.[6] With the passage of time, however, it soon hardens into the closely-guarded fence that starts among "leaping patrol boats"[7] in the Baltic to the east of the (Western) resort of Travemünde, bisects a "pleasant" beach on a spit named Priwall (a British observer would later find a nudist beach pressed up against the Western side of the frontier[8]), and then advances south after the crossing point, gathering up the brutal paraphernalia of wire, pre-cast panels, control strips, crossing points and observation posts as it stretches all the way to Czechoslovakia. The shorter border surrounding West Berlin was also permeable in the early post-war years: penetrated by the S-Bahn trains that allowed people from the two sides to mix on a daily basis, until it was abruptly sealed up on 13 August 1961 when the GDR started erecting the Berlin Wall, thereby creating the fully divided city investigated in Johnson's third novel, *Two Views*.

Johnson gives us the concrete and wire, and the difficulties of passing or even telephoning through the frontier. He was interested, and not only for the sake of his fictions, in the increasingly organised systems of escape: the failed attempt to drive a low-riding sports car under the barrier; the American marine who hid escapers in a secret compartment in his car; the student activists — Detlef Girrmann and Dieter Thieme — who were among the "escape helpers" he interviewed in exacting detail about the operations they carried out to smuggle hundreds of people through the frontier from the GDR (starting with fellow students who lived in East Germany and suddenly found themselves cut off from their classes in the West, and eventually including Johnson's wife-to-be, Elisabeth Schmidt, who was brought West by escape-helpers in February 1962).[9] And yet one doesn't have to read far to realise that Johnson also understands "the border" to involve more than the physical frontier between opposed economic and political systems: more, indeed, than an embodiment of the bloc-dividing "Iron Curtain" with which it became synonymous, and which ensured that a small event at a Berlin checkpoint could cause the entire world to shake. Johnson surveys the schism as it shapes many domains of human experience — sport, aesthetics, historical memory, claims to nationhood, even the German language, which is shown to have split into different jargons on either side. He maps the psychological, cultural and ideological gulfs squeezed into a few yards of physical space, pursuing "the border" as it runs between polarised mentalities and propagandas, as well as between different varieties of state power and employment of technology.

The border also has implications for Johnson's characters, who may have depth and even charisma to the extent that they are not fully reconciled to either of the warring ideologies. The Eastern ones especially remain mysterious, possessed of potentialities that may glimmer suggestively through the words they are prepared to speak as they try to correlate their existence with the slogans all around them. Some seem to testify to possibilities that find no realisation in the present — indications of a "moral utopia" that might one day find expression in a more authentic kind of "socialism", which did not sanction lies or, as happens in *The Third Book about Achim*, drive farmers to hang themselves rather than face enforced collectivisation of their land: a socialism, in other words, of a different order than that being constructed in the GDR, which existed "solely in the institutions which try to establish it"[10] and which had built a stately cult around the figure of the "administrator".

The border also had formal implications for Johnson, provoking some of the often noted "difficulty" of his novels. This may reflect his refusal to take sides within the terms of the division or to tell his readers what to think: his books are, so the young Jean Baudrillard suggested in 1962, works of "an artisan of language" not a "manager of conscience".[11] English translations could hardly capture the Low German or even Kashubian idioms with which he challenged official discourse (linguistic equivalents of the backwaters in which he and his young friends in Mecklenburg had liked to swim, canoe or sail). We could, though, hardly miss Johnson's avoidance of conventional forms of narrative. That necessity had become particularly evident in the divided city of Berlin. In the months before the GDR set about constructing the Berlin Wall, Johnson had toured America, lecturing about Berlin as the "Border of a Divided World". In an exceptional essay, translated and published under that title in *Evergreen Review*,[12] he described in some detail how the border between East and West had worked when it was still permeable in the years before the East German authorities had "sunk the division into the ground", and when the city transport system — the S-Bahn — still ran across the divide. Johnson, who would later republish his essay of 1961 as "Berlin Transit (Out of Date)", explored the literary implications of a transport system that allowed people from both sides to mix, and where the most prosaic object or occurrence — he gives the example of a man stepping off a train and walking towards a station exit — might therefore exist simultaneously in contrary perspectives. As he wrote, "there is no such thing as: Berlin. There are two cities of Berlin, comparable in population and developed footprint. Saying 'Berlin' is vague, or rather it is a political claim, of a kind the Eastern and Western blocs have been making for some time, insofar as each one gives the half in its respective sphere of influence the name of the whole region as though the other half either did not exist or were already included within its own."[13]

Exploring the same theme a few years later, the French author and critic Maurice Blanchot identified Johnson as the writer who had done most to demonstrate "the truth of Literature" in the context of a city that had been thrown into "abstraction" by the division and could no longer be grasped definitively in its "complete" reality.[14] Divided Berlin was, so Blanchot suggested, a place that had no use for "omniscience", nor for the panoramic survey through which writers elsewhere or in different eras might seek to capture reality. Berlin was a "situation" in which the concrete and the abstract were strangely combined. It was a predicament in which no given particular could be singled out without the risk of falsification, but which nevertheless could only be grasped by singling out particulars.

Under more conventional circumstances, a writer who chose to concentrate on "fragmentary" phenomena might be considered guilty of beating a "sceptical retreat" from reality or of a "lazy renouncement of a complete synthesis".[15] However, the shattered and then torn again city of Berlin, which the wall had turned into a "symbol of the division of the world", *required* a fragmentary approach. There was, Blanchot ventured, no other way of articulating the new fact that "the entirety of meaning is not to be found immediately either in ourselves or in what we write". Countless words had already been written about the split yet, for Blanchot, Johnson's first two published novels, *Speculations about Jakob* and *The Third Book about Achim,* proved that literature offered "the best approach to the situation".[16] He commended them as works by a writer who had adopted an "indirect" approach in order to articulate the "impossibility" of writing "books in which the division is put into play". Johnson, in short, was aware of the "gap" and the "dark unrelenting tension" between reality and "the literary grasping of its sense".[17]

The central character both in *The Third Book about Achim* and in a related later story, published in English as *An Absence,* is a divorced West German journalist named Karsch who lives alone near Hamburg and one day gets a call from an actress named Karin, a former girlfriend who now lives in the East. Having known one another in Berlin, they had agreed to communicate if anything important came up. So Karsch makes his way through the border, meets her, and stays to write the biography of Karin's new boyfriend, a "noted racing cyclist" named Achim — a commission that is put his way by GDR officials hoping that this "third" biography of their loyal trophy athlete will make a useful impression in neutral countries and West Germany. Karsch accepts partly out of a love of biography: he enjoys "matching a conscious past with the actual past, guiding a person's memory back to forgotten things, seeing them surprised at themselves".[18] During the course of his research, he finds himself surrounded by a new version of the German language — featuring "strings of genitives"[19] much citing of statistics and reliance on words like "dissemination", "shortage", "bottleneck" and "distribution". He also encounters a popular avoidance of "official terminology"[20] on the part of people who had developed their own subtle and inflected ways of checking out one another's attitudes to the regime.

The project does indeed turn out to be "impossible". Achim wants his biography to look as if his life had taken a turn for the better when Soviet soldiers turned up in his country, while Karsch is more interested in exploring other possibilities: that this revered communist hero may actually once have been a young Nazi thug, that he may have broken currency regulations by going West to buy a set of French gears for his bicycle, that he may even have been among the protesting workers who took to the streets in the tank-crushed Berlin uprising of 1953. Karsch has to give up as he realises that the truth about Achim lies beyond his reach. In the absence of any consensual reality, there is only the dull, thudding battle between embedded ideological assumptions. Achim cites some of the Western attitudes he has encountered while visiting to compete in cycle races. In the Federal Republic he met people who believed that Russia ruled the East directly, and that everyone in the East is starving ("Dig in, boy. For once in your life eat your fill"[21]). In Austria, he had been expected to stand for the West German anthem, the organisers apparently not understanding that the GDR possessed an anthem of its own — a "melody", as Karsch drily notes, intended to turn its long-suffering singers "away from the ruins altogether toward a future where the sun would shine over Germany more brightly than ever before".[22] There is a moment in *An Absence* when Karsch tries to "talk Achim out of his 'warmonger capitalists of the Ruhr'". He wants to confront these slogans with a more generous sense of reality but finds himself "hampered by being able to evoke no more about the Ruhr district, say, than the night express between Dortmund and Cologne, on its way to

Italy with cars and a corridor in which Karsch stood next to a girl who smoked sleeplessly against the November-black, coke-illumined window pane. Any young fellow with a sad face would have done alright there"[23]

4. PRAISE AND DENUNCIATION: A PAIN FOR ALL ZEALOTS

However challenging they may have been to "the perceptive faculties of the general public" these three novels made Johnson the subject of considerable international discussion. In the USA, the German-born historian Joachim Remak hailed *The Third Book about Achim* as "a great book" and its author as "a writer of genius".[1] John Updike would come out more quietly in favour of *Two Views,* announcing in the *New Yorker* that "the perfunctory liaison and nearly accidental reunion of Dietbert and Beate serves, at least for me, as a moving parable of human love and as a sufficient indictment of the political systems that separate us".[2] Another reviewer appreciated the "disciplined parataxis"[3] of *Two Views*. Others, however, got nowhere at all. "I am still not clear as to what was happening", said *The Nation* of *Speculations about Jakob,* leaving the *Christian Science Monitor* to complain more explicitly about the difficulty of finding a way through the "labyrinth of confused, devious, and often contradictory incident" that was *The Third Book about Achim*.[4] Johnson was also scolded by American Cold Warriors for refusing to take sides. Far from just condemning both systems, Johnson plainly needed to recognise that there was a "real difference" between East Germany and the Federal Republic. Melvyn Lasky, editor of the CIA-backed magazine *Encounter,* was disdainful of *Speculations about Jakob:* "As for his vaunted self-liberation from East-West clichés, what could be more sloganized and platitudinous than his trite picture of Jakob in the land of 'juke boxes and poisonous neon lights.'" Overlooking the fact that the offending scenes were actually written as imagined by a Stasi agent in the GDR, America's steaming partisan suggested "A little more cool tentativeness here too would have been in order".[5]

In France, there was rather less sneering about the "difficulty" of Johnson's writing. Jean Baudrillard, who published his essay on Johnson's first two novels in Jean-Paul Sartre's journal, *Les Temps Moderne*, appreciated the "Faulknerian" influence he saw in Johnson's sensitivity to a fundamental and pervasive "discord" — not between black and white, as in Faulkner's American South, but between the two German states.[6] He was impressed by Johnson's meticulous observations, whether of transport or communication systems or of nature ("a tree may even be a tree beyond the border"), by his refusal to dictate rather than describe, and by his insistence on the "unsurpassable distance" that lay between himself and his objects or characters. He hailed Johnson as a decipherer of "political man", who seemed to associate the possibilities of socialism, not with position-taking, slogans or dogmatic views, but with the increasingly "technical character of the world".

In both Germanies, however, Johnson would find himself being "unmasked" and harshly condemned as a renegade or worse. He was aware that the Stasi may well have been keeping an eye on him in West Berlin, apparently even poking around in his flat in the Friedenau district. The level of official mistrust in the GDR is indicated by the questions raised when Johnson started a spell of work at the Brecht Archives in East Berlin. Hearing that he had been appointed to edit Brecht's *Me-Ti: Book of Changes* for Suhrkamp, Manfred Wekwerth, a theatre director associated with the Berliner Ensemble who was later revealed to have Stasi connections, wrote to Brecht's widow and archivist Helene Weigel protesting that Johnson was both a "mediocre" opportunist who would use Brecht to elevate himself and also "an anarcho-Trotskyist — avantgardist — pluralist — existentialist, brilliantly eccentric (what do I know) scatterbrain".[7] Johnson, whose novels were never published in the GDR, would also be judged harshly by some Eastern émigrés in the West, including the writer Gerhard Zwerenz, who had met Johnson when he himself was studying under the philosopher Ernst Bloch in Leipzig in the Fifties. At a meeting of Group 47, held at the Bavarian alpine resort of Elmau in 1959, Zwerenz tried, unsuccessfully, to persuade the just emigrated Johnson to take up the cause of dissenting intellectuals, many of them closely associated with Mayer and Bloch's circle in Leipzig, who had recently been jailed as "counter-revolutionary" conspirators.[8] Zwerenz, whose suspicions may have been shared by others associated with the Leipzig circle, judged Johnson's refusal harshly, and appears never to have abandoned his belief that he must have been some sort of GDR agent.

There were those who took offence in the Federal Republic too. That Johnson had arguments with some on the Western left can be seen in a splendid typescript entitled "Conversation on the Novel, its uses & dangers, recent degenerations, indignation of the audience etc." and dated February 1973.[9] Written in English, presumably for use in lectures, this defends the novel against a voice that is young, educated and well-versed in sociological expressions: a voice belonging to those who find many reasons for condemning the novel: for not being "a revolutionary weapon", for being too expensive for workers who can hardly even afford breakfast, for taking up time that might otherwise be used to change the world, for demanding quiescence of its readers by ripping them out of their "community of interests". These militant voices objected that the novel's "personnel" tend to be affluent, and that readers need a bourgeois education if they are to stand a hope of understanding the nuances and multiplicity of a novel that prides itself on never issuing clear and simple instructions as to how one should act or behave. In short, the novel is nothing but an "instrument of well-meaning fools playing into the hands of the enemy". We heard faint echoes of this call to arms as students in England too, where a blunt instrument was being made of the suggestion, attributed to the British documentary filmmaker Ronald Grierson as well as to Bertolt Brecht, that "Art is not a mirror; it is a hammer".

In the perspective Johnson was working to establish, the novel was neither: it was, as he put it, a "world of its own" rather than "a mirror or reflection of the world", and you should throw it out if it was really just a stretched-out slogan telling you what to think or, even worse, what it was "trying to say".

Yet the most formidable onslaught faced by Johnson in the Federal Republic of Germany came neither from a handful of oppositional leftists seeking to turn the novel into their own kind of (Western) Marxist instrument, nor from suspicious members of the harassed and extinguished Leipzig circle.[10] The bitterest attack was launched by anti-communists who disliked Johnson's critical portrayals of the West as a place of rising consumerism with barely contrite former Nazis in positions of power, and who considered it scandalous to portray the GDR as a state that had its own constitution and terms of existence, and was not just a conquered, oppressed and illegitimate vassal of the USSR.

The worst period for Johnson began on 11 November 1961, when tensions between East and West were much aggravated by the GDR's recent construction of the Berlin Wall. The trouble started in Milan at a conference connected with the Italian publication of *Speculations about Jakob*. Hermann Kesten, a sixty-one-year-old German-Jewish author who was also an influential champion of the luminous works of Joseph Roth (and a member of Group 47 who had himself been forced into exile by Nazism in 1933), delivered a lecture in which he condemned the wall, claiming that it marked a "caesura" in German literature — an end to the "post-fascist" period and the moment for a return to the humanist tradition of earlier German authors. He also described Bertolt Brecht as "one of your dictatorship".[11] Johnson opposed this view, declaring that the GDR's sudden closure of the border in Berlin the previous August was neither a literary watershed nor a surprise. The wall was indeed "wretched" but it was also a rational and predictable response to a challenging situation: more than three million East Germans had already gone West, and the GDR's economy was imperilled by the flight. He also defended Brecht, and reiterated his view that the novelist's job was to tell a story — which was surely not the same as trying to "usher readers into illusions" of the kind that might serve official policy on either side: far from being a compliant fable, the novel should be seen as a kind of "reconnaissance" which invites readers to make their own sense of whatever might be revealed. Committed to the pursuit of Enlightenment and truth, he was emphatic that "mixing history with moral accusations" was to be avoided.

Twenty years later, Johnson would remember his alleged "defence of the wall", still somewhat grumpily, for a documentary on BBC Radio 4: "I stated that the East German communists didn't want to commit a moral act by erecting this barrier but they just wanted to defend themselves and their state and their economy, and this was taken by a lot of people as a sort of okaying of the wall and I had two or three unhappy months in the press".[12] The trouble began when Kesten used the pages of the Springer-owned paper *Die Welt* to further his misrepresentation of what Johnson had said in Milan, asserting that the writer had defended the wall as "good, reasonable and moral", and effectively accused him of being Walter Ulbricht's poodle in the West — as well as an author of no talent whose work was just a "pot-pourri" of stylistic tricks borrowed from Brecht, Faulkner, Robbe-Grillet and others in order to make a mannerist efflorescence of attitudes that, if expressed more plainly, might stand revealed as a GDR tourism brochure. A recording of Johnson's contribution to the Milan conference supported his claim that Kesten had, as the traduced writer told *Der Speigel*, turned him into a "lunatic" and "gunman", attributing words to him that he would never have uttered even if they had "made him unconscious with alcohol".[13] Apologies, however, were not forthcoming. Indeed, Johnson's counter-arguments appear only to have convinced his already decided accusers that he had something to hide.

Shortly afterwards, the "character assassination" that Johnson had suffered in the Springer press was repeated in the West German Parliament by the Foreign Minister. Dr Heinrich von Brentano had already won himself a place in Johnson's *The Third Book about Achim* by brutishly comparing Brecht's pre-war lyrics, written for works such as Kurt Weill's "The Rise and Fall of the City of Mahagonny", to the "storming" Nazi anthem composed by the pimp and thug Horst Wessel,[14] and he now demanded that the Federal Republic stipend recently awarded to Johnson for his approaching year at Villa Massimo in Rome be withdrawn. Brentano failed to apologise when it was pointed out that Kesten had misrepresented Johnson's talk, and Johnson remained a target of anti-communist hate from figures such as the Austrian Kurt Ziesel, whose own record as an unapologetic Nazi did not prevent him from mocking the Western literary establishment for getting down on its knees to worship this "incomprehensible" writer who refused to denounce the barbarity of Bolshevism. Another former Nazi, Wolfdietrich Schnurre, denounced Johnson as a "camouflaged communist". Books and readings were boycotted and, as he himself would remember at Darmstadt, he was accused of being a "trojan horse" and, indeed, "a Communist pig".[15] As Colin Riordan writes, the man who had arrived in West Berlin to be hailed as a "champion of freedom" had, within only three years, been branded a "traitorous communist" and put to work as the whipping boy of the West German right.[16] Even without the threatening and insulting nocturnal phone calls he received at this time, this was a considerable shock to Johnson, excoriating and even "devastating" as Riordan suggests. Johnson may have told the BBC that his difficulties extended over two or three months, but their memory was still raw in 1979, when he recalled the events in close detail in his Frankfurt lectures on poetics. Here he railed against "Senator McKesten"[17] and remembers resigning his membership of the German Academy of Language and Literature because it had refused to withdraw misleading references to the "Kesten Affair".

Johnson's exasperation at the reception of his own efforts as a novelist to "establish the truth" and "come closer to actual life"[18] is reflected in the story that was translated as *An Absence* and published as No. 35 in the mind-opening series of assaults on British insularity that was Nathaniel Tarn's beautiful collection of "Cape Editions". Here, the West

German journalist Karsch returns from the East having failed to find a way through to the actual human being behind the cyclist Achim's promoted image as a faultless hero of the GDR. In the spirit of an ideological wire-cutter, he starts challenging Western myths about the GDR, and not just those of the children who are convinced that the police in East Germany "went after ordinary passers-by with machine-guns".[19] He quickly gets into trouble for his efforts. Things come to a head after a television discussion in which he uses the word "recognition" in connection with East Germany — a provocation to those Westerners who saw the GDR as an illegal Soviet regime squatting on stolen German soil.

Assailed for his efforts, Karsch says to himself, "why go on trying to make the two German provinces better acquainted with one another, why get involved in the low and petty terms with which they took each other's measure, as though the year 1960 ceases to be shared at the border, why write, answer letters, give information, when these affairs terminate in applause and beer-drinking as after any old entertainment and tales from abroad, when the supposed 'Jew swine' finds best regards from the Wandsbeck execution squad in his mail, when gradually the smaller newspapers begin questioning whether this unknown journalist stands for anything representative or morally right, when what you get out of it is having almost every evening to turn down a call to partisan political leadership, thereby winning the contempt of nineteen-year-olds for this cowardly citizen who wouldn't stand up for anything but his reporting, not for any recommendation".[20] Karsch bales out shortly after the West German police arrive to search his flat on suspicion of treason, landing in Italy, where he abandons his search for difficult truths and lives by supplying West German newspapers with bland "page three"-type features of the kind he had hoped to get beyond with his failed biography of Achim. In 1962 Johnson himself left West Berlin for Italy where he would spend his state-funded year writing in the Villa Massimo in Rome. By that time, however, a different city and country had also laid claim to his attention.

5. NEW YORK CITY: BEGINNING ANNIVERSARIES

"America was a rumour", so Johnson told the *New York Times* in December 1966: "I came here to verify the rumour."[1] He had made his first visit in 1961, during which he gave a lecture at Wayne State University, in Detroit, Michigan, attended a seminar at Harvard, and also passed through San Francisco, New Orleans and Oxford, Mississippi, where he sought out a disappointing encounter with his literary hero, William Faulkner ("I am not a literary man", was just about all the elderly Southern writer was willing to say when his East German admirer eventually caught up with him in Charlottesville, Virginia — that and the deflating observation that "I come here only to go huntin' and fishin'"[2]).

Johnson returned to America for a brief tour in 1965, giving readings alongside Günter Grass, and then moved to New York for a much longer period from 1966–68, a visit that was made possible by his German-Jewish expatriate publisher Helen Wolff, who employed him to produce his textbook *Das Neue Fenster: Selections from Contemporary German Literature*. Keen to participate in the ordinary life of the city, and not to haunt universities as a subsidised ghost in the corridor (he would describe academic life as both a "golden cage"[3] and a "nature conservancy park"[4]), he went to work every day in his office at the publishers and lived with his family in a flat looking out over the Hudson River: Apt 204 at 243 Riverside Drive on the Upper West Side. It was a creative time, in which Johnson got to know some of Wolff's friends, including the philosopher Hannah Arendt, who lived nearby on Riverside Drive, and researched New York City with the energy he had previously applied to Berlin. He travelled about extensively on the trains and ferries, visiting the night courts as well as the bars, and, with Helen Wolff's help, joined a couple of City of New York police detectives in their unmarked car as they patrolled the midtown east side area. As Wolff had explained to the Chief Inspector while making this request: "His work is in the tradition of the disciplined realist novel, and he is particularly concerned with the life and problems of ordinary men and women".[5] He took part in readings and discussions too, joining Hannah Arendt to talk about Walter Benjamin, for example, or speaking to members of the American Jewish Congress, whose agonised and accusing response confirmed something he already knew very well: that no German could escape guilt for the holocaust.

Johnson had never been anything like as ignorant about America as the Polish spy, Pawel Monat who, on first flying into New York City in 1955, had scolded his wife for failing to understand that the air conditioning boxes sticking out of the apartment windows were "obviously dovecotes".[6] Johnson would play a more sophisticated game with that particular misrecognition, placing it on the "dark ravine" of West End Avenue and attributing it to the perceptions of a young bride from South Dakota who is reluctant to move to the area: "but the cages in the windows are not for birds", he would write, "they're for air conditioners you have to pay for yourself".[7]

Unlike Monat, who may have been a source here, Johnson had lived for years in the West by the time he arrived in New York. He too, however, was fighting false stereotypes: "I am destroying beliefs that everyone has tried to establish in me", so he informed the *New York Times's* Harry Gilroy (who had reported for the paper from Berlin in the late Fifties). Among his independent discoveries, Johnson cited the fact that "people on New York streets are not hurrying, one is not robbed of dignity in a subway crush, people here are remarkably patient — more than I think they would be in Germany". Having visited Harlem — "without being molested, or even noticed" — he was also, the reporter noted, "profoundly distressed by the inequalities suffered by Negroes":

"I don't really understand the attitude of whites to Negroes", he said. "Whites leave their children in the hands of Negroes. They ride in subway trains confident that the Negro driver will get them there safely. There cannot be repulsion."

He added that there were good signs of progress in race relations: "Practically everyone I know is for equal rights for everyone".

Johnson plainly had some catching up to do in this area. In the GDR, the so-called "Negro" had been a rare visitor — a technician or soldier undergoing training, perhaps, or a refugee from McCarthyism, such as the classically-trained African-American baritone Aubrey Pankey, who moved to the GDR in 1956 after being refused permission to stay in France or Britain under pressure from McCarthy's House Un-American Activities Committee. Johnson, however, would make that effort, both in his commentary for *Summer in the City*, a film formed around his experience of New York City and directed by the Berlin-born American Christian Blackwood for West German television in 1968, and also in *Anniversaries*, the vast four-volume New York novel he would write over the following fifteen or so years. Michael Hamburger, the poet and translator who had met up again with Johnson in Massachusetts and then New York in 1966, remembered how

Uwe Johnson at Michael Hamburger's house, South Hadley, Massachusetts, October 1966.

he studied the city with "a minuteness particular to him".[8] He also describes him as unusually fearless for a white man as he set off to explore the streets of Harlem — perhaps defended by his "heavy frame", which combined with cropped hair and leather jacket to give him the "tough" appearance of a Hell's

Angel or a skinhead — a look that had astonished Hamburger when he first met the writer.

We can gain some sense of the ambitions Johnson held for *Anniversaries* by returning to the typescript entitled "Conversation on the Novel...". Here he explains that he sees the novel not as a miniature or model world but as "a version of reality" that readers are invited to compare and contrast with their own experience. He suggests that its primary cause and justification lies in the basic human need driving people to want to overcome their separation — whether this be caused by frontiers, historical time or social codes. Aware that they live on "an unsafe planet", readers want "news from their partners", whether the latter are found in a faraway land, in the distant past or, indeed, just around the corner as neighbours. While they might continue to use chronology as a way of organising his material, the late-twentieth-century novelist must also try to articulate new forms of understanding. He or she should seek to capture not just the appearance of beauty but also the material processes underlying its production: "a rose is a rose is a rose", Johnson quotes from Gertrude Stein, yet the flower must also be understood from the point of view of the parks section of the gardeners union. Having cast an eye over the usual texts that might be found on a first-year reading list, Johnson dismisses Abel Chevalley's otiose definition of the novel as "a narration in prose of a certain length", and then dispenses just as quickly with E.M. Forster's unambitious ruling from Bloomsbury that to qualify as a novel it should have at least fifty thousand words. Not so, Johnson told the students: the novel that tries to speak the truth of our time will need a good two million words, and

Christian Blackwood,
Summer in the City.

scores of characters. Far from hiding in a single room, or even a considerable country house of the kind Jane Austen might have taken as her setting, it must step out onto the sidewalks, visit police headquarters and find its way into all the world's hiding places too. It must range widely through cities and countries, taking the entirety of space and, for that matter, of yet-to-be-discovered dimensions as its proper territory. Throughout, it must persist in the pursuit of truth in the understanding that the reader is just as responsible for this effort as the writer.

Johnson got going on *Anniversaries* in New York, where he stayed for a second year, assisted by a grant of $7,000 from the Rockefeller Foundation, paid through the New School for Social Research, to keep him over the seven months he needed to "complete work on his fourth novel".[9] It would grow into a vast and barely containable monster, fit not just to be "read" in the page-turning manner of the book-buying "consumer" to whom Johnson referred teasingly in his talks, but to be inhabited over a decade or two. Johnson began by releasing some of the "invented persons" from his earlier novels into the American city, and then following them into the work that would become his masterpiece. Various of these semi-autonomous characters from his earlier novels reappear in these pages, included the frustrated journalist Karsch, who, having failed to establish the truth about the GDR's cycling hero Achim, now turns up in America researching and writing a book about the Mafia. The major part, however, goes to Gesine Cresspahl, earlier encountered in *Speculations about Jakob*, where she was living in Düsseldorf in West Germany, having left her Mecklenburg home in the GDR, and working as a secretary for NATO. Johnson would speak of having caught sight of her one day in Manhattan — "on the southern side of 42nd Street heading for Sixth Avenue"[10] — and of gaining her reluctant permission to reappoint himself the chronicler of her story.

By 1967, when Johnson renews their acquaintance in Manhattan, Gesine is thirty-four years old, and living in a three-roomed apartment that appears actually to have been

Johnson's own on Riverside Drive. She has been in New York since the spring of 1961, and lives with her ten-year-old daughter Marie, the child of Gesine's brief relationship with the late railwayman Jakob Abs. She has a visiting lover named Dietrich Erichson, a professor who works in defence-related radar, and she herself is now a "foreign languages correspondent", employed by a Manhattan bank that draws up plans, as the novel develops, to assist the ongoing Prague Spring in Czechoslovakia by advancing hard currency to Alexander Dubcek's reforming government. For her own sake, as well as that of her smart and already partly-Americanised daughter Marie, Gesine also finds herself wanting to understand more about the traumatic twentieth-century history that has made her what she is. As Johnson remarked in an interview, "Gesine Cresspahl tries to rediscover herself, her parents, her countryside, her language".[11] The conversations in which Gesine and Marie review their family's history are central to the architecture of the new work.

Anniversaries is not structured like a conventional novel. Determined to use fiction as an instrument with which to investigate the reality of his age, Johnson employs a calendrical form to organise *Anniversaries* along two intersecting vectors of time and place. In the first, which has been described as "the time of narration",[12] the novel follows Gesine and Marie as they proceed day by day through a year of their life in New York, starting on 20 August 1967, and moving forward through a further 366 dated sequences, one for every day (the translator, Damion Searls, reminds us that Johnson had chosen a leap year), until it closes on 20 August 1968. Along this vector, Johnson provides detailed and close-grained accounts of their everyday life in the city — school, work, the street with its shops, cafes and bars, the parks and the subway, encounters with friends and neighbours, and vacations too. Germany had been divided two ways, but *Anniversaries* is the book of a city where almost everybody comes from somewhere else, and in which people are learning, or not, to live in the knowledge that others have a different experience both of the city they share and of the world beyond its horizon: "home" or just murder? — as Johnson's Jewish neighbours on Riverside Drive demand that we keep asking of Gesine's remembered Mecklenburg.

Gesine's "days in the year" are richly augmented by her scrutiny of the *New York Times*, which brings — and sometimes deluges — her with news of the wider events throughout this momentous year, shaped as it is by the Civil Rights Movement, the murders of Kennedy and Martin Luther King, and the ongoing war in Vietnam. This is history-in-the-making, told as it registers in Gesine's sharp, sceptical and very Johnson-like eye. She respects the paper — as close as America came, perhaps, to an embodiment of Jurgen Habermas's idea of the "bourgeois public sphere"[13] — but also takes stock of its omissions, biases and silent adjustments of the record. Made into an "omnidirectional ironist"[14] by her own experience of displacement, she notes the welcome accorded to Stalin's daughter, Svetlana Alliluyeva, when she defects in India and moves to New York, and also the moment when the paper silently introduces a smaller font for the swelling list of young men killed in the Vietnam War. She closely follows the paper's reports of the ongoing Prague Spring, a momentous upheaval that becomes an increasingly dominant presence in the book — and an encouraging source of hope, too, since it promises the recovery of the political aspirations that Johnson had seen violently crushed in East Germany in 1953 and again in Hungary in 1956. Encouraged by the Dubček government's apparently honest and accountable response to the death of an American Jewish aid worker, who had ended up floating dead in Prague's Vltava River, Johnson writes, "then this might really be Socialism — with a functioning constitution, with freedom of speech, with freedom of movement, with the freedom for even an individual to decide how to use the means of production".[15]

While remaining attentive to the consequences of the post-war Iron Curtain both in Europe and in Asia, the so-called "poet of the divided Germany" finds a new fault line to investigate in America and New York City itself. As Gesine and Marie go about their business, the "border" that had divided Berlin in Johnson's earlier novels is augmented by the "colour-line" cut deep into American experience. His interest in this abiding wound is evident in the many newspaper clippings he made while living in New York, now held in the Uwe Johnson Archive at the University of Rostock. It is also embedded in *Anniversaries* from the very opening scene — set at a coastal resort "on a narrow spit on the Jersey shore" a couple of hours from Manhattan, where "dark-skinned" people are allowed to work as servants but definitely not to buy or rent houses or (thanks to a proscription that is also applied to Jews) to make use of the "coarse white sand"[16] reserved for White Anglo-Saxon Protestants. Gesine has been aware of this fault line since she was looking for somewhere to live at the very start of her residency in New York City. It is there in the high rents demanded for mean and shabby apartments that are, nevertheless, "free of Negro neighbors"[17] and she confronts it again when she grabs Marie and fiercely walks out of an office in Queens, slamming the door on a property broker who has tried to tempt her with the assurance, "Don't worry we keep the shwartzes out."[18]

Over the course of the novel's year the *New York Times* teaches Gesine how this division plays out in the politics of the city. Through her eyes, we read of the African-American singer Eartha Kitt coming under fire for presuming, on the authority of her own experience of living in both ghetto and gutter, to tell President Lyndon Johnson's wife why young Americans might be turning to crime ("Because they're going to be snatched from their mothers to be shot in Vietnam"). We also see the African-American poet Leroi Jones (soon to rename himself Amira Baraka) spitting his fearless contempt back at the white judge who is jailing him for three years on account of the hostility to the Vietnam War expressed in an allegedly inflammatory poem published in *Evergreen Review*. Gesine notes the reported murders, which may or may not have been fired by racial hatred, and she is also far too attentive to miss the publication of a survey revealing how very few, if any,

African-Americans hold significant positions in the media — even the august, superior and liberal-minded *New York Times* itself can only count three among its two hundred reporters.[19]

Gesine and Marie also make their own more personal attempts to cross the colour-line. They do what they can to befriend Mr Robinson, the Black elevator operator in their apartment building (he turns out to have done his military service in West Germany). They risk the disapproval of neighbours by providing for Marie's Black school friend Francine, who comes to stay with them for a time after her mother is taken off to hospital following a stabbing. When Francine disappears back across the colour-line, they set out to look for her on the streets, only to make a more general discovery. "Our slums", Johnson notes of New York City, "are around the corner, and a foreign country". By the time he wrote this, in the second volume of *Anniversaries*, both he and Gesine understand "the slum" to be the product of a system of exclusion and discrimination that is actually more mobile than his statement may suggest. Unlike those quarters or estates that may have been deliberately created to house the poor in Europe, "the slums of New York weren't built as slums; here the slum is like a jellyfish in society, it moves around".[20] He goes on to describe how the "jellyfish" can turn luxury "brownstone" residences, built with fine interior panelling, oak floors and impressive fireplaces, into hellish barracks of degradation with African-American and Puerto Rican families squeezed into single rooms. By this stage in the process most white-skinned immigrants have fled, leaving the place to, say, Mrs Daphne Davis, a slumdweller in Brownsville, Brooklyn, who is reported to have found her infant daughter playing with a rat. "It was so big the child was calling: 'Here

This kind of slum may contain a whole world — a world made up of different worlds.

Christian Blackwood,
Summer in the City.

kitty, here kitty".[21] Recognising that "the slum is a prison into which society deports those who it itself has mutilated",[22] Gesine concludes that, while there may indeed be "individual whites who register the sound of a bottle exploding" next to them on the sidewalk, "the whites as a group do not get the message":

> When I hear "the whites", I often think of figures in sheets, ghosts, corpses on their way to the cemetery. Since the whites as a group refuse to help, why not stick a knife in an individual white person's heart and get what you need from his briefcase, his cash register, his apartment. Since people trapped in the slum have all their ways out to a worthwhile life blocked, why delay escaping into the illusions and sickness of drug addiction? Since society has put up a fence around this life, why follow the norms of that society, why treat a social worker as anything other than someone bringing a check, why not send the kids out to beg, why live under a roof. Since the bonds with society have been broken, why not rip out public phone cables, why leave a forwarding address when you go somewhere else, under a bridge, onto the Bowery, into jail, off to the war in Vietnam.[23]

The second vector shaping *Anniversaries* enables Johnson to raise a longer twentieth-century history into the Cresspahls' experience of New York City through the chosen year of 1967–8. This far-reaching trawl of the remembered past is largely located in Mecklenburg and Western Pomerania but with some closely observed episodes set in England where Gesine's carpenter father, Heinrich, lived for a period from 1925 to 1933. This dimension of the novel is opened when Gesine Cresspahl begins to tell her already partly American daughter Marie about her parents' and grandparents' lives in the small Mecklenburg town of Jerichow, which Johnson places a few miles inland from the Baltic coast, where the actual town of Klütz can be found. Whether or not Suhrkamp was right to advertise the first volumes of *Anniversaries* as proof that "the story is back", it was due to its exploration of the Cresspahl family history that *Anniversaries* was taken to mark a break with the earlier novels from which some of its characters were admitted. In a study published in 1989, the Belgian writer Pierre Mertens would describe the work as a "family saga" — "*Dynasty* a la sauce Cresspahl", so he suggested the menu might read, or even "*Dallas* mecklenbourgeois".[24] "All the stereotypes are here", so Mertens alleges, "the very same ones of every soap opera: disappointed ambitions, lost illusions, sordid intrigues, loves arranged or broken, enigmatic deaths". Although here, as Mertens admits against his own comparison, they are set against the "debacle of ideologies" and explained by "the division of a country, the rupture of the world".

As Gesine unfolds the past for her bright, opinionated and at times impatient daughter, that "rupture" is traced back through the division of Germany in 1945. The Mecklenburg narrative touches on the anti-revolutionary Kapp Putsch of March 1920, the political and economic struggles of the Weimar Republic, the rise and murderous triumph of Nazism, the Second World War, and, following the division of defeated Germany, the engulfing Cold War that extends into 1968 and includes, on the day after the novel's very last entry, the Soviet suppression of the Prague Spring. Johnson raises vast areas of twentieth-century history into view but not in a unified or panoramic manner. Much of the work of the novel lies in the way it uses the calendar to bring together its two narrative vectors — a single day pivoting past and present on the coincidence of a date. The novel tells the story of a family, to be sure, but it also dramatises an ongoing reflection on history and the ways in which the twentieth-century past may persist in the present as blight, burden, warning, and perhaps sometimes as a source of hope and inspiration too.

Johnson was definitely not seeking to advance a clockwork idea of history of the predetermined kind favoured by Stalinist ideologues or Western triumphalists. Neither was he using his evident pleasure in coincidence to trace out a mysterious gyre of time of the shaky cosmological variety that the Irish poet W.B. Yeats imagined in the early years of the twentieth century.

His engagement with history in *Anniversaries* is much closer to Walter Benjamin's understanding of "montage", in which past and present are brought together to produce the sudden and illuminating flash of a "dialectical image"[25] — revealing a "correspondence" which the reader is invited to participate in understanding. These moments of connection between now and then may well reveal the catastrophic barbarity of the twentieth century, an age that continues repeatedly to expose its own claims to enlightenment as a sick joke, but they can also encourage the utopian yearning that Johnson makes central to Gesine Cresspahl's divided experience of the world. Far from being an otherworldly fantasy or an allegedly redemptive blueprint to be imposed on reality by zealots, her utopia, as Gary L. Baker has put it, "manifests concretely in small ways"[26] Its moments of revealed potentiality may be fragmentary, fleeting and imperfectly realised, but they nevertheless testify to "the possibility for genuine positive change that would bring the human community closer to the ideal principles it sets for itself in the constitutions and moral codes that putatively guide its societies". For Johnson as well as for Gesine Cresspahl, one of the primary instances of "concrete utopia" at that time was the Prague Spring.

As he searches through twentieth-century history in *Anniversaries,* Johnson also reveals himself to be fundamentally concerned with both the importance and the limits of memory in a century fractured by so much trauma. As he told an interviewer for the *New York Times*, "In each man's life there exists a conscious past — what you think of yourself — and there is the real past that actually occurred and there are tensions between the two".[27] Like his uprooted and incurably homeless character Gesine, Johnson was himself capable of feeling nostalgic about Mecklenburg — not just an actual place in his book but also an unattainable past that can seem further distanced by the acts of memory that attempt to recall it.

In a tougher and more analytical register, however, memory becomes an instrument vital to the project of recovering and holding to the truth of a given situation. Sometimes that may

Bush beside Bodstedter Bodden, Darss, Western Pomerania.

have been a comparatively simple matter of insisting on the Nazi past of leading post-war politicians in West Germany, including the second president of the Federal Republic, Heinrich Lübke, who remarked, in response to accusations originating in the GDR, that he couldn't recall signing ("nor not signing" as Johnson notes drily) blueprints for concentration camp labour blocks built on the German Baltic at Peenemunde.[28] It is more difficult when Johnson brings Gesine up against the unfathomable question of whether her father, Heinrich, may have been blackmailed into becoming a British spy. Did he really take his five-year-old daughter abroad for six weeks shortly after Kristallnacht in November 1938, and if so, why did he return to Germany afterwards? The latter question confronts Gesine with the impossible task of working out whether the fleeting and imperfect sense of familiarity she has experienced when passing through certain places were truly examples of déjà vu rather than retrospectively assembled "fake memory".[29] Johnson also leaves his readers to wonder how fully this uncertainty is resolved by the apparently indisputable fact that a British halfpenny, minted in 1940, was found among her father's possessions after his death in the GDR.[30]

All this may help to explain why the German writer who was incubating this project in his mind seemed a puzzle to some who came across him in America. The novelist Richard Stern, who greatly admired Johnson's "beautiful" novel *Two Views,* remembered him coming to talk to his students in Chicago in 1967. He describes "a cryptic, witty fellow, with a long, fair, mostly bald head and an eye-glassed, owlish, Dr Cyclops look".[31] He sensed a "strange graveness" about his visitor: "He always smoked a pipe, but he was no comfortable pipe-smoking fellow. His fist gripped this complicated pacifier and puffed out what concealed him. But what was it?" Günter Grass, who had visited America on a lecture tour with Johnson in the mid-Sixties, told Stern at a PEN conference that the younger writer had "remained a stranger in the West" and, indeed, that "being a stranger was of great importance to him".

6. LEAVING BERLIN

After two years in New York City, Johnson boarded a Pan Am plane with his wife and their questioning daughter — "Why isn't England in Europe? / Why is Germany behind Scotland?"[1] — and brought his thoughts, notes and newspaper clippings back to West Berlin, where he would continue writing the novel that now stands as his greatest contribution to twentieth-century literature. Suhrkamp published the first volume of *Anniversaries* in West Germany to much acclaim in 1970. The second, which covered the second four-month period of Gesine's New York year, won Johnson the Büchner Prize when it appeared in 1971. Johnson's plans for the completion of the work had drifted by 1973, when the modestly delayed third volume was published. That volume had originally been intended as the last, but the book that came out covered only two months of 1968, leaving the remaining two for an originally unanticipated fourth volume in which Johnson also had to account for a long span of directly remembered history stretching from 1946 to 1968.

Anniversaries was a vast undertaking, yet if Johnson had slowed as he worked on volume III, this may also reflect the fact that he was stalked by difficulties that would eventually see him abandon once again the wired-off city in which he had appreciated the "silky light" and "the weight of colours in November".[2] Some of these troubles had occurred while he was still in New York. In November 1967, his sister-in-law Jutta Maria Schmidt, who was living in his flat in the Friedenau district of Berlin, had died in a fire thought to have been caused by a fallen cigarette. This disaster followed an earlier awkwardness. In February 1967, both his Berlin studio, which he had sublet to the poet and editor Hans Magnus Enzensberger's brother, and his family home, in which Enzensberger's separated wife Dagrun was living, ended up housing members of Kommune 1, a hairy and energetically left-wing group formed by the former Situationist Dieter Kunzelmann that included Rainer Langhans, Dorothea Ridder, Dagrun Enzensberger and her nine-year-old daughter Tanaquil. Like the fellow member Fritz Teufel, Kunzelmann would progress to more violent forms of terrorism, but Kommune 1's war against "bourgeois ideology" was also directed against the family, seen partly in Reichian terms as the root of many if not all evils.

Those who remember the period will have little trouble imagining the scenario: mattresses on the floor, women no longer so willing to wash the dishes while this or that revolutionary patriarch holds forth in a Mao jacket, ardent meetings to plot the theatrical acts of "fun terrorism" that would soon enough bring a new notoriety to the collective. In April 1967, various members of Kommune 1 were arrested for planning the "pudding assassination" of American Vice President Hubert Humphrey during a state visit to West Berlin. The weapons to be employed in this never enacted venture were only plastic bags filled with flour and yoghurt, but the resulting scandal was reported in the *New York Times*. Never tempted by Western Maoism, Johnson was horrified to find his name in the news and, having failed to get a satisfactory response from Enzensberger, asked Günter Grass to get the Kommunards out of his properties.

Johnson did nothing to heal the breach by including a withering attack on Enzensberger in the second volume of *Anniversaries* — dedicating one of Gesine Cresspahl's days to ridiculing the West German poet for posturing about the Vietnam War in an "open letter to America", published as "On Leaving America" in the *New York Review of Books,* and then heading off to "make himself of use" to "the people" in Cuba.[3] He'd had similar things to say outside his fiction too — not least in a short piece entitled "Concerning an Attitude of Protesting", written in English and published in a volume entitled *Authors Take Sides on Vietnam* in 1967. Here he launched into the "good people" who opposed their country's participation in the Vietnam War in the name of civilisation, Geneva, dignity and morality, while in their own lives quietly continuing to "eat of the fruits their governments harvest for them in Asian politics and markets".[4] Johnson denounced these liberal-minded westerners as self-aggrandising hypocrites who actually stood in the way of political change. They "want a good world; they do nothing about it". Having remained silent during the long preparations, their objection to the war was really only that it had become too visible. Convinced that these good people "will also soon, with embarrassment, describe their protests against this war as their juvenile period", Johnson urged them to "kindly shut up" and stop talking about a "species of good they help to make impossible" (an early critique there, of the sanctimonious liberal bubble that the Glaswegian housing activist, Sheila McKechnie, used to mock as the "Rightonosphere").

Johnson found his own way of falling out with some of the leading personnel as well as the political and ideological orthodoxies of the Western left at that time, but his remaining friends knew him to be in trouble in a much closer sense. An unattributed and (at least) double-exposed photograph from this period shows Johnson in full-swing at a composite literary lunch or dinner, possibly in Fritz J. Raddatz's place in Hamburg: glasses, bottles and cutlery everywhere, and several animated conversations going on at once.[5] It's a fetching portrait of intellectual life in the Sixties — lively, fearless and, like the image itself, potentially disorderly too. That photograph is neither the first nor the only indication of Johnson's volatility. In 1964, when he was working as chief editor and deputy publishing manager at Rowohlt publishing house, Raddatz had invited Johnson to a dinner also attended by the African-American writer James Baldwin. During the course of the evening, Baldwin said something that irritated Johnson, who dismissed him as "not a writer". When the wife of the publisher, Jane Ledig-Rowohlt, scolded him for this offensive remark, Johnson, who was a large man, had struck back furiously, causing her expensive jewellery to fall off her like so many "balls from a Christmas tree".[6]

This is by no means the only account of Johnson's alarming unpredictability, which could be greatly intensified by drink. The poet and translator Michael Hamburger, who knew Johnson in Berlin, New York and London, remembered many moments in which his friend had shown unusual consideration and kindness towards himself and also his family. He also recorded various "nasty incidents" associated with alcohol. A child's sense of these had been communicated to Hamburger by his daughter, Claire, who had first met the Johnsons in America in 1966, when her father was teaching at Mount Holyoke College in Massachusetts. Johnson had come to stay with the family in their house in South Hadley, and they later met up in New York over Christmas. Claire remembers Johnson taking her around the Bronx Zoo — deserted, knee-deep in snow and freezing cold — and also the Empire State Building.[7] Eight years old at the time, she recalls feeling grateful for the attention and kindness he showed her: "he was", she writes, "one of the few of my father's literary friends who even acknowledged the existence of his shy, awkward children, let alone actually engaged with them!" When she was eleven, Claire, who by then felt "a great fondness" for Uwe and his family, joined them for a week's holiday near Bülk in Holstein:

I remember being ... with them all on a windswept beach on the Baltic Coast. Grey sea, monochrome landscape, nondescript beach huts and houses circling the beach. There was a biting wind and, as usual, my main recollection is of being cold.

Uwe drank. He laid out bottle after bottle of beer on the table in front of him, in a long straight line, and proceeded to drink the contents, one after the other, in regimented style. He struck me as being very changeable, on the one hand being kind, generous and thoughtful, and the next minute being angry and withdrawn. His wife and child tiptoed round him, always placating him, and, when I stayed with them, I did as well.[8]

Upset by the "rigidity of Uwe's family's life", which could hardly have contrasted more with the Hamburgers's way of going about things ("I was used to chaos"), by the quarrelling, the heavy eiderdowns and the unfamiliar breakfasts — "a kind of apple puree and a type of raw bacon that I found impossible to stomach" — she asked to go home early. Johnson was "offended and upset" but took her to Hamburg airport, where he bought the unhappy English child something she would eat before putting her on the plane to go home, feeling "very guilty", as an unaccompanied minor.

This foreshortened trip was by no means the Hamburgers' only experience of Johnson's habit of lining up a long column of bottles on the table, and then steadily drinking his way through the lot. Michael Hamburger's wife, the poet Anne Beresford, remembers being dismissed with a terse "Why not?" when she cast her eye along one of these grim arrays and asked Johnson, "Are you really intending to drink all those?" To Michael, these joyless and "terrifying" drinking sessions seemed to be the writer's only way of escaping his own "puritanical rigour" — a characteristic that Hamburger, who was then seeking to maintain an "open" marriage, would later identify as "the main source of the tensions between us".[9] He considered Johnson's nightly drinking to be "not a social act at all, but a private ritual of immersion in those depths which all his conscious activities denied". He also entered a guarded plea of mitigation, registering how "cruelly intransigent" Johnson could be "towards himself" as well as "those closest to him".

We may detect a sympathetic nod towards Johnson's wife and daughter there, but Hamburger had also seen "vehement quarrels" on the wider literary front in the late Sixties, when he would meet up with Johnson and Günter Grass in Berlin, "especially when Uwe had been drinking".[10] There had been more "unpleasant scenes" when he met Johnson again in Berlin in May 1974.[11]

While Hamburger, who was writing shortly after Johnson's death in 1984, chose not to dwell in too much detail on this aspect of the novelist's life, the Swiss author Max Frisch had earlier recorded his own concerns in his Berlin diaries. Trying to get the measure of his brilliant but also testing younger friend, Frisch notes his pronounced formality, which extended to using "Sie" — a formality that seemed "like a reef" in a loosening world where everyone else was using "du"[12] — and also the highly idiosyncratic cast of his thinking. Johnson was often "impossible to understand; his system of associations (especially after the second bottle of white wine) remains a mystery to me".[13] On top of that were his cryptic formulations: "he speaks in crossword puzzles, plunges headfirst into commentaries on subjects that he has barely introduced". Frisch describes Johnson as a "logician" who could nevertheless be "completely irrational": a man of "facts, facts, facts", who "suddenly makes things up"; and a "Northman who doesn't take anything lightly". Noting his sudden fits of "moral rigorism", be they about the conduct of married couples or work and income, Frisch judged his sometimes impossible young friend to be "a puritan" who was "anything but small-minded" and all the more unyielding for the fact that he passed judgement without anger. Johnson was often accused of arrogance, but Frisch reckoned that his self-esteem was actually far from secure: a fact that manifested itself "in his standards, which have not been taken from anywhere else, but are a part of him".

Frisch was by no means hostile to Johnson and less exasperated than Gerhard Zwerenz, another migrated writer from the GDR, who described the more fêted author not just as "a statue of lost cultures" but as "the brazen edge of our crazy world".[14] Yet he knew that introducing this hardened-off human monolith to others could be dangerous. "Everything went wrong, very wrong"[15] — so Frisch recorded after taking Jurek Becker, the East German author of *Jacob the Liar*, to see Johnson on 1 May 1973. As a child, Becker had survived both the Lódz Ghetto and Ravensbrück concentration camp before settling in the GDR after the war. Unfortunately, he had "no idea" who Johnson was and made the mistake of trying to inform him about the location of Oranienburg, both the town and its concentration camp. Johnson rapidly became "frightening" — at first refusing to speak to Becker at all, then claiming to be Swiss and berating Becker as if he were to blame for the alleged fact that "the drugs from the Orient came over via the GDR". This disconcerting encounter was followed, later that same night, by an accusing phone call from Johnson to Frisch, who sensibly advised "against having the conversation now, after a fair amount of alcohol".[16]

It would be the same again when Frisch, who was fighting his own battle with drink, turned up at the Johnsons's home in Friedenau, Berlin, at about 8.30pm on 26 February 1974. This time he found the writer spinning arcane allusions and setting hostile word traps for the East German author Günter Kunert — he writes of "sharply serious crossword puzzling with the character of an interrogation".[17] Unyieldingly fierce about the GDR, Johnson was red-faced and impossible — interrupting incessantly while also raising his hand as soon as someone else was speaking "as if he couldn't get a word in". Kunert was one target, but Johnson didn't spare his other East German visitors, the novelist Christa Wolf and her husband Gerhard, who were attacked that same night as if they were personally responsible for the GDR, and regardless of the "fundamental" criticisms they themselves made of the "usurping power of their government". Frisch notes Johnson's "apodictic" manner and his wife Elisabeth's "exacerbating smile", attributing the whole vexatious package to "some combination of homesickness and hatred". As Frisch saw it, Johnson's discomfort about his own decision to quit the GDR was aggravated by Wolf's decision to stay. "Something like a guilty conscience; he demands that the others should have a guilty conscience. That's how it seems at times. Trauma".

Trauma, then, together with a remarkably sympathetic intelligence sealed off behind a face of stone, and a drinking habit that nobody could challenge without risking an explosion. The latter may have predated all Johnson's novels (Zwerenz alleges that there was already a bottle of schnapps in his pocket when he was attending lectures by Ernst Bloch at the Philosophical Institute in Leipzig in the mid-Fifties). By the time Frisch got to know the author of the unfolding work named *Anniversaries,* alcohol had fully entered his being: "He needs alcohol, a person under the excessive pressure of his conscientiousness. What comes to light through alcohol (three or four bottles of white wine over the course of the evening) doesn't expose him: he appears as someone wounded, but no smaller for it". In some respects Johnson seemed to remain fully in possession of himself on these occasions. Frisch notes "his appearance, the robustness of his body, the discipline of this thought, his immense sensitivity". The trouble came when

> he switches based on delusions, taking his own associations for the other person's statement. And his memory too: because he has a better recollection of secondary matters (where one was standing, when it was, etc.), this solidifies his assumptions, his interpretations; he composes and interpolates — so cleverly that I am no competition for him with my gap-filled memory. I only know that I didn't experience it in that way. He magnifies. A trifle (trifle for me) gains weight, often glamour too; he creates meaning which he then supports with a quotation, and the quotation might be accurate enough... When he goes out for a moment, I cork up my bottle to avoid drinking any more, and put it behind the television; as soon as he comes back, he says: There's a bottle missing. A first-class detective.[18]

A lot has been said about the association between intoxication, melancholy and artistic inspiration:

the "beautiful alcoholic conflagration"[19] that Jack London carried around with him and which fired so many twentieth-century writers, including Faulkner, Dylan Thomas and Jack Kerouac too. Johnson burned the same fuel, but there is little of the frothing fountain about his exactly plotted and closely observed novels. No florid "heaven-storming"[20] of the sort that the American writer Donald Newlove remembers trying to squeeze into the tiny "nutshell" of his own sodden book reviews, and not much sign of the collapsing "apocalypse of self-pity"[21] either.

So it was, though, that Johnson came to the point of leaving West Berlin. Reluctant to watch his younger friend drift further, Frisch, who had the means of a commercially successful writer, decided to help him gain some distance from his life in that politically islanded city. As he wrote in *Montauk*: "a younger friend, whom I much admire, does not ask me for a loan. All I know is that he does need a substantial loan and I am in a position to give it to him — and without interest, for it is wrong that my friend should have to work for me, when I am a rich man".[22] The sum in question was DM 120,000 and the idea was that it would enable Johnson to buy a house, not in Switzerland or Frankfurt, as Fritz J. Raddatz had suggested, but in England, where he might recover himself and concentrate on writing the fourth and final volume of *Anniversaries*.

So that is how it happened. The Belgian writer Pierre Mertens, who doesn't flinch from diagnosing Johnson a victim of "the old Pomeranian melancholy",[23] alleges that one of Johnson's last social acts in Berlin was to invite some friends round to celebrate his birthday in July 1974. In this retrospectively informed account, they turned up to find him already drunk: pretending not to recognise them and apparently "astonished to see them still alive". That same month, Johnson sent the first few completed "days" of *Anniversaries* IV to his publisher in Frankfurt and, on 19 July, set off for London to search for a house in southern England, where he — to the satisfaction of his editor at Suhrkamp, Siegfried Unseld, who was paying Johnson a considerable monthly advance — looked forward to completing the eagerly awaited fourth volume in a matter of months. It would be a while before German critics and readers started to wonder what had possessed their brilliant author to cast himself away "like a man shipwrecked at the end of the world".[24] And longer still before Johnson finished the final volume, in which a New York bartender named Wes declares, with some concern for his customers, that "All bartenders hand out medicine".[25]

Uwe Johnson, 1 March 1974.

PART II.

THE ISLAND: MODERNITY'S MUDBANK

I will merely say, it was there.

> — Robert Smithson, "Monuments of Passaic, 1967", *Artforum*, December 1967.

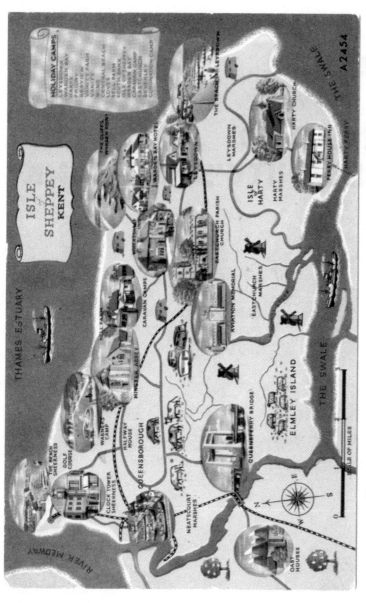

"I am enjoying myself trying to put the garden to rights as well as mixing cement for Harry. It's a lark". Hankie to Millie, Valentine & Son's postcard, early Sixties.

7. 1974: LOOKING OUT FROM BELLEVUE ROAD

- And what kind of job can you get with a degree in English?
- Teacher.
— Anniversaries IV, p. 1,636.

The walls around the staircase at No. 5 St Radigund Street, Canterbury, where I was living at the beginning of the year in which Uwe Johnson moved to England, were papered floor to ceiling with a poster produced by the Labour Party for the general election of 1970. Designed by Alan Aldridge, then still famous for his work with the Beatles, this huge billboard image showed painted Plasticine replicas — savagely rendered things that hindsight turns into prototypes for the puppets in ITV's later satirical series *Spitting Image* — of the Conservative leader Edward Heath standing alongside Alec Douglas-Home, the recently sacked Enoch Powell and four other members of his shadow cabinet. Headed "Yesterday's Men" and subtitled "they failed before", it was a portrayal of such arresting harshness that it would be cited among the reasons why Harold Wilson's Labour government had so unexpectedly lost the election to Edward Heath in June that year.

I still struggle to convince myself that I ever lived in "the bucolic, gorgeous English 1970s" remembered by the New York-based artist Cecily Brown.[1] Despite the economic and political strife racking the country, however, the early years of that decade do now seem a fine moment to have been a student in Britain — a time, in Annie Ernaux's phrase, of "consummate lack".[2] In 1970/1, the academic year I joined three thousand or so others at Kent, only 6.06% of English school leavers went to university. We had no tuition fees to pay and, unless from a well-off family, received a local authority maintenance grant too. The county of Kent, meanwhile, had responded positively to the creation of a new university in Canterbury, seeing improved status as well as commercial advantage in the prospect. Protesting students tried to confound this expectation, but their demonstrations, which would include a two-week occupation (encouraged by a coinciding performance of "Out Demons Out" by the Edgar Broughton Band) in February 1970, were less threatening than the actions of the "pudding bombers" who had taken over Uwe Johnson's flat in West Berlin a few years before. Remnants of the initial welcome survived, and not just among the room-farmers of Whitstable and Herne Bay, for whom "students" meant a handy increase in demand for seaside lodgings outside the summer season. Canterbury City Council even maintained a casual employment scheme for students staying in the city over the summer — contenders were invited to turn up at a depot to be equipped with a sickle and a forked stick of hazel, and then driven to a park or an old people's home, where we would spend a largely unsupervised day drinking freely-offered cups of tea and swiping at long grass until a van came to collect us. Students who found that prospect too taxing were free to sign on the dole during the vacations (Easter and Christmas included). On graduating, you could place your name on something called the Professional and Executive Register, thereby obliging some unfortunate civil servant to try to find you *appropriate* work. A new graduate only had to write something like "I want to be the editor of a literary magazine" on the form to gain another undisturbed period of subsidy from the British taxpayer. Seven years later Margaret Thatcher would reveal, while justifying one of the least opposed cuts of her first year as Prime Minister, that only one in twenty-five people registered on the PER had secured jobs.[3]

All this, to be sure, was grinding to a halt. During my time at the university, which ended a few days before the administration building collapsed into the disused bore of the world's first ever railway tunnel,[4] the new campus's modestly futurist hillside became oddly reminiscent of the Victorian poet Matthew Arnold's vision of "Dover Beach". Even though miles inland, one could still hear the shingle rattling as the crashed wave that had once seemed full of promise and ambition was sucked back into the sea. The British class war had continued despite the settlements sought by successive political leaders. Like Harold Wilson before him, Edward Heath had struggled to out-manoeuvre the "terrible twins" of British trade unionism — Jack Jones, General Secretary of the Transport and General Workers' Union, and Hugh Scanlon, President of the Amalgamated Engineering Union. These powerful barons, the second of whom has an insecure place in our story, had set the country's course in May 1969, when they went to Chequers to frustrate Barbara Castle's attempt to introduce a regulated system of industrial relations under the title "In Place of Strife" (it was at this encounter that Harold Wilson is said to have asked Scanlon, reputedly practising his golf swing at the time, to "Get your tanks off my lawn, Hughie"[5]).

In December 1970, a "work to rule" action by electrical workers had cast large areas of Britain into darkness, and filled the *Times*' letters page with the affronted call to arms noted by the historian E.P. Thompson: "May I, writing by candlelight, express my total support for the government".[6] More disputes followed, with Hugh Scanlon promoting, in June 1972, a composite bill at the TUC to bar affiliated unions from signing up to the emasculating measures of Heath's 1971 Industrial Relations Act. The strikes rotated from one unionised occupation to the next — coal miners, gas workers, civil servants, firemen — and a general sense of deadlock filled the air. These economic challenges were accompanied by other tensions on the domestic front. The template had been set in 1968, the year not just of Enoch Powell's "Rivers of Blood" speech but also of the less often remembered discriminatory law, introduced earlier by Labour Home Secretary James Callaghan, revoking the British passports held by Asians in Kenya. Enoch Powell was still finding widespread support in the early Seventies, not least during the rush of anxiety and aggression that followed Heath's decision to admit Asians being expelled from Uganda by Idi Amin in August 1972.

The international situation was also testing. Sterling came under immediate pressure after August 1971, when President Nixon, faced with the enormous costs of the Vietnam War, unilaterally freed the dollar from the gold standard. Meanwhile, the ongoing tensions of the Cold War were augmented by new forms of terrorism. In Italy, the Red Brigades emerged in a climate where "autonomist" and neo-fascist groups had been fighting it out on the streets. In West Germany, the "pudding bombers" had given way to Baader-Meinhof and the Red Army Faction, and a grouping of the Palestine Liberation Organisation had staged the Black September massacre at the Munich Olympics in 1972. Closer to home, we watched the unfolding "troubles" in Northern Ireland, where the sectarian division galvanised tit-for-tat pub bombings — with the IRA murdering three in Belfast's Red Lion Pub on 2 November 1971, and the Ulster Volunteer Force killing fifteen in McGurk's bar a month later. Tensions were increased at the end of July 1972 when, as part of "Operation Motorman", the British government used Centurion tanks to break into republican "no-go areas", thus producing self-defeating images of tracked vehicles being deployed against citizens in a manner that evoked Soviet behaviour in East Berlin or Hungary. We also followed the more distant antics of the Shah of Iran, a Western puppet who crowned himself King of Kings at a grotesquely extravagant party at Persepolis in 1971 and presided over the torturers of the "Savak" secret police force: one that, as we saw quite plainly at the University of Kent, felt no need to hide the watch it kept over left-leaning Iranian students at British universities.

By the close of 1973, Edward Heath was following Harold Wilson in running out of time — although not before his government had successfully implemented the measures thanks to which, as a *Daily Mail* historian recently announced, "Britain lost its soul".[7] In February 1971, it had presided over decimalisation of the national currency (it was hard at the time to see the end of the world in the passing of those heavy, pocket-shredding coins, some of which were, thanks to what was then called "galloping" inflation, worth more than their face value as scrap metal). It had begged and squeezed the stricken country into the European Common Market at the beginning of 1973. It had survived, more or less, the ongoing violence in Northern Ireland: with its paratroopers getting away with murder at the Ballymurphy Massacre of August 1971 and then again on "Bloody Sunday" in 1972. It had also endured through IRA bombings in England as well as in the six counties — Aldershot barracks in 1972, Euston Station in 1973 and, in 1974, worse outrages in which bombs were met with grievous miscarriages of justice: the M62 coach bombing, followed by the Guildford and Birmingham pub bombings.

On the economic front, meanwhile, every day confirmed that we were well past the end of the "long boom" of growth and prosperity (meagre as it had been in comparison with other countries) secured, since 1950 or so, by centralised planning, industrial policy and the tripartite "corporate" state. Few may have anticipated the enormous future consequences of the 1971 deregulation of the banking sector, but that wasn't the only financial story of the times. In June 1972, Heath's Chancellor of the Exchequer, Anthony Barber, had floated the pound only to watch it sink like a stone. He had printed money, thereby feeding inflation and the waves of industrial unrest that overwhelmed the government's attempt to maintain a firm incomes policy. Some may have sensed the coming of a new kind of "whizz kid" politician in Barber's failed manipulations.[8] Not for long, however. The oil crisis that began as an outcome of the Arab-Israeli war of October 1973 had strengthened the case for future offshore production in the North Sea, but a quadrupling of prices also proved overwhelming for the government. 1974, which has fairly been described as "the apocalyptic year of the British Seventies",[9] opened with a miner's strike, the imposition of a three-day week designed to conserve energy, and a general election that Edward Heath lost. In the following year, he would reluctantly yield leadership of the Conservative Party to his Secretary of Education and Science, Margaret Thatcher, a figure who had been widely reviled as "the milk-snatcher" after she withdrew free school milk from many British children. Nobody I knew at the time had recognised the "potential greatness" that the poet Douglas Oliver diagnosed from her televised contributions to the election campaign that brought Heath into 10 Downing Street in 1970.[10] However, the *Belfast Telegraph* was by no means alone in fearing for the future: "Food parcels, ration books and soup kitchens. Are these the basics we will all be getting back to as the swinging Sixties give way to the slump-bound Seventies in a bankrupt Britain?"[11]

*

The country really did seem to be tearing itself apart by the beginning of 1974, the year in which Germany's praised and excoriated searcher after "concrete utopias", Uwe Johnson, would choose Kent as the county of his English residence. I was by then a teacher at the Sir William Nottidge secondary modern school in Whitstable, on the coast seven miles to the north of Canterbury. Latterly, Whitstable has become notorious as a favourite habitat of prosperous media wraiths who come "Down from London", buy the best of the seaside properties and then get lonely and start commending their investment to others like themselves. ("The perfect place to escape", and "The coffee and cakes are delicious".[12]) There were precious few "DFLs" in the Whitstable of 1974 — although the actor Peter Cushing, well known from Hammer Horror's *Dracula* films, was an established resident, whilst the town was also rumoured to be favoured by south London villains associated with the Richardson and Kray gangs. As

I remember from parents' evenings in that sometimes unlit year when Harold Wilson followed Edward Heath in losing the alleged "Second Battle of Britain"[13] against inflation and trade union militancy, Whitstable was well-supplied with inhabitants who could be rugged in defence of their (and their children's) customary way of life. And that was by no means the limit of the town's cultural distinction.

At the end of the nineteenth century, the young Somerset Maugham had lived there, growing up orphaned and miserable in the care of an elderly uncle, the otherwise childless Vicar of Whitstable. Maugham later drew on his memories to create the "Blackstable" of his 1915 autobiographical novel *Of Human Bondage.* The Whitstable he knew was "a fishing village", with a small harbour that was also used by ships bringing coal from the north-east — a coincidence of industries that could lead to ferocious altercations on windy days. In the early Seventies much of Whitstable still conformed to Maugham's description. The streets could indeed still look "shabby". Some of the houses along the seafront were still occupied by "fishermen and poor people", a few of whom may even have frequented the non-conformist chapels on the High Street and, therefore, been "of no account" to the Church of England vicar.[14]

By 1974 Whitstable's writer of moment was surely Terry Harknett, who lived at the eastern edge of town. He was one of the so-called "Piccadilly cowboys", named after their habit of meeting up in central London pubs to drink and talk about the Western novels they confected by pulling motifs, landscapes and situations out of Spaghetti Westerns and lifting their weapons from catalogues and magazines of the *Guns 'n Ammo* variety. Writing under the pen name of George G. Gilman, Harknett came up with a hero named Edge, a Mexican-Swedish "halfbreed", with a limitless capacity for violence and a distinctive technique with a razor too. Both deplored and admired for their extreme violence, the "Edge" stories were distinguished by their brazen lack of moral compass, and by the fact that things just did not come right in the end. ("The only thing you have to be careful of is to get your guns right: if you get your guns wrong you get in terrible trouble", Harknett is reported to have said of the stories he turned out at such an incredible rate.[15])

"The Nottidge", meanwhile, was a troubled secondary modern school, named after an already forgotten former Chairman of Kent County Council, which had, as I have been surprised recently to discover, been opened in 1952 to much local enthusiasm (a memorial website recalls the first impressions of two witnesses: "As a kid, I marvelled at the sheer extent of Sir William Nottidge"[16]; "Going up there after being in the old Whitstable Endowed buildings was brilliant"[17]). Although I knew nothing of this when I began my stint as an uncertificated supply teacher (it was a case of interview one day, start work the next), "the Nottidge" had been conceived as another improving vision on a hilltop. Designed by an architect who had started his career in collaboration with the University of Kent's defeated master planner William Holford, it too had once been filled with the promise of a better world to come.

This time, the visionary architect was F.R.S. Yorke, a pioneer of English modernism whose first house had been made of reinforced concrete and designed with Holford for the 1934 "Modern Homes" exhibition at Gidea Park (the recent Pevsner guide to East London describes it, accurately, as "a rectilinear concrete box"[18]). In the early years of the Second World War, Yorke had once again worked alongside Holford, this time on larger projects — ordnance depots, factories, camps — connected to the munitions industry. In 1944 he teamed up with Czech and Finnish modernist friends to form the practice Yorke, Rosenberg & Mardall, which would, as Holford himself testified, grow into one of "the largest and most effective architectural practices in Britain".[19] During its first decade, YRM's output was, in the words of the influential critic Reyner Banham, so "characteristic of the Welfare State" that it might be expected to loom "far larger in histories of our time than architects who currently monopolise all the praise and blame that is going".[20] YRM was among the practices invited by the planner Sir Frederick Gibberd to design housing at new town Harlow in Essex. Yet much of the firm's bread and butter came from producing schools, in accordance with the selective system of free secondary education established by the Butler Education Act of 1944.

Like the yet-to-be imagined University of Kent, Whitstable's new school was built on open land above its town. The site, as the *Architectural Review*'s contemporary report testifies, was "high and very exposed but with extensive views in all directions". The school plan was consequently both "extended and open" in order to make the most of those views. At its centre stood a pair of two-storey teaching blocks, one with "normal classrooms", the other with more specialised rooms for science, domestic science,

Tank tower, Sir William Nottidge School, Whitstable.

woodwork, metalwork and needlework. The blocks were steel-framed structures, incorporating pre-cast concrete panels finished with white spar. And yet Yorke had specified more traditional materials too: London stock as well as local brick; areas of red cedar panelling on exterior elevations; and even some old-fashioned walls of rough-hewn local stone placed just inside the main entrance. The silhouette offered to the town of Whitstable was never going to rival that of an ancient Italian hilltop town, but the Nottidge was purposefully enhanced by a dramatically raised "tank tower": no match for the famous medieval bell towers of Siena or Urbino, but it did incorporate a concrete chimney as well as a water supply for the boiler house below.

Despite the sense of optimism that once inspired YRM's building, it's carefully chosen interior details — West African mahogany block floor tiles in the classrooms, brightly painted lockers in the corridors, Peggy Angus tiles in the dining area — lacked the power to sustain the school as an advertisement for the Conservative county of Kent's selective education policy. Some teachers worked hard on behalf of children with few second chances, but "the Nottidge" had its share of defeated figures too. One was on long-term sick leave and only present as part of the absence I had been employed to fill. Others sat in the staff room silently listening, or perhaps not, as a science teacher rehearsed his daily fantasy of placing some or other troublesome child under a bell jar and slowly suffocating the miscreant with the help of an oxygen tap. After a couple of terms of this, I left for the far side of the world. It was there, in Vancouver, that a new friend would introduce me to the first two volumes of Johnson's *Anniversaries* in the truncated translation published by the New York publisher Helen Wolff at Harcourt Brace Jovanovich in 1975. Remarkably, as I would discover shortly afterwards, this extraordinary writer, who had done so much to re-engage the novel with post-war realities, had by then chosen to quit West Berlin and to settle with his wife and daughter not just in Kent but on the offshore island I had looked out over from Whitstable's all-but-failing secondary modern school.

8. NEITHER ST HELENA NOR HONG KONG

No oracle, while the island lies at a distance.
— Douglas Oliver, "An Island That is All the World", 1990.

The Isle of Sheppey from an upstairs bedroom at 32 Bellevue Road, Whitstable.

The Nottidge has since been demolished and replaced, but there is a house not far along Bellevue Road that preserves the view around which Yorke, Rosenberg & Mardall organised their north-west facing classrooms. Unlike those in so many Victorian schools, the Nottidge's windows weren't mounted high in the walls to ensure that children who strayed from their lessons saw nothing but brick. Indeed, they were so revealing that it sometimes seemed as if there were no separation at all between the interior and the world outside. On clear days, your eye was encouraged to float out over the flat-roofed Portakabins in front of the already outgrown school, and then to drift down the slope occupied by allotments and the town cemetery, past Canterbury City Council's twelve-storey block of sheltered housing — Windsor House was then only five years old and not a disintegrating tower block of the kind that nowadays provides such arresting images of social dereliction in the songs of Wild Billy Childish and the Chatham Singers.[1] Beyond that lay the lower town and then the sea.

Looking north-east over a North Sea that had, as Uwe Johnson would soon be pointing out in letters to friends, been commonly known as "the German Ocean" before the antipathies of the First World War forced that name into retirement, an idling child or teacher might watch ships passing in and out of the wide Thames Estuary, or test the day's visibility

West-facing classrooms, Sir William Nottidge school.

by trying to distinguish the gun towers of the old Red Sands army fort, placed on stilts above a submerged sandbar seven miles offshore in order to intercept German bombers during the Second World War. To the west of this abandoned relic, the long view across the estuary towards Essex is interrupted by a thin tongue of land, which rises gently from flat salt marshes to culminate in a muddy headland marked by a white crater that, were it in Sussex or Dorset, might be an ancient chalk quarry rather than the caravan park — "Warden Springs" — that it will actually turn out to be.

The *Financial Times* recently announced that "the island is always a dream".[2] The fellow who made that statement lives by selling Mediterranean or Caribbean islands as "trophy assets" to oligarchs and other insufficiently taxed individuals. The point applied differently in north Kent forty-five years ago, when the island to which Johnson moved towards the end of

1974 had briefly become entangled with my own deliberations about leaving the country. On days that were clear as well as educationally challenging, the island outside the classroom window seemed not just to shimmer across the water, but to hint at the better future that surely awaited anyone prepared to put a stretch of water between themselves and their present situation in Britain. This alluring land had a proper name, of course, but, for all I knew about the removed place that beckoned from across a widening arm of the sea, the Isle of Sheppey only needed to be "Elsewhere" to cast its spell.

On the one occasion when I visited the island that year, I encountered little beyond my own sense of disorientation. I remember queueing while a ship passed through the raised Kingsferry Bridge separating Sheppey from the mainland, and then crawling in a line of lorries through an industrial wasteland that culminated in a beaten-looking town named Sheerness. I recall glimpsing the High Street in passing, and pausing at a weird pub named the Ship on Shore before driving on past sprawling bungalows and caravan and chalet parks, all of them waiting for the opening of a summer season that threatened to be as chimerical as the unattainable land I had imagined while looking across the Swale from the Nottidge's windows. That, more or less, is how Sheppey registered in my mind during the spring of 1974: an inviting prospect, to be sure, but also, as I had concluded by the time I looked back towards Whitstable from the desolate out-of-season resort named Leysdown-on-Sea, a perplexing oscillation in which paradise kept collapsing into the bleakest kind of slum. I may not have known it then, but I was by no means the first to see the island in this acutely polarised way.

*The Ship on Shore, Sheerness. Pub grotto made
from salvaged ship carrying barrels that turned out,
disappointingly, to be filled with Portland cement. Postcard
("Bad weather here"), September 1913.*

The view of Sheppey across the water from the seafront has
long formed one of Whitstable's best attractions — especially
when augmented by a lurid sunset. By the early Seventies, the
combination was a seasoned favourite on picture postcards:
the island as a low band of darkening purple stretched out just
to the west of the sinking sun. The same view is still enjoyed
by the drinkers who, now as then, tend to drift out of the
Old Neptune (aka "The Old Pub on the Beach") on summer
evenings to gaze out as the sun makes its final descent. In 2012
the much-pictured outlook would be commended in Brian
Barnett's unofficial town song, "Viva Whitstable", in which the
Girl from Ipanema joins the migrants seeking asylum in this
part of the world:

With a drink at the Neppy
She could see the Isle of Sheppey
And the sun falling in the sea.[3]

That choice of attraction will also be familiar to surviving admirers of the appropriately-named north Kentish "prog rock" band Caravan, whose members used to practice in a church hall at Graveney, a village on the marshes a few miles west along the Swale. These pioneers of the retrospectively named "Canterbury scene" invoked the Swale's sunsets when they named their most admired LP, *In the Land of Grey and Pink* — leaving the cover artist, Ann Marie Anderson, to replace Sheppey with a Tolkien-esque fantasy world that quickly became an emblem of Kent as "a stoned shire of winding cobblestone streets and patchouli-scented head shops where zonked out hippies on a diet of dope and mung beans created 18-minute song suites".[4] That faded vision is unlikely to have convinced those who understood Sheppey to be a prosaic, and predominantly working-class island where there is nothing weird about the clustered caravans — nearly all of the "static" rather than "touring" variety nowadays.

*

A small, low-lying and, over much of its extent, watery world of some thirty-six square miles, the Isle of Sheppey lies on the eastern shore of the river Medway, where it flows out into the wide, outer reaches of the Thames Estuary. On its western side, it emerges from the water, in a marshy and noncommittal kind of way, not far from a bone-strewn mudbank called "Dead Man's Island". To the south, once you get past the landfill site at Ladies Hole Point, the island is dominated by marshes and separated from the mainland by a tidal strait known as the Swale. The northern shore is formed by a ridge of London Clay, which rises towards the east of the island and reaches its highest point of some seventy-six metres above sea level at Minster, a village at the early Christian site where St Sexburga, the widow of a Kentish King, established a convent in 664 AD.

Such basic facts are true, and yet, like so many offshore islands, the "Isle of Sheep", as Sheppey's originally Saxon name "Sceapig" would have it, remains various and prismatic in its separation from the mainland. Not yet buried under solar panels, it may appear primarily as a natural habitat, thanks largely to the marshes along the Swale, now one of the primary wetland nature reserves in northern Europe. It may be seen as a bastion of British naval history, a status owed to the centuries during which Sheerness and Queenborough on the island's western shore served as outlying elements of the naval establishment based further up the Medway at Chatham. This view was espoused by the bicycling correspondent for the *London Daily News* in 1899. He advised Londoners undertaking a "circular" (and surely rather strenuous) Saturday excursion to the Isle of Sheppey to pause at a carefully identified vantage point before crossing the Swale to see "the Might of the Mailed Hand of England" moored off the island's Medway shore: "Gazing here, down upon these evidences of power, you feel that it is good to be an Englishman".[5] Those who prefer more ancient history must ignore the bungalows and caravan and chalet parks in order to glimpse the island of the complete Bronze Age foundry excavated at the remote settlement (once an island of its own) of Harty in 1879, or of the Danes who raided and overwintered here in the ninth century, ravaging the island, and allegedly firing St Sexburga's abbey as they went about it.

While some of Sheppey's antiquarians struggle to pull indisputable facts out of the swirling "mists of time", others have been quite at ease with legend. This is how Sheppey features, still appropriately coated in "the majesty of mud",[6] in *The Ingoldsby Legends*, a once highly popular collection of fables written by a Kentish vicar named Richard Barham and published pseudonymously from the 1830s onwards. The atmosphere of "fog and fantasy" has persisted to yield the recent claim, made by a Kentish archaeologist and enthusiastically welcomed by some on Sheppey, that Beowulf, the warrior hero of that Anglo-Saxon epic, landed here rather than in Scandinavia, as knowledgeable medievalists continue strongly to insist.[7] The mural adorning the wall outside Brian's Euronics, a white goods store overlooking Beachfields Park in Sheerness, invites us to imagine this Old English hero striding up past the amusement arcades of Leysdown-on-Sea to fight it out with the monstrous Grendel somewhere in the neighbourhood of the ancient marshland church of St Thomas the Apostle at Harty. On Sheppey, as elsewhere in Britain, legend can couple with living memory to bring time itself to a halt. That is how the island lingers in the memories of many who holidayed here in the Fifties and Sixties. Perhaps the same glamour of backwardness touched the island on which the singer Billy Bragg found himself playing alongside a band named the Chords during the brief "Mod Revival" of 1979/80: on Sheppey, he suggests, that particular "revival" may not have been strictly necessary, since the inhabitants appeared never to have given up on their parkas and scooters in the first place.[8]

Meanwhile, it was by no means only in my own initial perceptions that the island has alternated between paradise and a slum. Some have indeed looked across the water and seen a sea-washed island utopia. That is how it appeared both to the Rev. Turmine, author of the early Victorian guidebook in which "Sheppy" is identified with the enchanted "Fary Land" of the Elizabethan poet Edmund Spenser's epic *The Faerie Queen*,[9] and to Sir Charles Igglesden, the "sauntering" editor and proprietor of the *Kentish Express* who, nearly a century later, in 1937, hailed the place as "The Island Jewel of Kent".[10] Sheppey was also touched with serendipity for Father Paul Hennessy who, in 1983, took up his ministry at the Roman Catholic church of St Henry & St Elizabeth on Broadway in Sheerness. Father Hennessy sensed the world-to-come in the realisation that, many years earlier, he had walked along the beach at Seasalter, just west of Whitstable, looking out at the "magnificent" view of Sheppey and thinking, "now there is a place I have never visited".[11] Eight years later, Iain Sinclair allowed a different redemptive possibility to glimmer through the closing chapter of his novel *Downriver*. At an unexpected moment of remission owed partly to the island vision of the expatriated Anglo-Scottish poet Douglas Oliver ("Redrawing the map, I take out harm, restart in the centre"[12]), Sinclair's character Joblard, who has come here from Whitechapel to seek out traces of his unknown mother, suspends his jabbering chronicle of deformity and dereliction and allows Sheppey to emerge in a transfigured, almost prayerful light: "This is an island that is *not* the world. It is removed, discrete; one of those transitory border zones, caught in uncertain weather, nudged, dislocated by a lurch in the intensity of the light. A special place where, I'd like to believe, 'good persists in time'."[3]

The mainland knockers and snobs, meanwhile, are careful to see only the slum. Over the decades, the denigration of Sheppey as the "septic Isle"[14] has been read all the way back into the island's geology, which consists of slimy mud, gravel and clay rather than load-bearing, nationally prestigious, upper-class rocks such as limestone, granite and even chalk. The two world wars may have encouraged the view that Sheppey should be honoured as a beacon of British liberty, but it has by no means always been displayed as a trophy in the procession of national history. No British patriot has found a great deal to say about the island's performance during the second Anglo-Dutch War of 1667, when Sheppey was conquered by Dutch invaders (assisted by English Republican deserters), who had the uncontested run of the island for a week or so before leaving in their own time having loaded up on the livestock. In 1815, and for a brief moment before the more genuinely remote island of St Helena was chosen, Sheppey was judged sufficiently miserable for the fort at Sheerness to be rumoured as the possible place of Napoleon's confinement after his defeat at Waterloo.[15] It was in a similar spirit of denigration that the island appeared in the Irish press when Hong Kong was ceded to the British Crown at the end of the First Opium War against China in 1841. The *Sligo Journal,* a paper that was fierce in its belief that the only "diplomacy" understood by the Celestial Empire and its Imperial Commissioner Qishan was the British bayonet, judged the settlement ludicrously inadequate. Hong

Kong may have possessed a "very good harbour" but it was "nearly out in the ocean" and hardly represented an adequate concession for the victorious British Empire.[16] It was, so this contemptuous scribe concluded, "scarcely so large as the Isle of Sheppy".

This long history of slighting condescension, in which the sea becomes an isolating rampart rather than the "great common" Herman Melville had imagined it might one day become,[17] continues to weigh on the island and its population. Sheppey is still the butt of stupid jokes in mainland pantomimes as well as at Remainer dinner parties. As Mayor of London, Boris Johnson saw only improvement in the thought of floating a new international airport just offshore. Mouthy celebrities find the island an easy target too. A few years ago Jeremy Clarkson used his column in *Top Gear* magazine to sneer that the Isle of Sheppey was "mostly... a caravan site" where there are "thousands and thousands of mobile homes, all of which I suspect belong to former London cabbies".[18] As for the inhabitants, they tend, so Clarkson went on, "to be the sort of people who arrived in England in the back of a refrigerated truck or clinging to the underside of a Eurostar train".

Some of the nastiest mainland jokes dwell less on the chalets and caravans than on the reproductive choices of the island's supposedly indigenous population, people whose alleged inbreeding is assumed to have thrown human evolution into reverse. Sociological surveys of mobility may suggest otherwise, but mainland prejudice against this island of working-class liberties is reluctant to surrender its view of Sheppey as the (un)natural home of a two-fingered English aborigine known as the "Swampy": an inbred mutant who nowadays lurks in the metropolitan imagination as the Brexiteering native of a hostile estuarial country that European cartographers might, if they heed the reports of returning migrant workers, soon be mapping as "Fuck-off England" ("Sheerness", as was indeed announced by one street scrawler in the approach to the Brexit referendum, "is not the capital of Poland").

The islanders, who are well aware of the stigma that has for so long been attached to them, can be understandably quick to detect a slight. Here, as elsewhere on the Thames Estuary, however, they have also developed creative ways of defusing and redirecting the insults reflecting a wider metropolitan abandonment of the English working class. Ray Pahl, a sociologist at the University of Kent who did much to counter these false allegations, noticed that islanders were inclined to "adopt a mocking, self-deprecating tone often hiding a fierce pride".[19] This was the pre-emptive spirit in which he was told several times, sometimes with the help of a rough drawing of the Thames Estuary, that "Sheppey was a piece of shit in the arse 'ole of England". I remembered that in January 2015, when the words "Welcome to Hell!" were sprayed in large letters on a concrete pier supporting the bridge leading across the Swale to Father Paul Hennessy's Heavenly Island. "Turn back now", said the words on the subsequent pier. Perhaps somebody wasn't wanted.

*

And Uwe Johnson? It is safe to assume that this particular European migrant knew nothing about Sheppey or its conflicted status in the Kentish imagination when he decided to ignore the warnings of his English friends and move there with his wife and daughter towards the end of 1974. The Belgian writer Pierre Mertens invites his readers to imagine Johnson as a "German Crusoe" who, having tired of the political and ideological battles of his time, finally chose to shipwreck himself on an island that was all the better for being "without historic references".[20] He would live there, Mertens suggests, as a "double dissident", who had rejected both sides of the Cold War schism, and now "finds his destiny where it nailed him, outside the history of a people, a state, an era. Does contemporary literature count many 'incarnations' of this kind?"

In reply to that question, we must surely wonder whether contemporary literature actually counts even one such example. Johnson had indeed decided to remove himself from the literary scene in West Berlin, but there was never any possibility of him finding a place — whether a desert island or a "moral Switzerland" of the unattainable sort for which his character Gesine Cresspahl sometimes yearns — outside the history he carried with him. In this respect, Johnson, who had already demonstrated himself a penetrating investigator of historical environments in Germany and America, was well prepared for a populated English island that was full not just of "historical references" but also of physical resemblances to the landscapes of his past. In a famous passage of his book about Africa, *The Shadow of the Sun,* the Polish writer Ryszard Kapuściński remarked that "Our world, seemingly global, is in reality a planet of thousands of the most varied and never intersecting provinces. A trip around the world is a journey from backwater to backwater, each of which considers itself, in its isolation, a shining star".[21] Johnson too had an eye for struggling and apparently abandoned "backwaters". Writing before globalisation had done so much to reduce the grounded experience of place to a mocking consolation prize for left-behind losers all over the world, he was also interested in the historical currents, both personal and wider, that could bring far-flung "backwaters" together.

When Johnson first saw Sheppey from the air (in the summer of 1978), he registered it not as an island but as "a spit of land between the Medway and the Thames".[22] "Spit" (*die Spitze*) is a suggestive word, given the importance of topographical memory in Johnson's imagination, and it aligns Sheppey with a series of other "spits"

Baltic Resort, Dievenow, postcard, mailed 1940.

Inner German frontier on Priwall spit, from the west, 1960.

that he remembered: from Dievenow on the Pomeranian Baltic, where he had watched haymaking in watery meadows as a four-year-old staying with his maternal grandparents in 1934, to Fischland further west along the Baltic, and on to Staten Island and several other examples he had registered on the east coast of the United States. Forty years later, we can allow his chosen word to hint at the sense of estranged familiarity he encountered on the Isle of Sheppey: no homecoming, to be sure, but a fleeting sense of recognition that would only be available to one whose sense of place and landscape was neither entirely desolate nor locked, Brexit-like, into a singular idea of national identity. The word "spit" also suggests an appropriate landing point on the island. Not Heathrow followed by a taxi driven by his friend Frank, as it may actually have been for Johnson when he flew back to England on that day in 1978, and not yet the capital town of Sheerness, at the island's north-western point, where he had chosen to live across the road from the beach. We will opt instead for the often truly deserted spit at the island's south-eastern corner and then make our way north, picking up English echoes of the history explored in *Anniversaries* as we proceed around the coast to the house in which the Johnsons were living by the close of 1974. I have placed three warning notices at our starting point in memory of the forbidding signs that once marked approaches to the inner German border.

9. SHELLNESS: A POINT WITH THREE WARNINGS

The Isle of Sheppey, looking north from Shellness Point.

For a closer sense of the island on which our alleged "German Crusoe" chose to beach himself together with his storm-tossed wife and daughter, we must force a descent on the eye that glides so easily across the shining surface of the Swale from Whitstable. We can thicken those superficially tranquil waters by remembering not just the native oysters once harvested in such abundance from the seabed here, but the four coastguards who set off from Whitstable beach shortly after 4pm on Wednesday, 11 December 1844.[1] They had been despatched in "the four-oared gig on duty" to watch over the "various craft that might be rounding Shellness Point", and then to land at the coastguard station at Shellness, where they were expected both to communicate with the chief officer and to deliver their passenger, the thirty-three-year-old Mr Henry Pym, who had recently "retired" to Bridge, near Canterbury, having run an "extensive" farm near Leysdown — a little further north along the coast of what remains, so we are assured by a plain-speaking fish-and-chip operator of our time, definitely "the back end of the island".[2]

It was a routine trip and the coastguards were experienced sailors — all of them, as the coroner's inquest would affirm, "steady and careful men" and "sober" too. They understood exactly what the North Sea tides could do to the waters of the eastern Swale but they still failed to reach their destination. Five bodies were eventually found on or in the vicinity of the Pollard Sands, as was their boat, "lying on her larboard side" nearby. Various witnesses spoke at the inquest, including Charles Foreman, a dredger from Whitstable who, at the time of the accident, had been out wildfowling in a punt near the Pollard oyster grounds: he had seen the coastguards' gig travelling fast towards Shellness and assumed the men must have lowered their sails after passing out of his view. Since there were no other vessels to cause a collision, it was concluded that the boat had been capsized by "a heavy swell of the sea; which often takes place by the meeting of the two tides near the place where the bodies were found". The inspecting officer for the district, Captain Blair R.N., confirmed that "at times the crossing was a difficult one", arising from what was termed by the seafaring men of Whitstable a "hollow" or "counter sea" occasioned by the general tide, and by the water flowing through the "East Swale". Reassured that there had been nothing about the weather that might imply culpability on anyone's part, the Coroner returned a verdict of accidental death.

You would search in vain along the gravel beach at Shellness for a memorial to the "melancholy catastrophe" caused by the unusually deep troughs of that "hollow" sea. No one, however, could miss the derelict two-chambered concrete pillbox surviving as the southernmost structure on this flat and desolate point, a relic of twentieth-century warfare that must have accommodated a few raving Lears before the day in 2016, when Robbie Williams came to this deserted place to film the video for his single "Love My Life". Not a palm tree in sight, but that has not discouraged the fifty million YouTubers who have so far watched the singer sauntering about, while a cluster of young women wheel around him, their cameras and clothes as black as the trails of smoke with which steamers carrying excursionists back and forth between London, Herne Bay and Margate once filled the air over the waters here.[3] Forty years before that brief manifestation, Uwe Johnson's copy of the island's weekly newspaper invited a different authority to explain why the southern end of this sand and shingle spit was being added to the Swale nature reserve. An obliging spokesman from the Nature Conservancy Council explained that Shellness was "an excellent example of a hooked peninsula resulting from longshore drift accumulation".[4]

I. In the Pink Again: A Bird for Mr Johnson

Above Riverside Park, a brightly colored bird gave off a swishing swinging sound. Then it lifted its tail and hung in the wind over the Hudson and cried arr-arr. It was not an ABC TV copter, sir, it was your escaped electric razor, whose motor has had just about enough of its casing.
— Anniversaries I, p. 207.

On less hectic days, Shellness Point settles back into its existence as part of a grazing salt marsh managed with the interest of wild birds in mind. The wildfowlers who may, for all I know, sometimes still be allowed onto the marshes, pay more attention to the grazing geese than the waders — dunlin, knot, sanderling — that can be seen creeping along the exposed mud banks as they follow the tide up towards the shelly beach. The bird watchers also understand that the marsh harriers, curlew and redshank have been beneficiaries of EU subsidies paid to the marshland farmers who take care of their breeding grounds along the Swale. They may also get more excited by the oddities that sometimes turn up on the wind: a cluster of eight twite, perhaps, a shore lark or a Richard's pipit, or the pomarine skua seen coasting past Shellness Point that same year.

While Sheppey has always owed a lot to erratic visitors, washed up or blown in, it's characteristic "spirit of place" has also been shaped by the human interventions that can make such an implausible thing of nature in this repeatedly used and abandoned part of the world. There may be nothing here to match the helicopter-bird that Johnson imagined from Gesine Cresspahl's high apartment on New York's Riverside Drive, having crossed the grinding of an electric razor with reports from the Vietnam War drifting through the wall from a neighbour's TV set and possibly a hangover too. Yet there was one spectacularly unusual fowl that sought refuge on the Sheppey marshes towards the end of July 1873, a specimen that surely offers a fitting avian emblem for Uwe Johnson's adopted island.

Some Islanders must have wondered about the brilliant creature that briefly found refuge on the Isle of Sheppey's wilder marshes. Its plumage was said to be "perfectly white, excepting the wings, which are tinted with a beautiful rose colour".[5] What was this unusual incomer? Where did it come from? And how would it fare in its unlikely new habitat? The answer to the last of those questions was quickly provided by a labourer named Heathfield. On Saturday, 2 August 1873, this otherwise obscure fellow made his way across the Swale from his home at Murston, then just outside Sittingbourne on the mainland, tracked the marvelous firebird down to an inlet named Sharfleet Creek on Sheppey's Elmley marshes, and shot it.

News of Heathfield's Swaleside bag was sent to the *Field* by another local man, Mr Arthur John Jackson, who wrote from Sittingbourne to claim the "Flamingo in the Isle of Sheppey" as a first for the country.[6] Sheppey's rare bird was female and "full-winged" and measured four feet six inches in height.

Identified as a specimen of the type *Phoenicopterus ruber*, the dead flamingo had since been placed in the hands of a "naturalist" of Sittingbourne, for the "purpose of being stuffed and mounted". The *Field*, which plainly had its suspicions from the start, added an editorial note reassuring readers that another correspondent had confirmed that "the bird in question showed no traces of confinement". It also corrected an egregious error in the report, suggesting that "if the bird really is a flamingo, as it would appear to be from the description, we should imagine that it would prove to be the European species (*P. antiquorum*) and not the American species (*P. ruber*) as stated by Mr Jackson". It was left to the Kentish papers to record that the enigmatic vagrant, which was by then being eviscerated and stuffed by Mr George Young, of 17 High Street, East Sittingbourne, had also changed hands in another sense: it was "now the property of Mr T.L. Dene of Hollybank"[7] near Tonbridge.

The grazing marshes on which the bird claimed as England's first flamingo was shot for pennies may, for the while, remain much as they were. The bird itself, however, was not at all what it seemed. Within a few days, the *Field* published an addendum to the story in which the editor of its "Poultry and Pigeon Department",[8] Mr William Bernhardt Tegetmeier, insisted that "the immediate destruction of any scarce bird that puts in an appearance in this country is lamented by all true naturalists".[9] Were this not so, he suggested, "the Hoopoe, the Stork, the Golden Oriole, the Bustard, and other rare birds might be as common here as they are in the adjacent parts of the Continent". Unfortunately though, no sooner had such a bird decided to take its chances in England than "some wretched pot-hunter

Phoenicopterus antiquorum.

destroys it." The "sapient editor" of the local paper would then dignify this gun-happy wretch with the title "naturalist", even though he was, perhaps, only "some village skin-stuffer, who would destroy the last remaining pair of a species if he thought he could sell the skin for a sovereign".

Shellness from the west.

As for the unfortunate bird that tried its luck on the salt marshes here, Mr Tegetmeier had an authoritative witness to justify his caustic assertion that "the history of the flamingo shot in the Isle of Sheppey strongly illustrates the intense love of natural history which is characteristic of the British boor". He had recently received a letter from Mr Abraham Dee Bartlett, the revered superintendent of the Zoological Gardens at Regent's Park in London, who had described how, "on the 19th of July last we lost a fine, healthy, and perfect flamingo (*Phoenicopterus antiquorum*). The wing of the bird not having been cut since its moult was the cause of its loss, for it rose on the wing like a wild bird, and went away at once. I see by the last *Field* that a bird of this species had been shot at Elmley, Isle of Sheppey, on the 2nd of August. I have no doubt whatever that the bird mentioned was the same individual that made its escape from these gardens". Tegetmeier finished by aiming his own volley at the so-called "naturalists" of north Kent: "to have captured this bird alive and returned it to its owners would have evinced some skill and tact: any fool could have shot it". One hundred and fifty years later, it would be a small thing for the Sheerness Golf Club (founded 1887) to restore the island's forgotten firebird to its proper place alongside the sheep and rising fish (or are they porpoises?) that already frolic on its crest.

II. An Island Word for Mr Johnson

As readers of *Anniversaries* soon discover, Johnson respected the regional dialects of the German Baltic: including a West Slavic variation of Polish known as "Kashubian" and the Low German "Platt" favoured by the Mecklenburger and socialist carpenter Heinrich Cresspahl — as in "my father didn't talk about bombs, he talked in Platt about 'dropping shit'".[10] His employment of regional idioms — grounded words which are never, in Seamus Heaney's phrase, simply "escapees from the lexicon"[11] — has been counted among the many reasons why *Anniversaries* is so hard to translate into English or, for that matter, any other foreign language. Sheppey had unconventional offerings for its author in this regard too. We might begin with a dialect word that quickly shows the divergence between poetic and prosaic perceptions of the island. The *Oxford English Dictionary* traces the word "cotterell" to the much expanded and posthumously published 1748 edition of Daniel Defoe's *A Tour through the Whole Island of Great Britain*. Here it is stated that "at Sheppey Isle", there "are several Tumuli in the marshy parts all over the island, some of which the inhabitants call Coterels: these are supposed to have been cast up in memory of some of the Danish leaders who were buried here; for the Danes have often made this Island the scene of their ravages and plunder"[12] This story has been augmented in other accounts of Sheppey's mounds, not least those alleging that these inconsistently spelled hillocks actually mark the corpses of people murdered by English patriots during the St Brice's Day massacre of 13 November 1002, when Aethelred the Unready ordered the slaughter of all Danes living in England, later justifying his decision with the help of an organic metaphor that may leave him qualified to serve nowadays as an early ancestor of encroachment-hating Brexiteers: these illegal immigrants had, in the phrase attributed to Aethelred, been "sprouting like cockle amongst the wheat". Yet the *Oxford English Dictionary* also contains an entry that deflates such fanciful conjecture and brings Sheppey's enigmatic mounds back to earth. It cites a *Dictionary of Kentish Dialect and Provincialisms* of 1887, alleging that a "coterell" is neither more nor less than an eminently practical structure: "a little raised mound in the marshes to which the shepherds and their flocks can retire when the salterns are submerged by the tide".

Moving inland from the salt marshes along the Swale, the clay soil of the arable land around the Sheppey prison cluster, near the village of Eastchurch, was described as "stone-shattery and friable"[13] in an early Victorian survey of Kentish agriculture. This, however, is not the language with which those gently sloping fields, a couple of miles inland from Shellness, confront the sensibilities of the "new nature writing" pursued by present-day English followers of the American geographer John R. Stilgoe. In his founding text, *Shallow-Water Dictionary: A Grounding in Estuary English*,[14] Stilgoe rows a bilge-bottom boat through the vast, empty and, given rising sea levels, doomed salt marshes of Massachusetts, having already burrowed through old dictionaries and forgotten nineteenth-century memoirs to recover the "quiet, almost mute vocabulary" of this watery terrain's historical existence. He identifies words such as "creek", "gutter", "flotsam", "wrack", "skiff" (here traced back to the German "*Schiff*") and also "guzzle", the latter meaning a low dip in a dune or bank over which the high tide pours, and identified as an import from the "Kentish marshland dialect" of immigrants who reached this part of America in 1633. Given the appropriate light and a little mist, people in the salt-marshes along the Swale may still "loom" indistinctly as their seventeenth-century forebears had sailed off to do in Stilgoe's Massachusetts, and there may still be colours in the marshes at Elmley that are largely lost to the contemporary eye — although it is not impossible that one of the English revivers of traditional paint, Rose of Jericho or Farrow & Ball, may one day rediscover shades such as "manila" and "chartreuse", both of which, as Stilgoe tells us, were evicted from Kodachrome's spectrum during the post-war years when that since crashed company concentrated on the commercially more attractive colours of skin, sand, sky and sea. There is, however, nothing elegiac, subtly nuanced, nor, unfortunately, moribund about the "landmark" word that is said, once again by the *Oxford English Dictionary*, first to have been recorded in the fields around Eastchurch.

Towards the end of August 1837, the *Times* reported a "desperate affray" that had broken out one recent Saturday night in this inland village, when "resident labourers" came to blows with "strangers who have come onto the island for harvesting".[15] The summer "influx" had been larger than usual that year and it was said to have consisted chiefly of "gems from the Emerald Isle", who tended to live in tents by the roadside or under hedges.[16] This year's migrant harvesters had included several "pugilists" who, having finished their work on the evening in question, walked around the meadows "tossing up their hats, as is the custom with such people" and challenging the best men in the village to fight. When nobody reacted to this provocative invitation, the Irish itinerants were said to have gone into the village and "molested several labourers in order to provoke a fight". The villagers may have been shy of single combat, but forty or fifty of them later combined and, at about midnight, "went about the roads and fields demolishing the tents of these men, and wreaking their vengeance on men, women, or children that might come under them". It was a small incident in a normally overlooked location, but it would bring the Isle of Sheppey a place in history all the same. The *Times* followed the *Kent Herald* in calling the Irish strangers "'pikey-men', as they are termed", and the compilers of the *Oxford English Dictionary* would later register this as the first recorded use of the word "pikey" in the English language.

Sheppey's claim to originality may be doubted, not least because only slightly later usages employ "pikey" not to describe vagrant types who might hang around at turnpikes, but as a name for the gatekeeper, whose job was to collect money from travellers as they passed through.[17] We may also regret that the word first netted in the fields and hedgerows of Sheppey is by no means a "lost word" of the kind that the nature writer Robert MacFarlane has recently recovered in his popular series of "Spells".[18] On Sheppey, as elsewhere, "pikey" has survived into the present day unaided, still sufficiently vigorous in its insulting application to "travellers", to appear in the adolescent tweets that, in April 1991, cost a sixteen-year-old resident of Sheerness her job with the unforgiving Kent police as the county's newly appointed "Youth Police and Crime Tsar".[19]

III. An English Priest for an East German Atheist

- *Brüshaver without his biretta was a sight you did not want to see. The remains of a wound were still visible on his temple — a reddish indentation the size of a walnut.*
- *What was the Old Lutheran Church?*
- *Idiosyncracies about justification, atonement, the trinity. If you ask me, a dispute about the right of association.*
  — Anniversaries IV, p. 1,402.

"On the streets, the Salvation Army has emerged from its lairs: trumpets and handbells".[20] For Johnson, that was part of the "visual assault" called Christmas in Manhattan, but what sort of salvation did the Church of England offer to anyone — believer or not, washed up incomer or proud resident — at the sparsely populated "East End" of the Isle of Sheppey in the Seventies? How much, if at all, had things improved since the late 1880s, when, as Somerset Maugham remembered, the vicars of the isolated parishes on the marshes near Whitstable were a pitiful bunch of abandoned and twisted souls. "Every kink in their characters had free play",[21] so Maugham said of the drunkards, tyrannical wife-beaters and indebted incompetents who would sometimes cross the lawn at his uncle's vicarage. Johnson would find good reason to suspect the same of the vicar in charge of souls at Leysdown, a mile or so further north along the coast from Shellness, although we have to understand a rare word of ecclesiastical jargon to comprehend why. "Ultramontane" means "beyond the mountains", and there are none of those on the Isle of Sheppey. In church history, however, we are talking about the Alps and the separation between the papal authority of Catholic Rome and the Protestant north. That is how things were for Father Peter Blagdon-Gamlen, the "ultramontane" Anglo-Catholic ritualist who, since 1968, had been rector of Leysdown and Harty, as well as of his principal church of All Saints in the inland village of Eastchurch.

Among those of High Church persuasion, Blagdon-Gamlen is remembered for his *Church Traveller's Directory* (revised edition, 1973), an inventory of the ever-shrinking number of Anglican churches offering full or partial Catholic Privileges, which is said to have been embraced as a spiritual companion to the *Good Food Guide* by some of its more sybaritic admirers.[22] He was also a man with a record of controversy that extended far beyond his insistence on using incense, processing the Sacraments around the streets, performing Marian devotions and sticking to the officially redundant English Missal. Father Blagdon-Gamlen had opened his battle for "the Catholic Faith" as the "birthright of every Englishman" when still a lay member of the Anglo-Catholic Party during the Second World War.[23] In 1954, when leaving for Yorkshire at the end of a two-year stint as an assistant priest in Evesham, he had urged the grateful friends of All Saint's Church to "continue the fight for Catholic privileges".[24] By 1957, as vicar of St Bartholomew's in Derby, he was taking the message out into pubs and factories while also using the regional press to pour vitriol on the "cranks" who wished to see criminals treated by psychologists, and leading a campaign to use "block votes" in every constituency, thereby forcing MPs to yield to the demand for the sterilisation of sex offenders and the "rigorous imposition of the death penalty on murderers".[25] In 1959, he recommended that the Church of England should "consider encouraging football pools as a way of raising money for church funds". He was already doing this in Derby and he urged the church to consider "moving with the times" on a larger scale and thereby to "put those enormous football pool promoters out of business".[26] In January 1961, while still at Derby, he had protested publicly after being refused a curate (the Bishop denied making a "whipping boy" of Blagdon-Gamlen and justified his decision by pointing out that this uncompliant vicar was using "certain services", including the Benediction, that were not in the Book of Common Prayer).[27] A few months later, Blagdon-Gamlen had called for the formation of a trade union for vicars. Hoping this body would campaign for a living wage and also a pension for widows, he explained, perhaps unnecessarily, that "The bishops would not be in the union, for they are more like the employers".[28]

Blagdon-Gamlen's war against liberal progressivism was not confined to skirmishing with bishops who espoused the rising secular creed of management and perhaps even took the Bishop of Woolwich's doubting book *Honest to God* seriously. In 1962, *People* condemned this outspoken vicar of Derby for allowing an article he'd written for his parish magazine to be reprinted in *Combat,* the magazine of the British National

Party.[29] The views expressed in the offending article were proudly racist: "When I pass through the Dairyhouse Road and Arboretum areas, and see these folk lounging about, often on National Assistance, and knowing that decent English people cannot get jobs, it makes my blood boil." He would repeat his views on immigration, and also his judgement of liberal-minded bishops, after Enoch Powell's "Rivers of Blood" speech of 20 April 1968. By this time, he was the vicar of Harrold, near Bedford, and using the pages of the *Acton Gazette* to support Father Wills of St Thomas' in Acton, who had backed Powell in his parish magazine.

Blagdon-Gamlen cheered him on, declaring that "the idea of a multi-racial society was 'nonsense'", insisting that "it is generally admitted that about 97 per cent of English people support Mr Enoch Powell including a large number of churchmen, both laity and clerics".[30] Unfortunately, "a few anti-British and anti-white agitators who happen to be bishops and canons of cathedrals have been loud in their integration pleas, but many of us priests feel that the pulpit — as well as the sports field — is not the place for politics … Surely the lowest depth has been reached when St Paul's Cathedral, St Martin's in the Fields, and Coventry Cathedral can be used for memorial services for a neo-Communist political agitator and commemorative stamps issued".[31] The suddenly deceased "agitator" in question had indeed been likened to John Bunyan's Mr Valiant for Truth by the Dean of St Paul's at a memorial service on 10 April, and hailed as "the most authentic black Moses of our day" by an African-American Baptist, the Rev. David Rice, at a parallel service in Glasgow Cathedral.[32] The South African provost of Coventry Cathedral, Dr H.C.N. Williams, had only joined the hymn of praise a couple of weeks later: hedging his address with repeated and vigorous condemnations of the "parrot cries" of British protestors against the Vietnam War and nuclear submarines, but admitting that the non-violent Dr Martin Luther King was "by any measurement … a 'prophet'".[33]

Father Blagdon-Gamlen, who may still be remembered

in Eastchurch for the green pom-pom he used to wear on his biretta and for employing the full arsenal of "bells and smells" even when hardly anyone turned up for the service, certainly hadn't used his rustication as an opportunity to adjust his views about liberal bishops or the immigrants they were sometimes inclined to defend. Indeed, by the time Johnson moved to Sheerness, the vicar of Eastchurch and Leysdown had found a new evil to add to his lurid host of modern encroachments on the English way of life. In July 1975, he would make an appearance in Uwe Johnson's copy of the *Sheerness Times Guardian,* justifying his decision to make the National Front's *Nationalist News* available to the church-goers of Eastchurch on the grounds that he agreed with "the anti-Common Market views expressed".[34] In case anyone missed his point, it was reiterated by a letter writer who praised the National Front for its policy of "putting Britain first" — its slogan during the 1975 referendum campaign had actually been "Make Britain Great Again" — and declared that "the putting of the foreigner and his outlandish ways first has brought this once-respected country to the verge of bankruptcy and perdition".[35]

In 1973/4, Max Frisch noted in his journal that "It is not only God who sits in the local details but also fascism".[36] Johnson, too, knew what to make of this sort of talk. In the second volume of *Anniversaries,* he had registered the murder of Martin Luther King as it inflamed white minds in New York City:

- There's going to be white blood on our streets tonight.
- We're trapped here like in a cage.
- The Negroes will be able to block all the trains by tonight.
- No whites'll get out of this city alive.
- ...
- Well maybe they are overdoing it a bit.
- Flags at half-mast! It's not like he was Kennedy.
- The blacks need to be smoked out, block by block!
- Maybe it was one of them that did it themselves.[37]

The National Front's anti-Common Market slogan — "Make Britain Great Again" — may since have been admitted to America under Reagan in 1980 and then again under Donald Trump, but Eastchurch continues to be a place of outspoken views in our time too. In April 2019, there was outrage on Swale Borough Council, thanks to the discovery of a Facebook post by a UKIP councillor for Sheppey East named Padmini Nissanga. A self-styled English "patriot" of Sri Lankan origin, this former care home owner had denounced Remainers as "traitors" who must "face the death penalty" in the Saudi-Arabian style. She had also insisted that, thanks to arch-traitors such as Tony Blair and Michael Heseltine, "hundreds of children were abused by Muslims every single day".[38] The answer, as Cllr. Nissanga had earlier decreed, was to hang Remainers and finish off their voters with "huge machetes".

10. COINCIDENCE ON ENGLAND'S BALTIC SHORE

Had he really been shipwrecked at Shellness Point, Johnson would have found himself on a flat, bare and flood-prone shore that remains littered with the debris of a twentieth century that repeatedly broke over the island and then melted away, leaving its residues scattered through the encompassing emptiness. To walk north along this scarcely elevated spit is to feel the truth of an observation that the Polish photographer Pawel Starzec has recently made in connection with "repurposed" sites of atrocity in Bosnia and Herzegovina. "A point on the map stands still," he writes, "but the context moves".[1]

Uwe Johnson knew how that had worked in Germany. As he evokes the remembered geography of the

"We have fine weather", postcard of Fischland, mailed by "Grete", 31 June 1955.

GDR's Baltic coast, he insistently recovers the presences of the Nazi era — prisons, slave-labour barracks and armament factories, concentration camps — that may have been removed, converted to new uses, or forgotten, more or less systematically, since 1945. He of all twentieth-century novelists knew that, besides being "a point on the map", every truly historical landscape is also a slipping catch in remembered time. And that would prove as true on the Isle of Sheppey as on the different sandy "spit" he had known and loved during his years in East Germany. Situated at the traditional border between Mecklenburg and Pomerania, Fischland stretches out under similarly vast skies between the Baltic and a shallow inland lagoon named Saaler Bodden. Johnson had spent the summer of 1956 here with his wife to be, Elisabeth Schmidt, working on the manuscript of his long unpublished first novel, *Ingrid Babendererde*, and, as some witnesses are said to have recalled, swimming alarmingly far out to sea, much further than anyone else in that young company dared to go.[2] It was in pages written on Sheppey that he would have Gesine Cresspahl remember Fischland as "the most beautiful place in the world".[3]

Just to the north of the blockhouse at Shellness Point stands a terrace of cottages, still recognisable as part of the coastguard station to which those drowned coastguards from Whitstable were sailing. As late as 1934, a "sauntering" Kentish topographer could convince himself, if not all his readers, that Shellness was "once an uninhabited spit of land save for the hut of a fisherman who also acted as watchman when foreigners poached the oyster beds".[4] In 1827, when Trinity House installed permanent buoys in the East Swale, the "Southernmost dwelling-house at Shellness Point" was still known as "Bell's House".[5] By that time, however, this remote spot was destined for service as the "watch house" of the armed "Coastal Blockade Service" set up after the end of the Napoleonic Wars by a government determined to put an end to smuggling along the English coast from Shellness Point all the way around to Beachy Head in Sussex. The coastguard station that stood here through much of the nineteenth century — photographs from 1909 show a terrace of houses to the north of "Bell's House" with a handful of additional buildings — was augmented in the twentieth, not least by the military authorities which took the place over in time for the First World War and later built more houses, a couple of single-storey but still barrack-like accommodation blocks, and a control tower that now looks like a gimcrack trial run for the new international airport that the former Mayor of London, Boris Johnson, once wanted to impose on the Isle of Sheppey. These days, the "Shellness Estate" is a privately-owned holiday "hamlet", the various residents of which enjoy their own tennis court and swimming pool and get by without incorporated roads, mains water, sewerage or other publicly-funded services (including sea defences). The "Private" notices posted along their perimeter fences initiate a series of forthright and occasionally menacing warnings that can be followed north along the coast from here, culminating in the example — perhaps a souvenir from Donald Trump's America — stuck on the high gate of a private bastion on the slope up to Warden Point: "Trespassers will be shot", it says, before adding that "Survivors will be shot again".

Shellness with twentieth-century additions, looking north, February 2019.

"There I saw the sunset, many times..." (Gesine Cresspahl in
Anniversaries *IV), Ahrenshoop, Fischland, June 2016.*

Shellbeach, February 2019.

Directly to the north of the otherwise quite undefended
"hamlet" of Shellness, the spit briefly widens into an open
dune, a narrow slice of which is now designated a nudist beach.
Beyond that, the low ridge is occupied by a line of fifteen or
so individual cabins. These various and in some cases much
reconfigured improvisations are what remains of a makeshift
resort known as Shellbeach. A few of its surviving shacks are
still recognisable as "bungalettes" of an early twentieth-

century type that English Heritage has yet to classify as the Thames Estuary's contribution to vernacular architecture. Like the more solidly built structures of Shellness, they survive as DIY havens. One of the more picturesque examples may somehow have made the cover of *Country Living* in August 2011, but they remain pleasantly ramshackle structures, only a few of which show signs of the aesthetic double-take pioneered by Derek Jarman at "Prospect Cottage" in Dungeness. The adjacent road running down to Sheerness has long remained untarred: little better, indeed, than the "rough shoreward track" described in 1913.[6] Here, as on the point, the beach is made of billions of seashells, banked up in such profusion that many of the island's paths and tracks have traditionally been surfaced with them. The plastic flotsam that more recent decades have added to the mix is matched by now illegible fragments of concrete, metal and wire remaining from other installations that have been and gone.

In the last years of the twentieth century, Shellbeach would find its literary witness in Nicola Barker, whose 1998 novel *Wide Open* is set on this watery, windswept and definitely wide-open edge of the island, with its peculiar colony of black-furred rabbits (specimens are allegedly still seen dodging marsh harriers in the old salt-workings on the marshes), its yellow-horned poppies and the sometimes overwhelming sense of abandonment that seems to enclose its few out-of-season inhabitants: damaged, twisted and existentially ship-wrecked characters, getting by under huge skies with the help of a caravan or, in the word Barker uses to encapsulate what is actually a variety of structures, a "prefab". *Wide Open* is the inventive vision of a car-boot *Prospero*, who once told the *Daily Telegraph*, "An island is like a little world. You can control it. It has its own logic".[7] According to an Irish journalist who described Barker's novel when it turned up as an unexpected guest on the shortlist for the £100,000 Impac Dublin Literary Award in 2000 (it won), *Wide Open* showed "the bizarre Isle of Sheppey" to be "a forgotten zone which possesses little more than a small nudist beach, some chalets, a boar farm and a cast of glorious characters" who are "extraordinarily insane".[8] A few aggrieved residents may have spurned Barker's novel as yet another insulting misrepresentation of island life,[9] yet Barker surely does catch something of the spirit of this offcut place in the last years of the twentieth century, by which time the North Sea had several times already announced its intention of permanently claiming this low and officially undefended shore.

The collection of Sheppey newspapers saved by Uwe Johnson reveals that unconventional things were going on at Shellbeach in his time too. By the end of 1976, No. 18 Shellbeach was owned by a fellow named Stan Northover. This handsome young embodiment of a Sheppey-type known locally as the "rough diamond" was the son of a showman, also named Stan Northover, who had been hailed by the *Stage,* some twelve years previously, as "one of the best known personalities on the Isle of Sheppey".[10] In 1974, when the Johnsons first moved to Sheerness, Stan the younger was running a private drinking establishment known as the Cellar Club at 9 Neptune Terrace, scarcely more than a stone's throw from the Johnsons's house. Since then, Northover, who was never proved to have been a "fence" for the island's stolen jewellery as a pair of robbers among his club members once encouraged police to believe,[11] had decided to "opt out" of society. Rather than seeking "an exotic hideaway on a foreign island" or joining "a more fashionable hippy-type commune", the former manager of the Cellar Club had bought a burned-out chalet with a fifty-foot stretch of private beach here in "the wilds of Sheppey" and set to work creating the island's own answer to the improvised castaway lairs that the American sailor and author of *Moby Dick* Herman Melville had claimed to have found on the Galapagos Islands — including the one housing a "wild white creature" named Oberlus, who survived "beastlike" and diabolical among crawling tortoises on "McCain's Beclouded Isle".[12]

In December 1976, a *Sheerness Times Guardian* reporter found this unlikely outcast in residence with his wife and three children, insisting he had "never been happier", living in rarely interrupted solitude with "no income" and a diet of rabbits, pheasant eggs and fish. From "dawn to dusk" this pioneer worked on rebuilding and strengthening the "remote island retreat" that had been named "Tides Time", perhaps at one of the "family conferences" in which, so Northover declared, all his household's decisions were now made. Asked to explain why his property, No. 18, was the first building standing in Shellbeach, he explained that "The other 17 were washed away with the winds and tide and my main concern is that the same fate does not befall this one".

If Northover's retreat seemed vaguely Spanish in its *"adobe hacienda"* style, this was, he suggested, an unintended consequence of the fact that all its materials had been salvaged or, in some cases, retrieved as they were washed up on the shore. He knew that his recycled six-foot-high windows would look "ridiculous" in a low chalet wall so, having installed them, he set about masking them with "artificial curves. The effect softened the regimental look, and I liked the feeling of space the curves created". The interior had started out as a single room built in the first summer to meet the family's need for simple shelter — just a roof for everyone to sleep under, with a stone fireplace for heat and cooking and a chimney stack and canopy made of old oil drums. The case for a second floor was sealed by the acquisition of an "ancient staircase". Low-pitched and full of light, the upstairs extension included a studio of sorts and, as was remembered by one visitor (Martin Aynscomb-Harris, to whom we will return in due course), a four-poster bed that Northover had somehow managed to squeeze into a "bedroom" that seemed only to measure about four feet from ceiling to floor. While Stan raised money, allegedly by selling wooden carvings, the eldest child, Beverley, went off to art college and the two younger children got used to the long walk to school in Minster or Halfway. Life here was good. The family read "everything from encyclopaedias to sauce bottle labels" and also had the advantage of a battery TV and radio. Meanwhile the sea kept giving — fish, driftwood and the lengths of oiled rope with which Northover framed the doors of his house. To the *Sheerness Times Guardian's* appreciative feature writer, Northover's retreat was "like a Utopian paradise right here on Sheppey".

Like many such projects, however, this one would also be short-lived. On 20 January 1978, Johnson's paper had reported that, like other parts of Sheppey, Shellness had been utterly devastated by the storm-driven floods that had hit the island a week or so earlier. The road past Shellbeach was quite washed away, and the hamlet of Shellness, which happened to have been sold to its new owner only a month earlier (contrary to the wishes of the council, which had hoped that it might be turned into a "nature park with camping facilities"[13]), was drowned after its rudimentary sea defences were smashed and the entire place left covered in slime, gravel and mud. Stan Northover returned "from holiday" to discover that his "Self-built Beach House"[14] had taken "the brunt of the storm, which gashed a hole in the sea wall 100 yards across. The only sign that a house had ever stood there is a pair of net curtains swaying gently in the breeze". According to Bel Austin, who wrote that article, Northover gave up on "Tides Time" and moved to Waverley Avenue, an inland street further around the coast in Minster, where he knocked two bungalows together to create his next island retreat.

Before ourselves moving on from Shellbeach, we should recognise that storms and floods are not the only hazards that have threatened summer residents here. We can follow the shifting context of Sheppey's south-eastern spit further back into the century that weighed so heavily on Johnson with the help of an incident that took place here one summer day between the two world wars. In the calendrical structure of *Anniversaries*, 15 August is shared between the years 1968 and 1952, the latter being the day on which Gesine Cresspahl had said farewell to her father in Jerichow ("Make sure ya wear yer scarf"[15]), and set off for Halle on the Saale River, where she would study English Literature through the official Marxist prism at Martin Luther University. We, though, are concerned with 15 August 1933. In Germany, that was the day on which the newly empowered Chancellor of Germany, Adolf Hitler, survived a car crash while motoring in the mountains near the Bavarian village of Reit im Winkl.[16] There would be no such luck for the seventeen-year-old Jean Chesterton or, for that matter, for her older sister Joan, with whom she had crossed the Thames from Ilford in Essex to spend the summer as usual in the family's holiday home — a shack variously described as a "bungalette" and a "bungalow hut"[17] — overlooking the sea at Shellbeach.

After breakfast that bright morning, Jean and Joan noticed a small girl crying as she watched her large yellow beach ball, which had been caught by the wind, vanishing out to sea. Already clad in bright swimming costumes — one green, the other blue — the Chesterton sisters jumped into the family's wooden rowing boat and pulled out to rescue the ball. Catching up with it about a quarter of a mile from the shore, they noticed little splashes in the water around them and realised, helplessly, that they were being machine-gunned from the air. Five Westland Wapiti biplanes had suddenly materialised overhead, and the gunner in one of them, a civilian from the Midlands named John Boahemia, was practising "splash tactics" for the first time during a training week with the 605 County of Warwick Bomber Squadron of the Auxiliary Air Force. Hit twice, Jean slid down into the boat and was dead by the time Joan had managed to row back to the shore. "The water", as Johnson's Heinrich Cresspahl would say while imagining British bombs falling into the Baltic, "is as hard as stone."[18]

"The rowboat nearest to the water is the one in which the girl was shot". Shellbeach, 22 August 1933.

It was established at the inquest that the Chesterton sisters, who were enjoying their fifth summer holiday in "one of the first"[19] bungalettes to be erected at Shellbeach, had not strayed into the RAF's buoyed-off danger zone immediately to the south as some horrified airmen had at first alleged. In reality, aircraftman Boahemia, who complained of the day's fierce "Sea-glare",[20] had opened fire too soon, having mistaken the Chesterton's wooden boat for one of the target buoys anchored a few hundred yards beyond. Everyone behaved as well as they could under the circumstances. The girls' father, Mr William Chesterton (a partner in a firm of manufacturing furriers, Chesterton and Hancox, in the City of London), shook hands with the mortified aircraftman after the inquest, and Boahemia sent a wreath extending his "deepest sympathy and regret" to the funeral in Manor Park. The officiating congregationalist minister offered the respectfully absent gunner some words of reassurance, insisting that "the man who was also afflicted by this tragedy" could "walk with head erect, knowing that those who have been so deeply bereaved were without bitterness and able to recognize the innocence of his activities".[21] The *Daily Herald*, a Labour paper that had long opposed the War Office's insistence on grabbing land for military use all over the country since the First World War, preferred the less forgiving judgement of one of the dead girl's less reconciled brothers: "One would think that, during August, when the bungalows are occupied by 200 or more people the R.A.F. would practise as far away as possible".[22] The Air Ministry would, of course, stay put. They did, however, mark the perimeter of the "danger area" with larger noticeboards and brightly painted pylons.

As for the "bungalows", two hundred may have been a round count of residents, but there is no question that things had changed along the once "isolated and shut-off" spit leading down to the point at Shellness, and not for the better according to the dismayed assessment provided by Sir Charles Igglesden, who came here the following year, in 1934, and found the seafront at Shellbeach "covered with numberless bungalows".[23] Meanwhile, Shellness "at the extreme point [was] a mass of other buildings, the residences of members of a London club. The difference is so great that you would never recognise the Shellness of today as the same place ten years ago". And that, as anyone walking further north along this coast soon discovers, was by no means the extent of the changes the twentieth century would bring to this no longer quite so remote shore.

11. LEYSDOWN: THE "ON-SEA" SCENARIO

When I'm alone on my island
Surrounded by the sea
There's no more need to close my eyes
'Cos it feels like home to me.
— Dave Sinclair, "Island" (*Stream*, CD Crescent Label, 2011)

Uwe Johnson wrote a lot about trains and other systems of transportation, studying their routes and timetables and allowing parallels to emerge between their progress through space and the attempts made by his characters, or "invented persons", to achieve a different sort of transit through remembered time. In the judgement of a recent critical essay about *Anniversaries,* he associates modern transit systems with "shocks and jolts" that reflect the traumatic past of displaced Germans living in New York City.[1]

Jean Chesterton died due to an accidental collision between two not easily reconciled bids for the future, both of them introduced to this part of the island's south-eastern coast after the opening on 1 August 1901 of the Sheppey Light Railway.[2] This service ran for nearly ten miles east-west across the island from the South Eastern and Chatham Railway Company's existing station at Queenborough on Sheppey's western Medway shore, passing through four intermediate stations and two less formal halts before reaching its eastern terminus at Leysdown on the "uttermost verge" of this "remote and little known" place.[3] The Sheppey service was one of sixteen built in rural areas by an engineer and Territorial Army colonel named Holman Fred Stephens (he owed his Christian name to the fact that his father, Frederic George Stephens, was a Pre-Raphaelite critic and artist who had been taught by Holman Hunt). Colonel Stephens's moment came thanks to the Light Railway Act passed in 1896, with its aim of encouraging the creation of cheap lines in remote places, often with a view to bringing agricultural produce to markets from rural districts beyond the reach of tramways. Sheppey's line, however, was built with a different aim in mind. It was envisaged from the start as "the means of developing this part of Sheppey Isle".[4]

Leysdown, which would benefit from the "Sheppey Light" until the service finally went out of business in 1950, lies a mile or so further north along the coast from Shellbeach. As the operating South Eastern and Chatham Railway Company also explained (while justifying the decision not to run trains as far as Leysdown on the light railway over the winter months), there was barely even a village here before the train came. Indeed, at the beginning of the twentieth century, the place would have seemed the epitome of the obscure Kentish settlements that Arthur Mee described as "like the end of the world, with a lonely church and not a living soul about".[5] The Rose and Crown Inn served as a coroner's court when it came to adjudicating deaths that occurred on land or sea. There was a declining church of St Clements, once known to mariners for its leaning tower, another coastguard station on the shoreline and a small manor called Nutts, a lonely place whose eighteenth-century owners included Mr Edward Jacob, a surgeon with antiquarian and naturalist interests, who twice served as Mayor of Faversham and has also been claimed as the first person to suggest that the young William Shakespeare may have had a hand in writing *Arden of Faversham*, an anonymous late-sixteenth-century play in which Sheppey features as a cut-off land lost in a perplexing mist.

There was also, as the 1897 ordnance survey map shows,

a small rural school, across the road from Nutts farm, where a few may have noticed the energy of supplementary teacher Violet Clara McNaughton (then known as Violet Jackson), who taught there for a few years before quitting England at the age of twenty-nine in 1909 and emigrating to a homestead in Saskatchewan, Canada. Once there, she would rapidly emerge as a champion of "agrarian feminism"[6] and co-operative enterprise of the sort she had learned about from her late fiancé's grandparents in Sheerness. McNaughton may be long forgotten in Leysdown, but in Canada this determined woman, who had been rejected as too short for entry even into the lowest ranks of the British civil service, is remembered as the "Mighty Mite" who carried ancestral memories of Kentish radicalism with her as she campaigned for and among women farmers. She has recently been hailed as "one of Canada's greatest and most formidable adult educators and co-operators of the twentieth century bar none".[7]

Visitors to the huge car boot sale nowadays held at Leysdown on Sundays will find other ways of recognising how much has changed since the light railway came. By the middle of the twentieth century the village had been converted into a seaside resort: optimistically named "Leysdown-on-Sea" but already struggling against decline, degeneration and the local authority. In 1958, a group of Leysdown chalet owners had contested the council's valuation of their properties on the grounds that they received so very little in the way of public services. They cited the absence of water, electricity and mains sewerage, the unchecked crime, the flooding, the suspension-wrecking condition of the unmetalled roads, the lack of reliable rubbish collection, and noise from the disturbing forms of "commercialisation" that had been permitted to develop nearby. The claim that their much-burgled chalets were outrageously "over-rated" was rejected. The Valuation Officer stated that there were at that time 1400 separately rated bungalows on twelve or so camps in Leysdown, and that, "as every occupier of these bungalows knows", they could command a rent of between £3 and £5 a week from holidaymakers during the summer. The chairman of the East Kent Valuation Panel sourly told one objector that he was surprised, given the dump this dissatisfied fellow plainly judged Leysdown to be, "that he had bothered to build his bungalow there at all".[8] That characteristic dispute took place in the claimed Golden Age of "Leysdown-on-Sea".

Over the years to come, it would often be the consequences of that allegedly chaotic "commercialisation" that brought Leysdown into the news. By 1960, the "rowdyism" of disorderly summer visitors was an established problem, with a Sheerness magistrate who fined five young offenders for smashing up a café in Leysdown ("It was Hell broke loose", testified the owner), also telling them that "we are determined to stamp out this hooliganism. The only pity is these detention centres are so full we cannot send you all there".[9] In 1962, local residents organised a public meeting to demand action before the rough "type of customer" attracted by the "outrageously commercial development" — which, as the reporter asserted, the residents had foolishly allowed and even encouraged into existence — drove the "family holidaymakers" away from the Leysdown "Shanty", thereby killing the goose that had laid the golden egg.[10]

By 1971, the island's own newspaper could surprise nobody by admitting that Leysdown was "a declining holiday backwater".[11] As for the "commercial" enterprises that had been brought into the place, often against the wishes of the county planners, many of these have since closed. The betting shop, which a punter in 1964 likened to "The Black Hole of Calcutta", may survive under different ownership,[12] but the jazz, funk and soul venue, Stage 3, was lost to a fire in 1989. The pub on the seafront, the Talk of the Town — appreciated by one *Tripadvisor* witness as a "Spit and sawdust pub" with karaoke or "a guy singing", and deplored by others as "the worst pub in Britain" where "stabbings are quite normal" — was boarded up through my investigation, and, in October 2018, Merlin's Entertainment Complex, a larger venue once played by the likes of Dr Hook, Chas 'n' Dave and Jim Davidson, was put up for sale as a demolition-ready site onto which, so the agent suggested, eight or nine "sea-facing" houses might be squeezed if anybody wanted them and the planners consented.

The chalets, bungalettes and caravans of Leysdown-on-Sea have never been targeted by "Down from London" incomers of the well-off sort who have been buying places in Whitstable, Margate and other more favoured resorts along Kent's recently designated "creative coast". Yet this embattled settlement has continued to attract the eye of literary visitors, who come here to shake their heads in horror. "This is the end of the claims of civilization",[13] says the Sheppey-born Joblard, pre-empting them all as he sweeps through in the closing chapter of Iain Sinclair's east London novel *Downriver*, to register Leysdown as the last outpost of an east London that is finally being blown out of the city by government policy and development: "Leysdown-on-Sea is the ancestral dreamsite of a Lost Tribe: all the aboriginal cockney characteristics, celebrated in fiction and in song, have migrated here — and have been buried alive in pitches of caravans, mobile homes, wooden sentry boxes (inner-city privies), and upturned tin boats, veterans of Dunkirk".[14]

In the same year, 1991, the modernist gourmet Jonathan Meades also passed through. He arrived as a self-declared enthusiast for the bleakness of the estuary landscape who appreciated the informal charms of many of the DIY shacklands that sprang up as Londoners found cheap holiday spots on both sides of the Thames Estuary in the early twentieth century. Leysdown-on-Sea, however, managed to smash its way through his signature dark glasses and jab him rudely in the eye. This, wrote Meades in retaliation, is "terminal England, the last resort, the nadir of bungalow development. It makes Hayling look like Biarritz".[15] He found Leysdown's human inhabitants no better than the fenced-off chalet parks and trashy arcades. "The English can be terrifying", he muttered, citing the "double Doberman families", the "beery croak" of the bingo-caller, the ferocious-looking white men who drive their Escorts at "sixty miles an hour anywhere".

His prize exhibit was a family that practiced synchronised spitting, allegedly issuing a perfectly timed "buccal explosion" of jellied eel bones as he slipped by without revealing that he was actually the *Times'* restaurant critic.

By the end of the twentieth century, the forlorn condition of Leysdown-on-Sea may have been taken as grotesque evidence of the politically induced "unmaking" of the English working class — a backwater of the betrayed and abandoned kind from which Brexit would soon come. That, however, would have seemed too grave a theme for Tim Moore, the "comic travel writer" who has more recently credited Leysdown with providing the opening inspiration for his book *You are Awful (But I Like You): Travels Through Unloved Britain*. Prompted by his remembered astonishment at discovering, during a disorientated drive from London in the Seventies, that "a fog-smothered mudbank in the Thames Estuary had ever become a holiday resort in the first place", he opens by coming back forty or so years later to take another look at the static caravans and "garden-shed holiday chalets". He reads the signs on the all-but-deserted seafront announcing that the levels of "faecal" coliform and streptococci in the sea water could be considerably worse. He shrinks from the fish and chip shops and the sunbeds bearing signs announcing "Max Weight of 16 stone". Stepping into the Rose and Crown, this misplaced travel writer, who has since revealed his preference for the wilder regions of Iceland ("the desolation was thrilling: no building, no trees and, most conspicuously, no people"[16]), is greeted with the cry, "Fuckinell, wossat stink?" His reception is barely improved by the barmaid who volunteers that a nearby farmer must be spreading muck on his fields. Although far too much of the British periphery may well have come to resemble Leysdown by the time Moore passed through, the fact that his book — hailed by the *Daily Telegraph* as "funny and squirmingly vivid" — was published by Jonathan Cape also suggests a loss of ambition among literary publishers since 1969, when Cape issued the American translation of Uwe Johnson's novella *An Absence*. The visiting West German journalist at the centre of Johnson's story had definitely noticed the failure of the communist utopia in the GDR but he didn't go there to strike metropolitan smirks off the surfaces of other people's degradation.

It is, though, not just roaming writers who register the fallen condition of Leysdown-on-Sea. Notices posted on reviewing websites leave no doubt that this sense of dismay is shared by some who, far from just passing through with the aim of recoiling in horror, have actually come here on holiday. They too declare Leysdown to be the crappiest of all crap towns, filled with rackety caravan and chalet parks, equipped with foul toilets and blood-stained sheets and populated by people who swear, take drugs, yell all night and can themselves be as terrifying as the Staffordshire Bull Terriers they allow to roam free around the chalets. Leysdown, so I have read, is "the tackiest place in Britain", one that makes you "feel embarrassed to be British". "Derrum", who stayed in one of the parks in August 2015, employs the same comparative trope as Jonathan Meades, condemning Leysdown as "just a dump that makes Jaywick look like Malibu". The Leysdown shudder has even become a going concern for the Kent Film Office, which has learned how to trade on estuarial bleakness and takes pride in the fact that Leysdown-on-Sea was chosen as a location for "The End of the F***ing World" in the first series of Jonathan Entwistle's Channel Four drama of the same name ("I'm James, and I'm pretty sure I'm a psychopath") in October 2017.[17]

A Baltic contrast might help us turn the tide on this desolate commentary. Whatever may be said about Leysdown, the place was never as dismal as the colossal resort of Prora built in the late Thirties as part of the Nazi government's "Strength through Joy" initiative. Conceived as one of five vast "Sea Baths" proposed for workers following the destruction of Germany's trade unions, it consists of a series of huge six-floor concrete blocks placed along the 4.5 kilometre length of a magnificent Baltic beach on the spit — situated between those known to Johnson at Diewenow and Fischland — connecting the resorts of Sassnitz and Binz on the east coast of the Pomeranian Island of Rügen.

Prora, Rügen.

Robert Ley, the Nazi head of the German Labour Front (Uwe Johnson allows him a brief appearance as a "drunken pig"[18]), imagined Prora as a Nazi answer to Butlins that would provide compliant workers with a week of indoctrinated leisure. Every room would have a sea view. There would be cinemas, swimming pools, canteens and, at Hitler's insistence, a central arena in which twenty thousand joyful workers could be addressed as a concentrated Sieg Heiling mass. In 1991 this never-completed line of Aryan barracks (construction was interrupted by the outbreak of war in September 1939) emerged from GDR military control as a set of disconcerting ruins. When I last visited the site, however, some of its reinforced concrete was acquiring an unexpectedly luxurious shine. The developers who had bought some of the blocks, themselves now listed for conservation, were bringing them to new life, although not as the centre for refugees that some critics have suggested might be appropriate. Two-bedroom apartments were being offered at €600,000 and upward. It was a relief to come across some old-fashioned graffiti written in

English on one of the still unrefurbished blocks: "Heaven ain't close in a place like this".

*

Leysdown-on-Sea is indeed a chaotic mess, and perhaps also, as planners have suggested, proof of what can go wrong when decisions are made too locally. It was, though, a better resort than Prora. And who, meanwhile, are the knockers really laughing at? It is by no means just the shopkeepers, arcade operators and yobbos in the pub who have opposed the sense of horror with which refined onlookers may scrutinise the place. Asked to describe his earliest memory, the actor Eddie Marsan replied: "Hearing George Harrison's 'My Sweet Lord' on a caravan site on the Isle of Sheppey when I was about four".[19] Marsan, who was born two years before George Harrison's song became the biggest hit of 1970, is joined by another contrary witness in Chris Difford of the band Squeeze, whose song "Pulling Mussels (from the Shell)", released in 1980, is drawn from memories of a week spent in a Leysdown caravan park one summer in the late Sixties, having driven to the Sheppey "Riviera" with his family from Deptford (the song memorialises both the pleasures of the beach and the "pulling" that went on "behind the chalet"[20]). The Sheppey websites also contain many testimonies to the freedom, the light-heartedness, the simple attraction of cockling in the muddy sand or collecting shells on the beach, and the innocence of a time when a child could roam the island without fear or hindrance and the carcass of an old bus could make a perfectly adequate holiday home, as, indeed, might recycled carriages from the Light Railway after that service finally expired at the end of 1950.[21]

These memories reach back to the early Sixties, when Leysdown-on-Sea was still enjoying its modest prime as a "boom town" resort for east Londoners: a time when the chalet holiday camps were finding it difficult to cope with demand,

and when the "streamlined", "motel-like" and undeniably "with it" enterprise that was the Island Hotel and Country Club was owned by a former bingo operator who had become famous as the "King of Leysdown".[22] That informal monarch was none other than Stan Northover the First (father of the man who would build his family a shack utopia at Shellbeach in the Seventies), and his combined hotel and private club is said to have boasted more than two thousand members. The place was run by the former variety artist Harry Green who, together with his "blonde wife, 'Skid'" was reported by the *Stage* to be "putting zip into their business with variety bills of a high order". People in those days were said to be flocking to "this little Southend", where variety shows by early TV stars and female impersonators was giving bingo a run for the holidaymakers' money. Indeed, King Stan was said to be building a five-hundred-seat theatre in order to drive the "boom" further. Played by the Drifters, P.J. Proby, Joe Brown and Bill Haley, the Leysdown of that time is remembered as an agreeably "old-fashioned" party town that, as the websites attest, had a lot more to do with drag artists and wide-boy liberties than with the people-smuggling, drug-dealing and paedophilia of the world as it is today. A popular Golden Age, then, adequately represented by a photograph taken at the Leysdown Holiday Camp on 8 August 1957. It shows Neville Wood, a former fireman turned variety entertainer, frying an egg on the raised and flaming backside of his partner, Francis Capsoni.

There may be a lot of rose-tinted nostalgia about these invocations of the Leysdown of old — and in some instances a thick coat of retrospectively applied whitewash too. Yet there is more to be said than that. The attractions of Sheppey as a Cockney Arcadia were recognised by Somerset Maugham, who is likely to have remembered Victorian Whitstable's view over the sea to Sheppey when he wrote his final stage play. First produced with Ralph Richardson in the leading role, *Sheppey* opened at Wyndham's Theatre in London on 14 September 1933 — a month after Miss Jean Chesterton was accidentally shot through the heart at Shellbeach. Maugham evokes the world of a London hairdresser who lives in Camberwell and works at a salon in Jermyn Street. His name is Joseph Miller but everyone knows him as "Sheppey", since he was born on the island, spends all his holidays there and won't stop going on about it: "To hear him talk about it you'd think there was no place like it", says the manicurist Miss Grange.[23] "The garden of England, that's what it is", replies Sheppey: "I know the very 'ouse I'm going

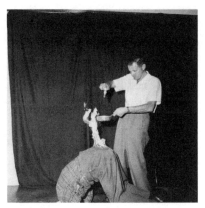

Neville Wood fries an egg. Variety at Leysdown Holiday Camp, 8 August 1957.

to buy when my ship comes home. Two acres of land. View of the sea. Just the place for me and my old woman". Although Maugham's hairdresser goes on to win a fortune on a horse in the Irish sweep, he never quite gets around to buying the "dinky little 'ouse" to which he has long dreamed of one day retreating.[24] Instead, he starts reading the Bible and finds it like "a great white light" illuminating the path he must follow to achieve "peace and 'appiness".[25] The rich, so Sheppey generously observes, may need to keep their vast fortunes for themselves, but he himself has no expensive habits to maintain. Fired by an entirely literal reading of the scriptures, he resolves to use his money to "Clothe the naked and visit the sick, give food to 'im that is a'ungered and drink to 'im that is athirst".[26] He becomes so busy loving his neighbours and giving away his money (Sheppey always "'as liked people"[27]) that he never gets round to buying his imagined retirement "'ouse". When the Grim Reaper finally turns up at his bedside, he can only remark, wistfully, "I wish now I'd gone down to the Isle of Sheppey when the doctor advised it. You wouldn't 'ave thought of looking for me there".[28]

A more systematic attempt to get to the roots of Sheppey's twentieth-century reinvention as an island of freedom, independence and convivial retirement for people who aren't oligarchs or lottery

Plotland house, Sheppey.

millionaires was made in the early Eighties by Colin Ward, the anarchist writer, journalist and former officer of the Town and Country Planning Association. While Margaret Thatcher waged war on "socialism", the welfare state and the "enemy within", Ward was celebrating the practice of "mutual aid" as it survived, more or less, in various unconquered corners of British life (allotments, holiday camps, urban squats, new towns, etc.) that had yet to be regulated out of existence by the state or fully surrendered to corporate enterprise. Conservationists and others might have despised coastal developments such as Leysdown as ruinous sprawl, but Ward and his collaborator in this endeavour, the planner and historian of alternative communities Dennis Hardy, took a much more appreciative view of the scruffy, informal settlements that had emerged in such places before state planning controls were introduced. They at least understood that the Englishman's Paradise is far more likely to be a "bungalette" than a stately mansion founded on slavery.

Ward seems to have opened his investigation of Sheppey by enlisting the help of a fellow contributor to the weekly journal *New Society*. The sociologist Ray Pahl, who started probing Sheppey in the late Seventies, was already reviewing Leysdown and its seasonal employment practices for their contribution to the island's marginal economy and also, as he had learned from some Sheppey teachers, to the reluctance of some of the island's school-leavers to accept conventional forms of work discipline:

> Leysdown-on-Sea attracted hustlers and cowboys and provided apprenticeships in mild crookery for generations of school leavers who, in the Fifties, Sixties and early Seventies, went "down Leysdown" to work as cheap labour, cleaning the chalets in the holiday camps, serving in cafes and bars and minding stalls and (later) machines in the fairgrounds and amusement arcades. The holiday trade provided myriad opportunities for small business enterprises to start with little capital, and the regular flow of new clientele prevented the build-up of bad reputations. Fiddles could be perpetrated all summer; prices could be exorbitant; and high labour turnover prevented possible protest but spread bad practices. Some parents refused to let their sons and daughters go off in the summer to pick up bad ways. However, such seasonal employment also had the useful function of providing independence, some pocket money and the experience of a number of bosses, without any opprobrium resulting from having "changed jobs frequently".[29]

Having been shown around Leysdown by the sociologist, who remembered suffering a slipped disc while trying to lift his car out of the mud during a shared island "safari",[30] Ward and Hardy went on to appraise Sheppey's much-condemned DIY developments as examples of a distinctive kind of popular Arcadia that had emerged on both sides of the Thames Estuary during the early twentieth century. Where others saw only chaotic eyesores, they discovered a "unique landscape" that seemed closer to "the American frontier" than to cultivated ideas of what England should look like: "It was", they wrote, "a makeshift world of shacks and shanties, scattered unevenly in plots of varying size and shape, with unmade roads and little in the way of services".[31] You can see it in the early photographs of Leysdown — shacks, "bungalettes" and old busses parked up and allowed to settle, as the air leaked out of their tyres, into static holiday homes. The postcard chosen by a south-east Londoner named "Doris" in August 1921 and sent to her family at home from "Wild Rose Cottage" in Leysdown appears to show the conical frame of an improvised tepee planted at the head of the sands. Another, sent from the island by "Hankie" to "Milly" in the early Sixties, says: "I am enjoying myself trying to put the garden to rights as well as mixing cement for Harry. It's a lark."

A number of the happenstance "plotland" Arcadias surveyed so sympathetically by Hardy and Ward had been pioneered by a developer named Frederick Francis Ramuz (1855–1946), a land agent born in Leytonstone, east London, who initiated his estuarial activities in the new municipality of Southend-on-Sea (declared a municipal borough in 1892) on the Essex side of the Thames Estuary.[32] Ramuz's trick, which he pursued in partnership with his eldest son George, was to buy up depressed agricultural estates cheap, subdivide the acquired land into many small plots, arrange a quarterly payments scheme, and then auction the plots with the help of a marquee, free food and drink, and a special train or, sometimes, a Belle steamer chartered to bring potential buyers downriver from London.

Having started out at Southend, Ramuz, who was twice mayor of that recently established town, expanded his operations to include the north-east coast of Sheppey where, within weeks of the opening of the Light Railway, his "Land Company" was offering 275 "really ripe, safe investment" plots "adjoining" the new station at Minster, emphasising that there was now "unlimited demand" for small villas on the island.[33] Ramuz bought his first one thousand acres on the seaward side of the ancient village of Minster, a site that the *Daily Express* obligingly described as an "unknown paradise" consisting of a "semi-circle of grassy cliffs, swept by the breezes of the German Ocean".[34] He then applied his usual technique — putting in (or at least marking out) dirt roads, dividing up the land to create some three thousand plots, and offering working-class Londoners a free return ticket on the train that would bring them from Holborn Viaduct to his "sale party" in the no longer so isolated place he described, with what Boris Johnson calls "plausibility" rather than strict truthfulness, as "the nearest point on the Kent coast to London". By June 1903, Ramuz was offering "Minster-on-Sea" as "the new El Dorado for land buyers".[35] A Minster Development Corporation was formed, and the site was duly commended by compliant journalists ("a place to take one's summer rest. Here on the nearer coast of Kent is the ideal holiday home."[36]). In 1904, an illustrated advertisement about the "great enterprise" that was producing this "refuge for Weary East Enders" informed readers of the *East London Observer* that Sheppey was the most remarkable "find" in "the Garden of England".[37] While the illustrator showed happy children digging sand on beaches that were actually shingle, the Ramuzes's copywriter magicked Sheppey's crumbling mud and clay cliffs into tall structures of chalk, proclaiming them as "part of the White Walls of Old England".

Ramuz's "new Paradise" was to be built plot by "salubrious" plot, and considerable profits surely awaited the "pioneers" of the coming "peace-land". If the "clerks and artizans" of east London needed more encouragement, they only had to consider the duly proffered words of the island's medical officer. Dr Julius Caesar, F.R.C.S., L.R.C.P., had no doubt at all that Minster-on-Sea would prove a "bracing and invigorating" locale for Londoners. "You buy the land", said the company, and "we do the rest". Large plots were offered for aspiring poultry farmers, and the fine old seventeen-room Queen Anne mansion known as "Borstal Hall" would surely make a good boarding school or private hotel. The core of the offer, however, consisted of smaller plots of 20 by 160 feet on which a villa or bungalow might be built. These were offered freehold, and it only took an initial payment of £2 to secure a patch of paradise that could then be paid off at one shilling and eightpence a week over the following four years. The promise, made in the *East London Observer*, that the Minster Cliff's Estate was "going like wildfire" was repeated on the postcard with which the "Development Corporation" also publicised its "New Health Resort". This offered "miles of quiet and interesting cliff walks" and "splendid opportunities for bathing". The watercolourist responsible for the picture did manage to paint the cliffs of Minster the colour of raw mud rather than chalk, but those who received the card had to use their own powers of deduction to realise that considerable sections of the "interesting" cliff path appeared already to have fallen into what was also, now you mention it, a very muddy sea.

"Minster-on-Sea: the New Health Resort", the Development Corporation's postcard.

While Ramuz and his son George were busy selling seaside plots on both sides of Minster, a rival company of London land agents, F.G. Wheatley and Son, was running a similar speculation at Leysdown and Shellness. The redevelopment here began in April 1903, when Mr S.A. Gillespie sold the Manor of Leysdown by private negotiation "for immediate commercial development".[38] The lordship of this ancient manor was included, but it was the land that mattered to the purchasers: 2,740 acres in all, much of it "rich pasture and meadow land" but also the extensive foreshore — "a sea beach of over three miles of fine shell and sand" — and the same system of promotion was soon underway. "Facing the German Ocean" was among the slogans that had been launched by 27 July 1903, when 108 freehold plots were offered for auction at a marquee luncheon on the "Shellness-on-Sea and Leysdown Estate". Mr Wheatley, who served as his own huckster and auctioneer, promised "Free conveyances. Immediate possession, and payments by instalments extending over 10 years (if desired)."[39] He spoke of creating golf links on "a considerable proportion of the estate", and was confident that "the anchorage at Shellness Point" would "prove a benefit to yachtsmen". He promised that the new "Marine Parade" that would soon stretch along the coast from Leysdown to Shellness would be nearly three miles long when completed: it was "suitable for bungalows, shops, and villas of all classes" and would have "an avenue and promenade 150ft. wide, fronting on the open sea, with an extensive lawn reserved for public use".[40] Repeated sales were conducted at the locality (the Shellness and Leysdown Estate Company is said to have maintained a base at a remote farmhouse close to the site known as "Mussell House"[41]), assisted by special trains from London and a free meal (complete with "Sheppey sauce") served in a large marquee. The latter amenity was especially well chosen considering how many of these events were challenged by mist, rain and delayed trains, which added considerably to the leap of faith required if purchasers were to believe in the promise of "profit", to say nothing of the motor track that Wheatley and Son generously tossed into the offer as yet another encouraging prospect.[42] Here, as at Minster, buyers might build immediately, but those who were not in a position to do so were encouraged to understand that plots allowed to lie idle had doubled or even trebled in value "in the course of a few years".[43]

By the end of 1904, the *Hendon & Finchley Times* was reporting that "very extensive purchases of building plots" had been made on the Shellness-on-Sea and Leysdown estate. Most of these sales had taken place in the summer "when a trip to the seaside is among the pleasures of the inland dweller".[44]

That December, however, the auctioneers had decided to "vary this order". On 2 December, they attracted two hundred guests to a "sumptuous well-served dinner" at the Holborn Restaurant in London, and then launched into a sale in which "thousands of pounds were expended". Mr Wheatley led the toasts (to the King and "the success of the estate") but was assisted in the local pitch by a Colonel Peddar, who promised that "a great deal of money had been expended on the property in the way of road making, sewering, and other work". As for the vision of a new Marine Parade with houses and shops extending over three miles between Warden and Shellness, there may have been a hint of warning in the conditional nature of his promise that "if the plot owners would start building, the estate had a great future before it". It was said that exceptionally high prices were achieved at the Holborn sale — significantly above those paid for adjacent plots at sales on the site. The lucrative event was rounded off with an "excellent" concert.

Nuts Farm, Leysdown-on-Sea, February 2019. The site of Messrs. F.G. Wheatley and Son's promised Marine Parade.

The golden name of El Dorado had been bagged by the Ramuzes for "Minster-on-Sea" but at Leysdown-on-Sea and Shellness-on-Sea the prospect of a quick gain surely also animated more faces than were moved by the spirit of mutual aid, especially among the buyers who chose to pick up two or three or perhaps ten plots rather than one. For decades, however, time remained at least partly on the side of those who continued to think Leysdown and the low spit leading down to Shellness Point would be better left to the birds, the sea purslane and the yellow-horned poppies for which the area is still known. Some shacks may have been swept away during the emergency measures of the Second World War, when the Isle of Sheppey was largely taken over for military purposes, but one only has to try to walk along the seafront at Leysdown to realise that — perhaps in anticipation of the brave new world promised by the more excited pushers of Brexit — the three-mile-long Marine Parade Messrs Wheatley and Son had imagined stretching down towards Shellness never actually happened. Even in the centre of Leysdown itself, the "promenade", such as it is, only extends for a few yards in either direction, its potential route firmly blocked by the various private holiday camp operators, who have staked out their access to the beach and are plainly determined to maintain their "exclusivity" with the help of wire and railings as well as forbidding notices.

In reality, Leysdown never achieved a "Marine Parade" of any length, and the plotland world that did emerge was not created with brick houses and bungalows of the kind imagined by the auctioneers, even less with white modernist villas such as can be found at Frinton-on-Sea across the estuary in Essex. Messrs Saunders and Son somehow managed to squeeze the outline of their promised "new seaside watering place" onto the twenty-five-inch Ordnance Survey map when it was revised in 1906. This shows a network of "avenues" bearing names of the kind developers tend to come up with: "Dorothy", "Ingoldsby", "Beach", "Seaview", "Raleigh" and "Drake". All the daemons are there, locked into a grid behind a "Marine Parade" that stretches south along the seafront, just as promised by Mr Saunders, coming to an end across a marshy field from the farmhouse ("Mussel House") now known as Muswell Manor. In truth, this lucrative fantasy land remained unbuilt, leaving the Ordnance Survey no choice but to set about quietly rubbing out its streets in time for their revised map of 1933. There are some bungalows a little inland, but visitors looking for "villas" in which to stay would have to make do with chalets and static caravans in wired-off camps from which, by the Seventies, lurking murderers and kidnappers from London were (if the sociologist Ray Pahl is to be believed) sporadically being removed by the police.

So the transformation came, although perhaps not in the way anticipated by the *Sheerness Times* when it observed, on 1 August 1903, that "The rural portion of Sheppey bids fair to become thoroughly metamorphosed".[45] There would be no place in "Leysdown-on-Sea" for the ancient manor of "Nutts" that once ran down to the sea here. The local paper reports that many of the plots were bought in a single block in 1903: Nos. 91–99 went as a single package for £165.[46] The first developer of "Nutts Avenue" installed Arcadian bungalettes fabricated out of corrugated iron and cement or asbestos sheeting, and the metamorphosis continued after that. By 1930, when "Mummie" wrote a postcard from this "very nice" place to "Miss Bennett" in East Croydon, she put an X in the grass to show where "Mr J.'s" bungalow had been built since the photo was taken.

Nuts Avenue, Leysdown-on-Sea, postcard 1930.

*

"We are going to make it a success", so George Ramuz had said in 1908 of his development on the Minster Cliffs Estate, to the north-west of Sexburga's ancient abbey: "we are going at it hammer and nails".[47]

Yet his attempt to turn Minster into "a prominent water place" would also struggle over the following decades. An early indication of the difficulty he faced was supplied in October 1911 by a journalist from Richmond who, while claiming to be determined not to criticise a "new seaside resort" until it is "up (in other words developed)", nevertheless got a damning article out of a visit to "Minster-on-Sea".[48] Having walked up the hill from the station, he spent two hours being sent from pillar to post in an unsuccessful search for accommodation. After exhausting "the alimentary resources of Minster" by buying a pound of cheese and some crackers from the only grocer, he discovered even the chocolate machine at the station to be empty before boarding a train and fleeing to Whitstable, where he found the congenial fortnight's holiday he claimed to have anticipated. Twenty years later, Arthur Mee also recoiled from the "tasteless world" of bungalows that the Ramuzes had piled up around Sexburga's abbey at Minster, a site that surely deserved better as "one of the marvels of all England".[49]

Some of the bungalows may indeed have been strange and makeshift improvisations, but vacant building plots also limited the attractiveness of a claimed El Dorado that, even forty years later, would still be described as "a seaside resort in embryo".[50] The country house, originally known as Borstal Hall, never did become a hotel or boarding school. Indeed, by 1912, George Ramuz himself had moved into the unsold mansion, which would, in the words of a local historian, prove liable both to military occupation, through both world wars, and also "to mysterious fires", including the conflagration that finally cleared the site in 1948.[51] In 1961, Ramuz's son George, who had inherited the heavily mortgaged and still largely "unknown paradise" of Minster-on-Sea from his father, was interviewed by a local journalist who plainly thought the Ramuzes had made a terrible mess with their chaotic plotland strategies. "You don't build a seaside resort in five minutes",[52] Ramuz countered defensively, when it was suggested that his failure to entice enough shopkeepers and other small purchasers from London into buying and then building on plots had blighted Sheppey's chances of redevelopment for half a century. He admitted that the Minster scheme had been an "absolute flop" plagued by many difficulties: the lack of fast trains to Sheerness, the scarcity of fresh water, untraced buyers whose plots lay empty for years and even decades before falling back to Ramuz, the fact that the targeted Londoners "didn't like it", the squatters and gypsies — more "pikeys" perhaps — who had to be removed and seen off when they tried to claim squatter's rights over unused plots. Having inherited a paradise that wouldn't stop resembling a marginal, unplanned and gap-filled shanty town, he concluded with an English formulation that might have interested Uwe Johnson as he later tried to figure out how Sheppey's connoisseurs of environmental degradation categorised failed places. According to Ramuz, Minster-on-Sea had turned out to be "a dead end".[53] Hundreds of plots initially intended for self-building holiday makers had been (or were destined to be) compulsorily purchased by the council or sold into the hands of conventional developers by the time George Ramuz died in 1966, leaving an estate valued at £16,587. "Minster-on-Sea" plainly still hadn't happened five years later. In an editorial at the end of the year, the *Sheerness Times Guardian* admitted that "Sheppey is like a mini Costa Brava, where not only are the hotels unfinished, they are unbuilt".[54] In Hardy & Ward's more generous judgement, Minster-on-Sea had been "So long in the making that it never quite made it".[55]

12. ROLLS WITHOUT ROYCE: LEYSDOWN ALOFT

And the roads in Jerichow-Nord were built strangely wider in various places. And behind the wall of barracks buildings there was more land fenced off than you'd need for drill grounds. The fences ran for miles to the west. And the wide roads went on and on, they never stopped. And for a long time the children of Jerichow would learn the wrong word for air-plane, they learned: fighter, *and they learned:* bomber.
— *Anniversaries* I, p. 409.

I dreamed that I was standing in a very large meadow, situated in a landscape which I did not recognize. In this meadow a monoplane landed, crashing rather badly some fifty yards away.
— J.W. Dunne, *An Experiment with Time*, 1934, p. 51.

Shortly before midday on Easter Monday 1909, a French inventor named Alfred Bellamy climbed into the car of the *Daily Chronicle*'s balloon outside the Crystal Palace at Sydenham Hill in south London. Only a few days earlier, he'd had to jettison bottles, plates, fruit, a chicken and probably also the basket containing the airborne lunch he had been enjoying with a business friend when his own balloon, *L'Aviateur*, in which they had floated up from Wandsworth gas works, suddenly plunged into a "very exciting" descent on a "quiet corner of Buckinghamshire".[1] This time, however, the Frenchman who had laughed so "heartily" as he told that story made a different mistake. Concerned about "buoyancy", he decided at the last minute against allowing a "representative" of the *Daily Chronicle* to accompany him, and he lost his only two bags of externally placed ballast almost immediately as he struggled to disentangle the balloon from trees during his "clumsy" ascent.[2] Although Bellamy was thought to have assessed the weather and abandoned his original intention of flying this comparatively small balloon to Holland, he was seen at about 12:30, passing low over the marshes to the west of the Medway. A man at Cliffe watched him, apparently jettisoning even more weight as the balloon trailed a ribbon advertising the *Daily Chronicle* over the village and then being swept up and out over the Isle of Sheppey by a sixty-mile-an-hour wind. The marshes were searched when nothing more was seen or heard of Bellamy, including those along the southern shore of the Isle of Sheppey. The truth, however, emerged a couple of days later. At about 2pm on the day of the flight, the *Daily Chronicle*'s balloon had been spotted by the skipper of a French steam trawler fishing on the Sandette bank some fourteen miles north of Calais.[3] Captain Papotre, who had his nets down at the time, could only watch as the balloon passed his boat just above the water in driving wind and rain, and then crashed into a heavy sea not far away. Interviewed in Calais between fishing trips, he told a reporter for the *Daily Chronicle* that "even if the aeronaut had maintained his seat when the balloon struck, he would scarcely have been able to live out such a night".[4]

The late Monsieur Bellamy was not just a balloonist. There were also motorised inventions among the machines this forgotten engineer had tinkered into existence in the factory he rented on the Uxbridge Road in west London.[5] His propeller-driven "hydroplane" floated on two canvas-decked canoes, and thousands had recently gathered on Hammersmith Bridge to watch it "tearing up and down the Thames", belching flames and smoke but creating no discernible wash even when roaring along at forty miles an hour.[6] As for his aeroplane, M. Bellamy, who had registered plans for a propeller-driven flying machine at the patent office in Paris in January 1903, had recently told reporters that he hoped soon to be making trial flights at Richmond but had so far been stymied by "the lack of any shed on a suitable ground".[7] That consideration alone might have encouraged the "intrepid Parisian"[8] to glance down with a mixture of resentment and yearning as the wind swept him seaward over the Sheppey marshes, where a group of like-minded competitors were preparing to erect large tin sheds near an ancient farmhouse between Leysdown and Shellbeach.

*

The failure of the "on-Sea" scenario to unfold as easily as F.G. Wheatley and Son had promised in the first years of the twentieth century left this flat and no longer so disconnected stretch of coast open to other forms of exploitation. While the pioneering plotlanders were still awaiting the three-mile-long Marine Parade that never happened, the flat marshland reaching down towards Shellness was becoming famous for something quite different. "Altogether", wrote the *Eastern Daily Press* on 23 April 1909, "signs are not wanting that Shellbeach will soon be the popular rendezvous for all whose inclinations tempt them aloft, as well as those who are merely curious to see others fly".[9] Thanks to an association known as the Aero Club, formed in 1901 by a company of amateur gentlemen-adventurers with an interest in ballooning, an area of marshland in this "out-of-the-world-place"[10] would soon come to be recognised as "the birthplace of British aviation".[11] As Arthur Mee would predict years later, "in the long, long years to come, men will come to this place and say, 'this is where it happened'".[12]

To some early observers, the project was just a posh boys' jape. "A miscalculation would give them a bath", so a report in the *Daily Telegraph & Courier* joked a week or two after the first successful flight: "The Swale, perhaps, is not an ideal bathing pool, but a ducking here would be in sight of Herne

Bay, and that would remind one of a summer vacation".[13] Joking aside, however, respect was also considered due to the public-spirited engineers and would-be aviators who had stepped in with their private means as well as their own often "fantastic" looking contrivances to carry on with a dangerous project the War Office had chosen to abandon.

Impatient with the fact that Britain was "distinctly behind"[14] America and France in the development of flying machines of the kind that, in December 1903, the Wright brothers had first coaxed off sandy ground near Kitty Hawk, North Carolina, Britain's wealthy young exponents of "aero auto-mobilism" created a "flying ground" here in April 1909, using land at Shellbeach that the Aero Club acquired with the help of its wealthy members. The triangular site was found by Griffith Brewer, a balloonist and founding member. In 1908, he had become British patent agent to the Wright brothers and he knew that the Club must have a flying ground before the American innovators would license British construction of one of their flyers. Muswell Manor, the remote farmhouse that had previously served as the sales HQ of the Shellness and Leysdown Estate Company,[15] was acquired as a club house by the Irish engineer Frank MacLean, a would-be airman who was also interested in astronomy and solar eclipses. "It is Land's End", so one visiting journalist would allege "and Muscle Manor [sic] is the last house in the world".[16] Writing in the *Morning Post,* the motoring correspondent Hugo Massac Buist described the manor house more appreciatively as "an exceedingly picturesque and comfortable building... a great part of it between four and five hundred years old". Himself a member of the Aero Club, he enjoyed the "delightful contrast between the building and those ultra-moderns who now use it".[17]

The Aero Club launched its initiative after the War Office had stopped funding its own experiments with powered flight and rejected the Wright brothers' offer of collaboration.[18] It's members set about creating a private "flying ground" and also a plane-building workshop run by the Battersea firm engaged as aeronautical engineers to the Aero Club. Having acquired their licence to build a first flying machine from Orville and Wilbur Wright, the Short Brothers would expand their operations rapidly as they added the manufacture of six individually commissioned Wright flyers to the seven or so other types of plane on which they were also working. A grassy "street" of workshops ("a 'village' of tin sheds"[19]) is said to have gone up in no time at all ("like mushrooms, they almost spring up in a night"[20]), thanks partly to a south London manufacturer of iron buildings, who was happy to add "aeroplane garages" to his existing offering of tin chapels, school rooms, golf and tennis pavilions, bungalows, and more modest metal huts for shepherds and keepers. Indeed, it was speculated that W. Harbrow's hangars of timber, felt and galvanised iron, in which women were employed to stitch and sew the men's flying machines into existence, would soon be surrounded by a new clutch of "flight bungalows" too.[21] The Aero Club's secretary, Commander Harold E. Perrin (nickname: "Harold the Hearty"), expected his landing strip soon to be receiving planes from all over the country — since "hundreds of inventors", inspired by the success of the Wright brothers in America, were working "secretly and steadily" on many different types of flying machine, and all were free to join the Aero Club for a subscription of 10s. a year.[22]

By March 1909, it was revealed that the Club had also found a new use for the coastguard station at Shellness, one of many to be closed down as the Admiralty set about reducing Britain's naval-run coastguard force and passing its responsibilities to a smaller civilian service under the Board of Customs. In Ireland, the Women's National Health Association urged a policy of leasing redundant coastguard stations from the Admiralty and turning them into isolation hospitals and convalescent homes for patients with tuberculosis.[23] Shellness, however, now faced the different prospect of being "converted for sleeping and other accommodation"[24] as required by the Aero Club's people at Shellbeach. (According to Buist, these houses would be made available for members to rent at 5s. a week each.) An artesian well on the Club's property guaranteed plentiful water, and a phone line was being installed in the club house and

Shellness Coastguard Station from the north, Flight, 1909.

also in the sheds (callers were requested to ask for "Shellbeach, Minster, Sheppey"). Some club members were already talking about the pleasures of "canoeing about the waterways" on their newly acquired triangle of marsh. It was envisaged that drawbridges could be placed across the watery fleets, and that dykes might be added to make the club's futurist flying ground "entirely private" and, indeed, "a little island itself".

Yet the Aero Club had more serious work to oversee too. Griffith Brewer reported on Sheppey's emerging "Champ d'Aviation" in the *Field* of 17 April 1909. Noting the speed at which the flying ground was being created, he praised "the pioneers who are about to risk their necks in order to bring this country up to the level of those on the Continent in the science of mechanical flight".[25] As a member of one of the Aero Club committees responsible for the development, he commended the Short Brothers' first workshop (120 by forty-five feet with sliding doors and "a good wooden floor") and helped select the site for the additional "sheds" in which further planes would be built and serviced. The men had also pegged out the route of the two-mile flying circuit that their labourers would create by filling in hollows, bridging ditches and scything down "rank grass" before the mowing machine and roller could be applied. Considering that this had to be at least a hundred feet wide in all places, the airman could have done without the two drainage ditches cutting across their land, but the surrounding dyke would at least allow the Club to gratify the public's "natural desire to view the flights at a safe distance." Brewer also repeated that the flying ground should not be considered the preserve of a wealthy few. Any aeronautical adventurer could subscribe to use the Club's facilities and compete for the cash prizes with which the Aero Club hoped to encourage the rapid development of British aviation: £55 for the first four men to fly 250 yards at Shellbeach, for example, and a further £50 for the first three who stayed aloft for a mile.

By June 1909, the Aero Club was raising funds from its members in order not just to "take over" Muswell Manor permanently, but also to "acquire the golf course"[26] directly to the north of it (presumably the one promised in F.G. Saunders and Son's advertisements) and the shooting rights over an adjoining one thousand acres.[27] Should these additional facilities prove insufficient to the leisure requirements of the Aero Club's gentleman amateurs, it was estimated that a croquet lawn, tennis courts and a bowling green might easily be added to the "more or less ready-made" cricket or football ground within the experimental estate. Further comfort was promised by another of the first buildings erected on a site that would be increasingly occupied by hangars and factory sheds. Buist announced that Frank McLean's "pretty little bungalow", which was equipped with a veranda, a hot and cold running-water lavatory, a cooking stove and "a number of other little luxuries", had proved sufficient to tempt a French motorcycling enthusiast, champion skater and

The Marquis de St Mars: *"The amateur champion skater of France, at practice on the rink at Engelberg".* Tatler, *26 Jan 1910.*

accomplished grouse-bagger named the Marquis de St Mars to apply for the post of club chef on "board wages".[28] Little doubt, then, that the air-minded pioneers gathering between Leysdown and Shellness would find Sheppey more congenial than the French flying grounds at Châlons near Pau, where "the most violent dissipation" available to the bored aviator grounded by poor weather, was, so one experienced knight of the air complained, to "cook scrambled eggs and read newspapers some days old".

A reporter for *Pearson's Weekly* took the two-hour train journey from London at the end of that busy first summer. Arriving in September 1909 to explore the possibility of buying a heavier-than-air flying machine, he stepped off the light railway to discover that Leysdown was "not a town or even a village; it is just a terminal station, and a very small one at that. Beyond it are only sand dunes and the English Channel".[29] He found the Short Brothers' aeroplane factory at Shellbeach a mile or so to the south: "It consists of a collection of huge corrugated-iron sheds... these, I was informed, are aeroplane garages, constructed to the order of wealthy amateur aeroplanists, some of whom, at all events, are doubtless destined to emerge from obscurity in the near future". At that moment, "a clean-limbed young Briton" who was obviously one of these pioneers "bowled-up in his motor-car" in order to have a practice in his new pattern biplane "Albatross" — a cross between a French Voisin and a Wright flyer, with certain improvements introduced by the Short Brothers. Henry Short told the visiting enquirer that he preferred landing wheels rather than the sledge-runners used by the Wright brothers, and that, while he did indeed build monoplanes, he considered biplanes to be more stable and the best kind of flying machine so far evolved. He told the journalist he could provide these flying frames — "with 35–40 horsepower engines, water-cooled, and of English make throughout" — for £850 apiece.

The founding members of the Aero Club may not actually have been named Algernon or Biggles, but they were of the aristocratic daredevil type and well able to finance their interest in the skies. One of their company was Charles Stewart Rolls, who had made his way through Eton and Cambridge (Engineering) to become a pioneer of the motor car: he was the Rolls in Rolls-Royce and a record-breaking balloonist as well as a racing driver who, in 1906, had driven one of his firm's cars from Monte Carlo to London in just over twenty-eight hours. However, the man awarded the title of British Aviator No. 1 by the Aero Club was "a tall, broad-shouldered genial Irishman from Co. Meath" who had experimented with model gliders and become interested in the mysteries of internal combustion while at Harrow, before embarking on a soon-interrupted course of studies of engineering at Cambridge.[30] Known to his friends as "Brab", Charles Moore Brabazon, who was also a yachtsman and a "tobogganist" who'd repeatedly made his mark on the Cresta Run, had bought an Alfred Voisin biplane in France for £1,000. Having maintained "perfect stability" during flights of two, three and five kilometres at Châlons on 27 February 1909,[31] he brought the "Bird of Passage" to Leysdown, where he carried off the first British flight of a heavier-than-air machine on 30 April. There was nothing remotely lofty about his departure from *terra firma*, but he managed to stay off the ground for more than a

Charles Moore Brabazon's "Bird of Passage" at Shellbeach.

minute, and was considered lucky to have survived the crash in which his brief adventure ended.

Visiting Leysdown with his brother Orville in May 1909 (the bowler-hatted pair were taken for a "run" around the site in Rolls' six-cylinder Rolls-Royce Silver Cloud[32]), Wilbur Wright is said to have declared the Sheppey flying field "ideal" and "40 times better than the grounds upon which he had experimented in America".[33] Better than those in France too: latterly near Pau, and before that at Le Mans, where Wilbur had left one thoughtful woman in the ticketed audience wondering whether the "whirring locust" in which the American pioneer seemed content to fly round and round without ever soaring far above the ground really would banish "the armies and the navies of the world" into the "barbarous past" as the utopians of the air believed.[34]

It was in one of the six licensed flyers that Wilbur and Orville Wright had come to inspect in the Short Brothers' "Sheds" at Shellbeach, that, on 30 October 1909, Charles Moore-Brabazon went on to win £1,000 from Lord Northcliffe's *Daily Mail* as the first British subject to fly a circular mile in a plane "constructed in Britain, by British subjects, of British raw materials". (Conditions that had not been passed by the American wild-west showman, Samuel "Buffalo Bill" Cody, who had previously carried himself and some passengers into the air over various distances in his machine, built at the Army Balloon Factory at Farnborough and known as British Army Aeroplane No. 1). "Brab" further distinguished himself a week later, claiming to have made the first air cargo flight on 4 November 1909 (a piglet dubbed "Icarus 2" was carried aloft suspended in a waste-paper basket — in jocular defiance of the well-known adage insisting that the day "When pigs fly" would never come). A month or so later, the Right Hon. C.S. Rolls flew a full fifteen miles in a Short-Wright flyer, passing the coastguard station at Shellness and wheeling round to Eastchurch, where he made the first landing on the Aero Club's new landing strip

— unable, as he explained, to stay up any longer due to the cold numbing his hands.[35]

By the spring of 1910, both the Aero Club and Short Brothers, who now employed some eighty people in their sheds at Shellbeach, had realised the limitations of the low-lying and watery land that Wilbur Wright had commended as "a magnificent ground for experiments".[36] With the help of their wealthy members, they had acquired a second site on Stonepitts Farm, a couple of miles inland at Eastchurch. Charles Rolls won "universal attention" by flying his Wright plane from Dover to Calais and back at the beginning of June 1910. He went on to meet his end a few weeks later while flying in a competition at Bournemouth Air Meeting on 12 July: his tail-plane collapsed during his steep descent and he became the first British airman killed in flight. He was soon followed by a second Leysdown pioneer, Cecil Grace, the Chilean-born Irish son of a New York banker who had practiced the airy art with Moore-Brabazon's "Bird of Passage" and then improved on his prize-winning contribution to the burgeoning "sport of aeronautics"[37] by commissioning the Short Brothers' biplane in which he had recently performed stylish swoops over the warships moored in the naval harbour at Sheerness.[38] Grace "disappeared" in December 1910, when headed for Dover from a village outside Calais, where weather conditions had obliged him to curtail an attempt to win the £4,000 prize offered by Baron de Forest for the year's longest flight from England into the continent (Grace took off on his return journey after a good lunch but missed England, having lost his bearings soon afterwards: his disorientated plane was last seen passing to the east of the Goodwin Sands, heading further out into the foggy North Sea[39]). At about the same time, another Shellbeach pioneer (who had practised on and later bought "Bird of Passage" from Brabazon), A.E. George, an engineer and racing driver known for his performances on the Isle of Man, crashed a plane of his own design at a flying display in Newcastle and, finding himself unable to raise money to continue, withdrew from the aviation field. By Saturday 10

August 1912, it was the turn of a different Aero Club pioneer, Frank MacLean, described as "a tall, well-built man, fresh-coloured, and with the frankest of eyes",[40] to make the first flight up the Thames from Leysdown. "Soaring over Tower Bridge", he landed his "waterplane" by Westminster Bridge and came ashore to the cheers of a crowd who were actually awaiting the arrival of a French aviator Mr Beaumont, who had discontinued the last leg of his intended flight from Paris to London after the wind caused his machine to "turn turtle" as he took off from the water at Boulogne.

*

The Wright Brothers' patents were impressively all-consuming, but they couldn't capture every flying machine that made the move from Shellbeach to Eastchurch. While the Aero Club's aviators were "soaring aloft" in their Wright flyers, a man who owed his initial inspiration to H.G. Wells was to be seen "out on the plain" tinkering with a "heavy machine, which is shaped very much like a snowplough with the sides open".[41] This peculiar rig had been designed by Lieutenant John William Dunne, an Anglo-Irish soldier who, having been invalided out of the second Boer War in South Africa, had spent his convalescence experimenting with flight. It was reported in August 1909 that Dunne, whom Wells had first convinced of the over-riding importance of "stability" in any future flying machine, would "very soon"[42] be bringing his tail-less biplane to Sheppey for continued experimentation. The first version seen on the island's flying ground may have been the two-winged model developed from one of Dunne's first designs and made by the Short Brothers early in 1909 for Professor Alfred Kirkland Huntington, a polo-playing former balloonist who was also Professor of Metallurgy at King's College London.[43] In February 1910, Huntington, who continued to carry out his own customising adjustments to Dunne's plane, is reported to have made some "satisfactory runs"[44] after fitting a Wolseley engine to his contraption, but not yet to have attempted "free flight". By April, he had been photographed flying his "Dunne-Huntington" model a few inches off the ground.[45]

With their swept-back wings and their absence of anything resembling a tail, Dunne's "flying arrow" prototypes had seemed highly unlikely to early onlookers in Sheppey. Not so, however, to the *Daily Express* correspondent who interviewed Dunne at Eastchurch in the summer of 1913. Dunne had already let it be known that his planes were partly inspired by his study of the winged and gliding seeds of the Zanonia plant. He now added to the contrary charms of a story that was being fêted as a "triumph of dogged British pluck over official rebuff"[46] by attributing his design to the realisation that "big sea birds such as fight their way through storms are practically tailless. They balance themselves in the air by flexion of the tips of their wings. That is exactly how my machine is controlled."[47]

The first incarnation of Dunne's vision had been a glider designed at the order of the British army's balloon factory at Farnborough. Since 1907, Dunne had been testing his plane secretly, together with the American showman "Colonel Cody" and Lieutenant Launcelot D.L. Gibbs of the Hampshire Militia Artillery, at the Duke of Atholl's remote Blair Atholl estate in the Scottish highlands.[48] Unfortunately, the Army Council has pulled the plug on the initiative, leaving the Marquis of Tullibardine to complain that its officials had been too "apathetic" to finance a guard for the trial site or even an engine sufficiently powerful to lift Dunne's device into the air. Dunne himself was more tactful, explaining that the cancellation followed the military authority's decision to concentrate on "dirigible airships",[49] and admitting that his flying machine, on which he continued to work through a private company named the Blair Atholl Aeroplane Syndicate, was "at present" of "little use for military purposes" – incapable even of rising "out of revolver range".[50]

Having survived the withdrawal of the War Office and entered a partnership with the French Nieuport company, Dunne had followed the Aero Club's move from Shellbeach to Eastchurch in order to work with the Short Brothers on further models of his "inherently stable" design. Orville Wright and his vigilant patent agent Griffith Brewer were among the witnesses, when, on 20 December 1910, Dunne took his D.5 model for two short flights over Sheppey in order to demonstrate that it was possible to steer and bank correctly using wing flaps instead of the "three-rudder" system employed on Wright flyers, and also to show, when descending, that the "automatic stability"[51] of his design made it possible to stay in the air for a considerable time without touching the controls. Dunne's "flying arrow" — he himself would explain that it was shaped "like a broad arrow-head *minus* the shaft"[52] — may not yet have been ready to allow him to demonstrate its ability, when banked at a steep angle, to fly "in a circle of only 100 yards", thereby coming close to the much-desired "hoverer" of aeronautical fantasy.[53] He did, however, successfully make his point. It was reported that, even though he narrowly missed a windmill and momentarily mistook his distance from the ground when landing, the experimental aviator had nevertheless managed to keep his unruddered and tailless biplane in the air for long enough to take his hands off the controls and, on his second flight, to pencil some notes on sheets of paper provided for him by one of the observers while the plane looked after itself.[54] The latter task was carried out in support of Dunne's own belief that his machines would prove more useful for military "scouting purposes"[55] than Wright fliers, which required the full and constant engagement of the operator to maintain the plane's balance.

Dunne's first "Shock-resistant" prototype, in which stability was to be obtained by "automatic" means rather than by "the skill of the operator",[56] may well have appeared insufficiently scientific to justify continued funding from the Secretary of State for War, R.B. Haldane.[57] Yet Dunne had made his first cow-scattering flight in a Dunne biplane in 1910 ("the sensation was most extraordinary") and by August 1911 he was completing circuits above the Eastchurch flying ground in his "latest monoplane".[58] By 1913, one of his offbeat D8 biplanes which, as he had once told a correspondent for the

Times, worked "on the boomerang principle — that is, it soars in a circle"[59] — would be boarded at Eastchurch by the famous French military aviator, Major Felix, who took off, after some short experimental flights, with the aim of crossing the English Channel. "Despite a strong wind and frequent showers of rain", he successfully landed at Villacoublay aerodrome in north-central France — stepping down to predict that the "existing types" of aeroplane — i.e. those built along the lines of the Wright brothers' patented models — would have disappeared in two years' time, to be replaced by machines of the Dunne type. Going further, Major Felix anticipated that the pilots

Dunne biplane at Eastchurch.

who "safely guided" these new automatic machines, would "hardly believe that men could ever have trusted themselves in the three-control, tail-guided, straight-planed aircraft of today".[60]

The *Daily Express*'s "special correspondent" informed MPs that he confidently expected Dunne's tail-less machines to become "as easily within the reach of the average middle-class man as is the two-seater motor car to-day. A child or an invalid can fly it".[61] Just as the "modern roadster" had displaced the "bone-shakers" in which people had somehow been prepared to risk their lives thirty years before, Dunne's invention impressed this excited witness as an evolutionary leap thanks to which the Wright Brothers' primitive contraptions would soon be consigned to the scrapheap of history. Having previously abandoned Dunne's experiments, the War Office had by now ordered two models. The future also looked bright to Professor Huntington of King's College London, who had decided that even his own tinkered-up early Dunne prototype — now known as "the Dunne-Huntington Machine" — was "a very practical machine for service purposes".[62] Others, however, who remained committed to "the skills of the operator" and to the military possibility of firing guns from the air, resisted this wave of enthusiasm and continued to dismiss Dunne's alternative as the "mad scheme of flying".[63]

By 1914, versions of Dunne's D8 were being built and flown in the USA and Canada, but Dunne himself had withdrawn from the project, partly on account of his poor health, in order to devote his time to redesigning the trout fly and pursuing more "philosophical" investigations into the nature of time. In *An Experiment with Time*, published two decades later, he would explain how he himself had experienced "precognition" in dreams, seeing things that were yet to happen, and concluded from this experience that linear time was a mental construct imposed on a "Serial universe" in which nothing really dies and past and future would be recognised as continuous where it not for the "mentally imposed barrier" of the "present moment".[64]

A greater openness to the "serialism" explored in Dunne's *An Experiment with Time* might have benefitted those partisans of the Wright flyer who had laughed as the inventor tried to coax his all-British "Snow-plough" into the skies above the Isle of Sheppey. The twentieth century would see the aeroplane develop in ways that did indeed, as Uwe Johnson noted, soon require a new vocabulary from schoolchildren ("they learned: *fighter,* and they learned: *bomber*"), and elements of Dunne's idea were carried forward in the same procession. There was nothing arrow-like or "swept" about the wings of the Wapiti biplane from which Jean Chesterton was shot in her rowing boat off Shellbeach in 1933. In Germany by that time, however, the engineer Adolf Busemann was already thinking about the supersonic speeds that might one day be achieved by "swept wing" aircraft. A prototype of the Messerschmidt P.1101, a fighter jet based on his later researches, was still under construction at the end of the Second World War. There were definitely also "swept wings" on the eight-engine American B-52s which, as Uwe Johnson notes in *Anniversaries* (a book whose skies are crossed by precisely logged planes), did such damage after joining America's bombing missions over north Vietnam in April 1966. As for the tailless "flying wing" idea, this was also tested in Germany, as part of Reichsmarshal Herman Göring's frantic search for "wonder weapons" during the last months of the Second World War. A captured prototype developed by Gotha from the Horten brothers' Ho 229 was shipped to America (as was the incomplete Messerschmidt P.1101 and, by 1947, Adolf Busemann himself), where the flying wing idea would break into reality forty years later with the first flight of the B2 Stealth bomber in 1989.

In the early days of flight on Sheppey, one of the stunts favoured by the aviator C.R. Rolls, was to fly over the Royal Navy's warships anchored on the Nore off Sheerness, where he would be greeted by a chorus of sirens and cheers from the sailors on deck. By 1911, the pilots who enjoyed performing such tricks were qualifying members of the training school for naval pilots set up at Eastchurch on a voluntary basis by the now "Royal" Aero Club.[65] The scheme began with four trainees at first, but expanded soon enough thanks partly to the enthusiasm of the First Lord of the Admiralty, Winston Churchill, who came to Eastchurch to train as a pilot himself (a desire that was reduced if not extinguished by the end of 1913, after Captain Gilbert Wildman Lushington was killed crashing the biplane in which he had trained Churchill shortly before).

Eastchurch had by then become the operations centre for the Royal Naval Service School, while Shellness was retained as the "Aerial Fighting and Gunnery School." The combined establishment went to the newly formed Royal Air Force in 1918, by which time Short Brothers had quit Eastchurch for Rochester on the Medway in order to concentrate on building seaplanes. RAF Eastchurch, as the airbase came to be called, was used by Coastal Command, responsible for the protection of Allied shipping, while also serving as an Armament Training Centre for the RAF. During the early months of the Second World War, it was employed as a receiving and training centre for Polish airman entering service alongside British forces. Bombed repeatedly by the Luftwaffe and effectively put out of action during the Battle of Britain, it was brought back into use and the permitted residents of Sheppey got used to seeing a considerable variety of planes flying overhead, from Hawker Typhoons to American Flying Fortresses. The Air Armaments School's gunnery range at Shellness was not deflected from its national purpose by the death of Jean Chesterton in 1933 — nor, for that matter, by the loss of the trainee airmen who died after stepping on the wrong floor panel and falling from their plane or accidentally shooting their own propellers to bits. The range was used for bombing as well as gunnery practice throughout the Second World War, including the rocket-firing practice carried out here for Hawker Typhoon squadrons in 1944. You could easily miss any sight of this history at Shellbeach now, but the case for vigilance remains strong. In October 2011, naval disposal experts found no fewer than sixty-one items of unexploded ordnance — bombs, depth charges, shells — during a two-day trawl of the nudist beach.[66]

13. TWO WAYS DOWN TO THE SEA: THE TRADE UNION BARON AND THE SUFFRAGISTS

Now and then talk turned to the house with the sundial, so near the Shoreline Cliff. When would that crumble into the sea, do you think.
— At Ahrenshoop, *Anniversaries* IV, p. 1301.

Houses on the Shoreline Cliff, Ahrenshoop, postcard sent 1958.

In the winter of 2016, I visited the Warden Springs Caravan Park just south of Warden Point, the low cliff that forms the northern-most end of Sheppey as it is viewed from Whitstable.

I was intending to stand here — at the spot identified as "Land's End" on Edward Hasted's map of 1797 — and look back across the water towards the place where the Sir William Nottidge School once stood above Whitstable. The mist put an end to that idea, but I did come across a garden fork and spade sticking out of the ground at the edge of the cliff.

Rising to a fraction more than fifty metres above sea level, the cliffs facing the wide open North Sea at Warden Point are considerably higher than the crumbling sand cliffs along the shore at Ahrenshoop on Fischland. Both, however, can be classified as "active" as well as "soft". The one along the spit at Ahrenshoop is regularly reconfigured by storm surges and the currents that sweep a lot of sand along the coast in an easterly direction towards Darss Point. At Warden Point, the collapses are caused by events that Natural England describes as "impressive, deep-seated, rotational landslips",[1] produced as the sea penetrates and undercuts the London Clay. On the Baltic site, coastal protection works are carried out on a more or less constant basis. Not, however, at Warden Point, where local residents are expected to watch the ground disappearing beneath their feet under a policy the Environment Agency dignifies with the name "managed retreat". The workers at Warden Springs Caravan Park may have knocked off for lunch by the time I passed by, but they were plainly engaged in pulling their wooden fence back a few yards from the brink of the advancing void.

George Harrison had a less muddy idea of mutability in mind, but here at Warden Point, the understanding that "All Things Must Pass" follows from the unstable nature of the cliffs. Each slumping fall exposes new tranches of the London Clay, dropping a new crop of fossils onto the beach below. Collectors have long been coming to search the shore or, more likely, to haggle with those shore-walking residents of the ridge-top road, who once made their living by scouring the beach for unusual fossils after high tides and storms, and then offering visitors a chance to buy these relics from a time when the Thames Estuary was a steaming and tropical place

166

inhabited by palm trees as well as sea urchins, whales, and the biggest turtle whose head was ever found. In 1750, Mr Edward Jacob, of Nutt's Manor at Leysdown, had been astonished when he discovered the fossilised bones of a vast elephant sticking out of the cliff at Warden. The skull of that monster's avian consort — an alarming flying machine named Dasornis, which one expert has likened to an "ocean-going goose" with a five-metre wing-span and a ferocious saw-toothed bill — would not be disgorged from Sheppey's geological heart of darkness until 2008.[2]

For centuries then, Warden Road, which makes its way from Eastchurch to Warden Point, has been coming to an unexpectedly sudden end. A large stretch of planted field went sliding down in the summer of 1870, remaining sufficiently intact for the farmer to harvest his crop before this vast clod dissolved into the waves.[3] Three acres of land dropped seventy or so feet in 1883, prompting one paper to observe that while "each decade shows a greatly-diminished acreage in the island of Sheppey", the landowners preferred to suffer these losses rather than "spending large sums of money on 'defences'".[4] A smaller chunk sank away just after the occupiers had walked over it in the spring of 1890,[5] and another slid down in 1894, leaving the cliff at Warden Point "almost perpendicular"[6] and prompting observers to foresee a day when all of Sheppey would disappear under the waves just as the Goodwin Sands (said once to have been the Sheppey-like island of Lomea), off the Isle of Thanet at Deal, had done before it.[7]

In the last year of the nineteenth century, when the cottage-lined road leading to Warden Point still bore the "inelegant" name of "Mud Row", the oozing cliff struck the *London Daily News'* cycling correspondent with alarm. He warned that only a "rough bar" saved the curious cyclist from riding into "a scene of the wildest desolation. The cliffs… composed of dark, greasy and crumbling clay, have slipped and fallen in every direction, and the sea at the bottom is discoloured far out with the debris".[8] Most of Warden, an estimated eighty acres, had already been swallowed up by these long-running "encroachments by the sea". Once a well-known landmark for ships, the Parish church of Saint James had been taken down in 1832 and rebuilt further inland with stone salvaged from the old London Bridge (itself demolished and replaced by a distinguished engineering builder named Edward Banks who had come to Sheppey to work on the Admiralty dockyard at Sheerness). In 1877, it had to be pulled down again. Some of the more recently interred bodies in the churchyard were removed and reburied at Minster before the churchyard finally disintegrated in the landslip of 1883. That cycling columnist had seen children at the spot "engaged in the gruesome and morbid occupation of digging out skeletons for "amusement". And not the children of ignorant cottagers, for whom there might possibly be some excuse, but of "people of perhaps some pretensions to culture and right feeling".

The end of the road at Warden Point.

*

It was once thought that the great Baptist preacher, Charles Haddon Spurgeon, might have been among the Victorians who came to this insecure spot to gaze into the firmament[9] — perhaps during the years when William Higgs, the builder of Spurgeon's vast Metropolitan Tabernacle at London's Elephant and Castle, was lord of the manor here at Warden. Be that as it may, the encroachments would continue through the twentieth century, carrying off not just cottages and bungalows but coastguard observation points, redundant First World War pillboxes in which children had sheltered as they watched the Battle of Britain,[10] a curious concrete "sound mirror" intended to warn of approaching aircraft, and, a little further around the coast, the Royal Oak, an isolated pub used by excursionists, smugglers and farm labourers (two hundred of whom assembled here to form a Sheppey branch of the Kent Agricultural Labourers' Union during the nationwide "Revolt of the Fields" in June 1873).

There are still a handful of properties to go before time has to be called on Warden Manor itself. Dating back to the early thirteenth century, this ancient building was given to the non-denominational Christian organisation Toc H in 1933, and used as a holiday and conference centre by members of this branch-based movement which started out as a rest and recreation centre established for Allied soldiers at Poperinge, Belgium, during the First World War. Military ranks and hierarchy were to be left at the door and the principles guiding the fellowship within would be summarised as "to love widely, build bravely, witness humbly and think fairly".[11] After the war, Toc H sought to engage men of all classes in the work of remaking their communities in reaffirmation of the principles and ideals for which so many had died — an idea of service that, in the words of one advocate, came "straight from Flanders"[12] and, according to the later declarations of the famously dissolute Prince of Wales (who would go on to resign the throne as Edward VIII at the end of 1936), made Toc H "the War's truest, because most fruitful, memory".[13]

In 1988, a year after the retirement of the Anglo-Catholic rector of Eastchurch, the National Front-supporting Father Blagdon-Gamlen, Warden Manor was taken over by a group of "Transalpine Redemptorists", a similarly "ultramontane" group who blamed a "crisis in the liturgy" for the many problems besetting the Roman Catholic Church. They came here to establish a "Monastery of the Sorrowful and Immaculate Heart of Mary" in which they would follow the old Redemptorist Rules and celebrate the "Seemingly forbidden" old Mass. They kept it up for a decade, using garden sheds as well as a barn as cells for aspirants determined to save their souls by quitting the world for "the solitude of the desert",[14] before shifting their retreat to the more truly deserted Orkney island of Papa Stronsay, and leaving the manor to be sold back into private use.

Not everyone who has sought to hide out at this end of Warden Road has been able to make such a well-organised retreat. The "colossal landslide" that occurred here at 3.30 pm on Sunday, 21 November 1971, carried away "nearly three acres of clifftop land".[15] "We have lost everything" lamented Peter and Sheila Bryant, a young couple who were expecting their first child in three months' time. Half their home, "Cliff Cottage", had tumbled over the edge, including the kitchen in which Sheila had been working moments before disaster struck. A large chunk of the "adjacent landscaped garden" had gone, although it, like some of its predecessors, remained weirdly intact in its new resting place: "It was as if a giant had silently taken a large section of the cliff top 150 ft down". Over the following days other residents here would be "scared out of their minds" as they watched cracks appear in their walls. Mr Sidney Smith at the Post Office convinced himself that the gaps between his floorboards were widening, and quickly moved into a neighbour's caravan. He was among those who called for an immediate stop to the "loud bangs" that kept bouncing across the Thames Estuary from the government's weapons testing site at Shoeburyness in Essex. Suspected of destabilising the cliffs and widening cracks in the Post Office's walls, these demands would only be heeded after a second, smaller fall which occurred directly after a "terrific explosion" from Shoeburyness four days later, bringing the brink disconcertingly close to farmer Victor Wickin's concrete pig house.

Farewell to Hugh Scanlon's lawn, November 1971.

The onlookers who flocked to Warden Point risked their lives to peer down on the fallen section of neighbouring garden that had followed the Bryants' kitchen into oblivion. They could see that trees were "still growing in the same position" and that "even the summer house" was "absolutely unharmed". There could be no doubt, however, that Mr Hugh Scanlon, the Marxist trade union leader who had refused, two years earlier, to remove his tanks from Harold Wilson's lawn at Chequers, had now lost a considerable portion of his own at the Sheppey hideaway where he had been able to escape the press. The newspapers had, to be sure, watched his every move on the mainland, making an MI5-assisted meal of, say, the 61% pay increase he was said to have been

awarded in May 1970,[16] or his embarrassment at the hands
of the shop stewards at Ford who condemned him as a sell-
out when he agreed to the secret ballots that obliged workers
to vote for or against industrial action as individuals rather
than in the pressurised collectivity of smoke-filled rooms,[17]
or denouncing his inflammatory rhetoric at the TUC, where
he gave the delegates "the fighting stuff that makes them feel
good"[18] in order to win the day for his own composite motion
banning affiliated unions from registering under Edward
Heath's new Industrial Relations Act.

The golf-loving President of the Amalgamated Engineering
Union happened to be in Florida at the time of the landslip
that put an end to his clifftop retreat. His wife Nora, however,
flew back to England in time to witness its end: "Demolition
work on Mr Scanlon's home started on Thursday afternoon…
A distressed Mrs Scanlon watched as builders removed the
outdoor stairway". While she and her husband were "very
sad to see their home go", she made it clear that they did not
"contemplate another home in Sheppey". Neither would the
Scanlons linger to join their neighbours in fruitless arguments
about compensation (rightly considered "unlikely" from the
start), or about the possibility of getting the public authorities
to build sea defences that might at last put an end to the
continuing "encroachments of the sea", and perhaps also to
acquire the last seven hundred feet of Warden Road, clear it
of such houses, shacks and bungalows as may be necessary,
and grade it into a gentle and stable slope down to the sea.
Within a month, Hugh Scanlon, whose primary residence was
in Eltham, south-east London, would be leading a delegation
of worker golfers to Yugoslavia, where they'd been invited to
demonstrate that their sport was not, as was widely thought
in the Eastern Bloc, just a "bourgeois game" reserved for the
"management class".[19]

So the Scanlons vanished from the island (they would
eventually retire to a villa overlooking the white cliffs at
Broadstairs), leaving their former neighbours on Sheppey to
joke — in accordance with since confirmed suspicions that

Scanlon, who had long since quit the Communist Party, was being closely monitored by MI5 — that it was surely not just natural erosion that had undermined his clifftop retreat. Mr Sid Smith of the Post Office was not in any position to move on so lightly. As was reported in one of the earliest copies of the *Sheerness Times Guardian* saved by Uwe Johnson, he and his wife Lucy had bought the 140-year-old post office in October 1971, only a month before the landslip that left only sixty feet of unreliable land between them and the end of the world. A former motor fitter from Abbey Wood, Smith had at first tried to get permission to extend his bungalow in Minster. When the planners refused, he had made the purchase he now regretted so bitterly. The Smith's had hoped to run the post office and shop, and to rent out camping plots in the summer, but their fields were now poised to disappear and their house was unsaleable. Smith's opening skirmish with the military at Shoeburyness soon gave way to another more enduring battle with public authority, this time the Nature Conservancy Council, whose officers kept insisting that Warden's unstable cliffs were a recognised Site of Special Scientific Interest, and must be allowed to continue releasing fossils from the exposed London Clay onto the beach below. After three or four years of calling unsuccessfully for action, Sid Smith wrote a letter not to any trade union but to the Queen, pointing out how he and his wife were being victimised by the state, and insisting that it is "people not fossils that matter".[20] "Surely", he explained to the *Sheerness Times Guardian*, "by now the conservationists have sufficient samples without endangering the cliffs even further" with their digging.

Despite the struggles of that period, in which islanders found their own way of lining up against the impersonal powers of the state, the erosion along Sheppey's northern shore is set to continue into the future. Nowadays, the Swale Borough Council passes the blame on to the Environment Agency, which has diverse ways of insisting that there is no practical way of stopping it. On 13 December 2017, the Conservative MP for Sittingbourne and Sheppey, Gordon Henderson, who himself lives on the island at Eastchurch, raised the shrinkage of his constituency in the House of Commons, pointing out that both homes and holiday parks were threatened — with some pitches standing "now only feet away from the crumbling coastline".[21] He had supported the local farmer who recommended that waste spoil from "major infrastructural projects, such as Thameslink and HS2" should be brought here, and dumped in the sea offshore in order to "reclaim some of the lost land and create a country park along the north Sheppey coastline that would have stopped any further cliff erosion and, at the same time, boosted tourism". Even though this scheme was proposed as "self-financing" and capable of being carried out by private interests, the statutory bodies opposed it. "There we have it", concluded the scandalised MP as he urged the government to reconsider the SSSI status of the cliffs: "In Natural England's eyes, fossils and slumping clay are more important than the homes and livelihoods of my constituents".

Dr Thérèse Coffey, the fellow Conservative who replied to Henderson as Parliamentary Under-Secretary of State for Environment, had nothing useful to offer the threatened islanders, except to point out that she knew the area well: "I expect that the post office at Warden Point is no longer there and has gone into the sea, but I remember several childhood holidays there". As for the abiding expectation that there was more to come, this would be confirmed at the end of May 2020, when residents of Surf Crescent, Eastchurch, heard the ground "groaning" just before a chunk of road, an orange Seat Ibiza, a shed and then a house named "Cliff Hanger" tumbled away, leaving little more behind than a teetering swimming pool. In the words of a swiftly evacuated neighbour, "It's not right to have people's homes, their livelihood, falling into the sea".[22]

*

It isn't only Transalpine Redemptorists and engine-fitters, reclusive trade union leaders and Cockney types like Somerset Maugham's lucky barber or retired boxers such as Frank Bruno who have found their way to the easterly heights of the Isle of

Sheppey. Among the summer visitors in the first decade of the twentieth century was the American-born Alys Pearsall Smith Russell, a Quaker reformer who was among the founders of the School for Mothers in St Pancras, London, and also the first wife of the philosopher Bertrand Russell. She turned up here in August 1909, and reported on her experience in *Common Cause,* a paper formed that year to promote the campaign of the National Union of Women's Suffrage Societies. "Sheppey", she wrote, " though less than forty miles from London, seems very remote and out of the world, and is an ideal place for an inexpensive and unconventional holiday".[23]

Stepping off the Sheppey Light Railway at Leysdown-on-Sea, Russell and her little party found "a beach, a coastguard station, and a yard for building aeroplanes, but practically no population". Determined to combine their summer holiday with some political campaigning, she and her friends chose instead to hold their meetings in the "flourishing agricultural centres of Minster and Eastchurch". At the former, which surely had "a tradition in favour of women, as a Dowager Saxon Queen, Sexburga, founded an abbey there", they went round every house in the village inviting people to rally that evening on the "grassy slope" by the "beautiful old Abbey Gate House". A few ladies took the front seat while children, some from the village and others on holiday from London, "swarmed behind them". The assembly was chaired by a "cliff-cottage-holder of Eastchurch", Mr W.A. Jewson, described as "a member of the Men's League" whose wife, also present, was a member of the National Women's Social and Political Union and an "ardent supporter of our cause". A crowd of about fifty gathered as he spoke, "mostly sailors or trippers from Sheerness" but also the "venerable clergyman", the Rev. W. Bramston M.A., and his daughter. Alys Russell admitted that her own address was "rather curtailed" by "noise and dust and heat", but Miss Kate Raleigh, who was "a prominent member of the Uxbridge National Society", delivered "an impressive and dignified answer to the physical force argument". The meeting, which Miss Raleigh would later suggest was "as far as I know, the first Woman's Suffrage meeting ever held in Sheppey island", was also addressed by one Miss Dawson, described as "a Suffragist from Philadelphia, U.S.A."[24] The crowd had taken a while to gather (the fierce reputation of the radical "Suffragettes" had plainly reached Sheppey before these more moderate "constitutional" campaigners), but its members had listened "most attentively, and 2s. and 51/2d. was collected in a child's sand pail".

Alys Russell was delighted when some members of that audience turned up again, three evenings later, for a second rally at the more agricultural inland village of Eastchurch. This time the pleasant historical background was provided by fields, trees and the gatehouse of Shurland Hall, which Kate Raleigh at least knew to be the last surviving fragment of a mansion where Henry VIII and Ann Boleyn are said to have been received in 1532. The campaigners also had the use of "a 'real' chair", in the form of an old landau lent by a friendly publican, Mr Woollett of the Crooked Billet. Miss Raleigh regretted that some "most intelligent Eastchurch people" stayed away, apparently because "they could not spare time to be arrested". The constable turned out to be friendly, however, and about a hundred did show up — a crowd that, with the exception of the clergyman and a sprinkling of summer residents from Warden, "was composed almost entirely of labourers and of their wives, who had come into Eastchurch for their Saturday's shopping".

Some of these agricultural onlookers may well have wondered what exactly this summer visitation was all about. One or two may even have been descendants of the beered-up villagers who gathered to assault itinerant Irish "pikeys" as they slept in their tents in the middle of a Saturday night in the summer of 1834. In the event, however, they listened attentively for over an hour, "the only disturbance coming from an old man in a smock, Benjamin Bunk, who very evidently had already had his 'arf pint', and who, to our relief, soon went off to get another one". Russell insisted that she had "seldom addressed such a perfectly serious audience before: one very roughly dressed young labourer, in particular, standing immovable and rapt the whole time, only relaxing at the end to drop several coppers into our pail". The resolution in favour of votes for women was raised by Mr Jewson and passed with a "very good show of hands". A fleeting visitor, Mrs Russell had left the island shortly afterwards, but Miss Raleigh, whose family had a summer residence there, would remain to press on with the campaign. She would give her Sheppey address as "Cliff Cottage, Eastchurch" — not a mean clifftop cottage perched above the crumbling cliff at Warden, but a substantial property that has since been demolished and, like its grounds, replaced by a considerable chalet park — adding her "Home address" after a "PS" as 8 Park Road, Uxbridge. Reserving the 5s. 8d. raised at the two August meetings for the formation of a Sheppey branch of the National Union of Women Suffrage Societies, she and the Jewsons intended to "carry on this work among those friendly and intelligent island dwellers".

So it was that Kate Raleigh and her friends went into action again during the second week of August in 1910, holding a repeat round of "village meetings" in Minster and Eastchurch, involving members of four Suffrage Societies, and featuring Mrs Fagan and Mrs Beith, who were respectively Treasurer and Secretary of the New Constitutional Society for Woman's Suffrage,[25] and also Mr Sidley of the Men's League as speakers.[26] By this time, Miss Kate Raleigh was hon. Sec. of the Sheppey chapter, and the campaigners also travelled in sisterly association with the Women's Freedom League, which had broken away from the National Union under the presidency of the socialist and pacifist Anglo-Irish campaigner Mrs Charlotte Despard, who was herself in no doubt that "Seaside and holiday resorts are good recruiting grounds for new members" of societies working for the "resurrection of woman".[27]

Raleigh would report that the "not-yet-quite-enough-educated" constituency MP did not attend, and could therefore be trusted to persist in the ignorance revealed in his recent declaration that "If only these women could *agree* about what they want we might perhaps see about giving it to them". However, the meetings also had to face more serious challenges. The speakers were at pains to distinguish their "constitutional" cause from the "regrettable" antics of the more radical, law-breaking women around Christabel Pankhurst — there would be no running in front of race horses or burning down churches and powerful men's holiday cottages on the Isle of Sheppey. They declared that the present was "an age of social reform" and that the campaign for enfranchisement was an essential part of the wider struggle to "help those who cannot help themselves". They spoke of conditions in the potteries, where women worked for three farthings an hour and the lead poisoning was such that 264 children in every thousand died before reaching the age of one: conditions that were truly "a blot upon civilisation". They insisted that, far from throwing men out of work, equal pay for women would benefit everybody but a few exploitative "capitalists", putting an end to the days in which poorly-paid women were involuntary "blacklegs" used to throw men out of work, and creating conditions "where it was possible to bring a child into the world in decency". Whether the problem was the persistent and quite unnecessary use of "lead glaze" in the potteries — or, in the more rural example put before the people of Eastchurch, the fact that "there were many villages where there was no such person as a midwife" — the time had surely come "to stand for better things, and there was only one way — the vote".

This was enough to convince the man, identified only as "The Rambler", who wrote the "Notes & Comment" column in the *Sheerness Times*. Having never before "heard a Suffragette speak", he was relieved to discover that they weren't the mad harridans of popular reputation. Indeed, he could find no fault with "the ideals" expressed by these "much-abused Suffragettes" nor with the manner in which they placed "their views before the public".[28] Agreeing that the conditions under which so many poor women worked was "absolutely shameful", he jumped off the fence with a gentlemanly thump that surprised even himself: "I say that if women, by having a vote, can do anything to alter this state of things, then by all means give them the vote". This he added, was "the nearest I've ever been to politics in print".

The Eastchurch meeting wasn't all plain sailing. The fierce wind, which so frequently sweeps across the island, kept the women clinging to the railings as they struggled to prevent their poster from blowing away. They also had to deal with a boy who "announced very gory treatment in store for anyone who should class his mother with lunatics and criminals". This interruption, was noted by "The Rambler", who blamed the "older people" in the audience for "not preventing the unseemly conduct of a group of half-grown youths, who tried to ridicule what they were far from understanding".

Given the reputation possessed by "Suffragettes", attendance could be disappointing. In the village meetings with which they opened their "holiday campaign" of 1910, Raleigh's band of women found themselves addressing as "Friends" a tree, a cow, and one or two people peering out of a lane and trying to appear as if they were not looking at "those Suffragettes". This changed, however, when they made their descent from Sheppey's rustic uplands and headed down across the marshes to the military town and resort of Sheerness, on the north-west point of the island. They had chosen to make their stand on "Regatta day", on the calculation that this annual celebration of masculine prowess would produce "large crowds ready-made". The assault was carefully prepared over several days — "all on the nail", as Raleigh would recall. A time and place for the evening rally was agreed with the council. Banners were prepared, advertisements posted in the newspapers, and many notices distributed in the town. On the day itself, the women adopted a custom that Raleigh alleged to be "well known in the East". In order to "remind our guests at the last moment that we were expecting them", we "walked round the town and along the parade carrying a banner and an announcement of the hour". Through this "simple and practical" measure, they found the "spectators thrilled with the notion that 'those women were up to something'". The response proved that "a yard or two of bunting on a stick may be a symbol of the highest ideal which a man or woman can aspire to... Soldiers and sailors appreciate this fact, and 'neath the merriment in which we joined, we felt, we might say, with John Bunyan's pilgrims in the river, 'I feel the bottom and it is good'".

The advertisement Miss Raleigh had placed in the *Sheerness Guardian and East Kent Advertiser* was poorly repaid by the paper's reporter, who preferred to linger over the "Scene on the promenade", where "the ladies in their brilliant and multi-lined and delicate toilette provided a beautiful profusion of colour which was heightened by the more sombre garb of the masculine onlookers". The Suffragists, however, did what they could to turn the regatta into a side-show. Things were livening up nicely by 6.30pm, when they got their "waggonette" in position in its allocated space on the Recreation Ground: "men, women and children approached it at a run, and we had the pleasing experience of beginning to a full meeting".

Writing for the *Sheerness Times* a week later, Miss Raleigh declared: "Large audiences I have seen, but never a more appreciative one than that formed by the few hundreds round our brake on the spot assigned to us courtesy of the Urban Council. Everyone seemed to realise that we were 'up to good', that we were claiming a privilege with the fixed resolve to use it in an upright and reasonable manner. After some interesting arguments and information, the audience were asked to spread the new ideas (if they are new) among their friends. Many copies of *Votes for Women* and *The Vote* were bought, and back numbers given away". Miss Kate Raleigh reserved her closing word on the triumph of the Isle of Sheppey "Holiday Campaign" for readers of the latter journal: "We are pleased with our Sheerness meeting, the first on Woman Suffrage ever held there".

PART III.

THE FIVE TOWNS OF SHEERNESS (DEFINITELY NOT BERLIN, NEW YORK OR ROME)

Sheerness is not only a fortress, but a kind of town, with several streets in it, and inhabitants of several sorts; but chiefly such whose business obliges them to reside here.
— Daniel Defoe, *A Tour Through the Whole Island of Great Britain*, 1724-6.

A stranger visits the Isle of Sheppey in the mouth of the Thames and goes for a walk there, on the streets of Sheerness-on-Sea.
— Uwe Johnson, "Oh! You're a German", *Die Zeit*, 3 February 1978.

C 06 Sheerness

Abb. 1 **Sheerness** an der Mündung des Medway in die Themse mit Dockanlagen an der W-Seite. Der Ort wird durch eine Grabenanlage (a — a) von der Militärstadt (b) getrennt, die ihrerseits wieder durch einen Kanal (f) von der Insel Sheppey abgeteilt wird. Südlich Sheerness bei Queensborough mit T-förmiger Landebrücke (d) zweigt der flußartig gewundene Swale (c) ab. e sind Tanklager auf der Isle of Grain, h eine Funkstation, g ein alter Turm in der Medwaymündung. Beachte das von Deichen eingefaßte und von Prielen durchzogene einförmig-grüne Marschland im Gegensatz zu den höher gelegenen Feldgebieten (i)

Luftwaffe aerial photo of the "war harbour" at Sheerness on the Isle of Sheppey, 1943.

14. MOVING IN

As a poor and much denigrated town on a shore where England ends and the wider world no longer begins, Sheerness may never have been the easiest place in which to sell a house. In January 2012, however, Katherine Bishop had an unusual reason to feel modestly optimistic as she blogged about her "large family home" in the late-Victorian district known as Marine Town. The upper storeys of the four- or five-bedroom Victorian terraced house looked directly out over the sea, and the building retained attractive "original features" including "internal wooden shutters and parquet flooring". 26 Marine Parade had

26 Marine Parade.

also, as Bishop added to her list of the house's attractions, once been "home to German author, Uwe Johnson".

Bishop's post was soon attracting comments from across the North Sea. She was surprised by the suggestion, written in German, that there might be something indecorous about using Johnson's name to increase the value of her property, and also by the query seeking confirmation that the interior of No. 26 had been painted black in the writer's time. This vision, in which the house appeared to alternate between a gloomy melancholic's tower and the grimmest cell in a forced labour camp, didn't accord with her recollection of the family home in which she had lived happily with her parents and two sisters for over twenty-five years. Her denials prompted her German-speaking interlocutor to confess that he may have been taken in by "an urban myth circulating in German literature classes".

Having talked again with her mother, Bishop returned to admit that "the wooden panelling on the wall alongside the stairs leading down into the basement" may well have been black when her parents bought the house after Johnson's death in 1984. When we spoke on the phone a few months later, she remembered that the lower walls inside the front door had been covered with a very dark paper of black and red — "quite hideous really". She also explained that German visitors had kept turning up throughout her childhood — photographing the house from the promenade along the sea wall opposite, sitting on the steps, knocking on the door and asking to be shown inside. Sheerness was not on the conventional tourist trail, but Bishop even remembers the odd coach pulling up so that rows of unlikely pilgrims could peer in at the windows. Her father had tried to accommodate this interest for a while but it had all become a bit difficult. He was busy running his accountancy business from home and there was really nothing left for visitors to see. Meanwhile, the circumstances of Johnson's death in the house in February 1984 had, as the Bishops knew, been miserable. When some of the author's admirers in Germany sent Katherine's parents a commemorative plaque to mount on the wall, they'd decided against encouraging further attention and put it up in the kitchen they'd made on the lower ground floor inside. It would be the new owners who, having bought the house for a little less than Bishop's asking price, proudly granted the thing its intended place beside the front door.

Why England?

Johnson was by no means the only dissenting citizen of the GDR who felt drawn to Britain in the early Seventies — attracted by its modestly socialised liberal democracy, its sense of liberty and perhaps also by the comic potential of its anachronistic class system (there was copy of David Frost and Antony Jay's best seller of 1967, *To England with Love*, on Johnson's shelves). "England" offered an alternative both to state communism and to the strident capitalism of America and West German cities such as Düsseldorf. Even in the very worst of its years as the crisis-ridden "sick man of Europe", England was attractive as "a land of silver rather than gold", as one researcher remembers being told by an incoming East German writer at the time.[1]

Johnson may have owed much of his own "initiation"[2] into Englishry to his landlady in Rostock: born to an English mother and a German father in 1900, Alice Hensan had become an abiding friend during the two student years in which he had a room in the lower ground floor of her house at Sankt-Georg-Straße 71. Meanwhile, the idea of England as a "haven" or a "safe hiding place" has also been found to feature in Johnson's work "since the earliest known instances".[3] Much of his posthumously published first novel, *Ingrid Babendererde,* is set in a school derived partly from his own experience of Güstrow's John Brinckmann Oberschule, at a time in 1953 when the official communist youth organisation is implementing the state's attack on the Christian youth movement *Junge Gemeinde.* One student, Klaus, opposes this policy, whereas his friend Jürgen supports it. Their discussion takes place in the class of an English teacher nicknamed "Sir Ernest", an old-fashioned and gentlemanly chap said to have been modelled on an Oxford-educated man who had taught Johnson at the school before he saved the increasingly Stalinist state the bother of sacking him by retiring. Under the cover of parody, so Colin Riordan has suggested, the English language becomes the free medium in which Klaus is able to float dangerous views, citing things that happened during the reign of Elizabeth I to condemn the ongoing persecution of a Christian student named Elisabeth Rehfelde, while Sir Ernest confines his comments to matters of pronunciation and usage.

An often ironically presented idea of England features in the early volumes of *Anniversaries* too. Given the late-twentieth-century trials of the British textile industry, some readers may be touched to learn that in the early years of the GDR — a state that would soon be encouraging its citizens to sweat in revolutionary materials (including, as Johnson notes,

185

"Dederon, the miracle synthetic fabric of the East"[4]) — England was associated with enduring traditional cloths. After the end of the war, a different teacher, the battered and compromised Ottje Stoffregen, lives in a room above Jerichow's pharmacy, wearing clothes made of "English tweed" that "wasn't shabby even after having been worn for ten years".[5] Durability, then, and, by the time Johnson gets to New York, a certain sartorial dodginess too: as in the "gorgeous trench coat of British manufacture"[6] the author wraps around a nosey and perhaps unreliable Polish-Russian émigré who is now doing very nicely for himself as a sociologist at Columbia University. Meanwhile, an expectation of old-fashioned British restraint is extended to Johnson's primary character, Gesine Cresspahl, by a news vendor who one day shows her *Time* magazine's latest splash of lurid colour photos documenting the ongoing slaughter in Vietnam, and is surprised by this regular customer's "tasteless" suggestion that people need to know what the war is like: "You're all about tact and reserve, it's almost English, and now you are telling me this?"[7]

Johnson's employment of the clichés of Britishness recognises that the assumed fixtures of national identity can, like displaced individuals, themselves suffer homelessness, dereliction and historical redundancy. Not content with registering the British ancestry of the hypocritical old aunt he makes of the *New York Times,* he lodges microfilmed back issues of the *Richmond and Twickenham Times* (with the help of which Gesine reconstructs her carpenter father's pre-war life in England) in the archives of an "Institute for the Preservation of British Customs", which he places next to a high society funeral parlour on Madison Avenue and 83rd St. The first translator to try bringing *Anniversaries* over into English, Leila Vennewitz, was so taken by Johnson's evocation of this shabby-genteel bastion, where the leather armchairs look like they have been imported from a gentleman's club in London and the staff behave as if they are in a country house only open to the plebs because of its owner's unexpected "impecuniousness",[8] that she set off to find it. Was the author perhaps thinking of the English Speaking Union? she asked, after failing to discover anything like it on the appointed corner. Her query prompted Johnson to confess: "I am loath to admit that this institution exists only in my book".[9]

And Sheerness?

Johnson enjoyed playing games with the ever more eroded trappings of Anglo-British identity, but these had precious little obvious bearing on the struggling downriver town in which he and his wife had now chosen to settle. Writing to his benefactor, Max Frisch, on 13 August 1974, Johnson describes the "Reconnaissance trips" that lead them to choose a house here for their English residence. He reported "a certain lack of attraction to Bexleyheath"[10], a town at the southeastern edge of Greater London, where they were based during the search. They'd found "hardly a hint of heath... the area is covered with terrace houses in barely four different designs, traversed by a Broadway that creates a community existing merely as a shopping centre; beyond that the foreign visitors' prejudice and ignorance is revealed in the diagnosis 'suburbia'". Admitting that they may have been blinded by memories of "another Broadway", the Johnsons decided against joining the folk who spent their weekends up ladders with "paint brush and soldering" or "faithfully advancing the cause of their landlord's love for roses of his very own, secateurs and twine in hand". Other English places on their list of rejected options had proved almost as off-putting. The Austrian writer Ilse Aichinger would soon declare Dover "impossible to improve",[11] but the Johnsons only had to watch a collection of English youths on the breakwater at the harbour — catching fish and then shoving them into plastic bags to suffocate, or running them over with their bicycles — to decide against stopping there. In Croydon, they watched as a distressed woman got off the train having just been molested by a man, only to confront the salacious interest not just of the conductor but also of a lady passenger who appeared to delight in "her enjoyment of it and having been spared it herself". In Bournemouth, on the south coast, they'd seen firemen, police and spectators converging on a blaze in the vegetation behind a row of bathing huts. Their decision was assisted by a male bather who just sat there, drinking tea and stubbornly keeping his back to the action. Johnson could not decide whether this potential neighbour "had had enough of fires" or "just wanted to keep his sunburn in the shade" but Bournemouth was out too.

Properties were also considered in Herne Hill, Herne Bay, Canterbury and Brighton, but it was the town known as "Sheerness-on-Sea" that changed the tone of Johnson's letter to Frisch:

⟨RECONNAISSANCES⟩

...I am reliably informed about a place where it seems to be no coincidence that a cul-de-sac in this country is not called that, or a **dead-end street,** but a **blind alley.** That would already be something. I am sure of it in Sheerness on the **Isle of Sheppey.** There is more than enough you could hold against this island, and such ample objections are infallibly expressed to me. It is, they say, really not at all lovely there. I admit that with surprisingly little resistance, since it is hard to dispute that on either side of the train the fruit orchards and rye fields with their charming fringe of foliage disappear as soon as the bridge over the Swale so much as comes into view. The chalky, swampy fields on the island are really not at all **Garden of England** (if indeed any tourist can stand this smug catchphrase any longer than from Dover to Canterbury). No, it is not pretty. But is that why we've come? It is also true that even the Romans did not build villas there, expeditions to the island on their part have only been alleged, never proven. It is true that Sheerness, pop. apx. 14,000, is clearly fringed all round with bathers who can afford only such pebbly beaches or else prefer to content themselves with trade and consumption along the stone sea-wall promenade (most of them in wheelchairs, an unjust voice reiterates). Sheerness does not in fact lie -on-Sea, as it tries to officially maintain: the north bank of the Thames continues to the opposite shore, one has to turn one's head slightly to the right if one wants to glimpse the open ocean. My opponents concede this, as well as the two hours by train to Victoria Station and the three to Heathrow. But it is not pretty, they say, and even less so during the other nine months! I could have taken them unawares by converting that timespan into an argument in favour — but I refrain. The life of the community is fundamentally, and then really and truly, influenced by a steel factory: there are labour conflicts with the workforce. A retiree, before the court over the theft of foodstuffs from a supermarket, accepts his punishment and says, in his closing statement, that the government payments leave him **not too well off**. On the other hand, the town park on Broadway.

A house on Marine Parade, comparable in construction to New York's **brownstones** but built around 1915 and likewise standing in a tight row, but cleaned and painted white, constitutes one helpful argument in favour. It has an enlarged basement storey under the front steps, lower than street level, with at best a view of strangely cropped passersby and cars out the front. There is a garden in the back, but for someone who wants to house a complete office there, and does not want to look out the window while he's writing, that doesn't matter. The storey to which the front steps lead up faces north, out at the railing of the promenade, with a thin stripe of sea (river) above it, and then nothing but sky. You can eat there; the view while you're cooking over the walled-in gardens at the distant rear facades of other buildings won't bother you too much. So there's that. The next floor up practically juts out over the water. So there's that. And by the time we get to the fourth floor, with the two mansard-roofed rooms facing north and south, it has already been decided that I will be barred from making use of them, if.

And so this If has commenced. Brokers telephone, **solicitors** prepare contracts to exchange with one another. Our cheque, deposited with Mr Börnii, will easily cover everything, including repair costs.

The current occupant has no objection to German successors. Another applicant is rejected and remembered without regret, since he once planned to turn a building like this one into a chest of drawers with mini-apartments. The **completion of sale** should be possible by August 20th.

⟨Letter to Max Frisch 4 August 1974[12]⟩

Johnson's spacious Victorian house was not built "around 1915" and one would struggle to find much chalk in Sheppey's mixture of gravel and clay, yet Sheerness was by no means an unfounded choice of residence. Having bought 26 Marine Parade and taken the transitional measure of placing Katharina in a boarding school named Oxford House near Croydon (pending transfer to Sheppey's new comprehensive school at Halfway), the Johnsons arrived in October 1974 to prepare the house for occupation. Writing again on 31 October, Johnson was pleased to inform Frisch that there had been "none of the cold, dark time, the time of no running water, which we expected on arrival."[13] The men from British Gas obligingly fired up the central heating boiler for them and the previous owners had left a light bulb in every socket and no junk lying about either: just a forgotten pair of knickers, a gold fountain pen, and three pennies lined up in what Johnson took to be a felicitous gesture of welcome on a window sill in one of the attic bedrooms.

The Johnsons had arrived in a year of acute political and economic crisis, and Sheerness was by no means immune from consequences that might, if some of the more polemically inclined British commentators were to be believed, have reminded them of life in the GDR. By 6 December 1974, Johnson would be writing as follows to Helen Wolff:

After the local papers have been enjoying to the fullest the prospect of catastrophe offered by an alleged impending sugar shortage, now we have one. The bread is almost gone from the shops. Lines snaking down the sidewalks, fifty feet long even here, and two people wide. Panic shopping for flour. And then they can't bake their own bread because there's no yeast. In any case, we have not joined the excitement, if for no other reason than that we would prefer sourdough. We also cannot agree with the amazement of the native critics who use the quality of British bread as an argument against the country's entering the European market. We are guests here, we eat Swedish bread.[14]

The Johnsons had already made certain adjustments to their house. They'd had double-glazed louvre windows installed in the bedrooms on the top floor and they got their builder to prepare the wall so that bookshelves could be fitted to make a library of the rear ground floor living room. Johnson, who appreciated the historical fabric of the property, wrote of somehow managing to break two hammers while refitting the communicating doors dividing the front and rear living rooms (they had been removed but not thrown out, by the previous owners who must, so Johnson guessed, have found them "too venerable"). He installed an office in the front basement or "lower ground" floor — a work room, with tiled floor, shelves for books and box files, a large table made for him in Berlin in 1965, which was so long that it had to be brought into the basement through the bay window at the front, and a smaller one for an IBM electric typewriter that might, as he himself would later wonder, have to be considered a "luxury" of the kind forbidden to writers in the fourth of Walter Benjamin's "Thirteen theses" on "the Writer's Technique".[15]

The Johnsons's first German visitor may have been Uwe's editor at Suhrkamp, Siegfried Unseld. He arrived from London by train on Saturday, 26 October, when the Johnsons were still readying the house before returning to West Berlin the following month to pack up their stuff. A week or so before his visit, Johnson had written to Unseld, sending greetings from Elisabeth, who was then perched up a ladder with a paintbrush in her hand. He had also warned his publisher that there was still precious little in the way of furniture, so that sitting anywhere in the house to talk would be difficult. They would have to walk instead, and Unseld should understand that "it can be quite windy here" and also that there is often "plenty of rain in the wind".[16] It would be sensible to bring a good scarf, a "true comforter" as Johnson advised. In his own note about that first visit to Sheerness, Unseld was still looking on the bright side. He recorded that No. 26 fitted nicely into its terrace facing the Thames Estuary and that the long walks through the cool sea air were pleasant if also tiring. He was pleased to discover that, while Johnson was reluctant to give him an exact date, his author anticipated that the fourth volume of *Anniversaries* would soon be completed, perhaps even in time for the full four-volume work to be published with all appropriate razzmatazz as the centrepiece of Suhrkamp's twenty-fifth anniversary celebrations a couple of years hence.[17]

Sheerness looking West towards the Medway, photo by
George Poule, c. 1975 (from Johnson's collection).

Undeterred by Johnson's warning that he and his wife were hardly in a position to accommodate four people overnight, the émigré German poet and translator Michael Hamburger visited the Johnsons over a day two months later, at the very end of 1974. He came with his wife, the poet Anne Beresford, and the East German writer Günter Kunert and his wife Marianne. In a letter following a phone call about the impending visit, Johnson had told Hamburger that "the house is not only inhabitable for a telephone but also, in some parts, for human use, too".[18] No surprise, then, that Hamburger's party found 26 Marine Parade barely furnished and, with the exception of Katharina's bedroom, which was full of "ornaments and mementoes", entirely lacking in signs of domesticity or comfort. The office Johnson had built for himself in the basement seemed similarly "austere" to Hamburger — metal shelves as "impersonal" as those in a public library, maps and charts on the wall but no pictures, and the only personal object a "little antique writing table set aside for Elisabeth's use".[19]

The house may never have acquired much in the way of "soft" furnishings, but it wasn't entirely bare once the Johnsons had settled in. There were lots of books, to be sure, and a very large round wall clock hung in Johnson's office, as well as an eighteenth-century map of the famously backward province of Mecklenburg. There were two reclining chairs by Charles and Ray Eames, a painting by the West German artist Hann Trier, and a cast of a carving of two "sleeping Vagabonds" by Ernst Barlach, the great expressionist sculptor (and, until the Nazis bullied him out of the town shortly before his death in 1939, a long-standing resident of Güstrow in Mecklenburg) about whom Johnson had written a dissertation while at university in Leipzig. The Johnsons also had a large black cat, carved from a piece of ebony in Polynesia, and presented to them by their friend, the West German journalist and author Margret Boveri (1900–1975), who is said to have found it on a market stall.

The front garden was really just a few feet of tiled yard that kept the house a merciful distance from the road. The larger area at the back was the usual walled rectangle with a gate leading into a narrow alley behind. This garden had been carefully tended by the two women — were they retired teachers, perhaps also a couple, as one former neighbour thought he remembered? — who owned the house before

Johnson. They'd introduced trellises, roses and other plants too. The Johnsons may have shuddered at the thought of joining the rose-pruning suburban tenants of Bexleyheath, yet they quickly came to appreciate their own piece of ground after the walled-in feeling of West Berlin. By February 1975, Johnson would be informing Fritz J. Raddatz, the well-known columnist and literary editor of *Die Zeit* (who had hoped Johnson might join him in Hamburg rather than burying himself in England), that Elisabeth — "the person with the secateurs" — would be happy to extend a hand of greeting in his direction were it not so covered with earth.[20]

Aware that this new interest might cause some arching of eyebrows in West German intellectual circles, he assured Raddatz that theirs would remain a "spartan idea of a garden". In a further attempt to dispel suspicions of an unlikely collapse into English domesticity, he added that, when they walked past the "overgrown, weedy, entirely untended yard" between the sea and the buildings of Neptune Terrace, diagonally across from their house, Elisabeth would declare this wilderness, still capable of sprouting like a post-war bombsite, to be her favourite "garden" in all of Sheerness.

The Case for Backwaters (Sheppey, Staten Island, Mecklenburg)

The Johnsons's early visitors were inclined to recoil from Sheerness and its island surroundings, if not also from the house they had chosen there. After Johnson's death, Michael Hamburger, who was almost certainly among those who had counselled the Johnsons against moving to Sheppey, declared that the writer's choice of Sheerness demonstrated that he had no desire to have anything to do with another "literary scene".[21] It was, he concluded, to be "the most thorough-going of self-imposed exiles". It would also be some years before Unseld admitted to his true thoughts about his author's English retreat: "Every time I arrived and left, my feeling was the same: how can one live here, how can one write here, in this run-down town, with little or no possibility of preserving what makes the outer life worth living?"[22]

The East German novelist Günter Kunert, a former protégé of Bertolt Brecht's who had come to England for a year as writer in residence at the (new) University of Warwick, shared the Hamburgers' assessment of the desolate place in which they had found the Johnsons. Having taken the train from Victoria Station, the party had changed at Sittingbourne, as travellers still do to this day, and boarded the short three-carriage train that would carry them across the Swale. As Kunert recorded in his *An English Daybook*, the seats inside British Rail's shabby conveyance were a poor advertisement for the attractions of "Sheerness-on-Sea". Their headrests were "enormously patinated" — so much so that one was stuck with tufts of white hair as if an old man had struggled to "tear himself from his seat on arrival".[23]

The world these visitors glimpsed as their train crawled along the western coast of Sheppey proved an "adequate" match for this dismal interior. Michael Hamburger diagnosed "rural slums". "Decay all around", agreed Kunert as he surveyed the wintry scene: "hills of wrecked cars in front of smelters, every now and then a few cows, a few horses on the flat surface". (They missed the dismal "parade of skeletons"[24] that Dutch Elm Disease had made of some of the island's already few trees, the remnants of the industrially obliterated settlement of West Minster, and the "Juggernaut" lorries that were driving locals crazy as they ground their way along inadequate roads leading to the industrial harbour estate at Sheerness.) Reaching the end of the line at the station that still announces itself as Sheerness-on-Sea, the four visitors detached themselves from their seats and picked their way through "a deserted coastal town" that seemed distinguished by absolutely nothing except for the recent arrival of "a German writer" who had chosen, for reasons best known to himself, to move his family into one of the "glued together" houses making up the forlorn "endlessness" that was Marine Parade. As he'd earlier done with Unseld, Johnson took Kunert and the rest of the party out for a walk on the promenade before waving them off from his doorstep in time for the evening train back to London. Kunert glanced back from the pavement to see the distinguished "German writer" standing motionless next to his waving wife and daughter, a teetering "Colossus" who looked as if he might at any moment fall on his wife and break into large pieces of stone.

Marine Parade, c. 1974, Neptune Terrace on lower right.

After Johnson's death, the director of his archive, Eberhard Fahlke, would try to deter those who saw only a fatal mistake in Johnson's decision to move to Sheerness, insisting that the relocation was neither "any kind of political or aesthetic statement" nor a desperate "plunge into exile". It was, he wrote, only an attempt to find "a roomy house with a view of the open sea far away from the hustle and bustle of Berlin" — one that would allow "the relaxation, concentration, and patience that were indispensable for his style of writing: faithful to historical fact and underlain with irony".[25]

Johnson's own letters suggest there was actually more to it than that. Within a few weeks of arriving, he was writing to describe his new home to Hannah Arendt, the German Jewish philosopher he had befriended while living in New York City. He admitted that the life of the town, if not the whole island, was "determined by a hulking lump of a steel factory where chopped-up cars are transformed into sheet metal for cars to be chopped up at a later date".[26] He didn't dispute that Sheerness was a one-horse town, its people insecurely dependent on "this one employer", but he praised it for being "an ugly, living community"and, as he had also informed Max Frisch, definitely not a "sleepy suburb like the scattered developments in the stockbrokers' belt in Surrey, with their charming prosperity". In Sheerness, so Arendt was informed, the people "say *'plice'* for the fish but correct the foreigners' pronunciation attempts with the proper form: *'plaice.'* They are the kind of people who say *'ta'* for 'thank you' and *'tada'* for 'bye' — and are opposed to the Conservatives to boot. We are already speaking to them, even though we say goodbye with a *'thank you,'* to be safe". By no means a bad town, then, for a displaced East German who still carried a puritan "socialist morality"[27] around with him. Nor for one who would insist, as Johnson did when a visiting American scholar eventually reached his door in 1982, that he, as a writer, believed in "individual truth, private truth".[28]

Part of Johnson's own truth was that he appreciated Sheerness for the very qualities that caused others to worry on his behalf. "He loved it",[29] remembers Anne Beresford, adding that she herself had failed to detect any charms in the wintry town Johnson had chosen: it seemed, as her husband Michael Hamburger agreed, to be both "peculiarly inaccessible" and "a rather bleak place at that time of year". Kunert, meanwhile, had suggested that this obscure English backwater might have appealed to Johnson because it "reminded him of his home on the Baltic coast".[30]

"He likes it there. It reminds him of home", agreed Johnson's friend, the Austrian-born Helga Michie, speaking in the present tense, as if Johnson was still there, when I phoned her at a London nursing home on 22 July 2015. When I asked how that could be, Michie, who had lost much of her family to the Nazis (but not her twin sister, the writer Ilse Aichinger) after herself escaping to England as a child on one of the last *Kindertransport* out of Vienna in July 1939, explained "it's the landscape — sea, sand, marsh". I could grasp that. The large skies over a flat and watery land were easily transferred to the Baltic coast. Sheppey knows both the high white light Johnson remembered there and spectacular sunsets that may match and, given the prismatic enhancements provided by the clouds of pollution over London, perhaps also exceed those he had seen from the shores of Mecklenburg and Pomerania. As for the marshes, I have yet to find anyone who can immediately distinguish photographs of the Swaleside marshes of Sheppey, from those on the flat and watery terrain between the Baltic and the shallow inland lagoon known as Saaler Bodden near Ahrenshoop on Fischland.

Had I phoned a few years earlier, Michie might have been able to help me understand other ways in which the struggling industrialised island of Sheppey resonated with the GDR. The large landowners may not have been quite as deplorable as the now dispossessed "Junkers" of Mecklenburg, but they had long known better than to live here, relying instead on tenants, bailiffs and "lookers" to take care of their unhealthy marshes and fields. There was little sign of a resident bourgeoisie in Sheerness, and, notwithstanding the colour TVs and G Plan furniture advertised by some shops, precious few invitations to conspicuous consumption along the High Street, where family-owned outlets battled on alongside chains like Boots and Burtons (the latter since retreated). The people of Sheerness had never lived under the Nazi or Soviet jackboot, but theirs was a military town (as the Luftwaffe had correctly noted on their aerial photographs) and several centuries of co-existence with the Admiralty and the Army Ordnance Board had, as Johnson would also point out, provided them with ample experience of the apparently arbitrary decisions of remote power.

Having grown up in the GDR, Johnson will surely also have been intrigued by the buildings — co-operatives, working men's clubs, masonic halls, chapels as well as churches and, of course, pubs too. These revealed the influence on the town not just of working-class conservatism but also of an English strand of socialism that predated Lenin and Walter Ulbricht too: a non-statist and more organic variety that in March 1913 had led G.K. Chesterton to assure readers of the *Daily Herald* that the trade union was "the only really English institution of modern times"[31] and which, in 1920, caused one dismayed member of the first Labour Party delegation sent to examine conditions in the USSR to announce, with more than a trace of affronted British presumption, that a new verse should now be added to the famous socialist song "The Red Flag", acknowledging that the Bolshevik upstarts had stolen the movement's precious totem and bleached it "the palest pink".[32]

If the landscapes of the Isle of Sheppey reminded Johnson of Dievenow, Ahrenshoop and other places on the Baltic coast, it's run-down charms as a human habitation were remarkably similar to those this no longer East German writer had associated, a few years earlier, with another derided industrial, flood-prone and largely working-class island he had got to know while living in New York City. In the third volume of *Anniversaries*, Gesine Cresspahl is taken there by her daughter Marie, who plans, one day (perhaps in 1982 as she will suggest later in the novel[33]) to repay her mother's self-sacrifice by setting her up in a home of her own. With this in mind, she shows Gesine around Staten Island, commending it as a place where this uprooted Mecklenburger might one day come to feel at least a bit at home. "Or go live with the poor, Gesine", so Marie says of this retirement option as Johnson runs through the contrary charms of this low-lying island, known for its stinking landfill sites as well as for linoleum production and fig trees planted by Italian immigrants. Several years before Michael Hamburger and Günter Kunert had surveyed the "rural slum" surrounding their train to Sheerness, Johnson had given his own version of the view from a train heading south across Staten Island:

> After the wasteland of single-story brick on the north coast of the island, finally some trees and landscape... Electrical lines on rough-hewn poles that are often tilted, from an age of modest technology. Grass growing between slabs of the sidewalk, weed and shrubs high and rampant around the stairs...

> a jerky rattling suburban line...

> crippled houses huddled together, collapsing, draped with pieces of plastic...

> Construction rubble, oil barrels, junk on the beach, splintering posts in the water, and, farther out, backlit pleasure craft and fishing boats. Everywhere, vegetation reclaiming the sick land, covering the scars and wounds of the ground...

> A living cat, white, with deeply blackened eyes, wants to be noticed, there is something it knows...

An unexpected wide field of high grasses, wild shrubs growing everywhere. A steam freighter so close to the shore it seems grounded...

On the sandy roads, covered with puddles of water, lonely cars drove as if cowed by field and thicket so far from eight-lane highways and apartment buildings. Marshlands, no longer traversable due to broken bottles and rusty tin cans. A colony of summer houses falling apart. Children who stared at strangers walking by...[34]

As a borough of New York City inhabited by half a million people, Staten Island is no mere mudbank. Even so, there is little in this extracted inventory of its qualities that couldn't find its equivalent on the Isle of Sheppey, another place where truth and dishevelment have run together in not always melancholy ways that repay reflection. The correspondence extends to the fact, used by Marie to clinch her case for New York's island borough, that its flat and watery landscape resembled the Mecklenburg to which her mother, like Johnson himself, could never return. Both of these low-lying places — Staten Island and Sheppey — were derided as backwaters, and that would surely be the start of something in Johnson's imagination (it was only after six or seven years in Sheerness that he described his fictional Mecklenburg settlement of Jerichow as "this windy backwater that called itself a town"[35]). Both were scarred, eroded and variously blighted places where people made their own kind of society out of an experience that more "successful" observers might fail to distinguish from abject failure. Both were places where historical memory may be more associated with wreckage — washed-up, stranded or just derelict — rather more than formal monuments. On that latter point, as Johnson came to know well, there was an exception to be made for the stone war memorial that has stood across the road from Sheerness railway station ever since 1922. Surmounted by the female figure of Liberty, who holds a scroll and torch over the names of civilians as well as serving soldiers and sailors who died during the Great War, it is carved with the words:

TRUE LOVE BY LIFE — TRUE LOVE BY
DEATH — IS TRIED.
LIVE THOU FOR ENGLAND! WE FOR
ENGLAND DIED.

That couplet, which would later be attributed to a retired classics master from Eton College named Arthur Campbell Ainger,[36] had been printed under the heading "For a Memorial Tablet" in the *Times* on 16 February 1918 (it would be carved into war memorials up and down the land over the following few years). When I passed at the end of July 2013, I found a photograph of Fusilier Lee Rigby, hacked to death by Islamists in Woolwich a couple of months earlier, placed against the railing in front of Ainger's words.

Sheerness War Memorial, with Fusilier Lee Rigby.

15. BLUE-FACED AND SHIVERING: A NEW TOWN ON ENGLAND'S FATAL SHORE

Jerichow was not in fact a town. It had a town charter dating back to 1240, it had a municipal council, it purchased electricity from the Herrenwyk power plant, it had an automatic telephone exchange and a train station, but it belonged to the nobility whose estates surrounded it.
— Anniversaries I, p. 25.

Marine Town from Johnson's back window.

As he looked south from the rear bedroom at the top of No. 26, Johnson will have noticed a high-walled footpath — Telescope Alley — emerging at a slant from Marine Parade at the lower left of his field of vision and drawing his eye away towards the Heights of Alma. Though named after a high redoubt overlooking the road to the Crimean city of Sevastopol, the pub at the end of Alma Street actually stands across the alley from the Ebenezer chapel, opened by Bible Methodists in 1861, and, directly beyond that, the Alexandra Road boarding school for infants built some thirty years later. These larger buildings stand in a dense network of late-Victorian terraced houses: some, like Johnson's own, still roofed with slate, but others already gone over to red cement tiles of the grant-aided "council" variety that became ubiquitous in the Seventies.

Marine Town, as this easternmost stretch of Sheerness is called, was built in an expansion that took off in the mid-nineteenth century and continued, in fits and starts, into the twentieth. If Johnson could glimpse fields beyond its roofs and gardens and, beyond them, the Kentish downs forming a low horizon on the far side of the Swale, this was only partly because the houses inland are smaller and more tightly "glued together" than the sea-facing terraces of Marine Parade. The land on which the back streets are built also stands lower. It is a slight difference, so easily overlooked that Johnson's artist neighbour, Martin Aynscomb-Harris of 24 Marine Parade, used to clinch the case for its existence by citing years of experience jump-starting exhausted Jaguars on the almost imperceptible slope that brings Marine Parade down into the Broadway to the west. The existence of those vital inches had been more painfully proven on the repeated occasions over the previous century when tidal surges brought the North Sea flooding in, filling the houses behind without reaching those at the western end of Marine Parade.

The view over the Johnsons's back garden prompts other questions beside the one vexing those in Germany we have heard wondering what can have possessed this brilliant author to cast himself away here "like a man shipwrecked at the end of the world".[1] Johnson appears to have put that question to himself. When a puzzled local asked him what had brought him to Sheerness, the writer replied, "That is what I am trying to find out".[2]

Johnson's record as a searching investigator of historical environments — be they in Mecklenburg, Carinthia, New York or, for that matter, further up the Thames in Richmond — invites us to follow him in turning the question back on the town in which he would spend the following nine years. What made it conceivable for even a "small" town to be built on this ground, which one of the more appreciative of the local studies that Johnson would gather onto his shelves during his decade in Sheerness admits was really just a "watery morass"?[3]

It was not just the threat of flooding that placed Sheerness on the wrong side of a "contour of death"[4] that had for centuries made the estuarial marshes such "insalubrious" places to live or even visit. Both shores of the Thames Estuary were affected but, by the beginning of the eighteenth century, Sheerness was especially cursed as "the most fever-ridden place in the whole of England".[5] Typhoid and cholera would do their work here, but the abiding affliction was a native form of malaria known, before this mosquito-borne disease was scientifically understood, as "ague" or "marsh fever". This pestilence may largely have died out by the beginning of the twentieth century, but it could always come back.

"His address was Sheppey",[6] so a government official declared of the *Anopheles atroparvus* mosquito in September 1917, while admitting that the island's extensive population of these insects had been re-infected during the ongoing Great War by soldiers and naval ratings bringing the malaria parasite back from Salonika, Mesopotamia and Egypt. A member of the Royal Army Medical Corps, Major Angus McDonald, who looked into the situation in 1918, confirmed that, of all the coastal saltmarsh areas affected in England, Sheppey claimed the "first rank" in the "order of menace", thanks to the year-round stagnancy of its often untended dykes, its marshes being "close to the homes of people and the people being of a class amongst whom malaria carriers from abroad are likely to be many and frequent".[7] Major MacDonald confirmed that reinfection of the native mosquito had already happened — there were sixty-one known cases of indigenous malaria on the island in 1918. Army researchers had found the offending mosquito, here identified more generally as *Anopheles maculipennis*, in huts at Eastchurch aerodrome and the military camp at Holm Place, in dwelling houses and also bell tents at Leysdown and Shellbeach. The larvae, meanwhile, were thriving in grass, pools and overgrown ditches. While the war lasted, it had been possible to remove human carriers of the malaria parasite to France, where

Anopheles Maculipennis on a bedroom wall in Kent, 1918.

No longer "a quagmire of vegetation and probably the chief breeding place of local maculipennis". Drained dyke at Holm Place, Sheppey, 1918.

treatment had been more successful, but this convenience was no longer available after the Armistice of November 1918. McDonald then had to rely on other measures, including the screening of huts with cardboard strips and butter muslin. When it came to the *Anopheles* larva, he favoured drainage and clearing of dykes but had to admit, given the negligence of farmers and landowners, that "perhaps the most valuable enemy of *maculipennis* in the estuarian dykes is the stickleback".[8] There were, he concluded, eleven "infective foci" on the island,

and some five or six hundred "carriers" living in its various settlements, including Sheerness.

Against that background, it is hardly surprising that the Medical Health Officer responsible for Sheppey in 1949 should have worried that post-war conditions were once again ripe for a fatal outbreak.[9] An expert at the government's Malaria Laboratory at Horton Hospital in Epsom did nothing to dispel his fear that Sheppey's mosquitoes might become carriers again, thanks this time to the "Families Camp" at Eastchurch, where the military authorities insisted – despite previous warnings – on accommodating the Indian, Anglo-Indian, Cypriot, and Maltese wives of men serving with the British Empire's forces overseas. The expert in question, P.G. Chute, who claimed to have examined three cases of native malaria a little further east along Marine Parade in Sheerness immediately after the Second World War, urged Dr. Crichton to consider spraying the infested saltmarshes behind the pub named the Ship on Shore with DDT – an experimental measure that was, he admitted, still an entirely untried method of mosquito control.[10]

1667: A Tough Year for Sheep

How, then, as we may imagine Johnson and his visitors wondering, had a town of some fourteen thousand people come to exist on this notoriously infested swamp that, for centuries, as Johnson soon found out from his copy of William Lambarde's *A Perambulation of Kent*, had been known primarily for its sheep? By 13 January 1976, he was telling his Rostock friends, Alice Hensan and her daughter Dorothy, that the Romans had marked the place on their maps as "the island of Ovinium", and that Lambarde too had reckoned it "greatly esteemed either for the number of the sheepe, or for the finessese of the fleese ... (which passeth all other in Europe at this day; and is to be compared with the ancient delicate wool of Tarentum, or the Golden Fleese of Colchos, it selfe) and for the abundant store of flocks..."[11]

The small town in which Johnson had landed himself and his family turned out to be the creation of a modern history that opened in the first year of the Second Anglo-Dutch War, a conflict provoked by British aggression against Dutch ships and imperial possessions in America, the Caribbean and West Africa, and formally declared by Charles II on 4 March 1665. A British fleet commanded by the Duke of York may have "trounced"[12] a Dutch squadron off the Suffolk coast at Southwold that spring, but further preparations against Dutch attack were considered necessary, not least at the mouth of the Medway, a river that was then the primary home of the English fleet. So it was, as Johnson was soon informing his friends abroad, that, on 18 August that year, Samuel Pepys, the diarist who was also Clerk of the Acts of the King's Ships, joined a party that included the navy's chief engineer, William Brockman, and sailed down the Thames from London:

> Up about 5 o'clock and dressed ourselves, and to sayle again down to the Soveraigne at the buoy of the Nore, a noble ship, now rigged and fitted and manned; we did not stay long, but to enquire after her readinesse and thence to Sheernesse, where we walked up and down, laying out the ground to be taken in for a yard to lay provisions for cleaning and repairing of ships, and a most proper place it is for the purpose.

Ten days earlier, the dockyard at Chatham, a then plague-stricken place some twelve miles further up the Medway, had been ordered to "equip Sheerness with the requisites for cleaning ships' hulls".[13] The new dockyard would be particularly convenient thanks to its proximity to the Nore, a submerged offshore sandbank that was already in service as a naval anchorage, and also to the existence of deep water close to the shore at Sheerness (the increased size of warships was combining with the shoaling of the rivers to challenge more sheltered dockyards in Deptford, Woolwich and Chatham). The land acquired may have been "unhealthy marshland of little value", but it is said that a certain Colonel Edward Vernon, whom Pepys later described as "a merry good fellow", was paid a fortune for it by Charles II — a fee that would be judged sufficiently "improper" to be successfully reclaimed under Charles' successor James II.[14]

Preparations for the new dockyard took place alongside other measures intended to increase the security of the English fleet in the Medway. *The Victoria County History of Kent* cites a "consultation" held at Garrison Point on 20 March 1667 to consider defensive measures that might improve on the circular artillery fort — "the old Bulwarke Sherenasshe"[15] — built here during the reign of Henry VIII. It was decided to create a garrisoned fort alongside the new dockyard, and also to establish a battery of eighteen-pounder guns to help repel any hostile fleet that might try to advance up the Medway.

Not for the last time in the history of Sheerness, these preparations would prove too little and too late. Neither the dockyard nor the fort had been completed when Sheerness was attacked by a squadron from the Dutch fleet in June 1667. The force of seventeen ships that sailed into the Thames was commanded by Lieutenant-Admiral van Ghent. Having failed to capture an assembly of frigates and Barbados merchantmen moored near Gravesend, Ghent sailed back downriver to try the Medway, attacking the fort at Queenborough and "conquering" much of the Isle of Sheppey, before proceeding to bombard the unfinished outpost at Sheerness and then landing eight hundred marines under the command of a "renegade English Republican"[16] named Colonel Thomas Dolman, to finish the job. "The enemy hath possessed himself of that place; which is very sad, and puts us into great fears of Chatham",[17] so Pepys wrote on 11 June 1667. He returned to the humiliating story on 30 June: "it is said that the country soldiers did first run at Sheerness, but that then my Lord Douglas's men [Scottish soldiers of the so-called 'Dumbarton Regiment'] did run also; but it is excused that there was no defence for them towards the sea, that so the very beach did fly in their faces as the bullets come, and annoyed them, they having, after all this preparation of the officers of the ordnance, only done something towards the land, and nothing at all towards the sea".

The conquest and plundering of Sheerness fort under Colonel Dolman, Romeyne de Hooghe after W. Schellink, c. 1669.

The Dutch account confirms that the defenders of the unfinished fort at Sheerness were easily routed: "Our cannon so stormed the place that the enemy left it before Colonel Dolman, who had been sent for by some messengers, had arrived".[18] This Dutch witness adds, "Our people found there an entire royal magazine, with very heavy anchors and cables and hundreds of masts. Our people took on board the ships as many of the cables, masts and round woods as they could, and they also acquired fifteen heavy pieces shooting balls of 18 lbs. The rest was destroyed or rendered useless, and the magazine burnt. The damage done to the English at this island was estimated at more than four tons of gold". While these events were unfolding, the 1st Duke Albermarle, whose gilded flagship the Royal Charles was at anchor in the Medway, was still in Gravesend, awaiting the Dutch fleet together with "a great many idle lords and gentlemen".[19] Like Pepys, who saw them there, these commanding fellows had yet to learn of the conquest of Sheerness, and we can't trust the Conservative myth-maker Sir Arthur Bryant, who asserted in a book published in 1933 that they should have known, since "the offals of sheep borne up the river by the flood showed all too well what the Dutch had been doing" on the Isle of Sheppey.[20]

Having laid waste to the unfinished fort at Sheerness,

Ghent's squadron advanced up the Medway on 12 June, allegedly with the help of renegade English pilots (who may, like Colonel Dolman and his force of realigned English soldiers, have been Parliamentarians who had gone over to the Dutch in reaction against the Restoration of the monarchy in England). Breaking through the defensive chain placed across the river, they unleashed havoc on the English fleet, which they found laid up and largely unmanned at Chatham and Gillingham, thanks partly to the financial difficulties of Charles II, who was struggling with the combined consequences of the Great Plague and the Great Fire of London. Before withdrawing in triumph, taking the Royal Charles with them as their trophy ("nothing more costly has been made in England"), the invaders further humiliated the English by proving themselves exceptionally well-mannered.

The Dutch marines who landed at Gillingham did not kill, loot or wantonly destroy — unlike the English force that had fired the town of West-Terschelling during Rear-Admiral Holmes' raid on the Vlie estuary the previous summer. And also, so Pepys testifies, unlike Lord Douglas's twelve thousand-strong English force, which came to chase the Dutch out of the Medway: a savage rabble that is said to have "plundered and took all away" as its members advanced through the Medway towns. On 30 June 1667, Pepys recorded the words of a waterman, who repeated the local conviction that "our own soldiers are far more terrible to those people of the country-towns than the Dutch themselves". As Johnson told Hannah Arendt, the contrasting Dutch account of the conquest praises Sheppey as "a beautiful and fruitful island" where little if any lasting harm was done to the natives: "Everyone was strictly forbidden, on pain of heavy punishment, to injure the inhabitants in life or goods".[21]

Work on both fort and dockyard at Sheerness went ahead with greater urgency after the polite Dutch sailed off with their prizes. New fortifications would be built, along with defensive ditches and canals on the landward side. In May 1673, the "clerk of the cheque" noted "the beginning of something like a yard here", including a store house going up on ground enclosed the year before. In a contribution entitled "Of the *Arsenals* for the

Royal Navy in Kent", prepared in the 1690s for a new edition of Camden's *Britannia,* Samuel Pepys described Sheerness as an "appendix" to Chatham and "a *Yard* furnish'd for answering all occasions for the same upon Ships of the *Lower Rates,* resorting thither in time of Action".[22] The previous year, on 7 June 1672, which is to say little more than a week after the Battle of Solebay (the first encounter of the Third Anglo-Dutch War), Charles II sailed downriver to Sheerness to inspect the new fort, the mere existence of which had already proved sufficient to dissuade the Dutch fleet from trying a repeat of its humiliatingly successful raid on the Medway.

Time for the Engineers

For more than a century, just about everything required by the dockyard and garrison was brought to Sheerness by sea. Even fresh water had to be shipped in at considerable cost in barrels from Chatham, Queenborough or even Gravesend. Various attempts had been made to sink wells under the jurisdiction of the Admiralty, but the ground turned out to be an unstable swamp of mud, gravel and quicksand, through which salt water would filter in apparently limitless qualities before digging had reached more than a few feet.[23] This difficulty was not resolved until after 1778, when the Master General of the Ordnance, Lord Townshend, realised that the government was unlikely to pay for improvements to the defensive fortifications along England's east coast unless each defended area was possessed of a reliable supply of fresh water. The engineer called in to achieve this, Sir Thomas Hyde Page, had been pensioned off after suffering serious injuries while fighting at Bunker Hill during the American Revolution. He set to work at Sheerness in April 1781, using a "very ingenious" engine-maker called Cole from Lambeth.[24] When his excavation was flooded out almost as quickly as earlier efforts, Page and the Board of Ordnance were mocked for making "not a well for fresh water, but a sink for the money of the public".

For his next attempt, Page chose a site within the army garrison and employed a certain Mr Hooper from Margate, who made a horizontal windmill for powering a water-removing chain of thirty-six-gallon buckets. This time, they marked out a circle of twenty-two feet across, and dug down in five-foot stages, lining the opening with vertically braced "ribs" of wood that locked into one another to close the circle. On reaching a solid layer of blue clay at thirty-six feet, they marked out a smaller circle inside the larger one, created another circular frame, built a double brick lining inside it, and then filled the space between the two frames with rammed earth. This inner cylinder, eight feet in diameter, was then sunk down into the ground without great difficulty — except for a "piece of tree" found at a depth of three hundred feet. The ground started to ooze at 328 ft, and the bottom of the well blew inwards at 330 ft, filling so quickly with torrents of water and quicksand that the well-diggers only just managed to escape. The water proved to be of "very soft quality" and "perfectly good for every purpose". The duly christened "King's Well" at Sheerness was soon being praised as "the most extraordinary Structure of its Kind in Europe".[25]

The quest for fresh water was by no means the only thing that called for exceptional engineering in Sheerness. The dockyard that Charles II ordered into existence in the seventeenth century was small, modestly equipped and, despite considerable growth encouraged by Britain's far-flung imperial wars and adventures through the eighteenth century, increasingly inadequate to requirements. It was this situation that brought the founder of the modern town of Sheerness to the island. Born in North Yorkshire in 1770, Edward Banks had started out as a day labourer but subsequently become one of the great engineering builders of his age. He would count three London bridges among his works, all of them designed by the Scottish engineer John Rennie (Banks and his partner William Jolliffe completed Waterloo Bridge in 1817, Southwark Bridge in 1819 and London Bridge in 1824), along with diverse lighthouses, prisons, canals, locks, and also the docks at Goole. It was the decision to build a new sixty-acre dockyard to Rennie's plans that had brought Banks to Sheerness. The first phase of this prodigious £3 million scheme involved creating a new granite basin on "quicksand, nearly forty feet deep".[26] The walls fronting the sea were composed of "hollow masses, standing upon inverted arches" which were themselves supported by numerous piles some thirty feet long. This ingenious "mode of building" was considered "in a great measure new in this country", although Rennie, who would die during the early stages of the work at Sheerness (the project was taken over by his son, John Rennie the Younger), had previously used a similar method at Great Grimsby.[27] The basin had iron gates of seventy tons each, and a steam-powered pumping system that could clear it of water in a few hours. Adjacent to the basin were three dry docks, and there were plans to build a new one thousand-foot length of river wall with a low water depth of twenty-seven feet and a great many more facilities within the site too.

Northeast corner of Rennie's dockyard.

The construction of Rennie's dockyard was begun in February 1815. Two months later, on 22 April, the First Lord of the Admiralty, Lord Melville, boarded the Admiralty yacht in London and sailed downriver to Sheerness with a bevy of commanding figures. This time the visiting party included the First Naval Lord and member of the Admiralty Board Sir Joseph S. Yorke, and also the first secretary to the Admiralty, John Wilson Croker. These well-appointed men stayed for long enough to express "much satisfaction" at the "improvements" underway, and then sailed back to London.[28] Another of Melville's flying visits to this remote construction site, made only a few days after Napoleon had surrendered to Capt. Maitland on the deck of *HMS Bellerophon* on 15 July 1815, gave rise to hectic rumours that "this fortress is fixed upon as the place of confinement of Buonaparte".[29]

Rennie's new basin was formally opened in September 1823. London was said to have been emptied as the people who mattered in such estimates climbed aboard the vessels that would bring them downriver to witness a development that had been hailed as the largest engineering works in Europe. The occasion was judged "a truly national fete", despite the abiding difficulties of the location. Two steam ships, the *Royal Sovereign* and *Venus*, which had collected their passengers from Tower Stairs at 6am,[30] arrived too late for the ceremony; and the *Lord Melville*, a steamer on which Sir Edward Banks (he had been knighted in 1822) and Jolliffe hosted "a very large party", considered it wise to leave Sheerness for the return journey at 3pm, three hours before even the Duke of Clarence had departed.[31] A general insufficiency of boats left many of the estimated fifteen to twenty thousand visitors stranded on the Isle of Sheppey without accommodation, obliging them to find their own way back to London via Chatham and other inconvenient places. While there, some of them might have registered both the "sallow, unhealthy complexions" of the natives and the "multitudinous array of new-formed graves in the church-yard". Some may also have felt the mud seeping into their shoes and wondered, as "W.R." would do in the *Morning Chronicle* five years hence, what "folly" can have induced the First Lord of the Admiralty "to construct the finest dockyard in England, or, perhaps, in Europe, in the centre of a pestilent marsh, where multitudes are carried off yearly by the remittent and intermittent fevers arising from its noxious miasmas..."[32]

Hulks Before Hovels

How, meanwhile, was a dockyard on such a dismal shore to accommodate its workers? The practice of incarcerating convicts on hulks in British waters had been introduced in 1776, when "disturbances in America" necessitated changes in the British system of penal transportation (America having preceded Australia as the customary destination for British convicts). At this point, as a parliamentary committee explained in a report of 1810, it had been decided that any offender might be put to work "raising sand or gravel from the river Thames, or in any other benefit for the Navigation of that river."[33] Other naval rivers were soon added to this dispensation. Convicts who might once have been shipped across oceans instead found themselves undergoing hard labour in the "hulk establishment" at home. They might receive a considerable reduction in their sentences for their pains, and the Crown was also empowered to spare those under sentence of death on condition that they served "a term not exceeding ten years" on the hulks. Above the overseers, there was an "Inspector of the Hulks", the first incumbent being a Mr Graham, whose improvements included separation of decks, close constraints on communication, the introduction of a chapel and the replacement of fixed barrack bedsteads with hammocks.

From the beginning of the "hulk establishment", there was much concern with "moral amendment" and saving the young offender especially from being rendered "more vicious" by confinement. Bad things had followed from the fact that prisoners were left "entirely to themselves" from the moment of evening lockdown within the decks to the opening of the hatches in the morning. The consequences of this lack of oversight were not limited to "gambling, swearing, and every kind of vicious conversation"[34] Rumour also imputed "the most atrocious vice" to the hulks. Indeed, letters had been received alleging not just that prisoners did indeed commit and suffer this unnameable sin, but that it had "ceased to be held in detestation" among the convicts. The captains of the hulks concurred in "disbelieving" the existence of such a thing, and the deniers worked hard to convince themselves that "this vice appears to be held in as much abhorrence on board the Hulks as in other places, and any person suspected of having been addicted to it has invariably met with ill-usage from the rest of the prisoners". The letters in which some convicts had alleged such goings-on were dismissed as the manipulations of devious men who considered their accusations to be "the most effectual means of exciting compassion" and stimulating friends into "exertions on their behalf". And yet the blizzard of rules that various inspectors brought down on the hulks in those early years leave little doubt that those in power recognised that something should be done.

In Sheerness, where "the local situation" made it exceptionally hard to procure labour, the convicts had been found "all the more valuable" in the years immediately before Rennie's reconstruction of the dockyard. Adult convicts had been lodged on the *Retribution*, a demasted seventy-four-gun frigate formerly known as the *Zealand* and stationed there as a hulk in 1810.[35] Boys under sixteen were accommodated, allegedly with the appropriate Christian discipline, on another third-rate man-of-war, the *Bellerophon* (known to sailors as the *Billy Ruffian*), which, having served in the Battle of Trafalgar and received the surrender of Napoleon after his defeat at Waterloo, was brought to Sheerness to be "fitted up" as a convict ship.[36]

There were escape attempts long before Charles Dickens created Magwitch in *Great Expectations* in 1861. In October 1810, seven convicts had stolen the *Retribution*'s "hulk boat" and sailed across the Medway to the Isle of Grain, where they were pursued and hunted down — two of the fugitives escaped, one was said to have drowned in a fleet and four were captured and returned to the disciplinary regime that a condemned murderer from the *Retribution* had recently described, while proclaiming his innocence just before being hanged in front of a baying Kentish crowd, as "the lash of tyranny".[37]

The difficulties of maintaining order among the five hundred or so convicts housed on the *Retribution*'s three decks were aggravated by the fact that, before work began on Rennie's new dockyard in 1815, there really hadn't been sufficient "hard labour" in the Sheerness dockyard to occupy them all. The work of loading and unloading, and of pumping water out of the old dock, was irregular and dependent on the fluctuations of the tide. With the exception of "a few shoemakers and tailors employed in keeping the shoes and clothes of the others in repair", those who remained on the ship were allowed to be "idle", or to "work for themselves, at their own pleasure; the materials for their work are procured on their own account, and they dispose of the articles made, either by sending them up to town, or selling them in the Dockyard". Attempts to improve the situation included the introduction of a school at which some convicts might learn to read, and also the decision to remove some of the "most refractory" of the five hundred for further "transportation" to New South Wales on 14 August 1811.[38]

It is possible to sense how much had been going wrong on the hulks by reading the detailed instructions prepared for John Henry Capper, who became Superintendent of the hulk establishment in 1815. These stipulated that overseers must "constantly reside on board",[39] and that "all healthy convicts" must be sent on shore to work, with the exception of those engaged in shoemaking and tailoring. A "Character Book" was to be kept in each hulk and the Chaplain would be expected to group the convicts into classes, using a scale of six categories ranging from Good to Bad. Food allowances must be published for the convicts to see, and the food itself should be weighed and measured in their presence. Overseers must use "justice and humanity" and attend the services in which the chaplain was expected to preach and read prayers every Sunday. A great many of the rules introduced in 1815 were plainly aimed to prevent the overseers setting up despotic regimes on their hulks. On disciplinary matters, they were to try "mild and persuasive means" first, and only resort to punishment on board if this fails — and the punishment was always to be carried out in the presence of the surgeon as well as the other convicts. They must understand that the hulk's boats should never be "employed for pleasure", that there were to be no fees or gratuities, and no pigs or chickens kept on board by overseers for selling to convicts. Cards and dice should be taken away from convicts. Temperance was to be the rule of the day, and officers supplying "spirits or beer" to the convicts must be dealt with.

The chaplains of the two hulks in Sheerness were assisted in their battle for redemption by the Sheppey Auxiliary Bible Society, whose members were delighted, in 1817, to hear the Rev. Mr Edwards of the *Bellerophon* report that the prisoners were attentive to "the reading and learning by rote" of "large portions of holy writ".[40] Speaking to the Society at a meeting in Sheerness, Edwards ventured that it would be hard to find less "swearing and profane language" being used in "any like number of labouring men". Among his homilies was the story of a convict who had found twelve shillings while working on shore and immediately taken it to the officer, asking him to "adopt means to find the owner" (who turned out to be "a labouring youth, whose whole week's wages did not amount to that sum"). The Rev. Mr Price of the *Retribution* had also reported great improvements since the government adopted new measures, themselves believed to have been first suggested by Price himself. He too spoke of the convicts' "attention to religious instruction", noting that "a considerable number had, unknown to him started a prayer-meeting among themselves". One poor fellow had even composed some appropriately pathetic lines of verse — no mention of the "atrocious vice" here nor, indeed, of any lash other than that of the evangelically awakened conscience — that were duly presented at the Bible Society's first anniversary celebration:

To the British and foreign Bible Society, by a Convict on board the Retribution Hulk, Sheerness

When torn from friends — imprison'd on the deep,
The wretched Convict bends his head to weep;
When burning tears in plenteous streams are shed,
And black despair sits brooding round his bed,
Where can he turn — to who for comfort go —
But to that Word, which comfort can bestow?
Though we are outcasts, fast in mis'ry bound,
We gladly hear the gospels joyful sound;
Not only Hear, but feel its pow'rful sway,
And humbly bend our sinful knees to pray,
The word of God has pierc'd our darkness through,
And said, though fainting, 'Ye shall still pursue.'[41]

Perhaps there was a harsh kind of relief to be found in the reported fact that, even before the opening of Rennie's vast new basin in 1823, the work his rebuilding had brought to the dockyard was no longer sufficient to employ all the men on the two convict hulks. Another "early embarkation"[42] for New South Wales would that year help to correct the surplus on the *Retribution*. The *Bellerophon*, meanwhile, had been "wholly appropriated" to accommodate "the juvenile convicts of the country", who were to be taught "useful trades" such as shoemaking and tailoring by adult convicts: it was hoped that in time they would make clothes for "the whole establishment of convicts throughout the kingdom".[43]

From "Sea Breakers" to "Blue Houses"

It wasn't just convicts who lived aboard derigged hulks at Sheerness in the early years. In November 1767, the Christian revivalist and founder of Methodism John Wesley, who visited Sheerness no fewer than nine times in all, had found himself in a "town" of a kind that "is scarcely to be found again in

England". As he wrote in his diary, it consisted of six old men-of-war in the dock beside the fort: "These are divided into small tenements, forty, fifty, or sixty in a ship, with little chimneys and windows; and each of these contains a family. In one of them, where we called, a man and his wife, and six little children lived. And yet all the ship was sweet and tolerably clean; sweeter than most sailing ships I have been in". [44]

Some of these floating "tenements" lasted into the early nineteenth century. According to the *Morning Post* the "Old Sea Breakers," [45] which would finally be buried under Rennie's new jetty, had been laid out along the shore of the Medway directly to the south of the dockyard. Having served in grander days as "the wooden walls of England", these hulks were placed by the sea wall in an attempt to reduce the force of tidal "surges", which the government of the day had been warned were both increasing and threatening to break through.

Once the "Breakers" were in position, it had been decided to "convert their internal capacity to some useful purpose". Their decks were surveyed and "speedily fashioned into public streets, skirted with convenient dwellings from head to stern, for the habitations of the workmen belonging to his Majesty's dockyard adjoining; and this proved a most salutary relief to the industrious, who, before, for want of local habitation, were forced to resort to their labours from unpleasant distances, greatly to their loss of time and health". The "marine village" that emerged on these hulks had "many entrances on the land side, and bridges from the main deck of one ship to the other. They had their King Street and their Queen Street, their George Street and their Princess Street, with a variety of other names for distinction. Out at the port-holes were their hanging gardens, where many things were cultivated for the use of their families. A great portion of the workmen in his Majesty's yard at Sheerness, are natives of the Breakers".

"Hulks at Sheerness", etching, Henry Moses, 1824.

A billet on these tide-breaking hulks may have been a lot better than nothing but there had from the start been voices clamouring for improved arrangements. As far back as 1675, the dockyard workers had petitioned for "houses, a market, and a minister", saying they were "living in a manner like heathens".[46] The first landed settlement emerged to the south and east of the dockyard, and just inland from the "Old Sea Breakers". Formed early in the eighteenth century it was, according to the Pevsner guide, a "do-it-yourself development".[47] Unlike the successive "new towns" of nineteenth-century Sheerness, it had no proud and powerful men who claimed to be its founder. Some of the first buildings may have been planned by the military authorities but many were built with "recycled" naval timber (Admiralty dockyards customarily allowed workers to take home "chips" of wood, and successive government inspectors would worry about the extraordinary size of the "chips" being hauled out of the gate[48]). First known as "the blue houses" on account of the fact that, as Uwe Johnson explained to his Dresden friends the Menzhausens in 1980, "the Royal Navy ... has a preference for blue paint and slowly but surely

… almost every worker's house was prettied up with the colour they'd swiped",[49] this English shanty grew into Blue Town — a densely packed warren of alleys, courts and lanes with many shops and pubs filled with soldiers and sailors, a small Jewish community with a synagogue and a nearby burial ground, and, by the 1780s, a large non-conformist chapel too.

Inside the wall: The Superintendent's House, Sheerness Dockyard.

If the garrison's cannons pointed out to sea from Sheerness, there were powerful moral forces that, having been incubated in the dockyard, aimed their cleansing fire inland. A town cannot be built with "chips" or, as it had become by the early nineteenth century, bricks alone, and the modern English town that emerged after Blue Town, on the landward side of the military establishment's moat, would be made of softer materials too: patriotism, to be sure; and a reverence for naval warfare, not least as the guarantor of employment; and quite a lot of speculative greed too. That, however, was by no means the end of it. During the hardship that followed the end of the Napoleonic Wars in 1816, a group of dockyard workers formed the Sheerness Economical Society as a co-operative venture that acquired flour, meat and other foodstuffs, and brought them to the island by barge for the use of members otherwise faced with excessive prices. The men leading this exercise in collective solidarity, which is likely to have been informed by knowledge of the co-operative mill set up by dockyard workers at Woolwich and Chatham in 1760,[50] crossed the moat to rent their first shop on what is now Sheerness High Street, and eventually took on further properties across the island (including a large warehouse that still stands beside the railway track in modern Sheerness). The Society remained a major force in the island economy into the 1960s.

Some of Sheerness's first co-operators will also have been followers of non-conformist Christianity, represented not just by the Methodism of John Wesley but also by the small congregation of dockyard workers who had started meeting to read the scriptures after Sunday services in the 1720s, and who went on to find their leading preacher in a young shipwright named William Shrubsole. Born in Kent and raised as an apprentice in the Sheerness dockyard, Shrubsole became a devout defender of his fellow shipwrights. In 1770, when the shipwrights in the Royal dockyards were suffering under cuts imposed after the close of the Seven Years War against France and Spain, he had published a pamphlet defending their appeal for a pay-rise and testifying that, thanks to the cancellation of overtime and associated economies, "those that had families saw, with terror, Poverty, like an armed Man, making hasty strides towards them". Convinced that poverty and moral dissolution ran together, he urged respect for his fellow shipwrights — "artificers",[51] as he insisted, who had developed their own most extraordinary integration of intelligence and skill, of reasoned calculation and practiced technique, born from years of shared learning and experience. Far from being viewed with "contempt" for the size of the "chips" they brought home, these men should be celebrated and rewarded for having perfected irreplaceable skills that were demonstrated in the final assembly of every one of the King's ships: "To see the various and multiform pieces of timber that compose a Ship's frame, taken from their scattered situation in the dock-yard, and placed in their proper order [to be assembled into] a 100 gun Ship &c. and with such exactness as not to require one quarter of an inch to be taken off with the adze; this to a mind capable of reflection is at once an argument for the IMMORTAL REASON of MAN, and a strong plea for the encouragement of those ingenious Artists".[52] Shrubsole insisted that the great warships built by these men were equal to the great country houses of the age. If the Royal dockyards lacked a Palladio, an Inigo Jones, or a Vanbrugh to personify their genius, this was because the "miraculous machines" they built, and which had conveyed "an idea of the glory of Britain to the remotest parts of the World", were the products of a more social and collective kind of production. There were, to be sure, men of genius in the Royal dockyards, but they were "only part of this respectable body of men: they served a regular apprenticeship for a title to it; and rose by the gradual steps of merit to the exalted Station in which they now shine".[53] Like weapons manufacturers down the ages, Shrubsole praised the Royal Navy's warships as bringers of "peace" to the world.

It was Shrubsole's urgent search for redemption that would lead him and his congregation out into the world beyond the dockyard. In the 1770s, he had written and published the first edition of a Kentish retelling of Bunyan's *Pilgrim's Progress,* a devout "allegorical narrative" entitled *Christian Memoirs,* in which Blue Town, like the rest of the human world, becomes "Darkland", a benighted kingdom full of perversion, destruction and Godless rebellion, while Sheppey's marshes are converted into the "Slough of Despond:" a "filthy bog" covered with a thick eye-stinging fog obscuring the stones on which the faithful pilgrim must step if he is to escape "the dissolution of the world" and reach the Celestial city he seeks.[54]

One of the stepping stones on Shrubsole's own pilgrimage still stands in Blue Town today. His congregation's first premises, created in the wake of an inspiring sermon delivered by the prodigious evangelical preacher George Whitfield in 1756, could accommodate three hundred in the upper floor of a brick house on Blue Town High Street. By the 1780s, however, members of the "great congregation" and their masonic brethren had built a larger chapel of Zion, known as the Bethel Chapel, which soon went through further enlargements to accommodate the swelling congregation. It remained in service until the congregation relocated to new premises in modern Sheerness after the First World War. Having survived nearly a century of industrial use since then, it now accommodates Blue Town's best known local industry, a cement gnome and garden ornament factory founded by a rag-and-bone merchant in 1974 and run by his son, Andre Whelan, who knows a lot about the shipbuilding methods used in the creation of the wide roof of the Bethel Chapel, and has also employed his own familiarity with moulding techniques to cover the entire imperilled structure with fibreglass (an effective conservation measure under the circumstances, although not of the kind normally recommended by English Heritage).

While something of the chaos that could be Blue Town surely reverberates in William Shrubsole's onslaughts against drunkenness, the surviving records of the Sun Insurance Office remind us that there were people with material as well as spiritual things to lose in "the Blue Houses" by the 1790s. A considerable number of "victuallers" appear among the policyholders living here, but so do grocers, bakers, a pawnbroker, a surgeon, a dealer in china and glass, a watchmaker (he lived in the garrison), a trader in hats and a number of self-declared "gents" too.[55] These were among the people who found themselves in "great anxiety of mind" when, 120 years after the Dutch invasion of Sheppey, history came ashore once again in 1797. That was the year of the famous "Mutiny of the Nore" in which sailors aboard the warships anchored offshore from Sheerness took control of much of the fleet, demanding an improvement in conditions and blocking traffic on the Thames. The people of Blue Town, mindful of the terrifying things they'd heard about the French Revolution a few years previously, feared that the rebels would come across the water and burn their ramshackle settlement to the ground. According to one eye-witness, the mutineers landed for the first time on 13 May, parading through Blue Town and the garrison with a large red flag and a band of musicians in tow. On hearing complaints at the "Old Swan", where sick people were kept, the mutineers are said to have interrogated the doctor, Mr Saffery, with such ferocity that he was "thrown into a fever" and proceeded, during a fearful "paroxysm", to cut his own throat.[56] Despite the evident moderation of their elected "President" — by many accounts a thoroughly decent fellow named Richard Parker, who would soon enough be hanged from the yard arm for his troubles — the marauding mutineers were said to have behaved in a manner that was "sufficiently threatening to try the stoutest hearts". They visited three hospital ships, approving two but not the third, the *Spanker*, and ducked, flogged and beat up both the steward and the butcher against whom complaints were also raised. Such was the panic that, by the time talks broke down and the soldiers in the garrison started firing the fort's cannons at the mutinous fleet, Blue Town had emptied in a rush: "mothers were carrying their suckling children at their breasts, and disconsolate husbands carried their little property down to the Chatham boat".

The Bethel Chapel, Blue Town.

The warren of ale houses, hotels, shops, shacks and alleys forming Blue Town was only the first phase of landed settlement at Sheerness and, by the early nineteenth century, a lot was running against it. There were still fewer than one thousand people living there in 1821, when the *Morning Post* commended the idea of "throwing down the blue houses"[57] and laying out a new town on the far side of the moat as the builder Edward Banks proposed to do now that his work on Rennie's new dockyard was approaching completion. By 1827, indeed, it was reported that "the greater part of the old dilapidated houses which flanked the dockyard at its eastern extremity have been pulled down, and others are still destined to share the same fate" as the dockyard was expanded and the point at Sheerness turned into "an almost impregnable fortress".[58] More of Blue Town was razed to make way for the high dockyard wall that still runs along the north side of its High Street, and further destruction was caused by a huge fire in 1830.

Less drastic forms of improvement were also tried. In 1847, Blue Town's unruly denizens were confronted with a new County Court House, planted among the public houses in a building previously known as the Emporium (at the first session, Judge James Espinasse, Esq., heard a colourful assortment of cases in which unpaid debts were the prevailing cause of offence, including one owed by a defendant who "rejoiced" in the name of Thomas Wellington Waterloo Spiers[59]). The evangelical voice of Christian redemption continued to oppose the chaotic vitality of Blue Town, insisting that even the most debased might find "fields of delight" in the scriptures. The unsanitary nature of the marsh on which Blue Town actually floated was also still attracting condemnation, by now based on considerably more scientific terms than were possible in the days when "marsh fever" may have contributed to the passing of William Shrubsole: his demise, in his sixty-seventh year on 6 February 1797, is said to have started with "a shivering aguish fit", after which he took to his bed, fell into sleep, and died without waking, even when "his whole frame agitated with convulsions".

The Humanity of Drains

The population had risen to little short of four thousand by 1858, when a long and closely informed letter to the *London Daily News* condemned Blue Town as a deplorable threat to the fighting power of the British Navy.[60] The writer, who wrote under the name "Sanitarius", was reacting not to the allegedly lawlessness of the haphazard settlement beyond the dockyard wall, but to the fact that a quarterly report from the Registrar-General of Births, Deaths and Marriages had revealed Sheerness to have "the highest average of death and disease in ... the valley of the Thames".[61] London was showing definite signs of progress, thanks to ongoing work to improve sanitation and water supply, but the Isle of Sheppey, which actually shared its distinction with other places on the Thames Estuary, was singled out as "a type" of the marshy districts, in which mortality was raised from seventeen to twenty-four in one thousand due chiefly to "the noxious emanations from a rich ill-drained soil".

Extracted in the *Morning Post*, the Registrar-General's report had described how the people of Sheppey showed "that pallid blue aspect which characterises aguish districts; they frequently suffer from ague, and sometimes from typhoid fever". It had also noted that "a considerable number of men in the Sheerness dockyard and in the ships on the station have been struck down and disabled by fevers during the present year". This was, so the report had declared, a consequence of the fact that much of Sheppey consisted of "marsh, drained imperfectly by ditches containing stagnant water and putrid vegetable and animal matter. The owners of this property are absentees, and the tenants mostly commit their farms to the care of a bailiff. No effort is made at improvement by the small occupiers, although experience has shown that the investment of money in the deep effectual drainage of the marsh is remunerative in a high degree".

The accusation here levelled against landowners and farmers was supported by a statistical analysis proving beyond doubt the value of improvements of the kind achieved over the previous four years — with the help of funds from the Government Drainage Fund — at the 439-acre Rayham Farm on the Isle of Sheppey. Without such commitment, the owners of marshland on both sides of the estuary would continue to "prejudice the health of the inhabitants, and deter people from building in the neighbourhood". It was evident to the Registrar-General that "a large portion of our naval reserve may be paralysed by ague and fever at the very time that it may be called upon to fight. A force that lives in an aguish atmosphere is necessarily enervated, and loses some of its courage. It cannot be always ready to meet the enemies of England at the gate with the Thames and the Medway". Although four decades still had to pass before Sir Ronald Ross established (through investigations carried out in India) that malaria was actually spread by *Anopheles* mosquitos, enough was known about the "miasma" emanating from stagnant water for the

Registrar-General to declare it a matter of national interest that "Sheerness should be immediately drained and supplied with pure water".

Drain, Blue Town, Sheerness, 2016.

"Sanitarius", whose letter was published in the *London Daily News* nineteen months later, on 28 December 1858, was in no doubt about the lessons to be drawn from the Registrar's warning. In his view, the scandalous "insalubrity" of Sheerness stemmed from a complete failure on the part of government authorities to exploit increasingly well understood principles of sanitation (he was thinking of the arguments associated with the reformer Sir Edwin Chadwick, and turned into policy by the Public Health Act of 1848) in "the humanity of preserving life".[62] The "perquisites of science and common sense" had been applied at Windsor, to ensure that Queen Victoria, who had recently been evacuated for her own safety, was able to return to her upriver castle without being poisoned by "deleterious gases", but nothing at all had been done for the poor and blighted downriver souls of Sheerness. Here, indeed, "the public service has actually caused the evil".

The justification for that assertion was provided by the condition of Blue Town, which "Sanitarius" plainly knew well:

There is no efficient outfall for drainage in Blue Town. Surface open gutters along the middle of narrow lanes and alleys are the receptacles for all household slops; the water slowly flows down them in wet weather, at other times the obstructed moisture lies, throwing up its miasma to crowded (often half-ruinous) two-storey houses; a few cabbage stalks make an overflow for yards. Oozing cesspools lie beyond, and the barriers of dock wall on one side and ramparts on the other keep off sun and sea breeze. All is squalid and unsightly — a crowded den for humanity, inferior to habitations of Arabs, nay, even Kurds, marsh and sea-bank with one single aperture for storm water close in the rear, but no system of drains and sluices, as found everywhere in Holland and Belgium ... In Blue Town the one public well has been useless for years. Three thousand people and more positively have no water but that given them on sufferance by a tap to the dockyard Artesian well, allowed to run under protection of a sentry, for one hour at noon and one in the evening.

It was true that water could be bought at the cost of a penny for three buckets, but this meant that it was kept in pans in rooms "to the great injury of house dwellers". No wonder, then, that "children are dirty and floors unwashed". As for the possibility of creating common wells, there was no point trying to sink them in the area — they merely filled with brackish sea water — unless they, like the dockyard well, were sufficiently engineered to penetrate through the London Clay "200 or 300 yards below".

Illness was endemic given "the old island ague-breeding marsh", but the lack of adequate sanitation in Blue Town had added typhoid to the lethal mix. Whichever version he contracted, "the fever-struck dockyard labourer had little chance of recovery". His home rendered it impossible. "After sundry attacks he is discharged, or he leaves of his own accord. Even the record of death is not allowed, as a warning in Sheerness. In the narrow rooms dames' schools become nests of disease, and children come home pale and haggard. A ragged school has latterly been started with apparent good hope, but hospitals, dispensaries, clubs, savings' banks — even a magistrate are English luxuries unknown."

"Sanitarius" conceded that the climate was disadvantageous and the population devoid "of the protection of the upper classes", who knew better than to live in such areas. "Three-fourths of the evil" was preventable, however, and there was an additional reason why the situation must be addressed by the government. The high incidence of "fever and ague" in the dockyard revealed that the squalor of Blue Town was "sapping the strength of men who are often called on for sudden exertion". Considering the nation's reliance on its dockyards — not just the labourers but also the riggers, shipwrights, engineers, firemen, and A. B. seamen — it was fair to conclude that "our neglect of justice and humanity will otherwise recoil upon ourselves as it has often done before".

16. FRITZ J. RADDATZ'S PERAMBULATION

Sheerness, Ordnance Survey map c. 1865
(dockyard and garrison blanked out top left).

Johnson was well settled by 1977, when he wrote to the chief
literary critic of the West German newspaper *Die Zeit,* providing
a "description of the route" this flamboyant man of letters should
follow when he joined the select list of intellectual and literary
figures who came from both sides of the divided Germany to
visit him in Sheerness.[1] Fritz J. Raddatz was to start by taking a
taxi to Victoria Station from outside his London hotel (Johnson
recommended Brown's in Mayfair partly because William
Faulkner used to stay there, and no doubt also on the safe
assumption that Raddatz would be travelling on an expenses
account). Johnson then detailed every stage of the journey until
Raddatz stepped off the train that had hauled him past the
"great hulking steel mill" then standing on Well Marsh, south
across the track from Blue Town, before finally depositing him
at the terminal named "Sheerness-on-Sea". After leaving the

station, Raddatz was to cross the road and "walk towards the notice board with the city map that you will have long since noticed diagonally across from you next to the phone boxes. Then all you have to do is go right on the High Street, then left on Broadway until it turns into Marine Parade. It's number 26, you have to knock because the bell is broken".

A short perambulation, then, during which, we are free to hope, Raddatz may have registered more of the history written into the town's buildings than Johnson's earlier visitors appear to have done. As he left the railway station behind him, he entered what may be the only authentically Georgian town in England that remains unbothered by tourists. Step out to photograph a building here, and you risk an unexpected response along the lines of the one I once got from a group of young mothers on the pavement: "Are you from the council, then?"

Starting just across the road from No. 1 High Street, once a free-standing hotel (and one of several island addresses at which Horatio Nelson is said to have stayed), Raddatz set out along streets that still testify to the vision, industry and founding ambition of Sir Edward Banks.

Having completed the new docks, to which various architects would add notable buildings over the following years, the late John Rennie's builder set about laying out a new town on the considerable acreage of land he had acquired across the moat to the south-east of both Blue Town and the dockyard. In the respectful words of Sheppey's early-twentieth-century historian, "it was owing, in a great measure, to his commercial acumen and foresight that many unsightly old rookeries were demolished, and in their place rows of elegant terraces and streets erected, imparting much of the charm which pertains to this healthful seaside resort to-day".[2] Whatever the success of Banks' attempt to create bricks from the clay beneath the "salts, or wastelands" lying next to the beach on his newly acquired Sheerness estate,[3] his transformation of the town remains unmistakeable. Not content with founding the settlement that Victorian speculators would further expand, Banks initiated Sheerness's longstanding and, to some, preposterously unlikely quest for reinvention as a fashionable seaside "resort" rather than just another dependent barrack or, in the words William Cobbett had used to deplore the war-funded expansion of Chatham a few years after Napoleon's defeat at Waterloo, another rash of vile "white swellings" and "odious wens"[4] thrown up at public expense to accommodate soldiers, sailors, dockyard workers and their families.

The Broadway from the Crescent.

Thanks to its proximity to the dockyard, the first new town here came to be known as Mile Town, and Fritz J. Raddatz can hardly have failed to notice that the shops, pubs and cafes on its High Street had escaped anything like the so-called "economic miracle" that had transformed bombed-out towns and cities in West Germany over the post-war decades. Unaware of the guidance provided by the appropriate Kentish volume of the Leipzig-born German émigré Sir Nikolaus Pevsner's survey, *The Buildings of England,* he may still have been surprised, on reaching the Crescent, by the grace with which the buildings here curved back to reveal a well-defined semi-circular space that reaches out of the past to counter any more recent sense of desolation. The neo-classical Crescent retains the ornate iron clock tower that Johnson cited as both a landmark and a seasonal target for drunken climbers on New Year's Eve (the most recent edition of Pevsner's *Kent: North East and East* dismisses this implant of 1902 as "showy but stunted"[5]). Although the gentleman's outfitter Burton has long since withdrawn, the windows abandoned by this once design-conscious company — founded in 1903 by a Jewish refugee from pogroms in the Russian Empire who went on to thrive as Sir Montague Burton — still promise Sheerness its place on a gilded roster of more prosperous towns and cities around the British Isles: Dublin, Bristol, Southampton, Edinburgh, Newcastle, Birmingham, Leeds, Manchester...

Turning left off the High Street at the Crescent, *Die Zeit's feuilletonist* had already entered a district known as "Banks Town" in its early days, which extended east along a street called "Edward Street." The three-storey flat-fronted terraces on either side of "The Broadway", as this spinal street was later renamed, are modest in comparison to Adelphi Terrace, the Adam brothers' neoclassical development off the Strand in London where Banks maintained his London address. They do, however, and as is duly registered in the Pevsner guide, persist in "the classical idiom" initiated by the Crescent.

Like John Newman, the peppery English architectural historian responsible for Pevsner's two Kentish volumes, Raddatz may have felt inclined to shield his eyes as he walked along the Broadway. It was, as this hunter of Kentish monstrosities had warned, on the north side of the street that "the choicest specimens of the town's secular architecture are arrayed. None is good and most are exceedingly bad."[6] First up was the "pompous" porch and "colossal" windows of the "ebulliently self-confident" redbrick and terracotta Conservative Club, a men-only bastion in a gross version of the Queen Anne style, where members might at least take a bath even if they could not afterwards sink into deep leather armchairs of the type Uwe Johnson had placed in his Institute for the Preservation of British Customs in New York. Dated 1897, and opened a decade after the club itself was inaugurated "under very auspicious

circumstances"[7] by the Under Secretary for War, there is certainly no mistaking this grandiose monument to the conservative political culture of the dockyard (as one dockyard worker explained to the sociologist Ray Pahl in the late Seventies, "the Tories are the people for war, they support that kind of thing and they were the people for a big navy, big army, you see, so you'd have a job to get the people in the dockyard to vote Labour"[8]). Banks Town resumed after that disruptive late-Victorian implant, but the return to earlier modesty was not necessarily a consolation. Newman found Holy Trinity Church, a commissioners' or "Waterloo" church on the south side of the street, to be "unimpressive", "most uninteresting" and built in "a wretched lancet style".[9] Designed by G.L. Taylor, previously responsible for the "exceedingly grand" Garrison Church outside the entrance to the dockyard, this lesser building stood on land provided by Edward Banks and had been consecrated by the Archbishop of Canterbury on the last day of August 1836.[10] A few more paces brought Raddatz to another redbrick interruption on the north side, this one still named the Royal Hotel but actually a late-Victorian replacement for the considerable and, of course, roughly neoclassical mansion that Edward Banks had built here in the 1820s.

Edward Street, Sheerness-on-Sea (postcard sent August 1910).

Known at first as Kent House, Banks's sea-facing version of the Royal Hotel had sat back from the road a little to the east of its successor, with the six fluted columns of its portico (a loose version of "Greek Doric", so the present editor of the *Pevsner Architectural Guides* informs me[11]), facing extensive gardens stretching down to the sea. In April 1827, it was reported that the Admiralty were buying the recently completed building with its ten acres of grounds as a residence for the Port Admiral of Medway, who was to be moved from Chatham to Sheerness.[12] This arrangement never came off and, on 11 June that year, Banks would advertise the building briefly known as "Kent House" as available for lease with its original purpose once again in mind. His notice in the *Morning Post* described it as a "new, large, and commodious hotel, with coach house for four carriages, stable for sixteen horses, large garden, with green and hot houses, and every convenience".[13] He also assured applicants brave enough to consider buying into his speculative vision that "a steamboat will run from London to the above hotel every day". Banks had over-reached himself with that last promise. The military authorities may have helped to ensure that the new pier he had apparently imagined building out into the sea directly in front of his hotel never happened, but the steamboats were by no means an idle fantasy. In 1824, he and his building partner William Jolliffe had founded the world's first General Steam Navigation Company, and both of the company's first vessels, the *Lord Melville* and the *Royal Sovereign*, had visited Sheerness a year previously for the opening of the new dockyard basins. Although a daily service to Banks Town was not to be, it would be reported three and a half years later that the Royal Hotel's winter balls, where aspiring guests were encouraged to look forward to meeting an admiral among other senior officers from the dockyard, were "rapidly rising in estimation."[14]

"Benevolence" Carnival assembly at the Royal Hotel, Banks Town, Sheerness. Photo: Robert Israel Hider, c. 1890.

The General Steam Navigation Company would soon concentrate its efforts on the more profitable business of sailing excursionists between London and Margate. Banks, however, had established himself in local reputation as both the entrepreneurial founder of the new town and a generous benefactor who, in a cruel winter, would in the most "handsome and liberal manner" produce £100 to be distributed among the poor of the neighbourhood in the form of "warm clothing".[15] His vision of "Banks Town" as a resort for respectable Londoners had won influential supporters on the island, including the self-declared "inhabitant of Sheerness" who, in August 1833, cited the coming of gas lighting among the increasingly civilised charms of a town that could surely be made into "one of the finest watering places in the kingdom". It only remained for the residents to "bestir themselves" a little more vigorously by, for example, campaigning for a bridge to be built across the Swale or setting up a company that really would run steamships into the town.[16] There was further praise for Sir Edward's new resort a week or so later, when his son Delamark (who may conceivably have been that very same concerned "inhabitant") went to the Wellington Inn in Mile Town to chair a meeting of two hundred people, who resolved to establish a "Sheerness and London Steam Packet Company" (shares are said to have been "taken with spirit"),[17] which promised to take up the unfulfilled challenge of bringing visitors from London to the pier that was by then about to be built out into the Medway from Blue Town.

Only fifteen years previously, so a self-described "Citizen of the World" informed readers of the *Kentish Gazette*, Sheerness had been "a dirty bustling sea-port" with its streets "(if such they could be called) full of drunken sailors and their partners".[18] That, however, was not to be the story in "Banks Town". As proof of the town's ongoing transformation from a disease-infested military "wen" to a resort for urbane visitors, both the *Kentish Gazette* and the *Morning Post* quoted heavily from a description of the now "considerable" town provided in the publisher Samuel Lewis' *Topographical Dictionary of England*. Looking out from the low cliffs near Minster, Lewis' witness ignored the mosquito-infested marshes behind him, inviting readers to concentrate instead on what was surely "one of the most splendid and interesting views in the kingdom — the German Ocean on the east; the Thames and Medway bearing innumerable vessels of all sizes, with the town and harbour of Sheerness to the north and west; and the fertile valleys of Kent, with the Medway winding through them, and the towns and villages interspersed, towards the south, combine in presenting diversity and sublimity of landscape *rarely excelled*".[19] There were by now bathing machines on the beach in Mile Town, and the "great scarcity" of fresh water was also being remedied. "Subscription wells" had been sunk to a depth of 350 ft, requiring their workmen to burn their way through a "complete prostrate forest" discovered at two hundred feet, samples of which were welcomed by learned museums as "a remarkable confirmation of the history of the Deluge". As for Sir Edward Banks's Sheppey home at Red House Farm, which stood on Halfway Road to the south-east of the town, he had by this time replaced it with Sheppey Court, thereby giving the no longer so thoroughly shunned island a two-storey country house in Greek Revival style.

As the central institution of "Bank's Town", the Royal Hotel would remain open for business through much of the nineteenth century. By 1843, when Mr J.T. Smithson was the proprietor, it was commended for being fitted up in "a very superior manner", for having splendid views on both sides that a sensitive guest might spend many happy hours sketching, and for possessing its own "omnibus" with which to convey guests to and from the pier in Blue Town. No less a figure than the Bishop of Nova Scotia was said to have declared himself "highly gratified" with its comforts after a recent visit.[20]

The nineteenth-century proprietors of the Royal Hotel tend to appear in the local papers on two accounts. They feature positively as stalwart and welcoming hosts in advertisements designed to attract visitors and continue the work of pressing back against the dismal impressions created by Blue Town. The good things were still in place in 1863, when a new proprietor advertised the "Extensive and Well-arranged Premises" as "a cheap and comfortable Hotel to sojourn at … The Hotel faces the Sea, and the excellent beach for bathing is approached from the lawn".[21] They also feature in court reports thanks to troublemakers from the other Sheerness, who might rob the place, smash its windows or, if still just unruly boys, rampage about in the proprietor's ten-acre garden and hurl clods of earth at any gardener who tried to see them off.[22]

By that time, both Sir Edward Banks and his son Delamark were long gone. Their best tribute may be the one paid by the president of the Gravesend Mechanics Institute, the Rev. Dr Joynes, while speaking at that organisation's first annual meeting on 19 January 1839. Having made his stand against those who seemed to consider it wise to keep the working class ignorant and, indeed, to abandon its "mechanics" to the ruinous attractions of "the gaming table and the tap room", he asked the assembled company to consider the case of the late Sir Edward, a great prodigy who had surely proved by personal example that "knowledge is power".[23] Having started out as a humble labourer, Sir Edward had "risen to rank and wealth by the exertion of his own thoughts upon the substances around him". Joynes also praised Delamark as the loyal son who actually lived on the island and was "liberally using the riches acquired by the skill and industry of his parent, and gladdening the hearts of the poor on the very soil where his parent worked". The President's words were commended by the assembled mechanics: "'Hear, Hear' and loud applause".

Marine Town and the Battle over England's Most Notorious Ditch

The ongoing economic slump and the dust and yellowish grime from the Blue Town steel mill being what they were, Fritz J.

Raddatz may hardly have noticed that — having avoided "Blue Town", as people arriving by train now do, and passed through the remnants of both "Mile Town" and "Banks Town" — he had entered a fourth new "town" as he walked east along the Broadway. By the time he reached the junction with "Berridge Road", he was in a district known as "Marine Town". This Victorian extension of Sheerness was created by a later generation of developers who may be said, no less than Sir Edward Banks and his son Delamark, to have exercised their will on "the substances around them". There was, however, less likelihood of the feuding founders of Marine Town being praised for their virtues by vicars in nearby estuarial towns.

Berridge Road, Marine Town, Sheerness.

Having once lived near Rochester on the Medway, Richard Berridge did have some Kentish connections to start with. Like Sir Edward Banks before him, however, he conducted his affairs from smart addresses — 36 Bloomsbury Square and later 18 Great Russell Street — in London. He was managing partner in the brewery of Sir Henry Meux, whose father had owned the Horse Shoe Brewery where the Dominion Theatre now stands in Tottenham Court Road (the firm was notorious for the "London Beer Flood" of 1814, in which a vast deluge of beer escaped from collapsing vats, drowning at least eight people as it engulfed surrounding buildings in the poor area of St Giles). Berridge and his managing partner Henry Bateman Jenkins (the son of an engraver, who was also in the employment of Meux and Co.), acquired a great deal of the marshland on which modern Sheerness now stands at the sale of Delamark Banks' estate in Sheerness in August 1852. Their timing was fortuitous, since the Crimean War, which opened the following year, brought a great boom to the dockyard and, by extension, to the rapidly developing eastern quarter that would become Marine Town. Sheerness would never match the California gold rush, but there was definitely money to be made, and all the more safely so given the government's reliance on the dockyard and garrison.

Marine Town, so the *Sheerness Times* declared in 1873, had "the date of its origin indelibly fixed upon it". It owed everything to the boom brought to the Admiralty dockyard by an Anglo-French expedition against the Russian Empire that required — as Uwe Johnson might have gathered from his copy of Denis Judd's *The Crimean War* — separate British fleets in both the Baltic and the Black Sea. To this day, the memory of this war, during which Sheerness gained two prison hulks full of captured Russian soldiers[24] as well as greatly increased demand for more conventional accommodation, was inscribed in the names of the area's streets, terraces and pubs too: the Hero of Crimea, the Napier Tavern, and the Heights of Alma, which Johnson could glimpse from his back window. Such was the momentum that the rising town gained from this victorious conflict, that the patriotic inhabitants of Marine Town had been joined by the *Sheerness Guardian* in renaming the entire area "the Crimea".[25]

"Marine Town" appears to have started out as little more than the Napier Tavern and, teetering on the seafront opposite, the exuberantly ornamented Neptune Terrace, which Pevsner dates rather approximately to the 1840s. Four years after Berridge and Jenkins acquired large areas of the "One-hundred-acre Field" on which cricket matches and agricultural shows had customarily been held, the *Kentish Independent* advertised an auction of new Marine Town properties to be held by the London-based estate agent Mr H.W. Rowlstone. On the evening of 7 October 1856 he would come to the Napier Tavern, then a free-standing building on a track that had yet to become part of The Broadway, to auction off fifteen "brick-built cottages" in Green Street, all of them let to "very respectable tenants" and in much demand, together with five "brick-built houses" in Napier Terrace, directly to the east of the tavern.[26] It was anticipated that the houses would prove "most desirable for small capitalists". They would be offered on ninety-nine-year leases, thereby "avoiding the fines and expenses resulting from the objectionable practice of leases dependent upon lives, so much the practice in Sheppey". The town, meanwhile, was "rapidly improving", and prospective purchasers were also made aware of "the great increase of families consequent upon the important, and permanent enlargement of the Government Establishments",[27] which rendered such housing "most valuable". Further sales followed in March 1857, when Mr Rowlstone returned to auction off another clutch of new houses, including fourteen in Constantia Terrace (built by Berridge and Jenkins on open ground directly to the south of the Napier Tavern), and more in both Napier Terrace and Green Street, now known as Berridge Road. By this time, "the great scarcity of housing in the area" had been further increased by demand "consequent upon the ongoing construction of the Sittingbourne and Sheerness railway".[28]

Looking West from Marine Parade, with Neptune Terrace to the right and Marine Terrace to the left (postcard, sent 1910).

Two years later it was announced that, having already disposed of some of their land for building purposes, Berridge and Jenkins, the latter now well-established as Berridge's man on the ground in Sheerness, proposed to lay out the remainder in streets on which "several hundred houses"[29] might be built. By this time, the new railway line was in service, having carried its first train to the terminal at Blue Town in time for the official opening on 19 July 1860. This transformative connection with the mainland is said to have been welcomed in "an exceedingly enthusiastic manner" by thousands of islanders. There were ovations and toasts. A band played on the platform and a "magnificent *déjeuner à la fourchette*" was laid on for the visiting dignitaries, some of whom were still reeling from "a most unpardonable piece of negligence" committed by the 13th Kent Artillery Volunteers, who had been invited to fire a welcoming salute over the arriving train. Unfortunately, one of the amateur "gunners" had aimed his cannon too low and fired "point blank" into the carriages full of important personages, so that "one gentleman was thrown from his seat, and a second was injured in the face, a third had his head 'twisted round', a fourth suffered a severe cut in the forehead, and many others were exceedingly annoyed".[30]

THE SEA VIEW HAS ME AGAIN

This embarrassment did nothing to slow the development of the town on the far side of the dockyard moat. By 1861, things were going so well that the auctioneering estate agent, Mr Rowlstone, had himself bought into Sheerness, becoming the new proprietor of the late Sir Edward Banks' Royal Hotel. By this time Berridge's partner, H.B. Jenkins, was arranging for the construction of "a number of small tenements" that would "adjoin 'the Crimea'" on the western side and lead into Mile Town High Street.[31] It was, however, as they pressed on to the east of Napier Tavern that Berridge and Jenkins came up against their most formidable local rival. As Melville and Co.'s *Directory and Gazetteer of Kent* for 1858 had declared of the area in which Johnson's house appears to stand, "there are many new buildings springing up, which form a separate district called Ward's Town."[32]

If Berridge and Jenkins achieved a reputation unlike that of the "heart-gladdening" Bankses, this may partly have been due to their habit of using the courts, rather more than good works and charitable donations, to advance their interests. In their early dealings at Sheerness, they could reasonably have assumed the sympathy of better-off residents as they set about squashing the claims of a bunch of desperadoes in Blue Town. In July 1856, a judge at the Kent Assizes in Maidstone heard a case concerning two cottages and a beer-shop named the Fishing Smack.[33] Messrs Meux and Co., the brewery with which both Berridge and Jenkins were already associated, had bought the properties for £120 from an indebted owner named John Benstead in 1849. They then sold them on for £150 to a Sheerness innkeeper named Nathanial Woodhard, who had never been able to get the Bensteads to vacate the premises. Indeed, John Benstead's son, Robert, had subsequently claimed to be the true owner of the properties, declaring that he, rather than his father, had bought them in 1839 with money made by various means including "hovelling" (i.e. assisting — although the *Oxford English Dictionary* suggests that this Kentish word could also imply

248

activities indistinguishable from looting — distressed ships) with the help of his "whaler".

By the time the Fishing Smack had been recovered, Sir Henry Meux, the prodigiously wealthy Hertfordshire MP who had inherited the brewery Meux & Co. on his father's death in 1841, was providing the nation with a different kind of entertainment. In 1855, and somewhere far from Sheerness, his eye had fallen on the nineteen-year old daughter of Lord Ernest Brudenell-Bruce. He had married Lady Louisa Caroline Brudenell Bruce in January 1856 and a son was born not long afterwards. Sadly, though, Sir Henry had also started to behave strangely. His young wife claimed that the first sign of his distemper only occurred in September 1856: while stalking deer in Scotland, Meux had developed certain "delusions" about the number of stags he had bagged.[34] Other reports suggest that he also peppered a fellow sportsman on a shoot in Cambridgeshire. In 1858 a Commission of Lunacy declared him insane and incompetent to manage his affairs: a verdict delivered after a long and very public hearing in which his three disgruntled sisters tried unsuccessfully to push the origins of his madness far enough into the past to invalidate a recent codicil to his will, in which he bequeathed his vast fortune to his infant son and, should this beneficiary die, to his wife — without so much as a penny retained for them.

After Sir Henry's withdrawal, Berridge and Jenkins fought their battles over Sheerness under their own names. Their primary antagonist appears to have been Mr James Ward, the solicitor who was trying to turn his stretch of marsh to the east of "Marine Town" into "Ward's Town". As the owner of land directly adjacent to Berridge and Jenkins's property, Mr Ward claimed that these London extractors had no right to assume public use of the track — Marine Parade in the making — crossing his land towards Minster. This claim was also a matter of controversy for the Local Board of Health, the elected governing body that was responsible for paving the public road that some of its members also wanted to see along the shore between Marine Town and Cheyney Rock to the east. At a meeting of the board in December 1859, Jenkins had informed the Chairman — none other than Mr James Ward himself — that he would not allow residents and owners of the "new town" he and Berridge were creating to be inconvenienced by Ward's outrageous claim. "It was", he said, "a monstrous pretence for any man holding a public position, and an unparalleled act of presumption, to lay claim to a portion of a public roadway".[35]

Ward lost his case as a private land owner in "Ward's Town", but he found another way of attacking Berridge and Jenkins. Founded through an election of qualified property-owning ratepayers on 29 August 1849, Sheerness's Local Board of Health governed the developing town under legislation designed to prevent cholera and other waterborne diseases.[36] At first, the two brewers may have felt encouraged by reports not just that the members of this new local authority had resolved to spend £10,000 on "extensive operations" to improve "this place, which has so long been notorious for its agues, arising chiefly from the want of drainage", but also, that "the government" was likely to bear "a portion of this expense", since "the population consists almost entirely of the military artisans employed in the dockyard, and others in government employ".[37] They would surely also have approved of some of the board's later decisions — including its determination to stop "night soil" being gathered in Blue Town and spread on the ground between Constantia Terrace and the Royal Hotel, i.e. in the heart of their new developments at Marine Town.

Drains, however, could cause disputes, especially in a booming town where powerful men were already squared off against one another. While the Local Board of Health was responsible for their efficiency, the ongoing development of Sheerness actually required the filling in of a considerable number of drainage ditches (the maps of 1860/1 are full of examples marked "ditch filled in"). It was in the tension between these two undertakings that James Ward found a new front for his feud with the hated imposters from London.

In 1860, the Local Board of Health had decided — the matter

was clinched by Chairman Ward, at a very lightly attended meeting — to launch a Chancery Suit against Berridge, his partner Henry Bateman Jenkins and also the Secretary of State for War, Sidney Herbert. All three stood accused of "stopping up a certain ditch butting the High-street", and thereby interfering with the Board's right to use it as "a ditch for sanitary purposes".[38] The ditch in question was said formerly to have served to take waste from Mile Town. However, the Commanding Royal Engineer, Lieutenant Colonel Montagu, had decided to fill it in, judging it to be a source of "malaria" that was injurious to the health of soldiers stationed in the neighbourhood. The case of Sheerness's "Chancery Ditch" would become a source of wonder and amusement all over the country as it dragged on — and so, more locally, would the "surly, snappish, irascible, abrupt, and unpardonable"[39] manner in which Chairman Ward conducted meetings. According to one witness, he ran the supposedly democratic board as nothing less than "a Star-chamber of the nineteenth century". His response, when confronted about his tyrannical tendencies, was characteristically blunt: "I've power, and I will use it",[40] he told a Board meeting on 5 January 1860.

The ditch in question had, as the Solicitor to the War Office would explain, originally been cut in 1829 to differentiate the Board of Ordnance's land from that being sold to Sir Edward Banks. It stood on the Board of Ordnance's side of the division, but Berridge and Jenkins were included in the action because of their more recently acquired interest in the adjacent soil. Ward had plainly not learned the lesson of Charles Dickens' novel *Bleak House,* published nearly a decade previously and plotted around an endlessly protracted Court of Chancery case known as Jarndyce v. Jarndyce. His intemperate action in going to the Court of Chancery was deplored by a minority of members of the Local Board of Health, including the former chairman Richard Brightman, who was well disposed towards Berridge and Jenkins. Having previously proposed Jenkins for election to the Board, only to find that chairman Ward had written the word "disqualified" next to his name on the voting papers,[41] Brightman now dissociated himself from this "most suicidal act", claiming that Ward was "involving the town in an expensive lawsuit from which no good could result".[42] Demanding that the action be withdrawn, he also insisted that a simple conversation with the admirable Colonel Montagu, would have seen the matter sorted out quite amicably for a few pounds. Ward, however, was not to be deterred from the ruinous adventure into which he had launched the town's increasingly horrified ratepayers — not, he swore, for as long as he "had a shilling in his pocket, or a shirt on his back". He insisted that Colonel Montagu was "treating the Board as a set of nonentities",[43] and that this was exactly what they would prove to be if they buckled and withdrew.

James Ward had no time for the "memorial" these dissenting ratepayers duly presented to the Board, accusing at least one signatory of being "the worse for drink",[44] and dismissing their accusations of "trickery" as a disgrace. One of his allies declared that Mr Jenkins himself was probably the "chief author" of the memorandum and Brightman's demand that the Chancery suit be withdrawn was thrown out by eight members to two. By this time the board had heard from the Solicitor to the War Department, who had written to insist that, since the Secretary for War, Sidney Herbert, could only be sued by petition of right, he would not be "putting either the plaintiff or the public to the expense of his appearance in this litigation". The discovery that he had "no interest whatever" in the result meant that the case became a contest between the Local Board of Health and Berridge and Jenkins alone.

The battle dragged on through the next four years, racking up huge legal fees as it went. At first, Ward and his camp felt reinforced by the Board's Inspector of Nuisances, who reported the ditch in question to be "an intolerable nuisance", overgrown with weeds and with the pipe "leading from the High Street, half-full of 'sullage'".[45] Jenkins and Berridge, meanwhile, had no intention of building a "covered drain" as the board had demanded. They would also benefit from a growing revolt among the ratepayers who convened to condemn the Local

Board of Health for pursuing this "much to be regretted" course after "intrenching themselves behind their imaginary dignity".[46]

The longer the case extended, the higher the cost was going to be for the losers. The ratepayers of Mile Town were definitely at risk, yet battles between absentee owners and the people of Sheerness had not invariably gone well for the offshore interests. This was the lesson of the Sheerness Gas Company, one of the first initiatives funded by outsiders who had hoped to profit from the emerging town. When the company collapsed towards the end of 1862, the shareholders had lost everything and then incurred additional liabilities when the works had to be sold for less than the outstanding mortgages on the property.

Montague Road, West Minster near Sheerness. Isle of Sheppey.

The Gas Works at West Minster: "That's me standing by the fence in a tam o' shanter". "Winnie" to her aunt, "Mrs. Pass". Postcard sent 2 May 1910.

For the *Sheerness Guardian*, the moral of that defeat had been plain to see. The shareholders of the busted company were all "strangers" who suffered "a want of local influence". Despite local remonstrations, they had continued to fleece the townspeople by charging "exorbitant" rates for their gas.

253

This may indeed have been a foolish strategy in a coastal town that could easily get cheap coal from Newcastle, but there was another characteristic of Sheerness that these offshore extractors might sensibly have borne in mind. Ten years previously, in 1852, there had been complaints to the Admiralty about the co-operative ventures through which dockyard workers were provisioning themselves, thereby curtailing the profits of conventional traders in the town. Not content with creating non-conformist chapels and building societies, the workers had established coal clubs, a baker's shop, a flour store and a grocer's shop, the latter turning over "upwards of seven thousand pounds".[47] Thanks to these co-operative initiatives, so the objectors had declared, "private trade is very greatly injured, and the value of property much depreciated; in fact, they bid fair to ruin the trade of this place altogether". The absentee owners of the gas company had eventually dropped their prices but too late and only after "the consumers" had taken the matter into their own practised hands, using their superior "local influence" to form their own rival company, the Sheppy Gas Consumers Company, which went on to take possession of its defeated rival's much "depreciated" works in West Minster at a very agreeable price (the new company was still selling gas on Sheppy when the industry was nationalised in 1948).

Berridge and Jenkins would not suffer this fate. They proceeded both to divide opinion in the town and to maximise the Local Board of Health's financial embarrassment. The two developers did what they could to extend the hearing in the Court of Chancery, thereby increasing the costs that would eventually fall on the ratepayers. They did this by their now familiar means: disputing the affidavits of the Board's witnesses, trawling up other locals prepared to speak on their side of the case, and then submitting contrary affidavits that would necessitate yet more expensive weeks of examination by lawyers. As the already extended case of the Chancery Ditch looked as if it were finally drawing to a close, they produced no less than twenty-five such affidavits, submitting them on 21

October 1863. This act, which took place after the counsel for both sides had accepted the Lord Chancellor's suggestion that no further evidence should be produced, provoked Thomas Morton Rigg, the founding owner and editor of the *Sheerness Guardian,* into an explosion of fury.

Like everyone else in Sheerness, Rigg knew about Mr Ward and his cronies on the Local Board of Health. He admitted their lack of process, their failure to prioritise or negotiate, their shifty way of publicly berating their own surveyor and accusing their clerk of cooking the accounts. He was, nonetheless, firmly on the side of the ratepayers of Sheerness and therefore also of the all too flawed Local Board of Health in its battle with these incoming London developers. "Thus we see", he wrote with Jenkins rather than Ward in his sights, "what a local curse an evil-disposed person, seeking to set his will above the law and for his own profit setting public rights at nought, may become". Berridge and Jenkins were plainly loathsome extractors bent on screwing the town from outside, but Rigg was even more excoriating about the "simpletons" who had provided affidavits for them, claiming that the ditch had actually been improved by being filled up "so as to leave only a small 'grip' for the passage of water", and that the sides of the grip were actually of "stiff clay" and not silt as the Local Board of Health's surveyor had declared. Such blockages as occurred when the sides collapsed were nothing to do with structural inadequacy, so these gullible fools had suggested, but the fault of "children jumping on them".

Rigg published the names of the twenty-five affidavit-producing offenders (including Jenkins), listing them as they had been read out and mocked by Chairman Ward at a meeting of the Local Board of Health, where Ward had taken aim at "the parties themselves" rather than their comments. The affidavits had "the very questionable merit of cleverness in making the worst appear the better side. They are artfully concocted, so as to entirely pervert the true merits of the facts they profess to elucidate". Some of the signatories had since admitted that they had only written what they were told to say, or that they had "only signed what they were asked to sign". Rigg called these men "gulls", "tools" and "traitors to the public interest", who had given their support to "an enemy of their town", without apparently realising that, in doing so, they were landing the cost of the Chancery Suit upon themselves and their fellow ratepayers. He recommended that, when the case of the Chancery Ditch was over, the town should "erect a monument on the site thereof", bearing the names of each and every one of Berridge and Jenkins's "simpletons" so that posterity could continue to pay tribute to the memory of these men who "did all that it laid in their power to do, to saddle the town with ruinous law costs, and to assist the evil-doer who forced the town into the Suit that he might evade the just desserts of his conduct".[48]

The owner of the *Sheerness Guardian* fell victim to his own fury. He was found to be in contempt of court for his comments about Berridge, Jenkins and some of their affidavit providers, and spent thirteen days in Whitecross Street prison in London before he was released at the end of January 1864, having reluctantly published an apology of sorts and agreed to give £50 to the accused to cover their costs.[49] Once at home in Sheerness, he went on to publish extracts from national papers condemning the decision to find him in contempt, insisting that "To call a man a gull is no more a slander than to call him a goose", and that the radical Liberal politicians, Bright and Cobden, would prove themselves to be motivated by "mere party spirit" if they did not rise up against this "flagrant outrage" against the "freedom of the press".

By that time the case known as "Chancery Ditch" had been decided against the Local Board of Health, and the Sheerness ratepayers were coming to terms with their liability for costs that would, as feared, turn out to be crippling. Faced with having to extract a sum that might well rise to £5,000 from the ratepayers, dissenting members of the Local Board of Health, continued their condemnation of their chairman Mr Ward and, in some cases, gave loud voice to the relief they found in the fact that they themselves had joined the board after the fatal decision to embark on "this miserable affair".[50]

Slight consolation was provided by the defeated board's much harangued surveyor, who reported at the meeting of 1 March 1864 that there was plenty of water in the well his contractor was then drilling on the board's orders — "ample to drown Sheerness" as he reassured (or threatened) the residents of this flood-prone place where the high tides had already demonstrated their ability to reverse the flow of sewage in the Local Board of Health's drains. This was another problem in which chairman Ward had a personal interest: at the board's first meeting of 1864, he had demanded that the surveyor give priority to sorting out "the inconvenience and damage arising from drain pipes which ran through his back garden, when the tide got into them".[51] Berridge and Jenkins, were not sympathetic. Having humiliated the board, they went on, in March 1864, to send the authority a bill for £250 in "compensation" for sewers passing through their land, a demand that the board rejected as, in the words of Mr Thomas, "only another money-making job out of ratepayers' pockets".[52]

The case of the Chancery Ditch can be registered as a founding moment in the development of the Isle of Sheppey's libertarian mistrust of the improving potentialities of the reforming state. It was as a direct result of this affair, in 1868, that the town's recently formed second newspaper, the *Sheerness Times*, felt obliged to defend the new approach to local government against a strong tide of contrary opinion: "There are some people who appear to think that the existence of a Local Board of Health in a town is an evil and a misfortune, to be deplored alike at all times and under any circumstances".[53] The people who had pressed for this form of local government, including the social reformer Edwin Chadwick, were loudly reviled for their interfering creations, and the wildest accusations abounded in the town: "so blind is this prejudice that we have but recently heard it gravely contended that our present Water Supply is worse than it was in the historic days of donkey-barrels and small buckets". People seemed to delight in knocking the Local Board of Health, without being troubled by, or even aware of, the fact that they as ratepayers were likely to find the bill arriving on their doorstep. The problem, concluded the paper, was not with the system, but with Mr Ward and the other incompetent men who had been elected to office thanks in part, so it was suggested, to the manoeuvres of a "partisan" returning officer who had no conception of the duties of his office.

Berridge Exposed

Jenkins cut a familiar profile in Sheerness but where, as people may have wondered as the case of the Chancery Ditch dragged towards its dishevelled conclusion, was his senior partner Richard Berridge? Before the Chancery Ditch fiasco was over the people of Sheerness had seen this remote speculator engulfed by a scandal that may have done quite a lot to raise spirits even among the town's disgusted chapel-goers. "Very fair, rather stout, with large whiskers and moustache, and his hair beautifully combed and parted down the back".[54] That is how Marine Town's absentee developer was described, in December 1862, by the landlady from whom he had earlier rented lodgings at Dorothy Cottage, Highgate, for the use of a certain "Mrs Faulkner" together with her new born daughter. "Mrs Faulkner" was said to have described Berridge as her "guardian and banker". He was actually, as would be admitted in one of the most widely reported divorce proceedings of 1862, her lover and the father of her baby.

As the hearing continued, it emerged that "Mrs Faulkner" was actually the wife of Major William Forster, who had been born in India and spent his life in the Indian Army, and she had been sent to England with her four surviving children for reasons said to be connected to her own health. Arriving in London in 1854, Mrs Forster had met Richard Berridge at 40 Bloomsbury Square, where they both lodged in the house of Mr and Mrs Dove (Mr Dove was said to be "connected with Sir H. Meux's brewery",[55] of which Berridge was then a junior partner). Berridge continued to visit her when, after six months or so, she moved east to 12 Heathcote Street, a detached house near Mecklenburgh Square. In the summer of 1858, he found lodgings for her at Gravesend, roughly halfway to Sheerness, before moving her back to Highgate. A servant who worked for Mrs Forster in 1858, claimed to have seen them "lying on a sofa" together.[56] She had also found the door to the drawing door unexpectedly locked on occasions when he was in the house. Ditto the bedroom — where the couple were said sometimes to have dined together.

Major Forster's counsel claimed that, having seduced his client's wife, Berridge had abandoned her as soon as the child was born — an unutterable dog, in other words, whose own former butler was happy to testify about the confrontations that followed. Thomas Sandolf told the court how the outraged Mrs Forster used to turn up unannounced at Berridge's house in Bloomsbury to berate him for the "niggardly way he was a supporting the child". She plainly made a proper nuisance of herself, pushing her way into the dining room when he was entertaining, returning to engage him in his counting house as he was preparing to attend the Derby, and not leaving until she had ripped his shirt. Another lady, a former friend of Mrs Forster's who was dining there at the time of one of Mrs Forster's unwanted visits, ended up "hiding in a closet", from which she could only be released when, after many hours of wrangling and recrimination, Berridge was persuaded to leave the house on the accurate expectation that Mrs Forster would follow him out of the door to continue accusing him in the street.

While not denying the charges, Berridge and Mrs Forster chose to pursue an aggressive line of defence, claiming that their behaviour had been provoked by "desertion, wilful neglect, adultery, and other conduct" on the part of Major Forster himself. Their counterattack rested on the allegation that the unhappy Major, while sailing from India in order to prosecute this case, had become friendly with an allegedly invalid and less than entirely vigorous Lieutenant Ellis and his wife, and then started his own affair with Mrs Ellis. Berridge and his lawyers had mustered some unlikely witnesses to support these charges, having persuaded Major Forster's own sister and daughter to attest that they had heard him commend Mrs Ellis for her beauty. More lurid details were contributed by various wide-eyed servants, who offered snapshots of the Major volunteering to lace up Mrs Ellis's dresses as tightly as only he could, or eyeing her charms through an open door while she faced him, "quite naked" in a hip bath. These witnesses failed to convince the judge that they had not been paid for their testimony, and Mrs Ellis was not obliged to testify. Firmly directed by the judge, the jury found against Berridge, who was ordered to pay not the £10,000 demanded on behalf of Major Forster but the still considerable sum of £5,000 in damages — the same as the estimated cost that fell on the ratepayers of Sheerness thanks to the loss of the Chancery Ditch case.

However badly things may have gone for Mrs Forster and her daughter, the London developer whose name adorns "Berridge Road" survived this scandal, and would continue to rise, as his various businesses flourished, through an ever improving series of addresses — from Bloomsbury to a splendid house named The Cedars overlooking the Thames in Putney, and then, apparently, to Knowle Hall near Bridgewater in Somerset. In 1873, some five years before he finally retired from Meux and Co., Berridge bought Ballynahinch Castle, a vast sporting estate in Galway, which he and later his son would improve and redevelop. By the time of his death in 1887, the developer of Marine Town had become the largest landowner in Ireland, where his 170,000 acres dwarfed the mere seventy-nine he held in Kent.

Berridge's partner, Henry Bateman Jenkins, had died in 1871. On his side too, though, upriver people would continue to benefit from the streets Uwe Johnson could survey from his back window. Jenkins left his property to his brother, Joseph John Jenkins, also of 5 Newman St, off Oxford Street.[57] An engraver as well as a long-standing member of the Old Society of Painters in Watercolours, Joseph Jenkins achieved some reputation as a painter of domestic and theatrical subjects (he captured the young actress and abolitionist Fanny Kemble before she moved to America) as well as bucolic rural scenes. He was unmarried, and after his death in 1885, his share of Sheerness freeholds and ground rents was divided between three of his artist friends. So it was that the respected maritime painter Edward Duncan of 36 Upper Park Road, Haverstock Hill, the painter of landscapes and "idylls", Thomas Watt Café, and the much travelled orientalist artist Edward Angelo Goodall of 57 Fitzroy Road, Regent's Park became beneficiaries of Berridge and Jenkins's adventures in Sheerness.

Lest we form too negative an impression of these metropolitan inheritors, we should acknowledge that in 1888, a year after Berridge's death, his trustees and those three artists, gave the Minster-in-Sheppey school board a plot of land on Alexandra Road directly to the south of the Ebenezer chapel so that its officers might build the school — since made over into flats like the chapel itself — that Uwe Johnson could glimpse from his back window upstairs.

17. BECOMING "SHEERNESS-ON-SEA": THE SCRAMBLE FOR A SECOND HORSE

The architectural historian John Newman had no praise for the Rio Cinema — a fantastic 1600-seat Art Deco building with a frontal "fin" that soared up to a circular look-out tower — which had been opened at 27 the Broadway by the Kay Brothers chain in 1937. Indeed, Nikolaus Pevsner's English deputy deplored this "vicious modernistic"[1] imposition, which had long since fallen into industrial use. He didn't really compose himself again until, further east along the same street, he found some reassurance in the "well composed W. front" of the Roman Catholic Church of St. Henry and St Elisabeth, with its "row of five lancets and a rose window rising to a typically steep bell-gable".[2]

As for *Die Zeit*'s Fritz J. Raddatz, Johnson had said nothing to encourage him to pause at either building. Had he been following cues from their earlier correspondence, his visitor from Frankfurt might have more inclined to glance past the church and adjacent presbytery to make out Neptune Terrace where, as his relocated friend had once told him, Elisabeth's favourite bewildered garden lay between the building and the sea. He may also have been musing more generally about Johnson's enquiry about the summer months in 1931 that Kurt Tucholsky, the already exiled anti-fascist writer of Germany's Weimar Republic, had spent in a rented farm cottage half an hour's drive away on the Kentish mainland at Ashford.[3] Neither Raddatz nor Johnson were in any position to realise that, if you turn a nineteenth-century British riot into a church, you could well end up with something like the one in which Newman had been pleased also to discover a "lofty, taut interior".

Designed by E.W. Pugin and situated next to its presbytery on the Broadway just to the east of the stump of the old One-Hundred Acre Windmill preserved in the car park of the Sea View Hotel, the Church of St Henry and St Elizabeth was built in 1863–4 on land originally leased from the Admiralty. It was financed by a Major

Church of St Henry and Elizabeth, seen from the East, with the Sea View Hotel beyond.

Henry Mostyn and his wife Elizabeth in response, so one Catholic website claims, to the quartering of the Tipperary Artillery Militia at Sheerness in 1860.[4] This decision is said to have brought some eight hundred soldiers to the garrison beside the dockyard, and also to have quite overwhelmed previous arrangements for Roman Catholic worship in the town.

The Tipperary men had been commended by the London *Times*, which observed their conduct during an outing to the Crystal Palace at Sydenham. The reporter praised the "freshness of look, breadth of shoulder and the roundness of limb" of these well-behaved soldiers, raised as they had been from "the heart of once lawless Tipperary", and counted their strict discipline proof of what could be done with a diet of "British beef and beer".[5] Two years earlier, by contrast, members of the North Cork Rifle Militia had rioted in Sheerness. In English accounts of their uprising, the trouble started on the evening of Thursday, 7 October 1858, when a group of riflemen chased a seaman through a shop in Chapel Street and into a private room at the back, where they used their belts to "inflict severe wounds on his head and face".[6] Having smashed up chairs and tables for weapons and torn strips off sheets to create slings, they had gone out looking for more trouble. When one of the rioters was apprehended, a picket of riflemen from the North Cork Regiment arrived on the scene. Far from restoring law and order, they are said to have advanced with their "Cork blood"[7] excited, using "drawn bayonets" to force the release of their countryman. Sheerness's entire force of three local policemen soon withdrew and the inflamed militia had the run of the town for an hour or so, causing traders to flee and confronting all attempts to calm them with volleys of stones and bloodcurdling cries reported as "Brain the -----, Brain 'em".

The riot went on, more or less unchecked, for five nights in a row, with hundreds of militia members marching out of their barracks to gather stones (an easy task given the new kerbs and paving then being laid in the town) and attack "the inhabitants wherever they saw any number of them assembled". The riflemen also chased their own officers, forcing one to "take shelter in the Fountain Hotel" in Blue Town, where many windows were smashed, shutters were torn off houses, and residents attacked and threatened. This mayhem was said to have been accompanied by a chorus of terrifying threats: "We'll have the ----- town down, and do for all hands". Eventually a detachment of men from the Royal Artillery force at the garrison combined with an incoming detachment from the Kent county constabulary to get the situation under control. Outraged commentators hoped the disgraced North Cork militia would be removed from the garrison and, perhaps, also be "disbanded at once".[8] The force was promptly removed to Aldershot in order to "restore the tranquillity" of Sheerness.

That was the English version of the story and yet, as the Irish papers were quick to note, a Court of Inquiry held at Sheerness concluded, with the full support of both the Admiral and the garrison chief, that the Cork rifles were "not the original aggressors in these riots which have acquired so unpleasant a notoriety"[9] and that their record of conduct before this provocation had been entirely flawless. This news was no surprise to the *Cork Examiner*, which remembered its own experience of having the English Royal Elthorne Militia "domiciled amongst us" during the years following the Great Famine (the main activity of the privates seemed to be "robbing their officers or the public"). Unlike the English press, in which the cause of the outbreak was little discussed, this paper pointed out that the violence began when the wife of one of the North Cork Rifles' sergeants was "grossly insulted, and the men themselves annoyed and provoked by offensive allusions to their country and religion".[10] It had no hesitation in condemning the "calumnies", so damaging to the "Irish character", which had been "diligently circulated" about the "otherwise excellently-behaved" North Cork regiment in England. The imperial British press might have enjoyed excoriating the "Cork ruffians",[11] but the *Cork Examiner* turned the tables to declare the people of Sheerness "utter savages" with "less feeling of the influences of civilization than the inhabitants of the wildest part of Ireland. They have only one feeling in common with the more cultivated of their fellow countrymen, that of a detestation of the 'Irish papists'"

In Sheerness, the suggestion that "the inhabitants" of the town had any responsibility for the riots was roundly repudiated at a meeting, allegedly attended by over six hundred townspeople, who gathered to insist that they were blameless for a dispute that had broken out between different "branches" of the service at Sheerness, and that "resident working men" had only congregated at the top of streets and courts in order to "prevent the belligerents forcing their way out of the High-street and injuring their property or the persons of their families".[12] No such plea would change the mind of the *Cork Examiner*, which had declared the Court of Inquiry's finding a proper repudiation to "the brutes of Sheerness", whose "mental picture of Paddy is drawn, with a shillelagh [a weighted club of blackthorn or oak] in one hand and a whiskey bottle in the other".

An awareness of the troubles drink could bring to an

isolated garrison town was also reflected, nearly twenty-five years later, in one of the first decisions made by those in charge of the Victoria Working Men's Club and Institute, an imposing, four-square building standing a couple of hundred yards back along the Broadway.

Victoria Working Men's Club.

Built at a cost of £3,000 on land acquired from the War Department, the club, which is likely to have spurred on the men responsible for the more grandiose Conservative Club built some five years later, was opened on 8 July 1882 by Mr Hodgson Pratt, secretary of the Working Men's Club Union, with delegates from the principal clubs across Kent, and some five hundred of the club's six hundred members present with their wives.[13] Created without patronage in accordance with the Union's motto ("self-help") and the wider conviction that, as Pratt declared, "the future rested with the working classes", the Working Men's Club — which Pevsner's largely unimpressed investigator granted another exceptional reprieve as "pure vernacular, and good fun"[14] — had stone (or cement) lions reclining on either side of its entrance and individually dedicated rooms for chess and cards, billiards and bagatelle.[15] It had a Committee Room, a Conversation Room, and also an Assembly Room in which events of the sort once offered by the town's allegedly "moribund" literary institute, might take place. Baths were to be added as soon as funds were available. Like other working men's clubs this one would promote the "interchange of opinion" between people of diverse parties and thereby "multiply the intelligence" of their class around the country. It would provide its members, many of whom were employed in the dockyard, with a sober as well as improving alternative to the town's many pubs. The "moderate" drinker would be allowed to join the virtuous teetotaller in working towards the "new era" promised by the national boom in working men's clubs, but not everyone was welcome. As soon as they had securely bought the initially rented land on which the Victoria Club stood from the War Department for £300, its founders had passed a resolution barring "military men" from "entering the precincts", either as members or as a member's friends.[16]

Meanwhile, military requirements continued to govern the pace at which the at first free-standing "terraces" of Marine Town were joined up to form streets of continuous housing. The Admiralty might suddenly announce, as it had done in the late 1850s, that several hundred new jobs were to be added. At such moments property owners and landlords stood to benefit from an acute shortage of stock that posed a moral danger to others, or so the *Sheerness Guardian* believed. A bad house, it explained, wrecks the "cleanly, tidy, thrifty mechanic's wife", who all too easily "degenerates into the 'slut' in both 'person' and 'place'".[17] The mechanic husband, meanwhile, senses the change at home and takes to the pub with such regularity that the house becomes "only his eating and sleeping place". In the *Sheerness Guardian's* view, the answer to this problem was not to be found in the manoeuvres of "small capitalists" of the sort attracted to the early sales of properties in Marine Town. The paper recommended that the working man of Sheerness should "make himself acquainted" with "the social, moral and physical advantages" afforded by building societies including the Sheerness Permanent Benefit Building Society, which had recently held a very well attended meeting in the Bethel School Room in Hope Street. Some readers might have been tempted further in that direction by an advertisement from "the Brotherly Unity Society", which was looking for a few young, healthy and respectable newcomers who might join its existing members in saving with the Sheerness Permanent (interested readers were invited to get it touch with the Treasurer, who turns out to have been Mr J. Ward, of 8 Alma St, Marine Town).[18]

Johnson, meanwhile, only had to glance at his own front

door to realise that Ward's Town, as this easterly stretch of Marine Town was briefly known, wasn't built only to service and improve the dockyard workers living in its humbler terraces. Each of the front door's two upper panels were fitted with cast-iron lattices through which freshening zephyrs might be encouraged to waft on balmy summer days. These ventilating fixtures, against which hinged interior windows could be closed during less exceptional weather, demonstrate that the sea-facing houses on Marine Parade had been erected with a seasonal diversification

26 Marine Parade.

of the local economy in mind. Together with the house's other "original features" — the shuttering and canopy work, the parquet flooring, the tiled bathroom at the back — that hygienic front door revealed No. 26 to have been among the "commodious" lodging houses with which later developers of the seafront had sought to advance the bid for a second horse initiated by Sir Edward Banks with his Royal Hotel, steamboats, and inviting notices about "Banks Town" in the more respectable London papers.

The people of Victorian Sheerness were well accustomed to the fact that the threat of collapse and inevitable retreat was contained within every incoming wave of growth. The town might boom as a "Royal Naval station and Dockyard" during times of war and imperial adventure. When peace intervened, however, it was rarely long before upriver politicians could be heard wondering about cuts or worse. William Shrubsole wrote his already cited defence of the shipwrights in the naval dockyards in 1770, during the reassessment that followed the Seven Years War, but Sheerness had actually been haunted by the threat of closure from the very first. Samuel Pepys may have sailed downriver to lay out the future dockyard in 1667. By June 1686, however, he would be in pursuit of "economy and efficiency" on behalf of a new monarch, James II, and convinced that the "disestablishment of Sheerness" was desirable. Since there was only a guardship and one other vessel receiving attention there, it was ordered that the workers should be sent back to Chatham and the officers posted to other dockyards as the occasion arose.[19] Doubts had also pressed in on John Rennie the Elder, the Scottish engineer who eventually designed and started construction of the new Georgian dockyard in the early nineteenth century. Visiting Sheerness in 1807, he had found the old dockyard to be "composed only of some old wooden ships imbedded in the mud, a few storehouses, a wretched basin lined with wooden walls, and some similar jetties".[20] He saw many reasons why the place should be "abolished" rather than rebuilt — it was on the lee or wrong side of the harbour, the foundation for new works consisted only of sand and quicksand, and the space available for rebuilding was "very confined" thanks partly to the haphazard adjacent settlement of Blue Town. Given the high cost of working on such a dismal site, Rennie had urged the government to abandon Sheerness, along with Woolwich and Deptford, and to concentrate on the creation of "a new complete establishment" that would, he believed, be far better placed further up the Thames, at Northfleet beyond Gravesend. He was over-ruled that time. A decade after the opening of Rennie's completed dockyard, however, the founders of "Banks Town" were galvanised by plausible rumours that the government was considering withdrawing ship-building activities from Sheerness, and using the site instead as a "depository for quarantine merchandise".[21]

As those lattices on Johnson's front door tell us, the great fear returned to stalk the streets of Sheerness during the years when Berridge and Jenkins were battling their way through the courts as they pursued their development plans. In the wake of the Crimean War, the Committee of Dockyard Economy, chaired by Rear-Admiral Robert Smart and appointed at the order of a Tory cabinet in the spring of 1858, found the Royal dockyards in a deplorable condition, filled with lethargic officers who were shockingly incompetent in their account-keeping, and all the more dysfunctional thanks to local systems of management in which unashamed favouritism triumphed over merit and efficiency. In the *Spectator*'s view (which echoed that of Captain Sir Adolphus Slade, who had complained in 1846 of "the absence of science in the dockyards"[22] and who refined and repeated his scathing accusations in 1859[23]), the problem was aggravated by the fact that the naval dockyards were overseen by a succession of senior captains, commodores, and admirals appointed to the position of superintendent despite knowing nothing at all about building, repairing or fitting ships. The obvious shortcomings of this situation were aggravated by rapid turnover (there were no less than five superintendents at Sheerness between 1846 and 1857), and by the Admiralty's all too apparent presumption that it was possible to manage such inconvenient and unhealthy places "by correspondence alone."[24]

Having been returned to power on a wave of popular acclaim in 1859, Lord Palmerston's second Liberal government responded to the uproar provoked by the Committee on Dockyard Economy by establishing a Royal Commission on the Control and Management of Naval Yards. Reporting in 1861, this body repeated many of the earlier criticisms, pointing to the "incompetence"[25] and "indifference" of many master shipwrights, calling for stricter management and clearer lines of accountability and also for the power to sack incompetent or corrupt members of the "established" staff, who had formed their own labour aristocracy and systems of preferment in the dockyards. As for the dockyard accounts, the Commission's summary conclusion relied heavily on the words "absence" and "want".[26]

The Commission had initially recommended the closure of dockyards at Deptford, Pembroke and Woolwich, but predictable jockeying followed and Sheerness, which the

Secretary of the Admiralty had at first described as "a station of great importance, especially for North Sea purposes", was soon rumoured to have replaced Pembroke and Deptford among the sites "destined eventually to be abandoned".[27] On that occasion, the defence fell to the Liberal MP for Kent Eastern, a baronet named Sir Edward Cholmeley Dering, who loudly rehearsed the "special advantages" of Sheerness — where, after all, large ships could be "brought up close to the yard" at all tides (aware of the coming ironclads, Dering emphasised that "at a trifling expense the largest ships in the navy might be docked in this harbour at low water"). He also invited the Secretary to the Admiralty to remember the words of a former First Lord of the Admiralty, Sir James Graham, who had suggested that "any Government that should seriously entertain the idea of selling or abandoning so useful a harbour as Sheerness would be trifling with the best interests of the country". A retiring Superintendent of the dockyard would later be more emphatic, reassuring apprehensive townspeople that anyone who conceived such an absurd idea "must be a lunatic" as well as, so he implied, a member of the Liberal Party.[28]

Dering's warning was issued in 1865, near the beginning of a "long, deep slump"[29] that brought the virtual collapse of shipbuilding on the Thames and heavy cuts to the dockyard workforce. The threat against Sheerness remained in September 1869, when "the 18,000 inhabitants of this rising town" once again sought reassurance from the Lords of the Admiralty that there was no truth in the whisper that their dockyard was, "most injuriously", to be closed.[30] The rumour was not killed off by the granted denial, and there was forceful feeling in Sheerness about the "constant reductions" in the town's dockyard (the Liberal MP for Pontefract, Mr Childers, won no friends in Sheerness when he declared that "a more extravagant yard in a more wretched place could not be conceived"). [31] By the following year, indeed, it was reported that twenty workmen were being discharged every week, and the dark cloud over Sheerness would not be dispersed by the announcement that "the eventual abandonment of that yard depends upon the completion of arrangements in progress and in contemplation at Chatham."[32] According to the *Sheerness Times*, "Sheerness has kept faith with the government." The guilty party was "the private ship-builders, and their desire that our vessels of war should be offered by private firms to be built by contract." This Victorian attempt at privatisation was "synonymous with jobbery and malversation of the public money."[33]

The town's defenders did what they could to secure the dockyard against Liberal reformers and commercial privateers. They urged those who maligned Sheerness as a most "wretched" place, to consider how great port cities such as Liverpool and Birkenhead might have looked in their early days, and they did what they could in their statements to thicken up the Medway fog that so frequently placed Chatham beyond the safe navigation of ships at times when the point at Sheerness remained "perfectly clear and accessible."[34] Keen to break their dependency on unreliable authorities upriver, they also looked for other ways of keeping the town afloat. So it was that, on Monday, 8 September 1873, the "principal residents" of Sheerness had gathered at the recently opened Victoria Hall on the Broadway and Trinity Road to form an association, through which they would renew the project of establishing their town as a convenient resort for "tired metropolitans."[35] As the *Sheerness Times* editorialised on 16 August 1873, this group of "public-spirited inhabitants" were determined to "assert very persistently" that Sheerness was quite capable of attracting visitors from London and, indeed, of rivalling "the attractions of Margate or other resorts as popular as Margate."[36]

Mainland "depreciation" was a familiar problem for Sheerness, but the association seeking to transform the town — "which the meeting agreed would henceforth be known as 'Sheerness-on-Sea'"[37] — also had to face up to the possibility that, despite the best efforts of Sir Edward Banks and the more recent pioneers of Marine Town to create a resort, public scepticism remained all too justified. In order to succeed in their task, the aspiring residents must, so a horrified recent visitor wrote from the safe distance of his home in Fleet Street, find some capitalists with the means to help them "'unSheerness' the place".[38] This job would involve removing buildings presently spoiling access to the town's only asset (the sea), constructing a proper parade along the beach, creating lodging-houses to which visitors might be willing to return, raising the sights of the recalcitrant local authorities, and doing something about the upsetting condition of the town's ill-treated cab-horses ("Poor dear dumb brutes!").

In the absence of the new town pier in which so much hope had been invested in the days of "Banks Town", there was no alternative but to use the existing one in Blue Town, which could hardly give the visitor a worse impression. The *Sheerness Times* described the journey that the ardently desired London excursionists would have to make if they were to reach the new watering place on the far side of the moat. The voyage from London might be congenial enough but "all pleasure was gone"[39] as soon as the visitor walked along the five hundred-foot pier and stepped down into the chaotic warren that was Blue Town. Fearing that she or he had come all this way only to stumble into "Wapping by the Sea", the apprehensive visitor "must, of necessity, turn back to the boat, and wait there the time of return". Frustrated excursionists would never discover that "beyond Blue Town, there is a Sheerness which is worth visiting. There is a good beach, quite equal to any to be found at more favoured watering places, and there is for excursions the whole of the very small but very interesting Isle of Sheppey. From the beach the visitor has an ever-varying panorama, for past him, and wholly within sight, must go the vessels, large and small, which make the port of London the wonder of the world". Sheerness had long had "a bad name as an unhealthy, slow, and neglected place". Thanks, however, to the improvements of drainage and water supply carried out since the highly critical report published by the Registrar of Births, Deaths and Marriages in 1858, Sheerness-on-Sea was actually now "about the most healthy town on the English coast" with a death rate "lower than at any other seaport resort, with the exception of Eastbourne".

The champions of "Sheerness-on-Sea", who plainly had their own ways of doing the new science of statistics, were determined that Marine Town rather than the dockyard or its immediate environs should become the centre of "Sheerness proper". Despite the "grim significance" the area held for the patriotic residents who still insisted on calling it "the Crimea", it was "to this new part of town that the visitor should hasten. There are already one or two commodious hotels, but nothing like the accommodation which such a place should have". Further improvements were essential if "Sheerness-on-Sea" was to become more than a cheating phrase that only provoked snorts of contempt from arriving visitors. Some amenities had already been pulled out of Blue Town and reconfigured as part of the town proper. The Bethel Chapel had retreated or, perhaps, advanced into Mile Town early in the century, and the post office moved into "commodious" new premises in the new town in 1876.[40] In order to create a more salubrious point of entry for the health-seeking Londoner, the active residents would eventually manage to adjust the railway too. Having arrived in Blue Town in 1860 it would be encouraged to keep going, turning east along a new spur that brought it to the still-existing new "central terminus" opened in Mile Town in 1883.

It was never going to be possible to convert the town's shingle beaches into golden sands that might truly rival those of Margate, yet other improvements were achieved. In the summer of 1876, an asphalted rollerskating rink had been opened by the lower esplanade, which promised to be a "fair success".[41] Plans been announced to add a Ladies Bath and also a Private Bath to the recently constructed swimming pool.[42] Marine Town could already boast a "handsome Public Hall", complete with reading rooms (the Sheerness Literary Institute had benefited from new public rooms at the Victoria Hall and theatre, opened on the Broadway in February 1870). Like Sir Edward Banks before them, the visionaries of "Sheerness-on-

Sea" wanted to see a "promenade pier" on the beach, and a new esplanade to help in "the erection of lodging-houses". The latter wish would be satisfied after 11 December 1875, when it was decided to proceed with the esplanade — partly to encourage the visiting promenader but also "to serve as a defence from the sea in Marine Town".[43]

Thanks to this independent effort, a resort named Sheerness-on-Sea really had come into existence by the end of the nineteenth century, even though, as the founders well knew, the odds remained stacked against it. The case for bringing the railway on from Blue Town to a new station in the heart of "Sheerness-on-Sea" may have been the only thing in the town that was assisted by the sinking of the paddle steamer Princess Alice on 3 September 1878. 650 summer excursionists drowned that night in water filled with recently discharged raw sewage after their ship collided with a collier in Gallion's Reach while returning to London Bridge

"The Girls are Very
Playful", Postcard,
Davidson Bros, c. 1910.

at the end of a "moonlight trip" to Sheerness. Johnson, whose house was no longer equipped with the venetian blinds or the overhead "gaseliers" that had once seemed as vital as indoor W.C.s to householders offering rooms to attract paying guests, will have learned about that too. It remains possible, however, that his visiting friend Fritz J. Raddatz had come all the way to his door without noticing that picking out the still undemolished residues of Marine Town's Victorian future, with its mixture of commercial, political and Christian visions of redemption, remains the primary attraction of walking east along the Broadway.

18. "BLACK TUESDAY": THE DAY THE WORLD ENDED

By the time Fritz J. Raddatz arrived at 26 Marine Parade and knocked loudly on the door as instructed, Johnson's bell was by no means the only thing in Sheerness that was broken. A year later, on 19 September 1978, the *Sheppey Gazette* would place the title "streets of Drabness" at the head of an article about Marine Town. Having explored the working-class streets directly behind Johnson's larger house, the journalist Martin Collier described the area as "very much in the mould of an old-fashioned community". It had many elderly residents, a selection of six "back-street pubs", and a strong sense of "community spirit" that could "perhaps only be sustained in an area with such a strong working-class tradition". The recent arrival of a Chinese takeaway in these "drab old streets" hinted at the changes that might come as younger people moved in. There could be no doubt, though, that the traditional community was dying. Featured as one of its heroic survivors, "Tubby Ward" was sixty-seven years old but still younger than many who had come to rely on him. Interviewing him in his front room, Collier noted that the ceiling was "so full of holes it looks like a pin cushion". This was the consequence, not of decay or infestation, but of Tubby's seasonal habit of buying Christmas presents for the neighbourhood's children, pinning them up with thread so that they would dangle temptingly in his front window, and then, as the day approached, inviting the passing children to come in and choose one for themselves. Tubby, whose seasonal generosity might nowadays expose him to dire suspicions, also ran errands and chopped firewood for older pensioners, delivering it to their homes in a long barrow. "People here just carry on smiling — it's all you can do. Helping other people and keeping busy is what keeps me going. Everybody knocks me up if they want anything".

Pauline and Harold Huggins in the local corner shop on the junction of Richmond Street and Alma Street were also practised in the art that the one-man blues band Duster Bennett had called "smiling like I'm happy". Friendliness and the "personal touch" still made a difference in their general store, little more than a stone's throw from Johnson's house. The elderly residents commended the shopkeepers, Tubby Ward, and the two women roadsweepers, thanks to whom the area retained traces of its traditional identity. They knew, however, that Marine Town was going to Hell. Mrs Florence Lee, who had lived in Clyde Street for thirty-five years, declared that "The area has lost its character. It is terrible here now". New "social problems" were partly to blame, but the incompetence of the council was a persistent source of grievances too. Marine Town had indeed been designated a "Housing Action area", a status that enabled the council, which was already providing mortgages of up to 90%, to offer improvement grants to some three hundred families who were still coping with outside lavatories and no bathrooms. In other ways, however, the local authority's record was poor — it was failing to repair properties or to rebuild on the derelict sites left when decrepit properties had been bulldozed. The old folk of Marine Town were by no means the only ones yearning for the past in James Callaghan's bankrupt Britain. In Sheerness, however, it was possible to name the day "The End of the World as We Know It" had arrived in town.

*

"Most of our people have never had it so good". So the Tory prime minister, Harold Macmillan, had told an enraptured Conservative Party rally at Bedford in July 1957. In Sheerness, as in other naval establishments around the shrinking

British Empire, people had been offered a different phrase to worry about. "Outline of future policy" was the title of a White Paper presented to Parliament some three months earlier by Macmillan's Minister of Defence. The defence budget had already declined as a percentage of GDP over the previous four years, but this had not been enough for Duncan Sandys, who horrified the service chiefs by demanding "the largest change in defence policy ever carried through in normal times"[1] and declaring it justified on many different grounds. The national economy was struggling, and there was an urgent need for capital and scientific expertise to be concentrated on the modernisation of industry. A few diehard imperialists might still be nursing illusions about Britain's singular role in the world, but the country was no longer likely to fight wars except in association with allies, including the USA, now that the breach caused by Anthony Eden's humiliated Suez intervention of the previous year was being patched up. The existence of NATO meant that Britain's armed forces were no longer required to be "self-sufficient and balanced in all respects". Meanwhile, both military planning and "world strategy" were fundamentally challenged by "sensational" changes in military technology: nuclear weapons and "rocket weapons" equipped to see if not yet think for themselves.

The largest of the savings demanded would be found by abolishing National Service in Britain, but Sandys'"Outline of Future Policy"also announced the end of a long era for British sea power. "Radical revision" would mean "basing the main elements of the Royal Navy upon a small number of [aircraft] carrier groups"and reducing the number of other large ships to a minimum. Determined "to prune to the utmost the elements which do not directly contribute to fighting capacity", Sandys demanded a reduction in the navy's historical accumulation of shore establishments both at home and abroad. It was too early to say exactly where the axe would fall, but it would not be possible "for the level of work in all factories, dockyards, depots and establishments to be maintained; and some will have to be closed".

"Wells drops dockyards Employment Bombshell". That was how the *Sheerness Times Guardian* announced the coming of the long-feared day of extinction on 14 February 1958. Percy Wells, the respected Labour MP for Faversham, had gleaned the news not from chums in Westminster or the Admiralty, but from trade unionists involved in the Admiralty Joint Industrial Committee. There would be cuts across the world. The East India Command would be closed. Hong Kong would lose its dockyard. The base at Trincomalee (Gokanna) was already being transferred to the Royal Ceylon Navy. The dockyard in Gibraltar would be maintained, but the one at Malta was open to offers.

It was, however, changes to the naval establishment at home that worried Wells most directly. He understood that 12,000 jobs were to be lost across Britain and also that the Admiralty committee charged with making the economies demanded by the Sandys report had resolved to merge all "yardcraft" services, cutting 25% and concentrating what was left at Portsmouth.

The news that Duncan Sandys' naval economies meant the end for Sheerness was confirmed to both Houses of Parliament a few days later on 18 February 1958. It had been decided to abolish the Royal Navy's Nore Command and to close Sheerness dockyard, together with the one at Portland in Dorset, the Aircraft Repair Yard at Donibristle in Fife, and "five other air establishments".[2] The First Lord of the Admiralty, the Earl of Selkirk, told the House of Lords that "the decline in naval repair work resulting from the planned reductions in the Fleet"[3] had to be faced. In order to allow for the development of other forms of employment in the area, Sheerness dockyard would be run down gradually, not finally closing until April 1960. The abolition of the Nore Command would be completed by April, 1961. Chatham dockyard would be retained, although the barracks and other naval establishments there would be shut by April 1961. The Scottish unionist and Civil Lord of the Admiralty Tam Galbraith regretted the impact this decision would have on the affected forces, and also among civilian employees, promising that "special employment services" would be set up under the Minister of Labour inside the affected establishments before the discharges began. £7 million would be saved by the cuts, which would entail the loss of 2,700 naval jobs ashore and seven thousand civilian posts.

Some Conservative MPs did indeed manage to keep smiling. Vice-Admiral John Hughes Hallett, MP for Croydon East, had planned and commanded naval raids across the English Channel during the Second World War, and he welcomed the "shift of expenditure from the tail to the teeth of the Royal Navy". Sir Frederick Burden, the Conservative member for Gillingham, emphasised the relief felt in the Medway towns at the announcement that the dockyard at Chatham would not be closed as rumour had suggested — even though the closure of the torpedo depot and the gunwharf workshops, the transfer of the mechanical training establishment and the Admiralty's withdrawal from the town's Royal Naval Hospital seemed elsewhere to justify the headline "Navy leaving Medway Towns".[4]

The Labour Party showed more vigour. Mr Thomas Steele, Labour MP for Dunbartonshire West, on the Clyde outside Glasgow, suspected an unstated political motive. He pointed out that, while virtually no new shipbuilding was going on the naval dockyards, the private yards, with which the Clyde was well supplied, had "full order books, and are finding difficulty in meeting their commitments". And what might come from the promised "consultation" with the President of the Board of Trade and the Minister of Labour given "the numbers affected, particularly in Sheerness, where no alternative employment is available?" Viscount Alexander of Hillsborough, a senior Co-operative and Labour Party politician who was now leader of the Labour opposition in the House of Lords, informed his fellow peers. "I know of a co-operative society that was founded by the first naval dockyard employees in 1815 and which is now an enormous establishment in the Island of Sheerness". It was, so this geographically confused fellow concluded, "an exceedingly grave and difficult situation for these people to face" and it may be necessary to consider "whether Sheerness should be made a special area. Except for some agriculture, the whole area lives on the dockyard".

Emanuel Shinwell, the seventy-two-year-old MP for Easington, Durham, was among the Labour doubters. After serving as both Secretary of State for War and Minister of Defence in Atlee's post-war Labour government, this erstwhile Glaswegian revolutionary had opposed the deployment of American nuclear weapons on British soil and he was not much inclined to lament the passing of one of the naval dockyards from which Britain's own first atom bomb had been shipped to the Montebello islands off Australia, where it was detonated in October 1952, irradiating large numbers of onlookers. Shinwell applauded the government's effort to reduce "public expenditure". He also sought reassurance that "appropriate measures" would be put in place to find "other occupations" for the dockyard's displaced workers, not just the "established" but more casually employed as well.[5] That question was also emphasised by the Labour MP for Faversham, Mr Percy Wells. Having informed the Commons that the decision would be "received with dismay in Sheerness, and with a feeling of callous betrayal", he too moved on quickly to ask what the Government would be doing "to prevent the Isle of Sheppey becoming a distressed area".

The *Sheerness Times Guardian*'s reporter was in London to put the first question to Lord Selkirk at the press conference following the announcements in Parliament. He wanted to know why Sheerness had not been treated like Malta, where the Admiralty was reportedly already receiving offers from commercial firms interested in the dockyard, no longer required by Britain now that the American fleet was becoming the commanding presence in the Mediterranean. Selkirk explained that no such interest could be sought before the decision had been presented to Parliament, but that new employers would be vigorously pursued over the two years leading to the closure. Indeed, as Lord Mountbatten added, the Admiralty had written to the Shipbuilding Conference that very morning.[6] The Sheerness reporter was also informed that the rapid pace of technological change had helped dictate the decision. Selkirk pointed out that even "visual firing — above or below water — is ceasing". Lord Mountbatten, who believed the Admiralty was presiding over "the rebirth of the navy", admitted grievous losses were entailed but then went on to talk about himself: "what we are doing in the Chatham area sent a shiver down my spine", he said, adding, "It was very painful for me, as the last three ships I commanded were all Chatham ships".

While the decision was under discussion in Westminster it was also being communicated in Sheerness. Notices were posted and the officer in charge of the dockyard, Captain P.M.B. Chavasse, broke the news to the Dockyard Whitley Committee (a joint industrial council in which both trade unions and employers were represented). Chavasse also met the Chairman of the Sheerness Urban Council, Mr W.C. Butterworth, to convey his personal regret that "this drastic step" had been considered necessary.

At a council meeting held a few hours later, Butterworth named the day "Black Tuesday", while others anticipated that the town would be "callously left to rot". The wider implications of the decision were already crashing into view: the baleful prospect faced by the Sheerness and District Co-operative Society, which reckoned 50% of its business was directly connected to the dockyard; the likely closure of the technical college; the halting of the council's long promised redevelopment (largely conceived as a bulldozing exercise in "slum-clearance") of Blue Town; the dismal implications for the island's school-leavers. The Water Board's plan to get a supply from the mainland suddenly seemed threatened, and there were concerns, too, about the Sheerness & Gillingham Building Society, which had helped many dockyard workers buy houses in Sheerness, and would soon be placing advertisements reassuring depositors that it had long been diversifying its asset base and that only 20% of its properties were now on the Isle of Sheppey.[7] "We must go on living", said one councillor, as the air was sucked from his lungs.

The council went on to organise the public meeting attended by Percy Wells and representatives of all Sheppey's three councils. Intended to unite "all the island" behind a deputation that would ask to see the Prime Minister, the meeting was announced for the following Sunday afternoon (28 February 1958). Held with Essoldo's permission in Sheerness's Argosy Cinema on the Broadway, it was attended by nearly one thousand people, many of them "standing at the back".

Speakers were asked to avoid party political argument in the name of the common interest. That was understood by the first speaker, Percy Wells MP, who had held the "weathervane" constituency of Faversham for Labour for thirteen years. Born in Kent in 1891, he had left school at sixteen to serve in the Royal Navy for three years. He had refused conscription in April 1917, and been imprisoned in Wormwood Scrubs as a conscientious objector.[8] He had moved to Gillingham in 1923 to take up his duties as District Organiser for the Transport and General Workers Union, an organisation that later appointed him General Secretary for Kent. He had confronted the Mayor of Dover during the General Strike of 1926,[9] and worked closely with agricultural labourers ("Farmers, as a class, were very pessimistic people", he told a village gathering in 1935, "and always thought themselves worse off than they actually were").[10] He had served as a local Labour Party activist in the county for some twenty-five years before winning Faversham in the Labour landslide of 1945. Wells was "one of us", so his election leaflet for 1959 would proclaim, and certainly not one of the "Here to-day and gone to-morrow" types his visiting Conservative rivals had proved to be over the previous four elections.

Even while acting as Parliamentary Private Secretary to the Foreign Secretary Ernest Bevin, Wells had remained conscientiously opposed to warfare: he was among the Labour MPs who voted against Attlee's "conscription" bill in 1947,[11] and he had a lot of history in common with Emanuel Shinwell too. He had, however, fought hard for Sheerness over the naval dockyard, even while gearing up for the wider general election campaign in which he would promise that Labour would increase the state pension, repeal the Rent Act, "slash" purchase tax on clothes and household goods, create full employment and a fairer distribution of wealth while also providing schools with smaller classes, more teachers and cancellation of the hated Eleven-plus exam. Unlike some of Sheppey's more recent Labour MPs, Wells was a Kentish man of the people who travelled up to London to

Percy Wells, MP for Faversham. c. 1960.

attend the House of Commons, and definitely not a Londoner coming "down" from the capital to visit his constituency.

At the meeting in the Argosy Cinema, Wells began by defending himself and the local council from the suggestion that they had not yielded sufficient ground to prevent this dire outcome: they had both, he said, loudly resisted any "whittling away" of functions carried out at the dockyard, knowing that successive small reductions would make it much harder to defend the place if and when the threat of total closure loomed.[12] He saw no economy in the plan to transfer a thousand men — the "established" workers to whom the Admiralty had obligations — to Chatham, and nor did he accept that the government's habit of giving naval work to private dockyards was genuinely motivated by economic considerations. In a move that must have been tough for a man of pacifist sympathies, he invoked the name of Sir William Penney, the Director of the Atomic Weapons Research Establishment who had earlier overseen the test explosion of Britain's atom bomb at the Montebello islands in 1952. Penney had grown up in Sheppey and got his educational start just across the Broadway from the Argosy at the Sheerness Technical School for Boys. Was it really a fair tribute, asked Wells, that "as a result of his efforts his native Island should be economically murdered?"

Wells was swimming with the local current, as were most of the speakers who followed him. As the only dockyard man on Sheerness Council, Cllr. J.G. Ward placed his own situation before the meeting: after forty years of working as an "established" man at the dockyard, he must either transfer to Chatham, paying his own travel or relocation costs, or surrender both his job and his pension rights. While he would share that prospect with other members of the "established" staff, he pointed out that the closure also represented a "breach of faith" with the "non-established" workers, who had built up a skill "peculiar to Admiralty employment", which the government appeared to have neither the means nor the will to replace. "They haven't one idea for bringing work on the Isle of Sheppey but they have carefully planned to run down the dockyard". The British people, in whose name the decision had been made, would surely not choose to "have it on their conscience that Sheppey should be reduced to a Jarrow, Durham or distressed area of Wales". John Coppins, who was Secretary of the Sheppey Trades Council and chairman of the trade unionists on the Dockyard Whitley Committee, had no trouble convincing the meeting that it should stiffen the proposed motion and demand, not just a delay in closure while alternative employment was established, but a straightforward reversal of the Admiralty decision and the retention of the dockyard as a going concern — a motion that was passed unanimously.

The citizens of Sheerness may have felt stunned by the government's announcement, but many at the meeting still managed to rise up furiously against the Conservative candidate for Faversham. Mrs Elsie S. Olsen was a self-described housewife and mother of four who would be running neck-to-neck against Wells in the general election to be held in October the following year. She had already campaigned unsuccessfully as the first woman candidate for Edmonton in 1951 and again in 1954, a year in which she had also come to wider public notice by asking the National Liberal Minister for Food, Major Gwilym Lloyd George, "what's happened to the lard?" at a meeting of Conservative women concerned with the easing of rationing.[13]

It was brave of this Conservative doctor's wife to turn up at the Argosy Cinema that afternoon, and her speech did not go at all well. She opened by declaring her sympathy for the stricken townspeople: "I felt I had to tell you that I am with you heart and soul in your great sorrow". Ignoring the rude fellow who shouted from the balcony "What do you know about it?"[14] and the hundreds who were already "on their feet, booing and jeering", she went on to express her hope that new forms of employment would soon be found and then started walking out along a plank of her own choosing, questioning whether the Labour Party really was putting the "well-being" of the community above party politics as the meeting's organisers had demanded. She took aim less at Wells than at Labour's former Secretary of State for War Emanuel Shinwell. He wasn't at the meeting, but Mrs. Olsen still tried to read from his apparently pacifist contribution to the Commons debate of 18 February, in which he had given the government's reduction of the armed forces his approval on the grounds that the decision was in accordance with Labour Party policy. She insisted that Shinwell had gone on to say, "We do not think the Government has gone far enough and we shall welcome further steps in this direction".[15]

Mrs. Elsie S. Olsen having a picnic lunch with her doctor husband before tackling an afternoon canvassing session in Sheerness, 6 October 1959.

By this time, though, Mrs Olsen was being booed, jeered and slow-handclapped: "five hundred men stood and hooted and howled. 'Go back to your

Tory tea-party', they bellowed. 'There are crumpets for tea today — it's Sunday'." Faced with this mocking hostility, Olsen was quickly reduced to muttering about fair play and good manners before making her escape through a side entrance. And there we will leave her. She may have been the first woman candidate ever to have stood for Edmonton in 1954, but she was no Margaret Thatcher in the making. She would be beaten by Wells in the general election twenty months thence, albeit not before shrinking the Labour majority in the "knife-edge" constituency of Faversham by fifty-nine votes to 253, and then be finally seen off by the Labour successor, Terry Boston, at the by-election following Wells' death in 1964 — despite, it was reported, having worn a different hat on each day of her eighteen-day campaign.[16] According to the *Sheerness Times Guardian,* Mrs Olsen's primary offence at the "Black Tuesday" meeting, apart from being a representative of the party that was closing the dockyard, was to have "introduced politics"when the common interest of the stricken community demanded "united effort". After her hasty retreat, Percy Wells, who had shared Shinwell's pacifist views during the First World War, pointed out that the former Glaswegian firebrand had also demanded that the government do something to create alternative employment for the redundant workers of Sheerness: he reiterated that this was hardly the occasion at which to start "fishing for votes"as Mrs Olsen had done.

Percy Wells also summarised his thoughts about the Argosy Cinema meeting the next day in the House of Commons. It was a debate about unemployment, in which various Conservative MPs expressed confidence that, despite the looming signs of a global recession, redundant servicemen and civilian workers could be absorbed into the civilian economy. Wells spoke directly after Hugh Fraser, Tory MP for Stafford and Stone, who had described the decline of the Royal Ordnance factories in Swynnerton as if their journey into "desuetude" had been a gentle and largely pain-free process. Referring to the previous night's meeting in Sheerness, he declared that had he called such a meeting in his constituency to discuss unemployment a week earlier, he would have been lucky if fifty had attended. As it was, he claimed that more than two thousand had shown up the night before, with many being turned away at the door: "These people see their jobs disappearing by 1960. It was that disclosure which had brought them there to protest against an action which they felt was absolutely unwise and unjustified".[17]

And that was how it went — the yard closed, as did the garrison and the Royal Navy's Nore Command. Many of the associated industries struggled and died as the ships melted away, and the people learned to get by in a town full of seafaring memories that may still have counted for something in the "well-stocked" public library, where Elisabeth Johnson would go, one day in 1976, to borrow a novel by Joseph Conrad. Discovering that all but three copies of the collected edition were out on loan, she was informed by the librarian that recent BBC films — both *Under Western Eyes* and *The Secret Agent* had been broadcast in 1975 — had piqued local interest in this great Anglo-Polish novelist of the sea. Perhaps, as Uwe Johnson suggested to Siegfried Unseld, the readers of Sheerness were unusually well-placed to appreciate Conrad not just as "the creator of a world seen through a temperament" but also as one with a "special knowledge of his consumers".[18]

19. FIRST MOVES ON THE AFTERLIFE: THE MODERNIST CHAIR COMES TO SHEERNESS

Though sparsely furnished, the Johnsons's house did contain a couple of striking lounge chairs constructed of "three elegant slabs of wood and leather" and designed by the famous American modernist Charles Eames. Johnson had feared for the future of one of these prized possessions after it collapsed beneath him. So local friends put out the call, and along came "Tony", a former guest or resident on the island and "probably the most skilled carpenter you could find", who drove off with the chair in pieces saying that he would "at least attempt" its restoration.[1]

Johnson might have fared better with a chair from the English designer Ernest Race's now much rarer "Sheppey" range of 1962: a simpler thing without moving parts but unmistakeably modern with its enamelled and exposed steel bar at the front of the seat, its hardwood side frames and upholstery that could be supplied in PVC, leather or the customer's own choice of fabric. To find the manufacturer of this award-winning work of mid-century English modernism, he only had to leave the ghosts of Mecklenburg in his office for a while, follow his usual route to the railway station, and then walk on past the large brick warehouse of the Sheerness Economical Society until he came to a semi-industrial street named New Road.

Anyone seeking a respectful perspective on the dreams of recovery once invested along this unprepossessing street could certainly have done worse than listen to the words spoken by the Chairman of Sheerness Urban District Council as he reviewed the condition of the town the end of April 1960. Repudiating the unhelpful judgement of Alan Whicker, who had recently come to Sheerness for the BBC's *Tonight* programme and blithely dismissed the place as effectively "dead", Councillor Jim Ward admitted that the announcement of the combined closure of the garrison, the naval dockyard and the Nore naval command had produced a "year almost of despair and certainly of very high hopes".[2] As he explained to the meeting, the thought of Sheerness and, indeed, the entire island, losing its livelihood had led the council to establish the "Development Committee" that was going into battle against apathy, demoralisation and the all too easy assumption that Sheerness might as well now be allowed to sink back into the sea from which its limited prosperity had come.

1960 was a dreadful year for the town — appropriately opened with the words of a visiting American sailor who, when asked what he made of Sheerness, had declared "It's as big as New York cemetery and just about as dead".[3] On 12 February 1960, the *Sheerness Times Guardian* reported that Industrial Aid had again been pledged for the island. Some of the planned new development would spread south along the Medway to Queenborough where the Pilkington Glass factory was to be found. In Sheerness, however, two sites were dedicated to the recovery of the island economy. The primary one was the former dockyard itself, sold in 1959 to a private company named "Building Developments Ltd".[4] Balfour Beatty had an interest in this acquisition but the primary mover was the country's leading post-war property developer Jack Cotton, whose company City Centre Properties had acquired the naval dockyard with the aim of creating a new "harbour estate" in which it would lease out buildings, old or new, as demand suggested, for engineering use. Reviewing his company's recent work in October 1960, Cotton announced of Sheerness: "I am confident that the Group's participation in the enterprise will be lucrative".[5]

By the following summer, Cotton, who that year merged City Centre Properties with two other companies to create the largest property company in the world, was no longer talking only of leasing out properties to industries in the "trading estate" he was establishing in the dockyard. He was also planning to establish a new deep-sea port at Sheerness, a "gateway from Kent to the Continent" that could, thanks to planned road developments (including the Dartford Tunnel and the M2), provide Midland industries with "a new fast road-sea link with Continental markets".[6]

The Kent Development Plan had also been modified to include the conversion of a second area of some 47.5 acres of land at the eastern edge of Mile Town, previously owned by the War Department but now surplus to its requirements. Sheerness Council had bought the land, rashly as pessimistic local critics moaned,[7] and the county's planning committee had agreed that it should be used for "light industrial development", a designation that would preserve the possibility of building housing on any unused areas.[8]

Within a short time, companies were beginning to declare their interest in "New Road". Among the first was the stationery manufacturing firm Twinlock, whose cast concrete factory was already being rushed into existence by a company named Atcost Ltd from Tunbridge Wells. Twinlock staff were informed that Sheerness "seems to have everything we have been looking for; plenty of land and people; and the most helpful municipal folk we have ever met".[9] Increasingly cramped at its Beckenham factory and apparently also used to poor local politics, the management declared itself pleasantly surprised by the reception its representatives had received in the town: "to be welcomed as manufacturers and employers is a strange experience for us", and one that encouraged the firm to defend Sheerness against detractors who saw it only as a marshy dump: "Scenically, it is nothing spectacular", the company's spokesman admitted, but when the sun was out and the tide high the town was "a very pleasant place".

Hopes were also rising and falling again over at the harbour estate. At the beginning of 1960, i.e. three months before the Admiralty finally vacated the dockyard, it looked as if the Cambridge electronics company Pye Ltd would be acquiring more than fifty thousand square feet of factory buildings, where they hoped soon to be producing electro-medical and naval communications equipment, as well as "high-fidelity sound reproducers". This expansion, which seemed likely to produce hundreds of jobs, was hailed as "wonderful news for Sheppey".[10] It didn't happen — for reasons that may have been connected to Pye's decision to merge with its competitor EKCO, across the estuary in Southend-on-Sea.

Next up was Associated Motor Cycles. This was going to be a huge amalgamated concern, reminiscent of a present-day army regiment into which many predecessors have been sent to die during a long history of cuts and mergers. AMS, as it was called, was actually an amalgamation of five different motorcycle companies — Matchless, AJS, Norton, Francis-Barnett and James — and it was already struggling against competition, from BSA at home, but also from BMW in West Germany and a far more effectively managed Honda in Japan. Its offer to make a government-assisted move to the harbour estate from Woolwich seemed to answer many problems in Sheerness, not least by creating one thousand jobs at a stroke. Everyone geared up for the opening, and the Board of Trade was so encouraged that it once again struck Sheerness off its list of scheduled development areas in which government loans could be used to encourage investment. There was some alarm in Sheerness in July 1961, when it was announced that AMS would not be making any profit that year, on account of a "steep downward curve in sales in Britain and the United States".[11] The share price fell sharply, but the Chairman still insisted that the move to Sheerness would help the company recover, since the low cost of the state-subsidised factory would surely ease its pressing financial difficulties. By 3 November 1961, however, it was apparent that AMS would not be coming to Sheerness after all, and the *Sheerness Times Guardian* was devoting its front page to the fact that the busy Labour MP Percy Wells was pounding the streets of Westminster and Whitehall, demanding that Sheerness be restored to the list of development areas under the Local Employment Act.

The coming and going of the public subsidy was bad news for smaller companies too. Paul Lassen, the managing director of a kitchen cabinet producer named Rossland Ltd, had moved his company to the harbour under the expectation of receiving loans from the Board of Trade: "We knew we would have to paddle our own canoe until such time as a loan was forthcoming from the Board".[12] The company had turned down other work, devoting all its resources to getting its new plant up and functioning, only to discover that the loan it had been encouraged to expect was not forthcoming now that "development area" status was to be removed. Lassen went down with his canoe, last seen railing against a government that had brought him to Sheppey "on false pretences".

Wadia Halim Murad kept up his fight with the government for a great deal longer, although it would almost certainly have been better for him had he not done so. Born in Jamaica as the son of a Lebanese Arab millionaire, Murad had come to England in 1921 to study at Manchester University, where he played a lot of cricket and left without a degree. By the early Thirties, he had become interested in wireless technology, producing a new kind of coil-former that helped to bring short-wave onto the mass wireless sets made by Pye, Plessey and Ultra. By 1939, he had returned to his primary interest in engineering, and was producing an improved capstan lathe through his Murad Machine Tool Company. His inventions had been widely used in the manufacture of munitions during the Second World War — Murad claimed to have both speeded up and significantly lowered the cost of manufacturing twenty-millimetre shells for Spitfires and Hurricanes. A self-declared admirer of the British Empire, he had helped to produce carbide armour-piercing shells used by British tanks in the north African desert, and also "spot-locating fixtures" for cylinder blocks and heads of the Rolls-Royce Merlin engines fitted in British tanks.

Wadia Murad's car, 2016.

After the war, Murad became determined to create "the best car in Britain". By 1948 he had produced a single working prototype of a 1.5 litre "Murad" saloon car. In 1982, he would tell the Sheerness journalist John Nurden that his car was "decades ahead of its time",[13] with its aerodynamic design, fitted radio and integral oil cooler. It had rear rubber-bonded springs and independent front suspension, leather seats and noiseless door locks that were said to have been the envy of the engineers at Rolls-Royce. The "Murad" was, he remembered, "a beautiful thing to drive, and so quiet. Wherever I went crowds would gather round". It was enthusiastically received at the Earl's Court Motor Show in 1947, and the ensuing positive trade press coverage of the car — which was "fully tooled and ready for production" — brought Murad advance orders from around the world worth an alleged £5.5 million. The "dream car" is also said to have drawn admiring crowds at every stop during a two-thousand-mile test drive around Britain in 1948. Unfortunately, however, the post-war Labour government was far from helpful when it came to initiating production. Murad had gained a government permit to develop an engineering factory on the Watford bypass, but this was suddenly withdrawn and he was ordered to move to south Wales. He refused and, after further argument, consented instead to open a foundry and factory in Aylesbury. More government wavering followed, costs rocketed unexpectedly during the ferocious winter of 1947, and the receiver was called in shortly after Murad had supplied a "Murad Bomilathe" for Sir Vivien Fuch's Trans-Antarctic expedition (the company's equipment is also said to have been used by the Royal Navy and in the laboratories of the Atomic Energy Authority).[14]

On 5 May 1960, Murad received a call from the Board of Trade, urging him to establish an engineering works in a government-designated Development Area. Declining a site in Scotland, he opted for Sheerness, where he was assured eight hundred skilled men awaited new employment. So, Murad and his prototype car moved to Sheppey, encouraged by the additional understanding that the Board of Trade would provide £50,000 to cover his removal costs. Unfortunately, by the time he started building his Whiteway factory and foundry at Queenborough, Sheppey was no longer on the list of potential recipients for state aid. Farewell, then, to the £50,000 and also to other anticipated subsidies. As for the eight hundred skilled workers who had lost their jobs in the Sheerness dockyard, Murad discovered that they had mostly been absorbed by the naval establishment at Chatham. "The labour was useless", he would tell Bel Austin of the *Sheerness Times Guardian*, so he had no choice but to spend £200,000 in wages to "indenture" forty apprentices and train them himself.

The new firm, Murad International Ltd, did not flourish. Production of the car was never a possibility, but demand for lathes of the kind for which Murad had become well-known during the Second World War was also declining, and the engineer was forced to diversify again. A former apprentice remembers that the wooden patterns Murad had once used to create machine tools lay rotting in the yard,[15] while the company tried to scrape along with simpler products: small, hand-operated paper guillotines, adjustable "Techni-Tables" designed for home use, a "NoTREST" desk stand designed to display an A4 sheet of paper at a convenient height for people using electric typewriters. Murad sold everything he could to stay afloat on Sheppey, mortgaging his five-bedroom house in Hertfordshire and surrendering his life insurance policies too. Try as he might, however, the enterprise just devoured what remained of his wealth and then failed. By 1982, when John Nurden caught up with the man he described as Sheppey's answer to John DeLorean, the bank had already obliged Wadia Murad to put his Queenborough factory up for sale for £90,000 (it went to a company named Wasos). He had nothing left but the increasingly vandalised and derelict machine shop he had later established on Montague Road, in the industrially obliterated settlement known as West Minster, on the island's Medway shore between Queenborough and Sheerness.

Having arranged to meet him there on one of his weekly visits, Nurden found an eighty-one-year-old widower shivering in an old overcoat, while the precision machinery that had been evicted from his lost Whiteway factory lay rusting in the "ramshackle junk yard" behind the machine shop — no longer fit for anything but scrap.[16] The precious prototype of the "Murad" car was stored inside the increasingly vandalised building, but it too was going nowhere, and not just because the engine had been stolen. During his decline, so Nurden reported, Murad had ended up sleeping across two chairs at his works, before being rescued by a former employee, Mrs Doris Palmer, who had taken pity on the old man and invited him to stay with her. By the time Nurden interviewed him, Murad had nothing to keep him going except the state pension of £30 per week. The phone at his machine shop had recently been disconnected and he'd just received a final ultimatum from Swale Borough Council ("pay your £2,000 rate arrears or go to jail"). A fighter to the last, he was preparing to sue the Department of Trade for the £50,000 removal costs he had been promised in 1960. "I shall fight them to the very end."

He was also planning to go and live with his better-off brother in California — "as far as he can go" from a country that gave grants to DeLorean and Volkswagen but had encouraged him to move to the Isle of Sheppey and then abandoned him. He would, he volunteered, "be sad to leave Britain. I have been here since 1921 and it will be a terrific break for me but I just can't take anymore." Or again: "What I did during the war was superb. It was magnificent. Now I brood. I am a very bitter man." Once resettled in California, he planned to restore his prototype car to working order and write a book about "how the British government hoodwinked him into moving to Sheppey". Calculating that he had lost £1 million thanks to that betrayal, he confessed that, while he hated acknowledging failure, he now had to face the facts. He hoped the *Kent Evening Post* would put him in touch with some of the forty people he had trained as apprentices, so that he could gather their testimony in support of his claim: "I am going to fight this bloody thing to the end of my life". Unfortunately he lost his case against the Department of Trade, and also, as may be presumed from the words Murad scribbled in the only surviving catalogue for his car, against the socialist "nit-wits" in Attlee's post-war Labour government who shouted "We are the masters now" and sang "'The Red Flag' in the Mother of Parliaments".[17] Murad died in Buckinghamshire in October 1989. His book never appeared, but his prototype car did recently turn up at auction. Allegedly found in an old farm building (some local opinion prefers the thought that it may never actually have left Murad's old workshop at West Minster), it was still engineless and by now also much dented and showing a fair bit of rust too. In its issue of 5 October 2016, *Practical Classics* reported that the car had gone for \$1,557 the previous month.

Ernest Race: A New Use for Kent's Fruit Trees

By the beginning of 1961, doom-struck Sheppey was also being urged to reinvent itself as a "brand". Mr A.W. Davies of K.S. Advertising in Canterbury even recommended a tagline — "I've discovered Sheerness and the Sunny Isle of Sheppey" — an implausible mouthful that was nevertheless briefly adopted as "Sheppey's favourite holiday publicity slogan".[18] On Tuesday, 10 January 1961, which records suggest was actually "Dull AM, becoming overcast and rain by afternoon",[19] Mr Davies came to the island for a "luncheon meeting" at which he was happy to cast his own reassuring beams over members of the Sheppey Rotary Club. "Advertising", he promised, "has a very full role to play in the future, both at home and in the field of international relations, for it is the support, and perhaps the very inspiration of free enterprise". He knew about the doubts of those who might be tempted to associate his profession with mere hucksterism, or the big business art of planting artificial desires into the hearts of their children, while at the same time wiping the floor with the "little man" whose shops battled on along Sheerness High Street. If, however, the island was to find a future, its people really must face up to the fact that "consumers choose branded and advertised goods in preference to unknown and unidentified goods".

Mr Davies had done his best but, in the year following the dockyard closure, Sheerness remained both unbranded and depressed, too sunken in spirit to be raised by a "sunny" slogan. Even the Royal College of Physicians' report revealing the link between smoking and lung cancer, to which a special *Panorama* programme was devoted on Monday 12 March 1962, had impressed the folk interviewed by the *Sheerness Times Guardian* as another cruel conspiracy against the island economy. One horrified Sheerness tobacconist reported a loss of 75% of his cigarette sales, while others invested slender hopes in a perceptible switch to pipes and small cigars. Smokers were definitely scared, as the manageress of the Sheerness branch of Lewis of Westminster conceded: "I never thought the public would be so silly".[20]

Thanks partly to the council's Development Committee, however, there had been at least some concrete reasons to feel less awful as 1962 dawned. On 5 January, the paper reported that the new year had opened with an optimistic industrial start. A company named Harris Engineering proposing to move their factory from Croydon to Sheerness harbour estate, and Pilkington were hoping, if they could get planning permission, to extend their glass factory at Rushenden, Queenborough. Encouraging developments were also underway on New Road. The clerk for the Sheerness Council, Mr Jack Griffiths MBE, reported that, since Christmas, the council had received two new enquiries from companies considering creating factories in the town. Arrangements were now in hand with Perox Chemicals, which had already taken a six-acre site on New Road, "the sale is now in the contract stage. Nothing should now go wrong".[21] Meanwhile, the Sheppey Shirt Company hoped to forsake their current premises on Blue Town High Street for a modern factory built on a three-quarter-acre site on New Road — and Abbott pharmaceutical company would also begin its island operations there, before shifting production to Queenborough.

The largest promise that loomed over the site in the first few days of the new year was provided by Kent County Planning Committee, which approved plans put forward on behalf of a firm who wanted to build a steel works on land in Sheerness. The company, Messrs Raine and Co. Ltd, proposed to construct a large factory on a twenty-one-acre site near New Road, creating jobs for between three and four hundred men. They envisaged using the new plant to melt scrap metal in furnaces, but they were confident that, even though some machining of steel would also be done on the premises, no excessive noise would emanate from their new factory. It would, as things turned out, be ten years before a steel mill opened on the Wellmarsh site directly to the north of New Road. Speedier improvements in the town's condition would be introduced by a smaller company that fully understood the importance of branding, even though it escaped mention in the clerk of the council's spirit-lifting new year announcement.

Towards the beginning of February 1962, Sheppey's valiant Labour MP Mr Percy Wells made his way to the Earl's Court Furniture Exhibition, in west London, in order to visit the stand of a company that was still settling into its new name, Race Furniture Ltd. Here he met the managing director, Mr J.W. Noel Jordan, his well-known director of design Mr Ernest Race, and also Mr Galsworthy, the office manager from the company's new factory at Sheerness.[22] Having admired some examples of the company's new line of "Sheppey" branded chairs, he reminded these newcomers that Sheerness had gone through a difficult time since the closure of the naval dockyard in 1959, adding that "Your arrival in the town has been most helpful at a time when we badly needed new industry here and new jobs".

The fact that Ernest Race Ltd would be joining the companies making their way to New Road had been announced with some pride by the *Sheerness Times Guardian* in June 1961: the paper was delighted to report that modern furniture which is exported all over the world and which has won a number of awards at design exhibitions was to be made in Sheerness.[23] The factory was expected to be ready by the end of August, and the company's existing works in Clapham would then be vacated. Ernest Race told the reporter that the new factory would eventually employ about one hundred in all, mostly men but also some women. Ten key workers would be moving to the island from Clapham, but the rest would be recruited locally, and the firm was prepared to train a limited number of local people. New Road would be the company's only factory, and 20% of its output would be shipped abroad, thus helping to increase the country's export trade. The design department, which was mainly responsible when a new model won an award, would be staying in Clapham. The firm had only encountered one snag so far, which Ernest Race described as the usual one of that time, namely the provision of council housing for the key workers. It was likely the ten would move to Minster, although it also appeared that Sheppey Rural Council, which also faced acute pressure from local applicants, would not now have the houses ready until the end of the year.

Race Furniture Limited had first emerged as a subsidiary of a light engineering company founded by Noel Jordan in 1939. During the war, the firm, called Enness Sentinel, had manufactured precision tools, jigs, davits for lifeboats and convertors that allowed busses and other vehicles to be powered by gas rather than petrol. By 1945, however, Jordan was exploring the possibility that engineering techniques and modern materials such as steel, plywood, plastics and aluminium,[24] might fruitfully be applied to the manufacture of furniture, an industry still dominated by craft techniques. He advertised for a designer in the *Times,* and found himself sifting through three hundred applications. It was at this juncture that Ernest Race, who had studied interior design at the Bartlett School of Architecture in London and then gone on to design and sell fabric woven in India, joined him as director of design.

Ernest Race Ltd, as the company was initially called, gained its licence to produce furniture at a time when the Board of Trade was seeking to increase the number of designs that could be approved under its Utility Furniture Scheme (a wartime measure that remained in place until 1953). Hardwood and fabric were not available to new furniture makers, so the company's early designs were constructed with materials no longer so urgently required for military production. The firm's first success was the BA 3 chair, made of cast aluminium alloy (some of it is said to have come from scrapped war planes) and with a seat upholstered in ex-RAF cotton duck.[25] Unveiled in 1946 at the Council of Industrial Design's "Britain Can Make It" exhibition at the Victoria and Albert Museum, the BA3 was taken up by upmarket modern-minded retailers including Heals and Dunn's of Bromley. Also used in restaurants and troop ships, it was well on the way towards selling 250,000 pieces by the time it was awarded a gold medal at the Milan Triennale in 1954. By then, the firm was producing light, upholstered easy chairs and settees, and also the Roebuck: a stacking steel rod chair with plywood back and seat, which has been described as a vertically shaped answer to Charles Eames's early LCM-1 chair. The Roebuck was launched in 1951, a year in which Race Furniture Ltd triumphed with two contemporary designs selected by the Council for Industrial Design for use at the Festival of Britain on London's South Bank. The Springbok was a stackable outdoor chair of white enamelled mild steel rod, with atomic ball feet of cast aluminium, and both seat and back made of springs covered in PVC tube. Also stove enamelled in white, the Antelope had a coloured plywood seat, and the same ball feet as the Springbok. A work of antic modernism that wasn't strictly modernist at all, the Antelope chair is said to have become widely regarded for its gaiety, elegance and wit[26] and to have encapsulated the spirit of the festival. Other chairs would be contracted from Race by larger clients, including schools, universities, hospitals and shipping lines. The foldable Neptune deck chair, made of beech plywood, was commissioned for P&O for liners on its Orient Line. The smaller folding Cormorant chair, also designed for use on liners, was sold domestically too. The company's first tip-up lecture theatre seating was made for the University of Liverpool Medical School in 1957, and then sold in modified form to many universities. It was partly with this sort of contract furniture in mind, that Ernest Race Ltd found itself looking at Sheerness as the possible site of a new government-subsidised factory.

*

Race's factory in Sheerness was designed in a frantic hurry — a Board of Trade deadline only allowed the architects forty-eight hours from start to finish — and then built as cheaply as possible by Atcost Factories Ltd of Tunbridge Wells. Consisting initially of four bays, but open to later expansion, it was constructed out of pore-cast concrete frames with walls of brick and patent glazing cladding, and a ceiling of glass fibre mat sandwiched between two skins of asbestos cement. Some of the equipment had been transferred from London, but the factory, which was intended to include all the processes involved in furniture production, contained new facilities too: descaling and derusting tanks in the stove enamelling department, along with new electrostatic spraying equipment and stove ovens, which would combine to secure a 70% saving in paint while also making it possible to dry a completed metal frame in just over a minute.

Back to the Marsh: preparing the ground for Race's factory at New Road.

Ernest Race Ltd had changed its name to Race Furniture Ltd by 30 March 1962, when the time came, just a day before the second anniversary of the closing of the dockyard, for its staff of some fifty workers to "down tools" for the official opening of their factory on New Road.[27] According to a company press release, theirs was "understood to be the third new factory to come into operation on the Isle of Sheppey since the closure of the Nore Command and Naval Dockyards brought heavy unemployment to the area in 1959". The statement also acknowledged that the new industries were "part of a Board of Trade drive to help the area with leased factories".

This was borne out by the Chairman of Sheerness Council, Cllr. A.H.R. Copeland, who used his introductory words to welcome Race Furniture to the island on behalf of all three Island Councils: "We are delighted to see them here, not only for the rates they will pay us, but because they are the type of firm Sheppey wants". Having commended the company for "helping us to bridge the gap" caused by the closure of the dockyard, he added: "they are producing wholly modern furniture which in itself is wonderful to have in Sheerness".

The opening was carried out by Paul Reilly, who a few years earlier had succeeded the furniture designer Gordon Russell as director of the Council of Industrial Design. Reilly, whose Council had been backing Race since the early days of the "Britain Can Make It" exhibition, was full of optimism about the factory: it promised work and skilled employment in Sheppey, but it also represented an internationally significant advance for British design. Hailing the company as a "text-book example" of what his own organisation had been campaigning for over the previous fifteen or so years, Reilly declared the meeting of Noel Jordan and Ernest Race to have been "one of the most fortunate occurrences in the story of British furniture". Jordan had shown courage as well as remarkable foresight in deciding to turn his wartime engineering company over to making metal furniture. He had quickly proved the "ideal" entrepreneur to open up this new line of business just as Race himself had proved to be the "ideal" designer.

Reilly declared Race Furniture to be one of "a handful of firms ... keeping the real traditions of British furniture alive". They were doing this, he emphasised, "not by reproducing our past, not by copying our foreign competitors, but by constant research, experiment and development and by a real understanding of the time in which we live". He commended the "unmistakable Englishness" of Race Furniture and its works — a robust and forward-looking Englishness that was achieved through "sheer, honest quality and common sense, coupled with the same modest good manners that were visible in the best of our 18th century pieces". Reilly commended both the courage with which the company had pursued its goals, and the "unmistakable conviction running through the Race catalogue. There is nothing opportunist, meretricious or fortuitous about Race designs". The company exemplified "design" as the Council of Industrial Design liked to promote it — i.e. "design in its widest sense, which includes design for efficient production as well as design for use and enjoyment".

Reilly insisted that moving to Sheerness should not be seen as a retreat into some sort of outer darkness. On the contrary, the relocation of the company's production facilities near the emerging new port impressed him as "a symbol of closer links with Europe and of further export effort". He was confident that the project would succeed, "for the very good reason that they have chosen to come to Sheerness". The assumption behind this schmoozing remark was that "there must surely be a natural, ingrained feeling for the well-found and the shipshape in and around Sheerness" since dockyards have long been good custodians of quality and of craftsmanship. "I believe that the people of Sheerness who work here, will soon sense the connection between past and present and will recognise in the precision and finish of Race furniture a worthy outlet for their skills".

Such then, was the promise coming to New Road: an exercise in contemporary Britishness, conceived as confident as well as modest, progressive and technologically adept in its carriage of history and tradition. Unlike the time-warped pieces Uwe Johnson had placed in his imaginary Institute for the Preservation of British Customs in New York, Race's furniture was "modern in materials, modern in method and very properly modern in conception".[28]

Mr Noel Jordan, whose company had been so generously praised as a furnisher to the world as well as a renewed England, accepted Reilly's tribute. Speaking at the Furniture Show in London, in early February 1962, he had remarked that, with his firm's new factory in Sheerness, he was already keen to make good use of old fruit trees from Kent orchards. He understood that large scale felling of fruit trees had been necessitated by blight, but insisted that cherry, pear, apple and plum trees did not have to be sawn up and sold as firewood. "We feel this is a pity, for these are fine timbers and very suitable for use in furniture which does not require very large sections. The trees are discarded because they are past their fruit production peak, but the timber is mature and sound".[29] If the timber were "utilised in English furniture" then the balance of payments problem would be helped, since less timber would have to be imported. For Reilly, as for Percy Wells MP, this confirmed the considerable virtues of the company: "From what I read about their plans to exploit the splendid fruit woods from the Kentish orchards — from the Garden of England that is — I do not doubt that the Englishness of Race furniture will continue to match the thorough Englishness of its two founders". We can safely assume that every one of these optimists trusted that the firm's Sheppey employees would respond to the demand for a more flexible, contemporary and outward-looking expression of Englishness than was described in one of the books on Johnson's shelves. *The English: Are They Human?* was the pre-war best seller in which the Dutch professor and long-standing Londoner, G.J. Renier, had cast an appraising continental eye over the unintellectual, hypocritical, prurient, animal-loving, trusting, sex-starved English and hoped for better days.[30]

In the firm's early months on Sheppey, modern furniture-making was portrayed as a natural diversification of the skills of the dockyard. As a trade magazine put it in May 1962, "welders are now using their craft again to make the metal frames used in so many Race chairs and tables, sailmakers are proving to be some of the best upholstery cover makers the company has had, and painters are adapting their skill to the electrostatic spraying equipment, which is new even to the furniture industry".[31] This was a fetching idea, but not always easy in practice. It is said that some of "the welders, boilermakers and chippies" who did try to make the adjustment struggled to get used to working on a scale that seemed more appropriate to watchmaking.[32] Meanwhile, the company found gaps in the skills that were available on the island: there were, for example, "virtually no skilled upholsterers from Sheerness, which was a long way from any traditional furniture making area".[33]

Eric Fuller joined the firm as an apprentice upholsterer in 1962, having just completed two years in the merchant navy and stepped ashore in Sheerness looking for work. It was, he thinks, his familiarity with discipline rather than any pre-existing skill that clinched the job for him and he had no recollection of working alongside veterans of the dockyard. The workforce he recalls had been hired locally and trained from scratch under iron discipline. "You kept your head down," he recalls. "You couldn't even stand with legs crossed." The foreman, a Clapham veteran named Fred Wright who used to turn up every morning with bowler hat and umbrella, made sure of that. Fuller's memory is confirmed by a man named "Jack" who was recently interviewed about his experience of leaving school on Sheppey. He described going along to "Ray's Furniture" [sic] to find work: "I walked in there and it was like going back to school. I said 'Oh God I thought I'd got shot of your lot.' Half my flipping class was there."[34]

As the first new range of furniture to emerge from Race Furniture's Sheerness factory. the "Sheppey" chairs and settees were designed for quantity production and constructed from "a standard set of interchangeable mass-produced components from which a number of alternative versions could be assembled."[35] The simplicity of the "Sheppey" range was considered appropriate for an English version of the "Swedish design" so much admired by Ernest Race since the Thirties. Technically less challenging to produce than Johnson's broken and disintegrated Eames chair, it was well adjusted to the limited skill base available to the firm during its early days on Sheppey.

Room setting with "Sheppey" chairs and settee. Design Council, London, 1962.

Intended for use in school common rooms and public seating areas as well as in domestic homes, the Sheppey range was promoted as proof of the company's ongoing determination to conceive design as closely connected to the manufacturing process and packaging too. Be they chairs or settees, the pieces were assembled according to the modular system of "knock down" furniture, introduced by the firm that had already come to epitomised Modern Danish design, France and Son, and adopted by Race Furniture Ltd many years before the "flat pack" system was popularised in Britain by Terence Conran's Habitat. Each item, be it chair or settee, came in interchangeable parts — metal frame, wooden end-frames, and cushions — that could be packed into two boxes and then assembled with only four nuts and screws per piece. The latex-foam cushions were side-seamed with, "for neatness", a single cross seam. They could be upholstered in a range of materials, depending on the decision of the customer. The front and back of the frame was made of sixteen-gauge 1.5-inch diameter steel tube and electrically welded to mild steel strips before being "electrostatically sprayed with a satin aluminium stove enamel" and fitted with British-made Pirelli Extraflex webbing.

An upholstered version of the end-frame was available, but bare wood was the intended form. It is possible that the end-frames of some of the first examples really were made with lengths of pear and apple from Kentish orchards, but the examples displayed at the Earl's Court Furniture Exhibition used yew and ash, the latter from trees "felled on the South Downs between Lewes and

Aluminium fillets in the arm of a "Sheppey" Chair.

Brighton — some from the site of the University of Sussex".[36] The visible joints in these end-frames featured a nice detail of which the company was particularly proud. Just as the famous Danish designer, Hans Wegner, would place signature details in his chairs (e.g. the oak fill over the screws in the teak backrests of the CH23 dining chairs designed for Carl Hansen and Co. in 1950/1), so the exposed corner of each "Sheppey" end frame featured two thin aluminium strips, which might have looked "superficially like inlay", but were actually triangular fillets held in place with Araldite glue. "The use of fillets is not uncommon in furniture construction but has rarely been used so successfully to give a decorative effect as well as extra strength". The woodwork was finally brushed with melamine lacquer and lightly polished to produce a "protective shine". It was a "Sheppey" chair made of ash that won the Design Award in 1963.

Ernest Race resigned from Race Furniture in September 1962, shortly after the "Sheppey" range was launched. He went on to work as a consultant designer to Cintique, Isokon and other firms before falling ill and dying aged 49 in January 1964. Having previously epitomised the "contemporary" at the Festival of Britain in 1951, Race Furniture Ltd did the same for the Sixties. After 1966, the products of its Sheerness factory, whose workers had by this time mastered all the techniques and contrivances required by a wider retinue of commissioned avant-garde designers, would be exhibited at the firm's stylish London show room at 15 Rathbone St, London W1, opened that year with a display of "Maxima" chairs by Max Glendinning — box-like things made of plywood and sprayed with bright melamine paint.

There was more work for university lecture halls and ocean liners too. Designed by Robert Heritage at the beginning of the Seventies, Race Furniture's "Q" range was first produced as seating for the *Queen Elizabeth II*. A chair called the "Tipster", which did what its name suggested and could also be ordered with a lifting armrest for right-handed note-takers, was designed for classroom use by Webb Associates in 1976. The theatres and venues equipped by the firm include the National Theatre in London, the Abbey Theatre in Dublin, and the Queen Elizabeth conference centre at Westminster. The troubles that put an end to the Sheerness factory started in the Eighties, when Race Furniture lost its long-standing contract with the Department of the Environment and entered a production agreement with Antocks Lairn, a company that ended up making Race Furniture in High Wycombe while the Sheerness factory got closed. On Sheppey, this was remembered as a very poor decision. Eric Fuller, who continued to upholster for Antocks Lairn for a while, and who, when I met up with him in 2015, was still working with the revived Race Furniture company at its present base in Gloucestershire, likened it to scrapping the Rolls-Royce and keeping the Mini.

As time passed, the workers employed by Race Furniture on New Road learned to make and upholster the strangest of chairs. It appears, however, that they had looked at their first works — the Sheppey range — with as much scepticism as "Tony" applied to Uwe Johnson's broken Eames chair. In 1966, the Council of Industrial Design's annual *Design Journal* published an article by Paul Reilly reviewing the first ten years of Design Centre awards. It also interviewed some of the winners in order to counter allegations, acknowledged by Reilly, that winning an award so closely associated with the peculiar tastes of the metropolitan elite might be more of a curse than a blessing for a product aimed at a wider market. The article in question insisted that, while contrary evidence was abundantly available, "perhaps the nicest effect of all was that on Race's Sheppey settees and chairs in 1963. The furniture was designed to mark the move of the Race furniture factory from London to Sheppey, but when the factory opened on the island, making mostly metal furniture, the reaction of the islanders was to say, 'And what do you call this?' All was changed, however, when the Sheppey furniture got its award. To the islanders, it was their furniture which had received national acclaim."[37]

*

And Johnson's broken lounge chair? One Saturday morning, nine weeks after he drove off with it, Tony reappeared: "sixty four years old, plentiful gray hair, dressed in his Sunday best".[38] He opened the boot of his car, and "there lay the cumbersome piece of furniture, whole once more". Tony muttered, "I have no idea what Charles Eames was thinking when he invented a chair with a vulcanite adhesive joint: he must have been a little drunk. Drunk in a good way, don't get me wrong, it's a nice chair alright".

Coming into the house, Tony looked around, commented on the sagging condition of a table while also declaring himself almost certainly too busy to fix it. Johnson poured some whisky, and the two men got talking, starting with the various tricks with which Tony had coaxed the chair back into existence: "If that monster ever breaks again it won't be in the place where I worked on it". As Tony went on to talk about his life, Johnson found himself transported, as so often, back into the world of the novel he had come to Sheerness to complete.

Tony, who plainly reminded Johnson of his own socialist carpenter Heinrich Cresspahl, had started his first workshop in Islington in 1937, quickly acquiring a number of distinguished American clients, who approached him with weird modernist projects: he remembered struggling to attach legs to an oddly semi-circular table in "such a way that they would definitely collapse". He had served in the medical corps during the war, following the allied advance from Normandy to Bergen-Belsen, where "the dead bodies didn't bleed. Just beaten to death, starved". Further disclosures followed, including the fact that Tony's late wife had come from Spandau... "I realized that Tony wants more than mere money for his work: he wants this too, conversation, if that's what you would like to call it".

It would appear that Tony was correct in his assessment of the Eames brothers' work. Designed to demonstrate that a modern chair could be at least as comfortable as the leathered thrones in English gentleman's clubs, the Eames lounge chair was first produced in 1956. It was, as New York's Museum of Modern Art had helpfully explained in 1973, composed of three plywood shells (rosewood in the original models), accommodating leather-covered cushions filled with down, latex foam and duck feathers.[39] Its arm rests were secured to the middle shell with experimental "shock mounts" consisting of glued rubber washers that allowed the various parts of the chair some freedom of movement, but which also, as collectors of vintage "mid-century modern" furniture keep discovering to this day, leave the chairs ever more liable to sudden collapse. The "Sheppey" chair might have been a bit low and long in the thigh but it wouldn't have done anything like that. A sensible option then had any refitter thought of making a forward-looking Institute for the Promotion of British Culture out of the sealed-up and mummified Institute for the Preservation of British Customs that Johnson had planted at Madison Avenue and 83rd St in New York.

Modern furniture and the export drive: Race Furniture van with a Jamaican freighter at the quayside.

PART IV.

CULTURE: THREE ISLAND ENCOUNTERS

I have hardly trodden your soil,
taciturn country, have hardly touched a stone.
I was raised so high by your heaven,
So dissolved in cloud, in mist and things even more remote
that I left you
as soon as my ship weighed anchor.

— Ingeborg Bachmann, "Leaving England",
translated by Michael Hamburger,
Modern Poetry in Translation, 3,
1967, p. 12

Gentleman outside the Belle and Lion, a Wetherspoon pub on Sheerness High Street, 8 July 2018.

20. ALL PRAISE TO THE SHEERNESS TIMES GUARDIAN

What a newspaper we have in this town!
— Gesine Cresspahl in *Anniversaries* I, p. 425.

At the end of October 1973, a year or so before he traded West Berlin for Sheerness, Uwe Johnson visited Klagenfurt, the capital city of Carinthia in the south of Austria and the childhood home of the poet Ingeborg Bachmann, who was born there in 1926. She had promised one day to show him around the town in which she had grown up. On the 17th of that same month, however, she had died in hospital following a fire at her flat in Rome. Johnson made his "Trip to Klagenfurt" alone, arriving four days after Bachmann was repatriated and buried there. His friend was gone but some of "the things that formed her life"[1] remained to be considered.

Picking up a copy of the *Carinthia Daily Times*, Johnson noted that the president of the Carinthian State Tourism Association had recently returned from a "goodwill tour of major German travel agents". Keen to promote Klagenfurt as a "bathing resort" with an "unspoiled environment", this booster reckoned the time had come for the city to develop a "winter image" to augment its already busy summer season.[2] Bachmann, who had left the city to go to university in 1945 and then spent much of her adult life in voluntary "exile" in Rome, had thought otherwise. She'd told Johnson that the province was being "completely ruined" by people determined to fill "Carinthia, Land of the Sun" with holiday facilities devoted to the exploitation of "'Rhein-Ruhr' tourist types".

Scanning the illustrated brochures, in which Klagenfurt was projected as a sleek destination packed only with "delights", Johnson ventured that "it seems impossible that anyone might be buried here". The tourist maps of this gleaming place had been adjusted to obscure the fact, pointed out by Bachmann herself, that "someone came up with the idea of putting the airport next to the cemetery". That, however, is where he found his brilliant, troubled and addicted friend's freshly dug grave: in outlying Annabichl, five or so kilometres from the city centre, and only partly covered by the ribbon-draped wreaths left by the governor of Carinthia, the mayor of Klagenfurt, and the National Minister for Arts and Education, all of whom had come to pay their respects to the poet who had so determinedly left town. Viewing the site from a nearby bench, Johnson remembers Bachmann's letter again: "above all one cannot have grown up here and be me and then come back". It was in order to account for the dislocation and departure of his late friend, who had written magnificently about her childhood in this "relinquished" place, that Johnson made his way to the city's newspaper archive.

Speaking on the phone from Rome in 1972, Bachman had informed him that *La Stampa* — though not unlike a fuddy-duddy old aunt — was still the most "objective" of the papers she might read there. That, as Johnson already knew, had not been a virtue of the publications of her childhood in Klagenfurt, when the German "tourists" had been different too.

The "official" paper of the Nazi Party, the *Carinthia Clarion*, gave Johnson a glimpse of the fervid celebrations the town mounted for Hitler's fiftieth birthday on 20 April 1939. Reading his way back into the pages of the *Clarion's* extinguished predecessors, he was able to verify the reports of locals who assured him, apparently without reticence or embarrassment, that Hitler himself had visited Klagenfurt after the widely welcomed annexation of 13 March 1938. The *Carinthia Daily* informed Johnson that, on 5 April that year, the Nazi leader had arrived from Graz at the end of a four-and-a-half-hour train journey through the mountains of Steiermark and Carinthia, where every station along the route had been "packed tight with jubilant people".[3] After shaking hands with the SS General Lorenz and other assembled strongmen, he marches down a street dressed in red swastikas to reach a square, formerly "New Square" but already "rebaptized" after the Führer himself. The Bishop fawns and the mayor crawls as he bestows honorary citizenship on the "Uniter of all Germans". Huge crowds, many dressed in traditional costume, sing and follow the children who lead the Sieg Heiling from their perches in trees outside the Sandwirt Hotel: "No end to the jubilation", notes Johnson.

Scanning the *Klagenfurt Times* he discovers that another batch of ecstatic dances and songs ("Little Girl, Way Down in the Valley", "No Country More Beautiful", etc.) were offered up on 19 July, when Dr Goebbels promised, during his own brief tour of Klagenfurt, that the Nazis would "hold the land and people of Carinthia steadfast and true in our German heart". On 24 July, Rudolf Hess came to announce that a memorial to "the fateful days of July 1934" (the month in which Hitler secured his standing as "supreme leader" with the bloody purge of the Nazi party known as the "Night of the Long Knives") was to be built at Klagenfurt. Such had been the populace's enthusiasm for the two earlier visitors that the District Propaganda Office this time asked the townspeople "not to throw flowers at the Deputy Führer (due to the risk of injury)".

It is hard to think of a twentieth-century writer for whom newspapers were more vital than they were for Uwe Johnson. He read them closely, searching their pages for the truth of situations, both past and present, whilst also noting their slants and omissions, their inconsistencies and hypocrisy. They could carry him, together with his "invented persons", far out into the world, yet they also enabled him to maintain an ironic distance from the reality he surveyed. At their best, they might challenge the powerful and embody the virtue of free debate, but they were also a useful medium for a writer whose desire was to read the world without necessarily revealing himself within it.

As every reader of *Anniversaries* knows, Johnson was a close scrutiniser of the *New York Times*, first in West Berlin and later in the two years he spent living and working in New York City from 1966 to 1968. Johnson shares the paper with his "invented person" Gesine Cresspahl, for whom it has become like "a person with a fixed place at the table".[4] As an "honest old Auntie"[5] of faded British origins, her distinguishing characteristics include an inability to "do something good without also discussing it",[6] a refusal, both high-minded and prim, to countenance cartoons and horoscopes, and a tendency to swell with pride (as well as sections and page-count) as she endeavours to "mirror" not just New York but the entire world — offering her readers "All the News ... That's Fit to Print",[7] together, of course, with plenty of "shopping opportunities" and places to live too.[8]

The GDR may have offered only a "chained dog"[9] named *Neues Deutschland*, barking crazily at everything beyond the chicken-wire fence, but the *New York Times* promised a nobler, more balanced alternative. We've seen that Johnson drew heavily on it in *Anniversaries*, holding it at a critical and sometimes mocking distance even as he threaded its efforts as a superior "supplier of reality"[10] into the fabric of his novel. Reading through the eye of Gesine Cresspahl, he notes how the self-proclaimed "world's best newspaper"[11] bolsters the serialised memoirs of Stalin's recently defected daughter Svetlana by printing photographs in which Comrade Joe was allowed to appear as a genial patriarch, gleaming back at the camera and even thumbing his nose at his bodyguard. On another morning he and Gesine, who like him has printer's ink in her veins, ponder the paper's silent inconsistencies. Having urged the King of Greece to "improve his country with a putsch", Auntie then "stayed true to her principles and immediately expressed revulsion at the torture of politically suspect Greeks".[12] He had a sharp eye too for the manoeuvres imposed on the high-minded paper by the need to maintain circulation while also staying true, more or less, to the impartiality proclaimed by Adolph Ochs, who had rescued it from bankruptcy at the end of the nineteenth century.[13] Hence, as Johnson notes, the recourse to "pedagogic compulsion", which enabled the *New York Times* to claim the excuse of "sociology" for a coverage of murders that, in less lofty papers, would be recognised as sensationalised "reader-snatching"."She sets our table with the latest developments", so Gesine explains: "we pay the higher rate and admire her civilized gestures".[14]

The News from "Where You Are"

On the Isle of Sheppey, a newspaper would, once again, turn out to be more than a useful source of local information. It would be a provider of strange stories to pass on to faraway friends who might enjoy an English freak show. It would also serve as a screen, or perhaps something closer to a crinkly net curtain, through which an unconvinced incomer might peer without giving anything away: a useful device, in other words, when it comes to keeping your perceptions "non-committal" and, as Johnson continued in a letter to Max Frisch, preventing them from "ascending into experience or judgement".[15]

For Johnson, as for the young Ingeborg Bachmann whose poem "Leaving England" was included in her first collection *Borrowed Time*, the experience of being in England may never have been entirely removed from the thought of departure. Unlike his late friend, however, he settled in with the help of a new assortment of newspapers. He would tell his New York publisher Helen Wolff that his reading in Sheerness included four English papers, two German weeklies and a daily paper from Frankfurt am Main.[16] The editor Eberhard Fahlke identifies the German papers as his usual ones — the *Frankfurter Rundschau, Der Spiegel* and *Die Zeit*.[17] Of the British Sundays, he read the *Observer,* and the *Sunday Times*, but his daily was the *Guardian* — not an "aunt" like the *New York Times* but "a strict old uncle", so he claimed, which rarely found stories from either Germany worthy of inclusion on the page reserved for "Overseas" news.

And the fourth English paper? The *Sheerness Times Guardian,* which dominates the collection of Kentish papers preserved in Johnson's archive at the University of Rostock, was an amalgamation of two rival papers, neither of which had, even in their Victorian heyday, quite managed to equip Sheerness with its own version of what Johnson, like any other reader of the German political philosopher Jürgen Habermas's book on the subject, might recognise as a properly bourgeois "public sphere"[18] — i.e. a free, rational and largely civil cultural arena that allowed citizens to push back against the powerful officers of government facing them from across the dockyard moat, or, for that matter, from the offices of the Local Board of Health that had become responsible for running the town in 1849.

In his first issue of the *Sheerness Guardian,* published on 10 January 1858, the printer and bookseller who also ran the post office in Blue Town, Thomas Morton Rigg, had proudly announced that "We are islanders", and that from this point of view "the mainland of Kent is a foreign land". As founder of the new paper, Mr Rigg was definitely not suggesting that Sheppey was a parochial backwater occupied by rooted natives with no interest in the world beyond their limited horizon. On the contrary, he was seeing off his competitor, the recently launched *Sittingbourne & Sheerness Gazette*, by conjuring Sheerness as a widely connected and outward-looking new town that had nothing in common with small-minded and tradition-bound mainland communities such as Sittingbourne. Sheerness was open to the wider world via the naval and military establishments that formed the primary reason for its existence. As a place that hadn't existed before their coming, it was equipped with "scarcely any aboriginal race". It was instead "a colony of emigrants from all parts of England, Scotland, Ireland and Wales" and "to such a society, the affairs of the neighbouring country are, in most cases, about as interesting as the local policy of Timbuctoo".

As we have seen from the case of the Chancery Ditch, the *Sheerness Guardian* was launched in a town that had yet to acquire the habits governing polite public debate upstream. Indeed, the paper had carried its proprietor into a buffeting series of libel suits, personal threats and punch-ups. In 1861, Rigg felt obliged to sue Mr Joseph Henry Burley, landlord of the Duke of Clarence Hotel in Sheerness, who had bloodied Rigg's nose in the coffee room of the Lion Inn, Gillingham. Rigg had turned up to witness a meeting in which Burley was giving final instructions to the solicitor representing a group of thirty disgruntled ratepayers being taken to court by Sheerness's Local Board of Health for refusing to pay a private improvement rate. Burley, who had no illusions about the neutrality of the Sheerness paper, had warned his solicitor that Rigg was using his access as a newspaperman to "collect information for the other side".[19] On hearing this, so the *Kentish Gazette* continued, Rigg "became exceedingly excited, struck the table several times with his clenched fist, to the detriment of his knuckles, and called Mr Burley a 'liar'". Burley threatened to "knock his head off" if Rigg repeated the insult, and when Rigg did just that he "instantaneously tapped rather smartly the nasal organ of the plaintiff, causing the carmine to flow profusely".

Unbowed by the two weeks he spent in jail in January 1864 after refusing to apologise for his intemperate reports about "the Case of the Chancery Ditch",[20] Rigg would be back in court the following year to sue the landlord of the Oxford music hall in Blue Town, who had "threatened him" after objecting to comments printed in the paper.[21] In 1872, he was himself successfully sued for publishing a letter, written above the signature "General Fact", libelling a lawyer working in the interests of Mr Ward, the Chairman of the Local Board of Health, who was himself alleged to have got into the habit of ruling "Sheerness like a small king".[22] The entangled nature of Sheerness life in those years is indicated by the fact that, as Rigg himself pointed out, the offended lawyer in question, Mr Mole, was a good friend of his.

The *Sheerness Times*, meanwhile, had hoped to do rather better than its older rival. Launched on 15 February 1868, it announced its existence with an editorial in which the founder, a man of "progressive" views named John Cole, promised the people of Sheerness a properly local paper — "cheap, concise, and carefully prepared" — and that he was determined to criticise "public men" on behalf of the true public interest without falling captive to any one party or opinion. The paper had gone on to expose the town's closed and unaccountable system of local government as a form of "one-man" rule, and, under John Cole's successor, Samuel Cole, continued to attack the "misrule" imposed on the town by the Local Board of Health. His paper took sides in the controversies of this period, backing the members of the board who opposed the chairman. It did so with sufficient force to persuade Chairman Ward and his cronies to impose a ban on the *Times'* reporters attending local committee meetings, a proscription that Cole and his dissenting faction on the board ridiculed and campaigned against, eventually forcing the "exclusionists" to withdraw their own proscription. As a descendant would later recall, "'Scenes' were prevalent in those days".[23]

Much, of course, has changed since the time when Sheerness gave the Wild West a run for its money. In September 2012, a friend sent me a picture of something he had encountered after sailing across the Thames Estuary to Queenborough a couple of miles upstream from Sheerness along the island's Medway shore. Having moored in the creek, he stepped onto the High Street to find a stand for the *Sheerness*  *Times Guardian* — the town's rival papers were amalgamated in 1939 — emblazoned with the week's top headline: "Second escape from Cattery". No doubt the story mattered greatly to the owners of the cats, Nesta and Smokey, and also to those at the offending Appleyard Cattery in Sheppey's inland village of Eastchurch. This manifestation of local life nevertheless suggests that island horizons may have narrowed since its newspapers first went into action. It might also be taken to confirm the apprehensions of those among the BBC's national news presenters who don't always manage to hide the sense of relief with which they hand viewers over to the poor regional colleagues who will now report on events "where you are" — as if being local is only for losers in this globalised world.

Johnson liked cats, allowing these spies from the animal kingdom to run through his pages quite freely, and sometimes to acquire considerable significance too. His new paper, however, was plainly neither an aunt nor a sanctimonious uncle — more like a disconcertingly weird provincial cousin. The collection retained at the Uwe Johnson Archive in Rostock reveals that, for the first four years of his residency, the writer was punctilious in preserving his household's copies of the *Sheerness Times Guardian* — a fact that may confirm Eberhard Fahlke's suggestion that he was thinking of one day writing a collection of "island stories". The first issue he saved dates from 16 August 1974, a ten-page broadsheet that he must have picked up during a preliminary visit when he and Elisabeth were still considering the purchase of 26 Marine Parade. The collection extends into 1978, after which Johnson appears to have cancelled his subscription — he would complain of finding delivered papers and mail jamming his front door when he got home from trips abroad — and continued his scrutiny of the local press for free in the pub.

Johnson read the *Sheerness Times Guardian* with more distanced curiosity than he had applied to the *New York Times*: scouring its pages for English peculiarities, both humdrum and picaresque, that could be passed on to his friends in New York and Germany, just in case they weren't already sufficiently worried about his unusual choice of residence. Writing in March 1978 to the secretary of his publisher, Siegfried Unseld, at Suhrkamp in Frankfurt, he notes: "Here the poorer or more assiduous schoolboys deliver the papers in the morning, just like in fairy-tales. On Friday, the '*Sheerness Times Guardian*' arrives, and you couldn't possibly overestimate the excitement with which we await it".[24] There was the prosaic everyday stuff of local reportage — "clothes iron stolen, dog tangled in rebar, Susan and Colin married, relatives visiting from New Zealand" — but that was by no means the full extent of it. Johnson also invited his German correspondents to savour the monstrous stories that occasionally broke through the routines of Sheppey life. The following example was for Christa Wolf: "two young men, eighteen years old, were talking with a sixteen-year-old girl at a friend's house. One Paul says: *You want to have sex?* She just laughs, Ruth does. The other Paul says: *Let's go through with it.* The first goes into the kitchen, comes back with a bread knife, and stabs her with it in the heart, from behind. Now Mummy is sitting there weeping: the girl, yes, *God rest her soul,* but Paul is such a good lad".[25]

That may have been a fictionalised cameo but it draws on things that can be found in Johnson's collected copies of the *Sheerness Times Guardian.* The maternal assurance that one of these murderous Pauls "is such a good lad", doesn't stray far from the headline: "'He is a good boy' — mother", used to introduce a story about a sixteen-year old who had spent an entire term truanting from school.[26] Another of the copies Johnson kept includes an arresting account of a trial, in which a twenty-one-year-old man was sentenced for apprehending a fourteen-year-old girl from Minster, whom he had allegedly already abused during babysitting sessions, threatening her with a knife and taking her to the "grassy hill by the seafront" where he raped her: "I expect I just wanted to be loved", so the offender explained at Maidstone Crown Court, after prosecutors had drawn ample evidence of depravity from his mouth.[27] The alarming facts reported by the local group of Gingerbread (a charity for single-parent families) had also passed before Johnson's eye: the number of illegitimate births on the island was twice the national average; the frequent "schoolgirl pregnancies", which inclined Gingerbread to conclude that young girls on the island thought of babies as like having dolls; the case of the twelve-year-old girl — the paper counted her among the island's "gymslip mothers" — who'd become pregnant when babysitting with boyfriends and "didn't know which boy was responsible".[28]

To read through the papers Johnson collected between 1974 and 1981 is indeed to confront a number of persistent themes. There were, for example, very good reasons for not driving on the island. The roads were poor, neither incorporated nor tarred in some former plotland areas, but the drivers could be terrifying too. The frequency of reported accidents suggests that anyone taking to the roads risked sudden death or terrible injuries at the hands of men — young, old and often drunk — who didn't always confine the carnage they caused to members of their own wild fraternity. Considering that Sheppey tended to be an island of freeborn libertarians, there is an associated reflex of blaming all the ills of island life on the state, be it the water authority, the Department of Health and Social Security, or, thanks to the reorganisations of 1974, the now largely offshore local authority known as the Borough of Swale, which had absorbed the responsibilities of the island's three abolished district councils. There were repeated complaints about the problem of apathy and also about vandalism of the "mindless" variety that proved capable of undermining every attempt at improvement or basic safety. The lifeguards lost their outboard motor and other rescue equipment provided to help endangered swimmers. The signs warning of the dangers of the soft and claggy mud of the cliffs around Warden Point were uprooted and hurled over the cliff not long before a fourteen-year-old boy sank up to his neck while exploring during his first evening on the island and died in dreadful distress before rescuers could extract him the following morning.

When it came to the industrial disputes of the period, the *Sheerness Times Guardian* would also give generously. The very first copy that Johnson saved reported that ninety-five striking craftsmen at Sheerness Steel, as the plant was by then called, had forced the wholescale closure of "Britain's biggest private producer of reinforced steel".[29] They would not repeat the performance in January 1980, when they alone among British steelworkers refused to join what had been loudly trumpeted as the first national steel strike in the United Kingdom since the General Strike of 1926. This later dispute, among the first to take place during Margaret Thatcher's leadership, would prove a call too far not just for the workers, but also for their wives, who remembered the impact of combined closure of the dockyard and garrison on Sheerness in 1960, and organised to keep their men at work. Backed by a deputation of burly farmers who came to Sheerness to lend muscle to their defence of "the right to work", the workers and wives found themselves well supported during the "Siege of Sheerness Steel". The government saw to it that large cohorts from the Metropolitan Police who were on hand to control the hundreds of flying pickets bussed in from steel towns in the north, together with their militant wives who promised that more sisters were on the way from Scunthorpe to "sort out these local women".[30] The leader of the "Sheerness Workers' Wives", Christine Lissen, would soon be speaking next to Norris McWhirter, of the right-wing Freedom Association at Speaker's Corner.[31] While right-wingers saw a heroic stand against socialism in the scuffles and arrests around Sheerness Steel's plant on Wellmarsh, observers on the left remembered another momentous strike that had extended for nearly two years from August 1976, setting workers, mostly very low-paid Ugandan Asian women, against the unyielding owner of the film-processing plant where they had faced degrading conditions. As one said of the island's shame, Sheerness was now "a name worse than Grunwick ... whatever the outcome the name of Sheerness Steel will ring a bell for a long time to come".

Johnson may have remained silently "non-committal" when the nurses at Sheppey General Hospital's maternity unit likened their employment conditions to "working in a concentration camp".[32] He did, however, comment on reports of the action taken by the island's schoolteachers in 1978. "You could hardly be expected to know the curious variety of strike they've come up with here",[33] Johnson told Burgel Zeeh. In those inflation-ridden days, the National Union of Teachers was holding out for a rise of 10%, having rejected the offered 9% — and the *Sheerness Times Guardian* was reporting the

Sheppey teachers' decision to enforce their union's ban on voluntary meal duties. As Johnson explained of this unusually considerate English dispute, "the teachers want a higher salary. For the children not to receive instruction as a result is something they do not want to be responsible for. Supervising the children during lunch, however, voluntary it is true, and paid only with a free portion of school lunch: that they will not do. And since the children left to themselves might have mishaps that they would be responsible for, the little as well as the bigger of England's younger generation have to spend that time on the street, where responsibility for any mishap is easier to distribute".[34]

Ministers and "Zulus"

The *Sheerness Times Guardian* would also supply the Johnson household with a regular stream of material to "satisfy our attacks on religion".[35] Johnson's difficulties in the GDR may have followed from his defence of the rights of Christian students to participate in political life, but it was as a man of strongly secular outlook that he savoured the shots at redemption attempted by the Isle of Sheppey's ministers as they stepped up to pen uplifting homilies for the paper's occasional column "With Faith in Mind". This rotating festival of stretched metaphors was launched on 10 March 1978 by the Rev. Robin Murch. As the vicar of Queenborough, Murch likened Sheppey to a crowded train on which scrutinising and wondering about the lives of fellow passengers was a "fascinating way of passing time". Thanks to the new column, he promised, readers would from now on be provided with regular indications about what was really going on in the minds of the island's Christians.

Johnson might have hoped for an early contribution from Father Peter Blagdon-Gamlen, the anti-Common Market Anglo-Catholic vicar of Eastchurch, Leysdown and Harty, but he had stirred up a lot of controversy by backing the National Front in 1975, and was not among the Sheppey ministers who contributed to "With Faith in Mind". There was, however, a rich choice to consider all the same. Johnson might have quoted the Rev. John Williams of St Peter's Church, Halfway, who marked the approach of a new school year by stressing the importance of not planting "that most destructive worm called 'Failure'"[36] in the minds of the island's young people, or, indeed, the vicar of Queenborough himself, who returned a few years later to offer some accommodating English thoughts on the American suggestion that prayer was like chewing on "the Minty Gum Ball of life".[37]

In the end, however, Johnson chose the Rev. John Cockrell, minister of Sheerness's United Reform Church, as his primary representative. Overlooking the column in which Cockrell tried to convince readers that "the life of faith is in some respects rather like regular care of your car",[38] he asked the East German novelist Christa Wolf to imagine the minister seeking to advance God's cause with the help of no less than three fleetingly registered visual aids: a three-legged dog he had lately sighted on the east of the island, a submarine glimpsed offshore at Sheerness and a Japanese man encountered on the Canterbury Road, riding a unicycle in the direction of London. The fact that Cockrell's own wife had refused to believe his reports of any of these sightings, brought him, so Johnson informed the novelist he had got to know when both were students in Leipzig, to "one of the fundamental problems of the Christian church: We relate things whose truth we know, but disbelief raises its head, and when you look for the thing, it is gone. Different, how different, in contrast, is the world of God".[39]

The *Sheerness Times Guardian* provided Johnson with quite a lot to stand back from, whether in puzzlement, dismay or the distanced curiosity of a newly arrived anthropologist musing over G.J. Renier's famous question: "The English, are they human?" He was, for example, alerted to the existence of the "Sheppey Zulus" by the very first copy of the *Sheerness Times Guardian* in his collection. Announcing that "Carnival time is here again", the front page for 16 August 1974 showed the

"Zulus" preparing to invade the beach near the town recreation ground in four metal boats: on the approaching day, they would leap ashore with their spears and skull-adorned shields and go into battle against the "white men" from the Sheerness Round Table. They were back the following summer, brandishing weird clubs (worse than Irish "shillelaghs", perhaps), wearing grass skirts and necklaces made of teeth, and bombarding the Round Tablers with bags of soot and flour.[40] Johnson also saved a copy of the carnival programme from 1977, perhaps for the sake of the cover photograph showing a gruesome militia of some thirty "Zulus" mustered in preparation for the assault wearing "fuzzy" wigs, blackface and already brandishing their shields and spears. That year's performance was singled out for praise by a visiting couple from Rainham, across the estuary at the edge of Greater London, who told readers that "Sheppey should feel proud of their small but lovable tribe of Zulus".[41]

An old photograph (see p. 240) suggests that "blacking-up" was already part of the Sheerness Benevolent Society's carnival efforts at the time of the Anglo-Zulu Wars of the late nineteenth century. Latter-day participants, however, have claimed that the "Sheppey Zulus" actually made their first appearance on Carnival day in 1929, when sailors from the surveying ship *HMS Steadfast*, then being refitted in the dockyard between bouts of service in the Red Sea, blackened themselves before invading the town beach to inaugurate the annual tradition of kidnapping prominent townsmen and obliging them to choose between donating a ransom for charity and being tossed into the cooking pot. "All Sheerness Carnivals include an invasion of Zulus, who act as collectors throughout the day", wrote the *East Kent Gazette* on 30 August 1957: "this year the much boot-blackened young men came from the local dockyard school and they were so realistic that they frightened some of the children! And what a commotion there was when they encountered a contingent of 'prehistoric' campers dressed in sacks". Traditionally, those deplorable mascots were played by stevedores from the dockyard. In the year of the closure, however, the "Zulus" who "created disturbances all along the procession route" had been mustered from among the chalet-dwellers at Warner's Holiday Camp. They set to work alongside five elephants, enlisted from a travelling circus, which "trod carefully through the streets in a line, holding tails with trunks",[42] a vast replica of the wooden horse of Troy dragged through the town by a group of "slaves", and no fewer than five Beauty Queens who were rewarded with a tribal "Durbar" by the "Zulus" at the end of the day.

By the Seventies, the "Zulus" were already having some difficulty with the organisers of the carnival. They liked to launch their attack from the sea, but were irritated that the carnival committee refused to consider the state of the tides when choosing the day for the event. They feared that "the danger factor" had been glossed over in the interests of providing the public with "thrills". Indeed, they horrified members of the Round Table by suggesting that the battle might be more safely staged on a shallow inland water — little more than a pond, really — beside the miniature railway at Barton Point, along the road from Johnson's house.[43]

We hardly have to guess how this annual performance looked to the East German writer who had devoted so much of his unfinished masterpiece to revealing and understanding the consequences of racism in New York City. As a "guest" in England, Johnson was reluctant to pass judgement on the life and customs of his Sheerness neighbours, but he did record one sighting of this passing remnant of dockyard culture. On 6 August 1978, he used a moment on a Lufthansa flight to write a letter providing Helen Wolff, with a characteristically "non-committal" account of the carnival he had seen from his house the day before[44]:

As of yesterday, my annual ordeal is behind me — I mean the Summer Carnival parade, where the local beauty queens float by down the High Street, Broadway, and Marine Parade, lolling mostly in bedroom decor on flatbed trucks, together with the holders of the same office from the nearby towns of Maidstone, Faversham, and Dover.

They are punctuated by advertisements: floats from car companies, motorcycle clubs, or the British Royal Mail; musically adorned with troops of dancing girls in uniform; and ringed by dancing "Zulus", dockworkers smeared black with shoe polish, throwing lemons or bananas into the enthusiastic rows of townspeople. Every year I watch this performance with grave displeasure, because everyone in it is enjoying life; my favourite vehicle is the last one, the street-cleaning machine, neatly gobbling up all the streamers and confetti.[45]

The Incomers' Town

The Admiralty may long since have abandoned Sheerness but the sea had continued to provide islanders with opportunities to reflect on the difference between "flotsam", "jetsam" and sheer criminality. Some of these lessons were provided by objects washed up: a mail bag found in the sea off Scrapsgate in 1963 and sent to Scotland Yard on the suspicion that it might have been tossed into the Thames after the Great Train Robbery,[46] or, as it was in Johnson's time, two trunks full of "herbal cannabis" which had been dropped overboard by crew members on board a banana boat approaching the port from Jamaica but were inconveniently brought to the surface when they got caught up in the propellers of the Olau Line's Sheerness-Flushing ferry.[47]

As for human incomers, the Johnsons will have deduced from their weekly reading that they were by no means the only migrants living in the town that the

151 Blue Town High Street.

331

Victorian founder of the *Sheerness Guardian* had described as an outward-looking "colony of emigrants". They had arrived too late to pick up the trace of Irvine Boaden, a "Maori tribesman" who was said to be living at 49 Marine Parade in 1960. He had come to England in 1947, and served with the Royal Artillery at the Sheerness garrison. (When asked why he had chosen to settle in the town, he declared "Because when I was demobbed from the army, I liked it so much here that I decided to stay".)[48] The Cypriot barber, John Abramides, had learned his trade in Limassol and then opened a shop at Sheerness, also in 1947. He had obdurately refused to move from his premises as the council's "slum clearance" went ahead in the Sixties, thereby saving the only historical house that still stands at the Eastern end of Blue Town High Street. Abramides had insisted, as Johnson might have read in 1975, that the 130-year-old building was still "as solid as a rock".[49]

Josef Pyka was a much-decorated Polish naval officer whose ship had left his country to join the Allies the day before the Nazi invasion in September 1939. Having served with various ships and detachments of the Polish Navy in the west, he was honourably discharged in 1948 and went to work also as a barber in Victory Street: "I love the people", he said of Sheerness, "and they are kind to me". He had stayed long enough to see Nazism in Poland replaced by Soviet communism, and had no illusions about returning: "I love England. I feel here I have a right on earth. I feel I am an individual and not part of a vast organization".[50] There was nothing more to be said about Alexandro Pacitto, an Italian who, in 1975, turned up in court charged with attacking a policeman with a bread knife.[51] Johnson's paper also introduced his household to Gokyo Nikolevich, who worked as Russian tutor at Sheppey School. Having been betrayed, captured and sentenced to death as an anti-communist partisan in Yugoslavia during the Second World War, he had later escaped to Italy, and ended up in Charing Cross Hospital, London, where he met the woman who became his wife, later moving with her to Minster on the island he now praised as "his freedom".[52]

The incomers who came to the town during the age of the naval dockyard may have done so for associated economic, military or political reasons, but those who had landed here since 1960 had followed more individual currents to this island of last resort. Johnson will have learned from his paper that he shared the town with a much travelled "diplomatic correspondent" and former editor of *Illustrated* magazine named Arthur George Bilainkin. Respectfully described as a "Sheppey historian" by the *Sheerness Times Guardian* (and long-since dismissed as a "crank" by the philosopher Bertrand Russell[53]), Bilainkin was by the Seventies living in a rented flat in a no longer naval terrace within the former dockyard. His unusual choice of residence may have been connected to the protracted and, from his side, vicious custody battle he had fought and finally lost (with costs) in the Fifties against his former wife, a doctor whom he had accused of "sadistically injecting" their ten-year-old daughter with drugs.[54]

Bilainkin used his retreat on the island to look back over his life as a roving diplomatic journalist and editor. On 18 March 1977, the *Sheerness Times Guardian* reported that this former admirer of the semi-detached communist President Tito — he had once recommended that voluntary work brigades, such as those he had seen after the war in Yugoslavia, should be used to clean up British railway stations prior to the Festival of Britain of 1951[55] — would be speaking about the oil crisis of 1974 at the Athenaeum Club in London. His argument, so readers were informed, was that King Feisal, whom he claimed to have known personally, had only wanted the British to support a resolution obliging Israel to leave Arab lands in Egypt, Syria and Jordan. He suspected that the oil crisis was somehow due to the malevolence of an old enemy: "I fear old Germans have taken over, and are rushing us into World War III, with little bankrupt, bragging Britain, as Mrs Thatcher gaily put it, gaily obedient."

In August 1977, the *Sheerness Times Guardian* returned to hear about Bilainkin's friendship with the Cypriot leader Archbishop Makarios, describing the letters and Christmas cards he had received and circulated as souvenirs among Cypriot exiles now living on Sheppey, and remembering how Makarios had handled the protracted negotiations leading up to the independence of Cyprus: he had eventually made concessions ("for the sake of peace and avoiding more sorrow") to a British Foreign Secretary, Mr Selwyn Lloyd, who assumed there would be "an imperishable British Empire to go on ruling for decades or centuries" and kept demanding "slabs" of the island for military bases.[56] By July 1980, the rogue male historian sequestered in the former dockyard was writing to the *Kingston Gleaner,* in Jamaica, explaining that he was preparing a further volume of memoirs and would be grateful for news of certain people (names provided) he had known when he was news editor for that paper in 1924–5. Readers could write to him at 12 Regency Close in the former dockyard at Sheerness.[57] Perhaps some did, but Bilainkin died the following year and his book never appeared.

Meanwhile, Johnson only had to listen, or look to the side, when his taxi or train was approaching the Kingsferry Bridge to cross the Swale, to discover that, thanks to another unpredictable incomer, steel bashing on the island was by no means confined to cutting up cars in Sheerness Steel's factory. It was here, on a patch of open marshland overlooking the Swale, that a mixed-race Trinidadian named Michael Contant, whose family's activities were regularly reported in the *Sheerness Times Guardian,* could be found bashing on oil drums, which he had cajoled out of scrapyards or found washed up on the shore during his own walks along the seafront. "There is a long preparation needed", so he tells a reporter in one of Johnson's saved copies of the *Sheerness Times Guardian,* "before a drum is made musical".[58] So that was where islanders got used to hearing him as he went about the noisy business of making and tuning chromatic steel pans before carrying them back home to Delamark Road in Sheerness, where he would tell his wife Carol about the birds and other creatures that had come to investigate his unfamiliar sounds.

Had Johnson dedicated one of his apocryphal "Island

Stories" to this other exceptional migrant, he would have discovered that "Mike" Contant was already known as "the world's finest first pan man" when he came to Britain as a tuner with a large steel band formed by the white Trinidadian Curtis Pierre. A "college boy" band, the Dixieland Steel Orchestra had received a lot of mockery as a posh and probably also pale-skinned entrant into the field by 1960 when it triumphed in all categories at the Trinidad Music Festival and then embarked on the European tour that brought its members to London — they were advertised as "the second steelband to visit England" — in 1961. Audiences at venues such as Porchester Hall in west London are said to have gone wild for the music: the band received "a lot of fame", as Pierre has remembered, "but not a lot of fortune".[59] Some of the musicians had gone back to Trinidad when it proved impractical to sustain such a large company abroad. Pierre himself persisted, playing at the Savoy Ballroom and elsewhere with a smaller steel band. In 1962, however, he found himself in the dock at the Old Bailey on a firearms charge (the cricketer Learie Constantine and other members of the Trinidadian establishment stepped forward as character witnesses, and the jury accepted his claim that, while playing with his band in Düsseldorf, he had bought what he'd believed to be a starting pistol in order to scare off menacing German Teddy Boys).[60] Acquitted of the main charge but humiliated by a subsidiary conviction, Pierre had returned to Trinidad shortly afterwards.

Michael however, stayed on, eventually meeting his classically-trained wife Carol, who'd come to London from a well-placed family (her father was an accountant) in British Guiana in 1962 to study violin, viola and piano at the Royal Academy of Music. She had envisaged going home to work as a music teacher. The colony, however, had been hit by a wave of rioting and political disturbance connected to the rise of the more or less pro-communist People's Progressive Party in the run-up to the island's first independent election in 1964, so she decided against returning to the now-independent Guyana. Having met at a dance, the Contants married and

Mike formed the Golden Tones Steel Band, with which he and Carol proceeded to tour in Europe. They lived for a time in Newcastle-upon-Tyne where they had been invited to teach the members of a mixed Caribbean and white English band. The next opportunity came up in Spain, where they met two wealthy Americans who planned to develop a holiday village in the Canary Islands, and invited them to come over to form a resident band. Two years later, when the unrealised project finally fell apart, they found themselves broke and unemployed in Lanzarote with two small children and a third on the way.

Another hard-pressed family, then, hearing the call of Sheppey. In the summer of 1966, the Contants fell back on their own last chance: a chalet in Leysdown, a place that Carole now remembers as "all a bit beer and chips",[61] which they had bought for next to nothing in a fit of cautious enthusiasm when still living in west London. They stayed there while Mike looked for work and more permanent housing on the island. The council offered no assistance at all and problems had piled up impossibly by the end of October, when the chalet park turfed everyone out for the required winter closure. Carol was admitted to hospital to deliver their third child, Jeanette. Mike was sleeping in a car outside, and the two older children were taken into care. Home for a while was a single miserable room in a run-down house in Sheerness, but the family was reunited when they managed to buy a house at 7 Delamark Road, not far from the High Street between Broadway and the beach. The street was "kind of rough" — sufficiently so, as Carol remembers, to be nicknamed "Brixton Road" by some in the town.

We might fear the worst at this point, and not just thanks to an article entitled "Sheppey Memories are Made of This", published in the *Sheerness Times Guardian* on 30 March 1984, in which witnesses looked back on the days when a school teacher called Dickie Farren saw fit to lead his charges into a song called "Rufus Rastus" and the 5.30pm transport to London was known as the "Jews' Express". The Contants, however, pressed through all that to become a shining presence on the island. Michael resumed his career as a performer ("Nat-C"), teacher and supplier and tuner of pans. Carol, meanwhile, who was versed in Montessori methods, set up a family band using the set of tuned pans Michael made especially for his children. They rehearsed at home, employing muffled sticks to limit the noise, and enlisting neighbouring children to the cause. As Carol told a journalist, "they learned so quickly that they were soon able to perform publicly". They played as "Our Tiddlers Steel Band" at the Cinque Ports Mayors' banquet early in 1975 and, later in the year, relaunched themselves as the Rainbow Steel Band, drawing in other local musicians including the drummer Jim Enright, a veteran of a Sheppey beat group known as the Rebounds — recently feted as a pioneer in a Kentish study entitled *The Rise and Fall of the Beat Groups in Sittingbourne*[62] — who delighted in this unexpected music and remembers playing on a kick-set not just with the Contants and their three children but with other Caribbean performers who joined too: including a dancer named J.J. Johnson ("a Caribbean gentleman and quite a crazy character", as Carol also remembers), who became known as "the glass walker", thanks to his trick of walking across broken glass as well as hot coals.

The Contants' family steel band became an island fixture and the story of their enthusiastically received performances can be read in Johnson's collection of newspapers. They regularly played at the Little Theatre, recently opened in a redundant chapel Sunday school building in Marine Town's Meyrick Road, and, on Sundays at a large club for handicapped and disabled people up at Minster Cliffs. "Contant family makes rainbows"[63] read the headline when the Contants performed at the Catholic Hall in August 1975: "Their's was a colourful programme as the name suggests — a variety of songs to steel drum and guitar accompaniment". Carol played guitar and sang, while Dominique (eleven), Marcos (nine) and Jeanette (eight) played piano, drums and guitars. A couple of neighbours, Estelle Tunbridge (thirteen) and Beryl Macken completed the group. "Rainbow band steals show" — was the verdict after they outshone the adult competition at the Sheppey Entertainment Association's Christmas Show in December 1975: "This is not really surprising when they are expert enough to play the Warsaw concerto on a pile of tin cans!"[64]

By the time of their appearance in the Queen's Silver Jubilee celebrations of March 1977, they were "the band with lots of sunshine... such a bright, colourful and happy group that their gaiety can't help spilling over to the audience and a full house at the Little Theatre on Wednesday was bathed in their particular 'sunshine'". On this occasion, Mike, who usually stayed in the background during Rainbow performances, took a solo spot, producing "sounds so hauntingly beautiful on the 'ping pong' pans that his interpretation of 'Danny Boy' and 'Girl of My Dreams' needs no comment". When the Rainbow Steel Band delivered their version of Richard Addinsell's *Warsaw Concerto*, a rousing and unashamedly romantic work written for a British film about the Nazi invasion of Poland in 1939 and popularised in the Fifties by performers such as Mantovani and Liberace, it was said to sound as if a full orchestra was on stage. The band was hailed as an inspiring model in other ways too: "There are no 'stars' among them — each respects the others' talent and provides the back-up which makes for the most heart-warming and unpretentious acts". These unexpected local heroes also appear in Johnson's collected programmes for the Swale Festival, which, in 1978, was pleased to announce that "Sheppey's own family group of amazing musicians" would once again be playing "Music of the Caribbean" in the Little Theatre. Pictures show these radiant Sheppey musicians beaming from under the frayed fringes of more or less Caribbean straw hats.

Carol now looks back on this as a great time in her life. There were "hardly any foreigners in Sheppey", as she recalls. And perhaps there was some "not prejudice" exactly, but "suspicion and a kind of reluctance" too. This, however, "all broke down when we played". Music, she explains, is "the thing that breaks the ice [and] knocks barriers clear away". Speaking from her home in Florida, Jeanette, who had the added difficulty of growing up partially-sighted (as a consequence of which, she ended up as a state-funded weekly boarder shuttling back and forth between Delamark Road and the parkland of an austere private school in Maidstone), remembers a neighbour whose xenophobic tendencies evaporated once she and her daughter started playing with the band. Sheerness was rough and tough, to be sure, and life on Delamark Road was marked by the harsh determination of some families to keep their children from mixing with those whose parents were in and out of jail. It was, nevertheless a good place to live, a town full of people getting by, despite the scarcity of work and the poverty that was also part of the story: a community where good lives could be lived without piles of money. The Contants played in their band and they also became ambassadors, taking this highly accessible music into schools, colleges and communities around Europe. As a performer, teacher, tuner and maker of pans, Mike Contant travelled to Russia and South Africa and he helped bands emerge in Switzerland and elsewhere. In Britain, he took pans into many schools, including one as Carol remembers in Northern Ireland, which chose to start a steel band at the height of the Troubles after the head decided that he must find a form of music-making in which children from both sides of the sectarian divide could collaborate, and which did not belong to one side or the other.

The Contants brought an invigorating story to Sheerness, but there is one more foreigner who had lived in the town, and Johnson had particular reason to notice his story as it surfaced in his paper from sixty years earlier. His copy of the *Sheerness Times Guardian* from 24 January 1975 contained a letter from an elderly former townsman who wrote from Poole to say that, while watching *Upstairs, Downstairs* on ITV, he had found himself remembering the First World War as he had experienced it on the Isle of Sheppey. Mr Howell asked if anyone remembered what had happened to a man "who once had a photographic business near the railway station" in Sheerness.[65] This fellow's premises had been "close to the vast guns of the Coast Defence Battery and from the upper windows of the house photographs could be taken of naval ships using the harbour." At the outbreak of the First World War in 1914, "Mr Lozell" had been "whisked away. Rumour had it that he had been interned or that he had been arrested as a spy." Kids — probably boys from the nearby council school — subsequently broke into his business premises and found "hundreds of photographs of ships lying around and everyone was convinced that he was up to no good." Further details were soon volunteered by a reader who called himself "Sekona" and alleged that the patriotic young men who had "ransacked" Lozzell's shop found "thousands of marks in banknotes along with the photographs of war ships and planes."[66]

The *Sheerness Times Guardian* may never have known to inform its readers that Michael "Natsy" Contant had grown up as the illegitimate son of an absent and little-known German father named Schneider. There was, however, never any doubt about the origins of the vanished town photographer — his name was actually Franz Heinrich Lösel — who had come to Sheerness from Saxony when still in his teens in the 1870s. His motivation is not known but he had left home at a time when Saxony was being forcefully integrated into the Prussian state (a process that had introduced military conscription for young men), and, once in Sheerness, found work as "shopman" to an elderly High Street photographer named John Hunt. He stayed in the trade, eventually becoming a photographer in his own right, and acquiring a studio overlooking the park known as Beachfields — aka the town Recreation Ground — and the sea beyond that. As a photographer, Lösel offered "*cartes de visite*" portraits for customers, be they townspeople, members of the garrison or summer visitors. Surviving pictures, which still float by occasionally on the wide river of junk that is eBay, show family groups, portraits of men in uniform, practising choir boys, Christmas trees, babies and shopfronts. As for his work around the naval station and dockyard, the three surviving photographs that I have seen suggest that he was in the habit of taking his camera aboard warships, gathering a considerable portion of their crew to be photographed on an upper deck, and then returning a few days later to offer the men prints for sale.

Franz Heinrich Lösel, "Portion of Crew of H.M.S. 'Victoria' taken on Forecastle of Said Ship" (circa 1890).

Lösel was said to be scrupulously polite, but he discovered nonetheless what it was to attract suspicion as a solitary foreigner in an English naval town. When, one summer night in 1895 he and a friend — a fitter named J.J. Doran — interrupted a man who was in the process of assaulting a woman in the park, a witness for the culprit tried, unsuccessfully, to persuade the magistrate that Lösel the outsider was actually the assailant.[67] The cloud of suspicion thickened during the spy scare that attended the Anglo-German naval rivalry in the years leading up to the First World War. By the summer of 1905, a year in which tensions with Germany combined with an "alien" fear brewed up around the arrival of Jewish migrants fleeing persecution in the Russian Empire, the town's children had started taunting "German Losel" (Sheerness had long since deprived him of his umlaut) and throwing stones at his many-windowed studio overlooking Beachfields park. When, one warm day in June, he hastened out to chase two twelve-year-old girls home to Blue Town in order to report them to their parents, he was accused of indecency by their outraged father, having allegedly been "incompletely dressed" at the time of the disturbance.[68] He insisted on bringing the girls before the local police court, but was

Sheerness Times, 27 August 1910.

publicly humiliated by the magistrate, who sent the girls home with a minor ticking off but is also said to have told Lösel to ensure that he was "properly attired at all times".[69] A few days later, he was himself brought up before the magistrates for persistently refusing to pay the toll when he took his camera onto the pier in order to go aboard ships. [70] He knew better than to suggest he was being persecuted by the council or its pier commissioners, but he did try unsuccessfully to assert his right of access as a ratepayer, and to establish that the council had no right to charge people for possessing the tools of their trade. Less than a month after losing to the council over pier charges, on 10 August 1905, it was revealed that Lösel — identified as "a German subject, who has been in business at Sheerness for the past thirty years as a photographer" — had been back in court the previous Wednesday to face more serious charges under the Official Secrets Act. This time Lösel was accused of attempting to take a photograph of "the new Ravelin Battery at Sheerness".[71] He was acquitted, having successfully established that he was actually pointing his camera in the opposite direction to take photographs of Bridge Road for a tradesman who wanted them for post cards. "The whole thing", he declared at the time, "is preposterous".[72]

Worse came over the following years. Personally isolated and with local demand for his services declining, Lösel lived under constant suspicion — accused of having a telescope as well as his camera trained on British warships or the defensive batteries across the park from his studio, and mistrusted by townspeople as well as military authorities, whose suspicions would be intensified by the fact that in August 1910, a soon-to-be convicted spy for the German Admiralty, a man named Karl P. Hentschel, really was offering German classes in the town — on 27 August, the *Sheerness Times and General Advertiser* carried his advertisement, boasting qualifications likely to be attractive to naval officers and dockyard officials.

By this time, Lösel only had to show his camera in the town to risk being reported and arrested. In August 1905, the Treasury's representative had been obliged to drop its charges against him, but things did not go so well for Lösel after he was acquitted on a comparable charge on the first day of the Great War. Indeed, he was immediately taken into custody from the dock as a suspected spy. He was kept in various prisons — Maidstone, Brixton, Reading — without any hearing at which he might have tried to counter the charges of the journalists who so roundly condemned him. A surviving official note claims that he was sent back to Germany, perhaps through an exchange of prisoners effected via Switzerland, in August 1917. Within days of his arrest, his studio and photographic plates had indeed been smashed to pieces as the reader who called himself "Sekona" had informed Uwe Johnson and other readers, of the *Times Guardian,* leaving subsequent enquirers with the perhaps impossible job of distinguishing the truth about him from unreliable rumour.

Although there was surely something for Johnson in the story of "German Losel", it wasn't the memory of the First World War that confronted him as he stepped out into Sheerness sixty years later. He was much more likely to encounter painful memories of the Second, in which the island aerodrome at RAF Eastchurch, had been repeatedly bombed by the Luftwaffe. One of his articles about Sheerness, first published in *Die Zeit* on

3 February 1978, described an early encounter on Broadway in which his awareness of these historical sensitivities was very much to the fore:

⟨OH! YOU'RE A GERMAN?[73]⟩

A stranger visits the Isle of Sheppey in the mouth of the Thames and goes for a walk there, on the streets of the town of Sheerness-on-Sea. It is a small town; the residents know each other. How do they know he's not from here? He buys a map: he has to find his way around. He looks at buildings more than at people: he doesn't expect any conversations with acquaintances. He walks idly around on a working day: he is a visitor. Where might he be from? From the mainland, from London, from another county. So he is an Englishmen, like the people from here — he belongs here. Or he might have come on the ferry from Holland, so he's a tourist, and tourists are welcome in Sheerness. When will the people of Sheerness know for sure? When he opens his mouth.

The stranger keeps his mouth shut. He'd smiled when the man behind the counter handed him the map, because the man behind the counter had smiled. A friendly comment about the summer weather was spoken to him and he only nodded in agreement. Does he not speak English? He can get by in this language. But he knows where he's from. He has a German passport in his pocket. The war with the Germans was thirty years ago now, it's over, but he thinks about this war. There was Eastchurch Airfield on this island, which the Germans bombed; there are people who were killed in air strikes and these people will remain in the memories of the citizens of Sheerness. The Germans fired rockets at London whose flight paths passed over this island; the residents of the island will remember these deadly arrows. This particular German was a child then, and his father was not in the German air force; he remains a German, one of the enemy. He does not expect to be greeted on Broadway in Sheerness. He is startled when a lady speaks to him, because now he has to answer, she will realise he's German, and she will turn away from him, and that will be like a slap in the face.

"Excuse me, sir", the lady says.

He answers the way he has learned to answer in school; there are many words in the answer and one of them will sound German. But the woman's face remains friendly and expectant, and she asks: "Is it you?"

"You" in English, "you" can mean **Sie** or **du**. Formal for strangers, or informal, for people who are close. He hears the latter in the woman's voice.

"I am not who you think, madam", the stranger says, in the many words his school wanted him to say, thereby putting on display his whole nation's struggle with the English th sound. The woman looks at him, asking for something, and she says:

"If it's you, then your name is Charlie Baker, and you were at Eastchurch Airfield, and you know the year 1940, and then you had to go to Scotland, and I'm — you know who I am".

The stranger knows the year 1940: the year of the first bombs. In the woman's eyes, this German looks like someone who was eighteen years old during the war, and because he left her he is supposed to come back. She doesn't believe in the six years the stranger actually spent then, she doesn't notice his German accent, because to her he's someone named Charlie Baker, who looks like him, walks like him. She was a lovely girl thirty years ago and Charlie was a fool, because she's waited thirty years for him. Now the stranger has to tell her the truth, for Charlie and for himself.

"I am so sorry", the woman says. "You are a guest in our country, you're on holiday, and here I come up to you and disturb you. That is not how we usually behave — stopping a stranger on the street. Please believe me! It's just, we had an airfield, Eastchurch, and a young man worked there who looked like you... Will you forgive me?"

The German doesn't remember many words when he says goodbye to Charlie Baker's girl, and they are the wrong words.

"Some come back one day", she answers sadly, and then politely adds: "Welcome to the Isle of Sheppey! Welcome to England!"

21. A PAINTER OF OUR TIME

"We are on very good terms with our neighbours. We almost never speak to them".[1] Johnson quoted that brilliant fragment of Sheerness etiquette in a letter to the philosopher Hannah Arendt on 18 December 1974. Having moved into 26 Marine Parade a few weeks earlier, he went on to explain for the benefit of his friend and near neighbour in New York City: "That is true with someone in building number 24". Indeed, he joked, "we would not have carried out this decision had we known in advance that an 'artist' makes his home there (quotation marks by way of example, to indicate possible pronunciation). Those are just the types we were trying to get away from!"

Fortunately, as Johnson quickly found out, the "artist" in question was really not of the "type" he had mocked in *Anniversaries* and fallen out with so chaotically in West Berlin. The Isle of Sheppey's artist was formed in a different and, perhaps not just for the Johnsons, far weirder mould than might have produced a left-wing West German intellectual such as Hans Magnus Enzensberger. "Then again", as Johnson told Arendt in his next sentence, "we could always claim that the visuals misled us. He drives a Jaguar, even if he uses it the way other people use apple carts — shopping, transporting the kids. It's just that now, after only five weeks, he is scrubbing the spots of rust, oiling the stains, embalming it with varnish. And apparently he had a poster for the Conservatives in his window for the October elections. — That can't be right, we immediately counter, and then it's happened: We are speaking to our neighbours after all. We don't understand them very well, as one would expect with the refined language of a conservative artist".

On another occasion Johnson, who never developed a positive regard for his neighbour's artistic work, would describe Martin Aynscomb-Harris as "a bearded man who produces landscapes and abstractions for the summer tourists"[2] — an exponent of the "representational art" with which, so Johnson also informed Hannah Arendt, Sheerness tried and failed to match Margate or Ramsgate as a tourist destination. And yet, had either of them ever allowed their conversation to trespass into such matters, Harris, who was surely not an artist of any previously known "Conservative" type, might have taught the East German incomer a thing or two about the steps a creative person must be prepared to take in order to make a go of things on the Isle of Sheppey.

Marine Parade Nos. 26 (Johnson), 25 & 24, with windproof chimney belvedere (Aynscomb-Harris).

Although he could be quite insistent about his status as the only professionally trained artist on the island, Martin Harris (as he was known on Sheppey) did not espouse any of the approaches my friends saw emerging on the new Diploma in Art and Design programme at Canterbury College of Art in the early Seventies. The man who was then principal of this establishment, a Scottish painter named Thomas Watt, himself appointed from Leeds, espoused a post-Cézanne style of drawing and painting from the figure. He also spent a lot of time in his studio making sumptuous paintings with "splodges of colour", so one former student recalls, while the established staff tended, according to the same sources, to head for the pub at lunchtime and only reappear to repeat the performance on their next teaching day. If Canterbury was then among the most creative art colleges in the country, this was largely thanks to the younger teachers, including the Cypriot artist Stass Paraskos, who joined as a lecturer in 1970, and the part-time tutors. Geoff Rigden was a strong and original abstract painter — a long way, as former student Humphrey Ocean remembers, from being just another derivative "cadet in the good ship Hoyland". Ian Dury, who lectured at Canterbury between 1970 and 1973 (and who once characterised Rigden's students as "thrill painters"), represented the other side of the coin. Figuration and detail were his thing: his paintings offered a smuttier, more sequinned version of the British pop art espoused by Peter Blake, under whom Dury had studied at the Royal College of Art in London. Like Rigden, Dury impressed students by really putting the time in (most of the part-timers were around late on the days when they stayed overnight in Canterbury), and also in his ambition for serious work.

Some good painters would emerge from among Dury's students, as would the anti-prog rock "dance band" Kilburn and the High Roads, which Dury set up at the college, having realised with the help of his students — "we laughed at his jokes", remembers Ocean — that he was actually a better performer than he was an artist. A different forcefield had developed around another part-time tutor, Michael Craig Martin. Having returned to the country from America in 1966, he was developing a more "conceptual" approach than the painters. His own works at this time included "box" sculptures that weren't boxes at all, and a creation entitled *Oak Tree* (1973), now in the Tate collection, which an uneducated viewer might reasonably decide was actually a glass placed on a glass bathroom shelf with an attendant text asserting that it was an oak tree. One erstwhile student, who preferred the arts of etching and traditional sign-writing to conceptual manoeuvres of this kind, remembers disputing Craig Martin's suggestion that the yellow lines painted along the edge of the road were in any sense "like" the solvent flows to be found in the American Morris Louis' paintings. Another recalls his sense of disbelief when Craig Martin declared, more than a decade before he went off to implement his plan with the help of Damien Hirst, Tracey Emin and other future YBAs at Goldsmith's College in London, that he would like to raise a generation of artists unburdened by any familiarity with traditional technique.

These, however, were definitely not the conversations that were happening on Marine Parade in Sheerness. If Martin Harris, who lived at No. 24 with his wife Susan and their two daughters, represented any tendency within twentieth-century English art, it was the heroic school of offcut artists who have refused to lie down and die when the agents and galleries stop returning their calls.

Susan Harris remembers meeting the man she would eventually marry in 1966 when she was teaching dressmaking at the Nuneaton School of Art in 1959 or 1960. She herself had studied the craft in Birmingham, having severely tested her parents (her father managed part of the Midland Bank) by failing to make the grade in academic subjects. Martin, who also joined the staff, had lived a fetchingly rackety art student life, first at Wimbledon School of Art and then at Hornsey in London, and he had recently been doing quite well with his work. Susan remembers him using a palette knife to distribute large quantities of bright paint, entire tubes of which would be gone in a minute or two. In those days, the paintings were "big colourful things" improvised in a flurry of activity (sometimes while talking with people in a convivial studio), which Martin would then drive to London and sell through Liberty or Heals. He had lived in a houseboat at Hampton Court, as well as in a bursting basement flat in Stoke Newington, and everything about him exuded an attractive freedom of spirit — he was "all syncopation and jazz", as Susan remembers, and dancing through the night.

Things had gone fine at Nuneaton for a couple of years, partly because they managed to get a couple of friends appointed to work alongside them, but Harris found the teaching onerous and relations with the principal deteriorated once he and Susan became engaged. So they threw in their jobs, packed all Martin's equipment — "basically old rubbish" as he assured me — into his army truck and hit the road for Sheerness, where he would park in Jewson's yard and, early the next morning, hire three people from the Labour Exchange — including, as it turned out, a future friend who had studied with David Hockney at the Royal College of Art — to help him carry his stuff into new quarters above the National Westminster Bank. It was June 1963, and the man who would soon be hailed as "Sheppey's own artist" had landed.

*

Why Sheppey? Susan herself would quickly learn to appreciate the island's separation from the mainland. On the island, as she says, it was possible to live a good life without being rich, or having to claw your way to the very top of the tree, or feeling any the less because you didn't match up to conventional middle-class expectations. In her account, the island was a place of modest but also varied possibilities: you could "get by" on Sheppey, and gain the freedom to "do things" as you wished.

In driving to Sheerness Harris was, to be sure, placing himself outside mainland understanding of success and failure. He was coming home in a more literal sense too. His father, Dennis A. Harris, had become the manager of the National Westminster Bank on Sheerness High Street, and Martin had spent holidays there while attending boarding school at St

Lawrence College near Ramsgate and also during his time as an art student in London. In the summers he had worked as a waiter at Warner's Holiday Camp, opened in 1955 on a former caravan site next to a disconcertingly smelly council dump at Minster. The place had a rectangular boating lake, tennis courts and a "den" for teenagers. "New Faces — New Friends", promised Warner's brochure for 1960 as it touted Sheppey as "the Londoner's playground". The impression of popular glamour was enhanced when the owner, Jack Warner, dropped in for lunch in what the *Sheerness Times Guardian* reckoned must have been the first time anyone arrived on the island in a private helicopter. Harris remembers being paid £4 a week plus perks, and staying with other seasonal workers in little chalets at the back. It was, he recalls, the "first time I had even met girls and what girls do, I didn't know one end of.... And I learned that there, so this doubled my education". As time went on he would help his friends from art school get summer jobs at Warner's, so there would be quite a group of them. "I had a wind-up gramophone and we had a keen interest in early American jazz, King Oliver and people like that". He would go up to London to buy imported American records from Dobell's Jazz Record Shop at 77 Charing Cross Road — Bunk Johnson, George Lewis, Sister Lottie Peavey. Youthful summer scenes, then, of "dancing and jiving around".

All this, Susan confirms, was in accordance with the line of "theatrical Bohemianism" in Martin's mother's family tradition. Harris loved the example of his uncle, Henry Pettit, who had owned a considerable tract of Canvey Island, upriver and across the estuary on the Essex shore, when it was "nothing but a bog". Pettit had lived in an old bus, but his operational HQ was a gimcrack palace named "Bohemia Hall", in which he ran Canvey's first cinema, showing silent films to piano accompaniment. Martin's maternal grandfather, John Harwood, who had lived with the family in Kent during the Second World War, had produced musicals in London and on New York's version of Broadway in the Twenties. He was a close friend of P.G. Wodehouse, who remained one of Martin's favourite writers. He had also, as Susan points out sharply, been all too successful in frustrating his own daughter's desire for a life on the stage.

As part of his job, Harris's father had disposal of the three residential floors above the bank on Sheerness High Street. So the young artist had the top floor cheap and also took over responsibility for the bank's unreliable alarm system, rigged up out of a whole series of twelve-volt car batteries and far beyond the ken of the elderly police constable who used to turn up for tea on the many occasions when the thing decided to go off. His father was well-known and generally also well-liked on the island, and Martin, who had returned to Sheppey aged twenty-five, had quickly established himself as something of a "happening" on legs. He became known for his distinctive vehicles: the Second World War army truck which he had converted into a travelling home and studio; a butcher's bike he named "Mr Bones" and had cycled around London and Paris as well as Sheerness; an old Ford Customline, an American monster car from the mid-Fifties, which he had further "customised" with the help of a local welder, adding a kitchen of sorts and, so he claimed, accommodation for some six or so people — a shack-like English anticipation, perhaps, of the "paleo-futurist" vehicles imagined in the illustrator Bruce McCall's fine book of visions *The Last Dream-O-Rama: The Cars Detroit Forgot to Build 1950–1960*.[3] There would also be a string of E-Type Jaguars, including a sleek silver-grey example, remembered more vividly than some of its successors because Harris proceeded to paint it mustard yellow.

The activities of the island's recently returned artist were soon being followed by the local paper. In February 1964, when he opened an exhibition of fifty works in his studio above the bank, the *Sheerness Times Guardian* described him as a twenty-six-year-old art teacher who was now "more of an artist than a teacher".[4] He had, so the impressed reporter noted, travelled widely in his customised army lorry — visiting many places in Britain, but also Paris, Venice, Pisa, and various "beauty spots" in Switzerland too. He was said to have "wide experience in every field of art — posters, book covers, theatre sets, costumes and programmes, and also interior decoration". His exhibition in the Bank House included works in various media — watercolours, drawings and collages and a single sculpture entitled *The Crucifixion*. The latter was an arresting piece: the *Sheerness Times Guardian*'s photographer revealed it to be a moulded and partly abstract construction in which imaginative viewers might detect the figure of Christ hanging between two common thieves, while a grieving woman reached up from beneath each twisted and drooping figure. As for the paintings, "one of the most interesting and unusual" examples showed "a Yorkshire terrier, which he painted on a piece of newspaper while cleaning his paint brushes".

Harris had quickly developed a local reputation and his paintings and, more recently, giclée prints found their way into many Sheppey homes. I've seen Thames barges, trawlers and rural cottages, vintage cars and Concorde taking flight, Westminster Abbey and London Bridge as well as Sheppey views and panoramas of coastal cities and estuarial towns

Martin Aynscomb-Harris.

around the country. A large and, as some drinkers speculate, perhaps not entirely finished example showing the town clock tower on Edward Banks' Crescent has a prominent place on the wall of the Belle and Lion, a pub created by Wetherspoon, which spent the unprecedented sum of £1.2 million converting the old Brittain and Hobbs TV and Electricals shop into a large, popular, Brexit-promoting establishment named after the first pub to open in Sheerness.

For a time, as Susan Harris remembers, Martin (who claimed, when I talked to him shortly after the 2016 referendum, to have voted Remain in order not to offend his wife and daughters) also achieved some wider profile as "a very flamboyant artist" exhibiting in London, making works for corporate foyers and restaurants and, in the early stages, becoming modestly successful. Harris had agents in his prime, some better than others. His wife Susan also notes, in the light of their later separation, that male artists who manage to co-operate with their wives tend to do better than those who don't. Determined to help her husband turn his art into a living, she would load a portfolio of his work into her aged Citroen 2CV (quite incapable, as she recalls, of functioning in reverse), and set off in search of buyers. When she arrived somewhere — Leamington Spa, Leicester, Sheffield, south Wales — she would park and seek out galleries in the area, guided by the recommendations of a traffic warden if one happened to be at hand. She found it advantageous to call on twenty or more galleries in a day — and would pack several days into a trip. She had some success in the north of England but remembers East Anglia and Buckinghamshire as cold and unrewarding.

In the last years of his life, Martin was still speaking out in defence of his art. After one of my visits, he came to the front door and continued explaining himself from the top of the steps. I had committed the error of asking him, perhaps a little insensitively, what he made of the extraordinary expansion of London's Tate Gallery under Nicholas Serota and, more particularly, of the "contemporary" currents now dominating the London art world. Bristling, he declared himself a proud representative of "the 98% of artists who make pictures for people to have in their homes". He had sold thousands in his time, so he insisted as the cars swept by, and he'd done so in defiance of the curators and galleries, the fashion-following collectors and, of course, the complicit, bum-licking art journalists and critics ("what's your name?") who made their living by pandering to that world. He was happy to make an exception for Richard Hamilton, who had later painted one of the Harris's daughters, but he drew the line at the clutch of YBAs who eventually emerged from Michael Craig Martin's incubator at Goldsmith's College. Take Tracey Emin, he says. Over the years, Harris had accommodated and tried to help many school-failed youths like Margate's famous daughter, and he knew how to recognise the type. She is, he said in a tone of calm, unblaming, let's-face-it island realism, "a guttersnipe". Perhaps, as I failed then to suggest, a prolonged period like that is necessary to the proper formation of what Emin's former partner in Medway chaos, Billy Childish, would recognise as a true "backwater visionary".[5]

Sold under the signature of "Aynscomb", Harris's own work never formed the slightest obstacle to the fast-rising stream of megabucks art. Susan remembers one of Martin's agents encouraging him to realise that he had to attend to the market if he wanted his work to sell. Martin, however, went his own way — unwilling or perhaps psychologically unable to sustain professional relationships of the kind necessary to the pursuit of a successful artistic career. As Johnson himself knew well, a household has to live and though the Isle of Sheppey had no universities or art colleges to provide part-time teaching, it was by no means without opportunities for the cognitively diverse artist who is prepared to exchange his brushes for larger ones of the house-painting variety. Martin became a man of many projects, joining the informal economy in which he would often employ others to work with him, or enter partnerships with people who would not necessarily treat him well or even honestly. Some of his schemes involved the conversion and customisation of vehicles: Susan sometimes felt he had unfinished cars and caravans all over the island. He also went into business designing and making market stalls of fibreglass: she remembers going to the opening of a market in the Midlands, and meeting Ken Dodd, who had been hired for the opening performance, and who turned out to be "a very nice man". For a while he had a picture-framing business, run from a three-decker barge moored at Queenborough, a riotous setting as former habitués recall, on which Martin made the metal frames used by some of the more upmarket London galleries. Every week he would drive one or other of his cars to London, where he would sell his artwork and carry out other chores for local people, some of whom, as Susan repeated, were plainly taking advantage of his good will.

So it was to be with houses. When they got married in 1966, the Harrises had moved into Holm Place Farm, along Halfway Road, where they took over a derelict labourer's cottage on favourable terms from the owner. While living there, they bought 24 Marine Parade for £3,800, a comparatively modest price that Susan nevertheless remembered as "crippling". The idea was for Martin to get the house ready so that Susan and he could move in to raise their coming children there. Susan, however, was content at Holm Place, once Martin had finally got round to making the cottage habitable, so he rented the new house to some tenants, who turned out "troublesome" to say the least. Susan remembers them as a "rough lot", who left the front door wide open day and night, threw condoms and other rubbish into the front garden, and were highly intimidating all round. Martin admitted that he had handed the house over to "a bunch of yobbos" who used the banister rails as firewood and, indeed, completely wrecked the place. He couldn't bring himself to chuck them out completely, but he did eventually ease them into the upper floors of the house, so that he and Susan could have the basement and ground floor. Just as he employed lots of people on his projects, and infuriated his wife by loaning "friends" money out of his own overdraft, he would also accommodate many in his property over the years — an irregular kind of landlord, who put his children through private school but was reluctant to do anything when his tenants ripped him off, bullied him, or otherwise exploited his goodwill. Susan, who was trying to raise their two daughters in a property that Martin was also running as a chaotic boarding house, remembers that there was almost no behaviour that he would not try to excuse by saying that the tenant in question "hadn't had our advantages".

Meanwhile, No. 24 remained a permanent building site. Susan remembers making a "rockery" in the garden by reconceptualising a mountain of uncleared building debris, but that was just the beginning. "I will never stop", Martin told me in 2015, as he reviewed more than half a century's worth of adjustments to the house that had become his largest work: "It's my version of the Forth Bridge". And, as Uwe Johnson was to find out, No. 24 was not his only property on the street. Martin denied that he had been the rival bidder for No. 26, who once, as Johnson told Max Frisch, "planned to turn a building like this one into a chest of drawers with mini-apartments".[6] Over the years, however, he would buy the houses on either side of his home — Nos. 23 and 25, and also another next to the much-windowed "Glass House", originally the Victoria pub, facing the sea from two sides at a junction a little further to the east along Marine Parade. The lack of separation between family and tenants, friends and scroungers would eventually encourage Susan to acquire her own residence in Queenborough and move out when her situation changed in 1991, but for Martin the refurbishment was indeed like the event described by Pete Brown and Piblokto! in one of the best LP titles of 1970, "Things May Come And Things May Go, But The Art School Dance Goes On Forever".

By the time of my last visit, No. 24 did indeed seem a battered, multiple-occupied mess, which Harris, who by then had serious lung problems, was setting out to convert once again: this time into a "dust-free zone". Johnson, however, had known it at a time when Harris's disorderly visions of improvement and a more creative way of life still had time on their side. He kept a copy of the *Sheerness Times Guardian* from 21 February 1975, in which the Harris's property was praised as the Bohemian lair of the island's most creative householder. "Artists try fresh approach to urban living", was the heading under which Sheppey's feature writer, Bel Norris, told the story of the refurbishment. She kept quiet about the crazy belvedere, a fibreglass viewing platform for watching the sunset over an evening drink, that Martin had perhaps not yet mounted on the plinth he made of a chimney stack that "collapsed" during one of his refurbishments. She did, however, describe an interior that was "alive with colour" where "imagination has been given full rein to achieve individual, unconventional, and entirely practical modern living for this couple and their two daughters". After buying the house, the Harrises had secured improvement grants from the council and, perhaps more difficult, persuaded its sceptical officers that they really could do the work themselves. They had started by ripping out the basement bay window, strengthening the gap with a rolled steel joist and then digging out a drive to create the garage workshop in which Martin would continue to repair and customise his vehicles — including the thing that he called his "Jaguar Caravan". His other innovations included a raised stage made of railway sleepers so that his young daughters might see over the sea wall, a sunken bath, two kitchens, a huge split-level lounge and a first floor "studio" where he produced "pictures which find a ready market in London". Forty years later, Bel Austin, as she has since become, can still add to the list of remembered features — including, somewhere high up in the house, an upright piano that Harris had managed to sink into a pit so that one had to sit on the edge of the floor to play it. Overall, so she wrote at the time, "the ideas are as fresh as tomorrow". We can be sure that Uwe Johnson read her piece — not least because he, or someone in his household, has marked the name of "Mr. Jim Religious", a retired carpenter said to have assisted Harris with some of the more challenging joinery.

Looking back on that article now, and comparing it with the condition of No. 24 as it was at the end of Martin's life, we might be inclined to count Harris's renovations, which had obliged Susan to raise her daughters in "a constant state of chaos", as proof that Sheerness remained spectacularly resistant to "gentrification". Even with this Bohemian exception, the town had nothing yet to rival the gentrified Brooklyn brownstone that Johnson had found in the "Food, Fashion, Family, and Furnishings" page of the *New York Times* on 27 April 1968, and included as part of Gesine Cresspahl's daily reading in the third volume of *Anniversaries*. Having bought this alleged slum for $28,000, the owners had gone for renovation rather than demolition (the Scanlons and their two young daughters were especially delighted with their restored third floor bathroom with its "original bathtub on claw-and-ball feet, the marble sink, stained glass windows and a toilet complete with pull-chain").[7] Sheerness had no experience either of the systematic displacement of poorer people, or of the slithering movement of the colour line that Johnson had seen creating slums among the brownstones of New York City and would return to in the closing volume of *Anniversaries* ("In twenty years the blacks will have been driven out of Manhattan. We'll be living on a lily-white island surrounded by the black boroughs",[8] predicts Ginny Carpenter, a prosperous white liberal feminist resident of Riverside Drive). Although well aware that nobody had ever made a London-style killing out of rising property prices on his street, Harris still insisted on comparing Marine Parade with Cheyne Walk in Chelsea and staring at me defiantly when I showed surprise at the suggestion that the day might one day still come.

The point, he insisted patiently, is that artists are often the first to see the potential in rundown places. They get there before the money and also, as he has particular reason to know, before the planners and conservation officers have worked out how to limit and control their improvements. In the case of Cheyne Walk, he explained, it was the Pre-Raphaelites who started to lift the street into its modern configuration as the home of billionaire oligarchs and golden-booted footballers. Look now at Marine Parade, he says, pointing out at the sea view and the gentle curve of the joined-up terraces as the street tracks the shore east towards Cheyney Rock. There were, he noted, residents who had respected and maintained their houses as they found them, even without necessarily gussying them up to make "antiques for living in". Some members of this leavening minority had also done what they could for the community. They had their triumphs here and there but, as Harris claimed to have learned over four decades, they'd so far lacked the critical mass to lift the wider area, or, more recently, to see off the buy-to-let cannibals who have been turning so many Sheerness houses into what Johnson described as "chests of drawers of flats". It wouldn't happen in Martin's life, but he still looked forward to a time when Marine Parade's Victorian houses would no longer be among the cheapest in southern England and, for that matter, worth only half the price of a detached and free-standing former plotland residence down the road in Minster. As for Uwe Johnson, he may not at first have understood the difference between an English terrace house and a New York brownstone, but Martin counted he and Elisabeth among the incomers who looked after their properties on Marine Parade, living in the house as a historic structure that had its own right to shape the lives of its occupants. "And I", he concluded frankly, as we sat in his much pulled-about warren, "did not".

*

In March 2015, when the BBC Radio producer John Goudie and I went to interview Martin about his recollections of Johnson, he started by reading a prepared description of how they'd first met their new neighbour: "Uwe Johnson came to Sheerness, and introduced himself to me and seemed to warm to me immediately because I was using an E-Type Jaguar to tow a trailer containing around five tons of bricks. I expect there were three lengths of wood sticking out through the Webasto open roof. I received his congratulations for using a so-called prestige car for this purpose..." Martin knew nothing of how Johnson had treated the ill-fated "foreign" sports car in the opening chapter of his novel *Two Views* — a capitalist status symbol that is driven into a canal lock in Holstein, fished out, restored and bought as a "long-limbed racy creature" by an image-conscious photographer from whom it is then stolen when parked outside a hotel in West Berlin.[9] He did, however, go on to boast that the humiliation he inflicted on his E-Type was completed by the "trailer" he often towed behind it. This was all that was left of the heavy Second World War army truck in which he had arrived in Sheerness from Nuneaton.

By 1974, he'd had this relic cut in half by one of the island's oxyacetylene virtuosos so that he could use its rear half for carrying timber, rubble or old bricks. Proud of the fact that his "trailer" — which may even, in another configuration, have been his "Jaguar caravan" — exceeded the recommended towing weight for E-Types by many times, he was also happy to confirm that Johnson "liked the fact that I used a prestige car as if it were a donkey".

Harris can be counted among those who asked Johnson, "What brought you to Sheerness?" — a question the writer describes as "spoken in a tone of almost outrage, entirely in passing and definitely easy to miss", and which he would try to answer with "baffled honesty",[10] adding an italicised quotation suggesting that many islanders understood the challenge: *"We groan, we moan, we flee, we always turn back".*

"We didn't know who he was", Harris explained of the human enigma who had one day moved in with his wife and daughter two doors to the east. "Was he poor or rich?" The Harrises suspected the latter at first, since Johnson evidently possessed the means to get No. 26 repaired and sorted out before he and his family took up residence. There was nothing to explain Johnson's arrival, so "I assumed he was in hiding... on Sheppey, people do this..." Perhaps Johnson had indeed come with the aim of keeping out of view, although surely not in the manner of an MI5-monitored trade union baron like Hugh Scanlon, or of an East End villain gone to ground among the caravans and chalets of Leysdown, or even of Somerset Maugham's sweepstake-winning London hairdresser, who had long dreamed of acquiring a bungalow on the magical island where he might escape death itself. Johnson was more "like Mick Jagger", said Martin as he remembered his own first impressions, explaining that the Rolling Stone surely must have places he can go when he wants a brief reminder of what normal life is like. He may not have understood the situation much better when Johnson, who had indeed been concerned to stay out of sight of Stasi snoops and potential kidnappers after first moving to West Berlin, announced that he lived on the island "only because he is sure that no one is listening to his telephone"[11]

In the early years especially, the two households found ways of getting along. At home, the Harris daughters got into the habit of calling Johnson "Charley Farley" — after a character in *The Two Ronnies.* Susan remembered the Johnsons's daughter, Katharina. She was a little older than her own Emma and Louise, but they used to play together, and Katharina would sometimes look after the Harris children and also take care of the animals when they were away. Katharina was, so Susan remembered thinking, "very shy and very lonely" and they both felt concerned for her. Susan remembers worrying about the Johnsons's decision to trust their daughter to the island's new comprehensive school: a place with a progressive head and too little discipline, so Susan reckoned, insisting that it surely wasn't fair to leave young children to bear the responsibility for their own behaviour. Elisabeth, meanwhile, impressed her as a "lovely person", who used to leave fennel tea on the doorstep when the children were sick.

The two households had their political differences to be sure. Susan insists that theirs really wasn't a purely Tory house — indeed, she felt so inconsistent in her loyalties at election times that she was tempted to display posters for different parties simultaneously in the house's windows. Martin, however, insisted "I'm Conservative. I was pro-Thatcher", and "[Johnson] didn't want to hear that". Harris was in no doubt that he was also "a little bit too public school" for Johnson — not only had he been to one himself, but he and his wife insisted on sending their daughters to a private convent school, off the island, at Gillingham.

The Harrises got along with the Johnsons despite such limiting considerations. Johnson would borrow tools and then demonstrate that he didn't have much of a clue how to use them, so Martin found himself carrying out various tasks in No. 26. In one respect, Susan saw Johnson as a threat to her husband. Martin's customary beverage was tea and he had neither much experience of alcohol nor a practised head for it.

Johnson, meanwhile, was "a terrific drinker" — as the Harrises knew from the large quantities of wine they saw going into No. 26. Susan would worry whenever Johnson invited Martin in for a glass. It was, she felt, frankly "irresponsible" to keep her husband drinking until he emerged from No. 26, decidedly the worse for wear, and then climbed back up his ladder to carry on fixing a gutter or doing other work on a window or the roof.

Johnson lent them English editions of some of his earlier novels but only on condition that they made no attempt to discuss them with him. Both Harrises remember struggling but failing to figure out what on earth was going on in *Speculations about Jakob.* "I felt he was from another planet", Susan told me, adding that she herself was a "very immature person" at the time. In later years she would study English literature at the Open University but in the mid-Seventies she'd hardly read anything more demanding than the children's books she shared with her daughters. Johnson's novels actually gave her a headache ("very hard" as she repeats of *Speculations*). She was, she concluded regretfully, "too ignorant" to appreciate his work: "I felt I failed him ... I couldn't give him anything back".

If conversation about art or literature was avoided by mutual consent, Johnson could not, as time went on, ignore Harris' activities as a small-scale property developer. Writing to Burgel Zeeh, Unseld's secretary at Suhrkampf, on 26 August 1982, he reported on the latest development on this front:

Have I told you (many thanks again for the matjes herring) that the house to the west of this one, occupied up until now by a handicapped woman as quiet as the quietest of mice, was sold immediately after her decease to someone who wants to turn it into four apartments stacked one on top of the other? Now, during the renovation and construction, I realize with both ears and nerves that the wall separating it from me is only one brick thick. When the man next door takes a break with his hammer, I can hear his cheerful whistling. You never know when the next blow is coming, everyone is painfully surprised. Who was it who said that no situation was so bad that it couldn't get even worse? That will come true in my case when people move in behind this wall who enjoy a little upright-piano playing, who deem loud ruckuses useful for the unfolding of darling children's souls, who only know how to use one button on their boom boxes, the one for **volume**...[12]

Harris remembered Johnson's discomfort at his building work differently. On one occasion he recalls being up his ladder working on the upstairs windows or guttering of No. 25, when some debris fell on the steps of Johnson's house. Out walked the writer, peering up and remarking drily about the "mess" he had made. Harris apologised from his perch, only to have Johnson remark in his fluent but accented English, "It was a joke."

Martin describes Johnson as "not an easy man to get close to ... He was a mate and a neighbour, but I never got close." He also remembered the writer as "a verbal bully." Offer some passing pleasantry such as "Hello Charles, nice day" and you could expect an answer such as "In what respect 'nice'?" It seems likely that Johnson, who dedicated an entire article to Sheerness' frequent and varied use of the words "thank you", was actually researching the finer points of English usage at some of these moments, but for Martin the interrogation felt mocking and aggressive: "Everything you say to him is a challenge to be picked to pieces." He remembered Johnson once explaining his approach to the students he met when he went off to teach in America: "The first thing I have to do is to clear all their ideas out of their heads." He did, though, recall more convivial occasions, as when Johnson consulted him over what might be the appropriate English wording for a funeral oration. Harris remembered trying to explain that, to him, the phrase "sincere condolences" sounded far too formal and official and hackneyed: his own preference would be for something more direct and closer to what one might actually feel. He suggested something more along the lines of, "I'm very upset that we've lost you."

As he tries to describe the gulf across which he and Johnson gestured, not always successfully over the best part of a decade, Martin cited his favourite writer, P.G. Wodehouse, and an episode from the story "Jeeves and the Chump Cyril", written while Wodehouse was living at 375 Central Park West in New York City and first published in the *Saturday Evening Post* on 3 April 1918. The story is set in a large Manhattan apartment building and Bertie Wooster has been in trouble with his highly exacting English valet Jeeves, who simply cannot abide the lurid purple socks his master has taken to wearing. Eventually, Wooster discovers that Jeeves has given these offensively showy items to the African-American lift attendant in their apartment building. Surprised when the grateful recipient thanks him for the gift that had turned him into "a blaze of mauve from the ankle-bone southward", Wooster concludes with the words "Well, I mean to say, what? Absolutely!"

What, Harris asks pointedly, might Johnson, the probing linguistic investigator from Germany, ever have made of that phrase? He himself judged it to be perfect in every way, and communicative too, but only to someone instinctively at ease with the fact that, on forensic analysis of the type the German writer favoured, it may turn out to bear no meaning at all. Wodehouse's English would surely so Harris suggests, have seemed utterly inscrutable to Johnson — as obscure, perhaps, as the public-school slang used over the radio by British tank officers in the north African desert during the Second World War, which is sometimes said to have convinced German interceptors that they were hearing a new and as yet unbroken code. Being unfamiliar with *Anniversaries*, he was not in a position to realise that Johnson would have had little difficulty grasping the situation of Wooster's elevator man. Describing the apartment buildings of Riverside Drive as he had found them in the Sixties, he notes in *Anniversaries* that "Negroes are permitted to superintend them, keep them clean, operate the elevators, polish the brass" but not to live in these monuments of faded prosperity, where "old age... lurks like a neglected disease".[13] Indeed, the befriended lift attendant in Gesine's building, "Mr Robinson", is a Cuban refugee who definitely does not wear flashy mauve socks. As for using the word "Negro" to describe people "of African descent", this was only allowed entry into the first English translation of *Anniversaries* because it had, by then been reclaimed by those it had previously been used to reduce and insult (in January 1971, Johnson had told his first American translator to use "any equivalents that do not offend Negroes, and [which] betray a kind of solidarity with them"[14]). We can be confident, though, that the author of *Anniversaries* was no more likely than his primary characters, Gesine or Marie, to be entertained by racist stereotypes, be they explicitly converted into insults or treated as implicit sources of humour as they are in Wodehouse. The German writer who "looked like Goldfinger" remained a curiosity to Harris, keeping himself at a formal distance and preferring — this was admitted with a slight sense of injury — to get most of his English conversation from the "very working-class" people with whom he fraternised in the pub further west along Broadway.

22. A JOB FOR THE TOWN PHOTOGRAPHER

One day in 1979, Johnson received a request from a friend in West Germany. The artist Hann Trier was preparing the catalogue for a retrospective exhibition in Cologne and he asked Johnson to provide "a high-quality black and white photograph"[1] of a painting Johnson had in his basement office in Sheerness. Johnson's interest in the artist's work had developed in Berlin nearly twenty years earlier. Trier had been in the habit of lending Johnson paintings, which he would hang on the otherwise bare wall facing the desk at which he wrote in his flat in the Friedenau district. Potential buyers would come to examine and sometimes actually buy these loaned works, which would then be removed just as Johnson felt that he had broken them in, rather in the way a smoker might "'break in' a pipe".[2] The loss of these paintings, and the sudden interruption of their ongoing conversation with his own developing texts, had eventually become "too much" for the writer, so, some ten years previously, he had bought a painting that he could be sure of keeping.

With Trier's permission, Johnson had named his acquisition *Blackboard*. Like its predecessors, it was an abstract work, painted in 1961 by this famously "ambidextrous" artist whose interest in speed and acceleration encouraged him to paint simultaneously with both hands, moving outwards from a central axis to produce shapes that gestured towards a unifying symmetry while also remaining divided and in some respects irreconcilable from one side to the other. As Johnson had explained to Trier in a letter written on the occasion of his sixty-fourth birthday earlier that year, "the maelstrom there does in fact throw off, like some kind of kinetics problem, spirals of blue and gray symbols that arrange themselves on either side, in lines and groups of types: only in this case one was free to attempt a solution or not". In this, *Blackboard* was analogous to Johnson's incomplete *Anniversaries* project: "That fit my own situation, since what I was busy doing in front of your picture was attempting to get to the bottom of the similarly encoded, equally integrated sign-system of an invented biography". In Johnson's case, however, a "solution" — at least to the problem of completing *Anniversaries* — really did have to be attempted.

So it was that, one morning not long after receiving Trier's request, Johnson set off along Alexandra Road with the painting that had become so closely associated with his own compositional struggles tied up in black plastic and catching the "stiff northeaster" that made a sail of the object under his arm. Trier had anticipated that fulfilling his request in Sheerness "won't be easy", but that was to underestimate the man who ran a photography shop at the southern end of the High Street: an establishment, so Johnson informed Trier with a dry smile, that its proprietor — "let's call him Barrie" — "calls a 'studio' followed by his surely accidental house number. Quite the world-traveller!"

Having carried his painting into "Studio 137", the writer, who was by this time well-versed in the townspeople's use of small talk, ventures an "appropriate" opening remark about the wind: strong enough, after all, to "blow the high water into a flood". Barrie agrees: "Quite a bit of weather we are having!" After this exchange of cod English pleasantries, Johnson busies himself untying Trier's painting, only catching sight of Barrie's expression after he "had his surprised look behind him", having replaced it with "a hard-mouthed face" of the islanders' it's-always-best-to-look-life-straight-in-the-eye variety.

"What might that be?" Barrie can't help exclaiming, as he scrutinises Trier's "maelstrom". Perhaps he made the mistake of looking for resemblances in the turbulence, as if the abstract shapes might resolve, with a bit of blinking, into waves or a tree in a forgotten landscape, or the division of Germany, or the widespread wings of Walter Benjamin's ever more dishevelled angel of history blown all into nothing by a Sheppey storm. Soon, however, it became clear that Barrie had at least "accepted the thing as a painting" since he "refrained from further enquiries" once Johnson had fended off his first disconcerted question by explaining that the work was "untitled". The sight

Hann Trier, Blackboard (1961). Photo: Studio 137, Sheerness, 1979.

of Barrie's buttoned lip causes a "small shift in the attitude of the school-leavers who spend their days at Barrie's under the pretext that they were learning the art of photography". Having pulled themselves together, Barrie and his team get down to work.

The next quarter of an hour is spent clearing the cluttered table so that the picture can at least be laid out flat. During this preparatory stage, Johnson stands back at a distance of four or five feet, but he can't help moving closer as Barrie prepares to take the photograph. This entails clambering up onto "a swaying swivel chair, complaining all the way (it is hardly a long climb, rather quite a short one)", in order to align the painting with a large camera mounted high up on "a kind of gallows". One slip, so Johnson notes, "and he would fall with both knees through the canvas". Having survived this perilous ascent, Barrie reaches up as high as he can and, "with fingers stretched to their utmost length", just manages to reach the button of the camera's remote control. After numerous attempts, he realises that the gadget is "not working". Descending from his perch, "he stares at the broken black thing so suspiciously and comprehensively that I was tempted to ask him if he was familiar with its German nickname: ear drill". Barrie, who may well have been as mystified as the rest of us by this explanation, then "places the busted device on the edge of a counter (can't throw anything away!), from which one of the next customers will knock it onto the floor. Then he starts tearing open the packaging of various accessories set out for sale, since he suspects there might be a remote control inside". On the third try, he finds one, and the crew regroup for a second attempt:

> Let another half hour go by and you would find this view before my eyes: the gangly figure of Barrie's workmate swaying like a reed in the wind on the squeaking, increasingly shaky chair that keeps trying to swivel around; to his left, another helper is trying to hold a flash at a 45 degree angle to the painting, while Barrie, on the other side, flash bulb in his hand as well, keeps correcting him. You have to have a feel for it! (Meanwhile, dangling in the camera's field of view are the cords that are meant to synchronize the flash with the shutter. Or would have been meant to if this system had ever worked for Barrie.) Everyone is talking over each other, counting, giving orders, the springs of the chair are groaning, all under the watchful eye of an experienced shop cat who learned from her Grandma long ago that human beings are all a little cracked.

After an hour or so, Barrie and his various apprentices have produced two negatives and, this being an ordinary day in the life of Sheerness's photographer, Barrie has moved on to apply his "artistic ambitions" to "new clientele". "An implausibly young couple have come in with a baby as tiny as a two-pound loaf of bread, probably still living in its mother's belly as of the previous evening. They now requested, in very quiet voices, a picture of their baby. No, just the baby. Their quiet, absolutely inflexible stubbornness suggested a fear that their request might be refused, and so I straightaway invented a will — 'If there is no documentary evidence of an heir by January 1979, the inheritance will pass to ...' — or perhaps a letter to Australia, with photograph enclosed, saying: 'You can see from Baby that we have to follow our heart...' Baby, however, does not want to lie alone in the cold under the white but unfamiliar silk umbrella that Barrie has set up for portrait photographs; it resists Barrie's attempts to console it; and so now Barrie is struggling with the challenging assignment of photographing Baby in the young mother's lap in such a way that it looks like Baby is sitting on a park bench".

Barrie, Johnson continues, "doesn't have it easy". He proves as much by asking to be paid in advance, in cash. When Johnson questions this departure from normal practice, Barrie starts selecting examples from his box of photographs that have neither been collected nor paid for: "He shows me scenes from the intimate life of people I don't know, who do like to take photographs but then leave Barrie stuck with the pictures on his hands; a particular favourite of his is a horse, fairy-tale white, on a textbook green meadow: Whoever took that one, Barrie cries, may have a deep connection to this horse! but as for me, this white horse with the crooked croup, I don't give a damn! I don't care tuppence! No offence intended! he appends to our goodbyes".

An adequate black-and-white photograph did eventually emerge from Studio 137 to take its place alongside Johnson's account of its creation in the catalogue to Trier's retrospective at the Kölnischer Kunstverein. It took a while, to be sure. Asked to "give us four days", Johnson registers Barrie's "roguish slippery smile" and goes back after ten, only to find the "studio" closed with no visible explanation — "it is known, though, that Barrie occasionally takes aerial photographs, or earns money with news photos for the *Sheerness Times Guardian*". When Johnson returns again after two weeks, Barrie can only regret that the copying machine has broken, and that the only man able to fix it is down with a cold. Eventually, though, the job is done. Johnson picks up the print and two negatives from a man at the counter and, as he leaves, hears Barrie shouts "good luck" from the back of the building, using "a tone intended to encourage a young colleague or guild-brother". Only then does it dawn on Johnson that Barrie believes that he, Johnson, must have painted the picture himself. It was a forgivable error:

> Sheerness is a small town, you see, and two buildings down from my address lives a bearded man who produces landscapes and abstractions for the summer tourists. With neighbours like that ... with Barrie's memory, in which you can count on a mass of mistakes ... it would be ridiculous if he didn't think it".

*

So what is the actual basis for this story of everyday life in Sheerness? "Studio 137" was indeed based at 137 High Street, opposite a much rebuilt pub named the Old House at Home. The "gangly workmate" who perches perilously on Barrie's swivelling chair for the second attempt to capture *Blackboard* was almost certainly Tim Oxley. Now living at Harty, at the eastern end of the island, he is still an enthusiastic photographer although just as familiar on the island as the council's dog warden. He had started learning about photography while at the Technical School for Boys on the Broadway where the maths teacher, Colin Penny, had set up a small darkroom. After the technical school closed in 1970, he continued his education in the superior facilities at the new comprehensive school at Minster. He worked at Studio 137 from the mid-Seventies until 1985, and remains grateful to "Barrie", who trained him to run the studio and also showed him how to do industrial and commercial photography. Oxley has no memory of photographing *Blackboard* but he does remember Johnson as one of the firm's less regular customers — "quite tall, balding, with an accent", as he puts it. Beyond that, "we didn't know anything about him".

As for "Barrie", who presided over Sheerness's only photographic establishment, he was actually George Poule, who opened Studio 137 in January 1973. Sitting below a colourful and definitely not abstract painting of a lighthouse in his home in Queenborough Road, Poule explains that he is French, although now perhaps only half so, having lived on the island for more than forty years. He was born within sight of the Pyrenees in 1942, and grew up in Pau — a town that he remembers for its famous view of the mountains rather than for the flight demonstrations once given here by the Wright Brothers or for the grand English villas still lauded in the tourism guides. He learned photography at the Polytechnic of Central London, but left after six months, when he realised he already knew enough to start making his way. Early in his career he worked with "Edmond's Studio", a photographic concession on the top floor of Harrods, and also as a spotlighter at the London Palladium, where he lit and sometimes also photographed popular stars such as Jimmy Tarbuck and Engelbert Humperdinck. He was indeed a "world traveller" of sorts, having come into his own as a ship's photographer, sometimes doubling as an x-ray technician, on P&O cruise ships. He worked on voyages to New York and Australia ("in those days they paid them £50 to go"), and on luxurious liners gliding through the Canary Islands, the Caribbean, or the Panama Canal. If his press cuttings are to be believed, Poule cut quite a sharp profile on those "dream boats". Suave, chivalrous and seductively French, he confesses to having had a darkroom full of portraits of bikini-clad girls and a charming way of asking whether a selected young lady might like to step

Janet and George Poule at Studio 137, with an Asahi Pentax 6 x 7 roll film camera.

out for a glass or two of Dom Pérignon at the next exotic destination.

Poule remembers loving the work but the cruises tended to happen in the autumn and winter, which left the summers open. One day in the late Sixties, Warners advertised a seasonal photographic concession at their large holiday camp to the east of Sheerness at Minster-on-Sea. Poule took it on, acquiring an empty studio in a camp that was then still attracting over one thousand visitors a week. His talents now extended to both ends of the social hierarchy. In the winter, he would smile his way through five-star cruises, with elaborate menus, silver service and all the trimmings, but the summer months now found him in a "cockney" paradise full of banter and egg and chips, selling portraits at four shillings and sixpence each. He remembers the dance hall and the beer ("ha! ha!") and the wardens who used to say that you'd know you were drunk when you could no longer distinguish the glitter ball's lights as they shimmied across the dance floor. Setting himself the target of selling at least one photograph to every visitor, he filled his studio at the camp with colour technology, using Agfa-Gevaert paper that had to be imported from New York — an expensive decision, but one that added definite glamour to his Sheppey offering, and also brought him printing jobs from less well-equipped photographers working the camps and chalet parks at Leysdown-on-Sea.

Poule enjoyed five good years at Warner's, but everything seemed to slump in the early Seventies: the cruise jobs weren't getting any easier to find and numbers at Warner's were dwindling (the Minster camp would eventually go out of business at short notice in 1980[3]). Poule had thought of moving to London but the scene there was dominated by influential agencies, and, as he asks, "How could I have told David Bailey that he was now my competitor?" Friends, meanwhile, pointed out that there was "no proper photographic studio on the Isle of Sheppey", and he decided, like a true islander, that "To think small and be successful" must be better than "trying to be big and failing". By May 1973, when he married his wife Janet, whom he had met and wooed on a Fred Olsen cruise from Millwall docks, Poule had bought out a tobacconist selling "Woodbines, lollipops and sherbet fountains" and reopened the premises as "Studio 137".

Sheerness's photographer explains that he "did his homework", and knew from the start that "it was not enough to do pictures of babies". He wanted to bring real quality to Sheppey, so he bought everything necessary to do full colour and canvas printing too. His babies would look special, as would their mums and dads and, for that matter, the dogs and cats that also featured in his studio's portraiture. His eye, though, was also on larger possibilities connected to the industrial enterprises on the island. The stevedores used to come in from Sheerness port: men whose industrial muscle was already shrinking (although Poule had learned to respect it, having once nearly delayed the departure of a cruise ship by inadvertently breaking the rules by himself carrying a small photographic drying machine up the gangplank). He did work for Abbott Pharmaceuticals and Sheerness Steel, which commissioned him to take photographs demonstrating that they really had cleaned their furnaces as the regulations demanded. When I showed him three aerial photographs from Johnson's own collection — one of Marine Parade and two of the town and port, with the Isle of Grain beyond — he remembered taking them on the order of Messrs Dickson and Howard of the Medway Port Authority, using a Hasselblad SuperWide C camera and a helicopter from Rochester, which had conveniently picked him up on open land just beyond his back garden.

Poule counted artists among his friends and customers too. He is, for example, full of admiration for the works of Margaret Loxton, who lived on the island when her husband, Jerry, was Head of Education at the prison at Eastchurch. The Loxtons used to visit Studio 137, but Jerry, who once employed Poule to teach French to his prisoners, left the island to run a garlic farm in the Dordogne. Poule had watched as

Margaret found her own direction while raising the children — an Open University degree, part-time work teaching art and English in borstals and prisons, and writing grainy but still morally improving stories for teenage readers in which young male school-leavers find their aspirations frustrated and their sense of manhood challenged as they step out into a cold world of joblessness and early marriage in towns that may also be hemmed in by a sea that, having whispered of mobility and far-flung opportunities to earlier generations, has since become a barrier reflecting only closure, dereliction and despair. *The Job* (1977) tells of a young man named Lennie who is unable to find work even though he reluctantly stayed on at school for his CSE exams: exposed to temptation by his love of fast cars, he becomes driver to a company of ruthless and intimidating gangsters, and only starts to lift himself out of disaster when his loyal girlfriend, Julie, who has failed to get him to emigrate to Australia, persuades him at least to tell the truth to the police.[4] *Inside and Out* (1979) is about a young man who slides into thievery in the hope of escaping the dismal life of his father, but only graduates from borstal to detention centre,and then to the regular prison, where he develops a more sensible ambition thanks, once again, to the loyalty of his girlfriend, Anne.[5] *The Dark Shadow* (1981) is about an unexpectedly well-off tramp — harried by local kids as "Old Billy Beer-Bottle" and eventually found "mugged" or murdered on a Sheerness-like High Street — who embodies the temptations that eighteen-year-old Jimmy must resist as he finds a path through joblessness, terrible housing, drink and emigration to Australia, before finding employment as a hospital gardener and accepting his responsibilities to his good young wife and child.[6]

Loxton took up painting too. Unlike Hann Trier, she produced recognisable pastoral views of Sheppey in which sheep and well-rounded farmers go about their traditional business while the Elmley marshes join the Swale in stretching out scenically behind them, and all seems to be as conventional expectation says it should be in the world. After herself leaving the island for France, she applied her Sheppey-trained eye to the wine regions and her paintings, sold as "English to the core yet inspired by France", have travelled far. Her cheering renditions of local life in Provence have illustrated the words of Peter Mayle and her bicycle-assisted *Travels in Burgundy* have been introduced by Alan Coren. Like her contented peasants, her skating and skiing nuns have adorned posters, pillow-cases and shower curtains around the world.

If Loxton impressed Poule as a "fabulous" artist, so too did Martin Harris, the artist responsible for "Barrie's" mistaken assumption that Hann Trier's painting was an attempt of Johnson's own. Poule had indeed been asked to photograph Harris' "brilliant paintings" before they were sent for exhibition or sale in galleries. He also used to accompany Harris to London to photograph some of his larger panoramic pictures — sometimes eight foot in length — showing them in situ in hotel or office reception areas or, as was the case with his series of four large panels of St Katherine's dock, actually painted on doors, in Marks & Spencer on Oxford Street.

Poule doesn't at first remember much about Uwe Johnson, but a glance at the photograph on the cover of *Inselgeschichten* starts him off. He looks at it, weighing up the pipe, the spectacles ("rather NHS, don't you think?"), and the glum unyielding expression: "I don't think I took him seriously", he says of this "not talkative" customer. He later confirms that Johnson was introduced to the studio by Martin Harris: "He liked being called Charlie, and he visited the studio a few times for other photographic needs. He was distinctive as he always smoked his pipe or cigars (in those days it was allowed) and had a German accent. He was a gentleman, but with no sense of humour". As for *Blackboard*, faint memories are stirring there too. He doesn't recall feeling shocked or disconcerted when it was unwrapped in his crowded studio, nor assuming that Johnson must have painted it himself. "It didn't look anything wonderful", he says of Hann Trier's painting, diplomatically, but in a tone that made it clear that he would not have chosen a Trier over another Harris or a Loxton to join the lighthouse on his own living room wall.

At the same time, he confirms the accuracy of various details in Johnson's account. For his studio work, he used a Linhof large-format camera and five-by-four-inch sheet film for copying. And the young school-leavers? "We had a YOP programme", he says, referring to the Manpower Services Commission's Youth Opportunities Programme, which had been launched under the Labour government of James Callaghan in 1978, with the aim of helping sixteen to eighteen-year-olds into employment. Like Race Furniture and other employers who set out to make manageable and productive workers of Sheppey's youth, Poule was strict on matters of discipline. His policy was to recruit young and insist on "proper rules" from the start. One unbreachable edict declared that "the customer is always right". Another decreed that you shouldn't start sneering or swearing until after the customers have left the shop. As for what he calls "the dancing chair", there was, as he later emailed to explain, more to this than the crazy swivelling structure than caught Johnson's eye:

I had made a modified revolving chair, to use as a platform to get height and position to capture an object, sometimes even with a tripod attached! I used to stand on it and sometimes it did swing a bit. Obviously he must have thought this was quite funny and he must have been worrying about his painting getting damaged more than me falling off.

So it must have been a funny situation: let's try to imagine the YOPers holding the studio lights and learning to spot them at the right place and myself with a 3 kilo camera swinging on a rotating chair and trying to focus on his painting. Mr Johnson, by now, must be having some concern about his painting and at the same time nervously smoking his pipe/cigars and watching every movement we made through his circular glasses.

It must have been a bit of a comedy show (like Frank Spencer in *Some Mothers Do 'Ave 'Em* — Michael Crawford visited Studio 137 in the old days). Happily we must finally have succeeded, as he did not make any complaint after all that. Our only problem was that the whole studio smelled of tobacco afterwards.[7]

Poule notes Johnson's account of being asked for payment in advance: "I cannot remember for sure, but I must have asked how he would make the payment. I asked because I had previously photographed some pictures for local farmers and one of them was of a white horse/s in a field, which was still hanging on the wall because he/she never collected or paid for the print" After reading Johnson's description of the episode, he repeats that Trier's painting was simply "not charming enough" for his liking, and if he gave priority to the baby and aerial jobs mentioned by Johnson, this may indeed have been because he was not convinced he would ever "get paid for something so basic".

Studio 137 carried on into the mid-Eighties, with Tim Oxley increasingly in charge. In 1980, George Poule started a new business, Travel World, based in a shop on the Broadway, which included a VIP Cruise Club and became one of the biggest travel agencies in the south-east. However, the days when it took art and expensive equipment to make a good photograph were passing, and he eventually sold the photography business. When I spoke to him at the end of 2015, the building, which George described as his "pension", was tenanted by the Direct Pizza Company.

PART V.

SOCIETY: "I DON'T WANT TO GET PERSONAL"

You have another suggestion for me: the neighbours. I have close to fifteen thousand of them; only nine hundred and eighty of them occupy my imagination, since they are unemployed and some of them are ashamed to live off the dole.

— Uwe Johnson, "Consider Yourself Many Times Thanked", *Die Zeit*, 13 June 1980.

PART V.

SOCIETY: "I DON'T WANT TO GET PERSONAL."

23. BECOMING "CHARLIE"

I share in the lives of the people here, I want to be part of it and understand it.
— Uwe Johnson in a letter to Erika Klemm, 31 January 1976, *Inselgeschichten,* p. 101.

The air ticket receipts preserved in the Johnson Archive at Rostock show that Johnson never really settled for the life of a marooned castaway. There were trips to America (two in 1975 alone) and he frequently flew back and forth to West Germany for readings, award ceremonies, and meetings with his publisher or the Academy of Literature. Johnson may have been content to leave Michael Hamburger's Suffolk home to the younger German émigré, W.G. Sebald, who would later feature Hamburger and his apple trees in *The Rings of Saturn,* but there were offshore excursions in England too. He would cross the Swale to visit London, and not just to make occasional contributions to BBC radio documentaries about the divided Germany. He visited the far side of the Thames Estuary in Essex, and also explored the Kentish mainland: the cathedral at Canterbury, Dover with its "Shakespeare Cliffs", and the coast path around the Isle of Thanet to Ramsgate from Broadstairs, where he was keen to show the Dickens house to Rudolf Augstein, a West German journalist who had been among the founders of *Der Spiegel* magazine.

In between his travels, however, and despite the rising impatience of his publisher Siegfried Unseld, who sometimes accused him of wallowing in the miseries his English exile imposed on him, Johnson really did find a world for himself in Sheerness — much of it concentrated along a few hundred yards of the Broadway, built as the proud spine of Marine Town but struggling to survive in the Seventies. The Catholic Church and the Victoria Working Men's Club held out on the north side of the road, as did both the post office and the stationary and book shop, run by the local publisher A.J. Cassell (and well used by the Johnsons) directly to the west of it at No. 31. However, a number of the institutions that had defined the street for earlier generations were dying or already gone. The Rio Cinema endured and so did the Argosy across the road from it, which had converted to Bingo in 1968. The Hippodrome, located in a building erected as Victoria Hall Theatre in 1870 and said to be the place where the local comedian Rod Hull began his career after the Second World War (at that stage allegedly without his emu), had recently given way to a nondescript bank. Despite a last-ditch introduction of nude girls on stage — according to one disapproving witness these figures, who were also obliged to remain motionless to stay within the law, "stood there on pedestals ... starkers but covered in a veil"[1] — the site was cleared in 1970.

The schools in the area had also fallen into redundancy when the island's new comprehensive school opened at Halfway in 1970. By October 1974, as Johnson learned from the *Sheerness Times Guardian*, the long-empty and increasingly vandalised Technical School for Boys which had prepared many of its charges for apprenticeships in the dockyard and its associated industries, was leased to a company seeking planning permission to convert it into flats and community facilities. The decision finally to demolish the building — already condemned in the Pevsner guide as "anaemic neo-Wren by *W.H. Robinson*"[2] — was announced in May 1975. "The outside is attractive", admitted the chairman of the responsible planning committee, "but the inside is diabolical", and "not suited" to any of the council's purposes.[3] By August, the local paper found nothing to show but a pile of rubble soon to be cleared to make way for a temporary carpark. "It had the appearance of a country estate which was in the wrong place", remembered the reporter Bel Norris, before placing it on record that "Even with the continuous drone of traffic and the distraction of sea views, students had managed high marks in examinations".[4]

By the time the Johnsons landed in Marine Town, efforts were already being made to check the slide into dereliction and newbuilt mediocrity. The case for restoration and reuse of buildings was being asserted by civic-minded members of the leavening minority Martin Harris described as both admirable and too small really to lift the town out of its difficulties. These local activists did, nevertheless, have some achievements to their credit. The Sheppey Entertainments Association may not have made it onto the council's list of the island's rich array of voluntary associations (a copy of which Johnson had on his shelves), but it had nevertheless been set up in the late Sixties to raise the funds to buy a hall that had once been the Sunday School of a long-since burned-down congregationalist church, and convert it into the Sheppey Little Theatre, which was opened, thanks partly to a frantic last-minute bond-selling campaign, as a 130-seat venue by the left-wing Labour Minister for the Arts, Hugh Jenkins, in October 1975. The *Sheerness Times Guardian* kept the Johnsons and its other readers informed about the events held here, although its reviewers would repeatedly note with regret that touring shows from the far side of the Swale were poorly attended, unlike the performances of the Contant family's Rainbow Steel Band.

The "blight" fought by these local citizens also extended north of the Broadway to the sea wall where the prospect of demolition had long hung over one of Marine Town's earliest and most singular buildings, Neptune Terrace. Here too, however, public policy was changing in accordance with the new mood. In January 1975, a previous plan to flatten Neptune Terrace and associated buildings complicating the promenade here was finally dropped by the council planners.[5] The residents who expressed relief at this decision included Mr Stan Northover of the Cellar Club — a late-night boozer's den at 9 Neptune Terrace whose ceiling and walls are said to have been adorned with hanging chamber pots. He and his wife would be moving on shortly — he explained that the family needed more space — but he commended the terrace as "beautifully placed, solidly built with stacks of character".[6] Mr and Mrs Barry Norman were only in their second year as proprietors of the Dolphin Café next door, although they understood that "this part of the terrace has been a café for about 25 years".The eighty-five-year-old resident Albert Tyler also welcomed the planners' change of mind, confirming that Neptune Terrace was "historic" and should indeed be saved, despite its highly exposed position on the sea front, and properly recognised as "a tourist attraction". So this rashly-placed terrace survived to be commended as "a wonderfully amateurish piece of stuccoed classicism" in John Newman's revised edition of Pevsner's *Kent: North East and East,* published in 2013.

Neptune Terrace (detail).

Both the county planners and Swale Borough Council, the wider district authority that took over from Sheppey's three local authorities in 1974, had got the message by the end of 1976, when Johnson's local paper printed an editorial confirming their acceptance that "Marine Town was well worth saving".[7] The Housing Action Area, promised in April that year (as long as enough residents in the working-class streets behind Johnson's house raised themselves sufficiently to apply for "bath and basin grants"),[8] was welcomed as a rejection of the "pull it down" approach that would have flattened not just Neptune Terrace but the "friendly community" behind the Johnsons's house, where Victorian terraces might have gone to make way for "soulless, featureless boxes". "There are too few places left in the country where pubs nestle amidst the rows of houses and where you don't have to go to the concrete shopping centre with its vandalised water fountain and piece of misunderstood sculpture to buy a loaf of bread and a packet of tea". The *Sheerness Times Guardian* hoped to see Marine Town saved as "a memorial to the time when senseless demolition came to an end".

*

Such was the little offshore world in which Johnson established a daily routine for himself. On 6 March 1979, he informed Helen Wolff that he ordered his hours "tidily" in the hope of encouraging progress in his work, and creating a skeleton on which the hours of each day might be hung.[9] Having cleared all correspondence from his desk by 1pm, he would walk across the road to the Dolphin Café, one of several businesses holding out on the promenade above Marine Parade — all of them, as is remembered by Ian Lambeth, who grew up here in the Seventies, "hoping to catch whatever was left of the tourist trade".[10] There was a seasonal beach store that sold buckets, spades, inflatable lilos and other "classic seaside paraphernalia". There was a pool and snooker hall (which appears to have joined the migration to bingo by the early Eighties) and also an amusement arcade — K's Kasino — with its traditional collection of coin cascades, one-armed bandits, a mechanical horserace, and a food service of the "ice cream and chips" variety. According to Lambeth, who remembers the place from his present home in Florida, Johnson is likely to have heard the thin whining of the arcade's sirens as he made his way to the easternmost house in Neptune Terrace. The Dolphin Café was "a pretty generic 'caff'" with a "serving counter at the back of the room, small tables, fried breakfast, fried everything, there may even have been handwritten signs in the windows advertising the available combinations". Johnson regularly came here for lunch, secure in the knowledge that "Denise" would have his black tea ready by the time he reached the counter.[11] Over the years, he would sympathise with the proprietors he saw struggling to make a living from this marginal outpost of seaside capitalism while also registering the systematic and inevitable nature of their defeat. In a letter written after the close of the summer season in 1980, he described the place under an ironically adjusted name for a couple of East German friends (both by that time working as art historians in Dresden) from his student days in Leipzig:

⟨DIAGONALLY ACROSS FROM MY WINDOW, TO THE LEFT⟩

Diagonally across from my window to the left, improbable as it may seem to you, begins a row of houses named Neptune Terrace and containing the Dauphin Café, where I get a hot meal of **bacon** and **egg** around noon. A few working men, gas-meter-readers, drivers, are there too, and they can eat heartier meals than that because they are less fat than I am. A misfortune occurred there this weekend. The fifth crew manning the café (since I've been going there), a married couple with two developmentally disabled children, has had to give up. They'd really tried. They wanted to make the establishment — basically just a single, rather dingy room — more attractive with a fancy curtain over the shop window. For every single one of the eight tables, they purchased new salt and pepper shakers, plastic, stainless-steel-looking, and probably at least ninety pence each. They greeted every guest, upon their entrance and also their departure. They noticed and remembered when someone regularly ordered the same thing. But only rarely were more than seven of the nineteen wobbly chairs occupied, and when the family huddled together at a table during quarter-hour spans of time without much of anything to do, they seemed to be taking refuge with each other. There were probably fights from the stress too; one time, the woman, some portion of disaster already present in her unwieldy, misplaced corpulence and her insistence on wearing black clothes, was seen running through the town in a state of excitement, in tears, out of control, passing people and not even noticing one of her regular guests, me. They had placed their hopes on next summer and its tourists, but in vain; on Friday, she stacked the furniture crying, and an awkwardly written note asking to be excused for the early closing hung in the window. On Monday, a new family took over, their predecessors having vanished from the island into a void that I picture to myself as a bare, dark, expensive room in a slum — all because there wasn't enough money on one occasion for the thirty pounds rent that someone in Gillingham has the right to rake in just because at some point in the past he was able to buy the building.

⟨Letter to Lore and Joachim Menzhausen, 29 October 1980[12]⟩

Having lunched at the "Dauphin", Johnson would complete whatever shopping or errands he had in the town, taking care to be home by 2pm so that the next spell of "sitting in front of a blank white sheet of paper in the typewriter can start punctually."[13] In the evening, he would walk along the Broadway to the pub, either the Napier, on the junction where Alma Road comes in from the south, or, in the earlier years especially, the Sea View Hotel across the road a little further along:

The two hours I spend with people in the "Sea View" every evening offer a kind of substitute for socializing. The conversations are strictly limited to the weather; since the floods at New Year's, they could be extended to cover the relationship between the published high tide and the direction, also the strength, of the wind. On the other hand, the prices went up again yesterday so there was a little discussion of the economic union with Europe (they were against). And if someone explains a bandage on his hand after all — thereby expanding the scope of the topic of conversation to his job, the ride to work, the behaviour of the attending physician — he will end by thanking me for my interjections, emphasizing the conventional behaviour: **Thank you for the company, Charles.** This game of stock phrases and silences never lasts longer than two hours for me, and then, from all sides: **Tada, Charles!**[14]

By 6 March 1979, when he gave Helen Wolff this account of his daily routine, Johnson was no longer a newcomer revealing his foreign status by walking around looking at buildings rather than people. His interest in joining the life of the town, or at least, as he insisted, of the 980 among its inhabitants who were unemployed, had also required that he create a new identity for himself. Having quickly discovered that the English tongue was quite unable to utter the name "Uwe" (to this day people tend to prefer "Yewy" to the slightly more accurate approximation that can be achieved by taking the brand name "Hoover" and knocking the H off it), he had, as he explained in a letter to Burgel Zeeh at Suhrkamp, allowed his English neighbours to come up with an alternative: "I was baptized 'Charlie' in December, 1974. That is how everyone knows me here; only the postman refers to me with my last name."[15] A new name, then, but also an alias that kept everything about his actual life and work hidden from those among whom he now lived.

According to the recollections of friends and acquaintances tracked down by Tilman Jens, a West German literary commentator who came over to look about in Sheerness for the mass-market news magazine *Stern* immediately after the discovery of Johnson's death in March 1984, the writer's English "baptism" took place on the Broadway. "Here in the pub we called him 'Charles',"[16] explained the eighty-seven-year-old former fireman Louis Miller, when the visiting reporter coaxed some comments out of him in the Napier Tavern. Everyone had their nickname, he explained, and "Charles" had gained his at the very beginning of his decade in Sheerness, on Christmas Eve in 1974. In Miller's reported version of the story, the seasonal party was well underway when the door opened and this "heavy, powerful man" walked in. "Oh there's Charlie", yelled one of the regulars. Johnson had laughed, appearing to accept the name, although not, of course, without trying to establish a more formal version. "No, Charlie is wrong, he said. The name is Charles. Actually, even Charles Henry although that may be a bit complicated in this setting". "That was the birth of Charles", said Miller, adding a detail with which Jens would variously sadden and horrify Johnson's admirers in the Federal Republic of West Germany: "from then on he let Ron pour a small glass of whisky over his bald head every Christmas as a symbol of his baptism".

The controversy prompted in West Germany by Tilman Jens' despatches from Sheerness leaves me grateful for a brief telephone conversation I had in the late Nineties with a man who had worked as a potboy at the Napier Tavern in Johnson's time. Scraping up everything he could remember from that already distant period, this fellow pictured the German writer sitting on a stool in the saloon bar, drinking Hürlimann lager and smoking French cigarettes — Gauloises plain, perhaps, or on reflection, maybe the filter-tipped Gauloises sold as Disque Bleu (and favoured by some of the more Bohemian students at the time). This witness may not have detected the "bell jar of strangeness"[17] with which Günter Kunert reckoned Johnson surrounded himself, but he did remember that the German incomer could be an awkward customer, who had little time for small talk or trivial disturbances — especially when he was engaged in animated conversation with a visitor from abroad.

I mention this fleeting description because it corroborates much that Tilman Jens gathered from the drinkers at the Napier more than twenty years previously. He informed his West German readers that these folk did not share Johnson's taste for Hürlimann, insisting that this suspiciously foreign, light-coloured lager — which the Faversham brewery of Shepherd Neame had started making under license from the original Swiss brewery in 1968 (and which it nowadays proudly advertises as "the first lager ever brewed in Kent") — was the strongest of the beers on offer in the Napier. "It's a brain-damaging beer," they assured Tilman Jens, "it will kill you." Johnson had been stimulated but not persuaded by their insistent warnings about his chosen brew, which Kentish pub-goers had, as I remember from Canterbury, already got into the habit of calling "Hooligans." Characteristically determined to establish the truth of the situation, he had written to the brewery in Faversham for confirmation that he was not drinking poison. Armed with the brewery's assurances, he would reply that the beer (which Shepherd Neame now reckon to have had a comparatively high alcohol content of 5.4% in Johnson's time) was brewed in voluntary accordance with Germany's ancient beer purity law forbidding anything but hops, barley, water and yeast. No question at all, as Johnson was pleased to reply to his English critics, of any "chemical additives."

The publican Ronald Peel — he's the "Ron" of the annual "baptism" story — told Jens that Johnson had always turned up at the same time in the evening, stepping into the Napier Tavern's saloon bar with a brief "Good Evening" — or "Good heavening!"[18] as Johnson himself imagines them registering his pronunciation — and then taking his customary place on a high, wooden barstool with a seat upholstered in red synthetic leather of the type Tom Waits was in those days hymning as "Naugahyde." He allegedly always wore the same distinctive garb too: a black peaked watchman's cap, a black jacket, black trousers, black leather boots, and sometimes a thin black tie — the same gear, in other words, that had shocked Michael Hamburger, who had been astonished to find this highly regarded and sensitive writer going about in such garb.[19] Even the ashtrays on the bar had to be black at his request, and "to make matters worse," he would insist on having two: one for stubs of the French cigarettes that "stank so disgustingly" to Peel's frankly English nose, and the other for the matches which Johnson, in a gesture that confirms other accounts of the exactness with which he measured his progress along the road to ruin, would line up in an orderly row as he made his way through the carefully counted cigarettes he allowed himself over a two-hour visit. Eleven cigarettes, eight pints of Hürlimann and also, just before returning home, "a double vodka with tomato juice, ice and lemon — but without Worcester sauce. And served in a large glass".[20] Such was the alleged tally by the end, Peel told Jens, rounding off his betrayal by adding not just that he'd been obliged to order in a special supply of Gauloises cigarettes for Johnson, but that he'd had to return the entire stock to the supplier after the writer's death since none of his other customers would dream of smoking these pungent foreign things.

Johnson's bar stool, long preserved as a relic at the Napier Tavern, in action with Big Fish and friends at the Little Theatre, Sheerness, 5 March 2016.

We gather from Jens that the drinkers in the pub came to terms with Johnson's unpredictable way of alternating between rudeness and friendliness: the way he might cut someone off at one moment and then take him or her suddenly to heart in the next. They learned that he could become sentimental about accordion music, and might even shed tears at the sound of the song "Lili Marlene". They had seen him "become the entertainer" too — dancing "like an elephant" or, going arm in arm with Muriel Adams, to sing Kurt Weill and Bertolt Brecht's song "Mack the Knife" — he in German, she in English: "see the shark with teeth like razors".

And yet Jens also reveals that, even after nine years, they knew almost nothing about the man who had sat in their midst. The "grand old man" of the Napier, the former fireman Louis Miller, was still astonished to have discovered that Johnson was "a famous man" from his obituary in the local paper. "We talked a lot here in the Napier", said the newspaper publisher Bill Harvey, before admitting that, while he himself may have revealed intimate details of his own life in these conversations, "Charles" definitely did not. Another of Jens's interviewees, Muriel Adams, had deduced that Johnson "felt a little bit guilty about being German". After returning from a short holiday in the Birmingham area, she and her husband had mentioned their visit to Coventry Cathedral. Johnson went quiet as she described how this blitzed monument had been rebuilt under the architect and designer Sir Basil Spence. He then closed the subject with a terse observation: "This cathedral would never have had to be rebuilt had Germans not reduced it to rubble".[21] "I think", so Adams told Jens, "he had a real guilt complex"."He looked like Kojak", someone else added to Jens's collection of graveside scrapings, "with a two-day-growth".

None of these pub-goers had known enough about Johnson to recognise the man who was destroying himself before their eyes, nor, for that matter, to grasp that his fits of costiveness and aggression were like flames flickering behind the windows of a vast and irreplaceable library. None of them were in a position either to confirm or counter Michael Hamburger's observation that Johnson was "not merely reticent, but almost morbidly averse even to such intimacies as are considered usual and decent among friends", or to assess the truth of Hamburger's further conjecture that Johnson may actually have drunk in such "terrifying" quantities in order to "break through", or at least to "loosen up", the "puritanical rigor" and strict "socialist morality" that seemed to weigh on him like a helmet of lead.[22] They did, however, know that the man who also deputised as their walking encyclopaedia could be a cussed sod. "I was not always happy with him", confessed the publican Ronald Peel, explaining that Charles could be "obnoxious" — as when he turned up with lots of "junk" from home, occupying about five places as he spread it out over the bar or table, and then objected to some speck of dust that nobody else would ever have noticed. There had been occasions, Peel admitted, when Johnson's "tyranny" made him and his fellow publican Col Mason incandescent with rage, "and then I had to call him to order". Sometimes these confrontations drove the writer to stand up and insist, quite emphatically, that he would never enter the pub again. The next day, however, he would be "back in his usual place" and "ready for reconciliation". According to Jens, Peel felt that, by the last few years, he and Mason had got Johnson adequately trained in their Kentish way of doing things. No question either, about his fits of generosity. Though not rich himself, "Charles" paid for a dignified funeral for an impoverished lady he had got to know. He gave some German mattresses to Frank Mathew Baker, the taxi driver who used to ferry him back and forth between Heathrow and Sheerness. When John Forster, a docker at the port, had a falling out with his wife, "Charles" had offered him a bed in his house.

This retrospective testimony encourages Jens to suggest that the drinkers in the Napier had handled Johnson none too badly. They were quite capable of growling back at the morose outsider they knew as "the owl" as well as "Charlie". They handled his sometimes pedantic-sounding questions about local culture or, particularly, their use of the English language, and they left him in no doubt when he breached the limits of acceptable behaviour. Without straying far from their customary repertoire of shrugs, jokes and grunts, they had looked after Johnson in their own way. It was in their company that the writer found not just a driver but someone to help tend his garden or to look after his daughter when he and

Elisabeth were away, or to joke about his plan to counter the effects of Dutch Elm Disease on the town's trees by planting a potentially vast, Mecklenburgian "white poplar" in the small garden at the back of his house. When they hadn't seen their resident alien for a while, the people of the pub, who never really knew when he was off on one of his trips abroad, would despatch a party along Marine Parade to knock on his door, as happened after his heart attack in 1975, and they did these things while also leaving him alone. "I don't want to get personal" is among the English phrases Johnson noted with approval, along with other collected gems — "We want you to stay as you are: handsome and poor","All gone to buggery" and no doubt others of a more local nature, such as the present-day example, "There's money on Sheppey but nobody knows where it is."

It is likely Jens was right to suggest that the "common people" in the pub coped with Johnson better than the intellectuals who'd recoiled from his impossible outbursts in the literary world of West Berlin. They also handled Jens in their own obliging way, offering their testimony in the deadpan catastrophic tone characteristic of the more abandoned towns around the Thames Estuary. We can't crawl back into the bar to count up the rounds Jens may have bought to lubricate his enquiries, but he managed to get the cardiganed publican Ron Peel to oblige his attendant photographer, Nomi Baumgartl, by acting out Johnson's movements during his very last appearance at the bar. He'd come in unexpectedly in the afternoon on 22 February 1984, sweating and looking completely overwhelmed. Having knocked back a pint, he'd left the bar and then returned later, taking off his glasses and rubbing his eyes, as Peel himself went on to do with an appropriately ghoulish expression, and then, after swallowing another three pints, finally stepped out into oblivion with a silent nod.[23]

Fortunately, Johnson can still speak for himself. A few years before that dismal night, he had provided another East German writer, Walter Kempowski, with his own account of his encounters with the people of Sheerness, on the promenade but also, to be sure, in the pub:

⟨A GERMAN AMONG THE ENGLISH⟩

It is also high time to answer your question about how the German is doing here among the English.

As my first witness, I call a retiree whom the gentlemen his age respectfully call "Major", who noticed my accent straight off and wanted to know more precisely where I came from. — From Berlin, I offered, keeping in mind the people in Berlin whom he had every reason to want to impugn. — **Berlin, what a splendid city!** he cried. He'd spent his honeymoon there, in 1921. And he wanted to buy me a round — **be a dashing young fellow tonight!** he encouraged. What I learned from others was that he had marched into Berlin with the first troops, in 1945, and that ever since then he had expressed an unshakeable opinion about the Germans as a race, but making an exception for me, the individual, the guest.

As my next witnesses, I present people on the promenade, passersby, neighbours. We open the conversation, as one does, with the weather. Gray weather we're having, dampish, makes for long nights; it surely is annoying how there's nothing on the telly. — Nah there's something tonight, someone says, and I know the program he means, since he says the time it's on: 9:25. A documentary about Auschwitz. But he looks right past me and says peevishly: Oh, just an ol' story from the war.

Another one takes the spot next to me and tells me outright that I have a German background, immediately transitioning to the comment that I was lucky, geographically speaking, since if I was from the Ruhr he would have helped bomb me to **ducking bits,** possessor as he is of the **Distinguished Flying Cross.** But that's all over now, he says, and he says he forgives me, as far as he's concerned. Says it and that's that. I never saw him again, because he was banned from the bar for breaking the rule in force there: talking about politics is indelicate, and private attacks are not allowed.

In sum, they are unanimous in never forgetting the German's nationality and history while the majority have decided not to talk about it, in order to leave him in peace, since he clearly prefers coming to terms with it in silence.

This can be taken to the point of protecting him from other people with that same background, Germans on holiday comparing their respective native cities a little too loudly with this one, which seems to them ugly, cramped, poor, and dirty. They try to convey in English that they desperately need to find a roof over their heads, a bed under their backs, and breakfast included. The locals know that there is a German sitting right there with them, who could ease these visitors' accommodation and orientation problems straightaway in their own language. But since they can see from his whole demeanour how little connection he feels or wants with such countrymen, they conceal him in a conversation in English and watch the tourists leave as if they had something urgent to say on the tip of their tongues that they would nonetheless refrain from saying, at least to me. And I think I might have some idea what it is.

⟨Letter to Walter Kempowski, 3 August 1981[24]⟩

*

Many of the stories Tilman Jens gathered in the Napier Tavern recounted events that had actually taken place in a different Shepherd Neame establishment on the other side of the Broadway. The now demolished Sea View Hotel was a considerable Victorian building that stood next to the Catholic Church and only a hundred or so yards to the west of the Napier, and it was here, in the bar on the southern side of the hotel, that Johnson had first become familiar with the joint publicans Ron Peel and Col Mason. It was also here rather than in the Napier, which Peel and Mason only took over in 1981, that his first Christmas Eve "baptism" as "Charles" had taken place: thanks, according to Johnson's version of the story, to the initiative of "a man known as Joe".[25]

For Jim Enright, who remembers the Sea View as it was in the Sixties, the room that mattered most in those days was on the first floor and called the "Rose Room". It was here that

Enright, or "Stitch" as he was known at the time, started running a dance music club. As described in *The Rise and Fall of the Beat Groups in Sittingbourne*,[26] Enright was drummer with the Rock Spots and then with the Rebounds, which he had founded as the first beat group in the area in 1959. He'd launched the Rebounds Dance Club after the people running the previous trad jazz nights in the Rose Room had thrown in the towel. He remembers pushing the fights out onto the sea wall directly to the north of the hotel, and being commended by a Sheerness policeman who declared himself pleased to know where all the island's villains could be found on a Saturday night. As for hiring bands, Enright had a system of asking aspirants to perform for free on an audition night, and inviting them back for a paid engagement if they made the grade. The bands that passed through on these terms included the Lower Third from Maidstone and Margate, whose recently employed singer, David Jones, would shortly change his name to Bowie.

Enright, who was still in and out of the Sea View in 1974, remembers Johnson as an unexpected, perhaps rather lugubrious presence in the ground floor bar, asking questions which were not always welcome or, for that matter, taken seriously by the younger customers who may only have registered the writer as another of the town's washed-up boozers. The Sea View was by then being given new life by Peel and Mason. Having met while on naval service in the Second World War (their engagements had included the Battle of the River Plate at the close of which the German cruiser *Admiral Graf Spee* was scuttled outside Montevideo harbour), they had gone on to run the Admirals Walk in Blue Town. Remembered as the first openly gay couple to run a pub in Sheerness,[27] they were also ahead of the council in seeing the case for the recovery and renovation of Marine Town. In October 1974, as may be read in one of Johnson's earliest saved copies of the *Sheerness Times Guardian*, Ron Peel was happy to lend the paper a photograph of the area as it had been when "The Sea View was the place to reside", and when music hall stars "like Marie Lloyd played the

Hippodrome and stayed here".[28] For him the Sea View was "steeped in nostalgia and history", and the joint licensees had become the devoted custodians of all its memories: "I love it here", said Peel, "it isn't too difficult to imagine the place when it boasted four bars, attracted the best clientele, and was the finest place in town". Peel had recently paid £10 for a stone cider jar bearing the hotel's name; it was so thickly encrusted with barnacles that he reckoned it must have been in the sea for a century. A week later he was sent an identical one that someone had dug up in a garden in Gillingham: "Call it coincidence, but there is an atmosphere about the hotel that defies description, and I can't help feeling there is a connection between the two 'finds'". So Peel and Mason were engaged in a providential as well as contrary project: trying to make a going concern of the past, pushing back against the dereliction and demolition gripping so much of the area, while also fund-raising for local causes in concert with other members of the Sheppey Licensed Victuallers and Beer Retailers' Protection Association. In November 1974, Peel claimed that "By such efforts we've helped to provide bedside radios for the sick, aid the lifeboat and to lay concrete paths to the new church".

Unfortunately, the Sea View's customers hadn't always proved worthy of the licensees' determination to keep this venerated Sheerness institution on the right side of oblivion. In February 1975, Peel and Mason were robbed by a group of men on a stag night pub crawl. Before moving on to trouble the next publican on their path, the celebrants had nicked an "oak plaque" the two naval veterans had commissioned to mark their war service on the cruiser *HMS Ajax* and the convoy-escorting destroyer *HMS Kempenfelt*. "We are getting sick of this pilfering", said Peel: "Every week something is taken, not only ashtrays and ornaments, but even the chalk and darts from the board... This crowd only took the plaque — they threw the darts at an aspidistra plant and speared the leaves".[29] Of course the two publicans kept going. By November 1976, when the scaffolding that had covered the building for eight months (and confined its operation to the smallest bar) was removed, the hotel would open two bars: "sleekly modernised" but furnished in traditional style, as was promised: "We wanted the hotel to resume some of its former grandeur".[30] Aware that the place once had fourteen bedrooms and a ballroom capable of accommodating 150 guests, their dream was "to put the Sea View once more in the five-star bracket".

By that time Johnson was already finding his place among the Sea View's regulars: a generous supplier of coins to the Salvation Army, he also bought tickets for the lotteries run by the pub, and in some quantity despite his fear that one of his numbers might come up. In December 1975, he had won an unwanted Christmas cake in a raffle held on behalf of the Royal National Lifeboat Institution: it was, as he told Alice and Dorothy Hensan in Rostock, "a veritable Alpine landscape, that cake, with ski-jumps, mountain cabins etc., and weighs about five pounds",[31] and he'd rashly bought ten tickets ("when the boys showed it to me I could read the challenge"). A few years later he would find himself pulled into a photograph that would be printed in the *Sheerness Times Guardian* on 15 September 1978. Col Mason, is handing a cheque for £184 to Mr Larry Larsen, the chairman of the local Kidney Unit Fund. The money for this vital hospital service had been raised by the pub, "mainly from very generous donations from customers", although £60 had been brought in by a raffle that very night in which the winner, a lady from the Rushenden estate near Queenborough, had won a bedspread. The mayor is in attendance, complete with his chains, and so too is Johnson: an uncaptioned figure standing alongside others at the back. He looks neither well nor particularly keen to be included, but he is definitely there:

⟨WELCOMED INTO THE COMMUNITY⟩

Now, I wanted to win that bedspread for you. Further details can be found on the two enclosed raffle tickets, and as for this white monstrosity's weight, I will say only that the ladies' knees buckled slightly when it was placed on their two arms for them to admire it. I would also like to mention that I had in my possession the next four numbers consecutive to each of these, in other words ten chances in all to win.

The night of the draw, Norman (second from the left) was only slightly more excited than Ron (fifth from the left), the donor for this lottery. For Norman's wife had spent more than a year knitting the bright white lump in the foreground — knitting, stitching, weaving, knotting, sewing, what do I know — and as he told a man he didn't know, a foreigner, living on Marine Parade (third from the right), he already had three people picked out in case he won the blanket himself. Now it turns out Norman's daughter sold the ticket

— I could kick myself! she says to one Mrs Stanton, but she is related to Norman's family, and so off he went with the thick bale to take it to her.

If it had gone to me, you would have received quite an amazing package in the near future.

⟨Letter to Alice and Dorothy Hensan, 15 September 1978[32]⟩

And that wouldn't be Johnson's only appearance in the island media. Two months later, he featured as "Mr U. Johnson" in the *Sheppey Gazette*, this time as the spokesman and scribe of the group of Sea View customers who had nominated Col Mason for a "Local Life Award" offered by the national Brewers and Licensees' Association and open to pub landlords who had made a significant contribution to their community.[33] In his commendation, which the paper in turn commended as the first ever gained by a Sheppey publican, Johnson mentioned Mason's work for charity, including his successful fundraising for the hospital kidney machine (the appeal had gone ahead in a fit of broadmindedness even after a doctor came to the island to explain that the NHS unfortunately lacked the facilities to station the device in question actually on the island), and also his kindness to his competitors in the trade, who knew him as a former chairman of the Sheppey branch of the Licensed Victuallers Association. Johnson's central point, however, was that Mason understood exactly how a publican should treat his customers:

> "He provides a sanctuary for the time between the strain of work and family's demands to follow and he does it in a friendly, quiet sort of way", says Mr U. Johnson, of Marine Parade, Sheerness, who leads a band of regulars who believe Mr Mason to be one of the best "mine hosts" in the business.... Mr Mason will blush with pride when he hears that Mr Johnson has this to say of him: "strangers, even foreigners, feel welcome ... It's a place you like to live in for one or two hours ... he does not force the customer into conversation, but is always quite ready for it. He remembers customers and their habits even after they have been away for three years. He is concerned about his customers' affairs once they are brought to his attention ... he never gives away confidential information."

Such, then, was the largely male society in which Johnson occasionally let his "non-committal" guard drop. A well-kept pub may have been full of well-maintained distances, but the Sea View and Napier were also places where he was tolerated as well as mocked and sometimes even liked too. A letter written to one of his old school friends in Güstrow reveals that he knew just what he — this curious visitor from Communist Germany — might look like to the Englishmen with whom he now rubbed along "as friends":

⟨SO THAT CHARLES CAN WRITE THE RIGHT THING TOO⟩

Since the previous Friday, too, had turned to evening, after weather that was partly sunny but mostly blasted through with a cold wind, we'd gathered together in our male society, referred to as a beer department store, due to the prices, for we had things to discuss...

Charles comes in, the foreigner, I've probably told you about him already. Real name's something totally different but who can pronounce German names like that, so we rechristened him, suits him pretty well by this point. — Gd'eevenin, Charles! **Good heavening!** As we expect from him, he sits down on the far left stool, which we keep free for him til at least seven, and since the evening paper for Sheerness and the region was laid out for him there as usual, he dutifully starts reading: windows broken in, TV stolen, gold watch for so many years of service..., until he notices a new sign hanging behind the bar:

DO NOT THROW / CIGARETTES ON THE FLOOR / AS PEOPLE LEAVING ON / THEIR HANDS AND KNEES / WILL BE BURNT

We know what's coming next. Charles pulled out his notebook and writes it down. Embarrassing to him but we're used to it. It's one of those phrases that's hard to remember, and Charles apparently can't let that happen in his line of work, whatever it is, something to do with writing. Still, he does find it embarrassing to write in public, so he hurries to get it down and stick the notebook back in his pocket, so that we'll forget about it. That's when he finally realizes that we were all talking at once, talking like crazy.

- Just cut em off. Cut their hands off!
- Chop em off!
- Right here, at the wrist.
- As a taxpayer I represent the view that —

- Right you are! They just live off the dole. Just don't want to work!
- I say chop em off only for repeat offenders. The first time they should just break their arm.
- Under doctor's supervision.

   By this point Charlie had understood enough to realize that we're batting around a philosophical question — the ethics of the penal code — and he asks us the nature of the crime in question.
- **We've been turned over!** said one of the victims, in an almost enthusiastic tone. They'd had a break-in.
- They broke open the jukebox, the one-armed bandits, drank all the bottles dry —
- And the telephone? Charles asked. Did you report any calls to the phone company?
- What? we say. What are you talking about, Charles.
- They could have called Yokohama on your phone.

   We just have to shake our heads at that. Only Charles could think of something like that. That's just how he is.
- They were just amateurs, Charles.
- Young people, out for a good time.
- I'm not saying anything about anyone specifically, but the boys knew their way around, one of them could be standing right here in the room with us.
- Damn right!
- I have my ideas, I'll tell you that.
- They took all the rum, all the martini, vodka, eggnog, but left a bottle of whisky untouched. That tells me something.
- A clue. Someone who couldn't drink whisky!
- Chop his hands off!
- Nah, another of the victims said. If they'd only have put the empties back on the bar, though, they could've washed up a bit. That's the only thing I hold against em.

But we are for chopping off, breaking, and otherwise mistreating the offending, thieving hands.

   ...
- Children! Children! the publican finally says — ominous,

the patriarch in full possession of his householder's rights —
but it was too late, Charles had already taken in a whole heap
of thought-provoking material. True, he acts like he was just
reading his carefree way through the newspaper for the Isle
of Sheppey and its surroundings, but we can see right through
him. The truth is, he's trying to retain and remember everything.
Want to bet that when he got back home he writes it all down?

That was why we tell him, quietly and casually of course,
our good wishes for Lady Di too, for 29 July namely, or rather
for the morning after the wedding night: let her be in such a
good mood that she says to the man in bed next to her, in a
sweet voice: **Oh my Royal Highness dear ... do the poor get
this?**

So that Charles writes the good stuff down too. Because
he's going to write a book about this island of ours someday,
how can you doubt it. He won't be able to help it. Just look at
us. How we're put together. How we say whatever comes into
our heads, can't keep our mouths shut.

⟨Letter to Heinz Lehmbäcker, 16 April 1981[34]⟩

The drinkers in the pub found ways of making their own
use of Johnson's writing habit — his papers included the
typescript of a letter, written as a member of "The Oversights
Committee" to be sent to a miscreant member of their company,
John Jakaley, of 56 Marine Parade. As Johnson notes in a
scribbled comment, this fellow was born in 1920, the son of a
Russian sailor named Jakovlev who had jumped ship in 1917.
He was instructed, in this communication of 9 October 1982,
to buy himself a frying pan, get his eyes examined for glasses
and leave his body to medical science, wrongly assumed to be
pursued at the University of Kent at Canterbury (phone number
provided). The fellowship of the Sea View and Napier would
sometimes also include their East German friend in their trips
to other hostelries on the island, and Johnson reciprocated by
inviting them to join him in on longer excursions:

⟨AN INVOLUNTARY TRIP⟩

In my letter from a good month ago I told you I would be taking an involuntary trip to New York, and in fact no strike has prevented me from doing so. I had prudently invited a companion to come with me, a man known as Joe who earlier gave me my nickname on the island, Charles, and who, in the present state of consumer society, is up for any sort of small task and particularly for keeping the keys for the various businesses, from the hair salon to the funeral home. He once deflected my offered thanks for support he'd offered with the words: **I did it as a friend,** and perhaps we really are **as friends.** It was his first time taking an airplane, his first time leaving the country at all, and his experience of New York started off in an "overwhelming way", namely with the New York Airways Sikorsky helicopter in which he was suspended for nine minutes before the crazy towers on the southern tip of Manhattan and above the parched quadrangle of Central Park. We had to do a lot of tourist things for his sake: walk across the George and Martha Washington Bridge, take a pleasure trip to Staten Island on the South Ferry (usually a ship only commuters take), drive for fun across the Verrazano Narrows Bridge, go see Coney Island (in April!), and avoid Harlem because he does have a family. But I did have something to do on Upper Broadway, in Riverside Park too, and when we walked by under the windows of the building where we, this is a different we now, lived years ago, he praised the view. So it was nice to have someone along, not to be forced to be alone with the other contents of my mind, which were, of course, present enough just then, as indeed on every other day.

So, back to Sheerness: runs the answer. Here is where my taxes are paid; here stand two rooms full of material for the conclusion of **Anniversaries.**

⟨Letter to Erika Klemm, 4 May 1977[35]⟩

Johnson arranged a different trip for a seventy-four-year-old — "one of the aboriginal inhabitants of the island" — who is also named "Charlie". This fellow, whom Johnson would describe as "the only new friend of my later years",[36] had long since appointed himself to the job (although he won't take money) of caring for the roses in Johnson's garden, "bringing to bear the convincing argument that he is just better at it".[37] By April 1979, however, Charlie has fallen ill. As Johnson goes on to explain, he has:

⟨A GOOD IDEA, CHARLIE⟩

... "a sudden painful lump" in his stomach area ... For weeks now he has not been able to keep down any food, and he has gotten so weak from weight loss that he walks unsteadily. He is stubborn too, so he has only recently requested an x-ray. He is obviously in very bad shape but they've put him at the end of the waiting list anyway — it will be his turn in three weeks.

"Yes. What you're thinking is what I am afraid of too".

On days when the swelling goes down and he is "almost pain-free" Charlie, who lives alone having managed with much difficulty to get a divorce, talks about what he would like to do when he is healthy again:

"He will take a trip to the Isle of Man.

What can his visitor say? Nothing comes to mind except: Good idea, Charlie.

Yesterday he asked me (-Excuse me, Charlie, I don't want to get personal) what I had planned for June, and I told him. I did not have a single workday free.

-- Too bad, he said. If?? In June I really do want to go to the Isle of Man, and it would have been a pleasure to ask if you would care to come with me".

⟨Letter to Burgel Zeeh, 4 April 1979[38]⟩

It may not have happened in June, but Johnson did respond to the request, organising a trip, negotiating it into reality by presenting it as "one of my whims"[39] and then accompanying the older "Charlie" to the island that, for reasons that remained mysterious, he yearned to see. The trip would prove almost more than the gravely unwell old man could handle, but Johnson went through with it: "We spent many afternoons practicing mutual silence across two big teacups; everything that needed to had long since been said."

24. SHEERNESS AS "MORAL UTOPIA"? (ON NOT MEETING RAY PAHL)

One of Johnson's most complete "island stories" was written in October 1978 for an edition of a German literary journal concerned with "Exemplars". Entitled "An Exemplary Case", it describes the events that befell "Jonathan", the name with which Johnson masks a man who has only consented for his experiences to be recorded on that condition and "since they're not about me".[1] On the evening in question, Jonathan had been in the pub with "Charles" and three others. He had set off for home a little earlier than usual, apparently at his wife's insistence, leaving fellow drinkers feeling "a little bad for him".

By the time their discussion had moved on to the recently imposed ban on using garden hosepipes, thanks to which Johnson's parched lawn was unlikely to be improved by the "capful of rain the wind was scattering across the island at the moment", Jonathan was driving along what he took to be "an unfrequented road" a couple of miles to the east. Suddenly, "his car conked out, throwing him through the windscreen, and across several yards of jagged cement that ripped open his skin". Jonathan had lost consciousness when his head hit the ground, and "much to his relief, since a second car was unexpectedly there on the street, occupied by a woman and numerous children and now lightly dented by Jonathan's; he would not have enjoyed waking up with such a memory. He could rely on our obituaries, his wife likewise: He'd only had three half-pints, we say, and: It must have been this cloudburst.

The usual sort of thing one tells a woman who might be half an hour away from a widow's fate. Here, with the ambulance and police hurrying to the scene, is where the story would end in many another part of the world".

"Not so", however, "on the Isle of Sheppey". Instead of "preparing a statement and exploring the possibility of pressing charges against Jonathan", the driver of the other car "calls the ambulance for him and stands faithfully by as he is loaded into it". She picks up one of Jonathan's shoes, which she finds some fifty feet from the wreck, hoping that it might still be fit for use. "Neither her children's bewilderment nor her own rain-ruined hairdo is enough to make her husband decide to bellow pre-emptively at Mrs Jonathan, rather he gives her his card and promises to help her however he can with the insurance company. So Jonathan's wife has something in her hand as she is driven off to casualty with the nearly lifeless man".

The hospital is on the mainland, ten miles away in Gillingham, but Jonathan's wife soon has "someone at her side" as she waits outside the operating theatre in which her husband "might well be dying under the doctor's knife". The man in question had been standing next to Jonathan at the bar, and knew how to be helpful: "he lied the three pints down to one and a quarter, applied the worthy adjective 'brilliant' to Jonathan's driving abilities, and above all assured her that the children in the other car may, at the very worst, have had a hair on their heads bent out of shape". By the time of the second emergency operation, at around midnight, he is still there, failing to distract the nearly widowed lady from thoughts of "how handy a trust in God sometimes was, in case there should be one", by pointing out "the blind smile" that could surely be seen, oxygen mask permitting, on Jonathan's face.

Jonathan would later marvel at the persistence of this particular friend: "he had spent almost the whole night lurking in the hospital corridor? On his feet? Without smoking? Well if they'd had a chair there ... he retorted, almost snippily". Before that, however, his wife had to deal with a different challenge.

The surgeon had at first left it open whether Jonathan would ever speak again, or, indeed, be anything other than "a total write-off like his car". So how was she to get back to the hospital to visit him? It was a long way off and the "less-than-rapid" train was expensive. The answer was provided by the driver of the car Jonathan had crashed into, who called "not lusting for revenge but rather offering to lend her his second car!" "How embarrassing", then that "Jonathan's wife does not even know how to drive, she has him for that. Not now. From that morning on there was a private taxi service for her, she could call upon neighbours, friends, and acquaintances round the clock and she sat at Jonathan's bedside twice a day". At home, meanwhile, there was "help with the children, with shopping, with staying by the phone — all of that was casually included in the net of assistance that had been woven around her". Despite the penalty points that eventually appeared on his licence, Jonathan remained adamant that the blame belonged to the used-car dealer who had obviously unloaded a car with "defective steering" on him. "Asked in an official capacity whether he was feeling any pain, he [had] answered like the legendary Indian nailed to a tree with a hail of arrows: *Only when I larf*."

*

Two years earlier, in October 1976, Johnson had described the events behind "An Exemplary Case" in a letter to the German writer Hans Joachim Schädlich, then living under increasingly difficult circumstances in the GDR. Having outlined the story of "Jonathan's" accident and community-assisted recovery, he manoeuvred around the unspoken question of drink-driving and its advisability or otherwise to declare that he could think of no place in the world where one might rely so completely on friendship and solidarity as the Isle of Sheppey. He went further, suggesting that, by moving to Sheerness, he had found his way into a "moral utopia".[2]

Sheerness as a "moral utopia"? Definitely not for Mr Eric Nicholls, the publican at the Brewery Tap, on Sheerness High

Street. Johnson's newspaper tells us that, during the night of 10 December 1974, he was knocked about and tied up by a pair of bungling Sheppey brothers who, in the course of a burglary, locked him in the lavatory where he was discovered the next morning in such a traumatised state that he died a few days later.[3]

And not for the TV "psychic" Mia Dolan, who grew up during these years in Minster, a mile or two east along the coast from Sheerness. Her father was a former merchant seaman who had gone into sales, while her mother came from a family that "stretched its roots between Italy and Lancashire" and had settled on Sheppey after her grandfather was posted to an army barracks there. In her memoir, *The Gift: The Story of an Ordinary Woman's Extraordinary Power*,[4] Dolan describes the simple pleasures of an island childhood in which she'd enjoyed the shingle beach and dreamed of becoming a classical ballerina after excelling in lessons at a local dance school. Unfortunately, her childhood was also disrupted by the molestations of "Uncle Arthur". The abuse had resumed when a man of twenty or so hit on her, still only thirteen or fourteen, at an under-sixteen disco at the Sheppey Comprehensive School. "Tony" stalked Dolan for weeks, hanging around her school and house, jumping out of bushes to grab her as she passed: he even followed her to Devon, where her worried parents had sent her to stay with a grandparent for safety, and trapped her overnight in a Victorian beach shelter. Six weeks after the Devon police dismissed her attacker without charge and sent her back to her parents on Sheppey, "Tony" caught up with her again at the Sheerness fairground, took her off at knifepoint ("the blade was a foot long") to an isolated and desolate slope along the seafront — local boys called it "the Greenhill Café", when they invited girls to join them there — and raped her.

After reporting the assault, which appears from Johnson's newspaper collection to have happened in 1975, Dolan discovered the dark side of island solidarity. She faced the accusations circulated by Tony's friends, who visited the accused on remand, believed his lying protestations of innocence, and put it about that she was "a slag" and a "prick tease" who had invited the approach. She was attacked by a gang of girls in the toilets at school and, when she struck back at them, falsely accused of being the aggressor by the supposedly progressive headmaster. Eventually, "Tony" was tried at Maidstone Crown Court and Dolan endured two days of interrogation in which his barrister tried to portray this fourteen-year-old child as a willing and experienced seductress. Her assailant got seven years, and Dolan went home to a family facing other difficulties thanks to her father's loss of health and bankruptcy.

In her memoir, Mia Dolan remembers the rape as the moment she realised, as her spirit seemed to split away and float somewhere above her assaulted body, that she possessed the psychic powers that would later bring her fame as a clairvoyant, while also drawing clients, including the derelict Royal known as "Fergie",[5] across the Swale to Sheerness, where they hoped to receive insights from the spirit world. Dolan may well have discovered unexpected potentialities in "ordinary" life, but her story hardly adds to the case for considering Sheerness a "utopia", moral or otherwise.

That, however, is really not what the German author meant. In a later letter to Schädlich, Johnson, who was well aware of the town's underside, admitted that his wife Elisabeth also reckoned that he had exaggerated the virtues of Sheerness when claiming it as such. And yet the idea of utopia was definitely alive in the Marxist literature Schädlich and Johnson had studied as students at Leipzig: repudiated in its totalitarian forms but also rehabilitated, not as a fantasy island projected across space into some remote ocean, nor as a programmatic blueprint to be realised through a power-grab and a Stalinist re-engineering of the human soul, but as the pre-figurative glimpse of a possible future in the present. This attempted redefinition of utopia, by now located in historical time rather than geographical space, could be found in various sources known to Johnson and his correspondent: in Ernst Bloch's idea of "hope", in the Hungarian philosopher György Lukács's identification of a "second ethics" opposed to the "logic of the institutions of the state",[6] and perhaps especially in the thought of Bertolt Brecht, particularly in the fragmentary *Me-ti* texts from the Thirties (recently translated as *Me-ti: Book of Interventions in the Flow of Things*[7]) which Johnson had edited for his and Brecht's publisher, Peter Suhrkamp, while living in West Berlin in the early Sixties.[8] Here, the utopian impulse is explored as an "intention" for the better, connected to the comparatively modest business of "drawing the conclusion from what already exists" while both ignoring the "priests" demanding the realisation of the *"Great Order"* and also leaving "as much as possible open".[9] It is possible, too, that, even without a few pints of Hürlimann lager, these moments of informal solidarity among people living largely offshore from the state and its regulating institutions somehow impressed Johnson as an unexpected Kentish echo of the suppressed capabilities he had seen breaking through at critical moments in Eastern Europe: the courageous Christian students he had seen jailed or driven into exile from their school at Güstrow, the worker's revolt in East Berlin in 1953, the revolutionary outbreak snuffed out in Hungary in 1956 and — Gesine Cresspahl's destination in the still unwritten closing days of *Anniversaries* IV — the "Socialism with a human face" promised by the Prague Spring of 1968.

"Charles" Johnson would surely have encountered rude English guffaws had he ventured the idea that the Isle of Sheppey might harbour any kind of "moral utopia" in the Sea View or the Napier. There were, however, some on the island who don't just laugh at the thought. I never asked Susan Harris what she made of her neighbour's suggestion, but we can deduce a possible answer from some of the things she did say about the island. She knew full well that Sheppey fell far short of perfection, but she also defended it repeatedly against the mainland knockers who derided the island as a sink of poverty and degradation where people and projects only went to fail. Her point in these defensive interjections, which she was quite capable of making in public meetings as well as in letters to national newspapers, was that islanders did what they could to watch out for one another: "there is", she declared, "a lot of humanity on the island".

And how did the idea sound to Carole Contant, who stayed in Sheerness until after her husband Michael's death in 2002? She has no recollection of Uwe Johnson and would not herself have used such a phrase as "moral utopia". She was, nevertheless, intrigued when I told her that the writer had claimed such a thing for the town where she and her family had lived and performed with their Rainbow Steel Band. Sheerness was poorly placed in conventional terms, and no stranger to failure, violence and grinding poverty. Yet it was also rich in sympathy and a broken-off kind of solidarity that may well sometimes have crossed the frontier of strict legality. Even the local police, she said while gathering up her memories on the phone, seemed "not too bad". All her children, meanwhile, had grown up as "people persons" — good at taking people as they were and finding possibilities in others, an approach they had learned during a childhood in which, even on the hard-pressed street that was Delamark Road, the door was open to everyone. Carole's daughter Jeanette remembers this quality of their life in Sheerness too — people of all sorts coming and going, mothers bringing children to stay overnight because their father had come home drunk. Blue Town was definitely rough, but there was a lot of good to be found among people who were only just coping or getting by. In one of her recent Bahá'í-influenced songs, Jeanette, who nowadays lives in Florida and performs as "Kiskadee", sings "I may not even like you, but you're my brother. One God, one religion, one human race".

*

There was another Sheerness householder who might have helped Johnson deepen his understanding of the situation gripping the people of this town, where a sense of abandonment and disintegration coincided with the defensive solidarity he had glimpsed from his observation posts in the Sea View Hotel and Napier Tavern.

By the mid-Seventies, Ray Pahl, who had been Professor

of Sociology at the University of Kent since it opened in 1965, was in no doubt that Britain was undergoing a chaotic transition from a planned economy in which full employment had seemed an achievable aim, to a far less predictable one that was already producing high levels of unemployment. Though the prospect of a "post-industrial society" alarmed many, it had also been welcomed with varying degrees of recklessness by followers of diverse alternative and oppositional creeds. From such perspectives, intimations of the coming scarcity provoked a sense of promise as well as fear. Though devastating in its impact on long-established communities, "deindustrialization" might also mean a welcome kick in the teeth for the bosses, just rewards for a country that had built its wealth on imperialist extraction, a preliminary step along the road to revolution, an end to dehumanising jobs and the manufactured needs of consumerism. For readers of the Californian prophet of counterculture, Theodore Roszak, we were living *Where the Wasteland Ends:* "*In that sense,* there is nothing to do, nowhere to get. We need only 'stand still in the light'." So this champion of "old Gnosis" concluded on the last page of his book of 1972, subtitled *Politics and Transcendence in Post-Industrial Society.*[10] The apocalyptic vision was shared by other green voices too: from Edward Goldsmith's *Ecology* magazine with its 1972 edition *Blueprint for Survival,* which disconcerted its more critical readers by failing adequately to distinguish its own recommended "back-to-the-land" movement from the variety pursued by Pol Pot in Cambodia, to the gentler anti-growth types who dreamed of fitting domes, solar panels and earth-closets from the *Whole Earth Catalogue* into a smoke-free English utopia that owed as much to the upper Thames visions of William Morris' *News From Nowhere* (1890) as to the Shire of Tolkien's Middle Earth.

There is nothing at all to suggest that Ray Pahl was personally tempted by the unstolen "wonders of being without"[11] — hymned by Spirogyra, an acid-folk band launched at the University of Kent in 1969. He was, however, intrigued by the idea that leaving behind the expectations of full employment and "affluence" may not be a matter of loss

417

alone. Indeed, he would offer several grateful nods to Marshall Sahlins' 1972 book *Stone Age Economics*, with its exploration of the "original affluent society" said to have been inhabited by our hunter-gathering ancestors: folk who don't appear, at least in Sahlins' pages, to have "worked" very hard at all for their survival (this view has since been much criticised, not least by Ted Kaczynski, the imprisoned Unabomber, who has taken Sahlins to task for grossly underestimating the work it actually takes, say, to turn a deer skin into something even a stone age being might consider wearing).[12]

Pahl started with the fact that "very little creative political thinking"[13] was being applied to the British economy's collapsing condition. Industrial manufacturing was in apparently irreversible decline, transformed by various developments including the "micro-processor revolution,"[14] which was already promising to undermine established habits of centralisation and nationalisation.[15] An average of 134,000 British jobs had been lost every year over the decade up to 1976. It had been anticipated that the gap would be closed by new openings in the service industries, yet by the mid-Seventies that expansion seemed to have stalled. It was with these facts playing on his mind that Pahl started visiting some of the coastal towns in north Kent, intent on exploring the implications of this decline in industrial employment "for the organisation of our society"[16] and to ask what might become of both "work" and "unemployment" in a society facing an apparently permanent dearth of jobs.

Uwe Johnson may have been in a league of his own, but Pahl wasn't an entirely easy man either, and he leaves little doubt that he was relieved to be escaping his colleagues as he climbed into his car and headed north to the Medway towns. Personal antipathies aside, he had wanted to break with the "Golden Age"[17] stereotypes pinioning too much sociological discussion of work in Britain. Although many of the students at the University of Kent knew better from their own experience, their lecturers were still influenced by an anachronistic notion of the "traditional" working-class community — an absurdly generalised idea, so Pahl claimed, which provided no way of telling the difference between, say, a Yorkshire mining village and an East Anglian fishing village, and which came encrusted with auxiliary clichés: the "typical image of the factory worker attending meetings of his union", for example, or the assumption that this industrious fellow's wife stayed at home cooking and looking after the children, and that "work" only meant "employment" as represented by the full-time male job.[18]

Pahl opened his search for reality in Chatham and Rochester, where he "sat around in cafés and visited people in their homes".[19] He found himself looking onto "a Dickensian, rather colourful stage where 'the characters' live in a world of second-hand cars and bikes and stalls at the market, and flitted from one derelict house to another". His interlocutors shared a "spirited and aggressive" view of the world — including one petty criminal who vanished into jail, allegedly sent down by the very judge "whose house he had recently re-wired 'for cash'". These initial encounters also seemed to justify Pahl's suggestion, made in an article published in 1976, that while "It may not take long for a nation of shop-keepers to turn into a nation of hustlers", it might also turn out that considerations of locality and community matter more than the post-war modernisers had grasped, and that, with conventional work giving way to less formal livelihoods, "a society based on *whom* you know rather than what you know, may be a more humane, pleasant and happy society in which to live".

⟨ONE OF MY FRIENDS IN SHEERNESS⟩

Since you have a son in the navy, I will add something that happened to one of my friends in Sheerness recently. Purser in the merchant marine by trade, employed by one and the same shipping company for the past thirteen years, he was suddenly, totally unexpectedly, fired for "incompetence". That's how he tells the story, but you never like to hear that someone you know is inept and bad at his job, so I asked various people in the know and discovered that it was probably because of his generosity: for example, he raised the pay for a Hong Kong-Chinese crew from the lower level it had been set at to the normal amount for European sailors, and as a not unexpected result received a warning for having exceeded the estimated expenses, and then another warning, if not the third that would have led per his contract to his being fired. This background, however, apparently lies farther back behind another background, in which shipping companies would rather spare the expense of a purser's salary altogether and replace his job by installing coin-operated machines that the crew members can use to obtain their own pre-cooked meals on the ships, reheated in microwaves, entirely without any selection, preparation, or service from a person who has learned how to do just that and is currently sitting around in Sheerness on dry land, forty-five years old and without much earning potential among three million unemployed. Admittedly, there are other negotiations taking place through his union, which in the best scenario will end with a hearing before an industrial tribunal, but the shipping company's plans and wishes are too well-known: he would be saying good-bye to the usual severance pay and possibly even his pension, which in any case it has been hard to claim due to his type of position. Due to **incompetence,** a Christian shipping company. The victim, formerly talkative and always ready with a laugh, is walking around gloomily, with only just enough of his former pride left to make so-called good (and actually stupid) encouragement repellent to him, no matter who attempts it.

⟨Uwe Johnson, Letter to Herr Ogrowsky, 5 July 1982[20]⟩

We might now regret that Pahl resisted the temptation to write a paper, or at least an article for *New Society* or the *New Universities Quarterly*, entitled "The Urban Pirate: A Contemporary Style of Getting By".[21] But not, surely, that this geographically-trained sociologist soon headed down stream along the river Medway to the Isle of Sheppey, by now assisted by the Nuffield Foundation, which funded him to carry out a pilot study of the transforming economy of the "industrial island" he would soon turn into his own "laboratory".[22]

Pahl's drive over the Kingsferry Bridge was not just a crossing from the "macro" to the "micro" level of analysis,[23] nor, in the terms that his PhD student and co-researcher Claire Wallace would borrow from the sociologist Basil Bernstein, from the "elaborated" code of middle-class language to the more practical and allegedly "restricted" code of working-class speech. For Pahl, crossing the Swale

KINGSFERRY BRIDGE, ISLE OF SHEPPEY.
THE BRIDGE, 650 ft. long, 50 ft. wide and the lifting span weighing 465 tons was constructed by John Howard & Co., Ltd. Opened by H.R.H. The Duchess of Kent, on 20th April, 1960.

Building the Kingsferry Bridge. Postcard, 1960.

also meant preferring "hard, obdurate reality"[24] against the "disembodied" theories gripping many of his colleagues at the university.[25] Sheppey was where Pahl would take his stand, seeking to go beyond the vivid but far from "scientific" investigations carried out by *Mass Observation* and by writers such as George Orwell and J.B. Priestley in the Thirties. As time went on, he would also claim common cause with E.P. Thompson, the Marxist historian and activist who asserted the case for experience, agency and the historically dynamic nature of social class against what he called the "poverty of theory" in a blazing English tract published in 1978.[26]

Arriving in Sheerness several years after Uwe Johnson and his family, Pahl found himself in a world where many of the changes associated with the coming transition to "post-industrial" society had already happened following the closure of the dockyard and garrison in 1960 — an event that, as Pahl counted the figures, had terminated or "displaced" all 2,500 jobs in the dockyard and also removed five thousand sailors from the local economy at a stroke. The closure had caused a severe rise in unemployment from which the island and its

33,000 inhabitants had never fully recovered. It had also turned the island into the site of an experiment that had been running for nearly two decades without anyone — neither politicians nor sociologists nor any of Britain's literary novelists — bothering to come over to see how the unfortunate guinea pigs were getting along. By the time Pahl and his fellow researchers finished their investigation in 1983, they had established that Sheerness was by no means just a busted town sinking into a marsh at the end of the world. It was also an accidental test-bed on which the "post-industrial" future was being pioneered.

One of the first things Pahl did was to make his way to Sheppey School to see how school-leavers were handling the prospect of going out into a world without the jobs, apprenticeships and domestic possibilities that had existed in the time of the naval station and dockyard. Situated at Halfway, between Sheerness and Minster, this was the largest school in Kent, set up in 1970 after a locally unpopular amalgamation of the Isle of Sheppey's three education authorities. The school, to which the Johnsons sent their daughter Katharina, was a rare comprehensive for Kent, although its first headmaster, Cyril Poster, may have been more inclined to think of it as a "community school" of the progressive kind he had extolled in a book published shortly after his arrival on the island. Poster was inspired by the example of the Danish Folk Schools, by the child-centred education espoused by the American pragmatist John Dewey and by his own experience of the village colleges set up in the Thirties under Cambridgeshire's Secretary for Education Henry Morris, who had seen the school as a way of countering the disintegration of rural life: engaging the rural population, combining "good government" with "self-government" and reaching out into its community as "one of the freest of our English institutions".[27] He identified the mission of the community school with the help of an American educationalist of the Fifties, who had declared that "What we once took to be the essence of community — the common purpose, loyalty, integration, solidarity — are no longer by-products of adjacent habitation".[28] Such was the primary challenge the contemporary school must address, and in doing so it should not waver in its commitment to the "relevance" of its curriculum — despite the contemptuous remarks of Kingsley Amis, whom Poster condemned for mocking that consideration as only fit for the lower circles of "vocational training".[29]

Poster held out with his liberal co-educational vision for six years, insisting that the only true discipline was self-discipline, defending his refusal to countenance corporal punishment while also admitting, as Johnson may well have gathered from his copy of the local paper, that "Hair-pulling and scratching were things I don't think I had seen before I came here".[30] His successor at the Sheppey school, Richard Barson, confessed to being a "disciplinarian" by comparison: "I am in favour of good order", he reassured the *Sheerness Times Guardian* on his appointment in December 1976.[31] He would soon be talking about introducing a school uniform too.

Barson permitted Pahl to devise an experiment that would help him investigate how sixteen-year-old school-leavers with poor (if any) qualifications were coping with the prospect of joining an island economy with "one of the highest levels of unemployment in the south east"[32]. With the help of teachers, he asked pupils who would be leaving in about ten days' time to imagine that they were actually in their sixties and about to retire, and to write the story of their working life as they imagined it might by then have turned out.

Having received ninety essays by boys and fifty-two by girls, Pahl informed readers of *New Society* that he was "staggered by the warmth and sensitivity which the youngsters revealed despite the rough and rather coarse first impression one gets from meeting them in a classroom".[33] Beyond the predictable fantasies of wealth, adventure and sexual prowess, he noticed that the essays showed a level of awareness and introspection that was both "impressive and alarming". They revealed a heart-rending expectation of disappointment and failure — epitomised by a boy who anticipated dragging himself through a sequence of dreary low-paid jobs in "a hearse of a life that would eventually lead me to the cemetery gates".[34]

Alongside this devastating sense of futility, Pahl noticed that the economic climate was putting both boys and girls in breach of traditional gender roles. The boys seemed to be placing more value in home, marriage and having children as sources of possible satisfaction, and also in the superiority of working for yourself rather than for an employer. They were heavily reliant on personal loyalties, and exhibited a fierce mistrust of the state, which they believed could only see them as a servant, informer or statistic.

The girls in this "isolated and very traditional working-class community, where the ties of kinship are strong",[35] proved to be clearheaded about the low-paid factory and clerical jobs they would eventually have to give up in order to care for their anticipated two children. Though struck by their "cruelly correct perception" of the lives awaiting them, Pahl nevertheless speculated that the island's girls might actually have "a more varied range of satisfactions" open to them than the boys. "For the girls to despair, they would have to despair of life itself." Allowing that biological assumption to pass, he suggested that the girls' awareness of children, household responsibilities, sickness and death might make it easier for them to place the difficulties of employment and money in a wider perspective: "Somehow the girls had the rich tapestry of life as a source of satisfaction. The boys were more dependent on their work".[36]

Pahl ventured that significant levels of domestic stress might be anticipated since the boys would not be out of the house as much as their fathers — who had almost certainly spent the day at work, and then perhaps the evening at one of "the many working-class clubs that flourish in the community".[37] Indeed, it seemed possible that these girls might manage pretty well without husbands. "I predict a pattern in the future in those working-class communities with high levels of unemployment, where female-headed households become increasingly common."

He also guessed that there might be "a switchover in traditional roles", with girls showing more interest, and even finding some relief, in the kind of jobs they might do, and boys relying more on their roles as "husband and father". These changes, which Pahl also sensed in his wider encounters around Sheppey, convinced him that women were likely to "play an increasingly dominant role in employment", while men were more susceptible to cynicism, and the belief that "I'd be better off on the dole". He imagined a future way of life in which "levels of unemployment will stay high, but much of it will be voluntary". Anticipating that "Home and domestic activities" would become "the central binding element in working-class marriages", he adopted them as a central point of enquiry for his later investigations into the way the "household", as distinct from the full-time and predominantly male job (of the type that had both "abstracted" the worker from his life and, as Pahl would later suggest, blinded sociologists, planners and civil servants from understanding what was really going on in the country[38]), was becoming the central institution of the new economic reality. "I admit that I am clutching at straws in the wind", repeated Pahl at the end of his article, but his reading of the school-leavers' essays left little doubt that "endemic unemployment does affect the relationship between the sexes and the nature of marriage".

⟨NOT AT ALL, CHARLIE⟩

Oh, I hope this letter can catch up to yesterday's! For I wrote you something yesterday that is not the way it actually was. Specifically, last night at the Sea View the reflective question came to me: Did "Linda Gibbons"'s husband really and truly take a hammer and... **Not at all, Charlie! He jumped up and down on the bonnet and everything, he is a biggish man, you know.** The rest is true: the car is now useless except to the Sheerness steelworks, where they melt down broken cars into sheet metal used to manufacture new cars.

We stayed on the topic of this "Linda Gibbons" a while longer. Since her separation from her husband, she's been working as a stewardess on our ferry... and now you are shaking your head. Yes, it's true, Sheerness has a car and passenger ferry, and I don't mean across the Thames to Essex, no — to Vlissingen in the Netherlands, which we Anglo-Saxons call Flushing of course, two departures from each location daily, seven hour trip. A little before six in the evening we see it diagonally across the wide mouth of the river bearing down on the port of Sheerness, in as much of a hurry as a fire truck and reminiscent in the distance of a brave little mail boat looking forward to its mooring. And it's at least as big as the Halberstadt, on which we left Warnemünde two years ago, for Gjedser, except ours in its modesty foregoes railroad cars and contents itself with busses. The woman works there, she makes enough to pay for someone to watch the children, who in any case are all old enough to go to school, and now the people from social security come, a kind of unemployment assistance, and they tell her she should give up her job and live on the dole, for the children's sake, who are in a better situation now though. What a thing to say! A lot of people do that in West Germany, Charlie says. Please, that's completely different! Joe Francis Adams, whom, by the way, Charlie's daughter is letting stay in his (Charlie's) house for the length of Charlie's trip to the continent (as we Anglo-Saxons are absolutely incapable of not calling it) — Joe has, in his very own street, a few houses down on the other side, a similar case: an unemployed man on the dole, the man goes for a walk in the morning with an umbrella (I mean really!) while Joe is driving to work. He would really like to whack him one every time, if that weren't so unthinkably impolite. So there we sit, taxpayers every one, and we wonder: **Where is it all going to end?** But that is a ritual; everyone has to answer, in chorus: **In the great big Shepherd Neame Beer factory up in the sky** — hallelujah!

⟨Uwe Johnson, letter to Erika Klemm,
24 September 1975[39]⟩

Claire Wallace, who joined Pahl's investigation as a researcher in 1979, would use different language than Pahl's to confirm that the closure of the naval dockyard had created a formidable "fracture" in "the island's processes of social and cultural reproduction".[40] Her point, which she would later elaborate with the help of various Parisian "theorists" including Pahl's despised Louis Althusser, was that the roles into which the young had been socialised were no longer there to be performed. The "fracture" was having a palpable impact on the experience of work in an island economy where full-time jobs and apprenticeships had been unsatisfactorily replaced with short-term state-funded youth training schemes. It made an aggravation of the rising pressure on the young to engage with "leisure styles and youth cultures", the branded trappings of which would surely be too costly for many would-be participants. It also increased pressure on the family, which was severely tested both in its expectation of traditional gender roles and in the now challenged assumption that "work" was dependable and normally took place outside the home.

This was a challenging prospect, and yet Pahl seems at first to have considered it with near nonchalance. He would claim to have gone to Sheppey with the aim of assessing "the possible importance of the informal, the personal, the small-scale and the slightly illegal as the basic ingredients of a new style in the next decade",[41] and he appears to have been encouraged by his initial findings. Repeatedly, in his early articles, he insisted that unemployment was now "different in some important respects from what it was in the 1930s".[42] He would justify this observation by pointing out that the post-war welfare state had removed many of the direst threats from the experience of unemployment, and that the availability of new kinds of devices — washing machines, freezers, portable power tools — made it possible for people to enter into various kinds of informal activity that should surely now be recognised as "work". The dawn of this imagined new Black & Decker age was being encouraged by two further considerations. The levelling of wage expectations was making it difficult to employ others to do things: "Hiring a cook or a chauffeur has always been limited to a minority" and the same was "now coming to apply to carpenters and glaziers".[43] Thanks, however, to the rise of DIY as a popular interest promoted by diverse magazines and television programmes, the much discussed "de-skilling" of the workforce in the formal economy was also being accompanied by a "re-skilling" in the informal one.

⟨WELCOME BACK⟩

. . . On Saturday a young man, unsummoned and unknown, rang the bell and announced that he had enough Sandtex (a patented plaster substance) left over from a job around the corner to be able to smooth out the façade of my house, badly dinged up by the sea wind, as good as new! Since he gave me a written guarantee, he's been hard at work scraping and painting since yesterday morning. You can pay cash and we'll both just forget about the VAT, agreed?

- And this D. in your name, what does it stand for? David?
- David it is.
- My name is Charles, I said, as one does.

One time last week, we were talking over beer about what a person really and fundamentally needs in order to get through the day, and when it was my turn I confessed: A tomato with morning tea, that's probably it. The next morning I found in front of my door a clear plastic bag full of tomatoes, grown and nurtured in a private garden, and I also know in and from whose they were.

In this part of the world, electrical devices are sold without plugs, and I said once, while purchasing such an object, seemingly helpless but sure of what would follow: Well I guess I could use a plug too. — I'll throw one in, the man said. First of all, we knew each other; secondly, the weather was really pleasant.

⟨Uwe Johnson, letter to Lore and Joachim Menzhausen, 2 September 1978[44]⟩

Initially consoled by this estuarial manifestation of the "cunning of history", Pahl illustrated the new ways of "getting by"[45] with the help of two case studies drawn from his pilot researches in Sheerness. "Mr Parsons" had been made redundant five and a half years previously, when the plant at which he had worked full-time closed down. The children had grown up and left, and "Mrs Parsons" worked in a wallpaper shop and made good use of the 40% discount available to her for purchases. He, meanwhile, was conventionally employed as a postman in the mornings but Pahl was interested to see that he had also improvised a lot of informal work as a gardener — growing his own food on an allotment, storing it in a freezer, and also working for others. Their new livelihood depended on possession of "capital equipment" (a deep freezer, pressure cooker, etc.) and "a familiar world of friends and relations". Mr Parson's home-improvement skills were enhanced by his army training as an electrician, and both his reputation and his list of clients were strengthened by the social standing he gained as a postman.[46]

Pahl's second Sheppey character, "Mr Simpson", was unskilled and, though only thirty-three, seemed unlikely ever to find conventional employment again. Yet he too was keeping busy and, together with his wife who was involved — sometimes with the help of their children — in various forms of home selling and manufacturing in the "hidden economy", making more than the household could expect from social security. Indeed, Pahl suggested that Mr Simpson "had reverted to a pre-industrial pattern of hunter and gatherer". He raised vegetables in an uncle's garden and did decorating for relatives, but he also lived by fishing, ferreting, poaching and, on occasion, buying a bullock from a Sheppey farmer and selling on the butchered meat. In doing this, he appeared to be resuming activities long-familiar to the working classes of coastal England.

As Pahl wrote, "Pre-enclosure traditions live on in some places where the power of the squire was less strong".[47] Thanks partly to the *Anopheles* mosquito, Sheppey was surely just such a place. "In the locality where I am doing my fieldwork the main landowner withdrew in the later seventeenth century and only smaller farmers actually lived on the land. Many of the workers in factory and steel mill come from farming backgrounds and preindustrial attitudes may linger on. Mr Simpson has been convicted of poaching." Questionable as this assumption of long-standing settlement definitely was, Pahl enjoyed the thought that Sheppey, which most middle-class visitors saw only as an "ugly and polluted industrial wasteland", was actually a place where the memory of pre-industrial England survived as a contrary resource: "it seems as though some workers are slipping out of their chains and walking out of the system's front door."[48]

*

In those early articles Pahl urged that the "informal economy" he had discovered on Sheppey should be recognised as "a viable 'culture of unemployment'"[49] and, indeed, that "appropriate public policies" should be contrived in order to harness it to "socially progressive ends"[50] These romantic speculations provoked a number of his academic colleagues into far from "theoretical" expressions of concern. In 1979, some of these emerged at a conference, chaired by Richard Hoggart, at which Pahl and his colleague at the University of Kent, John Gershuny, presented their findings. Written by a journalist from the *Times*, the report of this event claims that Pahl, in the course of drawing out the implications of his initial survey, had suggested that not everyone needed a nine-to-five job, and that people could cope with the experience of being thrown out of work in the formal economy by "resorting to domestic work at home and odd jobs for neighbours and friends in exchange for cash ... by growing food from allotments and hunting, and by gaining support from working men's clubs"[51]

This description of life as Pahl had imagined its possibilities on the Isle of Sheppey had been hailed by another contributor, Alec Dickson, the founder of both Voluntary Service Overseas and Community Service Volunteers. He commended Pahl's suggestion that many of the "psychological needs" once met through full-time employment, including "socialisation", could also be satisfied through the "informal economy". In a remark that may, once again, reflect Marshall Sahlins' influence, he also pointed out that Pahl's depiction of getting by on Sheppey was an "almost exact description of the life of a tribal community in New Guinea". There were more critical listeners, however, who mistrusted the political liquidity of the phrase "informal economy" and suspected Pahl was implying that it was "fun to be unemployed and working illegally". These respondents, some of whom may indeed have felt that Pahl needed less history and more rigorous "theory", rejected his apparent suggestion that the development of the informal economy was "a desirable trend" that would "substantially contribute to preventing mass unemployment".[52] They warned Pahl that "some people might suffer and be exploited" in what was inevitably an ill-regulated sector of the economy, and that the "informal economy" was close to the "black economy", with its perks and tax avoidance, and its tendency to "merge into crime".

"The black economy on wheels?" (Ray Pahl)

Pahl himself would become increasingly worried about the reception of his early findings. Indeed, one of the most engaging aspects of his 1984 book on the Sheppey researches, *Divisions of Labour*, lies not in the self-justifying and waspish stings he continues to aim at "theoretical" colleagues and some of his own collaborators too, but in the candour with which he admits his own early *naïveté*. As he acknowledged with some concern, his first articles on Sheppey were soon being translated and cited around the world. Indeed, as the translations and speaking invitations accumulated, he worried that his suggestion that people were learning to "get by" without "formal employment"[53] was becoming an excuse for complacency and, as a crude form of "monetarism" became the dominant economic creed under Margaret Thatcher, for just letting "deindustrialization" rip. "The idea", so he would confess, "that 'the informal economy' was a positive alternative to an ailing capitalism was the kind of good news people wanted to hear"[54] By 1980, which was still only the first year of "Thatcherism", he was feeling like "a character in a Greek drama who has unlocked something he cannot control". He suffered the same shock of recognition a few years later, when Patrick Minford, the right-wing economist who has recently been dug out of the past to declare how wonderful everything is going to be after Brexit, announced "that unemployed people 'can do useful things at home and even earn some small amounts legally while claiming benefits'"[55] By 1981, when Margaret Thatcher's Employment Secretary Norman Tebbit urged the unemployed to follow the example of his own father in the Thirties and "get on their bikes" to search for work, it was obvious that these were not the "public policies" Pahl had earlier imagined might make a positive force of the "informal economy"[56]

With this anxiety growing in his mind, Pahl resolved to dig deeper into island life. He raised more funding, latterly from the government's Economic and Social Research Council, hired the now-qualified Dr Claire Wallace as one of his research workers and, in 1980, bought and refurbished a house at 18

Delamark Road — a few steps from the Contant family at No. 7 — from which he and his assistants would conduct fieldwork when they weren't "overwhelmed with problems of damp, cracking plaster and marauding drunkards".

The new phase of investigation, which would reveal that Sheppey was not at all the same as a tribal society in New Guinea, was intended to go beyond his first "more unstructured and anthropological" investigations to produce "a more complete understanding of the social composition of households and their division of labour".[57] The plan was to investigate every activity on the island that might be construed as "work", be it done by young or old, men, women or children, and belonging as it might in any of three distinct spheres — formal, informal and communal/household.[58] As a central part of their investigation, Pahl, Wallace and their associates came up with questions about no less than forty-one different tasks and then interviewed 730 island households to see how they were carried out.[59]

By the time they had finished, Pahl's researchers had the data to strengthen his belief that understanding of work must be refocused around the household rather than only the full-time, predominantly male job. The fact that 32% of their respondents had made jam for themselves was among the results demonstrating the importance of understanding women's work, much of it going on within the household. A male form of self-provisioning was indicated by the discovery that 25% had mended the brakes on their own cars (Pahl and his assistants took photographs of men doing this sort of thing on the streets of Sheerness). A few, meanwhile, had engaged in activities that were not always on the right side of the law.

The survey revealed that various factors — he cites the plotland holiday industry, the dockyard, the availability of EEC mortgages for steelworkers — had combined with the island's low house prices, to encourage a remarkably high degree of home ownership. Pahl saw evidence of the latter in the skip-lined streets of Sheerness, in the upgraded plotland developments of Minster, Warden and Leysdown, and in the peripheral council estates, where he, like Tony Benn a little later, noticed the newly-painted front doors with which many former tenants would register their newly-possible access to the "housing ladder".[60]

One of the survey's most arresting discoveries in this connection was that as many as 14% of surveyed households claimed to have fitted a rolled steel joist into their own properties. For Pahl this was not to be understood only as evidence

"The collapse of the apprenticeship system means that some young people learn their trade in the street".

of a retreat into private life. As he pointed out, fitting an RSJ is standard procedure when it comes to upgrading houses in Victorian terraces such as are common in Sheerness. Noting that just over half his respondents had lived in three or more houses on Sheppey, while 15% had lived in "five or more",[61] Pahl concluded that many Sheerness households had incorporated buying, upgrading and selling properties into their financial strategies. It was a manoeuvre that Pahl himself carried out in Delamark Road (and also, he was not ashamed to admit, in Tuscany, where he restored the considerable hill-top country house in which he could accommodate some of his art collection — later donated to the British Academy — and write much of *Divisions of Labour*). In Sheppey, however, such preparations were often assisted by the availability of cheap holiday chalets into which families could move while working on their main property. This realisation represented a considerable novelty for those involved in the study of work. As Pahl himself concluded, "By emphasizing housing as much as employment, the narrow conception of a local labour market has been broadened to include the role of the state

434

and the rules and regulations that structure social relations in different contexts".

*

Pahl found a number of his early assumptions challenged by this later research. He had anticipated that the consciousness of the predominantly working-class people of Sheppey reflected their experience as long-term residents with "deep roots" on the island, and that the more he understood about the past, the more he would be able to share the experiences of the islanders. On the contrary, as he discovered, the majority of respondents had not been born on the island, and two fifths of those interviewed had moved there since the dockyard closure of 1960. Far from being grounded aboriginals — or "Swampies" as the mainland stereotype has it — still instinctively in touch with the traditions of pre-enclosure England as he had fondly imagined, the population was about as mobile here as elsewhere in Britain.

The survey also suggested that Sheppey may not actually have had a huge quantity of "informal" labour going on and that it would be wrong to assume this was particularly widespread.[62] The class structure of the island turned out to be broadly similar to that elsewhere in the country, but with a higher measure of home ownership and considerably more working-class "couple-based" households than elsewhere. Working-class women may have been somewhat better-placed on Sheppey (some employers on the island are said to have preferred to employ women), and it also became apparent that "household structure" was probably more important than social class in defining patterns of work.

As he considered how unemployed households in Sheppey were reacting to their situation, he also began to doubt there was actually anything "unprecedented" about the new situation of the British economy. Indeed, he came to realise that the boom years of the Fifties and Sixties, in which full employment had seemed an achievable goal, were actually exceptional: "The period of rising real wages, of demand for teenage and immigrant labour and of expanding state expenditure in health, social services and education has formed the base level, the conception of what is normal, for politicians, media commentators and many academics".[63] With the shipwrecking of that set of assumptions, his survey suggested the resumption of an earlier and longer pattern of activity as conventional jobs were withdrawn.

Pahl's widely distributed suggestion that the informal economy might convert "unemployment" into a more benign way of life would be an early casualty of his revisions — challenged not just by the finding that women were still doing the majority of domestic work in Sheppey households, but by the discovery that conventional employment and self-provisioning actually went together, and that the latter was not working as a simple substitute for the former. Indeed, the investigation suggested that "a process of polarization is developing, with households busily engaged in all forms of work at one pole and households unable to do a wide range of work at the other". Pahl now concluded that those with more skills and resources would be in a position to make the most of informal opportunities too. Households that were completely without formal employment found it difficult if not impossible to find other forms of work and could not be expected to make the leap. Opportunities for informal work appeared to be declining among the unemployed while those in employment were "better placed to engage in all other forms of work as well".[64]

Having found no evidence that unemployed men on the island did more or less "informal" work than the national average and, indeed, having discovered that more DIY-style self-provisioning was done in working-class households with multiple earners, Pahl recognised that unemployment was actually drawing the "informal economy" into new divisions of labour.[65] He saw an emerging pattern in which perhaps as many as 65% of households have become home-owning and consumption-orientated. These "high self-provisioners" were also "more privatized, inward-looking, home-centred and autonomous". They reflected higher levels of home and car ownership, were largely content with a "style of life based on small-scale domesticity" and were more likely to vote Tory.[66] Beneath them, however, was a "deprived" group of 20–25% living in poverty, and above a "well-salaried or capital-owning" bourgeoisie of 12–15%: "the new line of class cleavage is now between the middle mass and the underclass beneath it".[67] The sociologist who had gone to Sheppey full of optimism about the informal economy had discovered something quite different": "In so far as there is now structural unemployment, a distinctive form of poverty is being created".

In the end, then, Pahl's Sheppey was not a deeply-settled island populated by natives who had triumphed over the problems now facing many communities on the mainland by reviving older, pre-industrial, if not exactly "stone-age" ways of life. It was instead a place where "some of the characteristic problems of de-industrialising Britain" could be seen in a "particularly extreme form".[68] While it remained a prophetic land in which something of the world to come could be glimpsed, "the Sunny Isle of Sheppey" was a place of dark warnings rather than naïve utopian promise.

One of the most important messages relayed by Pahl concerned the importance of place, locality and "area" in the new economic reality. Then, as now, prevailing economic ideology was on the side of mobility. Pahl, however, took the opposite view. He ventured that, if the recession bit really hard, "strength in the labour market" might even become disadvantageous for some who found themselves out of work. His point, which was informed by consideration of some of the new "executive" housing being built around the country (although not yet on Sheppey), was that the "strength" of people with marketable knowledge had conventionally been linking with mobility — "any one locality is merely a staging post in the long haul up a career".[69] This sort of shuttling about had the effect of cutting its people off from any grounded community, and it might leave them particularly bereft when unemployment loomed and local connections became more important.

While rejecting the conventional distinction between (rooted working-class) "locals" and (mobile middle-class) "incomers", Pahl nevertheless insisted that the local context was rendered much more important by the new forms of household economy. Sociologists should "recognize that most people read their local newspapers with greater care than the national ones".[70] Physical separation made this "sharp disjunction between the national and the local" particularly evident on the Isle of Sheppey, but the gap would continue to loom elsewhere too. Pahl conceived this rising localism as a new form of "social consciousness" in which people would come to rely on local self-managed initiatives to "organize various forms of informal and communal work". He anticipated that ongoing economic developments would distribute "life chances" most inequitably between localities in the late-twentieth century. Some would develop rapidly, "with new jobs and capital investment", others would continue to decline, and it was in places such as these — nobody had yet thought to insult the inhabitants with names like "the left behind" — that "all the forms of work outside employment have their greater salience". Just as households in such places might go into internal retreat, local communities might also come to "look more within themselves". A sense of national abandonment was part of this story, but it also suggested the possible development of "greater vigour and determination to cope with social and economic problems at a local level". On Sheppey, Pahl saw signs of this "nascent localism" emerging "very vigorously". "It is not, perhaps, too fanciful to expect the rediscovery of local products, local crafts and ways of marketing local identity and historical associations". A defence of local memory would

also be part of this "nascent" social consciousness. Noting a rising interest in old photographs, old postcards, old people's memories, he ventured that "the stubborn concern of many people on Sheppey not to forget what they see as their 'past' should, perhaps, be considered seriously".

*

It is possible that Pahl was among the passersby who continued to peer down from the promenade along Marine Parade: hoping, even after Johnson had moved a shrub from his back garden in an attempt to reduce his visibility, to glimpse the uprooted East German writer sitting at the typewriter in his basement office. But did these two explorers of Sheerness society ever meet properly to discuss the town's claim to "utopian" qualities? When I put that question to Claire Wallace, who conducted a lot of Pahl's household interviews in Marine Town, she thought not — although she could just about remember "an eccentric German who lived on Marine Parade".

We can only hypothesise, in the subjunctive mood so much favoured by Uwe Johnson. The pub would have been the obvious place for a discussion, since both men treated these hostelries as informal research institutes. We can forget the smart establishment on the Leas at the beginning of Minster to the east of Marine Town where, so Pahl claimed, "a small elite of red-faced men with large stomachs, large Fords and tinselly wives with long fingernails patronize the Playa Club on Minster Cliffs and drink many gins before their steak or scampi and chips".[71] An encounter might surely have gone better in the Sea View or the Napier. Pahl, who was a comparatively urbane figure, would not have been required to share Johnson's enthusiasm for Shepherd Neame's Hürlimann lager, but who could predict which version of the German author he would come up against had he ever tried to join the displaced novelist in "the game of stock phrases and silences"[72] he played with the regulars? He might have been lucky and encountered the interested and sympathetic novelist who was capable both of discussing sociological theory and of exact observation of attitudes, behaviours and linguistic usage. The two investigators might have, for example, reviewed the precarious working conditions experienced by "John" who, as Johnson recorded in an unpublished note, was casually employed to drive 11 imported cars an hour from the belly of the just docked vehicle carrier to the car park three quarters of a mile away and then back by bus for the next one. He earned £2.46 an hour (after tax) on those days, and had to wash his hair every day due to the clinging stench of petrol. He had different problems when using hand trolleys to unload the banana ships. The refrigerated holds caused such dryness in his throat that he was in the habit of going to work with Thermos flasks full of beer.

Then again, Pahl might have been blanked by the "Charles" who preferred to skulk there, sullenly, inside his "bell jar of strangeness". Worse still, he might have been repelled by the more alarming version whose heavy head could swivel round at any moment in the manner evoked by the West German novelist Martin Walser some years later, "like a howitzer" mounted on a coastal rock. This was the Johnson who, as the publican Ron Peel remembered, would interrogate people with a ferocious battery of questions until he had them all squeezed out, who remained pedantic and insistent on accuracy even (or especially) when drinking, and who would stare at a stranger who dared try his luck in the pub with such hostility that the imposter left after a single hastened pint.[73]

No meeting, then, but we can still register how strongly the two men's findings in and around the pubs of Sheerness reinforce one another. Pahl provides a convincing sociological background to the evocations and encounters presented in Johnson's letters and stories: the rise of "self-provisioning" and other DIY initiatives, the difficulty of improvising a "livelihood" in the absence of reliable jobs, even the likelihood of marital stress and breakdown as gender roles changed. Both observers were interested in the ways in which the people of the island made sense of their situation. For Pahl, the prevailing attitudes, which are also captured in Johnson's informal despatches from the barstool, include a forceful and reactive patriotism combined with a libertarian mistrust and, where possible, disengagement from all branches of government. Both observers were familiar with the moaning and hand-wringing with which people expressed their "utter powerlessness in the face of forces based largely outside the island".[74] Both registered that this sense of helplessness was often mixed with a paradoxically fond regard for the employers that did produce jobs in the locality — as distinct from the council and the statutory authorities, which were more or less universally reviled.[75]

Like Johnson, Pahl saw the people of Sheerness as everyday sociologists and philosophers, vernacular raconteurs who had their own theories of history and society, their own polarised stories of "them" against "us". They were highly susceptible to "Churchillian pastiche"[76] and it was surely not only during the national steel strike of 1980, which the men at Sheerness Steel refused to join, that the attractions of a "'Passport to Pimlico' type of UDI" were loudly extolled on the island. The residents had variously stylised ways of looking up at the ceiling and groaning, in the phrase Pahl quotes from a local councillor, that "Enough is Enough". "Many islanders", he remarks, "cannot see the present except in terms of its decline from the past".[77] This tendency to see the world in terms of "before" and "after" is to be found elsewhere around the Thames Estuary. Canvey Island's well-known guitarist Wilko Johnson once told me that while people of his parents' generation living "in England" tended generally to employ the Second World War as the turning point, the decline and fall remembered "on Canvey" pivoted around the fatal floods of 1953.[78] On Sheppey, where nobody died in the inundation of 1953, it was the closure of the naval dockyard that formed the key break. So powerful was the sense of "the world we have lost" that, as Pahl was intrigued to discover, it was claimed as a personal injury even by people who had moved to the island since 1960.

Pahl offered a cod-sociological typology of "Islanders'

Ways of Making Sense of Their World" as he had encountered them when talking to people at home or in cafés, clubs and pubs — and here too his observations share a lot with those of Johnson. According to the "Durkheimian myth", the island had never recovered from the dockyard closure. Before that, they had enjoyed a "strong sense of social cohesion... built up over the centuries, based on the pride of craftsmanship, the patriotism associated with working for the Army and Navy, and the solidarity based on working men's clubs and the co-operative movement".[79] This particular "theory from below" was strongly supported by the *Sheerness Times Guardian,* which resorted to cavalier and bizarre invocations of history in order "to foster the dominance of an imagined past over the present". So strongly was this view felt that, in the wake of Margaret Thatcher's war in the south Atlantic, one correspondent urged readers to think of moving to the heavily subsidised Falkland Islands, where they would surely get looked after far better by the British government than on Sheppey.

Espoused even by pub-goers who had no time at all for any kind of socialism, the "Marxist myth" portrayed the islanders as members of an isolated and trapped labour force, a captive and characteristically docile "reserve army of labour" that had been profitably abused by capitalist extractors who came to suck the wealth out of Sheppey and, given the extensive involvement of foreign capital and companies in and around the by now de-unionised port, often out of Britain too.

The Weberian myth, alternately, emphasised the trials of people who found themselves helpless in the face of rationalisation and bureaucratisation. As Pahl writes, "Resentment against the apparently ever-expanding state was a common topic of pub conversation in working-class areas".[80] Island solidarity was inextricably connected to self-defence against bad council housing, insensitive social security officials "comprehensive schools that do not seem self-evidently good things",[81] and also, as Johnson's story of "Jonathan" invites us to add, the drink-driving laws and breathalysers introduced by Barbara Castle in the late Sixties. Whatever the issue, the decision-makers were always elsewhere, and the island "has always been victim of circumstances over which it has no control".[82]

A great deal of energy was also devoted to repudiating the "psychogenetic" theory, imposed on the islanders by visiting employers, officials of local government or welfare state agencies and, of course, by mainland observers who have long enjoyed cracking jokes about "Sheermess" or even "Sheernastiness".These mainland stories imposed various false ideas about the islanders' origins — alleging that they were the descendants of escaped convicts from the hulks once moored in the Medway, or the result of "substantial inbreeding" from "a small number of landless quasi-gypsy families" or cockneys relocated early in the twentieth century. It was also said that the IQ of Sheppey was lower than elsewhere in the county, and that there were more ESN pupils in the school. Pahl dismisses the theory as a "pernicious myth", which his own investigations had proved wrong in every aspect. Johnson knew that the sun sometimes shone on "backwaters" too. On a good day, he might even have agreed with the woman who betrayed no trace of irony as she told Pahl, "I like it here because it is so central: you've got London and city life in one direction and Canterbury and rural life in the other".[83]

While Pahl's islanders displayed "working-class solidarity" in abundance, this was not, so he concluded rather gleefully, of the kind approved by the academic Marxists who seem to have occupied a place in Pahl's outlook similar to the one Johnson reserved for the well-off and hypocritical New York liberals who made a mockery of the progressive causes for which they occasionally came out of their brownstones and apartment buildings to march about with such self-importance. Pahl suggested that his Marxist colleagues might usefully visit Sheppey and study "the pile of 'useful things' — old doors, planks, bricks, iron bars and the like — that accumulate in the gardens and yards of rural owner-occupied houses 'in case they come in handy one day'".They should then ask themselves whether they hadn't failed to "come to terms with the essence of individualism in ordinary English people" with their strong attachment to "homeliness, cosiness, domesticity".[84] Pahl defended working-class islanders against the fury of "socialists" who scorned "privatisation" and the sale of council housing and considered the desire for a home of one's own to be an act of class betrayal. He also suggested that international corporations might be more reliable employers than some of the homegrown alternatives. He might have dropped his early fantasy that some islanders had deeply settled roots reaching continuously back into a time before the enclosures, but he still placed them in the tradition of the freeborn Englishman, comparing their outlook with the "radical individualism" of the seventeenth-century Leveller John Lilburne.[85]

As he joined Raymond Williams and other contemporaries in looking forward — "Towards 2000", as the imagined future was in those days — Pahl concluded from his Sheppey investigations that the people may not be going much further with "municipal socialism and the teleological planners". It was Johnson who noticed that a negative opinion of Britain's membership of the EEC was already in place when it came to attributing the blame for rising prices ("detrimental" as he noted in a letter to Helen Wolff[86]). Johnson and Pahl may have passed rather than met one another, but they provide mutually reinforcing sighting of the island narratives that would, thirty years later, be mustered behind the cause of Brexit — although not necessarily, once again, in the manner assumed by the academics of our time. I asked one senior drinker in the Belle and Lion, Wetherspoon's thriving pub on the High Street, whether he counted himself among those whom a present-day Professor of Sociology at Kent, Matthew Goodwin, has so influentially dubbed "the left-behind".[87] He didn't need to know the word "agency" — nor, for that matter, to seek guidance from one of Tim Martin's Brexiteering beermats or house magazines — before robustly rejecting the appellation. Far from being a helpless victim of changed circumstances, he preferred, so he told me stiffly, to think of himself as a proud member of "the stayed behind". That may be one latter-day manifestation of the "moral utopia" Johnson imagined finding in Sheerness.

〈THERE SIT THE GUYS〉

Now I would like to tell you the story of fifteen minutes at the Sea View.

There sit the guys, where they've been jabbering away for forty-five minutes already, someone died, well, it's a sign, hard to say what it means, it came in disguise, or: The butcher at the Halfway co-op, filling in for the regular bloke, who decided after a week, at 2:30 on a Saturday, to make off with the week's takings, he was just thumbing his nose at the negligence of the main office not even checking if he'd done what he was supposed to do and deposited the day's earnings in the bank across the street, in which case he probably got the idea before Saturday between two and three, right you are!, and as for what will become of Mr So-and-So, they all give such staunch suggestions that none of them could be arraigned before the court. Now a couple comes in, and that changes the scene. Unlike when a lady walks in, when the word **bloody** and all its various direct objects disappear from the conversation, this couple demands more than merely following conventional morals — they require, without even fully realizing it, that we pay attention to them.

The woman makes the couple, even if her companion does the ordering — grapefruit for her, in small quantities; beer for himself, in large quantities — she allows him to, by coming up and standing inconspicuously next to him. In truth, at no point was she behind him. She is pregnant, and she feels it in her whole body. That's one thing: she already has to wear a dress that all but evens out the surface between her breasts and her belly. As she stands there she holds her hands loosely on her belly, she relaxes, she has something to protect. She is so full of her condition, visibly happy, her happiness increasing with every breath she takes. She is young — it's not about that. Her husband stands next to her, he is not a big talker, but there's no need for words now, she's here. That's another thing. She tells us the latest, and thanks to her they will be getting the key to their own home in a day or three, even if the mortgage payments look to be terrible, but they have escaped the impositions of the borough council and rent collectors. She speaks softly, but as though she is the one being asked, and no one has any doubt that everything important has to come from her. The husband, in his chubby stupor, acts almost sanctified, that is to say idiotic in his well-being, wanting merely to multiply and perfect this well-being at once by appearing with her and with that which he takes credit for and knows redounds to her credit too. She is masterful, discussing contractor problems with us, accepting respectful commentary and suggestions. Everyone is modest, almost shy; in such a way are idols created, as Bachofen says. It is clear on the faces of the bachelors young and old what they think: Best of luck to you both; I hope you can pull it off; don't worry about any envy on my count; ah if only I could be that young again; if I had been close to someone and she to me like that, I would have lived a full life. None of which is spoken, but by a kind of osmosis it is more real in the bar than anything else is, even if Joe does have a damned clever way of rolling himself a cigarette. The two of them stood next to each other, looking straight ahead, not at each other, and everyone there knew that they knew: I am with you, you are with me. We saw, without scoffing, that he reacts the way men do when she put her hand on the back of his neck, she reacts the way women do when he will later take her plate away because he's going to wash up, and their little fingers touch each other's. He knows it, he sees it, she can see it in advance; when she asks him to come with ⟨ = to leave⟩ he's already trembled in several parts of his body. It is no less affectionate, it comes from them both, when she says: Everything's fine Ron. Ron, I am all right. Cheerio, you all.

⟨Letter to Erika Klemm, 3 November 1975[88]⟩

25. "IT'S YOUR OPINION": A POSTCARD FOR THE KENT EVENING POST

"You should never read other people's mail, even if they show it to you".
— Uwe Johnson on Hans Magnus Enzensberger, *Anniversaries* II, p. 698.

In *Anniversaries* I, Gesine Cresspahl justifies her refusal to join her daughter's protests against the Vietnam War on the grounds that "I'm a guest in this country".[1] Johnson repeatedly gave the same justification for his own refusal to take public political positions in England, and he wasn't going to drop his "non-committal" stance for the very few British enquirers who made it across the Kingsferry Bridge to pester him on the Isle of Sheppey. He told Colin Riordan, for example, that he would not express a view on Thatcher's conduct of the 1982 war over the Falkland Islands. There would, however, be one occasion on which this expatriated East German could not resist intervening in an indisputably English political debate.

While the *Sheerness Times Guardian* concentrated its coverage on the Isle of Sheppey, the mainland Kentish papers that sometimes also caught Johnson's eye in the pub had a broader reach. Published from Chatham, the *Kent Evening Post* aimed to cover the towns of the entire Medway region, while also mixing its local reports with coverage of national and international events. Had he picked up a copy during his first year in Sheerness, Johnson might have learned that the former American GI and soul singer Geno Washington would soon be playing in Strood again, although without the support of the Ram Jam Band, from which he had recently split. A "Sheppey Supplement", printed on 29 April 1975, would have tried to convince him that the Isle of Sheppey's economy had at last recovered from the catastrophic closure of the naval establishment and associated army garrison at Sheerness in 1960 ("It was never so good" lied the headline of the "Industrial Spotlight" page, which also trumpeted plans to nearly double the island's population). Meanwhile, Medway council was exploring the possibility of addressing the housing problem by commissioning a cheap new kind of "plastic home" for newlyweds, and the domestic class war continued in line with inflation: the members of the National Union of Public Employees were demanding a 33% pay rise at their annual conference in Scarborough. All this was reported alongside the fall of Saigon, a ghastly collision of high-speed trains in Munich, which left forty-two dead (9 June 1975), and the termination of the Red Army Faction's murderous siege of the West German embassy in Stockholm.

The future kept leaning into view too — alternating between imminent catastrophe and implausible suggestions that the nation might actually benefit from scraping the mud of imperial history off its boots and seeking new life as a member of the European Economic Community ("a cooperative effort to build a just, peaceful and prosperous world" as the editor of the *Kent Evening Post,* Arthur Potter, had insisted at the time of the 1975 referendum[2]). As for Britain's other source of hope, the Johnsons were still in the first year of their Sheerness decade on Wednesday 18 June 1975 when Labour's Energy Secretary Tony Benn came to Kent by hydrofoil to join one hundred VIPs assembled at BP's oil refinery on the Isle of Grain, directly across the Medway from Sheerness. He was there to welcome the first loaded oil tanker to arrive from the British sector of the North Sea. Having turned on the discharge valve, and with ships in the Medway hooting in unison, Benn would "jubilantly" hold up a bottle of the "black gold" that promised to be "Britain's new lifeblood".[3] A dose of something transformative was direly needed. The pound was sliding to a new low, a railway strike was looming, and, that very day, even the power-broking golfer and trade union boss Hugh Scanlon was successfully ambushed by militant members of his own Amalgamated Union of Engineering Workers: the annual conference had passed a motion moved by Jimmy Reid, then well-known as the communist leader of the upper Clyde shipbuilders' work-in, rejecting any sort of "wage constraint" that might interfere with free industrial bargaining in accordance with Harold Wilson's Industry Bill.[4]

Entitled "It's Your Opinion", the *Post*'s correspondence column was maintained as a lively arena in which reasoning peacemakers had to shout if they were to be heard over the hectoring cries of zealots, the lamentations of civilisation's last-ditch defenders, and the groans with which defeated readers piled up conspiracy theories in an attempt to make sense of their worsening circumstances. The page burned with agitation about the failings of local government, the Christian (or not) virtues of the "public sector", and what was likely to happen to the already sinking country when Tony Benn's North Sea oil ran out.

The *Post* also provided Johnson with a kaleidoscopic array of English resistance movements to appraise. If Britain's place alongside the other six West European nations in the Common Market was a matter of abiding concern to the paper's letter writers, so too was the British state and its various apparatuses, national as well as local: the BBC, whose many crimes included a radio programme on "Modern Poetry" that spurned John Betjeman for stuff that neither scanned nor rhymed ("Poetry?" asked Mary Rankin of Higham: "I call it rubbish"); the public health lobby, which had somehow won Margaret Thatcher's support for the enforced "mass medication" that was fluoridation of the public water supply; and the Commission for Racial Equality, the mere existence of which had goaded one Kentish patriot to imagine that minority groups would soon be "taking our citizens to court for celebrating Trafalgar Day, St George's Day, maypole dancing, a return to Christian teaching... Is it against the law to boast of being English with hopes of retaining some of our heritage, such as family life, a moral code, self-respect and a sense of responsibility?"[5] After the general election of 3 May 1979, there were also letters about the early works of Margaret Thatcher — loved by some but not by Mr Ken Horton, a Labour councillor who regretted that, three months into her first term (and several years before she formally adopted the cause of "Victorian values"), the Prime Minister, who would indeed call time on the world as all these correspondents knew it, had already given new meaning to the saying "putting back the clock".

Occasional optimists fought back, as Johnson will have noticed from his bar stool observatory: writing to insist on the progress represented by the innovation known as the "fitted kitchen", or the possibility that the writer who had earlier stated that Rochester was nowadays only "fit for pigs" might be exaggerating a little: after all, this Medway town now boasted a new Charles Dickens Centre (recommended slogan: "back to the old days!"), which surely showed how the struggling economy might be revived by the coming new "industry" that was tourism.

By the beginning of the Eighties, when Uwe Johnson chose to intervene in this chorus of howling grievances, the *Kent Evening Post* was edited by a young journalist named Barrie Williams who saw the case for a wider perspective that might inform and perhaps even give ideological coherence to some of these passionate outbursts of local opinion. Williams opened his pages to an elderly political commentator named John Baker White (1902–1988), whose columns regularly stirred up controversy on the letters page, including the example that eventually prompted Johnson to break his self-imposed silence. By-lined as a former MP for Canterbury, Baker White, whose family had extensive farming interests in east Kent, had indeed held that constituency for the Conservative Party between 1945 and 1953. There was, however, rather more to say about him than that.

Baker White, who dedicated his maiden speech to

supporting a government bill that promised the restoration of the war-disrupted inshore fishermen of Whitstable and other small coastal ports,[6] had entered parliament as a seasoned anti-communist campaigner who had devoted a long career to the cause he'd adopted with the encouragement of Mrs Nesta Webster, a friend of his mother's who gained notoriety as well as continuing influence after 1917 as an anti-Semitic conspiracy theorist who attributed the French and Russian Revolutions and a great many other perceived ills to an alleged Jewish "plot against civilisation". White had embarked on his life's project shortly after leaving school in 1920, spying on the first meetings of the British Communist Party and then joining various organisations and groupings in the intelligence and propaganda fields. Having cut his teeth with the Industrial Intelligence Board, a shadowy blacklisting organisation formed by the Scottish agitator George MakGill, he had gone on to work with both the Anti-Socialist Union and the Economic League, another anti-subversive worker-vetting organisation, of which he was director from 1926–1939.

In his younger days, then, Baker White had moved in a world of anti-communist conspiracy and covert manoeuvres and covered traces of the kind that made an enduring mystery of the "Zinoviev letter", a forgery that did for Ramsay MacDonald's Labour Party when published by the *Daily Mail* just before the general election of 1924. Like others involved in the interwar "secret state", and as readers of the *Kent Evening Post* were not informed, he appears to have developed a soft spot for fascism, viewing it as a bracing response to the rising communist threat. Baker White was among the Britons who attended the Nuremberg Rally in 1937. Indeed, he stayed in Germany until April 1939, later claiming to have been there as a "spy" all along. He had continued his activities in the post-war years, both as Conservative MP for Canterbury and also as chairman of the National Freedom Association in Kent.

In October 1971, after the House of Commons approved British entry into the European Common Market by an unexpectedly large majority of 112, Baker White commended

Edward Heath both for winning this "great decision" against fierce socialist and nationalist opposition and for sticking to his guns with an unwavering commitment that had sadly not been shown by some vacillating members of his cabinet. He also remembered coming across Heath at the Nuremburg rally of 1937 and later meeting up with him again in his room at Balliol College: "We came back sharing the conviction that a dangerous and evil force was loose in Europe, something that one day had to be fought and defeated." That, so Baker White had informed readers of his "World Spotlight" column in the *Sheerness Times Guardian,* was the origin of Heath's vision of "Britain as part of a unified Europe." Unlike Enoch Powell and his followers, this Kentish right-winger had come to terms with the idea that Britain, which could no longer dominate the globe as an imperial nation, might use its new European affiliation to carry on giving the world "her accumulated experience, unique and inimitable, and her indefinable quality, known as the British way of life."

Johnson and Johnson

By the late Seventies, the *Kent Evening Post* was giving pride of place to Baker White's pungently expressed surveys of world events. Subjects that passed under his scanner included the history of Yugoslavia after Tito, and the coming of a new form of warfare in which "international terrorism" would be squared off against "ordered stable systems of society." In August 1979, it was the state of the shipyards and the claimed folly of the striking British workers who seemed too dim to understand that they would only lose their jobs to Polish yards on the Baltic. On 10 September 1979, at the time of the annual Labour Party conference, he denounced the admirers of "Soviet Communism" already in positions of power — he named Eric Heffer, Tony Benn, Frank Allaun — and reminded readers that the Labour Party was originally based on Methodism, not Marxism. On 21 January 1980, his pronouncements had been concerned with Afghanistan and how the West must act quickly to prove that the ongoing Soviet invasion of that remote and landlocked country was a terrible mistake. As for the debate that would eventually tempt Johnson to pick up his pen, Baker White kicked this off in January 1981, when he reviewed world affairs over the previous year and hailed the rising leader of Poland's Solidarity movement, Lech Walesa, as both "the man of the year" and, by implication, a proper hero of the political right.

The editor of the *Kent Evening Post,* Barrie Williams, may himself have stood close to Baker White in the camp of Thatcher and Reagan (he would go on to play a significant role in restructuring the regional press within the Northcliffe empire). However, he also knew that a lively and polarised letters page was good for circulation and Baker White was adept at drawing communists as well as soft-hearted but sometimes still shirty liberals into open view. One of Baker White's most persistent epistolary antagonists was a self-described shift worker named Bryan Johnson, a British communist whose views would definitely not have placed him among the reformers who gathered around the party's "theoretical" journal *Marxism Today* from 1977. While these modernisers were studying Antonio Gramsci's theory of "hegemony" and developing more sophisticated arguments about the emerging phenomenon they dubbed "Thatcherism", Bryan Johnson was with the hardline "Tankies" whose admiration for the USSR had survived successive post-war challenges, including those posed by Khrushchev's revelations about the crimes of Stalin, and the later uprisings in Eastern Europe that meant so much to Uwe Johnson. Having read Baker White's review of 1980, and his commendation of Lech Walesa as the man of the year, Bryan Johnson sat down in his house in Rainham to insist that it was a "total falsehood" to assert that 266 million people in the USSR were closer to the hunger line than they had been for half a century. Convinced that the Soviet people were thriving thanks to the five-year plan completed in 1980, the English Johnson condemned a Western reaction that seemed to consist only of "spreading falsehood" about the USSR and issuing nuclear threats.

These views were not welcomed by Mrs M.E. of Rochester, who had hoped that, with the coming of the New Year, she would be spared "the platitudes and Bolshevik rambling of Bryan Johnson". Speculating that no real person could really hold such absurd views, she wondered if "Bryan Johnson" really existed: "Perhaps, after all, you are just a figment of the Editor's imagination".The editor added a note assuring her that this really was not the case — as did Bryan Johnson, who came back railing against the cramped and confined outlook of Mrs M.E., which he likened to that of a caged bird: "All she knows and understands about the world is what she can see from her perch in Rochester". Her use of the name "Bolshevik" was "fifty years behind the times", he declared patronisingly, and she only had to consider the level of street violence in America or the coexistence of "food mountains in Europe" with starvation in Indo-China to realise that "It is Western Capitalism that lacks Humanity". As for the floundering British economy: "Our only growth industry is pornography".

Correspondents on Mrs M.E.'s side of this dispute assailed Bryan Johnson for his "red-tinted spectacles" and wondered how anybody who had not lived under the communist regime could consider himself qualified to "tell people how wonderful it is". One of her defenders introduced the secondary theme of tourism. There were, this correspondent observed pointedly, "not many Russian tourists" to Britain, "unlike American ones". Mrs M.E gave the discussion new momentum when she reversed the direction of this thought: "I would still like to see Bryan Johnson on the East side of the Berlin wall" — although "perhaps that too does not exist either since we are all such liars and believe those red bogy fairy tales".

When Bryan Johnson resumed his ironclad rhapsody about the workers' paradise, this time gloating over the fact that 2.5 million people were now registered unemployed in the country that was becoming known as "Thatcher's Britain", Barrie the editor started adding his own comments at the foot of Johnson's printed letters — each one a mocking judgement pinned to the chest of a man who was slow to realise he had stepped into the capitalists' pillory. His first note wondered whether Bryan Johnson had watched Malcolm Muggeridge's television programme *A Winter in Moscow* on BBC2 earlier that week. Muggeridge had been there in the early Thirties and was among the reporters who followed Gareth Jones in breaking news of the catastrophic famine Stalin had engineered in Ukraine. Another writer was less obscure, saying "I thought for a crazy moment that Bryan Johnson had finally gone to his Utopia in Russia, after all the stick he had taken here from readers". Happily, though, the useful idiot had stayed around to pen another load of "claptrap": "He must have done his 30 years of research in a nuclear shelter".

The suggestion that Bryan Johnson should be sent to Moscow to experience the land of his dreams hardly worried the man himself. On 13 March, in a letter published under the heading "Frozen mitt for Russia", he urged Barrie Williams himself to "Go there with a small delegation from the Medway towns": "enjoy the hospitality" and "see for yourself". He repeated his suggestion on 25 March 1981. In a letter headed "Russian dream is coming true", Bryan Johnson claimed that all the arguments of his critics were merely lies of the sort to be expected from "the media". Having pointed to the murders perpetrated by the US-backed junta in El Salvador, he returned to the Red Paradise he had praised so often before: "Go there and you will find no unemployment, no inflation, a healthy expanding economy, expanding industry, and ever rising standards of living for all. If some people prefer to bury their heads in the quicksands of Thatcherism that is their free choice but all the lies in the world can never change the truth and reality itself".

Mr Bryan Johnson may never have understood that he was exactly the sort of left-winger the *Kent Evening Post* liked to have exposing himself in its letter's column — a man of such dogged and simple-minded faith in the USSR could be relied on to incriminate himself and, by tabloid association, the democratic left too. As for the other Johnson, Uwe, who would soon be writing caustically in the fourth and closing volume of *Anniversaries*, about the well-dressed British Stalinists he had seen enjoying a holiday as guests of the GDR cultural authorities at Ahrenshoop in the early Fifties, he definitely noticed, as he followed this correspondence from his stool in the Sea View or Napier, that his namesake was not entirely alone in his illusions. The same day's paper included a letter, which the editor headed "Stop hating", from one J. Box of Pelham Green, Twydall, who also wanted to "dispel the hatred and fear this country has for Russia". Having reiterated that the "way to prevent war is not to spend massive sums on defence but to visit and make friends", Box went on to assert some "facts", which he had on the authority of a visit made by members of the National Association of Local Government Officers in 1960 and also, he freely admitted, of more recent pronouncements made by Radio Moscow. Unlike British workers, declared Box, Russians paid only 5% of their income on rent, and "no rates are payable. Old people are treated like royalty, paying half-price for fuel and travel". Under the "preventative health system", readers should know that "everyone has to be examined 10 times a year". This recycled propaganda was too much for Barrie the editor. Beneath this letter, he stated "For the information of Messrs Johnson and Box a one-way ticket to Moscow costs £264. Send us a card, lads — Editor".

Williams's comment offended some readers, including Mrs D. Simmonds of Gillingham, whose letter appeared on 30 March under the heading "My Russian Trip Impressed Me". She was disgusted at the *Evening Post* for treating two of its "Opinion Correspondents" so rudely, adding that not so long ago she'd been on a trip to Moscow and Leningrad organised by none other than the *Kent Evening Post* itself, which had printed pictures and news of "all the wonderful things we saw". This precedent did not justify an enforced relocation: "I love the Canary Islands, Norway and Switzerland but that does not mean I want to go and live there".

Two further letters appeared on 3 April. One came from

another of the *Post*'s more seasoned correspondents, B. Harding, who forcefully demolished the fantasy of the Soviet bloc as a "Red paradise" ("Try telling it to the prisoners behind the Berlin Wall and to the relatives of those murdered by East German [Russian puppet] border guards..."). The second, which was both shorter and more elliptical, was from Uwe Johnson.

"I thought it best to keep my mouth shut", Johnson had declared a couple of years earlier, when the makers of a BBC radio documentary asked about his reluctance to pontificate about the Berlin Wall in the early Sixties. We know from one of his letters to Christa Wolf, that Johnson had no intention of breaking his rule of silence in order to engage with the views of his British namesake — he called the Rainham Stalinist "Brian, unfortunately also Johnson"[8] — or of the second representative of insular English culture named Box. Yet he did feel obliged to comment on editor Williams's breach of a principle that might well have been taken for granted at the "Institute for the Preservation of British Customs", his imaginary New York establishment in the first volume of *Anniversaries*.

As Johnson explained to Wolf, it was the editor's comments that finally got to him, since they surely placed the paper "in breach of British fairness". The editor had mockingly asked "Brian" for a postcard, so Uwe Johnson, the "unacknowledged humorist", finally overcame his reluctance to interfere in British political life, and pulled one from his collection. He favoured interwar views of Sheerness street scenes but he might just as well have chosen a card showing the Olau Line's passenger ferry approaching Sheerness from the Dutch town the British insisted on calling Flushing: a service that Johnson was pleased to watch sailing back and forth to Europe, apparently undeterred by the fact that it had been condemned, shortly after it opened in 1975, by a Sittingbourne farmer named Michael Nightingale. A Conservative County Councillor who also ran rubber and tea plantations in the Far East, the latter had informed Kent's Planning and Transport Committee that "all the hippies in Europe" now invaded Sheerness railway station every morning", before moving on to Sittingbourne where they would "clog" the commuter train to London and "annoy ordinary travellers" with their rucksacks.[9]

Printed on 3 April 1981, Johnson's message appeared under a heading that proved that Barrie the editor, had at least got the joke if not the full point about his breach of British values:

Just the ticket!

REFERRING to the Editor's final argument against Messrs Box & Johnson (March 25).

Let the two of us find a country to disagree upon. On conclusion, he would owe me a one-way ticket to the capital of that country, and I might send him a card. — U. Johnson, Marine Parade, Sheerness.

Just the ticket!

Referring to the Editor's final argument against Messrs Box & Johnson (March 25).

Let the two of us find a country to disagree upon. On conclusion, he would owe me a one-way ticket to the capital of that country, and I might send him a card.

—U. Johnson, Marine Parade, Sheerness.

Having posted his card, Johnson had gone off on another trip abroad and forgotten all about it. When he returned to Sheerness he was, so he told Christa Wolf, "informed from all sides" that his message had been printed, together with his name and address. "But no one kept the paper. So now I am waiting in uncertainty for a public discussion of Tierra del Fuego or Canada, and looking forward to a ticket. I hope it'll end up being New Zealand."

26. IMPLOSION: TWO STORIES FROM THE SITE

The intended reader may have been lying on a beach, although possibly not in Sheerness, or any of the other struggling "on-Sea" resorts forming a "necklace of poverty" around London.[1] The story itself, however, opens on an ordinary Monday morning in just that sort of place, where a mother is struggling to disentangle the sound of the radio from her dreams. She drifts back to sleep for a moment before hauling herself out of bed to awaken the two children, who scramble for their clothes and the bathroom before rousing their father and heading down for the breakfast their mother is preparing in the kitchen.

In the midst of this hurried daily routine, the mother reflects that, although largely content with her life, she nevertheless still feels the desire for "a bit of excitement now and then". Nothing excessive, of course, but "just enough to prove we are not as dull and boring as we may appear on the surface". With this thought in mind, she glances out of the window and across to the back garden of a neighbour called "Gilbert", where a "splash of colour" catches her eye. "It was the most perfect rose she had ever seen. The pale yellow and pink of the petals exactly echoing the tints on the wispy clouds on the summer morning dawn sky. It was neither a bud nor yet full blown. It was at that in-between stage when roses are in their prime. The impact it made on her was so vivid that it was as if the delicate, flowery perfume was all round her, fresh and fragrant". Before she has time to think better of it, she hears herself telling her sleepy husband, "If you were full of passion instead of egg and bacon, you would get that for me". When he eventually comes round to the fact that she has spoken, she explains her impulsive proposal: "I just thought it would be rather romantic if you leaped over the wall and got it for me". The children are horrified, exclaiming "That would be stealing, Mummy", as they are packed into the car by their father, who drives them off to catch their train for school.

Once they are gone, the mother reflects on her sudden and impulsive remark, deciding that her husband, who was actually quite romantic already, had been kind not to point out how unromantic she herself looked at this time of day — hair unbrushed, no make-up, outdoor sandals on her feet. The assignment, meanwhile, would be challenging. Her husband would have to "climb over two walls and take a ladder with him" to be able to reach the rose. If he was seen as he clambered about in those overlooked back gardens, he might be charged with theft, of acting while drunk, of being a peeping Tom, or even of indulging in petty espionage in the hope of discrediting a different neighbour who was then standing in the local council elections. So the matter is forgotten until the next morning, when the mother wakes to find the plucked rose on her kitchen table: "The perfume was as lovely as she had imagined it would be. It was an exquisitely formed flower with a presence quite out of proportion to its size". The story ends with a final guilty glance at Gilbert's deprived garden, and a resolution: "One day they must tell Gilbert — she was sure he would understand".

Entitled "The Forbidden Rose", the story was written by Susan Harris for a competition run by *Woman's Own*. A winning entry, it was published in the magazine's "Holiday Reading Special" for 1982. While the narrative sits safely within the conventions of romantic fiction, it was also true to its author's life. The rear window, through which the rose was glimpsed across a neighbour's garden, was Susan Harris' own at No. 24 Marine Parade in Sheerness. The man she named "Gilbert" was actually Uwe Johnson, two doors to the east at No. 26, and the adventure with the rose had unfolded in real life more or less as she described it. Susan's husband Martin remembers her issuing the challenge, and also how the solitary rose was made more exceptional by the bewildered state of Johnson's garden, which had been allowed to wander during the year when the solitary author — unwell and ever more in debt to his publisher — was still failing to complete the long-awaited fourth volume of *Anniversaries*.

Woman's Own *Summer Reading Special, 1982.*

At first, when Susan put the challenge to her husband, Martin had offered to ask Johnson if he would mind giving them the rose, confident that the writer could hardly care less about the flower. For Susan, however, this was to miss the point. Her desire for romance would not be satisfied unless her husband did the thing properly: sneaking out in the middle of the night and struggling over walls and fences before reaching up to steal the solitary prize. By this stage in Johnson's residency the garden was, Martin recalls, an almost solid block of "thorns and weeds and ivy", held up by the side walls, and, towards the centre, by the now-rotting pergolas put in place by the women who had owned the house before Johnson. So there he was, as Martin remembers, late that same night, "up to my knees in the mud, fighting my way through all these thorns and ivy underneath the pergola arch, trying to think where's that bloody rose, got some secateurs in my hand and the ladder I'm dragging through … I said is he in bloody America, bullying the students over there, or is his head going to come out of the window saying, 'Vat are you doing in my garden at three in the morning?' But he didn't come through. I managed to fight my way up, and get well scratched doing it, snip this rose off, bring it back, find a nice vase, put it in the vase with a little note with a kiss in it. I got brownie points for that romantic thing". And, as Harris closed in his own plain-speaking way, "Susan wrote a story that you could only call the worst of Mills & Boon".

That verdict sounds harsh, yet Susan willingly confirmed that her effort placed her as far as it was possible to be from Johnson in the literary hierarchy. The German author, whose novel she had struggled and failed to understand, probably wouldn't have minded at all about Martin's theft of his flower, but she shudders to think how he might have greeted her "silly soppy story". There was never any question of her showing him the page on which she had made a "forbidden" flower of his rose. "That seems a pity", so Johnson's biographer Katja Leuchtenberger told me in Rostock, confident that Johnson — who was certainly capable of acts of kindness — would indeed have "understood" the situation.

*

As might be deduced from the wilderness into which Martin Harris was obliged to trespass in order to pick that bewildered flower for his wife, things had changed in 26 Marine Parade since the Johnsons had moved in and started drawing up optimistic plans for their garden. (In some "agricultural news" relayed to Max Frisch in March 1976, Johnson noted that the "ministry responsible" — i.e. Elisabeth and himself — had been trying to decide whether an "irreplaceable" rosebush should be cut back further, or otherwise rescued from the rampant honeysuckle already threatening to extinguish it.[2]) Although the Johnsons kept their private life very much to themselves, the Harrises knew about the serious heart attack the writer had suffered in June 1975, just as they recognised in later years that he drank far too much and remained unwell — "I could have pushed him over with a finger", said Martin of the large and sometimes challenging man whom Günter Kunert had also registered as a teetering "colossus" on the doorstep. They also noticed the tensions leading up to the couple's separation in 1978. When I talked with the Harrises over thirty years later, both were still pained by the memory of looking on as involuntary bystanders at somebody else's calamity: "They were as bad as each other", said Martin, as he recalled a situation he and his wife had been left to understand through its external indications. It was part of their unEnglishness, so Harris seemed to suggest, that neither of the Johnsons knew "the first thing about the art of compromise".

The situation leading up to the separation has more recently been described by the German academic Bernt W. Seiler.[3] In his account, which was published in 2006 and remains (as he observes) uncontested if not universally approved in Johnson circles, the crisis had indeed begun in the summer of 1975, when Elisabeth revealed — "unwillingly", as Johnson would later allege in a "Statement to my Executors" written on 21 February 1983, and "by a slip of the tongue" — that she had been conducting what Johnson called "a steady affair" with a man living in Prague.[4] Seiler, who claims to be the first to have publicly revealed the name of the man in question, dates the encounter back to October 1961, when Elisabeth Schmidt was twenty-six years old and studying Indology in Leipzig. She and another GDR student, Erika Jäckel, had travelled to Prague with their lecturer Eberhardt Klemm, a former student of Ernst Bloch's, who was then teaching musicology. While there, she decided to stay in Prague to study for a semester. Klemm's Czechoslovak contact, a historian of music and Mozart scholar named Tomislav Volek, agreed to take her to concerts and show her around the city. Volek, who was a few years older than Elisabeth and had learned German in school under Nazi occupation, is said to have been pleased to meet a German who had herself suffered some of the consequences of the Third Reich (Elisabeth's father and mother had died in 1944 and 1945 respectively) and a romance had developed between them.

Seiler notes that, while Elisabeth had been friends with Uwe

Johnson since 1956, this brief liaison took place at a time when the future was unpredictable. For the previous three months, the Berlin Wall had stood between the pair, and there could be no certainty how or when they would meet again. The matter was resolved in February 1962, shortly after her semester in Prague, when Johnson arranged for student "escape helpers" to smuggle Elisabeth through the closed frontier to West Berlin (they were married that same month). She and Volek continued to correspond. On a few later occasions, they also met up when Volek got permission to attend conferences in the West. Seiler mentions a day or two in Salzburg in September 1964: Volek was in the city with a delegation from the Czechoslovak Composers' Association at a time when Johnson, who by then had "many obligations as a well-established author", is said to have been travelling about in Holstein looking for a place in which to set part of his novel *Two Views*. Another brief meeting is said to have taken place in November 1965, when Johnson was on a reading tour promoting *Two Views*. That time, Elisabeth is said to have paid for a flight from Hanover so that she and Volek could share a visit to the opera in Berlin, thus putting a secret break in Volek's closely monitored itinerary. From then on, they maintained an intermittent and, as Volek recalled, largely "poetic-melancholic" correspondence. When the Johnsons were living in New York City, Elisabeth wrote about possibly continuing her studies at Columbia University, and also offered coded observations about conditions in Czechoslovakia after the suppression of the Prague Spring, or noted the contrast between the upbeat cheerfulness of New Yorkers and the fact that people were turning up at the city's hospitals more or less daily having tried to commit suicide.

Although it is not for us to join the journalists and lawyers who have, for better or worse, passed judgement on this situation in Germany, we may still suspect with Seiler that the liaison between Volek and Elisabeth was something that many partners would have been able to leave in the past. Seiler, who wrote after meeting Volek in Prague, also suggests that their ongoing correspondence was really just an exchange between friends — sufficiently innocent for Volek to think nothing of sending his occasional letters directly to the Johnsons's home address and, as Seiler also suggests, for Elisabeth to have thought little of letting her husband know about the situation in 1975. Even Johnson, who over the course of his life had come to place great emphasis on personal trust and loyalty, would later claim, in that same Statement of 21 February 1983, to have understood the matter as "a private and personal affair to the point of my forgiving her and attempting a reconciliation by going on to live with her". Be that as it may, he also registered the disclosed events as a grievous betrayal that continued to rankle in his mind. By the time he wrote to Hannah Arendt at the beginning of August 1975, Elisabeth had become "my dear wife Mrs Letsnotdiscussit".[5] Over the years to come, this private crisis may also have informed his expressions of sympathy for some of the men in the pub who had argued with or been kicked out by their wives. He might have offered help or even a bed for the night to some of these unhoused fellows, but there were limits to his sympathy. He had, for example, nothing to offer the misogynist who sat down next to "Charles" in the Sea View one night in 1977 and asked him what he thought about women. Having failed that test ("Oh, I replied, in the island manner: I am very much in favour of personal relationships"), Johnson politely declined the subsequent invitation to write the stranger's story.[6] He informed Helen Wolff that he was pleased to get home that evening without suffering an attempt on his life from this aggressive fellow: a "real blighter", so Johnson was informed by friendlier drinkers, who might have found an adequate summary of his outlook by taking a stroll down Black Griffin Lane in Canterbury where, as I recall from my brief spell as a milkman, a resident maniac had seen fit to daub the words "Woman is the n****r of the world" around the arch above his front door.

Seiler, who met Volek several times in Prague,[7] confirms that Elisabeth did what she could to settle the suspicions metastasising in her husband's mind. She is said to have written a confessional "diary" of her encounters with Volek in a notebook, and, at some point in the summer of 1975, to have written to Volek in Prague, asking for the return of her letters so that she could demonstrate their harmlessness. This wasn't easily done across the Iron Curtain, and Volek's reluctance may only have intensified Johnson's desire to see them. He tried unsuccessfully to involve Günter Grass's wife Anna in the attempted recovery, asking her to use their acquaintance with the widow of the translator Vladimir Kafka to help extract the letters. When that failed, he tried Erika Klemm (formerly Jäckel), the other Leipzig student who had gone to Prague alongside Elisabeth and her own husband-to-be in October 1961. She passed on Elisabeth's letters to herself and, in 1977, returned to Prague to do what she could with Volek.

According to Seiler, their meeting was unproductive, perhaps not surprisingly since Volek had difficulties of his own. He had been in trouble with the authorities in Prague ever since 1972, when he had refused to retract an article he had written likening Soviet condemnation of "formalistic music" to the Nazi pillorying of "degenerate art". Indeed, he had been sacked from his job at the Prague Academy of Sciences. Not an easy time, then, in which to deal with Johnson's next move in his bid for the "return" of Elisabeth's letters. At 1am, the phone rang in the small flat Volek then shared with his mother. He picked it up to hear the word "Johnson" uttered in a "funereal" voice. There were more calls like that, in which Johnson said little more that "Send me my wife's letters", with neither explanation nor argument by way of justification. Volek is said to have become both furious and uncooperative. The danger to which he was being exposed, at that time when calls from the West were closely monitored by the Czechoslovak security services, became all too obvious when he answered the phone to hear a man announce himself as "Jonsen" and then start talking in Czech about "letters of my wife". The caller, who was plainly not Johnson, ignored Volek's request that he speak in German but cursed and hung up when Volek reverted to Czech, dismissing him as a liar and an agent of state security.

In October 1977, so Seiler suggests, Elisabeth herself started calling, asking for the letters and explaining that they had become necessary to the continuation of her marriage. In desperate straits, she even offered to buy them from Volek, but he rejected this suggestion as an insult that destroyed whatever was left of their friendship, declaring himself "tired of having to deal with the obsessions of a forty-five-year old psychopath". He finally dismissed Elisabeth after a further call in which she said she would arrange for someone to pick up the letters from his home. Outraged but keen to resolve the situation, he is said to have left a selection in an envelope by the door and told his mother to give them to whomsoever turned up for them. No such caller arrived but the letters allegedly vanished all the same, presumably into the hands of the Czechoslovak state security service. That, in Volek's account, is where the exchange came to an end.

For three years, the Johnsons remained together in No. 26, but the situation worsened when news of the skein of suspicions ramifying in Johnson's mind reached literary circles in West Germany. Someone (fingers would be pointed in the direction of Fritz J. Raddatz) revealed the tensions they'd seen in Sheerness, and Johnson, who had a strong sense of personal privacy, felt himself doubly compromised as the story went into circulation. It had been bad enough that the literary world in West Germany wouldn't stop speculating about his apparently endless delay in completing *Anniversaries* but the new topic had, in his own interpretation, placed him in a situation like that faced by the Prussian Baron Geert von Innstetten, in Theodore Fontane's late-nineteenth-century novel *Effi Briest*. Innstetten has discovered letters revealing that his much younger wife has had an affair when the couple were living in Pomerania years previously. Such was the "paranoid logic of honour",[8] however, that he only felt obliged to react by challenging her lover to a duel once the affair was known by others.[9]

If no one had known about Johnson's suspicions, so the "Innstetten-reflex"[10] is said to have unfolded in his mind, he just might have been able to let the past go and achieve a reconciliation with his wife. As it was, he and Elisabeth separated in 1978 and, the following year, he condemned his wife out loud in the last of a series of five autobiographical lectures on poetics delivered at Goethe University in Frankfurt. In doing so, he also revealed that the "betrayal" of which he accused her had by this time spread into a new area of his life. Like his publishers, Johnson had been aware of the very real possibility of Stasi surveillance over his activities while he was living in West Berlin, and he was still watchful during his years in Sheerness. He had said as much to Martin Harris and he also asked Michael Hamburger not to give out his address or phone number to anyone at all. Indeed, the latter friendship was suspended for a year or so after Hamburger forgot this edict, thereby obliging Johnson to open his door one day in 1976 to find the Iranian poet Cyrus Atabay smiling into his face.[11] He and Atabay had met before in West Berlin, but the novelist's fury at this accidental betrayal of confidence was exacerbated by the fact that, as Johnson knew but Hamburger did not, the intruding poet was a cousin of the hated Shah of Iran.

By 1979, Johnson's suspicion of surveillance had entered his disintegrating marriage and started interfering with his writing too. In the book he would later make of his Frankfurt Lectures, *Accompanying Circumstances (Begleitumstände)*, he declared that he had "let himself be helped" in his work by the graduate of a Prague seminar whom he had "mistaken for his wife" and, looked on as a "co-worker" in the final volume of *Anniversaries*, which he intended to close on the day before Soviet and allied tanks entered Czechoslovakia to extinguish the Prague Spring. It now appeared that "since the autumn of 1961, she had been in close contact with a confidant of the STB, the Czechoslovakian State Security Service".[12]

Thanks to this additional "fact" about Volek, which Johnson would later claim to have discovered in the spring of 1978 ("not by my wife, but by accident" he would assert in his English "Statement to my Executors" of 21 February 1983), he had realised that "his dealings with the Czechoslovakian elements" of *Anniversaries IV*, were by no means as independent or free-spirited as he might have expected." In *Accompanying Circumstances,* Johnson blamed the shocking discovery for his heart attack, and also for his lack of progress on the novel. The revelation had caused "damage to the subject" of his unfinished book and brought about the "writer's block" that had prevented resumption of the project. A person in the "state of depression" that followed such a revelation might, so Johnson went on in his chosen subjunctive way, "sit down at the typewriter at the usual time, as soon as the doctors allowed him to do so." He would, however, "experience a complete inability to put anything on paper with which he wishes to address future readers." Undermined in his professional integrity as well as at the heart of his personal life, this "person" was immobilised for three years. Unable to re-establish contact with his primary character, Gesine Cresspahl, he had to teach himself "to write again at the age of forty-four, with two lines a day, five lines a week, but after three months seventeen pages."

Elisabeth Johnson had left the house as the idea that she was some sort of spy and literary saboteur gripped her husband's mind, moving to a smaller residence at 47 Unity Street, a couple of streets inland from Marine Parade, where Katharina would join her. The parents lived only a few hundred yards from one another but the break was final: there was to be no contact between them. In order to prevent accidental encounters, Johnson divided the streets of the neighbourhood between the two of them, also drawing up a schedule of times when they might safely use the same shops without bumping into one another. "It was bad," said Muriel Adams, who cleaned house for Johnson, "you didn't mention the name of one in the presence of the other. Last year, we almost had a terrible mishap when sending our Christmas greetings ... Charles would never have forgiven us for that." Susan Harris also told Jens of how Johnson had come to their house a few weeks after the separation. He wrote an address on a piece of paper and asked if it meant anything to them. "'Yes, Elisabeth lives there', I answered. Charles got up and left without a word." And that was how things remained until the end. "He wanted to forget her," Susan Harris told me thirty years later, but "was always in her tracks."

*

If the Harrises were representative, it may be that none of Johnson's acquaintances in Sheerness knew about the causes of the breach or, for that matter, about the coverage given to Johnson's accusations in the Federal Republic after the publication of *Accompanying Circumstances* in 1980. Some in West Germany may have leapt at the story, but others were horrified by Johnson's accusations and their implications for his wife and daughter. Günter Grass, who had been close to the Johnsons in Berlin, described his allegations about the still unnamed Volek and Elisabeth as a "gruesome fiction".[13] The East German writer and film director Thomas Brasch also discovered how impossible it was to check Johnson's descent into chaos. He had first met the writer at Siegfried Unseld's home in Frankfurt on 8 January 1977, during Suhrkamp's twenty-fifth anniversary celebrations. Brasch had made his own departure from the GDR only a few weeks before (he left following the GDR's decision to expatriate the dissident writer and singer Wolf Biermann while he was touring West Germany), and Johnson gave him some useful advice about the challenges of the transition to the West and, in particular, the importance of holding onto your independence as a writer and not allowing yourself to be made over into the grateful victim some Western observers expected you to be.[14]

Brasch, who had survived a hated British public school as well as the GDR jail to which he had been sentenced for demonstrating his support for the Prague Spring, would later look back with sympathy on the difficulties Johnson had faced in the West. He understood that the GDR was in some respects an easier place for a writer to work than the West, with all its demands and distractions. He also believed that Johnson had hoped to regain his focus by moving to Sheerness, where he had tried to recreate "Mecklenburg in England" so that he might follow his admired William Faulkner and concentrate on building "a new country through letters". In Johnson's defence, he quoted the "beautiful Jewish proverb" declaring "You may be paranoid but that doesn't mean people aren't out to get you".

The people out to get Johnson may not have been the Czechoslovak or East German state security agents, whose interest in his unfinished novel Johnson surely overestimated. He may, however, have been right to feel hounded by the literary gossips in West Germany who had given up waiting for the final volume of *Anniversaries*, and were now wondering out loud about the possibility that their brilliant, difficult writer had finally gone crazy on his English desert island. Brasch admitted that he had himself played the role of just such a "culture buffoon" when he and Johnson met up again in the slipstream of the Frankfurt Book Fair in 1982. He was aware that Johnson had by then convinced himself that his wife was a Czech agent trying to damage his work on *Anniversaries* IV by such unlikely ruses as getting him copies of the wrong articles from the *New York Times*. He knew better than to tell Johnson he thought this accusation "a joke" but he did, nevertheless, make the mistake of giving the author some uninvited advice about the unfinished novel that was obviously weighing so grievously on him. Like Michael Hamburger, who had similar thoughts about the condition of his apparently self-condemned friend in Sheerness, Brasch rashly suggested that Johnson might consider letting Volume IV remain as "a collection of material". His idea was that *Anniversaries* could be allowed to rest incomplete as literary modernism's last and perhaps most splendid installation: a "tripartite country on a high mountain" with the three already published volumes standing next to each other "and behind them a huge heap of paper" containing the drafts and research materials assembled for Volume IV. Johnson was predictably disgusted at the suggestion, accusing Brasch of thinking him unable to complete the work and insisting that, as a writer himself, Brasch would surely be just as insulted by such a proposition. Brasch wrote a poem entitled "Half Sleep", dedicated to Johnson and published in the *Frankfurter Allgemeine Zeitung* on 26 November 1982. After Johnson's death, a framed copy of the cutting was found hanging on the wall beside his desk.[15]

THOMAS BRASCH	THOMAS BRASCH
Halb Schlaf	Half Sleep
für Uwe Johnson	*for Uwe Johnson*
Und wie in dunkle Gänge mich in mich selbst verrannt, verhängt in eigne Stränge mit meiner eignen Hand:	And as if in dark corridors stuck inside myself, tangled in my own ropes by my own hand:
So lief ich durch das Finster in meinem Schädelhaus: Da weint er und da grinst er und kann nicht mehr heraus.	I ran through the dark in the house of my skull: There he sobs and he grins and can never escape.
Das sind die letzten Stufen, das ist der letzte Schritt, der Wächter hört mein Rufen und ruft mein Rufen mit aus meinem Augenfenster in eine stille Nacht; zwei rufende Gespenster: eins zittert und eins lacht.	These are the last stages, this is the last footstep, the watchman hears my cries and cries my cries with me out the window of my eyes into a quiet night — two crying ghosts: one trembling, one laughing.
Dann schließt mit dunklen Decken er meine Augen zu: jetzt schlafen und verstecken und endlich Ruh.	Then with dark sheets he closes my eyes: now to sleep and to hide, now rest at last.

*

Like the Harrises at No. 24, we may count the bottles going into a neighbour's house but who would presume to know for sure exactly what is happening between the people inside? After reading Seiler's account of the break-up, we must nevertheless suspect that Johnson turned his marriage into a Strindbergian inferno in which exaggerated and false significance could be attached to the tiniest event or gesture. Seiler, who writes primarily in order to challenge the accusation against Volek, accepts that Johnson may well have convinced himself of the truth of the conspiracy theory he derived from his wife's alleged confession. He insists, however, that Volek was not an agent of the Czechoslovak STB, and that Elisabeth, whom Seiler has never met, was therefore innocent of the same charge. He notes that, while Johnson never admitted his error, he did eventually row back a little from his accusations, conceding that Elisabeth may not have known she was being manipulated. And Volek? Having himself been an object of suspicion — not just to Hermann Kesten, who had denounced him as an "agent" in 1961, but to some who had known him as a student at Leipzig and continued to wonder about his apparently effortless emigration to the West[16] — Johnson might indeed have been more careful with his charges. He would appear, though, never to have paused long enough in his calculations to recognise that there was a real person behind the phantom he had made of Volek on the far side of the Iron Curtain, and one who may well have been endangered by his hostile and intemperate approaches.

We know, from August Strindberg once again, that an agonising marriage can keep people going even when an outsider only sees two people manoeuvring in a prolonged and demeaning "dance of death". We can, however, only speculate about the extent to which Johnson's allegations may also have endured for more or less instrumental reasons. It is conceivable that the story of sabotage and betrayal acquired some more or less conscious utility for Johnson, providing not just a weapon with which to punish his wife but an excuse for his own protracted delay in completing *Anniversaries* IV. Seiler notes that the accusation against Volek was allowed to stand after Johnson's death by some concerned to defend his literary reputation. At the head of his list stands Johnson's editor and publisher at Suhrkamp, Siegfried Unseld, who surely should at some point have corrected the record. It is conceivable that for Unseld, who continued to fund Johnson through his last solitary years in Sheerness, the alleged conspiracy worked to reduce any thought that the pressure he was placing on his writer to complete *Anniversaries* — as the publisher's advance grew into a huge and unsustainable debt — might have been among the causes of the final collapse. Such were the pressures placed on Elisabeth as the situation unfolded after Johnson's death, that she is even said at one point to have advised Volek, through a lawyer, that he should let the accusation against him stand and confine his denial, if he really felt one was

necessary, to a statement he might send to the Uwe Johnson Archive where it could be withheld from public view until a later date. For Seiler, who traces this story from Volek's perspective, a critical judgement of both Johnson's behaviour and Unseld's assent is inescapable: "To make such an accusation was as effective as it was free from risk in 1980 — there was practically no evidence to the contrary. Even if Volek had found out about the accusation at the time — and not, as he claimed to have done, by reading about himself in a newspaper during a trip to Berlin in the late Nineties — he would have been powerless against it ... where could he have been heard and who would have believed him against the testimony of Uwe Johnson and Siegfried Unseld?" It. was only after the raising of the Iron Curtain that it became possible

Desperate Dan as Easter Island monolith, Andre Whelan's gnome factory, Blue Town, 2016.

for Seiler to establish that there was "no basis whatsoever" for Johnson's charges.

*

As for writing of the searching, multi-voiced, scrupulously informed kind for which Johnson is known, this was surely irreconcilable with conspiratorial understanding in which all complexity and nuance is collapsed into an obsessive delusion. Johnson's work on the *Anniversaries* project may have been "blocked" after the summer 1975, but he did keep working on other texts, including a novella entitled *Sketch of an Accident Victim (Skizze eines Verunglückten)*. First published in 1981, but reputedly written in 1975, this is a disconcerting work in which Johnson pulls his reader into the mind of an émigré writer who has murdered his unfaithful wife. Arresting in its autobiographical resonances, the novella also retains a sense of complexity absent from the accusations the author levelled against his own wife.

The story opens with an extract quoted from the acceptance speech Johnson gave when receiving the prestigious Büchner Prize in 1971.[17] Here he describes an old man making his way through the streets of New York's Upper West Side to his customary restaurant. The place, which had once been his, is now run by Puerto Ricans, who have become used to this survivor's evening routine. He arrives at seven, takes up his regular position with his back to the window facing the street, and only ever orders coffee and toast, since that is all he can afford. He sits there, talking to himself or "to dead people" (although "the dead can't be Germans") and placing his order in a still strongly accented voice: "Ssänk ju", he says, in an English that Irish customers sometimes helpfully adjust and repeat on his behalf. The extract closes with something that American officials had said at his naturalisation ceremony in 1941. They had warned him against giving up his German citizenship. "He might get homesick after the war. Homesick."

So Johnson opens his story in an émigré Jewish world

he had himself come to understand with the help of the philosopher Hannah Arendt in New York City. In an article written immediately after her death in December 1975, he would recall taking Arendt, who lived as his near neighbour at 370 Riverside Drive, for a walk through a Jewish area in New York City. Here, she demonstrated a remarkable ability to "read" the faces of passersby, identifying the social position, occupation and former place of residence each had occupied before their world had been destroyed by the Nazis.[18]

As the novella develops, Johnson identifies his solitary diner as a German Jewish writer named Joe Hinterhand, who'd had to flee Germany as a young man in the Thirties. We next encounter this slyly named fellow as a younger man who has recently been released after serving ten years in a New York jail. Thanks to the kindness of old friends, Dr Hinterhand now sits in an apartment on Riverside Drive, looking out over the Hudson River, reviewing his life and the betrayal for which he had eventually murdered "Mrs Hinterhand", the otherwise nameless woman who had left Germany to join him in exile first in England and later in the United States.

Johnson has Joe Hinterhand born in the same year as Hannah Arendt, 1906, but there can be little doubt that he saw something of himself in the betrayed writer of his narrative. He emphasises the connection by announcing that Hinterhand — the name evokes hindquarters as well as the last player (who may also be the dealer) in a game of skat — had started out as a foundling called "Joachim de Catt", the pseudonym under which Johnson had at first thought of publishing *Speculations about Jakob* before deciding to leave the GDR for the West. No surprise either, in this claustrophobic theatre of associations, that the woman who is granted neither a voice nor any name except Mrs Hinterhand is described as a person who saves for holidays on the Baltic Sea, goes swimming as often as she can, and believes that the Russian Bolshevik Alexandra Kollontai is misrepresented by those who say she thought having sex was of no more significance than drinking a glass of water, and that "the ideal remains the monogamous union based on great love".[19]

The description of Dr Hinterhand's early married life in Kent also resonates with what we know of the Johnson's first months in Sheerness. Joe, who has been pleasantly surprised by his wife's willingness to leave Germany in the Thirties to marry him in exile, recognises "during an idle journey through the southern provinces of England" that she must be "compensated for the lost Baltic sea with another coast".[20] So he uses "his last" and also "borrowed" money to buy a house "in a residential village north of Folkestone", which then becomes more hers than his. Since "people liked her", Mrs Hinterhand proves a useful presence during the two months of renovation, talking to the builders, electricians and plumbers about their specialities and acquiring "considerable knowledge of fishing and angling" while also discussing the comparative merits of the radio symphony orchestras of London, Vienna or Berlin. She would be well-liked when she accompanied her husband to the pub, and less inhibited than him in repeating "Cheerio" on leaving. When asked what had brought them to England, it was she who answered: "My husband did".

No surprise either, that it is because the Hinterhands like "the sight of vast expanses of water"[21] that, at a later period of their life, they eventually leave New York City and move, most implausibly, to Gardiner's Island, just offshore from the wealthy Long Island settlement of East Hampton. It is here, in a village that Johnson imposes on this famously private island that is smaller, richer and a great deal more exclusive than the Isle of Sheppey, that readers are asked to imagine Joe Hinterhand deciding he would like to write his wife's biography as they slide into a shared old age. He mentions his plan in a radio recording, and his subsequent action soon makes suggestive evidence of his late wife's retort: "over my dead body".[22]

All has seemed to go well enough for Joe Hinterhand until, one day in 1947, he discovers that "Mrs. Hinterhand" has been betraying him all along with her Italian fascist lover: at first "carnally", and then in correspondence that has continued until 1947. From the moment he discovers this conspiracy against himself and his work, his consciousness had been "blocked against perceptions" and "new entrances". Like Johnson's own, it was "arrested, sealed, merely a container in which the past was rigidly administered".[23] As Johnson explains, a deceived man looking back on his feelings as an expectant father can expect to see nothing but his own delusions, which "should be deleted". Looking at old photographs, he sees his past life dissolving into a truth he had never suspected. The "ripple" on his wife's forehead in the picture he took at Folkestone Central Station as they set off for America in 1939 is suddenly a sign of "her annoyance at having to say farewell to the grand hotels of the European mainland, to her weekends in hotels, dirty weekends".[24] He remembers holding forth into a microphone in Chicago during the Second World War, confidently denouncing the policy of American isolationism being advocated by the former aviator Charles Lindbergh (whom he saw as the man who had wanted the Nazis to bomb Folkestone) and blithely unaware that he was, all along, wide open to objection: "But your wife is sleeping with a fascist".[25] As for the pleasure he had once taken at the Anglo-German internationalism implied by the name she had chosen for her (their?) son Anthony, that too is suddenly cancelled by the realisation that there are Antonios in Italy too. Everything is lost in this exactly rendered nightmare of "transverse" knowledge.

Though much of the novella's material is autobiographically derived, it remains a creatively revealing text, and by no means just a piece of displaced special pleading. Johnson wrote it partly in response to Max Frisch's story "Sketch of an Accident",[26] in which a Swiss surgeon, who is driving along the French Riviera squabbling with his girlfriend, eventually drives his Porsche into a truck at a crossroads outside Montpelier (the girlfriend dies but he, who appears to know his responsibility, is declared guilty of nothing since he had the right of way). It has been suggested that Johnson's novella testifies to his long-standing admiration for Bertolt Brecht, and the alienation devices with which he wrote of engaging apparently accepted and obvious meanings while at the same time "making them strange".[27] The novella has also been hailed as an autobiography of the "shattered self"[28] and, in a different strain, as a radically unsettling text that exposes "the weakness of male identity"[29] by turning the tables on the anachronistic writer who espouses enlightenment values and knows the world primarily through concepts and texts — Johnson's text is thick with quotations, mostly about marriage, drawn from Frisch but also Ernst Bloch, Kandinsky, Alice B. Toklas, the Austrian poet Marie Luise Kaschnitz, and many others — but who has no clue as to what is actually going on in his own life.

By the end, Hinterhand stands revealed as another "lonely" male writer who has reduced his voiceless and nameless wife to an assistant, who helps him revise his books and on whom he comes to rely as his only "connection with the world". He may even, as Johnson seems to imply, have persuaded himself that Mrs Hinterhand had "wanted the deed" to be done, since it involved the destruction of the "image" to which her controlling husband had sought to confine her.[30] Whatever else may be said about Johnson's disintegrating marriage, this novella, which Fritz J. Raddatz commended as a "gruesome day of judgement",[31] demonstrates that Johnson continued to exist as a writer. It is a complex and genuinely creative text, even though it may fall short of the high mission attributed to "the independent capability of artistic thinking" by Hannah Arendt's husband, Heinz Blücher, who had provided Johnson with impromptu "seminars" on politics, history and philosophy when the novelist stayed with Arendt and himself on Riverside Drive. While lecturing on Homer at Bard College, some fifty miles up the Hudson river in 1954, this former communist anti-Nazi German émigré, who claimed to have experienced five revolutions in his lifetime, had told his students that "Art is so mighty because it changes our perception of the world... If we love art and participate in the experience given there our entire being will be changed, so mighty is this experience and yet so harmless".[32] Art, in short, as something distinct from myth of all kinds — or at least, "as a myth we can live with, but in which we cannot live".

PART VI.

THE STORM OF MEMORY: A NEW USE FOR THE SASH WINDOWS OF NORTH KENT

It all revolved around the view. It was the view that was appropriated.

— Uwe Johnson on Riverside
Drive in "A Part of New York",
*Dimension: Contemporary German
Arts and Letters*, 1968, p. 333.

Looking north from the front bedroom of 26 Marine Parade, Sheerness, 31 August 2018.

27. UNJAMMING MARCEL DUCHAMP'S LARGE GLASS

"I am not dead. I am in Herne Bay".[1] So wrote Marcel Duchamp on a postcard to his German friend Max Bergmann in August 1913. Earlier that year, Duchamp's painting *Nude Descending a Staircase* had horrified critics at the Armory Exhibition in New York, but it is most unlikely anyone was bothered about that particular scandal in this popular seaside resort on the Kentish mainland, a few miles to the east of Whitstable. The rising French avant-gardist was there to chaperone his seventeen-year-old sister Yvonne as she attended English lessons at Lynton College, a private establishment on Downs Park, a couple of streets inland from the seafront. By day, he played tennis under clear skies. In the evenings, he enjoyed the electrically illuminated Herne Bay Pavilion, a huge hall with facilities for dancing and roller-skating, which had been opened on the town's pier only two years previously.[2] He was, so he assured Bergmann, quite "enchanted" by the place.

We know, too, that Duchamp continued to think about the project that, some ten years later, would yield one of the founding works of twentieth-century conceptual art: *The Large Glass*, also known as *The Bride Stripped Bare by her Bachelors, Even*. While in Herne Bay, he sketched various studies that would later be gathered into the work. He also clipped a photograph of the Grand Pier Pavilion illuminated at night, which would eventually appear attached to a note outlining the possible background to *The Large Glass*: "An electric fête recalling the decorative lighting of / Magic city or Luna Park, or the Pier Pavilion at Herne Bay".[3] In the same note

Duchamp stated, apparently for the first time, "The picture will be executed on two large sheets of glass about 1.30 x 1.40 m / one above the other (demountable)."

Grand Pier and Pavilion, Herne Bay. Postcard c. 1920.

These shreds of evidence were barely enough for those who organised the festival with which, in August 2013, Herne Bay marked the centenary of Duchamp's visit — and especially not for the man who had inspired their festival's most charming hypothesis. The artist and curator Jeremy Millar had surveyed every scrap of information he could find about Duchamp's stay, and yet he'd still had to resort to fiction in the film he made about the episode in 2006. Entitled *Zugzwang (Almost Complete)*, the film speculates in a spirit of "possible discovery" that Duchamp, who had indeed once said that he would like to refer to his work as "my windows" rather as a more traditional artist might speak of "my etchings", got the idea of making *The Large Glass* on two panes of glass, one placed above the other, from "the larger sash windows of the grand Victorian houses in the town". "Might he", wonders Millar, "have considered *The Large Glass* as a sash window?"

Millar ventures the possibility that Duchamp had never seen

sliding sash windows before coming to Herne Bay. Perhaps the man who would soon pioneer a new kind of "machine art" had been intrigued by their mechanism, to say nothing of the unexpected French devices that might, without too much effort, be flushed out of their English name: not just the "frame" that may found in the English "sash" (by courtesy of the French word "chassis"), but also the more menacing apparatus preserved in the French name for this characteristically English type of window, *"fenêtre à guillotine".*

Certainly, *The Large Glass* makes effective use of its two "windows". Duchamp referred to the upper one as the "Bride's Domain" and the lower as the "Bachelors' Apparatus", and the work suggests both attraction and polarised repulsion between the two. The bride and her mechanically rendered bachelors are at once close and separate, their figures drawn towards one another and yet eternally frustrated by the frame separating them.

The connection Millar is seeking to establish between *The Large Glass* and the sash windows of Herne Bay might have been more resoundingly clinched — and definitely more "complete" — had Duchamp included some sort of sliding movement between his "windows" so that the frustration of both the bride and her bachelors might be registered not just by their adjacency but also by the superimposition of the two separate frames. Unfortunately (and I sympathise as one of the many former students who have struggled with jammed and rotten sash windows in rented off-season rooms in north Kent), he can't get the things to shift at all. He does his best with the help of a photograph showing the two panes casually leant against one another while the work was still being assembled in Duchamp's studio. That, however, is as far as Millar can persuade his hypothesis to go. He may, perhaps, be glad to hear of another major European artist who, some seven decades later, came to terms much more explicitly with the sash windows of north Kent.

Towards the end of 1974, when 26 Marine Parade was still being repaired and decorated prior to the final move from

West Berlin, Johnson was pleased to inform Max Frisch that the front bedroom at the top of the house was being fitted with a double-glazed *"louvre window"*. The lower rooms, however, faced north across the estuary through large single-paned Victorian sashes. It was through their frame that Johnson glanced over an English sea view chosen at least partly because it reminded him of others. These apparently displacing resemblances inform and shape his most significant engagement with English realities.

*

Johnson was talking about the pub when, in October 1975, he informed Erika Klemm that "The Sea View has me again".[4] However, the view from his house across the Thames Estuary also acquired a sense of uncanny familiarity that would extend far beyond the quickly noted fact that the southern stretch of the North Sea, which filled the right hand side of Johnson's windows, was still occasionally described as the "German Ocean".

Views over water mattered greatly to Johnson, and so too did the windows through which he, together with his principal character Gesine Cresspahl, often observed them. It has recently been pointed out that the "framed gaze" serves as a constellating principle of *Anniversaries* – and one that prevents Johnson's evocation of New York City from becoming conventionally realist or "mimetic". As Thomas Herold describes it, the "framing" is connected to "the German past" that lurks at the edge of Gesine Cresspahl's field of vision, triggering "memories, hallucinatory daydreams, descriptive evocations, or symbolic references"[5] that press into and shape her experience of the American metropolis. The containing frame converts the view into an "image", which then goes on to evoke "corresponding images" from the unreachable past. This rising storm of memory serves to obscure the city, but it also enfolds the American present in recollections – often sudden, disconcerting and involuntary – of the unattainable

Mecklenburg "home" for which Gesine sometimes yearns (although without forgetting the genocidal murder and ideological violence that have permanently dislodged her).

Johnson shows how this might work in the first volume of *Anniversaries*. It is 15 October 1967, and the ten-year-old Marie Cresspahl is sitting by the window in her mother Gesine's three-roomed flat at 243 Riverside Drive, gazing out towards New Jersey on the far side of the wide Hudson River as she ponders her homework. Sister Magdalena, the teacher at her private school, has demanded an essay entitled "I look out of the window". Marie's options, which Johnson elaborates with characteristic precision, include describing "how the colours are tiered under the clear sky, with the blue terrace of the steep New Jersey shore between the softer colour of the vegetation and the sharper gray of the river, all sprinkled with sand-coloured boughs and sparse patches of foliage on the upper promenade, plus, along the lower edge of the view, the poisonous car paint next to the solemn gloom of a park fence deep in shadow".[6]

That "tiered" world (which young Marie spurns, preferring to describe the more dramatic events of the day she watched a building burn down through the window of "Charlie's Good Eats" on 96th Street) is derived from the "unassailable"[7] view Johnson had himself known while living in the apartment he later allowed Gesine and Marie to have for slightly less rent (as Herold also notes) than he himself had paid: a place "with five windows that all looked out onto Riverside Park, and in the fall you looked out at the Hudson".[8] The passage also anticipates the way Johnson would come to see the view over the Thames Estuary from his house on Marine Parade — a building, as he had explained to Max Frisch just after making his offer of purchase, with an upstairs that "practically juts out over the water". Given a "clear" day, which can by no means be taken for granted in north Kent, this view too is gathered in by the window and framed as a series of horizontally aligned bands of colour. The uppermost tier, which may be blue, white or grey depending on the weather, stands above a tiny strip of greenish brown produced by the distant Essex shore. Beneath that, a wide band of sea gives way first to a tawny layer of shingle, mud and sand, and then, although one may have to lean over to see it from the uppermost floor, to the heavier grey concrete of the sea wall on the other side of Marine Parade.

"There is no perception that is not full of memories,"[9] declared Henri Bergson, and so it was for Johnson as he looked out from his house in Sheerness. The sashes that framed this incomer's Kentish sea view as tiered bands also abstracted it to a degree: dislocating it sufficiently to open it, however unexpectedly and, indeed, fleetingly, to the coinciding memory of the earlier views across water with which Johnson would repeatedly map the course of his life. "Ultimately", as he explained while talking "About Myself" on the occasion of his election to the German Academy for Language and Literature in 1977, "it would be fair to say that I have a thing for rivers. It's true, I grew up on the Peene in Anklam, the Nebel flows through Güstrow, I have traveled to and in Rostock on the Warnow, Leipzig presented me with the Pleisse and the Elster, Manhattan is surrounded by the Hudson and East and North Rivers, I also recall a Hackensack River, and for the past three years I have had on offer outside my window the River Thames, where it turns into the North Sea".[10]

The sash windows framing Johnson's view over the Thames Estuary may have been sold to him as an attractive feature of 26 Marine Parade. Once he had moved in, however, they would start working almost as instruments for engaging the memory of those other watery views, thereby turning land, sea and air into the witnesses of a scarifying international history defined more fundamentally by war, murder and extreme ideological conflict than by pleasant days spent sailing, swimming, or strolling along the promenade — although these too had a place in Johnson's memories of Mecklenburg and the Pomeranian coast further to the east.

It was thanks to this sliding theatre of contrasts and resemblances that Johnson went on to sketch one of the most arresting and revealing of twentieth-century "views" of the Thames Estuary. His is not a view that will be found fully expressed in a single text or image that might be listed alongside, say, the opening pages of Joseph Conrad's *Heart of Darkness*, in which a sunset over the river is so brilliantly used to evoke the "dark" times and places of European imperialism, or for that matter, classic estuarial paintings such as Turner's *The Fighting Temeraire*, in which an ancient ninety-eight-gun warship, a veteran of the Battle of Trafalgar, is shown being towed upriver from Sheerness to Rotherhithe, where it will be scrapped, while a turned-round sunset burns luridly to the east behind it. Unlike these topographically engaged masterpieces, Johnson's sea view does not exist in a single, finally achieved work. Like so much connected to his unfulfilled "island stories" project, it comes down to us as a characteristic perspective: a partly autobiographical way of seeing that Johnson shared with Gesine Cresspahl and the other "invented persons" gathered in his empty basement office during his last years on Marine Parade.

Following the prompting of his novels, in which the responsibility for making sense of a situation is so deliberately shared with the reader, and picking up on threads and fragmentary observations in his occasional writings about Sheerness, we can understand Johnson's "sea view" as an approach in which exact observation is accompanied by this partly involuntary "appropriation" of a much larger remembered history. The tiered world beyond his windows would remind this expatriated citizen of the GDR that, while Sheerness was a long way from the Germany of his childhood and youth, it too lived — albeit with its own kind of dawdling somnolence — in the shadow of flood and fire.

View from the front bedroom, 26 Marine Parade, Sheerness.

⟨THE ESPLANADE RIGHT IN FRONT OF THE HOUSE⟩

Here I am speaking only of myself, and yet it may be not merely egotistical if I describe to you some views to be seen over the course of a few afternoon hours. Views, namely, out the window, and I wish you could have seen them: the two of us, next to each other, right in front of the house, where the poorer folks from London enjoy disporting themselves on a Sunday like this one, as tourists by the sea, visible only from the waist up to me and my dear wife Mrs Letsnotdiscussit, and yet still a valuable warning about the lack of, or taste in, leisure attire. Following them come the waves of the River Thames, sea-like here, beating against the stones as high or as low as the Royal Geographical Tidal Institute's calendar permits them to. For an ignorant observer such as myself, they are merely bright white a long way out, a little dirty-looking but choppy in any case; the last third of my visual field, though, is **as blue as blue can be,** magnificently changeable, from pale to gray to strapping within this color. Within and atop this blue, what is there to say to a lady from Königsberg: bathers in various stages of suffering from sunburn, boats with sails in fashionable colorations, some of them even classified and many of them well-suited to offer me certain memories, silent but critical, pertaining to the process of jibing. People paddling, those who let themselves be brought hither and thither by petrol engines, and on the horizon, where cartography would suggest that we should be able to detect the south coast of Essex, merely a difference: not a line but a smudge between water and sky, which educated people label as a horizon and which is therefore mine. And I've almost forgotten to admit to you the rude British Petroleum oil tanker that just now went pitching from right to left, from east to west, across the window — probably because I believe I share your opinion of such objects in one's field of view.

⟨**Uwe Johnson, letter to Hannah Arendt, 3 August 1975**[11]⟩

491

Bodsteller Bodden, Darß, Mecklenburg-West Pomerania.

View from the living room, 26 Marine Parade.

28. SEA DEFENCES: FROM GOD'S WILL TO "PUDDICOMBE'S FOLLY"

Remembered worlds would slide over one another in Johnson's sea-facing sash windows, yet his letters reveal him to have been aware of another dramatic feature of the outlook from 26 Marine Parade. As you descend through the house the relation between those tiered bands of colour in the sea-facing windows changes. Seen from the window in the main upstairs bedroom on the first floor, the rusty strip of shingle and beach has shrunk thanks to the grey sea wall, which has risen up to nip off the lower parts of any person who may just then be walking past on the promenade. The beach has vanished entirely by the time you reach the living room on the raised ground floor. From Johnson's office beneath that, the large expanse of grey concrete has cancelled everything except for a tiny strip of sky.

When I first looked out through the window of the "lower-ground-floor" room in which Johnson sat through much of 1982 — alone, unwell, ever more in debt and sustained, in the short term, by tea, tobacco and alcohol as he worked towards completion of the fourth volume of *Anniversaries* — I saw the wall directly opposite as testimony to his spiritual condition in these last years of his life. Things were bad enough, surely, without this blinding barrier rising up more than four metres from the pavement to press in on him like a cement sarcophagus. How, I wondered, could one not be shocked into silence by the brutal irony of the fact that the writer who had devised a new form of literature capable of articulating the division of Germany and, in *Two Views*, the experience of living in a city suddenly split by the Berlin Wall, should have spent his last days looking out at a vertical slab of concrete that did indeed seem to scream both "Dead End" and "Blind Alley", even if no local graffiti artist had yet got round to persuading those words to stick to its roughly-textured surface?

It was Holger Helbig, director of the Uwe Johnson Society in Rostock, who awakened me to the fact that the wall now standing outside Johnson's office wasn't actually there in its present form when Johnson took up residence in 1974. That said, however, the lower concrete rampart that preceded it — and which his visitors registered as a "smooth high wall"[1] despite the fact that it was topped with open iron railings and had garages below — was still sufficient to block the view from Johnson's office. He informed Max Frisch that he didn't intend to spend much time staring out of the window as he worked, and he would repeat the claim eight years later, reassuring a visiting interviewer that he did not make much use of his house's view over the water, tending rather to spend his days head down at his "metal behemoth"[2] of a table.

These may well have been evasive remarks but to see Marine Parade's wall only as a hideous English reprise of the Berlin Wall is not to understand it at all. The "Anti-Fascist Protection Rampart" dividing East and West Berlin had been built in a few days by the GDR, but the version blocking the view from Johnson's house was the outcome of a much longer struggle between a little town built on remote marshland which, even with the lower tides of the mid-Victorian age, was said by one concerned "inhabitant" of that time to have stood between five and seven feet below the high-water mark,[3] and the vast force of nature that Joseph Conrad would declare "farthest removed in the unchangeableness and majesty of its might from the spirit of mankind".[4] The unequal struggle between the marginal community of Sheerness and that vast inhuman sea had shaped the political, existential and religious life of the town from its earliest days. It had also ensured that, like the ocean they were intended to resist, the town's sea walls had come in successive waves, each one absorbing the materials of its defeated and collapsing predecessor. This fact was duly registered in Johnson's "non-committal" understanding and also in some of the old photographs he gathered into his archive.

The Victorian Version: "Nothing more than a mud-heap"

The town of Sheerness did not exist to suffer the "universal fright"[5] caused by the calamitous storm of 26–27 November 1703, which killed more than eight thousand people as it swept across the country, felling innumerable ancient trees, tumbling buildings, shattering ships and causing windmills to spin so crazily that they caught fire and burned to the ground. That disastrous visitation convinced the puritanical Daniel Defoe that "Storms and Tempests are Above our rules", acts of divine punishment, imposed on people who needed to understand that "'tis in vain we pretend to be Wall'd about by the Ocean, and ride Masters of the Sea".[6] Built well over a century after the "worst storm in British history"[7] and at first hardly walled about at all, the little town at Sheerness was also known for its non-conformist zeal, and its stricter chapel-going people shared Defoe's understanding that "In publick Callamities, every Circumstance is A Sermon, and everything we see a Preacher".[8] William Shrubsole, the dockyard shipwright and founding congregationalist preacher at the Bethel Chapel in Blue Town, offered his view of such catastrophes in a sermon delivered on 24 June 1787. "Often", so this ardent believer declaimed, "you may observe the righteous and the wicked perish together, in one undistinguishing calamity. The Earthquake overthrows and swallows up the crouded sacred temple, as well as the infamously frequented brothel! The pestilence breathes its deadly vapor on the good and on the evil! And the raging tempest, and the swelling waves ingulph or dash on the dreadful rocks, ships filled with religious refugees, or cruel pirates. The direful and devouring judgement makes no distinction between the righteous and the profane".[9]

The fear of inundation had haunted Sheerness from the start, and not just in the minds of those who attended the emerging town's more apocalyptic chapels. What were people here meant to think when the negligently managed Bilberry dam above the village of Holmfirth in the West Riding of Yorkshire burst in the middle of the night on 5 February 1852, washing away entire mills as well as houses, leaving eighty-one people dead and many others injured, orphaned and instantly pauperised? A well-informed correspondent drew the obvious, and far from theological, conclusion in the *United Services Gazette*: "Appalling as is the catastrophe that occurred at Holmfirth, one of a much more fearful nature threatens the town of Sheerness".[10] Sheerness lay "about eight feet below high water mark at the time of spring tide, and some parts more than ten feet" and an inundation here would surely sink "thousands" in a "watery grave". There were by that time already about five thousand people living in Mile Town and half that in Blue Town, and the houses, which were mostly made of wood, would be swept away, leaving the people to drown along with the "immense quantity of sheep and cattle on the marshes". Anyone visiting Sheerness at high water could already see the water rising to "within a foot of the top of the stonework of the dockyard and the beach wall", with the wind, if it came from the north-west, sending great splashes over the top. It would only take "a two-feet rise" above the usual height — i.e. a rise of the sort already known in other places — to produce "a calamity not to be described or equalled in the annals of history". Surely no inhabitant could avoid "shuddering for his own safety, especially when considering that [the influx] would extend for nearly two miles round the town, thus giving little room for retreat". Meanwhile, the sea walls on which so many lives depended were "weak, and require strengthening with good stone-work instead of mud". They needed to be raised "three feet higher at least" if the town and dockyard were really to be "safe from such an occurrence". There was, in short, a job to be done and — here again is the thin silver lining that

496

observers have strained to detect at the edge of so many dark and menacing clouds over Sheerness — it would "provide employment for many".

Steps were eventually taken. An undated photograph in Johnson's collection shows the view looking east along Marine Parade as it was towards the end of the nineteenth century. While the row of pink-stoned houses known as Shrimp Terrace is yet to fill the space before the last house on the inland side of the developing street, the terrace in which Johnson would live is visible to the right, as is the Victoria Hotel, a tall building that would come to be known as "the Glass House" on account of the many large windows it turned towards both the sea and the sunset upriver. Already taken in hand by Victorian reformers, the old sea wall has been turned into a promenade, surfaced with tarred gravel and, on the landward slope, faced with grouted stone. If later descriptions are to be believed, it has also been raised up from the pavement by a little vertical wall about eighteen inches high.

Marine Parade before 1890. From Johnson's collection.

Had he wanted to go back to the beginning of Marine Parade's sea defences, Johnson might have considered the experience of the English writer D.H. Lawrence's mother, Lydia Beardsall, who grew up in Sheerness as the daughter of a Nottingham-born engine fitter employed at the dockyard. An ardent primitive Methodist and lay preacher who had moved to the booming town in March 1858, George Beardsall settled his family in a small house, 10 Chapel Street, at the western edge of the emerging new settlement of Marine Town.[11] Lydia worked as a pupil teacher and governess until 1870, when her father, who had been disabled and impoverished by a fall at the dockyard, took the family back to Nottingham. Lawrence remembered his mother, whom he would later describe as a "superior soul",[12] as the model for Gertrude Morel in his 1913 novel *Sons and Lovers*: sensitive and intelligent but married to a brutalised and drunken Nottingham miner and inclined, in the midst of this life of "dreary endurance", to grieve for the girl who had "run so lightly on the breakwater at Sheerness ten years before".[13]

Photographs attributed to the year 1866 reveal the rudimentary nature of the "breakwater" along which Lydia Beardsall ran. In its first years, Marine Town was protected by a natural accumulation of shingle near the top of the beach and, on the landward side of that, a ridge of clay, raised up alongside the pavement to the height of a few feet.[14] "Nothing more than a mud-heap", as the *Sheerness Times* would scoff when reprinting the photographs of Marine Town's first sea defences some sixty years later, and "a quagmire for pedestrians" in wet weather.[15]

Looking at these images from Marine Parade's first decade, it is easy to grasp why, in November 1875, an "inhabitant" reported that "many residents" were still anxious for reassurance from "a competent authority" that they were not faced with the imminent prospect of "a breach ... and that at midnight, amid a slumbering population".[16] Two weeks later, during the night of Sunday 21 November 1875, the sea duly poured over the defences for more than an hour, and it was only a fortuitous change in the wind forty minutes before high tide that limited the damage to displaced kerbstones and holes scooped in the road. The following month a government enquiry came to Sheerness to consider the case — ardently pressed on the authorities in a memorial signed by nine hundred of the town's "working men" — for assistance towards the cost of building a more substantial sea wall and esplanade.[17]

"Nothing more than a mud-heap": Marine Parade's first sea wall, c. 1866.

A year or so later, in 1876, the council acquired the strip of land on which Marine Town's "clay bank" stood, and set about "battering" stone headers into its sides.[18] Even after the improvements shown in Johnson's photograph, Marine Parade's sea wall remained a consolidated version of the original "mud-heap". As such, it was quickly revealed to be more convincing as a summer promenade than as a barrier protecting "Sheerness-on-Sea" from the storm-driven winter or spring tides.

In November 1880, residents of some of the town's lower streets found the water two feet deep in their houses, prompting the *Whitstable Times* to declare that "the poorer classes are great sufferers by the calamity, which may prove fatal to many".[19] The paper also repeated local speculation that Sheerness's sea defences had been weakened by "the removal of large quantities of shingle for sale, and the neglect to provide proper groynes".[20] Worse floods followed during the gales and blizzard of 18 January 1881. This particular storm surge brought death and mayhem all over the country — many boats and barges lost at sea, piers swept away, entire trains lost under blizzards of snow, and chaos in industrial and working-class districts of south London (the water stood five-and-a-half feet deep in houses from Waterloo to Upper Marsh Street).

Sheerness suffered "great damage" too.[21] The sea broke through the defences in many places, including the eastern end of Marine Parade where the wall by Cheyney Rock was "entirely carried away".[22] This time, half the town is said to have been left under three feet of water and "the distress in the district is beyond description".[23] Within weeks, the Sheerness Board of Health had pressed forward a plan to improve Marine Parade's esplanade, and the *Sheerness Times* was canvassing the support of ratepayers, who it was thought might be interested in the proposal "either as a precaution of public safety or as a local improvement certain to be self-paying in the long run".[24] That same month, members of the town's Sea Defences Committee resolved to get a clause inserted into the Floods Prevention Bill to enable it to overrule the rights of the Lord of the Manor, a fellow named Polson, widely thought to have been endangering the town by extracting so much shingle from the beach along Marine Parade.[25] After protracted wrangling, the War Department accepted responsibility for the sea defences near the garrison and dockyard, sufficiently at least to repair overwhelmed stretches of the "mud wall" surrounding their land, and said that they would both build a three-foot concrete wall in the weakest place near the moat, and also introduce a series of groynes, intended to trap shingle in the hope that it would form a natural revetment between the town and the sea.[26] "Urgently needed" works under the jurisdiction of the town, however, were left undone because the local Board of Health claimed that the sea defences were government property and not its own responsibility.[27]

These were alarming facts for the town and its ratepayers to face. In the national perspective, however, public apprehension of the "fearful calamity" that might come with flooding gave priority not to Sheppey, Canvey Island or any other flood-prone site in the estuary, but to the City of London itself. Indeed, if Sheerness featured at all in the capital's deliberations about flooding this was, according to a prescient article in the *Builder*, because it surely had a role to play in the "early warning system" that must be developed to protect the capital rather than itself.[28] Believing that modern methods made it possible to calculate "to what height a tide will rise at London that has attained a certain height at Sheerness", the author considered it "requisite" that a tidal gauge be placed at "a proper spot near Sheerness" so that London might be given time in which to take hasty measures with planking, cement and similar materials to ensure that Lambeth and other riverside areas of the capital never flooded again". This was a flawed proposal, since no one in 1881 actually knew how to predict the surges that wind and storms might add to a rising tide.

In Sheerness, meanwhile, the struggle for an adequate sea wall continued to test local resources. A storm drove the high tide back to cause even greater calamity on 29 November 1897, sweeping away much of the Co-Operative Society's pier at Cheyney Rock, and drowning livestock and a farmer on the marshes at Elmley and Harty.[29] During this unusually extreme version of Sheerness's recurrent "Great Disaster" the sea smashed a "huge breach" in the breakwater by the Roman Catholic church on the Broadway and then poured into Neptune Terrace, flooding the lower rooms (including some that are now part of an old people's home). Townspeople gathered to stare at the "truly pitiable" sight of a brand new piano floating up to bang against the ceiling — touchingly unaware that the sea was at the same time pouring into their own encircled homes, a few streets inland. Not content with breaking through Sheerness's western defences along the Medway, it also poured over the Marine Town Esplanade "in considerable volumes"[30] rushing down Telescope Alley and Richmond Street in "one uninterrupted course"[31] and leaving three feet of water in Clyde Street and Unity Street. Once again, occupants retreated to the first floors of their houses, and the railway line was drowned, leaving Sheerness "completely cut off from the rest of England".[32] Viewed from the ruins of the sea wall at West Minster on the Medway, Sheerness "appeared as if it had been transported to the shore of a lake". It was given "quite a Venetian aspect" as people started rowing boats along streets...[33]

Rose Thomas's postcard.

Further adjustments to Marine Town's inadequate "breakwater" were carried out in the following years. By 3 July 1914, when a visitor named Rose Thomas sent a postcard home to Gosport, the promenade had acquired a bench and, on the seaward side, a little vertical wall. This "dwarf wall", which stood about two feet high, included a gap for "storm boards" at the traditional access point near Neptune Terrace. Although it may well have left the view from the houses along Marine Parade largely intact, anyone versed in modern coastal hydraulic theory would recognise it as a monument to prehistoric ignorance. It was shaped in a way that would simply fling breaking waves up into the air, where the driving wind would catch them, just as it was said to have done in 1852, and sweep them over into the road. It was also placed on quite the wrong side of the promenade, which should have been used to stretch, slow and exhaust the advancing wave before impact. A pitifully inadequate thing, it could do nothing to reduce the growing case for a thoroughgoing rebuild along the entire length of the street.

1933: "Something more substantial"

So it was that, by 1974, when Johnson moved into No. 26, the residents of Marine Parade had long faced a vast concrete rampart, conceived and planned in the year of the Wall Street crash, funded through a public works programme set up by Ramsay MacDonald's second Labour government, and built, not without difficulty, by Sheerness Urban District Council in the early Thirties.

Known locally as "the Garages", the concrete sea wall and promenade over which Johnson imagined looking with his philosopher friend Hannah Arendt was the product of a period of twentieth-century British history that Johnson had researched for the first volume of *Anniversaries*. It was in 1925 that Gesine Cresspahl's father, Heinrich, a guild-minded cabinet-maker and social democrat who had left an increasingly hostile Germany for the Netherlands soon after being locked in a potato cellar during the right-wing Kapp Putsch of March 1920,[34] moved again to England. He settled in Richmond, on the Thames upriver from London, where he lived in two rooms near the gas works and, from 1928, ran a carpentry firm, Pascal & Son, for an English owner who liked

503

to brag about his heroism in the Great War even though he had actually only ever "counted caps"[35] at Dartmouth naval supply base, and who also turned out to be an anti-Semitic follower of Oswald Mosley's British Union of Fascists. "Twenty per cent unemployed in England,"[36] Johnson had noted in *Anniversaries*, and he now only had to glance at the looming anti-sea protection rampart outside his window to recognise that the problem had weighed on Sheerness too.

Marine Parade's re-engineered promenade and sea wall was an indirect outcome of the First World War. Germany's submarine blockade had demonstrated the importance of protecting vital low-lying agricultural land from flooding. When it came to sea defences, it had also revealed "the obvious imperfections of the existing piecemeal and disorganised state of affairs throughout the country".[37] The problem was put to the Royal Commission on Land Drainage, established under Lord Bledisloe in 1927, which reviewed the nation's flood defence system, condemned the existing laws (some of which dated back to the time of Henry VIII) as "chaotic" and "obscure", and insisted that a matter of such obvious national importance could no longer be left to 361 under-resourced land drainage authorities, which only had the power to raise funds from the direct beneficiaries of any proposed defence works. Following the Commission's report, the Land Drainage Act 1930 created Catchment Boards in each of the main river areas, granting them the power to raise funds from county and borough councils throughout their river's catchment area.

The inadequacy of existing systems of tidal prediction also had to be addressed if early warning systems were to be improved. This work had fallen to the Meteorological Office and also the Liverpool Observatory and Tidal Institute, founded in 1919, which used data recorded at Southend to analyse the ways in which high tides might be increased by winds. It was this work that would eventually produce the theory of the "storm surge" caused by "the drag" of the wind on the sea, which was shown to be all the greater when the wind's "fetch" is long, and capable of wreaking havoc if it coincided with a high tide.[38]

The sea, meanwhile, kept coming. Sheerness had escaped the worst on Tuesday, 1 November 1921, when a north-westerly gale lifted the spring tide about three feet above expectation, raising the ships in the naval harbour high over the heads of disconcerted onlookers in Station Road.[39] It was only by rare fluke that the town escaped inundation on 6 and 7 January 1928, when a "tidal wave" nearly a foot higher than previously recorded reached London just after midnight and without any warning from downriver. Overwhelming the embankment, it drowned fourteen people in basements along the Thames and caused extensive damage (not least at the Tate Gallery, where the water wrecked important works of art stored in the basement, including sketches by Turner).[40] Despite some flooding in the dockyard and around the creek at Queenborough,[41] Sheppey was saved — allegedly thanks to the vigilance of the local manager of Queenborough Port and Contracting Company. Mr W.S. Fenton, who had responsibility for the dams on the island, happened to overhear men on the Nore lightship talking over the radio with colleagues having "a rough time"[42] at Goodwin Sands. Alerted by a voice predicting "they will be having some water up the river tonight", Mr Fenton had despatched his workmen to secure the dams. Aware of the happenstance nature of his decision, he joined those who demanded a more formal early warning system.

By the beginning of March 1929, Sheerness Urban District Council was also being challenged to do something about the dire condition of the town's sea defences by the highly concerned chairman of its Works Committee. Having forced the question onto the agenda despite the reluctance of colleagues, Councillor S. Carpenter insisted that the town was living in "a fool's paradise".[43] He declared the danger of flooding so high that he really "could not understand people travelling along the sea walls with perambulators".

There were all too many excuses for the council's inertia. Lack of resources was a familiar complaint for a town aware of the straitened condition of many of its ratepayers, and the difficulty of raising an adequate response to the threat was increased by the division of the island into three different local authorities, including the Minster Rural District Council which had tended, in the critical judgement of the *Sheerness Times,* to "stand aloof"[44] — its jurisdiction was placed on higher ground — from Sheerness's worries about flooding. The town's Urban District council was also hampered by the fact that the War Office, which owned the defences at the weak length near the battery at Barton's Point, was reluctant to repair the disintegrating groynes on the shore there or, indeed, to accept that the shingle so vital to the town's security really was being swept away by high tides.

Councillor Carpenter may at first have had to "accept the flogging" imposed on him by his more resigned fellow councillors, but his repeated insistence that Sheerness was in "real danger"[45] gained ground over the coming weeks. While the council continued to believe that the cost of sea defences was "becoming more than some of the coastal towns could bear" and should be made into a "national charge",[46] it was soon countenancing action along the lines suggested by Carpenter, who was by now also declaring that three or four large concrete groynes were needed to prevent the erosion of shingle between Neptune Terrace and Cheyney Rock.

By the end of March, more "definite" plans for a new scheme were being prepared.[47] Having admitted himself "no expert" on sea defences, Councillor Carpenter attended a conference organised by Lowestoft Council as part of the preparation for the Coastal Protection Bill (brought to the House of Commons on 29 October 1929). He also visited London to discuss his council's developing ideas with George Lansbury, the idealistic East End Christian socialist who was First Commissioner of Works in Ramsay MacDonald's minority Labour government, and also with officials of the Unemployment Grants Committee, responsible for loaning money to local authorities for public works intended to relieve unemployment in depressed areas.

Carpenter became the driver of the council's proposed scheme, and also of its application for a loan of £25,000 from that committee.

Introduced in 1929, the "Marine Town Improvement Scheme" would involve a great deal more concrete than was required by Councillor Carpenter's groynes along Marine Parade's seafront. As the clerk to Sheerness Council alleged at a public enquiry into the application, held in Sheerness under the auspices of the Department of Health (which supervised the Unemployment Grants Committee's schemes) in January 1930, the Victorian wall was a woeful thing, which the rising sea had repeatedly exposed as inadequate. Lacking even rudimentary foundations, it was, so Councillor Carpenter explained, really "only mud plastered over". The idea of "global warming" was for the future but, as Carpenter also pointed out, the town's high tides were already estimated to be nearly two feet above those of the 1890s. Since 1904, when Sheerness council had bought the foreshore from the Lord of the Manor, they had swept away much of the protective shingle from the beach and the water regularly now rose right up to the "dwarf wall" on the promenade.

The council's new scheme would extend along the full length of Marine Parade, from Neptune Terrace all the way east to Cheyney Rock. Made of concrete, both reinforced and mass, it would be thirty feet wide in all and five feet six inches higher than its predecessor. It would have foundations of shingle, varying from four to twelve feet deep, which would rest on clay upwards of two feet thick. It would include three if not four concrete groynes built out towards the sea to prevent the shingle drifting.

If keeping the sea out of the town was a priority, the Marine Town Improvement Scheme was also intended to help Sheerness cope with its oldest fear. As a naval town, Sheerness had boomed during the First World War. Once the armistice was signed, however, naval expenditure shrank as it so often had at such moments, and workers were being laid off in the time-sanctioned manner. By 1931, concerned residents would be urging the constituency MP to seek an official denial of rumours alleging that the shrunken dockyard and naval station, on which the town was still utterly dependent, might be closed altogether.[48] In this depressed post-war climate, the members of Sheerness Urban District Council had felt "forced", once again, to "develop their town as a seaside resort". Various steps had already been taken to make the place more attractive. These included the creation of new leisure facilities near the main beach in Mile Town and the intensification — in 1923 — of a longstanding campaign to persuade the County Council to abolish the hated toll on the Kingsferry Bridge across the Swale. ("Freedom is ours", the *Sheerness Guardian* would blaze when this discouraging "stranglehold"[49] on the island and its summer trade was finally broken in July 1929.)

As the council was pleased to note, these improvements had already enabled Sheerness to draw summer visitors from south and south-east London, as well as from nearer industrial areas such as Gillingham, Maidstone and Chatham. The local papers reveal that a new kind of "lost property" was turning up on the beach: a pile of clothes, including trousers and a mackintosh, left unclaimed in front of Neptune Terrace; or an old sock with £31 in treasury notes stitched into its toe, eventually reclaimed by a couple of Londoners who had not dared to leave their savings at home. More glamorous visitors were counted in too, including the recently married artist Frank Medworth, who passed through in September, together with his wife and the new baby whose arrival had kept them close to home that year. Though he would not deny his accustomed preference for Spain when interviewed over a cup of coffee by the *Sheerness Guardian,* Medworth was happy to declare Sheerness much improved since the summer visits of his childhood as the son of a Southwark joiner. The "natives" seemed "very pleasant" although "not easy" to approach by those they judged strangers:

He was stopped by a man who exclaimed, "You're a foreigner, aren't you?"

"Well", replied Mr Medworth, "we are cosmopolitan".

"Oh", replied the man, "I knew you weren't English".[50]

The Marine Parade Improvement Scheme would also seek to mitigate one of the remaining shortcomings of the developing resort — i.e. Sheerness's unpredictable weather — by providing three "ornamental shelters" on the new promenade, and more shelters and changing facilities in the space below. Thanks to the new bathing area at the western end, the council would also be able to sweep away the unsightly "wooden bathing huts" still littering the main beach. In the language of the town's publicity committee, the Marine Parade Improvement Scheme would clean all this up, thereby contributing to the "booming" of Sheerness as a resort.

But who was to build this prodigious, multipurpose rampart? With the dockyard employing a thousand fewer workers, and five hundred of the five thousand men on the town's national insurance register being unemployed, the Marine Parade Improvement Scheme was proposed as a labour-intensive two-year initiative that would, so the Unemployment Grants Committee had been assured, help to decrease "some of the suffering of a very large part of the population".

If anyone is still counting, Marine Parade's anti-sea protection rampart might rightfully be registered (alongside the bathing facilities on the Serpentine and other examples of "Lansbury's lidos" in London's parks) among the rare achievements of Britain's short-lived second Labour government. That, however, was not how some residents of Marine Parade saw it. They used the Ministry of Health's public enquiry to repeat objections previously articulated in letters to the local paper. They were worried, as Mrs Cole at No. 32 frankly admitted, about the impact on the value of their properties. They denied there was any genuine need for the "improvement", claiming that the sea had never flowed over the wall in living memory (on that score, Mrs Cole could only speak for the last nine years but her older neighbour, Mrs Beale of No. 33, had a full forty covered). They tormented themselves with the thought of the raised promenade, which surely threatened to confront them with an experience like that of the residents of Blue Town High Street, whose windows were blinded by the high brick wall isolating the dockyard. There was some dispute whether the council really intended to raise Marine Parade's defences by ten feet as Mrs Cole feared or only, as the surveyor insisted, by five feet six inches, but residents had reason to suspect that the height was determined primarily by the council's determination to create shelters for summer visitors beneath as well as on top of the esplanade. They anticipated that unruly "youngsters" would congregate in these shelters at night, and there were rumours — which turned out to be partly true even though they were vehemently denied at the hearing — that the financially stretched council, which had been far from forthcoming about its plans, secretly intended to build rentable garages and perhaps even shops on the landward side of its new rampart.

Although the residents of Marine Parade expressed their objections strongly, the majority in the flood-prone town welcomed the Marine Parade Improvement Scheme. It promised at least some work for the unemployed, a two-penny rate increase was not an intolerable price to pay for reliable sea defences, and the trade associations saw nothing but benefit in the prospect of a seafront that would complete the transformation of Sheerness into a summer resort that might at last hold its own against Herne Bay and Margate.

After the public enquiry, the scheme was adjusted to console the unhappy residents of Marine Parade by placing flowerbeds at both ends of the development, and also on the roadside slope occupying parts of the new rampart. Ornamental glass covers were added in places, and it was emphasised that the shelters would be locked at night to discourage loitering youths. These ameliorations would, it was promised, reduce costs as suggested by the government inspector, while also ensuring that there was nothing "sordid or severe" about the scheme.[51] As part of the drive for economy, it was decided to incorporate materials from the old Victorian promenade into its successor.

In May 1930 the government loan was approved, on the understanding that five hundred of Sheerness's unemployed men would be employed over the two years of the scheme.[52] A month later, a three-man deputation from the Sheerness branch of the National Unemployed Workers Movement brought their demands to a meeting of the Sheerness Urban District Council. This association was, as Uwe Johnson knew, led by Wal Hannington, among other British communists, and its members would be remembered for breaking the Two Minutes Silence on Armistice Day by singing the Internationale and for marching past the Cenotaph with pawnshop tickets pinned next to their medals. In *Anniversaries,* the sight of these economically straitened marchers has a disconcerting effect on Gesine's mother, Lisbeth Cresspahl, then living on the edge of the depression with her carpenter husband in Richmond. Fearing for the future in a country where craftsmen were increasingly advertising their products as "ONLY BRITISH MATERIAL USED. ONLY BRITISH LABOUR USED", she insisted on quitting this island of "crushed households"[53] and taking her reluctant husband back to Germany in 1933, where Gesine was born just as Hitler gains power.

Communist or not, the members of the Sheerness branch of the National Unemployed Workers' Movement appear to have been polite and, with one or two exceptions, quite restrained. Coming forward with "six points", they asked for the council's reassurance that the pick of the jobs on the new scheme would not go to already established council workers or to people who already had adequate pensions, and that priority would be given to those who had been out of work for longest. The jobs should be awarded in six-week periods to ensure fair treatment for all the local unemployed, and they strongly objected to the 2% pay increase awarded to the borough surveyor, Mr W.P. Puddicombe, who had agreed to take on supervision of the works, thereby saving the council from the allegedly greater cost of hiring an external civil engineer. Having made their points, the leader of the deputation, Mr Moore, thanked the council for the "courteous and kindly manner" in which they had been received.[54]

So the town had gone into action. Counting up reasons for the "prevailing note of optimism"[55] with which its inhabitants might look forward to the new year of 1932, the *Sheerness Guardian* gave pride of place to the anticipated opening of the new esplanade. The optimism was not to last, except, perhaps, among members of the town's Publicity Committee which, in March, would hold its own "boom week" to publicise Sheerness as a much-improved holiday resort. This, however, was to overlook the struggles of the borough surveyor, who had already failed to convince sceptical councillors that the works were "well within time"[56] and that the Marine Parade Improvement Scheme really would be ready to greet summer visitors in August. Like the incredulous councillor who asked for confirmation that he meant "August 1932", the *Sheerness Times* had by this time become scornful. The council had borrowed £25,000 from the government to fund the development, but the site was a slow-moving mess. The paper urged that the work must be completed as soon as possible. After that, further steps should be taken to "improve the inner slope by the cultivation of suitable plants and flowers to relieve the bare aspect of the concrete walls". Once this was done "a different view may be held" by those — "not a few" — who "openly avow that, in their view, the Council has spoilt the sea-front of Sheerness."[57]

August came and went without completion, and soon after that the council and ratepayers faced a worse problem than the hooliganism of those — locals or visitors — who had already started cutting into the wood of the new shelters, clambering onto their roofs, and defacing "the side walls of the new promenade with chalk drawings and figures."[58] By 17 November it was reported that the Sheerness Urban District Council had exhausted the loan, and been obliged to place the job under its own "general foreman" who, in order to lessen the consequence for ratepayers, would complete it using as many of the council's "permanent men" as could be spared for the task.[59] By December, Puddicombe, who also seems to have had enough of unemployed workers by this time, was blaming the delay on a lack of skilled carpenters. Councillors dismissed his excuse as "very watery".[60] The *Sheerness Times,* meanwhile, identified exactly how many unemployed carpenters had been available for work throughout the period in question and declared on behalf of the ratepayers, "the more we hear about this scheme, the greater the feeling of disappointment it creates".[61] By this time, the matter was being "freely discussed in the town" and the council invited further condemnation by refusing to discuss the situation except "in committee".[62] "Puddicombe's folly", as the development had come to be known, seems not to have been mentioned when, towards the end of 1932, George Lansbury came to open a new Labour Party hall and HQ on Sheerness High Street — a meeting that started with the singing of "Jerusalem", after which this long-standing pacifist and Christian enemy of the "merchants of death" spoke out in favour of the new forms of civil production that must surely be developed for the nation's naval dockyards and armaments factories.[63]

By 1933, when Marine Parade's controversial new rampart was finally ready to be photographed by Valentine's postcards, young Lydia Beardsall's "breakwater" had been entirely replaced by a vast inverted trench system which had the combined effect of tossing the beach back into the sea, lifting the promenade high into the air, and stealing the view from the private houses along Marine Parade in order to make it available as a public amenity for curious summer visitors sauntering along just outside their bedroom windows.

"Puddicombe's Folly", postcard.

Such was the esplanade over which Johnson imagined surveying the view with Hannah Arendt, and where he really did walk out, taking note of the beings encountered there: the dwindling number of summer tourists with their heroic optimism about the weather, the sheepish criminal doing an early version of "community service" by picking up litter from the beach, or an "overweight Labrador mutt", trotting along "in the wake" of an old woman, and clanking weirdly thanks to the bell she had tied round its neck.[64] The railings, meanwhile, would make a backwards belvedere for promenaders interested in scrutinising not the view across the estuary, but the sight of a man sitting at his electric typewriter in a basement room full of invisible landscapes and "invented persons", failing to complete the long-awaited fourth volume of *Anniversaries*.

29. BEACH, SEA AND "THE VIEW OF A MEMORY"

In June 1977, Johnson wrote to his friends Antonia and Felix Landgraf in Lower Saxony. "You have not been to Sheerness in the summer", he said, "and so I will tell you about a local custom that I have never seen anywhere else but which seems uncannily familiar to me. When it's hot, people leave their door open and drape a cloth over the opening, its pattern generally recalling an awning or the stripes on old armchairs. I involuntarily think when I see it: Warnemünde, and then immediately afterward: But that's impossible".[1]

That fleeting and "involuntary" recollection of the Baltic resort down the river Warnow from the GDR's hard currency raising port-city of Rostock was by no means unique. At the end of July 1980, Johnson wrote again to the Landgrafs, telling them about the "one day" that overcast summer on which Sheerness had managed to attract a handful of visitors from London.[2] The weather was very far from brilliant but these determined excursionists had "relied on hearsay" as they set off in the morning and they now "sat uncomfortably under damp morning clouds" on the beach. The locals, meanwhile, had "mistrusted the incident straight off", keeping their doors firmly closed and definitely not replacing them, as Johnson had seen done in brighter years, "with sun-blind curtains that are supposed to let in the wind to cool the house and leave the flies to fry in the heat". Johnson described looking out over the grey scene: "The curtain of the water's horizon was firmly drawn", but "the beach, loosely furnished with swimmers, deck chairs, and sun umbrellas, far below the seafront promenade, offered for an afternoon, the view of a memory, an unreachable one of course".

All memories are like that — of course — and not just those that are "unreachable" because they are also mistaken. Yet Johnson has very much more to say about memory than the fleeting comparisons in his letters may suggest. Indeed, *Anniversaries* would establish him as one of the great twentieth-century writers of memory and one who knew that, under modern conditions, this particular muse could be a dreadful curse as well as an inspiration. "A man", so Johnson writes, sees memory as "an ornamental trinket",[3] but that is not at all how it was for Gesine Cresspahl. As she goes about her days in New York 1967–68, her mind keeps throwing up "static, disconnected fragments" of the remembered past, which may evoke a longing, if only for the sake of a better understanding, while at the same time frustrating her desire that memory might be "not the storage but the retrieval, the return to the past, the repetition of what was: being inside it once more, setting foot there again. There is no such thing".

The same dissatisfaction is felt on 27 December 1967, when Gesine is looking out of window in Manhattan's Riverside Drive. The New Jersey shore is "white, bundled up high behind the bright icy blue river".[4] It reminds her of "a winter morning on Lake Constance, the memory of snow-covered gardens, children on the railway embankment with their hoods up, the church-tower tuber on the water, foreland and mountain range rising up through the headlights there, and the Säntis massif imaginable as hidden behind the new snow in the air". And yet despite that sudden impression, "the moment of recall, the fact of bringing it into present, corrodes both at once: past memory and present view".

At a wishful moment near the beginning of the novel, Gesine agonises over this frustrating fact at greater length, attributing it less to the traumatising impact of the history through which she has lived than to the psychology of memory itself:

If only the mind could contain the past in the same receptacles we use for categorizing present reality! But in recalling the past the brain does not use the same many-layered grid of terrestrial time and causality and chronology and logic that it uses for thinking. (The concepts of thinking do not even apply there. That's what we're supposed to live our life with!) The repository of the mind is not organized in such a way as to provide copies, or retrieve things that have happened. When triggered, even by mere partial congruence, or at random, out of the blue, it spontaneously volunteers facts and figures, foreign words, isolated gestures. Give it an odour that combines tar, rot, and a sea breeze, the sidelong smell from Gustafsson's famous fish salad, and ask it to fill the emptiness with content that was once reality, action, the feeling of being alive — it will refuse to comply. The blockade lets scraps, splinters, shards, and shavings get through, only so that they may be scattered senselessly across the emptied out, spaceless image, obliterating all traces of the scene we were in search of, leaving us blind with our eyes open. The piece of the past that is ours, because we were there, remains concealed in a mystery, sealed shut against Ali Baba's magic words, hostile, inapproachable, mute and alluring like a huge gray cat behind a windowpane seen from far below as with a child's eyes.[5]

"Blind with our eyes open." This sense of being suddenly captured by a remembered world that nevertheless remains inaccessible can be far from comforting for Gesine. "No, not homesick", so Johnson decrees about this largely involuntary experience: "But there is a waking up in the night, with a shock in the nerves, not wanting to recognize the thick gray light outside the windowpanes and looking for another window; even the April colours don't look right ... There are mornings when the glittering sun on the East River disappears in the shadow of the blinds, and Long Island becomes a different island. The smog turns the crush of houses in Queens into a soft rolling landscape, forest meadows, vistas of a church tower like a bishop's miter, the way I saw it once from the sea as the boat jibbed, obscured by furrows in the ground, eventually reachable not far past the shoreline cliff".[6]

Many things can prompt those "scraps, shards, and splinters" of past life to explode into the present. It might be the weather, a physical resemblance, or the way light moves in the glassy foyer of a Manhattan office block. Often, though, it will be a coastal scene or view across a river that comes to be ghosted by "partial congruence" with the memory of another one. The "river colours"[7] of the Hudson, glimpsed under an open sky from Riverside Drive, will do it for Gesine Cresspahl, and the water itself repeatedly proves to be an uncannily familiar medium too. At the opening of the third volume of *Anniversaries,* Marie is swimming alongside her mother at a summer resort named Patton Lake, a few hours north of New York City. At her request, Gesine counts up the various lakes in which she remembers swimming since childhood. Having learned to swim on Fischland or in Lübeck Bay, in a Baltic Sea that sailors from the Kaiser's defeated navy would call "the flooded field of the seven seas",[8] she moves on to various lakes and swimming pools in Mecklenburg before arriving at Wannsee outside West Berlin. Her survey then runs across West Germany, to Switzerland and France as well as America, where the lakes tend to have native American names — "And you came swimming all the way from Mecklenburg", remarks Marie, having allowed eighteen lakes before this one.[9]

So persistent is Johnson's attention to water and to views across it that *Anniversaries* itself comes to resemble the geography of Mecklenburg — sea-edged and filled with marshes, inland canals and lakes as well as rivers and the occasional swimming pool. Each of the first three volumes of *Anniversaries* opens with a watery scene. The first with a view of Atlantic waves crashing onto a beach "on a narrow spit of the New Jersey shore"; the second in a blue-tiled swimming pool — the "Mediterranean Swimming Club" — beneath the Hotel Marseilles in New York City's Upper West Side,[10] and the third with that scene at Patton Lake.

Gesine is very much Johnson's creature in this. We have already seen how, in the course of speaking "About Myself" at Darmstadt during his induction to the German Academy of Language and Literature, he told his life story by remembering the rivers beside which he had lived. He added to this inventory of remembered waters in the CV he typed up on 22 February 1984, which happens to have been the very last day on which he was seen alive in Sheerness. He had been asked for such a document by the German writer and educationalist Friedrich Denk, who was due to introduce him at a planned reading at the German International School in Petersham Road, Richmond. In this fuller version, a copy of which survives among Michael Hamburger's papers in the British Library, Johnson wrote out in capitals the names of the rivers in each of the places he had lived. Starting where he had grown up, in present-day Poland, he named the DIEVENOW (now the Dzwina) at Kammin (Kamien Pomorski), near the home of his maternal grandparents, and the OBRA outside his SS-run school in Kosten/Kościan. He added the RECKNITZ and the NEBEL at Güstrow, the TIBER in Rome, the HARLEM as well as the HUDSON and WEST RIVER in New York City, the HAVEL, SPREE and LANDWEHRKANAL in walled-off Berlin. Johnson's last expanded map of his life as a series of free-running rivers also includes the Isle of Sheppey, acknowledging the MEDWAY and SWALE beside the THAMES — rightly said by now to "beset" rather than smoothly glide past the low-lying town of Sheerness.[11]

Rivers and lakes figured largely in Johnson's unsettling storm of memories and so too did the sea, which we are invited to consider not only for the glinting or wave-shaped surface that might be seen from a beach or sea-facing window but also for the powers that lie hidden in its depths. Johnson engages the sea not as an engineer, marine biologist or nature writer might know it, but as a non-human force that is nevertheless the witness and even bearer of the murderous history that keeps troubling the surface of Gesine Cresspahl's consciousness. Early in *Anniversaries*, he permits her to tell her daughter about the day ("On a day like this, thirty-six-years ago. On a white day like this...") when her father proposed to her mother while strolling along the promenade overlooking the sea at Rande, a fictional Baltic resort derived partly from Boltenhagen. Yet he also interrupts her recitation of that seaside scene with the *New York Times'* present-day report of the death in prison of Ilse Koch, the notoriously depraved and sadistic "Beast of Buchenwald"[12] The incoming waves too are entangled: caught up both in Nazi imagery of national destiny and in the later Stalinist imagination in which Hitler appears as a "recurring type" in the "ebb and flow of history" — as demonstrated in the slogan painted on bedsheets and hung on town halls as a guarantee of the new socialist state's eternal identification with the people ("Hitlers/come and go/but/the German people, the German State/remains"[13]).

Johnson answers this deformation by returning the waves to the actually-existing sea. He was particularly attentive to the way in which each incoming wave peaked in a fold of white foam atop a momentary wall of blue or green, and then rolled forward to enclose a cylinder of air briefly before collapsing back onto itself. This restoration was already underway in *Speculations about Jakob*, where Jonas Blach remembers walking from the inland town of Jerichow to the beach at Rande with the young Gesine Cresspahl. It's raining, and there is a "hard wind" leaping up into their eyes from the sea, and they stand there, staring down at "the waves that broke under us over the steel jetty and froze, foamy, spraying, before they crashed and turned over and wriggled through the heavy pilings and unrolled full length, lazy and irresistible, onto the sand"[14] At that point Gesine speaks: "'On the crest of the waves,' said her voice, yes on the foamy crests — before they break".

Those cresting waves — each one unique, individual and exact yet bound to be almost instantly reclaimed by the whole — reappear in the very first paragraph of *Anniversaries*. By this time, they are beating in on the New

Jersey coast, but the sight of them quickly transports Gesine back to the Baltic:

> Long waves beat diagonally against the beach, bulge hunchbacked with cords of muscle, raise quivering ridges that tip over at their very greenest. Crests stretched tight, already welted white, wrap round activity of air crushed by the clear mass like a secret made and then broken. The crashing swells knock children off their feet, spin them round, drag them flat across the pebbly ground. Past the breakers, the waves pull the swimmer across their backs by her outstretched hands. The wind is fluttery; in low-pressure wind like this, the Baltic Sea used to peter out into a burble. The word for the short waves on the Baltic was: *scrabbly*.[15]

Like days in the calendrical structure of *Anniversaries*, Johnson's waves are singular and yet interconnected, discrete and yet part of a continuous series. They suggest an idea of history utterly unlike that imagined by the Stalinist dialecticians who believed in the "wheel of history" that "cannot be turned back" or in "History as a winch that winds up the past, irrevocably, for eternity. Onward!"[16]

*

If Johnson felt the play of distant but remembered tides as he looked out across the surface of the Thames Estuary, he also imagined his way down into the water, and here too his perspective is characteristically his own. Not for him, the surface-stripping melancholy of Jean-Paul Sartre's stranded protagonist Antoine Roquentin, who at one point in the novel *Nausea* gazes out at the sea with his hands gripping the balustrade at "Mudville" (an intellectual's vision of Le Havre), despising the promenading townspeople, and using his own corrosive bile to dissolve the view they so readily took for granted: "The real sea is cold and black, full of animals; it crawls underneath this thin green film which is designed to deceive people. The sylphs all around me have been taken in: they see nothing but the thin film, that is what proves the existence of God. I see underneath! The varnishes melt".[17] We may be confident that Johnson knew Sartre's caustic pre-war novel from the time he spent studying modern Western literature with Hans Mayer in Leipzig. Yet it is neither a crisis of language nor the inability of words to engage the world that drove his imagination down through the sometimes filmy surface of his "Sea View" in Sheerness. Johnson's sense of what lay beneath the surface was at once less contemptuous of common perceptions and more apocalyptic in its modernity.

We may start the descent with the pragmatic local knowledge of Johnson's friend "Charles", who knew the waters off Sheerness by the fish that might be caught in them. In summer, as Johnson recorded in a surviving note, it was possible to land eels, bass, flatfish, sole, mackerel, dogfish and skate.[18] In cold weather, the tide also brought cod and whiting.

If Johnson saw fit to record this prosaic list of the fish that might be taken from the waters outside his window, he also pursued his interest in the transformative powers that fable and mythology had long associated with the sea's depths. In 1976, he published his own "retelling" of "The Fisherman and his Wife", a German folk tale which Günter Grass would also take as the basis for his novel *The Flounder*, published in 1977.[19] The story opens on an ordinary, even pleasant day, when a poor fisherman leaves the "filthy shack" he shares with his wife, and walks down to the sea to fish from the shore. Casting his line into the deep and clear water he hooks not a cod or a whiting but a large flounder which proceeds to speak to him, claiming actually to be an "enchanted prince" who should be released rather than killed. The astonished fisherman puts the flounder back in the water and goes home to tell his wife, who is adamant that the fisherman must hasten back to the water's edge, catch the flounder again, and demand a gift for sparing the fish-prince's life: perhaps a "little cottage" for which they might abandon their stinking little shack.

The flounder is no sooner asked than he tells the fisherman

to go home, where he will find his wish already granted. As the fable progresses through its stages, the fisherman, who is compelled by the swelling ambitions of his wife, journeys back and forth to the shore, asking for a grander transformation each time the flounder is caught and returned to the water. The harried fisherman asks for a palace, and then for the vast domain of a king, and that is by no means where the matter ends. Meanwhile, the sea changes for the worse each time the fisherman returns to trouble the magical flounder, and not for the better. At the second request the water, which had started out so clear, has become yellow and green. By the third it is "purple and dark blue and gray and dense" and by the fourth it is "boiling up" from within. Ships are firing distress signals over the ruinous waves and the sky is a lurid red and blitzed by the most terrifying lightning storm by the time the fisherman's wife tires of life as an empress and despatches her husband to the shore demanding that she must live like the pope. Sadly, even that wish proves insufficient as soon as it is granted. Looking out over "great black waves as high as church towers and mountains, all capped with crowns of white foam", the fisherman pulls in the flounder and informs it of his wife's final request. Hearing that she now wants to be God, the fish closes the tale with the words: "Go home. She is sitting in her filthy shack again."

In the "Afterword" to his "retelling", Johnson explained that the tale had initially been collected by the artist Philipp Otto Runge, who had found it somewhere near Hamburg in the early years of the nineteenth century.[20] Runge, whose search had been inspired by the poet and fellow Romantic Achim von Arnim's insistence, stated in connection with his own collection of folk poetry, on the importance of preserving and passing on "everything that has kept its diamond-like hardness through the rolling onward of the years".[21] Recorded in its original Low German dialect as part of this "nationalist" project against France, the story was passed to the Brothers Grimm, who included it in their *Children's and Household Tales* in 1812. A version in standard High German, published in Berlin in 1814, would be widely read — so Johnson observes — as a "biography" of the over-reaching Napoleon. Johnson himself, however, kept his "retelling" as close as possible to the Low German in which, as Runge himself had stated, it had originally "blossomed". He notes that the Low German word "*Butt*", the word for "flounder", implied "blunt" as well as "flat",[22] thereby emphasising "the "ordinariness" of "the sea creature that is in a position to perform miracles". As for the "filthy shack" that was "the initial and final dwelling place of the stricken couple" this had been a "pisspot" ("*Pißputt*") in Runge's recorded version, but, for Johnson, who "strove for literalness", it is a "bucket" ("*Eimer*").

As for the wider meaning of the fable, Johnson opens his Afterword by saying that "For as long as helpless individuals remained unaware that they could redress their grievances with earthly social conditions themselves, they desperately wished for mysterious remedies and, at least in fairy tales, welcomed them in all sorts of guises".[23] He points out that, in many German versions of this kind of tale, the deliverance was provided by a fish — in this case "the totally nondescript flat fish which is not even a bewitched prince and yet has power over everything on earth". The fable tells of magical powers, but in many versions it also serves a more disciplinary purpose, demonstrating that "anyone who presumes and wants to be raised above his station must be punished". Some of the over-reachers fall from a ladder or tree, or from the gates of Heaven. Others find themselves at the bottom of a well, or their carriage suddenly turned into a pumpkin and their horses into a team of fleas. In the great majority of versions of "The Fisherman and his Wife", all the fault lies with the unreasonable wishes of the wife. It is, as Johnson declares, "the story of an unhappy marriage, presented as smugly as the invention of a gossiping neighbour". The fisherman warns his wife to resist the immodesty of her own demands, but he does not wish "to be against her" so keeps going back to the beach to ask favours on her behalf, fishing for the flounder as "he had earlier fished for her". Johnson scholars have duly puzzled over the extent to which the folk tale known as "Grimm 19" may have resonated with Johnson's own marital difficulties (unlike Günter Grass, Johnson does not set out to correct the tale's acknowledged tendency to blame all the ills of the world on the fisherman's wife).

By the time he came to Sheerness, Johnson was well prepared for the possibility that there might be something else, besides Charles's prosaic flatfish or Runge's magical flounder, lurking in the waters outside his window. Repeatedly in *Anniversaries,* it is danger rather than magical power that lies beneath the surface of the water. That is how it was for Gesine's mother Lisbeth, when she swam far out into the Baltic from the beach at Rande, a suicide attempt frustrated by a fisherman, who spotted her as night fell and hauled her into his boat. She was two and a half miles from the shore in water at least seventy feet deep, exhausted but still heading out and visible thanks to her bathing cap — "It was vanity. And I was punished for it", as the pious and self-punishing Lisbeth says of her unwelcome rescue the next day.[24]

The peril of sinking beneath the surface is also the "secret" of the "huge gray cat behind a windowpane", mentioned in Gesine Cresspahl's account of memory and its limits. That elderly Mecklenburg cat attends one of the primal scenes of Gesine's childhood. At the moment in question, it was actually sitting on the windowsill inside the Papenbrocks' kitchen. In order to approach it, Gesine, who was outside at the time, clambers up onto a leaky old water butt outside the window. The new lid made by her father does not prevent her from falling in. Her mother, Lisbeth, sees her disappear into the water but does nothing, merely standing there "as if rooted to the spot". The child is fished out by her father, who had come up behind Lisbeth, and watched her watching the disaster unfold — transfixed by the thought of having "the unjust suffering of her child to offer up to her God too" and making "the greatest sacrifice a person can make".[25]

Meanwhile, something unexpected also lies in "the depths" of the inky black water of Patton Lake at the opening of the third volume of *Anniversaries*. After counting up all the lakes in which she has ever swam, Gesine discloses that this particular example is not in fact a natural body of water but a "dredged-out basin", surrounded by "stunted" trees and a "chemically treated landscape set up for paying customers",[26] which had only been filled with water to create a resort after the Second World War. Go back to 1944, and the thick and inky water disappears to reveal heavy tanks, practicing "for the last assault on Germany".[27] These machines reduced "thick old trees" to stumps and left "the ground so churned up by caterpillar treads that the area had to be turned into an artificial lake, with trees having nowhere else to go and high yields from vacation rentals. From here came the Sherman tanks that measured out the market squares of Mecklenburg, too". History, then, as intermittently remembered trauma darkening the water from below.

Johnson himself had other memories that might have prepared him for the most arresting feature of the view over the Thames Estuary from Marine Parade. I learned about one example in 2012, when I first went to Rostock to talk about Sheerness with members of the Uwe Johnson Society. When I mentioned the peculiar object that would become the focal point of Johnson's English view, Siegfried Werner, who had known the writer during his school years in Güstrow, was reminded of a pond or small lake somewhere on the road between Recknitz and Güstrow, past which he and Johnson had cycled in the late Forties. This no longer existent body of water, which had been in the vicinity of two tiny settlements named Spoitgendorf and Glasewitz, was where unexploded ordnance found in the post-war clean-up was taken to be dumped. Werner remembered it as tempting as well as dangerous, and not just for curious children. Explosions did happen, he said. People got injured and in some cases, he thought, also killed. Here, if his memory was accurate, was another anticipation of the submerged hazard that drew Johnson's eye down through the horizontal tiers of colour in his window and into the silted waters of the Thames Estuary.

30. WHAT IS THAT THING? THE SS RICHARD MONTGOMERY

Johnson's most sustained Sheerness essay, "An Unfathomable Ship", opens with a description of one of the first things he noticed about the view from his upstairs window: "In the Thames, about two miles off the north coast of the Isle of Sheppey, a cluster of parallel diagonal poles catches one's eye".[1] These closely observed objects were "visible especially at low tide, but also when the tide is eighteen feet higher, because behind them tosses and pitches almost ten miles of the water's surface as well as, since the Essex coast in the distance quite noticeably veers off to the north, the horizon line under the quickly shifting illuminations of the sky".

Johnson goes on to suggest that, while anyone moving to Sheerness will be "struck by the reflections of the light on the multiply moving mouth of the Thames and North Sea", it was those tilted "poles" cutting upwards through the surface of the sea that had really caught this resident alien's attention, prompting him to ask: "what is that thing?" To begin with, and presumably guided by a Baltic memory of some kind, "he thinks those poles are fish traps, blown into a diagonal position by a ferocious west wind, since the eye is easily fooled about distances when looking out across a boundless body of water". On this assumption, it seems possible that "the black triangle that becomes visible between the poles at ebb tide" could be a fishing boat exercising certain rights over the sea bed in that particular area.

The upthrusting "poles" that break through the horizontal lines of Johnson's view may well be arresting in their slanted verticality — like the masts, crosses, wintry trees and net-draped poles that form such striking presences in the flat and sometimes moonlit landscapes painted in the early nineteenth century by the Romantic artist Caspar David Friedrich in Fischland, or further to the east on the Pomeranian island of Rügen. And yet fishing was the wrong Baltic comparison. After noticing that the "triangle" has not moved for two weeks, Johnson's newcomer realises that the "poles" are of unequal length and have a "strangely regular relationship with one another". Watching huge freighters pass by on either side of them, he concludes that they are too close to both the Medway and Thames shipping lanes to be fishing apparatus of any description at all.

The "native inhabitants" proved happy to confirm Johnson's rising doubts about "that thing". Putting down his hammer and gazing out to sea, one fellow declares it a pity to be wasting time on work when the weather is so good for fishing: "no matter how dark the cloud", he says, "it always has a silver lining". This Sheerness homily, which Johnson will dignify with a quotation from John Milton's "Comus", shows how the presence of "that thing" confronts the inhabitants of his adopted town with a choice between two catastrophic futures. The "cloud", as Johnson goes on to explain, is the memory of the flood that overwhelmed Sheppey's sea defences and swamped much of the island at the end of January in 1953. The fear of another such inundation had led to "the most thorough discussion, involving the best plans and resolutions" concerned with warning systems and improved sea defences. Yet not enough had been done to prevent Sheerness being flooded again in January 1978 — another round of dead sheep and wrecked furniture followed by the retreat (or costly advance) of insurance companies as they reviewed their coverage of properties in Sheerness.

If the continuing threat of inundation was the "cloud", the silver lining would be found in the thrice-pronged "thing", which promised to add a fiery End of Days to the flood that would one day wash over the "tufted grove" (Milton's phrase) of Sheerness. The protruding "poles" turned out to be the masts of the *SS Richard Montgomery*, an American Liberty ship that grounded on submerged sands a little under two miles offshore from Sheerness in August 1944, breaking up and sinking in two pieces shortly afterwards. Having since become wrapped in a thickly sedimented layer of local lore, the sunken freighter was known variously as "the wreck" or "the grand old lady of the Thames" or "our one sight worth seeing". It had the unusual distinction of being packed with unexploded bombs: huge quantities of them, stacked in the holds seven metres high and capable of blowing up at any moment.

Johnson's artist neighbour, Martin Harris, told me that the presence of this explosive hazard 1.8 miles from the sea wall made living in Sheerness like camping out "on the slopes of Vesuvius". Johnson was happy to embrace that idea. The closure of the dockyard and associated naval command may have contributed but it was thanks to "the wreck" that every inhabitant of Sheerness knew they were involuntary inhabitants of an experimental English version of the "risk society" that the West German sociologist Ulrich Beck would soon be describing as a "new modernity"[2]: living in perpetual danger, insecure, powerless to influence the forces menacing them, and yet somehow managing to hang on to the semblances of everyday life.

"What is that thing?" wondered the newly arrived Johnson as he glanced out through his window. Established residents were more likely to ask a different question: "Why on earth is it still there?" Ever since the stranding, the *Richard Montgomery* has been lending its own apocalyptic twist to life in the town. To this day, enquiring visitors are likely to be informed that if they look out from the promenade on a calm and clear night, they might see flames playing on the water above the wreck, allegedly caused by phosphorous escaping from smoke bombs and igniting on contact with the air. "Welcome to Sheerness", says the large mural painted by Dean Tweedy in 2015 on a wall overlooking Beachfield Park. It shows a sulky mermaid lying on the beach with her hand on a detonator and the masts of the *Richard Montgomery* protruding from the water behind her: "You'll have a blast". The *Daily Mail* got hold of that story, proving that residents of the "rundown" town were not unanimously pleased to embrace its destiny as a place of dark tourism.[3] Since Johnson investigated "our one sight worth seeing", its dangerous condition has also been invoked to see off Boris Johnson's attempt, when Mayor of London, to float a new four runway international airport in the waters just off the Isle of Sheppey. While literary visitors may now join the local artists who have embraced the *Richard Montgomery* as evidence that Sheerness really is "the end of the world",[4] "the wreck" has also continued to prove a more telling point about the widely condemned indifference of the public authorities upriver, which should surely have cleared this hazard decades ago. As one campaigner from Southend asked of the government in 1978: "How far down the river do you have to go before a dangerous wreck becomes acceptable?"[5] "That thing" had a history — fable-like yet also prosaic and tediously persistent — which Johnson's glancing essay encourages us to fathom.

*

Still in position as one of the Thames Estuary's more accidental historical monuments, the *SS Richard Montgomery* is one of nearly 2,750 "Liberty ships" built at great and increasing speed in rapidly expanded American shipyards during the

Second World War and used to supply American and Allied forces in Europe and elsewhere. The ships were modelled on a British design, itself derived from existing tramp steamers, which had been employed for an order of one hundred ships commissioned from American shipyards in the early years of the war. Manufacture was carried out on both American coasts, using increasingly rationalised techniques and an industrial "speed-up" that would eventually make it possible for a Liberty ship to be built in days rather than months. They were assembled from prefabricated sections and the conventional practice of riveting was replaced with welding, an economy that hastened production but also increased the dangers of sudden disintegration, especially in cold waters. Such were the perceived inadequacies of the mass-produced Liberty ship that it was condemned, in a book published in 1943 by the American Socialist Workers' Party, as "a jerry-built job, made to be sunk".[6]

Launched in July of that same year, with a gross tonnage of 7,225, the *SS Richard Montgomery* was the seventh of eighty-two dry cargo Liberty ships built by the St Johns River Shipbuilding Company at Jacksonville, Florida. It made several crossings to Liverpool and also to (and across) the Mediterranean, where it appears on one occasion to have shipped mustard gas bombs into the southern Italian port of Bari. On its last voyage for the United States Shipping Administration, the freighter had picked up a cargo amounting, according to one early report, to 6,876 tons of bombs (the numbers would be differently arranged to produce 8,687 tons in some later accounts), detonators and related munitions at Hog Island in Delaware, before leaving New York on 25 July 1944 and crossing the Atlantic in a convoy on which everybody understood the danger posed by enemy submarines. Having arrived at Oban on 8 August, it sailed round the coast of Scotland to Methil, in Fife. On 13 August, it headed south for the Thames Estuary where the master of the ship — an experienced fifty-four-year-old German-born American migrant named Friedrich Wilhelm Heinrich Willecke who, as Uwe "Charles" Johnson might have anticipated, would soon be converted into "Captain Wilkie" by the British press — had orders to await the formation of a convoy bound for the recently liberated port of Cherbourg in France. It's cargo of bombs were intended for use by the US military during the Allied advance into Germany following the D-Day landings two months earlier.

As it entered the estuary on 15 August, the *Richard Montgomery* came under the authority of Thames Naval Control at Southend Pier (then known officially as HMS Leigh). The King's Harbourmaster there, who would later be identified as Acting Lieutenant Commander R.J. Walmsley, "ordered her to berth off the northern edge of the Sheerness Middle Sand — part of the Little Nore anchorage — in about 33 feet of water at low tide".[7] According to one contemporary witness, the harbourmaster had chosen this anchorage because he knew the dangerous nature of the ship's cargo and wanted, understandably enough, to keep it away from other vessels crowded into the estuary. Given that the heavily laden *Richard Montgomery* was "trimmed to a draught of 31 ft, aft" (considerably lower than normal for a Liberty ship), the grounding, which took place after the vessel dragged its anchor in a rising northerly wind following a high tide in the night of Sunday, 20 August, might well be considered a predictable outcome of the harbourmaster's decision. Not so, however, according to the Board of Enquiry held in the ship's saloon a few days after the stranding. At this hearing, which is said to have been conducted in an "an all-pervading stench of leaking fuel oil",[8] both the King's Harbourmaster from Southend and the pilot who had guided the *Richard Montgomery* to its appointed anchorage pointed the finger of blame squarely at Captain Willecke. His German origins, which were reflected in his accented English, presumably did little to improve his reception. He was variously described — not least by those who found it convenient to blame him rather than the Harbourmaster — as a "cripple", a drinker and, by implication, a man so irascible that his own watchman had been terrified of waking him as the ship dragged its anchor. No one thought much better of the second mate, who had failed to wake Willeke when lookouts on nearby vessels sounded their sirens in warning as they watched the ship drift, and could only say "I don't know" when asked why. Willeke was found to have "hazarded his ship" and suspended for a year.

It would later be alleged that both Willecke and the Thames pilot had actually questioned the proposed anchorage at the time. The Assistant King's Harbourmaster at Southend pier ("HMS Leigh"), Lt Roger Foley, had also been sufficiently concerned to demand that the harbourmaster give him the order in writing. In a discussion that also involved the harbourmaster's commander, Foley had recommended that the *Richard Montgomery* might be safer if it exchanged position with a smaller vessel anchored in deeper water nearby. Having been chided for questioning the harbourmaster's decision, he left the room. Two days after the stranding, but before the enquiry held aboard the stranded ship, he had been conveniently "posted to another section".[9] As for Captain Willeke, having sailed back to New York as "Ex *Richard Montgomery* Cap" in December 1944, he is said to have gone back to work soon afterwards, and to have died of heart failure while being shipped home from Brest with US troops shortly after the end of the war.[10] By then, the *SS Richard Montgomery* had settled into its final position: an American possession resting on British Crown land within the area of the Sheerness dockyard port and also within the responsibility of the British Admiralty.

At first, it had been imagined that, if some of its explosive cargo were removed, the stranded *Richard Montgomery* might be refloated at "the next good spring tide" in a fortnight's time. This aspiration died almost immediately. Indeed, it was reported that at the time of the stranding, crewmen fishing from the *British Queen* over a mile away had heard sounds like gunshot as the strain placed on the heavily laden hull by the retreating tide caused "some of the welded plates to crack and buckle with an explosive snap".[11] Peering over, they saw the crew, who were "naturally apprehensive of the noise, and of the hazardous nature of their cargo, conduct an emergency evacuation of their ship via the lifeboats and rafts". Whatever the truth of that report, the *Lloyd's Register of Shipping* records that the *Richard Montgomery* itself signalled that the ship was breaking in two within only an hour or two of the grounding. This was followed by a further signal reporting that the holds were dry even though the ship had "a split from port to starboard side", and recommending "discharge as soon as possible".[12]

Under exceptional wartime "deeds of arrangement" implemented in 1941, the Admiralty had command of the Port of London Authority's responsibility for salvage and wrecks in the Thames Estuary and beyond.[13] So the PLA were acting as agents for the Admiralty when they mustered some brave men and launched an emergency salvage operation to remove the cargo from the breaking ship. Conducted under contract by Messrs. Watson and Gill, Shipbrokers of Rochester,[14] the work, which was underway when the Board of Enquiry met to deliberate over the situation in the saloon, was carried out by three gangs of stevedores who, having negotiated an encouraging level of danger-money, sailed out to the site from Sheerness, together with various tugs and barges, and also the ship's Chief Officer. Starting on 23 August, they altered the *Montgomery*'s derricks in order to power them with steam from a tug. Guided by an American "stowage plan" of the ship's cargo provided by the Chief Officer, they persevered despite the discovery that oil had leaked over some of the bombs, making them slippery and even more perilous to handle. The salvage operation suffered a major setback when the hull, already split but undergoing new stresses as heavy bombs were removed from the rear holds, cracked further just the following day, flooding the three still-loaded forward holds. The back of the ship finally broke on 8 September, but salvage work was continued until an estimated 3,170 tons of bombs had been cleared from holds four and five. The operation was not finally called off until 25 September 1944.[15] Although civil servants would later assert that the stranding was a "Marine (i.e. not war)" casualty, the Admiralty paid the Port of London Authority £16,200 for the discontinued salvage operation and returned to the overwhelming priority of fighting the Second World War. By now separated into two parts, the *SS Richard Montgomery* was left to the sea — together with the bombs remaining in the forward holds. These included many heavy general purpose and semi-armour-piercing bombs as well as smaller cluster fragmentation devices and phosphorous smoke bombs. For several years after the stranding, however, no one in Sheerness appears to have known exactly how much of what remained on board.

*

Clearing sea-lanes of wrecks left by the Second World War confronted the Admiralty with a "vast" challenge — it was estimated that there were three to four hundred off British shores, the majority on the east coast between Dungeness and Newcastle-upon-Tyne.[16] When, at the beginning of March 1946, the Admiralty once again adjusted its salvage agreement with the Port of London Authority, it stipulated that the PLA's use of Admiralty salvage vessels should be concentrated on seven wrecks. Since the dispersal of one of these — the destroyer *HMS Vimiera*, which had sunk off Sheppey with the loss of ninety-six men after striking a mine near the East Spile Buoy in January 1942 — involved blowing it up with the assistance of sixteen carefully lowered depth charges, it is scarcely surprising that the *SS Richard Montgomery* was left off that particular list. By 30 September 1946, the Admiralty had hardened this apparent oversight into policy, announcing that, while no attempt was to be made to salvage the *Montgomery* or its remaining cargo, a precautionary light would be placed on the wreck to reduce the damage of accidental collision. A beacon was duly rented to the Admiralty by Trinity House, and fitted to the wreck by men from Sheerness dockyard. The Admiralty also reassured the Port of London Authority that it was "most improbable that this cargo constitutes any danger provided that no big explosion (such as that of a depth charge) takes place in the immediate vicinity."[17]

From that moment until the present, the protruding masts of "the wreck" have served as the poles around which two reluctant parties have danced and slumped their way through the decades. On one side are the tight-lipped and unforthcoming men from the ministries — initially from the Admiralty and Port of London Authority and later, as statutory responsibilities were redistributed through the cuts and amalgamations of the post-war decades, from the Ministry of Defence and the Board of Trade. Whether wriggling or just inert, these officials have proved unwilling either to risk removing the hazard or, as soon emerged, to provide the people of the estuary with a convincing account of the dangers they were evidently expected to live with. Accustomed to the instrumental habits of "seeing like a state,"[18] they have remained non-communicative even when the deteriorating condition of the wreck has obliged them to fire brief statements of policy and decision down the estuary.

The other participants in this apparently never-ending gavotte are the people who have had no choice but to live within sight of "the *Monty*": downriver types who tend to mistrust officials, with their power, secrecy and assumed expertise, and have relied instead on local memory, speculation and the evidence of their own eyes as they try to understand the hazard to which they have evidently been abandoned. While stubbornly insistent on the facts as known in the locality, they have also been inclined to weave these partial threads of truth into all-encompassing conspiracy theories about the wreck and, especially, the motivation of the upriver officials who seem determined to leave this dangerous matter unresolved, kicking it down the road until the time comes for them to shuffle off onto their generous public sector pensions.

Two other parties have also been in attendance throughout. The first is composed of MPs from constituencies on both sides of the estuary: several generations of them, who have stood up as MPs should do, one after another and from both major parties, to raise questions in the House of Commons.

Then there was the press, which would delight in "discovering" the *Richard Montgomery* and its dangers repeatedly over the decades to come, filling the official silence with lurid exposés intended to aggravate fears of the coming Armageddon in a way that otherwise uninformative government ministers and civil servants would rarely hesitate to condemn as "sensational". The participation of these onlooking parties would ensure that the story of the wreck became a polarised fable about government and the people in post-war Britain — an allegory that may seem all the more compelling for being set along an estuary that served, five hundred years earlier, as the primary geography of the Peasants' Revolt. Uwe Johnson would make his own sense of this stand-off between downriver communities and the largely absent representatives of upriver power and official expertise, even while sparing himself all the details of the deadlock and exhaustion that have since found new resonances in the polarised time of Brexit.

In the early post-war years, which had yet to be recognised as the beginning of Britain's "long boom", the men at the Admiralty must have hoped that the wreck Johnson would eventually dub "unfathomable" would remain unregarded too. As they and their successors discovered, however, this potent war relic was never going to sink quietly into the past. Known to be highly dangerous even though exact information about its cargo was not forthcoming, "the wreck" quickly became the subject of local speculation and rumour. People clung to fragments of knowledge: the stories of those involved in the first salvage operation, for example, or the visit of an American who turned up in Sheerness at some point in 1948 to examine the wreck for a New York salvage company named Phillips, Kraft and Fisher, Inc. (it was said that he left town without discussing his company's interest in the situation, and was never seen again).[19]

Given the persistence of the semi-piratical form of salvage that islanders once knew as "hovelling", it may be no surprise that valuable materials disappeared from the ship — including, allegedly in 1956, much of the copper "degaussing" cable wrapped round the hull to reduce its attraction to German magnetic mines. These, however, were superficial as well as illicit reclamations and they did nothing to prevent the wreck swelling in local conjecture. By 1951, when Winston Churchill was returned to power having narrowly defeated Clement Attlee's post-war Labour government, "that thing" had already transmogrified into Sheerness's answer to the Kraken — a terrifying sea monster known primarily through fables but in this case also plain to see, its spines piercing the air less than two miles away from the town's far from perfect sea defences.

The authorities upriver were by this time also working out their position on the new hazard. The SS Richard Montgomery made its first post-war appearance in Hansard on 23 April 1952, when Dr Reginald Bennett, a former naval commander who was now the Conservative MP for Gosport and Fareham, received a written answer to a question in which he had asked the First Lord of the Admiralty to clarify his responsibilities for the wreck and to describe the actions he had and would be taking to ensure that the cargo did not blow up.[20] The reply to Dr Bennett's question, allegedly informed by discussion with the MP for Southend East,[21] came not from the Admiralty, but from the Parliamentary Secretary, Commander Sir Allan Noble, who dismissed the question, saying curtly that the Admiralty had no responsibility for the wreck and therefore no plans for it either. It was, as others beside Dr Bennett were plainly intended to understand, the Port of London Authority that held responsibility for salvage operations in the Thames Estuary.

This exercise in stately buck-passing did nothing to deter the Labour MP for Faversham, Percy Wells, who wrote to the First Lord of the Admiralty on 18 June 1952, expressing concern about the hazardous wreck on behalf of his constituents in Sheerness. He explained that he had already been in touch with the Port of London Authority about the matter, but they had declared themselves stymied by the Admiralty: "it has not yet been possible to obtain any definite information as to the state of the explosives".[22] In the absence of such basic information, let alone anything resembling what might nowadays be called a management plan, fears of a vast explosion were growing in the locality. Wells mentioned a "sensational article in a recent issue of a Sunday paper" thanks to which constituents were pressing him for information. He hoped that the Admiralty would provide him with some answers.

Following these inconvenient displays of public concern, powerful men and their ministries were soon preparing for battle in London. Among them was the Chairman of the Port of London Authority, who had recently been elevated to the House of Lords as an independent peer. John Anderson, as he had been known before becoming Viscount Waverley, was a Scot of considerable standing within the British state. After overseeing the development of the "Anderson" air raid shelter as Chamberlain's Lord Privy Seal in the late Thirties, he had gone on to serve as both Home Secretary and Minister of Home Security in Winston Churchill's cabinet during the first year of the Second World War, and again as Chancellor of the Exchequer in the months before the Labour election victory of July 1945. Having restrained himself from following his initial impulse to take the matter directly to Churchill for a quick resolution, he went, more appropriately, to the First Lord of the Admiralty, James Thomas, informing him that he'd been shocked by Commander Noble's "outrageous" declaration that the Admiralty had no responsibilities in the matter of the *SS Richard Montgomery*. At a subsequent meeting with the Admiralty, which was duly chaired by Thomas on 22 July 1952,[23] he repeated that the PLA had been "shaken" by the "complacency of the experts" who, having early forbidden the PLA from making any attempt to clear the wreck, now seemed to consider it tolerable simply to leave it as it was.[24] In his view, the hazard, which was surely getting more dangerous as the years went by, must be cleared and removed over the remaining weeks of the summer. He also pointed out that, as a self-funding public trust, the PLA lacked the resources to carry out this task unaided. Since the ship belonged to the American government, or perhaps to the

US salvage operator to whom they might have sold it, the PLA had considered the possibility of hiring private contractors to remove the obstacle, and then forwarding the bill to Washington – despite the Treasury Solicitor's Office, which had already pointed out that it would be "quite impossible"[25] for the British government to force the American authorities to pay.

Aware that the Admiralty had written to the PLA on 21 March 1952 warning that the submerged bombs might behave in a "very capricious" way, Waverley was also worried that it would not be possible to manage a private contractor sufficiently to ensure "100% efficiency" in such a delicate operation.[26] It was surely time, he argued, for the British state to accept responsibility and see that the increasingly necessary job was done properly. The case, as Waverley told the meeting, "appeared to the PLA to be like that of an extreme instance of an unexploded bomb and the Crown had never boggled in the past over removing unexploded bombs". Waverley also pointed out that the PLA had not been responsible for the wreck during the war, the Admiralty having taken over its salvage responsibilities throughout the Thames Estuary. Six years previously on 12 August 1946, the Admiralty had written to the PLA Salvage Department "telling them the wreck should not be moved". Its officials had now, so Waverley concluded accusingly, "decided to wash their hands of the wreck".

When they met informally to discuss the situation five weeks before the meeting, both Wavertree and Thomas had actually found each other inclined to favour the idea of clearing such bombs as could safely be removed and then "blowing up the vessel" without further delay. The Permanent Secretary to the Admiralty, Sir John Lang, had not been happy at the thought of this cavalier consensus. It may indeed have been normal Admiralty practice to dispose of unsalvageable wrecks by exploding them,[27] but Lang had been concerned both by the "complete uncertainty" over what bombs remained in the sunken ship's holds and by the impossibility, therefore, of establishing for certain that none had been packed with (dangerous) fuses already inserted.[28] He believed that this solution would only be "reasonable" if it were possible to confine explosions to a small part of the cargo. This was not the case with the *SS Richard Montgomery*. He told the meeting that, while "a mass explosion would be most dangerous to Sheerness", it was also likely to scatter "large quantities of unexploded bombs", leaving them lying around on the seabed in what the PLA had already been informed was a "very capricious" state.[29]

Lang and his officials went to considerable lengths to stiffen their First Lord against Waverley's arguments. Not content with presenting a strong case for leaving the explosive wreck exactly where it was, their briefing documents also suggested that the PLA was "shirking a responsibility", as had been implied by the curt response Dr Reginald Bennett's question had received from the Parliamentary Secretary, and that Waverley's advisers were seeking to "blackmail"[30] the Government into paying for the work, while he himself was strongly biased towards "shifting the cost onto the state". They denied that the Admiralty had taken over all responsibility for the wreck under the emergency measures of the war, alleging that the PLA had earlier welcomed the *SS Richard Montgomery* as "a useful job for their organisation, which was otherwise running out of work" and that its extreme reluctance to fulfil its responsibilities now might be based on "nothing more respectable than the view that 'Naval personnel are paid to risk their lives'".[31] Waverley might cite the fact that the Admiralty had written to the head of the PLA Salvage Department on 12 August 1946, specifying that the wreck was not to be removed, but it had really only meant "removed by them". The charges laid against Waverley by these evasive minions had irritated the First Lord of the Admiralty. Declaring that he had re-read the papers connected to the case, Thomas used red ink to mark up one of the briefing documents now accessible at the National Archives with the comment, "We are being petty and should get on with the job".[32]

*

Despite this interdepartmental manoeuvring within the state bureaucracy, it was the Admiralty's researches into the *SS Richard Montgomery*'s cargo that clinched the decision against immediate clearance in 1952. Discussion with the American military authorities in London helped the officials get a clearer understanding of the bombs remaining in the broken ship's holds.[33] It was confirmed that the heavy TNT-filled bombs were not fused, and consequently less dangerous than they might otherwise have been. The smoke bombs might well leak, releasing white phosphorous that would ignite as soon as it reached the water's surface. The major concern, however, lay with the remaining cargo, said to include 1,750 cases of cluster fragmentation bombs and perhaps 580 individually loaded twenty-six-pound fragmentation bombs. The likelihood that at least some of these comparatively thin-skinned devices were fitted with integral fuses was seized upon as a major complication.

Some of the deteriorating fuses might indeed get washed out and rendered innocuous as their cases were corroded. There was, however, and as Home Office explosives experts would confirm repeatedly over the years to come, a definite possibility that some might produce copper azide as they decomposed. This "capricious" substance would render them highly unstable and liable to sudden detonation if disturbed. It was considered entirely possible that a single cluster fragmentation bomb behaving this way might set off the entire cargo. It was estimated that the explosion would break most of the windows in Sheerness and also cause a tidal wave and seismic shock likely to do "severe" damage to buildings both there and in Queenborough, three miles further along the Medway. These findings seemed convincing to the men at the Admiralty, who drew the conclusion that has governed the site ever since: the *SS Richard Montgomery* was best left well alone. By 15 January 1953, the Port of London Authority had been brought into line with the Admiralty's policy of vigilant inaction, and the First Lord of the Admiralty could inform Mr Percy Wells MP that the situation had now been "exhaustively examined" and "the risk to life involved in any attempt to remove the cargo is appreciably greater than the risk to life involved in leaving the wreck alone".[34]

It would prove considerably harder to convince the public in Sheerness and elsewhere around the post-war estuary that this policy towards the *SS Richard Montgomery* consisted of anything other than irresponsible negligence that would not be tolerated in more prosperous places upriver. The Admiralty's refusal either to come up with a clearance plan or to communicate a factually justified explanation of their decision effectively abandoned the *Richard Montgomery* to hostile speculation. In Sheerness, the wreck quickly became an object of disbelieving and even taunting daredevilry as well as fearful rumour and speculation. It is said that people got into the habit of sailing over to "the *Monty*" to fish from it and, if the tide was low, to picnic on its decks.

The popular press, meanwhile, had quickly learned to delight in the masts and derricks of the all-too-visible wreck, polishing them up until they shone back at the town of Sheerness with a terrifying gleam. The article condemned as "sensational" by the Labour MP Percy Wells had been printed by the *Sunday Dispatch* on 11 May 1952. It was prompted by the news that, following Commander Bennett's question in the Commons, the Port of London Authority intended to "survey the wreck and decide what action can be taken".[35] The unnamed reporter described the stranding as "in the Medway estuary about a mile off the foreshore". His figures were on the rough side too: he claims the ship had been carrying 6,800 tons of American bombs, and that more than three thousand tons of these had been recovered immediately after the stranding and "shipped on to Normandy". He also claimed that "For eight years the 16,000 inhabitants of Sheerness... have looked out at the wreck" and wondered "what would happen to them if its cargo of 3,000 tons of bombs blew up". Throughout that entire time the Admiralty and the PLA had engaged in "mutual buck-passing" and it had "seemed to be nobody's business to remove the danger".

Contacted by the *Dispatch,* the MP who had first raised the question in the House of Commons, Commander Bennett, suggested that "If the cargo blew up probably half of Sheerness would be flattened and there would be some damage, too, in Southend". It was, he reiterated, "high time something was done and I shall be glad to see a move". While no one in Sheerness will have relished the prospect of being "flattened", this early forecast of the town's plight was overshadowed the following week when the paper gave its front page to an article about the "'Iron Curtain' of security" that had been lowered around Chatham dockyard, where a fleet of ships was preparing to receive "Britain's first atom-bomb"[36] before sailing for the Montebello Islands, off the coast of north-west Australia, to cause a twenty-five-kiloton explosion, far more annihilating than anything that might be feared of the Richard Montgomery, would be detonated on 3 October 1952.

By this time, as the *Sunday Dispatch* also revealed, the people of the estuary were already making the *Richard Montgomery* their own. In the apparent absence of official interest in the site, an offer had been received from certain "Thames divers" to inspect the wreck. The man behind this unofficial proposal, Mr J. Bentall, explained that "two colleagues and myself have volunteered our services to give a survey report. We have not been told whether our offer has been accepted". Meanwhile, Sheerness had already discovered that the increasingly notorious masts of the *Richard Montgomery* did at least provide the town with a new seasonal attraction: "in summer local boatmen run sight-seeing trips to her". For a town that had long been anxious about its shingle beach's failure to match the golden sands of Margate, here at least was a ride to compete with the artificial thrills of "Dreamland".

31. THE DOOMSDAY SHUFFLE

Sheerness's view of the *Richard Montgomery* would change after the closure of the Admiralty dockyard and the Royal Navy's Nore Command in 1960–61. As the other warships vanished, the remaining wreck achieved new significance locally as a symbol of the town's abandonment: an abiding threat of devastation, to be sure, but also a measure of the enduring indifference of governments that, having ripped the economic heart out of this patriotic coastal community, thought nothing of leaving such a dismal memorial to Sheerness's naval past poking up to disturb the view that was one of the town's few remaining assets.

The *Daily Sketch* published two articles about the "sunken ghost ship" in the spring of 1962. These were written by Desmond Wettern, a young journalist who had served with the Royal Navy (and would later become well known as the *Daily Telegraph*'s naval correspondent, persisting, through an ongoing age of naval cuts and restructuring, as a last-ditch champion of British sea power). In the first article, Wettern described what had happened when Sheerness Urban District Council's seafront controller, Lt Col H.R. McKechnie, wrote to the American naval authorities in London asking for "a brief history of the ship".[1] For better or worse, he explained, the wreck had become "one of the big local attractions", to such an extent that the council, which knew better than to look even this horrifying gift horse in the mouth, wanted to be in the position to inform visitors about it from "the main information office on the seafront".

After a few weeks, McKechnie had received an answer confirming that, according to the Maritime Administration in Washington, *SS Richard Montgomery* "went aground in 1944 and, since only the superstructure remained visible, was declared a maritime wreck". So far so familiar, but that could not be said for the following claim: "According to the record she was raised and scrapped and sold to Phillips Craft Fisher Co. in April 1948". Wettern ended the first part of his divided article by pretending not yet to have discovered "what was on board" this highly visible but allegedly non-existent ship: "Nobody knows — though one rumour says she was carrying a load of dynamite. Enough, it is said, to blow out every window in Sheerness".

On 8 May, the *Daily Sketch* returned to its story of the "ghost ship", printing a second article devoted to solving the "mystery" planted at the end of the first.[2] By now, as Wettern wrote, the US Maritime Authority was prepared to confirm what was plain as day to every holidaymaker who had paid for the summer thrill of a guided boat trip around the wreck: "Yes, she exists, alright". As for what was in the sunken freighter's holds, Wettern's telephone enquiry produced the following answer:

"'Bombs!'

'What sort of bombs?'

'Oh! Just bombs, you know. We can't say exactly what sort'".

Confirmation, and also further cause for alarm, was provided by a *Daily Sketch* reader, Mr Joe Gilhooley of Stoke-on-Trent, who remembered being part of the "Royal Navy boarding party sent to clear the bombs from the ship during the war". Explaining that they had only "managed to salvage half the cargo before the ship heeled over", he estimated that there were about three thousand tons of explosives still on board: "she is virtually an unexploded bomb. The authorities know this — that is why they have never dynamited her to clear the harbour of the wreck".

America's "ghost ship" had become a "problem ship" with which no branch of British public authority was at all keen to interfere. Looking for a positive end to his story, Wettern closed by repeating the Admiralty's statement that the best hope lay in a vanishing trick that the wreck might be left to carry out by itself. The *Richard Montgomery* was already "scouring out a hole" in the seabed, and it was possible to imagine that both the ship and its threatening cargo may "in ten years' time have disappeared into it." It was an absurd idea, but one to which evasive officials were nevertheless still drawn. Indeed, it would not be long before the responsible authorities came up with a reassuring phrase to replace their predecessors' use of the word "capricious" to justify leaving the cargo just where it was. They started finding consolation in the thick and muffling "blanket of silt" said to be covering the bombs as the tides continued to scour the hole that would carry the hull down towards Australia.

Two years after the *Daily Sketch* published Wettern's thoughts on the subject, local fears that the abandoned *SS Richard Montgomery* might actually threaten far worse than broken windows were inflamed by a long feature article written by David Lampe, allegedly after "many months of difficult, painstaking research", and published in *Wide World* magazine in October 1964.[3] On Lampe's pages, the *Daily Sketch's* "problem ship" became "the Doomsday Ship", laden with bombs weighing "more than seven million pounds" that were still "very much alive" and capable, as Lampe announced, introducing a phrase that would be much repeated over the years to come, of causing "the most catastrophic non-nuclear explosion in history." If the *Richard Montgomery* went up, as was considered entirely possible, there would be a "heavy fall of shrapnel on towns inhabited by 375,000 people and Sheerness, which was closest of all, would be wiped from the map: "every building and every thing — as well as all the 14,000 people who live in that town — would be destroyed. A tidal wave would inevitably follow the big blast — to wash away the last traces of the sorry debris that was Sheerness." By the time David Lampe had finished with it, the *SS Richard Montgomery* promised an apocalyptic day of reckoning to rival anything imagined by the most zealous of Sheerness's chapelgoers.

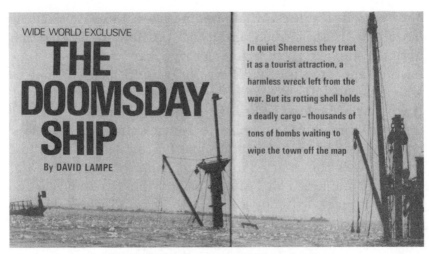

Wide World's view of Sheerness.

In the absence of a full and available official account of the situation, it may not be surprising that Lampe's reconstruction of the stranding of the *Richard Montgomery* was very far from accurate — not least in the suggestion that the sinking of the ship, which was actually caused by the splitting of the hull ("welded not riveted", as Johnson would correctly point out), was the fault of the British stevedores, wrongly alleged to have been unloading the stranded vessel at the approach of a storm, and to have left its holds open when hastily abandoning it. Other statements may be truer relays from local memory of the time. It was Lampe who captured Sheerness's recollection of the American who was said to have come over to Sheerness shortly after the war to inspect the bomb ship for a US salvage firm and then to have fled, never to return. He was also informed about a Dutch company, which considered the job in 1951, but pulled out after its man suggested — before he too scarpered — that the best solution might be to suck the sand out from under the wreck to encourage it to "sink into the ooze" more quickly. Viscount Linley, who was by then the Chairman of the Port of London Authority, had also bought the Admiralty line that the *Richard Montgomery* — which had become "How shall I say? A well-known landmark on the Thames" — would eventually "sink harmlessly into the mud".

When he talked to the local authorities, Lampe found men shrugging their shoulders on both sides of the estuary. In Southend, where people might be lucky enough to get away with broken windows, the town clerk seemed studiously indifferent to the threat. "We've lived with it for twenty years, and so far it hasn't blown up", he said, brushing aside Lampe's warnings with the words, "We're prepared to accept the advice of our government on matters like this". The official view in Sheerness was similar. Having made his own enquiries in the town living "in the shadow of death", Lampe concluded that "most people in Sheerness don't even realise that the bombs are there and many of the people who once knew about them seem to have forgotten them". Even the Sheerness Town Clerk, Mr J. Griffiths, seemed "unaware of the tremendous tonnage of bombs until informed by *Wide World*".

Lampe judged these local officials to be in dereliction of their duties, but he reserved a stronger condemnation for the men at the Admiralty, allegedly disgruntled at having been merged into the Ministry of Defence earlier in 1964, who had failed even to send down naval divers to review the state of the bombs inside the holds. He found it symptomatic that no official over the last twenty years had even asked to see the loading plan of the *Richard Montgomery*'s holds, an unexamined copy of which had only recently been thrown away by William Hurst Ltd., the company that had served as agents to the American Maritime Commission during the partial clearance of the disintegrating ship's holds (it seems not to have occurred to Lampe that the officials in question may long since have had the documentation from American sources). However much the authorities might invoke the "consensus of expert opinion", this was only "an excuse to do nothing" in the hope that the Thames silt would eventually suck the all too visible wreck into oblivion.

There is much about Lampe's article that may appear to prove one of the abiding lessons about British government that emerges from the story of the *Richard Montgomery*: the more secretive and unforthcoming the official authorities choose to be, the more speculative will be the press and its readers in their interpretation of events. Yet Lampe did, unquestionably, have an ace in his hand. The unconsulted "expert" he pitched against those claimed by the Admiralty was "Britain's foremost and the world's most experienced bomb disposal expert". Having served for many years with the Royal Engineers, Major Arthur Bamford Hartley, MBE, had used his retirement to write a book reviewing the bravery and ingenuity of his extremely heroic comrades in the Second World War. Not given to imaginative flights, he called it *Unexploded Bomb: The Story of Bomb Disposal*.[4]

Hartley had intimate knowledge of the dangers faced by those who had dug and crawled their way into "bomb shafts" that might turn and twist weirdly as they ploughed through as much as sixty feet of earth. He knew the many ways in which courageous "disposers" had died — blown to bits, drowned, lost under collapsing earth, gassed by a sudden release of ammonia or carbon monoxide, horribly burned by phosphorous catching fire as it came into contact with air in a confined space. His engagement in bomb disposal had extended into the post-war period, when as many as 1,400 German prisoners of war were "drafted to Britain" to help British sappers in the slow and "nervously exhausting" job of clearing beaches of mines.

Precious little in Hartley's book supports the Admiralty's hope that the TNT-filled bombs on the *Richard Montgomery* might gradually become more "blanketed" and less dangerous if left undisturbed. Indeed, the major recalled a conference convened by the Director of Bomb Disposal in the spring of 1945, at which it was unambiguously resolved that "old bombs were at least as dangerous as new ones" — a realisation that led to instructions that all discovered bombs should be blown up "in situ" unless "very special reasons" made this impractical. The instability could be caused by the degradation of fuses, but Hartley also remembered many cases in which the filling of an old TNT-filled bomb had become self-activating when excavated and "tampered with". "Chemical and physical changes" could lead to a build-up of gasses that might quickly asphyxiate a disposer if it escaped. His examples include a bomb dug up in Sheerness. Finding that internal pressure had already sheared off the baseplate, the officer in charge had quickly clambered out of the pit in which the bomb lay. Already keen to "escape the gas bubbling up from the rear of the bomb", Captain Wadsworth was hastened by the further discovery that the bomb-casing was getting warm.

Hartley was horrified to learn that the *Richard Montgomery* had been left on its sandbank for so long. Leaving the wreck there, he told Lampe, was "like finding a long forgotten bomb dump in a crowded suburb — and then walking away from it without bothering even to tell anyone. In my opinion these bombs are a major hazard. They won't make themselves safe. On the contrary, as time passes they may become more dangerous. A lot more dangerous." He trusted that the bombs had been packed very carefully, and without fuses. He knew from a huge specimen he had once fished out of Ipswich harbour that American bombs were painted with highly protective paint: "salt water might take a thousand years or more to penetrate them". Neither probability, however, justified inaction. Some sixteen different combinations of explosives had been used in American fragmentation bombs during the war, and it seemed that nobody knew which particular mixture had been used in the examples stowed on Sheerness's "Doomsday Ship". Moreover, production standards had fallen by 1944, and the *Montgomery*'s cargo came from manufacturers required only to produce explosives "with sufficient 'shelf life'" to last through the war. Who could be sure that the TNT hadn't crystallised and therefore become highly unstable, or that nitrates in the explosive fillings had not started to break down and generate gases which might in turn generate sufficient heat and pressure inside the bombs to set them off? It was entirely possible, he told Lampe, that the bombs might "explode at any time".

Considering that the wreck had apparently been left largely unattended and "well within the reach of anyone", Hartley also worried about an "endless" number of more external accidents that might trigger a disaster: the collapse of the wooden packaging around the bombs could do the job, as might the strength of the tide, the impact of an unpiloted ship losing control in the current — which was, according to local fishermen, very dangerous around the wreck — or of a shallow-draught vessel scraping its way across the deck as was said already to have happened. It was by no means a remote possibility that "an amateur frogman" might start poking about among the bombs: Sheerness boatmen claimed that at least one such had already dived the wreck and "carried away some of her brass fittings". It would be a few years before the IRA started bombing pubs, railway stations and bandstands on the British mainland, but Major Hartley already dreaded to think "what would happen if a malicious person began tampering" with the *Richard Montgomery*. "Sheerness Would Be Wiped Out" shrieked the headline beneath which the *East Kent Gazette* was pleased to report that the Faversham constituency's recently elected Labour MP, a barrister and former RAF flight lieutenant named Terence Boston, had already sent a copy of *Wide World* to Lord Jellicoe at the Admiralty.[5]

*

The articles published by the *Daily Sketch* and *Wide World* may have been viewed with entitled contempt by the authorities upriver, but their claims could not be wholly ignored. On 18 March 1965, in answer to a question by Boston, the Labour Secretary of State for Defence Mr Christopher Mayhew tried to demonstrate his grip on the situation. He informed the House of Commons that, following recent "sensational" press accounts, a working party involving the Ministry of Defence, the Home Office, the PLA and the Medway Conservancy Board had been set up in the autumn of 1964 to look into the "explosive risks in leaving the wreck alone or in attempting to clear it".[6] This had confirmed that the wreck should be left where it was on the grounds that it was no more dangerous than in 1952, and that "an explosion, although serious" would not be anything like the cataclysm imagined by journalists. The working party had also recommended an up-to-date survey of the wreck, which naval divers would carry out in the summer of 1965 "under strictly controlled safety precautions".

In the event, as Mayhew would inform Boston a few months later, the divers discovered that the two halves of the wreck had separated and sunk into the mud. They had not entered the holds but it was estimated that "heavy silting" had probably engulfed the remaining cargo.[7] The survey confirmed the Ministry of Defence in its view that, while the wreck must be left untouched, it should be identified more clearly as a hazard on the charts of the estuary, marked off by buoys, and also equipped with an automatic fog signal: "I think that is the best we can do". Hearing that various private parties were still showing interest in salvaging materials from the wreck, the ministry also added a light to the second buoy, and instructed the Medway Constabulary to arrest and remove anyone interfering with the site.

News of these modest measures was not enough to reassure the members of Sheerness Urban District Council, which wrote to Boston asking him to arrange for "an expert (or experts)" to come to Sheerness to "allay the fears of councillors faced with questions from the townspeople".[8] If the *Richard Montgomery* really could not be cleared and removed, the council expected more than a light on a buoy. Its members wanted the authorities to consider building "a suitable barrier around the wreck" to prevent even the remote possibility of a collision, and also to provide an "estimate" of damage to Sheerness "should the explosive be found to be unstable".

The Sheerness Urban District Council anticipated the requested encounter with cautious optimism. At a meeting on Wednesday, 16 March 1966, councillors congratulated themselves for having "prodded" the Ministry of Defence into admitting the danger posed by the "Bomb Ship" and declared again that a "speed-up" was necessary when it came to making it safe once and for all time.[9] "We have mixed feelings about this", admitted the Chairman, Cllr F.W. Roalfe, adding that he hoped "experts" were going to look at the ship and that the matter would be resolved "very shortly".

The men from the responsible public authorities in London prepared their case carefully, calling in various explosive experts to consider what scraps of reassurance might be offered to the awakened councillors of Sheppey. It was accepted that the explosives were still dangerous, and that an explosion was more likely to be caused by the "shifting of cargo" in tidal currents than by chemical interaction within the bombs.[10] Sheerness Council's idea of creating a barrier around the wreck was discounted on the grounds that the necessary pile-driving or drilling might set the whole thing off. They also considered the masts poking up into the town's view: some wanted to remove these on the grounds that they might "sheer and fall vertically into the holds", while others argued that they were still in "exceptionally" good condition, and that their visibility was useful to shipping. It was agreed that "a ring of buoys fitted with radar reflectors" could be supplied, and answers to anticipated questions and objections were prepared to prevent further concessions being squeezed out under pressure. Although a letter announcing the forthcoming meeting was sent to the MP Terence Boston, it was, as a civil servant explained in an internal document, kept "deliberately vague in the hope that he will not invite himself along".[11]

So the day had come, on 22 April 1966, when twelve members of Sheerness Urban District Council finally sat down to review the situation with those officials from the Ministry of Defence, the Home Office and the Board of Trade. The meeting wasn't held at the council's offices in Sheerness as members had initially imagined, but in the more impressive Admiral's Conference Room at Chatham Dockyard. It was chaired by the well-prepared J.M. Kisch of the Ministry of Defence's Shore Division (Naval) and it appears to have gone as well as the Ministry of Defence could have wished. The minutes, which are marked "Confidential", suggest that while some councillors insisted on their questions, there were also moments of resigned if not deferential acquiescence. The officials acknowledged that the "public attitude" in Sheerness might believe that the refusal to move the *Richard Montgomery* was based on reluctance to dedicate the necessary funds to safeguarding this poor, abandoned and comparatively lightly populated working-class area. The town's representatives were, however, strongly encouraged to understand that this was definitely not the case, and that money would willingly be found for the clearance if it were judged possible.

Like their predecessors in the Admiralty, the men in charge stuck to their claim that nothing could be done that would not be more dangerous than inaction. It was only possible to draw limited reassurance from the fact that the bombs were at least now buried in their "blanket of silt" and to introduce more security measures. Warning notices would be attached to the protruding masts of the ship — a draft of the proposed wording was distributed at the meeting — as well as to the safety buoys. There would be a notice for mariners and a stronger identification of the danger area on charts. Given that the decision had been made to leave the wreck where it was, "the real menace" was now not the ship but "the passer-by who spontaneously decided to reconnoitre the wreck". The Kent Constabulary were therefore ordered to remove, "by force if necessary", any trespassers and the Medway Conservancy Board would maintain a "constant radar watch on the wreck and conduct daily river patrols in the area".

Once again, the *Richard Montgomery* continued to lie there. Unsalvageable but also undeniable, it was by now adorned with prominent warning notices, each one like a postcard sent downriver as proof of official vigilance, each one adding to the Doomsday Ship's utility as a roost for cormorants and shags. Parsimony with information remained the official way: partly, it may surely be assumed, because the men upriver knew very well that a fuller knowledge of "the facts" as the Americans might one day reveal them, could hardly be relied upon to take the End of the World out of Sheerness. In the upriver world, where powerful people had the power of decision, the passage of time might be associated with eventfulness, development and rising prosperity, personal or otherwise. Downriver, as the story of the *Richard Montgomery* shows very clearly, it would be attended by a silted mixture of anxiety, helpless inertia and speculation — the tedious encrustation that builds up around problems national governments fail adequately to address. As Brexit would later show, we must find our history in that too.

*

A year after the councillors of Sheerness bowed to the Ministry of Defence, fears on both sides of the argument were confirmed by the explosion of another sunken "bomb ship". This one was a freighter named *Kielce*, loaded with ordnance intended for American forces in West Germany, which had suffered a collision in April 1946 and gone down in ninety feet of water some three or four miles offshore from Folkestone. On 22 July 1967, salvage divers, who had already cleared much of the cargo, are said to have fired a charge intended to open up the hull so that one hundred or so tons of bombs remaining under the bulkhead could be removed. They had already carried out two such explosions without unintended consequences, but this time the bombs went up. While the salvage workers sitting in a rubber dinghy some four hundred feet from the wreck were reported to have seen only "a small ripple and some spray",[12] a considerable crater was formed in the seabed and the seismic shock, which was registered in California, cracked chimneys, ceilings, walls and also some windows in Folkestone. There were reports of a "tidal wave", which had caused some alarm among holidaymakers on the town beach and is even said to have led to some successful damages claims, even though subsequent analysis found it unlikely to have been "greater than about 2 ft".

The explosion of the *Kielce* increased concern about the *Richard Montgomery*, which lay in much shallower water, considerably closer to Sheerness, and carried a very much larger collection of bombs. It was, however, a far worse event that stiffened the determination of Mr Freddy Burden, a former squadron leader who was now the Conservative MP for Gillingham in Kent. He asked Parliamentary questions about the dangers posed by the *Richard Montgomery* on 25 October and 8 November 1967, when the nation was still reeling from the disaster in the south Wales mining village of Aberfan, where a mountainous slag heap had collapsed on 16 October, killing 116 children as it buried their school. Spurred on by this avoidable disaster (the National Coal Board had long ignored pleas for action from people living in the grossly mismanaged slag heap's shadow), Burden insisted that the Ministry of Defence, then under Harold Wilson's Labour government, really must do something about the hazard threatening his town as well as Sheerness: "it is up to them to see that the danger is removed before the country is involved in another Aberfan".[13] He was informed by the temporising Under-Secretary of State for the Navy, Mr Maurice Foley, that the government was still awaiting a report drawing conclusions from an American reappraisal of the bombs aboard the *Richard Montgomery*, which, after all, remained US property.

The reality, as Foley knew, was altogether more complex. The Ministry of Defence had received the awaited American report in June that year (a month or so before the *Kielce* went up so serendipitously). Recently opened files in the National Archives reveal that the Ministry of Defence had also worked hard to win over the Americans, leaving them in no doubt that all the responsible British authorities considered it better to leave the ship where it was. They had argued this forcefully at a meeting with American army experts in 1966, and the civil servant in charge of the Ministry's Shore Division (Navy) had even written to the Americans with a series of leading questions that pointed unmistakably towards the British conclusion that vigilant inaction was the safest course.[14] Despite this pre-emptive strike from British officials, the American "boffins" had insisted in going off in quite the wrong direction. Their report insisted that it was still "entirely feasible to salvage the remaining cargo, provided qualified personnel are used and adequate equipment is available".[15] Recommending that the bombs be salvaged and dumped at sea in water of five hundred fathoms or more, they also declared themselves confident that the operation could be successfully accomplished — by British contract workers approved by the Ministry of Defence.

This put a big cat among the pigeons at the Ministry of Defence. Two British explosives experts whose views had been cited by the Americans in support of their conclusions were promptly instructed to produce letters stating unambiguously that the bombs were simply too dangerous and the condition of their fuses too unknowable to justify any attempt at removal. It then fell to Mr J.E.D. Street, the head of the Ministry of Defence's Shore Division (Navy) to draft and justify the British response rejecting the American proposal. In a "loose Minute" dated 27 October 1967, he insisted that the Americans "know a lot less than we do".[16] Reiterating that all consulted explosives experts warned of the danger of interfering with the bombs, which the Americans like the British were unable to detail precisely, Mr Street emphasised that recovery of the bombs would be "an enormous and expensive task". He also claimed to have detected yet more encouraging thickening in the "blanket of silt" with which his predecessors had sought to muffle the concerns of sceptical politicians and fearful residents alike, asserting that the bombs had been rendered less dangerous by "increased siltration" since 1964, when a survey had suggested that an explosion would only break windows and crack already weak walls in Sheerness. Aware of high levels of "public awareness" about the issue in Sheerness and elsewhere, and also the concern of various MPs from both sides of the Thames Estuary, Street recommended that news of the government's rejection of the American suggestion should be slipped through as a written answer to a supplementary question, and not announced in a ministerial speech to the Commons where a debate might "give probably unjustified prominence to the potential risks".

While the Americans accepted the Ministry of Defence's decision, this is more than can be said for the nation's amateur visionaries. In 1971, the Board of Trade, by this time under Edward Heath's Conservative government, was still having to brush off letters from private citizens offering their own steampunk schemes for the removal of the wreck.[17] Mr Persad from Selly Oak, wanted to enclose the thing in a vast steel dome riveted (not welded) to the seabed with a hole left in the top, and then to blow it up once and for all. H.N. Brunby of Doncaster thought it would be better to isolate and freeze the *Richard Montgomery* before using floating cranes to raise both the wreck and its unpredictable cargo out of the water in solid blocks of ice.

Pearl Ace, *a Panama-registered Vehicles Carrier, passing the* Richard Montgomery, *2017.*

Yet there were also pleas of a less technical nature. In October 1971, suspicions that high wind and tides were causing movement in the disintegrating *Richard Montgomery* drew new notes of alarm from concerned figures in Sheerness. Three of the town's ministers — Baptist, Church of England

and Congregationalist — came together to write about the "upsurge of anxiety" being felt about the hazardous wreck "so close to the beaches of Sheerness".[18] They cited many causes for increased alarm — the recent movement of the broken hull, such as it may have been, the increase of shipping in the Thames and Medway Channels, and the prospect of a new airport on Maplin Sands, across the estuary at Foulness, plans for which had been formally accepted by the government in April 1971 and which threatened to introduce a flight path that would bring low-flying planes directly over the wreck. The three ministers pleaded that, even if the bomb ship remained too dangerous to remove, something surely had to be done to reduce the "equally real risk" the wreck posed for the people of Sheerness. Looking back into the days of national service, they declared that "some of us can remember using sandbags etc. to muffle the explosive power of anti-personnel mines, etc.", and urged that "modern technology and experience" should now be applied to the search for a "marine equivalent". The Chairman of the Governors at St George's Church of England Middle School in Sheerness was also worried. He wrote to the Seretary of State for Education and Science, Margaret Thatcher, explaining that the families and children of the town had "grave cause to fear", and pleading that she should encourage the responsible departments of government to give more serious attention to the possibility of "rendering the effects of the blast less devastating" for the town and its children.[19]

By the time Johnson arrived in Sheerness, the *Richard Montgomery* was well-established as a generator of wild estuarial narratives of helplessness and official abandonment. Files now accessible at the National Archives reveal that the upriver authorities were by no means as idle as they seemed to downriver communities. The latter may not have been kept informed but, at the beginning of the Seventies, engineers at the government's Hydraulic Research Institute at Wallingford really had been commissioned to survey the possibility of constructing a barrier around the wreck, in order to protect it from collisions. Their investigation, which reported in January 1971, revealed that "turbulent eddies" had caused extensive scouring at the ends of the separated halves of the hull, raising the fear that bomb-filled parts of the ship might drop dangerously into the hole opened beneath them.[20] The idea of sinking blockships as protective measures around the wreck was discounted as both dangerous and useless — since they would sink into the unstable bank and probably also slide out towards the Medway shipping channel. It was considered safer to produce a "rubble dam", but this had its dangers too. Almost incidentally, the Hydraulic Research Institute's investigators noted that the forward half of the wreck had now itself split into two, raising the likelihood that bombs were already sliding out of the holds.

By November 1971, Edward Heath's government had given up on the idea of building any variety of protective wall.[21] That announcement prompted another flurry of alarmist press attention, and more public concern following an edition of the BBC television news programme *Nationwide,* which, on 1 March 1972, interviewed fishermen from Leigh-on-Sea, on the Essex side of the estuary: they spoke of having trawled up a bomb — or, as an official may have suspected, an old First World War shell — and claimed that many bombs were now scattered around the wreck.[22] The pressure was mounting on the upriver authorities whose strategy seemed to some critics to consist only of postponing the problem, together with the responsibility for deciding over it, into a bureaucratic version of Doomsday, i.e. a looming disaster that may, with any luck, not happen on the present incumbent's watch.

Documents in no longer closed files reveal that, following a meeting with the Department of Trade and Industry in March 1972 the explosives experts at the Ministry of Technology's Explosives Research and Development Establishment (ERDE) at Waltham Abbey were charged with forming a working party to look into the possibility of conducting an "experimental" explosion in order to establish the "hazards" posed by the *Richard Montgomery.*[23] In his paper for the meeting,

ERDE's researcher, S.J. Hawkins, admitted that his own initial enthusiasm for simply blowing up the wreck had been impractical, thanks partly to the necessity of evacuating not just Sheerness and the Isle of Grain on the southern shore of the estuary, but also Southend and Shoeburyness to the north. This would, he declared, be a very expensive operation, and the explosion would no doubt also be followed by innumerable compensation claims for damage and loss of earnings. In justifying his change of mind, he drew on the Atomic Weapons and Research Establishment's report (No. 0-36/72) on "The Kielce Explosion". He also cited his own earlier "technical memo No. 11", printed by ERDE in 1970 under the title "Effects of Detonation in the Wreck of SS Richard Montgomery off Sheerness".

In the latter investigation, Hawkins had sought to predict what would happen if the 1,400 tons of TNT on the *Richard Montgomery* exploded at low tide, with thirty-seven feet of water above the charge. Careful to confine himself to scientific forces — air blast, underwater shock, seismic vibration, ejection of water, tidal waves — rather than human consequences, this expert in "sonic bangs" anticipated that an explosion would produce a water column a thousand feet wide rising nine thousand feet from the sea. It would sculpt a crater of some five thousand cubic metres out of the sea bed, while perhaps also, as the Hydraulic Research Station had suggested, opening a north-south channel through the Sheerness Middle Sand and having other "deleterious" effects on the Medway shipping channel, while scattering unexploded bombs far and wide too. The impact would be worst for Sheerness and for ships in the Medway Channel, but not at all good for any planes that happened to be approaching or taking off from Southend Airport.

Having demonstrated that deliberate detonation was not a sensible option, the ERDE working party, which convened again on 29 November 1973, was asked to consider the possibility of salvaging the wreck with the help of a "dry dock" that might, so the Department of the Environment's Marine Engineering Division had tentatively suggested, be constructed around it.

The latter idea was to surround the wreck with an encircling dam. Built at a safe distance of two hundred feet, this would create a tide-proof "lagoon" from which the water might then be removed a foot or two at a time. The revealed cargo would be hosed down, treated chemically to remove rust accretions and barnacles, and then carefully removed. The operation would be repeated until the cargo was cleared, after which the ship itself would be cut up and lifted in pieces.

In his briefing paper, Hawkins assesses every aspect of this delicate operation. He gathers everything that is known about the cargo — using American information to establish exactly what bombs and fuses are involved. He allows for the discrepancy between the original loading manifest and the record of bombs removed during the salvage operation of August/September 1944, and takes into account that there may be some materials left in holds previously declared empty. He then plots every action necessary to the successful completion of this delicate operation — building the dam, getting access to the site, dealing with the dangerous fuses: both those already screwed into the M1A1 cluster fragmentation bombs and the separate AN-M103 detonators intended for the larger TNT-filled bombs but packed individually in waterproof metal cans and then stored in batches in wooden cases.

It would, Hawkins reckoned, be technically possible to construct such a "dry dock" and then to lower the water level gradually, so that the silt could be gently hosed off the top layer of bombs before proceeding further. Some cutting may be necessary to get access to the holds, but mechanical force had to be avoided in examining the fuses for copper azide. There were ways of doing this for the M1A1 fuses in the cluster fragmentation bombs, but the others might have to be left in their wooden cases and detonated once the rest of the ship had been cleared. Having outlined every step of the manoeuvre, Hawkins concluded that safe recovery was "a definite possibility". He admitted, however, that it would be hugely expensive with the dam alone costing a possible sum of £5 million. Perhaps that, rather than just the caution of bomb-shy politicians, was the reason why it was never attempted. That is how things stood when Uwe Johnson moved to Sheerness and saw the masts of the *Richard Montgomery* poking up from the seabed outside his window. Like unemployment, poverty and the flow of Hürlimann lager in the Napier Tavern, the Doomsday shuffle was set to continue.

32. BECOMING UNFATHOMABLE: THE BOMB SHIP AS "MURKY REALITY"

Perhaps, during his very first days in Sheerness, Johnson really did mistake "that thing" for a peculiar English fishing apparatus. Had he done so, however, the illusion was dispelled much sooner than might be deduced from his essay "An Unfathomable Ship". Within days of moving in, Johnson was using the apocalyptic wreck outside his window to add a punch to his friends' doubts about his new home. Early in December 1974, he wrote to Rudolf Augstein, the founder and head of *Der Spiegel,* insisting on the attractions he might expect to encounter on a visit: "Two and a half miles from the shore there is a munitions ship that sank in April 1945 [sic], which no salvage company dares to attempt; if it goes up, it'll knock more than ten feet off the buildings and they will hardly be able to rescue the inhabitants from their upstairs windows with rowing boats. Are there not a few words one could waste on this ship? There are. But you should see it for yourself."[1]

The East German writer Günter Kunert, who met up with the Johnsons at 26 Marine Parade a month or so after that letter was written, noted the apparent pride with which Johnson took this little party up to a higher floor to show them the "sinister panorama" that could be seen from the front bedroom:

> ... a monotonous expanse of water furnished with a tanker or freighter far out by the horizon, as though to give the eye something to rest on. In the middle of the reflected

verticals, a buoy marking where an American munitions ship went down in 1945 [sic], which, as Japanese divers have only recently confirmed, cannot be salvaged. If it were to explode, all Sheerness would go up. And yet no one had informed the buyer of this house, Herr Uwe Johnson from Berlin-Friedenau, of this fact before purchase. And yet he, for his part, told me about it with such satisfaction, almost pleasure, as though his purchase price had obtained him the right, which he could legally exercise in case of emergency, to a catastrophe.[2]

Johnson wrote the first version of "An Unfathomable Ship" at the request of the West German political philosopher Jürgen Habermas, who was preparing a collection of essays to be published as Suhrkamp's thousandth volume in 1979. Aware that the ideas and attitudes that had shaped West Germany through the post-war years were increasingly challenged by new realities, Habermas judged it timely to devote the book to an investigation of "the spiritual situation of the age". The phrase was taken from the philosopher and psychiatrist Karl Jaspers, who had used it as the title of an influential tract published in 1931, in which he had set out to review the condition of life in the years before Hitler's final rise to power and to analyse the adequacy, or otherwise, of Enlightenment values of reason and reflection to those seeking fully to understand and guide people under the new circumstance (the English translation was published as *Man in the Modern Age*[3]).

Johnson was among the fifty or so "critics, writers and social scientists" who received a letter from Habermas invited them to contribute to *Observations on "the Spiritual Situation of the Age"*.[4] Dated 15 June 1978, the commissioning letter reminded readers of Jasper's essay and suggested that the West German left was again at a moment of transition, indicated by the emergence of terrorism on the far-left and also by the state's draconian response to this new threat. The post-war past that was now threatened with disintegration had been shaped and informed by Suhrkamp Editions, which had gone into action as a literary house, publishing Adorno, Benjamin, Beckett, Brecht, Frisch, Grass, and Johnson himself before opening up to a wider and more international list of theorists, historians and commentators. Suhrkamp's endeavour had been "resolutely" affiliated with the idea of Enlightenment, humanism, bourgeois radical thought, and with "the aesthetic and political avant-garde of the nineteenth century". It was also, Habermas added, an expression of a post-war era in which the slogan "the spirit belongs on the left" had seemed closer to truth than before or since. With the rise of the "New Right", however, "All this is now over".

Habermas used his letter to encourage contributors to choose their own way of addressing the proposed subject. Their engagement with Jasper's work might be as tight or as loose as they wished and they were certainly not expected to mimic Jaspers by writing "in the language of *haut bourgeois* cultural criticism, and with the pathos of a nation's instructor". They should, however, heed one consideration that was surely not "obsolete" about Jasper's approach, namely, the "duty of intellectuals" to react to "movements, developmental tendencies, dangers, and critical moments". It was still, Habermas stated, "the task of intellectuals to make conscious a murky reality". Johnson's entire work may have shared in that aim as it applied to twentieth-century Germany but his contribution to this particular volume also fits another of Habermas's indications: "Perhaps you will take your theme merely from some singular phenomenon, an observation, or a symptomatic expression..." Johnson wrote the words "Richard Montgomery" on his copy of Habermas's letter of invitation, and set to work making his own sense of the bomb ship in an article that has been described as "his only serious piece on England".[5]

In a letter accompanying his contribution and dated 8 January 1979, he admitted that he may have been too free with the "lee-way" Habermas had offered his authors, and that he would understand if his piece was considered too far "off-topic" to be included. Habermas did indeed at first decline Johnson's essay as having very little connection to "our complicated fatherland". Keen, nevertheless, that the collection should include something from Johnson, whom he recalls having met "quite a few times" at Siegfried Unseld's home in Frankfurt and also at Hannah Arendt's apartment in New York,[6] the political philosopher asked for something else. By then, Johnson was busy writing the "Lectures on Poetics" ("that is a stony field for me"[7]) he would deliver at Goethe University in Frankfurt am Main and he declined the request. Johnson then revised his essay, which could certainly not be accused of avoiding "murky reality", and submitted the more recent version to *Merkur*, a "Journal of European Thought", which published it in 1979.[8] Habermas, however, held to his insistence that Surhkamp's thousandth publication really could not be published without something by Johnson, so the initially rejected earlier version was included as the closing item of the collection.

*

So what did Johnson bring to Sheerness's dismally abiding story of the Doomsday Ship? Having established the two futures facing Sheerness — drowning by flood or going up in a fireball — he commends the *Richard Montgomery* as the object of an enlightening investigation that he and the town's other residents might like to pursue while they waited for the final day of reckoning:

> Until we reach that point, might we be in a position to get to the bottom of this derelict, to recover the jetsam it has thrown off, historically, magically, biographically, sociologically, chemically, administro-scientifically, poetically, statistically?[9]

That was a larger project than Johnson himself could exhaust in a single article. He does, however, combine his invitation to others with a demonstration of the ways in which the "wreck" — which he insisted, with all due respect to the earlier memorial standing across the road from the railway station, was Sheppey's true "monument to the 1939-45 war"[10] — might be independently repossessed and the local predicament reconnected to a larger and by no means merely English understanding of history. He opens ironically, suggesting that, while all the Liberty ships bore the name of American heroes, the man who was Richard Montgomery would surely have been amazed to discover his name meaning anything at all two hundred years after his death. Born in Ireland in 1738, he was a "mercenary" who had entered the British Army at the age of eighteen and later "sold his services to the rebelling Americans". Appointed a Brigadier General in Washington's Continental Army in 1775, he had taken Montreal on 13 November that year, but died only six weeks later while leading 1,635 inexperienced men in a grossly miscalculated attack against "professional British soldiers" at the Fortress of Quebec. As a turncoat and a commander of limited competence who had proved a mortal danger to his own men (Johnson describes him as "a general, from whom people run away"), Montgomery had been obliged "to be patient when American ships were being named after the fathers of the Revolution". The first Liberty ship was launched in September 1941, but Montgomery's specimen had only emerged from the dockyard at Jacksonville, Florida in 1943 and here it was, as Johnson puts it, "barely a year later ... busted off Sheerness".[11]

Digging further down into the "magic of names", Johnson notes that the ships were named "Liberty ships" after an earlier "national emergency" of America's own. Historians may not doubt that the man who named the "Liberty Fleet" was the Chairman of the Maritime Commission responsible for their design and manufacture, Admiral Emory Scott Land — the designation was confirmed by the decision to name the very first to leave the slipway the *SS Patrick Henry*, after the patriotic American revolutionary who had declared "Give me Liberty or give me death". Johnson, however, who enters the story sideways, finds a different inspiration in "no less a symbol than the Liberty Bell", which was commissioned in 1751 by the Pennsylvania Provincial Assembly, made by the Whitechapel

Bell Foundry in east London, inscribed with a quotation from Leviticus ("Proclaim liberty throughout all the land unto all the inhabitants thereof") and, in 1953, hung in the Pennsylvania State House, in Chestnut Street, Philadelphia, to mark the fiftieth anniversary of the Charter of Privileges drawn up for the colony by William Penn.[12] Unfortunately, this great symbol of American liberty was miscast from materials that proved too brittle, giving it a "faulty, unsteady tone". Although recast at least twice, it continued to annoy the neighbours, who complained "as early as 1772" about the fact that its "celebratory din was being unleashed on too many occasions".[13] The Declaration of Independence was proclaimed to the sound of the Liberty Bell on 8 July 1776, and it had to be hidden in the countryside when the British invaded the city the following year. Restored to its place after the American victory, it remained there, "performing its patriotic duty", until it cracked apart again. There are various accounts of exactly when and how the fracture finally became irreparable, but Johnson followed the legend claiming it happened in 1835, when the bell — by this time also adopted as a symbol by abolitionists — was rung at the funeral of Chief Justice John Marshall of the Supreme Court. After that, it was retired to become a famous historical relic of the republic.

In Johnson's allegorical retelling of the story, it was the "crack" rather than any uncomplicated manifestation of "liberty" that America's miscast bell shared with the welded, and by now twice split, hull of the SS *Richard Montgomery*. The existence of this fatal flaw was not recognised by the organisers of the Cold War sequel that Johnson goes on to describe in a bracketed paragraph. In 1950, after the Red Army had "backed down from its blockade of West Berlin", seventeen million American citizens had donated so that a copy of the Liberty Bell could be cast and then shipped to West Berlin where it would be installed in the City Hall at Berlin-Schöneberg as part of a "Crusade for Freedom" shared with Radio Free Europe.[14] This was duly done and the replica — which showed no signs of the crack — had ever since been "rung for two minutes every day at noon (as well as at additional times on solemn or celebratory occasions)". In 1965, as Johnson remembered, "the loyal press of the West Berlin Occupation Zone" urged residents to donate towards the cost of miniature replicas of the Liberty Bell, which were made by a Berlin porcelain works and sent as anti-communist gestures of thanks to the families of American soldiers who had lost their lives in Vietnam. "Apparently, this reciprocation from Berlin (West) for the gift of 1950 was meant to provide an image, at least among grieving Americans, of that for which their men were dying in Southeast Asia too, bringing or defending with God's help the cause of liberty as symbolized by a little bell, from a porcelain factory in Berlin, on American mantelpieces next to photographs draped in black crepe".[15]

The bells of Marienkirche in Lübeck, preserved as they fell during RAF Bomber Command's night raid of 28–29 March 1942.

Johnson employs a more socialist perspective as he goes on to consider the impact of the "Liberty ship" programme on labour unions in America. He describes the rush to produce these ships, and the development of modular construction techniques in which prefabricated sections of the hull were joined by welding rather than the more laborious process of riveting. When the programme began, each ship took some sixty or seventy days to build. Under Henry Kaiser, whose primary shipyards were on the West Coast, it became possible to produce one in less than five days. Unemployment went down, women were drawn into the workforce, as were other workers with no experience of factories or shipyards. It was a climate in which "wages were frozen and heavily taxed" even as prices kept rising.[16] Unions entered a voluntary no-strike agreement, renounced overtime, and even supported Roosevelt's decree binding workers to their workplace: all that, Johnson notes, in exchange for a third of the votes on the War Labor Board. As the war progressed, it became illegal for workers to strike once the state had taken over a business, and the unions smiled at that too, as did the American Communist Party, which — and here Johnson sails close to the American Trostskyist denunciation of the Liberty ship programme — had called for "the speed-up" and backed the maintenance of the no-strike rule even after the end of the war. "The situation of the US labour movement in this period came down to the exact opposite of *Liberty*".[17]

Not so for Henry Kaiser, who became the personification of "another kind of American freedom", namely "a talent for using the work of others". The *Richard Montgomery* was not actually built in a yard owned by Kaiser, but Johnson had his own reason for fingering this epitome of the ruthless capitalist entrepreneur who had grown rich and powerful on the Liberty ship programme and continued to flourish in the post-war decades. In the opening pages of *Anniversaries*, he had described how, on 25 August 1967, the *New York Times* gave two hundred lines to the memory of this deceased industrialist, who had left school at the age of thirteen to work as a delivery boy for $1.50 a week but had now died leaving assets of $2.5bn.[18] So here in the waters off Sheerness was that rampant plutocrat once again: a peerless exploiter of "cost-plus" pricing on government contracts, whose memory Johnson adds to the "murky reality" of a wreck that shows the consequences of Kaiser's motto insisting that there was "no money in a long drawn-out job".[19] If speed of production was one priority in the manufacture of these so-called "Ugly Ducklings", economy was another. "All aesthetic considerations were absent, as were gyroscopic compass and radar. The vessel's one task was to move freight, escorted and protected by the watchdogs of a convoy, and never could affection or respect for this heavy labourer, as expressed in the fairy-tale nickname, transform it into a white swan".[20]

Ignoring the fact that the *Richard Montgomery* was actually an American ship in the service of the American military when it got stranded, Johnson concentrates on the more general point that Liberty ships were used to supply Britain and other Allied countries under the Lend-Lease law of 11 March 1941. From the East German perspective Johnson seems here to rehearse without irony, that assistance had certainly been a long time coming. He explains that Stalin, in the summer of 1941, had begged the Allies to open a second front in Western Europe and the Arctic. After Roosevelt's apparent promise to Molotov the following year, he had announced the imminent coming of such a front in 1942 — informing his own people and, by air-dropped propaganda leaflets, taunting Nazi forces on the Eastern front with the news as well. Humiliated by continued inertia from Britain and America, he had to wait through 1943, as excuses were made and Lend-Lease deliveries were reduced, allegedly in order to "ramp up for the Second Front which was still nowhere to be seen".[21] By the time D-Day finally came, on 6 June 1944, it was hardly surprising that Stalin believed the three-year delay reflected an Allied wish to have the Soviet and German armies "bleed each other dry first". The final insult came immediately after the end of the war in May 1945, when the category of Lend-Lease deliveries concerned with feeding the Red Army "disappeared overnight", thereby "adding ten million soldiers to the mass of an already undernourished civilian population". Johnson insists that this practice of "fobbing off Soviet bloc countries for too long with goods alone" must be considered "one of the earliest roots of the Cold War".[22] As a ship "whose production series is named with a word that does not exist for a Communist consciousness (Stalinist denomination): *Liberty*", the *Richard Montgomery* testified to that awkward fact too.

*

When it came to getting the measure of the *Richard Montgomery*'s English afterlife as a hazardous wreck in the Thames Estuary, Johnson relied heavily on newspaper articles published during the new wave of anxiety provoked by the announcement in August 1978 that the authorities would soon be conducting their four-yearly underwater survey of the ship. The operation, which began at the end of September, was supervised by Commander John Bingham, Deputy Queen's Harbourmaster at Chatham. The naval divers under his command would use underwater television cameras to survey the hull, but not the bombs, which they had been instructed to leave well alone.[23] By the time they clambered into inflatable dinghies to approach the wreck from a mooring and salvage vessel, the press was assuring readers that these brave explorers would be "playing Russian roulette on the grand scale".[24]

Some of the local journalism Johnson read as he sat in the pub appeared in the *Kent Evening News* and the *Sheppey Gazette*, but he also relied heavily on the *Sunday Times*, which had triggered the new wave of public alarm with a feature article entitled "The Thames Timebomb", published on 27 August 1978. The author, Jon Connell, opened by informing his readers that, while summer visitors on the Sheerness promenade might view the *SS Richard Montgomery* as "one of Britain's oddest tourist attractions", local residents knew this "well-known and trusted neighbour" rather differently.[25] Connell suggested that they were used to clambering about on the wreck, filming it, sailing between its masts, salvaging valuable materials from it and, if they were fishermen, using the site as a convenient dump for bombs and other "detritus" of war that turned up in their nets (better, after all, than losing a day's fishing while you wait for a naval bomb disposal unit to come and deal with the situation). Contrary to the "official line" claiming that the wreck was becoming safer as the sea washed, blanketed and buried its cargo, Connell revived the idea that it was actually becoming more dangerous every day, that the hull was breaking up and moving and, indeed, that the "Thames timebomb" might blow up at any moment.

He made these allegations on the authority of a new estuarial warrior from the northern shore, who had by then become well known as a tenacious and highly critical opponent of government policy regarding the wreck. In 1972, when he first took up the issue, David Cotgrove had been described as a Southend restaurateur "with links to the fishing industry". His brother John remarks that nobody should deduce from this that we are talking about any old fish and chips merchant ("You obviously don't know much about Southend",[26] he said when I phoned to ask about the establishment he ran with his brother). Founded by Cotgrove's grandfather in 1896, and therefore almost as old as the municipal borough of Southend-on-Sea, Cotgrove's Restaurant was well-placed at the southern end of the High Street near Pier Hill. Capable of serving a thousand meals on a busy summer day, it also managed, as one former resident remembers, to be "the go-to place for bourgeois respectability in the Sixties".[27]

At the time Connell approached him for the *Sunday Times*, Cotgrove was chairman of Southend-on-Sea Chamber of Trade and Industry's Local Affairs Committee, and it was in this capacity that he had formed a taskforce of three to discover the facts about the *SS Richard Montgomery* and to review government policy in the light of their findings. He recruited Cllr David Anthony Atkinson, a Director of Chalkwell Motor Company in Leigh-on-Sea, who had served, while training as an engineer a year previously, as a notably right-wing national chairman of the Young Conservatives (he would go on to become an MP well known for his opposition to sanctions against the apartheid regime in South Africa and then for the personal scandals that overwhelmed his later years). The third member of the Chamber of Trade's investigation was a journalist and performing musician who had been born into an east London family with a background in fireworks manufacture as well as in music hall and variety. Richard Anthony Baker (whose brother John pioneered electronic music with the BBC Radiophonic Workshop) was enlisted for his knowledge of Southend and the estuary as Hon. Secretary of the Rochford Hundred Historical Society.[28]

These men may not have been as wild as some of the pirate radio operators and anti-state secessionists who had colonised various of the estuary's abandoned anti-aircraft forts in the Sixties. They were, however, far from deferential towards upriver authority — and unlikely to be successfully overawed at a "confidential" briefing of the kind that, in 1966, the Ministry of Defence had laid on in the Admiral's ballroom at Chatham as they overwhelmed and reassured the members of Sheerness Urban District Council. Entitled "The Explosive Cargo of the USS Richard Montgomery", Southend Chamber of Trade's report on the "developing hazard" that "still lurks off the Sheerness shore in the full view of the communities which it threatens" had been launched at a press conference at the Institute of Journalists in London on 20 April 1972.[29] Reporters who turned up for this event were invited to recognise the "incredible" negligence of the secretive public authorities, accused once again of having done very little to understand the dangers posed by the wreck, and nothing at all to remove it from the estuary since Dr Reginald Bennett MP first asked for clarification in the House of Commons in 1952. The Southend report, and the journalistic discussion that followed its publication, set many of the terms on which Connell and, through his *Sunday Times* article, also Uwe Johnson came to understand the *Richard Montgomery*.

Having reviewed everything that might be conceived as an official public announcement on the condition of the *SS Richard Montgomery* and her cargo since the moment it ran aground, the Southend investigators were scathing about the jumble of inaccurate, defensive and contradictory statements made by officials and politicians since 1952, asserting that it revealed the state's indifference to the people on both sides of the estuary. Undeterred when the public authorities refused them access to the technical report they had commissioned from the Hydraulics Research Station on the possibility of erecting a barrier around the wreck, they set off along their own "lines of enquiry", relying heavily on "local knowledge" and talking with people involved in "various activities in the Thames and Medway" who were quite unlike the officials in being generous with "advice, information, and the loan of documents". It was noted, in an observation inherited from David Lampe's article for *Wide World,* that not one of these experienced witnesses had "ever been asked about the matter in any way" by the responsible public officials, who could therefore be judged wilfully ignorant of the situation and manipulative in the expertise they claimed to possess.

Deferring to no one, Cotgrove and his accomplices had cut through the various acronyms used on the American loading plan and set their findings against a second inventory they had managed to get hold of, this one listing the bombs salvaged in 1944. From an initial cargo estimated at 6,127 imperial tons they calculated that 3,552 tons remained. Nearly 90% of these were general purpose and semi-armour piercing bombs, with a combined weight of 2,770 imperial tons. The remaining cargo of explosive materials included white phosphorous smoke bombs, and also rather more than a hundred tons of cluster fragmentation bombs about which they had "received very little information", although they were understood to be "individually packed in wooden transit cases" and also to have "an integral arming system".

They also insisted that the wreck was resting on firm ground and not sinking into sand and mud as official advocates of the supposedly reassuring "blanket of silt" theory had once tried to suggest. Despite the notices posted on its masts, the wreck was by no means secure against disturbance, and neither was the risk of an explosion decreasing. Indeed, Cotgrove and his accomplices repeated Lampe's charge that the TNT in the large bombs had already lasted far beyond its "safe" period, and would long since have been destroyed under normal circumstances. Despite official assurances to the contrary, the chances of an explosion were definitely not remote "by comparison with absolute safety".

The continued official neglect of the wreck impressed these Southend campaigners as particularly culpable given the possible threats, which were by no means limited to collision with a passing ship or the impact of the *Richard Montgomery's* own decks, masts and derricks as the disintegrating wreck collapsed. They didn't mention the summer boat trips full of holidaymakers from Sheerness, but they personally knew of at least twenty-five people who had visited the ship, indicating that an "immense" number must have done so over the years. Some had gone to salvage valuable materials but they'd also heard of barges that had sailed between the masts and fishermen who'd got accustomed to using the site as a convenient dump for stray bombs that turned up in their nets. Writing only a few weeks after the IRA bombed Aldershot barracks in retaliation for the now officially admitted atrocity of Bloody Sunday perpetrated by British forces in Derry on 30 January 1972, they also noted the possibility of malevolent interference by a "determined individual" who might actually do what students from a northern university had merely threatened in January 1969.

By the time the Southend Chamber of Trade's report had gone into circulation, the circumstances surrounding the anticipated explosion were ready to be turned into the finger-pointing thriller published by Hamish Hamilton in 1976. *Blockbuster* is one of no less than sixty-one books that a man who published under the name of "Stephen Barlay" wrote in the thick cloud of cigarette smoke he housed, latterly, in an upstairs bedroom in Wembley. Barlay's interest in the *Richard Montgomery* may have been reawakened by the publicity surrounding Cotgrove's accusations, but he had known about it since David Lampe's article in the October 1964 edition of *Wide World* (the same issue included Barlay's own feature about the Soviet scientist Professor Vladimir Demikhov's disgusting attempt to graft the living head of a mongrel onto a sheepdog's back[30]).

Blockbuster revolves around the terrorist conspiracy of a blackmailer who threatens to blow up the *Richard Montgomery* if the government doesn't hand over £1 million. Using various formulaic devices, including grinning Chinese torturers, bent coppers and lustful, hyena-like sex, the author threads his story through what was publicly known about the wreck in the years following Cotgrove's report: from the warning-posted buoys to the cracks in the hull, through which Barlay's blackmailer duly squeezes his threatening charge. The plot revolves around a senior police officer, suspected of being "the Principal" behind the blackmail conspiracy but eventually unmasked as a hero who has actually organised the threat to blow up the *Richard Montgomery* in order to flush out genuinely corrupt officers, who have learned their criminal ways during earlier service with the Hong Kong police. This misunderstood hero's justification for the risk he is taking with the lives of people in Sheerness is that his plot might at worst oblige the "political midgets"[31] then occupying the Cabinet Room at 10 Downing Street to do what they should have done long ago, i.e. find and commit the resources necessary to dispose of the *Richard Montgomery* and its hazardous cargo for good. In this respect, the novel is a fictional tribute to the longstanding downriver understanding of the *Richard Montgomery* as a monument to the British state's indifference to the lives of ordinary people.

Johnson, who had learned of Barlay's novel from the *Sunday Times*, notes its existence with a few words that do nothing to suggest he ever read it: "Belletristic treatment: a thriller, *Blockbuster*".[32] Nobody in the Napier Tavern had been in the position to inform him that the author "Stephen Barlay" was actually István Bokor, a Hungarian Jew who had seen many members of his family murdered by fascists during the Second World War, and had himself survived to join the Communist

Party and then become a freelance radio journalist who had left the country in a hurry, having been in the broadcasting building that stood at the centre of the suppressed anti-Soviet revolution in 1956.[33]

*

Sunday Times journalist Jon Connell may not have known about "Barlay" either, but there was, as he did understand, more to be said about the authority of his primary witness. David Cotgrove was, so Connell announced, "a former government explosives researcher." His brother, John Cotgrove confirms the truth of this: before taking over the family restaurant in Southend, David Cotgrove had, as he described in a note among his papers, worked for some ten years as an "experimental officer" at the Atomic Weapons Research Establishment across the estuary from Sheerness on Foulness Island.[34] His job had been to assist scientists working on nuclear detonation systems there and also in Australia where he himself had gone to test various forms of "ironmongery"[35] that might be used to ignite Britain's atom bombs.

So Cotgrove, who also records having glimpsed the *Richard Montgomery* on the first day after the stranding and later sailing with friends to clamber aboard the unsecured and freely accessible wreck in 1949, also knew a lot about explosives. In 1973, the year after publication of the Southend Chamber of Trade's report, he had got in touch with an American expert, Major Theodore C. Chart, outlining the story of the *SS Richard Montgomery* and explaining the increased anxiety felt by "the communities on both sides of the estuary" now that the wreck was directly "in line" with the runways of the new international airport being planned for Maplin Sands. He sought Chart's confirmation that the high-explosive bombs remaining on the wreck might safely be recovered in a "properly equipped salvage operation" and that there was only a "very remote" chance that any of the cluster fragmentation bombs had been packed with the potentially dangerous fuses installed. In a letter dated 28 March 1973, Major Chart cautiously agreed that Cotgrove's analysis of the situation seemed "logical" and that an explosion seemed "highly unlikely" during recovery given the involvement of an experienced salvage crew. On 26 June 1973, Cotgrove took copies of this correspondence to the Chief Explosives Inspector at the Home Office's Explosives Branch in Horseferry House, London SW1. After hearing his case, E.G. Whitbread wrote an internal memo declaring Cotgrove's analysis "interesting and important". The Department of Trade was soon writing to the Ministry of Defence, warning that the Home Office felt there might be "some merit" in Cotgrove's theory, and suggesting that an early response from the MOD Ordnance Board would be welcome given that Cotgrove was by now also calling for a public enquiry into the *Richard Montgomery*.

Considering that neither a public enquiry nor any visible adjustment in the official position had taken place during the intervening years, it is not surprising that Cotgrove was showing signs of exasperation by 1978, when he gave his views again in the *Sunday Times* article that would serve as the primary source for Johnson's "An Unfathomable Ship". Once again he brushed off the official claim that the bombs were quietly getting safer, insisting instead that "every year the danger increases" while also reprising David Lampe's suggestion that the *Richard Montgomery* had the power to produce "the most catastrophic non-nuclear explosion in history".[36] The possibility of the explosion being triggered by low-flying planes taking off from Foulness may have died in 1974 when the incoming Labour government killed off plans for a new airport on Maplin Sands, but Cotgrove could offer other threats for Connell to list. The coastguard station at Warden on the Isle of Sheppey had by this time counted twenty-four near misses and one direct hit by a freighter, and there was every chance of worse to come thanks to increased use of both Thames and Medway shipping channels. Although Cotgrove wondered what might happen when the tide went out on a hypothetical oil tanker that had accidentally got stuck on top of the wreck at high tide, it was the "danger of deliberate interference" that was judged most worrying. The student threat of January 1969 had turned out to be a rag-week jape, but there remained a serious possibility that the wreck might be targeted by terrorists operating under cover of night or bad weather. That danger was not made any less alarming by the unnamed police sergeant who, when asked about his force's contingency plans, said "It'll be a question of calling for our harps and haloes and praying".

Speaking out to local papers after the *Sunday Times* piece appeared, Cotgrove repeated his claim that the management of the *Richard Montgomery* had been "bungled from the start". The Admiralty had brought the problem on itself by ordering the ship to anchor in a plainly inappropriate place. Not content with twice rejecting American advice that the wreck could and should be cleared — first in 1948 and later in June 1967 — the British authorities had "seriously misled the public"[37] about the dangers of inaction. The limited official publicity granted to the *Richard Montgomery* had been devoted to "perpetuating a series of myths" to justify the Ministry of Defence's "attitude", condemned as "essentially an attempt to convince people that the *Richard Montgomery* has settled firmly in the seabed and is thus free from any natural disturbance which might affect the bombs".

It was also thanks to Cotgrove that Johnson, who had become particularly interested in the "cracks" in the *Richard Montgomery*'s hull, could accurately declare in his essay that "In September 1978, the question was above all whether the wreck had come apart in a second place". The Department of Trade had announced that the approaching survey was intended to establish whether this was the case, but Cotgrove claimed to have warned them about it years before. He had deduced that the hull had cracked again by studying the angle of the masts and looking at an aerial photograph of the site, taken as part of a survey by the Medway Ports Authority in September 1971.[38] He had carried out further investigations the following year after being invited to discuss his allegations with a trade minister and a junior environment minister after the publication of the Southend Chamber of Trade's report. In the days before the meeting, which took place on 3 July 1972, he had gone so far as to commission a diver to inspect the hull. The unnamed investigator hadn't just found the new crack. He had "put his head and shoulders through it to inspect the bombs which were clearly visible."[39]

Officials might insist there was only a "one in a million" chance of an explosion, but Cotgrove believed the new split had created a highly dangerous situation that demanded urgent action. As he told the *Sheppey Gazette* in September 1978, the one-thousand-pound TNT-filled bombs were now actually "straddling" the eighteen-inch gap and "effectively keeping the ship together" as the tides poured back and forth between the separated sections. The movement of the fragmenting hull was causing the bombs to "grind over each other", exposing them to "a massive force like a vice". Cotgrove considered this more than sufficient to detonate a bomb, which was in turn highly likely to set off the rest: "they are being squashed and are gripping each other. Is this a safe situation? They are certainly not undisturbed, but maybe the Ministry does not want the public to know that."[40]

Various public officials shuffled out, as Johnson read, to reject Cotgrove's "scaremongering".[41] They also reported the words of the local Conservative MP Roger Moate, who had taken Faversham from Labour's Terence Boston in 1970. Although he had yet to come fully into his own as one of John Major's Eurosceptic "bastards", Moate was surely already a man who might have respected the endurance of an individual seeking to sustain a people's cause against powerful state bureaucracies. Not yet, however. He derided the revival of interest in the *Richard Montgomery* as "a typical 'silly season' story. We have seen many of them in the past".

Johnson, who drew orientation as well as information from this coverage, was closer to Cotgrove in his sympathies than to the jaded politicians or the officials who had claimed, following the underwater survey of September 1978, that "there is no significant change in the state of the wreck nor any additional spillage of explosives." This was, as Johnson noted drily from his barstool, a sentence "that contains explosives which have already spilled out through existing holes."[42] In his reading of the situation, the failure of official bodies to remove "the wreck" combined with the inertia of the public agencies that continued to leave the town exposed to the risk of flooding, giving a new dimension to the danger threatening Sheerness. While providing a clear demonstration of the powerless of islanders against the upriver state, the story of the *Richard Montgomery* also revealed Sheerness to be a place where Murphy's Law had spawned a host of subsidiary clauses. The basic premise that "if anything has even the slightest chance of going wrong, it will" was now attended by additional findings: that "everything takes longer than people expect"; that "if it is possible for several things to go wrong, then the one that will cause the most damage will go wrong first"; and that "the importance of a subject can be judged by the lack of interest in it."[43]

In the meantime, Johnson gathered up some of the "folklore" circulating among those obliged to live between Sheerness's sable cloud and its terrifying silver lining. It was said that Churchill had written to Roosevelt's successor, saying the time had come to remove his bombs, "but the Yanks said sorry, a gift is a gift."[44] Then there was the highly experienced, world-class salvage firm — was it Dutch or Japanese? — that had come to have a look but quickly backed off saying they'd "prefer not to touch this one." Even the Germans were said to have beaten a hasty retreat, raising the hope that "one good thing about the Common Market," might be that it would become possible to "trade this island for a West German city" — perhaps Dusseldorf ("I hear it's on the water already").

Under "psychological tidbits," Johnson notes that "the *Richard Montgomery* is present in everyone's consciousness, down to the level of common expressions" such as "I wish that ol' thing'd go up at last, then we'd finally have something goin' on around here."[45] He registers the curious fact that people remained strongly attached to their island despite the catastrophe that might engulf them at any moment. School-leavers rarely sought work on the mainland, and older folk even retired back to the island, choosing "to spend their twilight years here, in sight of a time bomb". Back behind his own window by now, he adds "Even foreigners settle here, separated from the likely prospect of an explosion by a single window-pane? What I'm trying to tell you, in a whisper: It's a death-wish".

Johnson collected some of his own local ephemera for "An Unfathomable Ship", including, we may assume, the islanders' ready answer to the parliamentary Undersecretary of Trade, who had recently reported that, in the event of an explosion, damage claims should be sent to the United States of America: "Right. But then we'd hardly be in a position to do it".[46] In other respects, he is content to replicate the British press coverage. So it is with his list of events that might cause a detonation: a bungled salvage operation, impact with a stray ship, a strong tide causing breakage of "an intermediate deck" so that bombs fall onto one another. He cites the possibility of a terrorist attack, shockwaves from low-flying planes and students on a spree ("as occurred" [sic] in 1969). To this recycled list of community favourites, "Charles" adds a couple of his own: "a suicide reluctant to go alone" and, "an intractable philologist who wants to test the saying according to which you've done a great thing if you've set the Thames on fire".

When it comes to describing the possible consequences of an explosion, here too Johnson follows the *Sunday Times'* Connell, who in turn follows *Wide World's* Lampe in mapping the impact over a series of concentric circles. The explosive experts at Waltham Abbey had confined their scientific analysis of a hypothetical detonation to measuring abstract forces, but campaigners as well as journalists preferred to offer a more concrete picture of the consequences. The *Sunday Times* illustrated Connell's hypothesis with a map headed "How a Blast Would Strike".This tracked the likely impact with the help of two circles. Being within the inner one, placed two miles from the wreck, Sheerness could expect "old buildings and unbuttressed walls" to collapse and "gas and water pipes" to fracture. Between that and the second circle, at seven miles, "windows might crack and insecure chimneys and roof tiles could topple". With the help of a second diagram tracking the damage that might be caused by "a fireball capable of hurling large chunks of debris more than a mile away", Connell noted that this would have worse consequences on a day of low cloud cover, since "the blast would be 'bounced' back downwards, increasing the damage on the ground".

The Kentish papers dreamed of a bigger bang than that. A few days after Connell's piece appeared, the *Sheppey Gazette* declared that "the shockwave would be felt throughout the island. Old buildings could collapse; gas and water pipes could be wrecked, windows within a seven-mile radius could crack and insecure windows and tiles would topple".[47] By this time David Cotgrove was losing his sense of restraint too. In one highly coloured version, he would be quoted as saying that an explosion would "take Sheerness, Grain and Southend with it".[48] In another, he promised that:

> The explosive force would be equivalent to that of a small nuclear bomb. It would have very bad effects. Old houses and perhaps new ones would collapse. It would be a disaster area. The roofs of factories and large buildings would be sucked in. The most serious effects would be felt within a two-mile radius. It would be a very unhappy situation... In addition the blast would send up a giant fireball, capable of hurling large chunks of debris a mile away.[49]

Johnson makes his own oblique entrance into this game. Although he relies heavily on the *Sunday Times*'s facts and predictions, his contribution is also fired by a sense of justice that, while both ironic and avowedly secular in tone, may still be allowed to resonate with the fiery Judgement Day harangues of Blue Town's great shipwright preacher William Shrubsole. So it is that Johnson augments Connell's comparatively restrained broadsheet blast with a "tidal wave" and does everything he can to bounce the explosion's impact as far upriver as possible in the hope of visiting just deserts on the negligent London powers that had allowed the *Richard Montgomery* to haunt the estuary for so long:

> An explosion of this mixture will be among the largest in human memory, not counting the nuclear ones. If you take the **Richard Montgomery** as the centre of a circle with a radius of two miles, the first land to be hit will be the north-west corner of the island, with the town and port of Sheerness. The older buildings and unreinforced walls will collapse, and the gas and water pipes will shatter. Within a radius of seven miles, broken glass and the collapse of any wobbly chimneys or loose roofs is likely. That circle includes half of the town of Sittingbourne, as well as the oil port and refinery complex on the Isle of Grain, west of Sheppey. The detonation may cause a fireball whose air pressure will fling heavy objects and debris more than a mile, perhaps into one of the supertankers with a hundred thousand tons of oil in its belly. (The **Richard Montgomery** lies near the extremely busy shipping channel of the Thames. A few miles farther north, Her Royal Highness's Ministry of Defence maintains and runs a naval artillery range in the ocean, whose detonations reach the windows of Sheerness like fist blows.) A simultaneous explosion of the whole cargo will cause a tidal wave to rush up the Medway and Thames rivers, destroying additional settlements near the banks. At low tide, the effects would be multiplied, due to there being less water to absorb the shock. The ultimate extent of the damage will be determined by the weather. Any heavy, low-lying cloud cover above the exploding cargo of bombs will bounce back ascending shock waves and the multiple ricochets will reach Canvey Island, ten miles upstream, where they will hit storage tanks with a holding capacity of almost forty thousand barrels of oil as well as chemical and methane gas containers. A chain reaction or domino effect could produce damage in the eastern suburbs of London, to a greater or lesser extent. It is unlikely that the House of Commons or Whitehall would be affected.

587

Mr. Tweedy, The Montgomery Mermaid, Recreation Ground, Sheerness, 2015.

33. EXPLOSION: FROM THE RICHARD MONTGOMERY TO THE CAP ARCONA

When I put a question about "The Unfathomable Ship" to the German sociologist Renate Mayntz, widow of the artist Hann Trier and a friend of the Johnsons over many years, she re-read the essay and described it as "very characteristic of [Johnson's] way of looking at reality: incisive, cold, as objective as possible, a camera that catches all details and even the legacy, the history inscribed in the present... I think in his passionate search for descriptive exactness, for 'truth' without implied protest or some normative 'message', he was a true representative of Enlightenment. There are things you don't have to say, you just need to show them".[1]

With that point in mind, we may wonder ("poetically") what brought the stranded *Richard Montgomery* to Johnson's mind in connection with the "spiritual situation of the age" Karl Jaspers had described in 1931. For Jaspers, that "situation" had been shaped by a secular equivalent to the "Death of God" imagined by Jean-Paul in his eighteenth century nightmare about the atheistic claims of the Enlightenment. Jaspers associated the modern epoch with a "shipwrecking" of enlightened ideas of truth, reason and reflection, which was causing a "widespread conviction" that "human activities are unavailing; everything had become questionable; nothing in human life holds good; that existence is no more than an unceasing maelstrom of reciprocal deception and self-deception by ideologies".[2] It was by no means only for the chapel-goers of Sheerness that the "shipwreck" of reason implied "the revelation of a depth which nothing other than Transcendence can fill".[3]

Jaspers' insistence on the "stranding" and "shipwreck"[4] that must be undertaken by philosophical reflection if it was to fully engage with the "historicity" of modern experience, was by no means the only parallel Johnson's text suggests but does not explicitly spell out. Given the evocative, if not strictly allegorical nature of his essay, we might also come to suspect that there is also more than is explicitly stated to his account of the crack, which he dislodges from the sunken and disintegrating hull of the *Richard Montgomery* and attaches ("magically") to America's Liberty Bell. Once cast into motion in this way, the crack may connect itself ("poetically" again) to other bells in the reader's mind: the cracked bell that sounded, to the mid-nineteenth-century Parisian poet Charles Baudelaire, like the "death-rattle" of his own broken soul in a poem titled "La Cloche fêlée" in *Les Fleurs de Mal*, or the one the American psychologist William James used, nearly half a century later, to describe the "irremediable sense of precariousness" suffered by the "sick soul", famously likened to "a bell with a crack; it draws its breath on sufferance and by an accident"[5]. From here, we may quickly come to suspect ("biographically") that the crack, now back in its actual place on the ship, turns the *Richard Montgomery* into a witness both to the trauma of its century, the evils it has made of some forms of enlightenment and also, as it pokes into his view from a "murky reality" that is actual as well as symbolic, into a dim reflection of Johnson himself: not a stone colossus any more, nor a man lost inside a glass bell jar, but a sunken wreck, traumatised and broken but still containing great force within its hull of encrusting steel. A "death-wish", as we may well be tempted to conclude, although Johnson discourages that thought by including it in his essay as a joke.

In the "historical" register, meanwhile, other explosions echo in the blast that Johnson could not quite persuade to reach all the way upriver to engulf the Palace of Westminster. For some, including David Cotgrove, the likely devastation had been dwarfed by the memory of Britain's atom bomb test on the Montebello Islands. In Sheerness, however, the primary supplier of remembered explosions remained the First World War. The term "great explosion" may remain attached to the disaster that took place on 2 April 1916, killing 106 people at the Explosives Loading Company gunpowder works at Uplees, across the Swale from Sheppey.[6] Worse things, though, had by then already happened in Sheerness's naval harbour: 741 men had died when the battleship *HMS Bulwark* (formerly commanded by Scott of Antarctica) blew up and vanished in seconds when moored alongside three other battleships just off Sheerness on 26 November 1914. Six months afterwards another vast explosion destroyed *HMS Princess Irene*, a liner built in Scotland for the Canadian Pacific Railway in 1914 but immediately requisitioned for war use as a minelayer. This vessel disappeared in a great sheet of fire on the morning of 27 May 1915 when its newly loaded cargo of mines were being primed in hasty preparation for a mission. Cases of butter, engine parts, severed heads and limbs were scattered for miles around. 352 men died this time, a much smaller loss than the *HMS Bulwark*, but one that ripped a far larger hole in the life of Sheerness, claiming no less than seventy-eight dockyard workers who had been on board the *Princess Irene* to reinforce the ship's decks.

Johnson only had to look at the names engraved on the town war memorial across the road from the railway station to know how faithfully Sheerness had remembered these losses from the First World War. Yet these were not necessarily the examples that resonated in his mind as he surveyed the masts of the *Richard Montgomery* through his sash windows. One Johnson scholar, D.G. Bond, has suggested that he might have found a precedent for his portrayal of the *Richard Montgomery*'s version of the "Great Explosion" in the writings of the German schoolmaster, churchman and dialect poet Johann Peter Hebel, whose early nineteenth-century "calendar" stories, collected in his *Treasure Chest,* included one telling of a ship loaded with over 37,000 lbs of black gunpowder which blew up in the

Steenschuur canal in French-occupied Leiden on 13 January 1807. Bond sees various "correspondences" between Johnson's account of the *Richard Montgomery* and Hebel's evocation of the Leiden disaster, which left 152 dead and over two thousand injured, and destroyed some two hundred buildings at the very heart of the town.[7] Both texts, he points out, combine historical research with an "allegory of the apocalypse". Both see the "little people" as providing "the moral and the hope", praising them for retaining "inner dignity" when faced with "outer historical barbarism". Both are concerned with the defence of "the good and the proper" against diverse degradations.

This is a suggestive parallel, to be sure, but we will find a different ship if we follow the example of the readers who sometimes wrote to Johnson describing how they had used his books as guides to the places in which they were set. One had thanked him for his book about Ingeborg Bachmann, claiming that it had helped her find her way around the Austrian town of Klagenfurt. He also had a postcard pinned up in the kitchen at Marine Parade from an American lady who claimed to have achieved good results by following *Anniversaries* around Staten Island, using the novel as if it were a weird kind of Baedeker or Pevsner guide.[8] Encouraged by these examples, I went back to Mecklenburg in order to test a similarity I had noticed when looking at maps of the Thames Estuary and the Baltic coast east of Lübeck.

From the resort of Travemünde, I took the ferry across the Trave, and then drove along the spit at Priwall to reach the place where, until 1989, "the fence" had divided the two Germanies. Various characters in *Anniversaries* pass this way and it may also have been to this checkpoint that Johnson brought Michael Hamburger's eleven-year-old daughter Claire and tried to impress upon her the importance of the division. Nowadays, however, the whole place seems benign, and there is nothing — no watchtowers, notices, wire, nor red-and-white poles — to interrupt anybody's walk along the beach.

I found a suitable viewpoint a mile or so east of the removed frontier, near a little village named Rosenhagen. Standing on

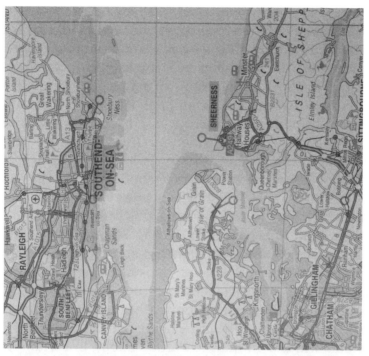

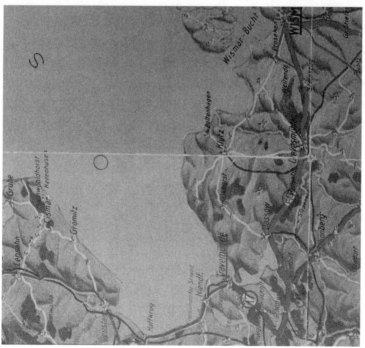

that no longer forbidden strand, with my back to a low sandy cliff inhabited by a teeming colony of sand martins, I looked out over the "scrabbly" Baltic waves and tried to compare this sea view with the one Johnson knew in Sheerness. Although the Bay of Lübeck is not really an estuary, the resemblances I had noticed when comparing maps of the two geographies persisted. In both views there was a navigable and working waterway coming into the wider sea from the left: the Medway in the case of the Thames Estuary and the Trave which enters the Bay of Lübeck between Travemünde and, on the eastern side, the Priwall spit. In both views, one could also see signs of land on the far shore. In Sheerness, this was the Essex coast at Southend and Shoeburyness. Here in Mecklenburg, the land across the water was West Holstein and the just discernible buildings were in and around Neustadt and the sandy bay at Timmendorf. The distances were not identical, but it was still easy to imagine how, under weather conditions that could indeed be the same in both places, the framed view from Johnson's window in Marine Parade might, in certain lights, have oscillated between North Sea and Baltic.

There were no masts sticking out of the water in Neustadt Bay, but it was the site of traumatic explosions that surely haunt Johnson's essay "An Unfathomable Ship" even though not explicitly mentioned. The unspoken parallel, as I already knew from *Anniversaries* III, lay between "Liberty" as the *Richard Montgomery* represented it in Sheerness and "Liberation" as British forces had brought it to this stretch of the now rapidly re-emerging "German Riviera" in the last days of the Second World War. For the child who was Gesine Cresspahl at this time, the reality of that disastrous arrival could still be counted in corpses washed up all along the stretch of Baltic shore on which I was standing: a horrifying glut in May 1945, followed by a slower stream that extended for decades after that — the last sea-washed skeleton is said to have emerged in 1971.

This horror had its origins in Nazi policy, as Johnson goes on to explain in a chapter that makes its own "montage" using information found in a book written by the German survivor Rudi Goguel and published in 1972.⁹ When it came to "evacuating" a concentration camp, the Nazi's preferred policy was, as Johnson reminds his readers, to obliterate all trace of the place, first putting gangs of prisoners to work — digging up the mass graves, grinding up remains and scattering the "bone meal" over the fields — and then murdering the prisoners who had been forced to carry out these hideous tasks. So quick was the Allied advance through northern Germany in early 1945 that they had no time to erase the camp at Neuengamme, twelve miles south-east of Hamburg, or, presumably, the "Mecklenburg branch camps of Boizenburg and Reiherhorst at Wöbbelin."¹⁰ Instead, having released Swedish and Danish nationals who had been concentrated at Neuengamme prior to being repatriated in the Swedish Red Cross's famous "convoy of ninety-two White Buses" in April 1945, they crammed the remaining six thousand prisoners into freight cars and took them to Lübeck harbour. Drawing on Goguel's account of an episode he himself had only known through fragmentary local memory, Johnson records that five hundred died on the journey, and that four car-loads of sick "weren't even loaded onto the ships, they were screaming with fever, they were shot, and anyone who didn't hear that in Lübeck's outer harbour might well have heard the festive sounds of the German SS in the adjacent grain silo, celebrating final victory with the finest cognac and delicacies from stolen Red Cross parcels". After some ten days, through which many remained confined in German Reich Railway cars at the quayside, the surviving prisoners, "whom the people of Lübeck knew absolutely nothing about", were crammed onto three ships, all of them "easily visible from land, and known to not only the fishermen". An estimated 2,800 were loaded into an already bombed freighter called the *Thielbeck*, which was then towed out into the Bay of Lübeck. A smaller motor launch, the *Athen*, was used to carry successive batches of prisoners out to a larger vessel, the *Cap Arcona*, already anchored in the bay off the town of Neustadt.

Built for the Hamburg-South America Line in 1927 and named after a chalky headland on the north-eastern shore of the Pomeranian island of Rügen, the *Cap Arcona* had gone into service as an exceptionally fast and luxurious liner: a "floating palace",[11] which became known — in Britain and other countries as well as Germany (where it had been launched as a symbol of resurgent national prestige) — for its grandiose facilities, which included electric lifts, a salon with Gobelin tapestries and marble fireplaces, a sea-plane mail service, and a full-sized electrically lit tennis court on the deck between two of its funnels. In the old advertising, a cruise to Rio de Janeiro or Buenos Aires aboard the *SS Cap Arcona* ("one of the most beautiful ships afloat", as a travel agent was pleased to advertise in the *Yorkshire Post*[12]), was presented as the ideal way to escape the northern winter for southern sea and sands.

Strauss melodies may still have been playing, but prospects had changed for some aboard the *Cap Arcona* by March 1939, when there was especially good reason to fear for the twenty-five so-called "wandering Jews"[13] who, according to a brief article syndicated through many of Britain's local papers, were found to have remained aboard the "Queen of the South Atlantic"[14] when the liner passed through Southampton on its return voyage from the south in March that year. These desperate émigrés had embarked in Boulogne a month or so earlier, hoping to find refuge in South America. Having been refused permission to land there on the grounds that the quota had already been filled, they were now uncertain whether they would be allowed to disembark at Boulogne (no landing was apparently offered in England), or find themselves obliged to stay aboard all the way back to Nazi Hamburg.

By the end of 1939, the *Cap Arcona* had been commandeered by the German navy, painted gray and put into service as a floating barrack at the Nazi port of Gotenhafen, now Gydnia, on the Baltic in conquered Poland. It had served in that role for the length of the war, with an unusual intermission in 1942, when it was employed as a set for a grandiose Nazi film called *The Sinking of the Titanic*. Things did not go well, despite the extravagant resources allocated to the production. The well-known director, Herbert Selpin, who is said to have rivalled Goebbels in his megalomania, was denounced by his own scriptwriter for having committed "verbal treason" as he railed against both the navy and the Nazi leadership: he is thought to have been murdered by "suicide" in his cell a day or two after Goebbels handed him over to the Berlin police.[15] As Germany's eastern front collapsed during the last weeks of the war, the *Cap Arcona* was used until its engines were destroyed during three desperate voyages evacuating German troops and civilian escapees west to Copenhagen from East Prussia across a heavily mined Baltic Sea in which Soviet submarines had free play. The dangers of these voyages were demonstrated by the sinking of the *Wilhelm Gustloff*, originally built as a cruise ship for the Nazi Strength Through Joy organisation, which was torpedoed at the end of January 1945 with more than nine thousand lives lost, an estimated five thousand of them children. After the first of these voyages the captain of the *Cap Arcona*, Johannes Gerts, shot himself while anchored in Copenhagen harbour, allegedly unable to face the prospect of making the same run again. With its turbines wrecked over the course of two further crossings, the *Cap Arcona* was decommissioned by the German navy in Copenhagen at the end of March 1945 and ordered to the Bay of Lübeck, where the catastrophe remembered by Johnson awaited.

Once the Nazi's had finished packing it with concentration camp victims, Johnson estimates that the *Cap Arcona*, which had been designed to accommodate 1,325 passengers, held 4,600 prisoners (other estimates suggest five thousand or more[16]). They were crammed below deck "with the sick at the very bottom (with no medicine or bandages) and the Russian prisoners in the banana storage hold (with no light, no air, and for the first three days no food); the dead were piled up on deck. The ship stank of the dead, of the disease and shit of the living — a putrid heap and not even moving". The *Thielbeck* was similarly packed and, although Johnson doesn't mention them, there were also Dutch barges near the *Cap Arcona* which had been filled with prisoners from the Stutthof concentration camp before the ladders were removed, and they were towed along the coast from Danzig.

The situation was never anything but murderous. "It took longer to die here than in the gas chambers", so Johnson writes "but it wouldn't be long before they were all dead". It is considered very likely, indeed it would be admitted in the later war crimes trials, that the Nazis intended to scuttle or torpedo these ships with their occupants.

In the event, however, it was thanks to the British that, some four days after Hitler had killed himself in his Berlin bunker and only hours before the surrender of German forces in northern Germany, "Freedom came across the bright sunny bay on May 3 in the shape of a squadron of British bombers". Ignoring the German submarines that were on the surface, allegedly preparing to send the three ships to the bottom of the sea, Hawker Typhoon fighter bombers from four RAF squadrons beat them to it with their rockets. These planes, whose crews may not have been among those who were trained to use Typhoons in this way at Shellness on the Isle of Sheppey, "started in on the *Athen*", on which a white flag was hoisted after three direct hits. The planes then turned to the ships in the outer bay. They sank the *Deutschland,* a liner that was empty and being refitted as a hospital ship. The *Thielbeck,* which was packed with prisoners, rolled over on her side and sank without trace after twenty minutes. The *Cap Arcona,* which is said soon to have had the captain's bedsheet tied to the mast, "took an hour, then it tipped onto its port side, slowly, faster and faster, until it was lying on its eighty-five-foot side, twenty-six feet of it above water". Meanwhile, as Johnson's Gesine Cresspahl tells her daughter Marie, "death was proceeding more quickly, and in various forms. The prisoners could die in the fire, in the smoke (the fire hoses had been cut), from the German crew's rifles (the crew had life jackets), jammed in by hoarded food supplies, crushed in the panicking crowd, from the heat of the glowing *Cap Arcona,* in the lifeboats plummeting into the water, from jumping into the water, of cold in the water, by being hit or shot at by German minesweepers, and on land from exhaustion. The saved numbered 3,100, the dead somewhere between seven and eight thousand. At around five in the afternoon the English took Neustadt, so it was in the British zone, same as Jerichow, and contact was permitted between the two places, and that's how we knew about it."

*

The sinking of the *Cap Arcona* stands among the worst maritime disasters ever. Why did it happen? The British military authorities would long be reluctant to face that question, which to this day challenges the version of the war installed in official remembrance or, for that matter, in the manoeuvres of those veteran-hunting bodysnatchers, from Farage to Patel, who have recently conscripted the memory of the Second World War into their appeals for Brexit. It is largely accepted that urgent warnings had been received by the British the day before the attack — from the Swedish Red Cross or the Swiss delegate in Lübeck, who had learned there were prisoners on board from a message placed in a matchbox and thrown at him from the *Thielbek*. Either this information wasn't passed on or it fell victim to a situation in which intelligence, like reconnaissance, was secondary to a policy of destroying shipping that might be used to service Nazi withdrawal to an imagined "northern redoubt" in Norway, and of finishing the war come what may before the Russians grabbed even more German territory.[17] Much later, eyewitnesses were still mortified by the consequences. In a letter to the *Daily Telegraph,* published on 18 March 1982, a troubled F.G. Parson, who had been aide-de-camp to General Sir Evelyn Barker (commander of the VIII Corps), described what he had seen walking along the Trave to the beach at the "pretty little holiday resort" of Travemünde: wrecked ships, stranded Dutch barges filled with dead prisoners from the east, and "thousands" of bodies including many, some of them children, who had obviously been shot or clubbed to death as they tried to come ashore.[18]

And it was not just at Travemünde that pale sands had been darkened. As Gesine Cresspahl remembers in *Anniversaries,* "The dead washed up on every shore of Lübeck Bay, from Bliestorf to Pelzerhaken, from Neustadt to Timmendorf Beach, into the mouth of the Trave, from Priwall to Schwansee and Redewisch and Rande, even into Wohlenberg Cove, as far as Poel Island and the other Timmendorf. They were found almost daily".

Johnson pulls this dreadful harvest into the heart of the remembered world of *Anniversaries III:*

Too many washed up on the coast near Jerichow — the finders couldn't bury them all secretly in the sand. The British occupation authorities had issued orders that all corpses from the water be reported, and they insisted that these orders be followed. The British took a truck and rounded up men who had been members of the National Socialist German Workers' Party. These men were driven along the beach, and wherever a black lump lay on the white sand the British stopped. The Germans were given no gloves for the loading, not even pitchforks or shovels. The British drank their whisky right in front of the Germans, despite this medicine, they too had to threw up. The British created no special cemetery for the dead from this watery camp. When the truck was full, they drove the load far inland, all the way to Kalkhorst, even Gneez. When they drove into Jerichow, they lowered the sides of the truck. The MPs made the Germans leave their houses to look at the cargo as it was driven down Town Street to the cemetery at a walking pace. Slower than walking. The cargo was not easy to recognize. It had been damaged by bullet wounds, charring, shrapnel blows. It was recognizable by the faded, split, clinging, striped clothes. The individual pieces of human being were often incomplete. There were limbs missing, or there were limbs on the truck bed without a torso, one day there was nothing but a piece of head. The fish had eaten a lot of that one. The British made the people of Jerichow gather on

Market Square. In the middle lay the first load of bodies. The commander handed over to the Germans the Germans' dead. He made them their property. He allowed them to place the mortal remains from the sea into coffins. They were permitted to close the coffin and carry them to the cemetery. After the dirt had been shovelled onto the mass grave, the British fired a salute into the air. At the cemetery gate stood a sergeant, holding a box in front of him, and on this box he stamped the ration cards. Anyone who had not accepted the dead would not eat."

Gesine's recollection of these events prompts the following exchange:

Marie: "And you still want to swim in the Baltic?"
Gesine: "We ate fish from the Baltic. The Germans eat fish from the Baltic to this day. There are almost three thousand prisoners lying at the bottom of the Baltic".[19]

For Marie, listening in New York City, this episode is the starkest outrage. "It was their own dead", she says. "Those English are utter scoundrels!" To the child that Gesine was at the time, it was indeed the British who had "made dead people public in Jerichow". And, once the British had withdrawn from the area, it was the Russian Military Commandant K.A. Pontiy who had gained her respect by putting an end to "the education of the German people by means of the overland transport of bodies". He had ordered that from now on "this particular flotsam had to be collected in the cemeteries of the coastal villages, outside the territory under his command". Gesine handles Marie's accusations more reflectively as she describes how the disaster was hidden under a blanket of silence:

- The British dropped the bombs. They saw the prisoners' camp uniform and fired at them anyway. That's the truth.
- The British didn't want that truth. You could be thrown in jail for less than that. There were German U-boats

above water all around the ships, and none of them were hit — that was too dangerous even to whisper.
- But you Jerichowers knew.
- It wasn't new information. You could already see prisoners in striped clothing in Mecklenburg (maybe not in Lübeck) — but they weren't to exist in language.

Gesine goes on to remark that the bombing of Lübeck Bay is not mentioned in the five volumes that the British went on to publish about the air war against Germany.[20] "Official history. Stiff Upper Lip", scoffs Marie, prompting Gesine to point out that it is also "official history that the British arrived before the German submarines had time to sink the prisoners themselves".

Johnson notes that the sunken ships remained in the water until the British authorities gave permission for salvage operations. The *Thielbeck* was raised, cleared of bones, and repaired: "Let's call the old tub the Reinbek and have her run till 1961, until it's worth selling her. Today if you happen to see a Magdalena flying the Panamanian flag, that's the Thielbek of May 1945". In 1946, the *Athen* motor launch, which had not been sunk, "became the Soviet General Brusilov". The wreck of the *Cap Arcona*, part of which had remained highly visible above the water, was scrapped in 1950. Only the bell remains, and that, as Johnson wrote, could be inspected at the Museum of Danish Resistance, in "Churchill Park", Copenhagen.

For years, the British authorities would remain content to combine their stiff upper lip with secrecy as thick as the Thames silt that never really blanketed the *SS Richard Montgomery*. The relevant military archives were closed for a century, and it was, reputedly, not until 1980 that the British pilots themselves were informed of the true nature of their targets or, for that matter, of the identity of the people they had returned, as ordered, to shoot up in the water. More than a decade after that, the Imperial War Museum in London would record interviews with British witnesses, including a medical nurse who visited Travemünde while on relief from Belsen, and remembered the shock of finding himself swimming among corpses.[21] As recently as 2004, one by this time American survivor of the *Cap Arcona* reiterated the claim of a German historian who had deplored the fact that "none of the important British books on RAF activities in World

Grave of 16 unknown victims of the Cap Arcona *and* Thielbeck *sinkings, in the Old Cemetery, Klütz, Mecklenburg.*

War II — books such as Max Hastings' widely known *Bomber Command* — mention the incident".[22] Benjamin Jacobs (born as Bronek Jakubowicz in western Poland), who had earlier survived in Auschwitz by working as an incompletely trained dentist, did what he could to fill the silence, offering his own account of the operation, and also of the young British pilots: men like the flying ace Johnny Baldwin DFC — "a dashing figure with curly brown hair, a clipped moustache and a wry grin", who was the first in Squadron 198 to dive on the *Cap Arcona*.[23]

We may register that gap in British official memory, even while also respecting the conclusion of the Dutch resistance leader Piet Ketelaar, who also survived the *Cap Arcona* attack and, in 1987, would employ the laconic phrase "tough luck" to suggest that the disaster was "one of those things that happens" in wars.[24] By that time some if by no means all RAF veterans were joining the English nationalists who would use various symbolic instruments including, in 1992, a new statue of Arthur "Bomber" Harris to redeclare the memory of the Second World War against both "Europe" and the limited domestic achievements of post-war social democracy in Britain. There was no place for the *Cap Arcona* in that simplified version of the remembered war, which, in 1989, would find its slogan in

Saatchi & Saatchi's poster for the Victoria and Albert Museum's exhibition of Prince Charles's "Vision" of British architecture: "In 1945, the Luftwaffe stopped bombing London. Two years later the Blitz began."[25]

As we think of Johnson standing at his Sheerness window in 1979, we should know that it was not only in West Germany that survivors of the *Cap Arcona* tried to sustain the memory and understanding of the disaster across Cold War frontiers. Long before Goguel and Johnson published their versions, news of an earlier attempt had reached Britain from the GDR. On 24 February 1965, a Scottish journalist named Jack Nicholls described a "call from behind the Iron Curtain" in his "Bon-Accord Gossip" column in the *Aberdeen Evening Express*. Quoting from a GDR publication named the *Democratic German Report*, he announced that the East German communist and actor Erwin Geschonneck (already well known for his films and his earlier stage work with Bertolt Brecht among others), was planning to make a film about the *Cap Arcona* disaster. Having himself been among the concentration camp prisoners crammed aboard the ship, he was now hoping to contact British witnesses: the RAF Typhoon pilots, to be sure, but he was most interested in finding a man he remembered as Captain Pratt of the 11th Armoured Division, who had appeared to be in charge of operations when the British arrived in the area shortly after the sinking and who, as Russian and German survivors attested, had done "all they could for both the living and the dead". Whatever the result of his appeal, the project did not go ahead on this apparently conciliatory basis. Years later, Geschonneck would eventually make a television film entitled *The Man of the Cap Arcona*, transmitted in the GDR in 1982, but Captain Pratt never stepped into its light.

The *Richard Montgomery*, meanwhile, continues to interrupt Sheerness's sea view even four decades later. It proved a useful hazard for those who campaigned against Boris Johnson's determination, announced when he was Mayor of London in 2008, to see a new international airport built in the Thames estuary directly to the north-east of the Isle of Sheppey. This idea, which quickly gained the name "Boris island", was to prove as fanciful as the Mayor's other vanity project, the "Garden Bridge", and the risk of detonating the *Richard Montgomery* was a strong card in the hand of those who successfully opposed it. It would be wrong to identify the memory of this defeat, rather than the risk of further collapse on the disintegrating wreck, as the primary cause behind the Ministry of Defence's subsequent offer, announced in 2020, to pay £5 million to any contractor prepared to remove the already trimmed and streamlined masts from the ship.[26] We may, however, still be tempted to see this new development ("poetically") as a reflection of the "Beast of Brexit's"[27] preferred form of government: it is easier, after all, to adjust the appearances — for Uwe Johnson, the three masts were spines of memory, history and unvarnished truth — than to address the underlying problem. This, however, wasn't at all how it looked to many of the islanders who read John Nurden's report on this recent development. Some may have regretted that the proposed action would deprive both Sheerness and Southend of a valued "talking point" for tourists. Others declared themselves well up for doing the job with a dingy and a hacksaw.[28] Surely not, though, after Beirut.

34. TRIUMPH OF THE SHEERNESS WALL

By October 1982, when the new Thames Barrier upriver at Silvertown was first raised against a high tide threatening London, Johnson knew that the lesser rampart outside his window was a decaying and inadequate thing. In "An Unfathomable Ship" he had coupled the weakness of Sheerness' sea defences with the vast wave threatened by the exploding *Richard Montgomery* to produce a fable in which the little people are repeatedly betrayed by heedless national governments. Johnson did not affirm the estuarial conspiracy theory claiming that the Thames Barrier was constructed with the covert purpose of protecting London from the coming explosion of the *Richard Montgomery*. He was, nevertheless, sympathetic to the suspicion that it proved the willingness of the metropolitan elite to defend the capital while abandoning downriver communities to face the increased risk of inundation caused by their new contrivance. By the end of 1982, however, and as he explained in a letter to Burgel Zeeh at Suhrkamp, Johnson would have preferred a bit more neglect so that he could get on with writing the long-awaited fourth and final volume of *Anniversaries*.

⟨THE HOUSE TO THE WEST OF THIS ONE⟩

There is a saying in vogue here, which runs: "I'm all right, Jack (pull up the ladder)". Jack here is the person in a safe boat who hangs out the rope ladder for his fellow shipwreckee. Once the latter is safe on board, he does not need to care who else might be swimming down there in the cold misfortune, so he says: I'm all right, Jack.

...

I have, no doubt, let fall a word or two about the inexorable pollution and impoverishment of the city of Sheerness. Now I am obliged to add the fact, impossible to make up, that the offices of Southern Water intend to protect this grimy, insignificant locale by raising the flood wall even higher in front of this row of houses. Preceding this undertaking must necessarily come the removal of the existing embankment with all its garages, storerooms, and the concrete wall on top, that is, a to and fro of heavy machinery from excavators to the wading crane with its fat cement noggin. As a result, Southern Water has sent representatives of a sworn surveyor's firm into every house to determine and record its architectural condition in anticipation of the claims they expect from residents as a consequence of the demolition and reconstruction. In other words, we have to reckon with the chance of collapsing walls, likewise of cracking windows. I mention all this in no way expecting that it will make me feel better to complain (a hypothesis all too amply disproven), but merely to discourage you for a time, say two years or so, from asking how I'm doing. You will know the answer already: Aggrieved.

⟨Letter to Burgel Zeeh, 26 August 1982[1]⟩

Siegfried Unseld read Johnson's letter, in which the author also complained about Martin Harris's building works in the house next door, to his secretary with impatience rather than amusement. Perhaps, he replied, it was time for Johnson to sell the house, repay the loan to Marianne Frisch and quit Sheerness for good.[2] Then again, as Unseld also said rather sourly, it was possible that his writer might, in some strange way of his own, actually relish the prospect of all this disturbance. The situation wasn't going to get any easier for

Johnson, who declined the suggestion, pointing out that the loan still had years to run and he would not be in a position to finish *Anniversaries* if he were out on the street.

The pre-war rampart known as "Puddicombe's Folly" had just about withstood the "Great Flood", for so long both "foreseen and dreaded",[3] that broke over the island, still without adequate warning, during the fatal storm tide of 29–31 January 1953. In the Netherlands 1,836 people died, and 307 lives were lost in eastern England, including considerable numbers at two of the plotland paradises on the north shore of the Thames Estuary (thirty-seven died at Jaywick and fifty-eight on Canvey Island). There were no fatalities on the Isle of Sheppey, but much of the island had found itself "under deep water" once again.[4] The Sheerness dockyard was properly drowned — a frigate capsized and a submarine sank — and residents in the town were once again awakened by the sound of their furniture knocking against the ceilings of downstairs rooms. Much of the water came through the town's western defences, but a thirty-foot breach was opened at Cheyney Rock, with "great slabs of concrete being torn away as though by a high-explosive bomb".

In "An Unfathomable Ship", Johnson had described how the devastation of that year still haunted Sheerness a quarter of a century later — a memory but also a dire prospect that "might well return, bringing its waterlogged homes, drowned sheep, flooded telephone connection boxes, short-circuited power lines, burst gas pipes, and disappointing valuations from insurance companies". And all that despite the reassurances of the Duchess of Kent, who had arrived on the scene a few days after the flood. Clad in a "clover pink fur-lined tweed coat, brown hat and trim Russian boots", she had stepped ashore at the Sheerness dockyard before touring the island and promising the impossible to locals who knew better: "I will see that things are put right".[5]

That job, as Johnson was now finding out, had been taken up more consequentially by one of the Kent River Authority's leading engineers. A modernist whose customary materials were shingle, marram grass and concrete rather than paint or words, Roland Berkeley Thorn was a pioneering figure in the rethinking of the county's sea defences following the fatal surge of 1953. He would draw heavily on his Kentish experience in *The Design of Sea Defence Works,* a textbook in which he set out to establish "a satisfactory theoretical basis" that would at last allow sea defence engineers to avoid the "costly failures" caused by the "trial and error methods" of the past.[6] Preferring the scientific "principles and findings of coastal hydraulics" as expounded and tested by, once again, the government's Hydraulics Research Station in Wallingford, he specified ways of calculating every aspect of a wave's movement, be it reflection, refraction or swash. He also tried to solve the key of all mysteries by establishing how waves might be calculated to conspire not just with tides but with weather systems too.

When it came to Sheerness, Thorn and his fellow engineers knew there was work to be done. Tim Kermode, who joined Thorn's team as a graduate engineer in 1974, remembers that they were at that time still operating in the climate established by the Waverley Committee on Coastal Flooding, set up by the government after the floods of 1953. This had restated many of the demands of the pre-war Bledisloe Commission, recommending higher standards of protection for sea defences around populated and important agricultural areas, the development of an adequate early warning system, and an increase in the maximum "precept" that river boards might raise from local authorities as a contribution towards the cost of sea defences. It had also demanded urgent investigation into the possibility of placing a barrier across the Thames to protect London. Since it was actually understood from the start that a closed Thames barrier might increase sea levels in the estuary, it was also accepted that the defences downriver from the barrier had to be both strengthened and raised on both shores

In Kent, the plan was to extend these improvements all the way from the barrier to the Isle of Grain. Although Sheerness lay further to the east across the Medway, it too was singled out for attention as a low-lying "cell" that could only be defended by provision of a more adequate sea wall running continuously for some six miles from Scrapsgate at the eastern end of Marine Parade, all the way round the town and former dockyard, and then south along the Medway, past the now extinguished settlement of West Minster where so many breaches had occurred since the nineteenth century, to Queenborough. By the end of 1974, when the Johnsons arrived in the town, the responsible bodies were already embarking on this Sheppey Sea Defences Improvement Scheme, announced by the Southern Water Authority a year or two earlier. £10 million would be spent defending Sheerness and Queenborough. The scheme, which was intended to proceed at an expenditure of £1 million a year, was approved for grant aid by the government in 1975.

Between Scrapsgate and the pub named the Ship on Shore, a mile or so to the east of Johnsons's house, Thorn's engineers were content to bolster the defences with a process known as "shingle recharge", in which split-bottom barges were used to release shingle onto the beach at high tide so that it could be bulldozed into position when the sea retreated.[7] In Sheerness itself, however, "massive sea walls" remained necessary even if some locals, including the residents of Marine Parade, disliked the prospect. The sea clinched the matter soon enough.

In January 1977, it was the turn of Mr Henry Bugden to find himself in the local paper: eighty years old and disabled, he'd been obliged to stand on his sticks in the dark in knee-deep water for two and a half hours before being rescued from his living room in Estuary Road.[8] A year later, on 6 January 1978, the Sheerness Times Guardian tried to reassure its readers with an article headed "Tide turns on Sheppey sea battle", which commended the progress being made on a £220,000 re-engineering of the sea wall near the Yacht Club by Cheyney Rock, further East along Marine Parade. Only a few days later, on 13 January, the paper was forced to return to the more familiar type of headline: "When the Sea Vented its Anger". "Forewarned by police, people had tried once again to barricade their doorways with anything that came to hand. Great chunks of concrete were chewed out of the sea defences near the town playground, and debris was strewn along the length of overwhelmed Marine Parade". Once again, the island's reporters searched up emblematic stories: such as the "distraught woman" who was seen "staggering away" from her ground floor flat in Short Street when the water reached the top of her cooker. They also tried to wring a few drops of humour out of the misery: who, for example, was the man who waded up to two *Times Guardian* reporters as they stood in three feet of water at 4am, and asked: "Can you direct me to the railway station?"

Johnson had described the aftermath in "An Unfathomable Ship": "After the flood of January 1978, the residents of Sheppey were given a promise by an elected official that the island would never again be flooded as long as he was in office, and if it did he would resign. They had almost twelve months to watch the sea promenade being made walkable again, for the sake of the daytrippers from London, and to wonder why the flood wall was being reinforced in such a secretive way, with construction work on it remaining invisible even to the keenest eye".

The flood of January 1978 had actually goaded the Southern Water Authority into speeding up their plans for sea defences on Sheppey, raising an extra £6 million from the government for works over the next two financial years. The engineers had decided to bring about some immediate improvement to the existing sea wall running along Marine Parade, and they were by no means just acting for the sake of the day-trippers as Johnson had suggested. Tim Kermode remembers there being an obvious risk of an exceptional tide simply washing over the promenade forming the roofs of the reinforced concrete garages facing Marine Parade below. The best the engineers could do in the short term was to solidify the railings running along the landward edge of the garages by encasing their lower part in concrete. This "dwarf wall" had to be light, given the poor condition of the garages below, but at least it would not be an ordinary vertical wall like the pitiful thing that had been stuck on the seaward side of the promenade in the years before 1914. Though temporary, it was designed on scientific principles with help from the busy experts at the Hydraulics Research Station.

If this "dwarf wall" really was constructed in a "secretive" manner, as Johnson suggests, this would have been to avoid irritating the residents of Marine Parade who, as Kermode recalls, strongly resented this further encroachment on their sea view. Writing from "Sheerness (Shivering-on-Sea)" to his American publisher, Helen Wolff, on 16 March 1978, Johnson revealed himself to be among the unimpressed: "Sheerness underwent a flood in January, and the residents of the low-lying parts of the town brought rescue, and milk, to each other in whatever boats the flood hadn't smashed to pieces. Our part of town, although not in as much danger, has now been given additional protection in the form of an almost two-foot high shoe for the promenade's railing. So you would not have a view of the sea from the guest room any more, and I must ask you to consider one storey higher".[9]

None of this, as Johnson would soon enough have reason to explain in "An Unfathomable Ship", would prevent the return of the sea:

On December 30, 1978, at 11 p.m., shortly before an unusually high tide predicted in advance by the official tide tables, water did in fact splash over the much-scrutinized little wall, and the authorities had learned so much in the meantime that the alarm was not sounded until two hours later — with loudspeakers, not the promised sirens. With a predictable storm behind it, the hale and hearty water went for a vigorous stroll about the island, made itself at home in more than five hundred homes and businesses, blew fuses, burst gas pipes, swamped telephone connections, and spoiled an enormous quantity of things that could otherwise have been used as food and clothing. And then, since it had had such an easy time of it, the water came back again on the 31st, in the afternoon, wiping out all of the morning's pumping and cleaning efforts and contaminating the farmland and pastureland even more thoroughly. This time, again, only sheep died as an immediate result. But the insurance companies withdrew from a region where they would have to fork over an enormous amount of money whenever the weather decided so. The affected parties will have to pay over a quarter million pounds more in property taxes as a result of the new damages, starting in January. And once again, an investigatory commission will ask how this could have happened, and numerous people will promise that this time they are going to learn a very important lesson from the whole affair. (That resignation? Hasn't happened yet.)[10]

In some houses in Sheerness, the damage from the floods of 1978 would remain visible for ages. Fifteen years later, the performance artist Ewan Forster, who was then preparing a never realised project connected to Johnson's residence in the town, had dealings with a woman who worked in tourist information on the island. Invited to the house she shared with her son (remembered as a composer of TV theme tunes), he heard of the pair's annual holidays in various Eastern Bloc countries. He also remembers that they had a collection of communist posters, brought back from these partisan vacations, which they had pasted over the lower area of their interior walls in an attempt to cover up salt marks left over from the flood.[11]

*

The floods of 1978 really were the limit for the Sheppey Chamber of Trade and Industry, which was not going to settle for makeshift or temporary solutions, even one as scientifically tested as the "shoe" Kermode and his colleagues had fitted to the railings along Marine Parade. As the president explained in that year's "Christmas message" to the people of Sheppey, the Chamber had been tireless in campaigning for an end to Sheppey's trials as "the neglected area for adequate sea defence."[12] Obviously, the flooding was bad for the residents, but it also hindered the island's economic development, since nobody wanted to move to a place that might suddenly find itself underwater. The Chamber of Trade had beseeched "all the authorities concerned" including the Queen. It was time for a proper wall, and in the New Year its leaders would be joining an island deputation to meet "the appropriate authority whose responsibility is the funding of such defences".

The situation was also judged unacceptable by Roger Moate, who represented Sheppey as the Conservative MP for Faversham. He may have tired, over the years, of the press-stoked alarms about the *Richard Montgomery*, but on 25 January 1979, he stood up in the House of Commons to declaim about the floods in Sheerness. He condemned the Meteorological Office for trying to justify their failure to issue any warning before the recent floods on the grounds that they were due to "unusual weather phenomena" causing unpredicted "wave actions".[13] The Right Honourable Member wanted both the House and the Minister to understand "what it is like for a town to live in fear, knowing that the only defence against the North Sea is a Victorian sea wall some 6 ft lower than it should be". Governments and Whitehall might dither, but "Alas, the cruel sea does not wait on committees". It must be recognised that "The one and only thing that will satisfy the island and cannot be refused in all humanity is the fastest possible construction of a sea wall". Given the rising sea level he could accurately note that "much of the land area of Sheerness" was now "2 metres below the level of the annual spring tide".

In support of his demand for a nice, big, reassuringly visible wall, Moate announced that he had received many letters describing the "suffering, loss, hardship and heartbreak" in Sheerness. One had come from the Bishop of Maidstone, who declared himself "desperately sorry for those who had only just completed the work of drying out and redecorating their houses and now have to begin all over again". The bishop also pointed out that it was the poor, elderly and vulnerable who were most affected, since "the roads affected house many in low-income groups who are unable to move to a safer place". In the past Moate had tried not to be too "alarmist", but the latest floods had "swept away" his inhibitions, and he urged his colleagues to understand that "hundreds of lives" were at risk and that "no other town of comparable size in Britain" was "exposed to such danger of flooding as Sheerness".

In answer to Moate's charges, the Minister for Agriculture, E.S. Bishop, had pointed out that other towns were also facing inundation: far from being completely exceptional, Sheerness was in the same category as Wisbech and King's Lynn in the fens, other towns on the east coast and, for that matter, parts of London too. Even so, this agitation did eventually produce results, which were in turn to be a nightmare for Johnson. Having complained about the inaction of the authorities, he now experienced the consequences of their awakening.

The new wall would enclose the often-flooded Georgian houses of Neptune Terrace, and extend east along the entire length of Marine Parade. Started in 1980, the construction continued through the last months of Johnson's life. It was given extra drama, as the artist Martin Harris recalled, by a discovery made in the garages and storerooms under the western end of the promenade opposite Johnson's house. Some of these spaces had been used by the council to keep deck chairs that might be hired out to visitors, a declining trade that had been taken over by a lone operator who stepped in, somewhat piratically Harris thought, after the council had abandoned the trade as insufficiently worth the time of its staff. Others, however, were found to be filled with unexploded ordnance left over from the Second World War — opening the way for further disturbances, as people started amusing themselves by "chucking the stuff about" and contriving noisy explosions on the beach.

Like the designers of "Puddicombe's Folly", Southern Water's engineers were aware of the tension between protection and amenity value, and how easily one could diminish the other. They started by demolishing and removing the existing wall with its garages and storerooms, and then preparing a new site for the replacement, which would at least be set further back from the road to create a wider pedestrian area along Marine Parade. On the seaward side the engineers integrated the new structure into the stepped revetment of its predecessor; on the landward side above Marine Parade the new wall was topped with a "wave wall" significantly higher than its temporary predecessor. The aim of this latest view-blocking product of modern hydraulic engineering was to force each incoming wave to roll back on itself as it crested and to do so within the height of the wall — enclosing a cylinder of air that was duly photographed and studied during the Hydraulic Research Institute's trials.[14] For the engineers, the rolled-back crest of these strictly managed waves may well have articulated the hidden principles of hydraulic mathematics, in which a wave is conceived as "a perturbation that travels in space and time".[15] It was not for them to consider the implications of their exactly theorised wall for the more poetic "secret" that Johnson had ascribed to the free and unrestrained crests of the Atlantic waves breaking forward as they approached the New Jersey shore in the opening paragraph of *Anniversaries*.

*

Even to the partisan enthusiasts at the Cement and Concrete Association, it was obvious that building "a prominent sea-defence wall in front of small-scale terraced houses of the Georgian and Victorian periods in the conservation area of a seaside town" could be a sure "recipe for disaster".[16] To mitigate this problem, Southern Water and its consultant engineers decided to bring in a firm of architects to work on the landward side of the scheme. The job was handed to Garnham Wright Associates, a firm chosen for its previous experience in designing and casting concrete in a manner that might improve the appearance of large blast-resistant buildings required by petrochemical companies. As Jack Garnham Wright's daughter Penny Pope remembers, their design for Marine Parade's wall was intended to address two problems. First, that a long surface of smooth concrete would be both boring to look at and very easily disfigured by graffiti. Second, that, even though a new pedestrian space had been created by setting the wall further back from the road than its predecessor, the wall would remain a looming and formidable thing, which should be encouraged, if only by visual trickery, to "step away" from the houses opposite.

Where an engineer might have settled for a "plain bleak uncompromising wall", as *Concrete Quarterly* admitted, Jack Garnham Wright's team had decided to give the surface a strongly "rusticated" pattern: a roughly textured surface, ornamented by a relief design that could be cast in sections as the wall proceeded along the road. This pattern was an attempt to "reconcile the ideas of inherent strength with the architectural scale of the terraces and the nautical and seaside associations of the location". The surface had to be rough and resistant to graffiti, but the design, which was intended to establish the wall as a "backdrop" to the new pedestrian area, was strongly formal, drawing on the visual language of "classical" architecture and incorporating patterns of the type found on the stuccoed exteriors of many Georgian buildings: in grand parts of towns and cities, to be sure, but also in seaside resorts where stucco had often been used to protect buildings from saltwater spray.

According to *Concrete Quarterly*, the idea was to create an "arcaded" effect, using smooth formwork in the recessed areas, and rough-textured concrete to create the illusion of outstanding masonry blocks enclosing them. Each simulated arch had a pronounced "keystone", inspired partly by the kind that might be found at the centre of a window arch in a Georgian house. The "rusticated" effect of the supporting "pilasters" was achieved by creating a shadow-catching "pattern of V-shaped grooves in the concrete to resemble masonry joints". Further tributes to the local streetscape were built into the new pedestrian area, which was planted with saplings and paved in a pattern of coloured bricks that followed the rhythm of the arcaded wall while also echoing the colours of Shrimp Terrace, built as it was in "red brick with pink 'stone' dressings and other elegant embellishments".

Not content with this, the architects pulled their wall into focus on the landward side by placing a more elaborate section midway along its length. This included two raised pedestrian areas, the fronts of which were faced in brick and shaped in a way that paid abstract tribute to the memory of the "garages" that previously stood here. Like their interwar predecessors, the architects tried to appease local objectors by including flowers in the scheme. The raised areas were capped with lintels containing beds that might be planted, while further plant boxes were sited on the pavement between them. Visitors may still be surprised to encounter the central item (the words "quirky" and "light-hearted" were used to describe it): an ancient ship's figurehead of "Titan", actually a fibreglass replica of one that had adorned the prow of *HMS Forte*, said to have been selected from the dockyard's collection. Gaily painted, possibly by Jack Garnham Wright himself, it was mounted on the new wall between the two raised areas — the scarlet of "Titan's" toga being repeated in the colour of the two nearby street lights. The entire setup was conceived as a jaunty tribute to Sheerness's history as a seaside resort: a Kentish answer, perhaps, both to the "unsophisticated arts" praised by Barbara Jones, the originator of English pop art, and even to the "seaside surrealism" Paul Nash had earlier detected in the strangely out-of-place iron street furniture to be found in Dorset's coastal town of Swanage, reused after being collected as ballast for stone-bearing ships returning from London.[17]

On 10 June 1983, the *Sheerness Times Guardian* showed a picture of the ongoing works. At that time, the completion date was set for early October and local opinion was now concentrating its arguments on the "beautification" scheme proposed for the enlarged strip of land between the road and the new wall. Should this really be planted with tree-lined walkways, equipped with "modern lighting" and turned into something resembling a linear park, as Southern Water, the architects, and the local planners were proposing, or should it be used to widen the road and provide car parking for residents? Mrs Beryl Sunderland at 40 Marine Parade leaned towards a wider road and may also have agreed with a former mayor, who considered the very thought of public flowerbeds a provocation to vandals. Mrs Janice Monday at No. 36 came out for beautification, but could, of course, see both sides: "It's a thorny problem", she said, "and I'm glad I don't have to solve it."

View from Living Room, 26 Marine Parade

It was not until 4 May 1984 that a collection of councillors and Southern Water officials gathered in the central area of the new sea wall in Marine Parade to watch as the Mayor of Swale, Councillor Hugh Curling, unveiled the black-bearded figurehead of Titan, declaring that, with Sheppey now "as safe as it could be from the risk of tidal flooding", residents could "look forward to many years of peace and prosperity untroubled by the waters behind us".[18] The assembled company, which included Jack Garnham Wright, admired "Titan", who to this day looks both surprised and surprising in his immobile role as the "focal point" of an "attractive landscaping scheme" that seems long since to have lost its point as well as such plants as it may ever have possessed.

Lawn and sea wall in snow behind the (demolished) Sea View Hotel, 28 February 2018

Johnson was gone by then, and there is nothing to suggest he suspended his enduringly "non-committal" stand on English political matters for long enough to take a position over the argument between beautification and parking. He did though, see enough of the wall to form a view of the architect's work. His artist neighbour Martin Harris was inclined to scoff at the thing, which he condemned as both "brutalist" and entirely unnecessary. He remembered, though, that Johnson saw something other than "brutalism" in the textured and graffiti-resistant surface with which the new wall confronted residents across the road. Recognising the classical language used in Jack Garnham Wright's "rusticated" design, Johnson declared it to be all too reminiscent of the monumental works of Hitler's preferred architect, Albert Speer. Johnson's death, aged forty-nine, towards the end of February may have been a grievous loss for literature, but it spared the writer the knowledge that Speer's rehabilitation was already being prepared in England — or that, largely thanks to the Luxembourg-born architect Leon Krier, whose book on Speer and his works would be published to a very mixed reception in 1985,[19] Hitler's architect would soon be installed as the inspiration for a British "classical revival" championed by Prince Charles.

AFTERWORD

A very dark night it was, and bitter cold; the east wind blowing bleak, and bringing with it stinging particles from marsh, and moor, and fen – from the Great Desert and Old Egypt, may be. Some of the component parts of the sharp-edged vapour that came flying up the Thames at London might be mummy-dust, dry atoms from the Temple at Jerusalem, camels' foot-prints, crocodiles' hatching places, loosened grains of expression from the visages of blunt-nosed sphynxes, waifs and strays from caravans of turbaned merchants, vegetation from jungles, frozen snow from the Himalayas. O! It was very very dark upon the Thames, and it was bitter bitter cold.
— Charles Dickens, "Down with the tide", 1853

"The East German novelist Uwe Johnson, known locally as 'Charles', was found dead at his home in Marine Parade on Monday." That is how the *Sheerness Times Guardian* relayed the news to its readers on 16 March 1984. The forty-nine-year old writer, who "lived alone in his three storey home" and had an exclusive circle of friends at his two favourite pubs, was thought to have died about two weeks previously, perhaps on the night of 22 February, the date of his last appearance at the Napier Tavern. The author, who was understood to have spent "a great deal of time away on lecture tours in America", was also reported to be separated from his wife, who lived nearby with the couple's twenty-year-old daughter and worked as a language tutor at Sheppey School Further Education classes. Registered that same day, the death certificate tells us that Lionel Skingley, the recently appointed Coroner for North Kent decided, on the basis of a post-mortem without inquest,

622

that the forty-nine-year-old Uwe Klaus Dietrich Johnson had died of hypertensive heart disease. It wasn't his job to record that Sheerness may have lost its most distinguished resident alien since Napoleon Bonaparte failed to take up enforced residence there after his defeat at Waterloo in 1815.

News of Johnson's death reached his publishers in Frankfurt on the day his body was discovered. Siegfried Unseld and his secretary, Burgel Zeeh, had for some time been trying to raise a response from their author. On Monday 12 March they had sent a telegram asking Johnson to get in touch, but the call came from Elisabeth Johnson, who told Unseld that "Uwe is dead".[1] Unseld and Zeeh were soon in the office of Johnson's Sheerness solicitor, Sevier and Partners, where Mr Clough showed them an article about Johnson in the national *Daily Telegraph*, before relaying what he had been able to find out about the accompanying circumstances.

Clough confirmed that his client was last seen alive on Wednesday 22 February, when he had told Nora Harris, who had for years been coming to his house three times a week to clean, that he wouldn't be needing her services until 8 March.[2] Arriving at the house on the appointed day, she had found the front door locked and chained on the inside and decided that Johnson must still have been too busy to face any disturbance. Unable to gain access the following morning, she peered through the letter box and saw letters and newspapers piled up on the floor and the light on. She relayed her concern to Col Mason and Ron Peel, landlords of the Napier Tavern, who decided to wait until after the weekend before investigating further: "perhaps Charles, as they called him, would return and you couldn't enter his house against his will".[3] On Monday 12 the two publicans went to the house, smashed a lower ground floor window at the rear, and climbed in to find Johnson lying on the bloodied parquet floor of his living room. They had, as Mr Clough also explained, noticed two empty bottles of red wine on the table. Such was the news that confronted Siegfried Unseld and Burgel Zeeh. Their brilliant author, who'd found so little satisfaction in the literary fame Suhrkamp had helped bring his way, had died unwell, alone and, in more than one sense, heartbroken in a wintry English seaside town. And he had apparently done so while struggling to bring about the exodus of a cork from a third bottle that Unseld and Zeeh would see for themselves when they entered the house, still standing upright on the floor next to the table on which Johnson had struck his head as he went down.

Before that, however, Mr Clough had something else to announce. A year or so previously, Johnson had ordered Sevier and Co. to draw up a new will, invalidating the one he had prepared jointly with his wife on 2 October 1975, when they were about to depart on a visit to America. Some of the revisions the solicitor was about to reveal might have been anticipated following a letter Unseld had sent to Johnson on 7 December 1982, a little over a year before the changes were made. In this, the publisher had informed Johnson that "we need to talk about your finances".[4] Unseld, who had for many years been paying Johnson a regular advance, stated that by the end of that December — when, in accordance with the most recently broken deadline, Johnson had been due to deliver the completed text of *Anniversaries* IV — his debit balance with Suhrkamp would stand at DM 230,094.89 (approximately £60,000 at the exchange rate of the time). The payments would continue until the end of March 1983. It was a short communication, in which Unseld stated three times, "we have to talk about it".

Johnson had spent a couple of weeks mulling over the situation before replying with a sketch of the course of action he proposed to follow in order to escape, or at least postpone, looming disaster. He accepted that, whatever Unseld might decide, future arrangements must "revolve around my obligation to reimburse Suhrkamp" for this debt (which had, as he pointed out with customary precision, actually grown a little beyond the sum Unseld mentioned).[5] As a preliminary step in this direction, he announced that he had already signed over his life insurance to Unseld and proposed that the publisher should draw up a contract specifying that he — "the landlord"

— would not receive any payments from his copyright after 31 March until the debt was cleared. He undertook to allocate his share of the joint-owned house on Marine Parade to the publisher. He offered to take on such editing work as Unseld might suggest, volunteering that a monthly proportion of the income from any such work should be set against the debt. As for his own writing, he intended to wrap up *Anniversaries* IV in a few months, and then embark on another book — a history of the Cresspahl family since the late nineteenth century — which he imagined completing over a six-month period. He hoped the time for the latter project might be financed from the sale of the manuscripts of his seven published novels, reserved for his daughter in the will of 1975 but now also put on the table for Unseld, who would surely, even under present straitened circumstances, be able to find a buyer willing to stump up six times Johnson's monthly subvention. By this means, Unseld might ("if you want to help") secure Johnson's "place at the typewriter" for long enough to bring both *Anniversaries* and the new work to completion.

Dated 22 March 1983, the new will now disclosed by Mr Gough followed this course of action through to its abject conclusion. In the will of 1975, Johnson had left everything to his wife, asking his executors, in the event of their early death, to ensure that funds were made available to help his daughter through university, and also to ensure that she received various of his possessions, including his collection of Mecklenburg maps and books, his typed manuscripts and author's copies of his books, and also his thirty-volume 1973/4 edition of the *Encyclopaedia Britannnica*.[6] In the new will, the encyclopaedia went to his wife, but everything else — including the collection of Kentish publications he had previously asked to be offered to the public reference library in Sheerness — was left to Suhrkamp.[7]

Clough also revealed a "Statement to my Executors", prepared on his company's advice in case the new will was ever challenged. In this declaration, which the author claimed to have "made in the trust that it will never be made public",

Johnson sought to justify the change by repeating and, indeed, magnifying the accusations he had made in his Frankfurt Lectures. [8] He also asserted that, thanks to his inability to work following his wife's alleged betrayal (which he also blamed for the heart attack he had suffered in 1975), he had run up "enormous debts" with Suhrkamp. Since he could not have survived "without their generosity", he wished to repay "the kindness and the steadfastness" they had shown "by bequeathing any money and property I have to them, as I may owe them a great debt at the date of my death". In the final paragraph of this awful statement against "my wife E.J. and her daughter", he asked his executors to take "all sensible steps" to prevent Elisabeth Johnson, whom he still recognised as the part owner of 26 Marine Parade, from entering the house or, failing that, of "laying hand on anything in the house including any of the contents".[9]

The cremation took place at Vinters Park in Maidstone on Friday 23 March. Siegfried Unseld justified his own attendance by explaining that he had promised the author that he would make sure things were done in accordance with his last wishes: "no music, speeches, flowers or any religious or other service whatsoever".[10] Elisabeth and Katharina Johnson were present, as were Johnson's sister, Elke an Huef, his friends and now executors Felix and Antonia Landgraf, and Mr. Clough, the solicitor from Sevier and Partners.

Although none of Johnson's English acquaintances had been invited to join those who gathered to see "Charles" make his final departure in this unceremonious manner, Unseld records that "two other people were present in the crematorium chapel, a man and a woman I could not identify".[11] The two in question were Martin and Susan Harris. They had been surprised to look out of the window earlier that day and see a hearse drawing up outside 26 Marine Parade so that the coffin could, as Unseld recalls Elisabeth Johnson wishing, start its journey from the house. The Harrises wanted to pay neighbourly respects to the man they had known for nearly a decade, so they pulled on some smarter clothes, jumped into their car and followed the little cortege as it made its way past Sheppey cemetery before crossing the Kingsferry Bridge onto the mainland. Having arrived at Vinters Park, they crept into the crematorium chapel and sat down in the obscurest seats they could find at the back.

What they saw struck them as overwhelmingly bleak. For a start, there was hardly anybody there. According to Unseld's record, the four women who were present sat in a row in front of the coffin, Mr Clough the solicitor sat near Dr Felix Landgraf behind them, and Unseld himself (whom Harris remembered as the busy fellow who must have been Johnson's "agent") remained standing throughout, perhaps worrying less about the presence of these two English interlopers at the back than about the flowers the crematorium staff had placed on either side of the chapel, and which he had not been in any position to remove. After some minutes of silence, which Unseld himself described as "long", the sky-blue curtain closed and Johnson was gone. More than three decades later, Martin Harris was still wondering about the things he had seen that day: "not a word was spoken" he said with a mixture of puzzlement and dismay. He and Susan had driven home perplexed and also worried that they may have been wrong to intrude on the event. They didn't know that everything they'd witnessed had actually been done in accordance with Johnson's wishes which, in this matter, as in the request that his executors discourage any future attempt to write his biography, had not changed between the wills of 1975 and 1983.

If news of Johnson's death brought Siegfried Unseld to Sheerness, it also brought Tilman Jens, the journalist who came to investigate the circumstances for *Stern*, a popular weekly news magazine based in Hamburg, which was then still notorious for its purchase and publication of Hitler's falsely alleged "diaries" a year previously. Nobody in Sheerness will have known that Jens was the son of the well-known West German writer and academic Walter Jens (a member, like Johnson, of the German literary forum Group 47). What they saw was a twenty-nine-year old reporter from a magazine that evidently had the means, as Martin Harris remembered thinking, to provide an expenses account as well as a photographer. He was among those who helped Jens pull back the shutters on the English life of "the unknown man of the Thames".[12] Not content with telling the ignorant reporter that the man he was talking about was actually "Charles", these informants also tried to explain how it was that Johnson had been allowed to lie dead or dying in their town for two weeks before anybody even noticed. "How could we?", they can be heard asking in *Stern*'s article, repeating Jens's question before trying to pass on their excuses to the magazine's legion of West German readers. In Martin Harris's answer it was the fault of Johnson's automatic light-switching device: installed to deter thieves when he was away, this contraption turned on the house lights at the strangest of hours, making it impossible to be sure whether the writer was at home or on the far side of the world again. Johnson's housekeeper, Nora Harris, mentioned the lights too, together with the fact that Johnson had so often "disappeared" without warning, only announcing his absence on postcards that would arrive from Germany, France or America a few days later. The unemployed shipwright, Jeff Lucas, told Jens that Johnson was probably the only person in "this God-forsaken nest" who drank his tea and coffee black. It was thanks to this foreign perversity that 26 Marine Parade had never sent out the classic English distress signal: a collection of unopened milk bottles accumulating steadily on the doorstep.

As we have seen, it was Jens who provided German readers with their first dramatized glimpses into Johnson's Kentish life as "Charles": the pub, the working-class folk he liked to hang out with, the incredible (and possibly exaggerated) quantities of alcohol they claimed to have seen him pour down his throat and his alleged willingness to have whisky dribbled over his head every Christmas as part of his annually renewed English "baptism". These were grotesque revelations for the novelist's admirers in Germany to assimilate, but they were only part of the story Jens dredged out of the Kentish slime for the readers of *Stern* magazine. Martin Harris remembered being irritated when he eventually caught sight of Nomi Baumgartl's photograph of a phallus scrawled on the lamppost outside Johnson's house (just another example, he had thought, of the media's habit of framing Sheerness as a dump). Some of the Johnsons's West German friends may have been more concerned about the much larger photograph, attributed to the Kent Press Agency, showing Elisabeth Johnson waiting outside 26 Marine Parade for the hearse to arrive on the day of her estranged husband's funeral. She looks uncomfortable, as anyone might when caught by an intrusive paparazzi-style snapper leaning over the new promenade wall to invade a desolate personal moment. Given the slant of Jens' article, the bought-in picture stood there as an accusation against which no defence was really invited. Accepting Johnson's allegations of betrayal from his book *Accompanying Circumstances* (*Begleitumstände*), Jens repeats them and then twice makes a free-standing paragraph of his own accusing words: "Elisabeth Johnson is silent. Does not defend herself." Muriel Adams did her best to defuse his charge, telling Jens, "She's never talked to me either... only at the beginning of July, she always reminded me of his birthday and bothered to send me a birthday card." That "silence" may have been entirely justified, and not just by the confidentiality owed to people in private matters. Jens, however, presented it as a sign of guilt, leaving Elisabeth Johnson dangling there for all to see on the gibbet *Stern* made of its invasive photograph.

Unfortunately for Jens' career as a journalist, his article also revealed that he had taken his photographer into Johnson's house so that she could select such targets as the *New York Times* tote bag hanging in the hallway, or the papers and other objects standing on his "metal behemoth" of a writing desk (including the desk diary, conveniently open beside the electric typewriter at the pages for 21-22 February). While Baumgartl snapped away, Jens himself had evidently gone poking about among Johnson's papers and possessions. When news of the fury provoked in Germany by this criminal intrusion reached Sheerness, the *Sheppey Gazette* added its own contribution to the coverage.[13] Tilman Jens was reported to have claimed that he entered the house with permission and in the company of a security man or policeman. Martin Harris rejected the suggestion that he had assisted in this act of trespass. Jens had, he said, approached him saying he was "keen to get pictures of the house". At the journalist's request, he had written to Elisabeth Johnson, explaining that Jens was "trying to do a tribute to her husband" and wondered whether she was happy for him to go in the house. When she told him not to have any contact with Jens, he had written to Johnson's literary executors, but the Wengrafs had also refused, excusing themselves on the grounds that they were "not empowered" to permit such a thing. He had, so he told the *Sheppey Gazette,* no idea how Jens and his photographer had got in to the house.

More than thirty years later, Martin Harris told me that he had in fact been an accomplice in Jens's raid — not on the first occasion, when Jens entered the house with Nomi Baumgartl, but later when he is said to have returned alone for a second visit, having phoned to say that he had accidentally left a roll of film in No. 26. Harris, who had quite liked the journalist, had seen no harm in the request and agreed, after some wavering, to help. This involved another nocturnal visit to Johnson's garden, not to steal a rose this time, but, as he remembered, to help squeeze Jens through the ground-floor window that had previously been used to enter the house by the publicans from the Napier Tavern. At this point, Harris's story became farcical. *Stern*'s reporter was on the "chubby" side and got stuck in the frame, which turned out to be so loosely attached that it started coming off the wall. Once this was sorted out, Harris found himself waiting outside in the garden for far longer than he thought it would take to collect a roll of film. He returned to his own house, where he spent a considerable time wondering nervously what on earth Jens was up to (at this juncture a miniature Minox-style spy camera appeared in Harris's recollection of the event), eventually going back to extract the intruder before the pair of them were arrested for breaking and entering.

Whatever the exact truth of this situation, and the above is only Harris's remembered version, there can be no doubt at all that Jens's article was a scandalous piece that brought *Stern* under fierce attack and caused Jens to be left without a job. Fritz J. Raddatz fiercely condemned *Stern*'s revelations, and repudiated the implied suggestion that it was he who had first spread the news about Johnson's marital problems.[14] Others, including Günter Grass, gave different accounts of their disgust at Jens's conduct, citing the high premium Johnson had always placed on personal confidentiality, and also the injury the article did to the surviving members of the unwell writer's shattered family. Jens's worst offence was to reveal the existence of a light brown notebook in which, so the reporter alleged, Elisabeth Johnson had, at her husband's command, described her meetings with the Prague musicologist Tomislav Volek. This trophy was presented as a confession of guilt, allegedly written in diary form on Johnson's demand, in some perverse echo of *Anniversaries*. Such, boasted Jens, was "the book from which she read to him" in the evenings. Although the latter statement may not be accepted with any certainty, there is little doubt that such a book did exist. Siegfried Unseld, who was not inclined to challenge Johnson's vengeful accusations, was careful to hint in his later account of Johnson's last days that he knew all about the book and its contents ("I knew what that was"), even though he also claims that, "at my request", the notebook in question was later returned to Elisabeth Johnson by the executor, Dr. Felix Landgraf.[15]

Those inclined to defend Suhrkamp's conduct through this shocking situation can point to various things Unseld and his company went on to do with the estate it had inherited: publishing Johnson's work, setting up the Uwe Johnson Society and Archive (now in Rostock), and more generally fostering the collection, editing and translation of the writer's work. This continues to be a major undertaking, to which readers and researchers are greatly indebted. From this perspective, Unseld's letter warning Johnson about his finances may appear no more than an extreme example of the type of letter publishers may still be inclined to send out as they approach the last resort: a brisk stimulant intended not to traumatise and threaten their sick and despairing author, but to encourage him into finishing the inordinately delayed final volume of *Anniversaries,* as Johnson had indeed proceeded to do over a few frenzied months. In retrospect, the arrangement that is now in place between Suhrkamp and Elisabeth and Katharina Johnson may also lend credibility to Unseld's claim that neither he nor his publishing company had ever intended to leave Johnson's descendants completely out in the cold, and, indeed, that Elisabeth Johnson had declined the publisher's initial attempt to reach an informal settlement on the principled grounds that any such arrangement would be in breach of her late husband's will.

Others, however, continued to see the situation very differently. A decade after the initial shock, Elisabeth Johnson, who had moved from Sheppey back to Mecklenburg following the reunification of Germany, went to court to challenge the will of 1983. After two hearings, in which much, including the accusations in Johnson's "Statement to my Executors", was exposed and raked over by lawyers, her claim was finally rejected by the Berlin Court of Appeal on 17 October 1995. The following year, the conviction that a grievous injustice had been done to Johnson's descendants was presented in a volume by Werner Gotzmann. In this light, Unseld looked more like a manipulative overseer than a long-suffering friend and saviour. Here, he was the man who had put Johnson under severe pressure, when he was already in desperate straits, effectively obliging him to produce a new will, and going along, for his own convenience, with his allegations about his wife and their daughter. In the eyes of Gotzmann and others who took Elisabeth Johnson's side at this time, the "betrayal" narrative had been allowed to stand because it served as a "legitimation" of Suhrkamp's breach of the wife and daughter's natural rights.

Unseld would repudiate these suggestions as unfounded slanders,[16] but he didn't directly condemn Elisabeth Johnson for her closing words on the matter. In her "Afterword" to Gotzmann's book, she remembered how Unseld had urged her to "mourn" when she contacted him after Johnson's death and then sought to discipline her by hinting that the allegations made in Johnson's "Statement to my Executors" might become public, as indeed they would eventually do, if the will was challenged in the courts. She criticises Unseld's text, "For When I am Dead", in which he presents his relationship with Johnson as testimony to "a beautiful friendship", suggesting that this involved both self-deception and a refusal to accept responsibility for the pressure that had been placed on a writer who was plainly far from well, had little understanding of financial matters or, for that matter, of the difference between business and friendship. She also offered a brief account of the "affair" that had become so magnified and distorted in Johnson's mind: "Once I was unfaithful to him; I told him in 1975. Three years later, I realized we couldn't live together. I left the house. I felt he had to change; he hoped I'd come back. And so we lost sight of each other. Everything else is fiction."[17]

It seems fair to say that news of this wounding dispute, which for many years continued to smoulder and sporadically blaze up in Germany, did not reach many in Sheerness, where people expressed their sadness differently. Susan Harris, for example, didn't need any news from abroad to feel pained by the fact that relations with Elisabeth (respectfully remembered by some islanders as the "Frau Johnson" who taught German evening classes at the local comprehensive school) had never been repaired after the events of March 1984. As for Johnson himself, the available evidence does not allow us to conclude with much certainty that the writer responsible for one of the most attentive and sympathetic accounts of a mother and daughter ever written by a male author achieved at least some understanding during his last months that his accusations were both exaggerated and made by one who was "de-ranged", which is not just to say, as Johnson got round to explaining in

Anniversaries IV, out of his "place in the world".[18] At another moment in that volume, he also demonstrates an understanding of the materiality of delusions. Set in Soviet-occupied Mecklenburg in 1946, the passage in question is concerned with the perceptions of a young communist leader Gerd Schumann, who has just discovered, as he prepares to give a speech in the October election campaign, that the town of Jerichow has by no means fallen in with the party line. Turned away by a thirteen-year-old girl (Gesine Cresspahl) when he knocks on a door seeking a place to rest for a few hours before addressing the rally, the agitated Schumann, whose failings will soon enough see him carted off into a Soviet prison camp, decides she is "crazy, feebleminded, a figment of his imagination." That's when Johnson writes, "A man can imagine things like that in moments of severe emotional strain. Mirages, illusions like that, do exist".[19]

In a Different Spot

Illness, drink and paranoia may have overwhelmed Johnson in his last months, but *Anniversaries* was completed before then. On 17 April 1983, he had mailed the last remaining days of Volume IV to Suhrkamp, announcing, in an accompanying letter to Burgel Zeeh: "at my discretion, a temporary closure. Although there are conversations with Mrs Cresspahl such as the following: Thank God it's over. We're done here. With this, yes".[20]

Johnson had continued to think of leaving Sheerness in the months since: options included West Berlin, where a position at the German Academy for Language and Literature seemed possible, or another spell in New York City, where Max Frisch's apartment might have been available. Yet the text of *Anniversaries* IV suggests he had actually settled for a different form of withdrawal, one that carried him into the richly populated world he had kept in the "cellar of memories"[21] in which neighbours and curious promenaders on the other side of Marine Parade could only see a sad-looking man failing to get down to work.

Johnson had long been bequeathing elements of his own experience and situation to his "invented persons", and in *Anniversaries* IV he continued to transfer his own life into theirs. The porcelain replicas of the Liberty Bell, which had had borrowed for his essay on the *Richard Montgomery,* are restored to West Berlin, whence newspaper publishers will forward them to New York as gifts for "families one of whose members has been killed trying to kill members of other families on the other side of the world in Vietnam".[22] A bad day in Sheerness gives way to the communist Gerd Schumann's description of walking into the fictional Mecklenburg town of Jerichow: "What a godforsaken dump, this is. If only he'd never set foot in it".[23] The "windy backwater" that had been so potently represented by the landscapes of the Thames and Medway estuaries finds its way back to north Germany, just as the "never-decomposing garbage" piling up along the "scabby" edge of a "putrescent river" belongs once again to the Hudson in New York City.[24] The thought that strangers can be identified by their habit of looking at buildings rather than people is lifted from its earlier application to Sheerness and relocated in the novel as proof that the unparented eleven-year-old Gesine Cresspahl was no longer a stranger in the town of Gneez, where she had moved from Jerichow in order to attend school in 1946.[25] Johnson's own habit of picking at words, which had seemed so pedantic and at times insulting to his English neighbour Martin Harris, is passed to a "top student" named Dieter Lockenvitz, who gladly receives the author's "linguistic stethoscope" and uses it to diagnose the corrupting language of official discourse in the GDR.[26]

Johnson also has things to offer Gesine Cresspahl's friend and lover, the US government's adviser on radar technology, Prof. Dietrich Erichson. Long ago, in *Anniversaries* I, "D.E." had installed Johnson's "metal behemoth of a desk" in a colonial house in New Jersey — together with his wine, two bottles of which his resident mother got out for him each morning so that, when he got home from work, he too could sit there as "a heavy, sorrowful figure in the night".[27] Johnson now hands his own funeral instructions to the much-travelled Erichson, who carries a piece of paper written in four different languages announcing his wish "To be cremated at the place or location of death with no music speeches flowers or any religious or other service whatsoever".[28] He requests this not out of anger or contempt, as Gesine explains, but "so he wouldn't put me to any unnecessary trouble". Since Erichson died when his plane crashed, his survivors were spared even that inconvenience. "Burned up n buried n now theres nothin", as his mother puts it in her blunt Platt dialect — to which Gesine adds: "That's how he wanted it".

In 1981, Fritz J. Raddatz told British radio listeners that Johnson had once written something very beautiful. He had said that nobody who ever left their country did so "without writing a letter, a letter to the country".[29] Johnson's entire work, Raddatz suggested, should be understood as "a long, long letter addressed still to the country, which means to the problems of the country". *Anniversaries* may yet be read as that sort of "reflection" in a reunited Germany thirty years after the Cold War. Thanks to Damion Searls' English translation of the full text, it is also being reactivated in the USA, not least in Nicholas Dames' brilliantly "delirious" essay showing how it speaks to the New York City of the COVID-19 lockdown.[30]

In the still more or less United Kingdom, we may notice that Johnson was found dead in his house in Sheerness on the day, 12 March 1984, when the National Union of Mineworkers embarked, under its President Arthur Scargill, on their year-long and eventually defeated strike against Margaret Thatcher's thoroughly prepared government. Although this coincidence tells us nothing about either event, it does serve to remind us that, by the end of Johnson's life on the Isle of Sheppey, deindustrialization of the sort unleashed with some regret and trepidation by Harold Macmillan and Lord Mountbatten in 1960, when they consigned Sheerness to a future without the naval station, garrison and dockyard, had come to seem a price worth paying to the later Tory ministers who, during Margaret Thatcher's leadership, urged the working-class victims of "change" — one of the words with which the once stately responsibilities of cause and effect were dissolved in this period — to eat fewer "chips", "get on their bikes", and prepare to embrace tourism as the new "industry" of the future.[31]

The triumph of that vision was claimed again on the Medway after the closure of the remaining naval dockyard at Chatham, completed a couple of weeks after Johnson's death, on 31 March 1984. There was, once more, a great sense of loss ("It's installed in you",[32] as one former worker explained of the dockyard at which British nuclear submarines had latterly been serviced), and talk of the heart being ripped out of a community. Former workers may remain convinced that Medway towns such as Chatham and Gillingham have never recovered, but that is not the considered verdict of one of the sociologist Ray Pahl's successors at the University of Kent. In a report commissioned by BBC Radio Kent in 2016, a "global business forecaster" named Professor Richard Scase concluded that the closure at Chatham had been very positive for the area. It had eliminated "unhealthy, unsafe and inefficient jobs" and put an end to "over-manning, pilfering and wastage", and also to a "highly unionised" situation in which "bigotry and sexism" were rife.[33] It had obliged the government to invest heavily in English Estates' redevelopment of the area, while also preparing the way for the emergence of the Historic Dockyard Museum, which is helping out "Dickens World" — which may not, let's face it, have managed to lift the town entirely on its own — and also the creation of a campus shared between the universities of Kent, Greenwich and Christ Church Canterbury.

There is no reason to imagine that, as a "guest" in the country, Johnson would have been prepared to express a view about the British miners' strike had he lived to watch it unfold. He definitely did, though, reveal a political perspective, as well as the distancing sense of irony for which his writing is known. In his typescript "Conversation on the Novel..." Johnson noted the comments of those who dismissed the novel as a decadent distraction from the revolutionary cause if not an outright "enemy of the people" and described himself as being "on the left but in a different spot". As the *Times'* obituarist rightly noted on 15 March 1984, he had spent much of his life "searching for an undogmatic socialism with a 'human face'" that might emerge as an alternative to the "conflicting ideologies" of the Cold War.[34] The unnamed obituarist also reports that he had persisted in such a position after 1968, even though the suppression of the Prague Spring, which starts immediately after the final day of *Anniversaries* IV, had left him feeling "increasingly gloomy about the possibilities of this being realised by any government". Johnson respected the values embodied in the famous manifesto, "Two Thousand Words to Workers, Farmers, Scientists, Artists and Everyone", a key document of the Prague Spring written by the then still communist writer Ludvik Vaculik, signed by various Czechoslovak intellectuals, athletes and artists, and published by some Prague newspapers in June 1968.[35] Indeed, he reprinted the manifesto in *Anniversaries* IV: a volume that, like the manifesto itself, could never have pleased "King Arthur" Scargill, who has condemned the emergence of Solidarnosc in Warsaw and continued to defend Stalin even in his more recent stance as a communist Brexiter who would like to see a workers' state reopening Britain's mines, mills and factories.

Scargill was the leader of virtuous people whose communities were fundamentally threatened. He was viciously hounded too — harassed by the state as well as by the rampant Tory press and its outriders. He alone, though, chose later to sue his own National Union of Mineworkers for failing to pay the cost of his fuel allowance, the preparation of his annual tax return and the rent on his flat in London's Barbican until the end of his days. I remember him alongside another unapologetic relic of defeated times, whom I encountered fleetingly in 2018 on a visit to Fischland with the filmmaker Shona Illingworth. We had stopped by the roadside at a T-junction in order to film a large military block that, like the Nazi pleasure-barracks at Prora, was being converted to new use. We had just got started, when an already rare pop-popping noise came along the road from a little resort town named Dierhagen. The noise was followed by a GDR-stickered Trabant, which paused while the unsmiling driver appraised us coldly, and then turned left in the direction of Ahrenshoop. The man at the wheel seemed oddly familiar, and it was a while before I realised that we may just have glimpsed the last leader of the GDR, Egon Krentz, who retired to this coast after serving his time in jail and, as I only found out later, now lives in Dierhagen — an allegedly uncontrite admirer of the more enduring strong man, Vladimir Putin. (The apparition felt unlikely to me too but that, in a sense, is the point: the GDR loyalist I saw was only another inflexible old man in a heritage car.)

There is nothing in *Anniversaries* IV that might seem reassuring to either of these fallen leaders or, for that matter, to Bryan "unfortunately also Johnson", who had praised the USSR to the skies on the letters page of the *Kent Evening Post*. Nothing for anybody who might believe that "socialism" was a matter of holding out in an ideological bunker, keeping quiet about the subsidised holidays you may once have enjoyed on the Black Sea or staying firm in your commitment to an ever more antiquated idea of industrial class struggle. No wonder Johnson stands far back, in *Anniversaries* IV, from the British communists and sympathisers who flit through his account of the post-war years in East Germany. We meet them as unfriendly freeloaders claiming to be artists in the official cultural retreat at Ahrenshoop, as the "socialistically inclined English girls"[36] who show up at the anti-imperialist Third World Youth Festival in East Berlin, and as the notorious Red Dean of Canterbury, Hewlett Johnson, who appears here being praised to the skies by GDR loyalists for his faithful hymns of praise to "The Socialist Sixth of the World"[37] — "a theologian ostracised in his own land" whose successors at the Deanery at Canterbury Cathedral are said to have discovered an abandoned menagerie of Russian animals in the attic: large folkloric toys that had been presented to this credulous Christian admirer's children by Stalin himself.

There are, without question, moments in *Anniversaries* IV when the creative compact between Uwe Johnson and his reader seems to fray, and one can glimpse the author, muttering among his characters in that empty basement office. *Anniversaries* IV has great days set in New York City, including 1 August 1968 when the colour yellow is traced across the surface of the city — the taxis, the smog, the butter, the gold, the painted kerbs beside the fire hydrants, the sign on the Metropolitan Museum, even the allegedly "manila" envelopes — before it is finally bundled up as a "national quality" and dropped as the colour of death over people with yellow skins in Vietnam.[38] And yet America seems more distant and faraway in this final volume, and so too does Mecklenburg, which is, by this time, so heavily suffused with nostalgia — a "painful virtue",[39] in Marie's words – that the yearning must strike some readers as a malady rather than a virtue of the post-war generation of German writers, and one that is not necessarily helpful in its bearing on twenty-first-century conditions.

At its heart, though, *Anniversaries* IV is a brilliantly observed analytical portrait of the first few years of the GDR as it moves towards the 1953 uprising witnessed by Gesine Cresspahl in Berlin, and the establishment under Walter Ulbrich of a regime in which "The party is always right".[40] Johnson reproduces the remembered atmosphere of the time, with the ubiquitous slogans and Picasso peace doves, the work brigades hunting for blight-spreading Colorado Beetles allegedly dropped on the GDR's potato fields from American planes, and a long inventory of the people arrested in Mecklenburg to be sent off to Russia and never seen again, or given long jail sentences for "crimes" that weren't crimes at all.

Much of this is told through events at a high school Johnson derives partly from his memories as a student at the John-Brinkmann school in Güstrow. *Anniversaries* being a novel, this requires the development of some new characters. So Gesine Cresspahl is moved aside sufficiently to allow the focus to fall on a classmate, Anita Gantlik, who has arrived in Mecklenburg, along a route known to Johnson, as a refugee from East Prussia.

Her mother, brothers and sisters were killed in the fields by the advancing Red Army in 1945, and she herself — aged eleven — was raped by three Russian soldiers who knowingly infected her with the gonorrhoea that has left her sterile. Having escaped west with her "bonehead"[41] father, who somehow managed to be a Polish Nazi sympathiser, she became a child day labourer, and then, by luck, a favoured translator for the Russian commandants. Thanks to that experience, she is able to impress her mates at the academic high school with her knowledge of Russian, which includes the obscure fact that, as she tells a teacher, "The Russian word for "train station", ma'am, *voskal*, is derived from the amusement park near London's Vauxhall station…"[42] A member of the persecuted Free German Youth, she leaves to become an escape helper in West Berlin, bringing people across the border from the GDR.

In that respect, at least, she fares better than a one-armed man named Johnny Schlegel, who is another educated representative of the socialism from "a different spot" that Johnson and other young anti-Nazis had watched being snuffed out as the GDR got into its stride. Following the Second World War, Schlegel turns his inherited farm outside Jerichow into a commune, having learned both his farming skills and his ideas of social organisation from the land settlement schemes he had known during the Weimar Republic, before the Nazis refeudalised the land in the name of "Blood and Soil".[43] Since the end of the war Schlegel had "handed out his inheritance in ninths to refugees from the lost eastern territories, so long as they were farmers or willing to learn to be".[44] These fugitives were treated with considerable hostility by the locals, but not by Schlegel, who granted them a share of the farm profits depending on the work they put in and the number of horses they had brought with them. This co-operative enterprise becomes an affront to the agricultural policies of the GDR: Schlegel's form of socialism extended beyond the use of land, draft animals vehicles and tools, to include household tasks, which were done in common, just as meals were eaten at one table. Johnny Schlegel's farm was assessed wrongly, obliged to meet quotas several times higher than those demanded of more compliant farms, and even to pay for cows that were already its own. Schlegel eventually falls victim to his own punctilious record-keeping, which enabled the authorities to establish that he had paid money into a foreign account when buying a piece of land in 1947. He was arrested in February 1953 and convicted on the evidence of his critical comments about state agricultural policy and his diary full of ill-advised remarks about the communist takeover in Prague. He gets fifteen years in prison. The farm is confiscated and the co-operative "cleaned out". The members who aren't jailed join the procession into refugee camps in the West.

The utopian impulse that Johnson claimed sometimes to have glimpsed in the working-class solidarity of Sheerness certainly takes a bashing in *Anniversaries* IV. Johnson shows it defeated in East Germany during the post-war years, and draws things to an end just short of its extinction in Prague 1968. Displaced from political reality, it finds refuge in the unattainable and nostalgically rendered landscape of Fischland ("Never again") while also retreating into the infantile fantasy of Marie Cresspahl who, as a four-year-old in New York in 1961, invents a "republic of children" named Cydamonoe, "a Kinder-Garten in the intended meaning of the word",[45] which is only accessible by air from specified places. Surrounded by water and filled with windmills and grass roads for pedal carts, tricycles and jump machines, Cydamonoe is a place in time as well as space, where the working principle is "help yourself" to anything you might want. "No child ever did without" in Cydamonoe, and should they develop a desire for something that wasn't already present, there was a "Want and Will building" where members could take their requests. Many vaccinations are required by those seeking to enter Cydamonoe, since it remains "the only country in the world that is worth living in".

For all the personal trauma and defeat, Johnson the writer who had learned his "irreplaceable method of interrogation and experimentation" under Hans Mayer in the GDR, is still very much at work in this closing volume. He is there with his persistent, sceptical search for the truth of changing situations, his sense of testimony, his curiosity, and his striving towards a kind of novel in which fiction serves historical enquiry, but not just by faking its way over inconvenient gaps in the record in the manner of so much historical fiction nowadays. On the wider political front, Gesine Cresspahl knows the dangers of narratives that simplify and schematise in order to arouse. She is pleased to have passed that scepticism on to her daughter in New York: "Marie is suspicious of stories where everything fits together — I've taught her that much."[46]

Johnson may have tested his approach against the sloganized reality of a since abolished communist state, but *Anniversaries* remains on the side of anyone seeking to challenge the "post-fact" world with a recovered art of "focused observation" and critical "information."[47] It is surely a good novel to read in this period when new techniques of narrative dissimulation have once again served to empower the far-right, and when the long discredited strategy of "socialist realism", with its Stalinist pretence that the promised future is already dawning in the present, finds a weird reprise in British government TV adverts showing the "New Start" that will surely follow Brexit (if only we islanders get our patriotism and paperwork in order). In this regard, *Anniversaries* IV completes a work that remains inspiring in its enduring visibility: resistant, contrary to expectation, and still there even after its world has dissolved around it — as arresting, perhaps, as the not yet sawn-off masts of the *Richard Montgomery*, and potentially a lot more useful.

NOTES

Uwe Johnson's *Jahrestage: Aus dem Leben von Gesine Cresspahl* was written and first published by Suhrkamp Verlag in four separate volumes (1970, 1971, 1973, 1983). Damion Searls' American translation, from which all English quotations are derived, was published as *Anniversaries: From a Year in the Life of Gesine Cresspahl* in a continuously paginated cased set of two volumes by New York Review Books in 2018. References to *Anniversaries* below use the pagination from this edition while also identifying the original volume with Roman numerals. All passages quoted from previously untranslated Johnson texts, including those gathered in Eberhardt Fahke's edited anthology of Johnson's occasional English writings, *Inselgeschichten (Island Stories)*, are from translations prepared for this project by Damion Searls.

COVID-19 and the associated lockdowns are at least partly responsible for the fact that some references are incomplete or, indeed, entirely missing.

Preface

1. Written in 1796 and originally published in Jean Paul's novel *Siebenkas,* "Speech of the Dead Christ" is here quoted from the translation given by Thomas Carlyle in "Jean Paul Richter Again", first published in *Foreign Review* in January 1830 and collected in Thomas Carlyle's *Critical and Miscellaneous Essays,* Volume 2, Boston: James Munroe 1838, p. 240

2. Gerhard Zwerenz, *Die Verteidigung Sachsens und warum Karl May die Indianer liebte Sächsische Autobiographie in Fortsetzung,* Folge 25. Accessed at

poetladen.de/zwerenz-gerhard-sachsen25-uwe-johnson.htm

3. Uwe Johnson, will dated 22 March 1983, quoted from Heinrich Lübbert, *Der Streit um das Erbe des Schriftstellers Uwe Johnson,* Frankfurt: Suhrkamp Verlag, 1998, p. 38

4. Uwe Johnson, *Anniversaries* IV, p. 1384

5. A Leslie Willson, "'An unacknowledged humorist': Interview with Uwe Johnson, Sheerness-in-Kent, 20 April 1982", *Dimension: Contemporary German Arts and Letters,* Vol 15/3, 1982, p. 410

6. "Novelist had been dead for two weeks", *Sheerness Times Guardian,* 16 March 1984, p. 3

7. Ingeborg Bachmann, *Darkness Spoken: The Collected Poems,* translated and introduced by Peter Filkins, Brookline MA: Zephyry Press, 2006, p. 617

8. Matthias Bormuth, *Die Verunglückten: Bachmann, Johnson, Meinhof, Améry,* Berlin: Berenberg Verlag, 2019

9. Eberhard Fahlke, "Auf der Suche nach 'Inselgeschichten'", in Uwe Johnson, *Inselgeschichten,* Frankfurt am Main: Suhrkamp, 1995, p. 175

10. Uwe Johnson, letter to Hans Joachim Schädlich, 3 October 1976, quoted in *Inselgeschichten,* p. 17

11. Uwe Johnson, "Conversation on the Novel, Its Uses & Dangers, Recent Degenerations, Indignation of the Audience etc.", typescript dated February 1972, Uwe Johnson Archive, University of Rostock, UJA/H/000918

12. "Motorboater Rescued after Circling Sheppey", *Yachting Monthly,* 28 April 2010

Part I: The Writer Who Became a Reef

1. Reading Uwe Johnson in Kent, 1970–3

1. Gordon E. Cherry & Penny Leith, *Holford: A Study in Architecture, Planning and Civic Design,* London and New York: Alexandrine Press, 1986, p. 203

2. Ibid.

3. Edward Hyams, *The Last Poor Man,* London: Longmans, Green and Co., 1966, p. 124

4. The lecturer, Ian Gregor, certainly understood that Forster's injunction, which came with the more interesting rider "Live in fragments no longer", was actually Margaret Schlegel's way of hoping for a passionate rapport with her husband to be, the desiccated businessman Henry Wilcox — a context that may not have been grasped by students who hadn't quite made it to chapter 22 of the novel.

5. Uwe Johnson, *Speculations about Jakob* [1959] (trans. Ursule Molinaro), New York & London: Grove Press, 1963

6. D. J. Enright, "Make it Hard", *New Statesman,* 6 September 1963, p. 290

7. Uwe Johnson, "Preface" in *Das Neue Fenster: Selections from Contemporary German Literature*, New York: Harcourt, Brace & World, 1967, p. viii

8. Ibid., p. vii

9. Paul Celan, "Speech on the Occasion of Receiving the Literature Prize of the Free Hanseatic City of Bremen", *Selected Poems and Prose* (trans. John Felstiner), New York & London: Norton, 2001, p. 395

10. Ibid., p. 396

11. Ilse Aichinger, "Dover", *Bad Words: Selected Short Prose* (trans. Uljana Wolfe and Christian Hawkey), London, New York & Calcutta: Seagull Books, 2018, p. 103

12. *Speculations,* p. 222

13. Ibid.

14. Romain Rolland, "An Open Letter to Gerhart Hauptman" (29 August 1914), in *Above the Battle* (trans. G.K. Ogden), London: Allen &Unwin, 1916, p. 19

15. Reinhard Baumgart, "Laudatory Address, Georg-Büchner-Prize, 1971", Deutsch Akademie für Sprache und Dichtung, www. deutscheakademie.de/en/ awards/georg-buechner-preis/ uwe-johnson/laudatio

16. *Speculations,* p. 224

17. Ibid., p. 221

18. Ibid., p. 209

19. Ibid., p. 147. For a critical discussion of the publisher Siegfried Unseld's post-war reservations about the treatment of nature — wrongly identified as "bordering on Blood and Soil" — in the first novel Johnson's wrote, the posthumously published *Ingrid*

Babererende, see Hugh Ridley, "'Nach einem Lenz, der sich nur halb entfaltet': Aspects of the Reception of Uwe Jonson's *Ingrid Babendererde*", in D. Byrnes et al, *German Reunification and the Legacy of GDR Literature and Culture*, Leiden & Boston: Brill, 2018, pp. 114–5

20. Ibid., p. 147
21. Ibid., p. 152
22. Ernst Bloch, *The Principle of Hope*, Vol. 3, Cambridge, Mass.: MIT Press, 1986, p. 1376
23. Roger Taylor, *Art, An Enemy of the People*, Hassocks: Harvester, 1978
24. Roger Taylor, "The Marxist theory of Art", *Radical Philosophy* 5, Summer 1973, pp. 29-30
25. Ibid., pp. 29-34
26. Alicja Iwánska, "Without Art", *British Journal of Aesthetics*, Vol. 11, No. 4, Autumn 1971, p. 406 Quoted in Taylor, "The Marxist theory of Art", p. 31
27. Ibid., p. 410
28. Stewart Home, "Art is like Cancer: Interview with Roger Taylor" [2004], www.stewarthomesociety.org/pol/Taylor.htm. See also Roger Taylor, *Beyond Art: What Art is and Might Become if Freed from Cultural Elitism*, Hassocks: Harvester, 1981

2. On the Move but Nobody's Refugee

1. Dietrich Orlow, *The Nazi Party 1919–1945: A Complete History*, New York: Enigma, 2008, pp. 405–6
2. Christopher Browning, *The Origins of the Final Solution: The Evolution of Nazi Jewish Policy September 1939–March 1942*, London: Arrow Books, 2005, p. 189
3. Max Frisch, *From the Berlin Journal* (trans. Wieland Hoban), London & Calcutta: Seagull Books, 2017, p. 163
4. Tomasz Blusiewicz, "Überseehafen Rostock: East Germany's Window to the World under Stasi Watch, 1961–1989" in Center for European Studies, Modern Europe Workshop, Harvard University; 2016. Blusiewicz is quoting from Christian Halbrock, *Freiheit heisst die Angst Verlieren: Verweigerung,*

Widerstand und Opposition in der DDR: Der Ostseebezirk Rostock, Göttingen: Vandenhoeck & Ruprecht, 2014, p. 51

5. Uwe Johnson, "About Myself: Acceptance Speech upon Induction into the German Academy for Language and Literature" ["Ich über mich: vorstellung bei der Aufname in die Deutsche Akademie für Sprache und Dichtung"] (trans. Damion Searls), Darmstadt, 11 November 1977, *Zeit Online,* 11 November 1977

6. Christa Wolf, *City of Angels or, The Overcoat of Dr Freud* (trans. Damion Searls), New York: Farrar, Straus and Giroux, 2010, p. 221

7. Victor Klemperer, diary entry for 17 August 1945, *The Lesser Evil: The Diaries of Victor Klemperer 1945–54,* London: Phoenix, 2004, p. 40

8. Gary L. Baker, *Understanding Uwe Johnson,* Columbia: University of South Carolina Press, 1999, p. 18

9. Uwe Johnson, *Anniversaries* II, pp. 968–9

10. "About Myself"

11. Dorothea Dornhoff, "The Inconsequence of Doubt: Intellectuals and the Discourse on Socialist Unity", in Michael Geyer (ed.), *The Power of Intellectuals in Contemporary Germany,* University of Chicago Press, 2001, footnote 38, p. 86

12. Peter Nicolaisen, "Faulkner and Southern History: A View from Germany", *Southern Cultures,* Vol. 4, No. 4, 1998, p. 34

13. Ibid., 40

14. Katja Leuchtenberger, *Uwe Johnson,* Berlin: Suhrkamp, 2010, p. 22

15. Harry Gilroy, "Author Who Left East Germany", *New York Times,* 4 December 1966, p. 171

16. "Now, sailing on the Thames, nigh its mouth, of fair days, when the wind is favorable for inward bound craft, the stranger will sometimes see processions of vessels, all of similar size and rig, stretching for miles and miles, like a long string of horses tied two and two to a rope and driven to market. These are colliers going to London with coal" (Herman Melville, *Israel Potter: His Fifty Years of Exile* [1855], New York & London: Penguin, 2008, p. 114).

17. Stephen Parker, *Bertolt Brecht: A Literary Life,* London: Bloomsbury, 2015, p. 541

18. *Speculations,* p. 161

19. Ibid., p. 221

20. Jean-Louis De Rambures, "Uwe Johnson, de l'Allemagne de l'Est aux États-Unis", *Le Monde*, 3 December 1971, p. 24

21. "Author Who Left East Germany", p. 171

22. Leuchtenberger, *Uwe Johnson*, p. 26.

23. Colin Riordan, "Reifeprüfung 1961: Uwe Johnson and the Cold War", in Rhys W. Williams et al (eds.), *German Writers and the Cold War 1945–61*, Manchester: Manchester University Press, 1992, p. 210

3. The Border: The Distance: The Difference

1. This label is said to have been coined in 1962 by the literary reviewer Gunter Blocker. See Deborah L. Horzen, "Past Meets Present in Uwe Johnson's *Jahrestage* and the *New York Times*", PhD dissertation, University of Florida, 1996, p. 6. The translator Damion Searls suggests that this cliché would be more accurately rendered into English as "the voice of divided Germany", since the word "poet", unlike the German "Dichter", implies someone who writes poetry rather than prose. See his "On Uwe Johnson: Poet of Both Germany's", *Paris Review* online, 15 October 2018 https://www.theparisreview. org/blog/2018/10/15/on-uwe-johnson-poet-of-both-germanys/

2. *Fire in the Phoenix* (presented by Richard Mayne), BBC Radio 3, 29 October 1979

3. De Rambures, "Uwe Johnson, de L'Allemagne de l'Est aux États-Unis"

4. Uwe Johnson, *The Third Book about Achim* (trans. Ursule Molinaro), London: Cape, 1968, p. 236

5. Ibid., p. 4

6. Ibid., p. 230

7. Ibid., p. 3

8. Anthony Bailey, *Along the Edge of the Forest: An Iron Curtain Journey*, New York: Random House, 1983, p. 6

9. Uwe Johnson, *Ich wollte keine Frage ausgelassen haben: Gespräche mit Fluchthelfern*, Frankfurt am Main: Suhrkamp, 2010

10. *Speculations*, p. 214

11. Jean Baudrillard, "Review of Uwe Johnson's *The Border:*

Toward the Seventh Spring of the German Democratic Republic." This review of the French translation of *Speculations About Jacob,* was first published as "Uwe Johnson: La Frontière" in *Les Temps Modernes*, 199 (1962), pp. 1094–1107. Thomas Kemple's translation is included in Gary Genosko (ed.), *The Uncollected Baudrillard*, New York: Sage, 2001

12. Uwe Johnson, "Berlin, Border of a Divided World", *Evergreen Review*, 5 (1961), pp.18–25

13. Uwe Johnson, "Berliner Stadtbahn *(veraltet)*", 1961, in *Berliner Sachen*, Frankfurt:

Suhrkamp, 1975, p. 9. Here quoted from Damion Searls' translation, "Berlin Transit"

14. Maurice Blanchot, "Berlin [1964]", *MLN*, 1099:3, April 1994, pp.345–64

15. Ibid., p. 348

16. Ibid., p. 352

17. Ibid., p. 354

18. Uwe Johnson, *An Absence* (trans. Richard & Clara Winston), London: Cape, 1969, p. 23

19. Ibid., p. 17

20. Ibid., p. 18

21. *The Third Book about Achim,* p. 231

22. Ibid., p. 233

23. *An Absence,* p. 28

4. Praise and Denunciation: A Headache for All Zealots

1. Joachim Remak, "Germany in Fact and Fiction", *Harpers Monthly*, August 1967, pp. 94–6

2. John Updike, "Two Points on a Descending Curve", *New Yorker,* 7 January 1967, p. 91

3. *Choice*, April 1967, Vol. No., 2, p. 165

4. Donald Heiney, *Christian Science Monitor*, 27 April 1967

5. M. J. Lasky, "Review of *Speculations about Jakob*", *New York Times Book Review*, 14 April 1963

6. "Review of Uwe Johnson's *The Border*"

7. Manfred Wekwerth, Letter to Helene Weigel, 25 May 1964. Quoted in Erdmut Wizisla, "Private or Public? The Bertolt Brecht Archive as an Object of Desire", L. Bradley & K Leeder (eds.) *Edinburgh German Yearbook 5: Brecht and the GDR: Politics, Culture, Posterity*, Camden House, 2011, p. 106

8. "Die Verteidigung Sachsens und warum Karl May die Indianer liebte"

9. "Conversation on the Novel, Its Uses & Dangers, Recent Degenerations, Indignation of the Audience etc."

10. Ernst Bloch, who had been forced into retirement in 1957, stayed in the West after the Berlin Wall was built in 1961. Hans Mayer crossed over in 1963, after enduring years of condemnation and pressure for refusing the orthodoxies of Ulbricht's Stalinist regime. See Dorothea Dornhoff, "the Inconsequence of Doubt: Intellectuals and the Discourse on Socialist Unity", in Michael Geyer (ed.), *The Power of Intellectuals in Contemporary Germany*, University of Chicago Press, 2001, pp. 59–87

11. "Reifeprüfung 1961", p. 214

12. *Berlin Wall*, BBC Radio 4, 13 August 1981

13. "Mauerschau" (Walter Busse), "Johnson", *Der Speigel*, 50/1961, 6 December 1961

14. *Third Book About Achim*, p. 229. Johnson also looks back on Brentano and his accusations in *Begleitumstände: Frankfurter Vorlesungen*, Frankfurt am Main: Suhrkamp, pp. 204–5

15. "About Myself"

16. "Reifeprüfung 1961", p. 216

17. *Begleitumstände*, pp. 206–51. The thoroughly damned "Senator McKesten" appears on p. 231

18. Eberhard Fahlke, "*Ich überlege mir die Geschichte*": *Uwe Johnson im Gespräch*, Frankfurt/Main: Suhrkamp, 1988, p. 244. Quoted in K. Fickert, "Martin Walser's Portrait of Uwe Johnson", *International Fiction Review*, 22, p. 5

19. *An Absence*, p. 44

20. Ibid., pp. 53–4

5. New York City: Beginning Anniversaries

1. "Author Who Left East Germany", p. 171

2. "Faulkner and Southern History: A View from Germany", pp. 31–44

3. *Understanding Uwe Johnson*, p. 6

4. *Anniversaries* IV, p. 1637

5. Bernd Neumann, *Uwe Johnson*, Hamburg: Europäiche Verlagsanstalt, 1994, p. 599

6. Pawel Monat with John Dille, *Spy in the U.S.*, New York: Berkley Medallion, 1963

7. *Anniversaries* II, p. 495

8. Michael Hamburger, "Uwe Johnson: A Friendship", *Grand Street,* Vol. 4, No. 3 (Spring, 1985), pp. 112 & 110

9. *Begleitumstände*, pp. 425–6

10. *Understanding Uwe Johnson,* pp. 116–7

11. Uwe Johnson interview with Dieter Zimmer, quoted in Mark Boulby, *Uwe Johnson,* NY: Ungar, 1974, p. 98

12. *Understanding Uwe Johnson,* p. 117

13. Jurgen Habermas, *The Structural Transformation of the Public Sphere: An Enquiry into a Category of Bourgeois Society* [1962] (trans. Thomas Burger), Cambridge, Mass.: MIT Press, 1989

14. Nicholas Dames, Departures and Returns, *N +1,* 5 June 2020. https://nplusonemag.com/online-only/online-only/departures-and-returns/

15. *Anniversaries* II, pp. 596–7

16. *Anniversaries* I, p. 3

17. Ibid., p. 14

18. Ibid., p. 15

19. *Anniversaries* II, p. 526

20. Ibid., p. 731

21. Ibid., p. 732

22. Ibid., p. 734

23. Ibid., p. 735

24. Pierre Mertens, *Uwe Johnson, Le Scripteur de Mur,* Arles: Actes Sud, 1989, p.31

25. Osborne, Peter and Charles, Matthew, "Walter Benjamin", *The Stanford Encyclopaedia of Philosophy* (Fall 2015 Edition), Edward N. Zalta (ed.), https://plato.stanford.edu/archives/fall2015/entries/benjamin/.

26. *Understanding Uwe Johnson,* p. 143

27. Phylis Meras, "Talk with Uwe Johnson", *New York Times Book Review,* 72, No. 17, 1967, p. 43 Quoted from K. J. Fickert, "Ambiguity and Style: A Study of Uwe Johnson's "Osterwasser", *International Fiction Review,* 9, No. 1, 1982, p. 21

28. *Anniversaries,* I, p. 703

29. *Anniversaries* II p. 683

30. Ibid., p. 703

31. Richard Stern, "Penned In", *Critical Inquiry,* 13. 1 (Autumn 1986), p. 26

6. Leaving Berlin

1. Uwe Johnson, "How to Explain Berlin to a Newcoming Child", *Berlin Sachen,* Frankfurt: Suhrkamp, 1975, p. 102

2. Ibid., 104

3. *Anniversaries* II, pp. 690 & 697

4. Uwe Johnson, "Concerning an Attitude of Protesting", Cecil Woolf & John Bagguley (eds.), *Authors Take Sides on Vietnam*, London: Peter Owen, 1967, pp. 108–9

5. Illustration 6. In R. Wizisla (ed.), *"Liebes Fritzchen" "Lieber Groß-Uwe": Uwe Johnson — Fritz J. Raddatz, Der Briefwechsel*, Frankfurt am Main: Suhrkamp, 2006, pp 168–9

6. From Fritz Raddatz's autobiography *Unruhestifter* (The Troublemaker), http://www.spiegel.de/kultur/literatur/fritz-j-raddatz-hauptsache-irgendein-licht-faellt-auf-ihn-a-431479.html See also Gianna Zocco, "Disturbing the Peace of 'Two Not So Very Different' Countries: James Baldwin and Fritz Raddatz", *James Baldwin Review*, Vol. 3, 2017, p. 94

7. "Uwe Johnson: A Friendship", p. 112

8. Claire Hamburger, informal note written for the author and the BBC radio producer John Goudie in 2016

9. "Uwe Johnson: A Friendship, p. 113

10. Ibid., pp. 113, 117 & 110

11. Ibid., p. 115

12. *From the Berlin Journal*, p. 19

13. Ibid., 147

14. "Die Verteidigung Sachsens und warum Karl May die Indianer liebte"

15. *From the Berlin Journal*, p. 103

16. Ibid.

17. Ibid., p. 156

18. Ibid., p. 148-9

19. Jack London in *John Barleycorn, or Alcoholic Memoirs*, quoted in Donald Newlove, *Those Drinking Days: Myself and Other Writers*, London: Junction Books, 1981, p. 133

20. Ibid., p. 60

21. Ibid., p. 62

22. Max Frisch, *Montauk* (trans. Geoffrey Skelton) [1976], Portland & Brooklyn: Tin House Books, 2016, p. 200

23. *Uwe Johnson*, p. 12

24. Kurt Fickert, *Neither Left Nor Right: The Politics of Individualism in Uwe Johnson's Work*, New York: Lang, 1987, p. 121

25. *Anniversaries* IV, p. 1533

Part II The Island: Modernity's Mudbank

7. 1974: Looking Out from Bellevue Road

1. Cecily Brown, interviewed in *FT Weekend Magazine*, 11/12 April 2020, p. 28

2. Annie Ernaux, *The Years*, tr. Alison L. Strayer, London: Fitzcarraldo Editions, 2008. p. 109

3. Hansard, HC Deb 04 March 1980 vol 980 cc 237

4. Built in the 1820s as part of the Canterbury and Whitstable Railway, the Tyler Hill tunnel is now Grade II* listed and described by Historic England as "the world's first modern railway tunnel on the first passenger steam railway". The long disused tunnel collapsed under the university's Cornwallis Building on 11 July 1974

5. Geoffrey Goodman, "Lord Scanlon of Davyhulme", *Guardian*, 28 Jan 2004

6. E.P. Thompson, "Sir, Writing by Candlelight", *New Society*, 24 December 1970, reprinted in *Writing by Candlelight*, London: Merlin, 1980, p. 39

7. Dominic Sandbrook, "The Day Britain Lost Its Soul: How Decimalisation Signalled the Demise of a Proudly Independent Nation", *Daily Mail*, 31 January 2011

8. "Terribly Seventies", *Times*, 4 Nov 1978, p. 8

9. Andy Beckett, *When the Lights Went Out: Britain in the Seventies*, London: Faber, 2009, p. 246

10. Douglas Oliver, *The Harmless Building*, Brighton: Ferry Press, 1973, p. 80

11. Michael Walters, "Smiling Through — 1975 Style", *Belfast Telegraph*, 3 September 1975, p. 8

12. "Janet Street-Porter's Whitstable", *Daily Telegraph*, 5 September 2012

13. Gordon Leak, "Now for Battle of Britain II", *Newcastle Journal*, 19 September 1974, p. 8

14. Somerset Maugham, *Of Human Bondage* [1915], London: Vintage, 2000, p. 23

15. Quoted by Ben Bridges, http://www.benbridges.co.uk/riders8.html. Accessed 29 February 2016

16. Dave Taylor, "Origins… In Law and Social Change", "Memories of the Sir William Nottidge", www.simplywhitstable.com. (Accessed 20 April 2016)

17. Carol Sims, "Life as Pupil and Governor at 60-year-old Showcase School", *Whitstable Times,* 3 September 2012

18. Bridget Cherry, Charles O'Brien & Nikolaus Pevsner, *London 5: East, The Buildings of England,* Yale University Press, 2005, P. 208

19. William Holford, "Letter to the Editor", *The Times,* 12 June 1962

20. Reyner Banham, "Introduction" in *The Architecture of Yorke Rosenberg Mardall 1944/1972,* London: Lund Humphries, 1972, p. 4. The documents connected to the Sir William Nottidge School are here quoted from the YRM holdings at the RIBA Archive held at the Victoria and Albert Museum, London.

8. Neither St. Helena nor Hong Kong

1. Hear, for example, "What's Wrong With Me" on Wild Billy Childish and the Chatham Singers, *Kings of the Medway Delta,* Damaged Goods, 2020

2. George Hammond, "The Beginner's Guide to Buying an Island", *Financial Times,* 32 March 2019, p. 1

3. https://www.youtube.com/watch?v=XaKZqMxdS7k

4. Paul Moody, "England's Dreaming", *Classic Rock,* No 161, August 2011 http://officialcaravan.co.uk/blog/2011/07/20/classicrock magazinejuly2011/ Accessed on 29 February 2016

5. "Circular Tours for Saturday Cyclists: Sheppey", *London Daily News,* 23 September 1899, p. 7

6. Thomas Ingoldsby, "Blue Dolphin: A Legend of Sheppey", *The Ingoldsby Legends or Mirth and Marvels,* London: Richard Bentley, 1858, p. 70

7. Paul Wilkinson & Griselda Cann Mussett, *Beowulf in Kent,* Faversham: The Faversham Society, 1998

8. Billy Bragg, personal communication, 2016

9. Henry T.A. Turmine ("Native of Minster"), *Rambles in the Island of Sheppy; containing many interesting and amusing incidents that cannot be found in any history or description hitherto published,* London: A. K. Newman and Co., 1843

10. This was the verdict of Sir Charles Igglesden, in the Sheppey volume (Vol. 28) of

his series, "A Saunter Through Kent, with Pen and Pencil", reviewed in the *Folkestone, Hythe, Sandgate & Cheriton Herald,* 9 June 1934, p. 17. Original quotation, Igglesden p. 10

11. Father Paul Hennessy SS, "With Faith in Mind", *Sheerness Times Guardian,* July 15 1983, p. 4

12. From "An Island That is All the World", in Douglas Oliver, *Three Variations on the Theme of Harm: Selected Poetry and Prose,* London: Paladin, 1990, p. 66

13. Iain Sinclair, *Downriver,* London: Paladin, 1991, p. 400–1. For Sinclair's source here— "I have no religion at all. I have only tentative belief that the good persists in time" — see Douglas Oliver's "An island That is All the World", in *Three Variations on the Theme of Harm,* p. 88

14. This phrase is noted by Claire Wallace, a sociologist who researched on Sheppey in the early Eighties. See Claire Wallace, *For Richer For Poorer: Growing Up in and out of Work,* London: Tavistock, 1987, p. 14

15. "The confirmation of the surrender of Buonaparte...", *Hull Packet,* 25 July 1815, p. 3

16. "Friday, April 16, 1941", *Sligo Journal,* 16 April 1841, p. 2

17. *Israel Potter: His Fifty Years of Exile,* p. 150

18. "Jeremy Clarkson Dubs Isle of Sheppey a Huge Caravan Site", *Guardian,* 12 January 2012

19. R.E. Pahl, *Divisions of Labour,* Oxford: Blackwell, 1984, p. 189

20. Mertens, *Uwe Johnson: Le Scripteur de Mur,* pp. 55, 65 & 47

21. Ryszard Kapuściński, *The Shadow of the Sun,* New York: Vintage International, 2001, p. 171

22. Uwe Johnson letter to Joachim and Ingelore Menzhausen, 2 September 1978, *Inselgeschichten,* p. 104

9. Shellness: A Point with Three Warnings

1. "Melancholy Catastrophe, *Kentish Mercury,* 14 December 1844, p. 1

2. Ron Wood of Leysdown, cited from Sue Nicholson, "The Isle of Sheppey: What Lies ahead for the Holiday Island", *BBC News,* 28 September 2012. https://www.bbc.co.uk/news/uk-england-kent-19715522

3. Charles Igglesden, *A Saunter Through Kent with Pen and Pencil*, Vol. XXVIII, Kent, Ashford, 1934, p. 96.

4. "120 More Acres for Swale nature reserve", *Sheerness Times Guardian*, 1 April 1977, p. 1

5. "Natural History: Flamingo in the Isle of Sheppey", *Bedfordshire Times and Independent*, 23 August 1873, p. 3. I owe my knowledge of this rare bird to E.H. Gillham & R..C. Homes, *The Birds of the North Kent Marshes*, London: Collings, 1950, p. 159

6. "Flamingo in the Isle of Sheppey", *The Field: The County Gentleman's Newspaper*, 16 August 1873, p. 190

7. "Elmley", *Kentish Gazette*, 19 August 1873, p. 3

8. F.W. Smalley, "William Bernhard Tegetmeier", *British Birds*, Vol. VI., No. 8, 1913, p. 249

9. W.B. Tegetmeier, "The Destruction of Rare Birds", *The Field*, 23 August 1873, p. 205

10. *Anniversaries* I, p. 428

11. Seamus Heaney, in conversation with the author, "Night Waves", BBC Radio Three, 16 September 1998

12. Daniel Defoe, *A Tour thro' the whole island of Great Britain*, London: S.Birt et. A., 1748, vol. I. p. 153

13. "Agriculture. The Farming of Kent. [From a Prize essay by Mr G. Buckland], Isle of Sheppy", *Canterbury Journal, Kentish Times and Farmer's Gazette*, 21 February 1846, p. 1

14. John R. Stilgoe, *Shallow Water Dictionary: A Grounding in Estuary English*, Cambridge, Mass.: Exact Change, 1990

15. "Sheerness", *The Times*, 27 August 1938, p. 6. An article making use of the same *Kent Herald* report appeared under the heading "Sheerness" in the London *Standard*, 27 August 1839, p. 1

16. We may register a certain pattern here. The English papers would note how many of Sheppey's agricultural labourers fled for a better life in America, often assisted by children who had already made the journey, and their departure would be reported in Irish papers, thereby informing those who might travel to Kent to replace them. See, for example, *Sligo Champion*, 3 November 1851, p. 3

17. See, for example, "Southampton Bridge", *Hampshire Advertiser*, 6 June 1840, p. 2

18. Robert Macfarlane, *The Lost Words,* London: Penguin, 2017

19. Danny Boyle, "Kent Youth Tsar Paris Brown Stands Down", *KentOnline,* 9 April 2013

20. *Anniversaries* II, p. 430

21. Maugham, *Of Human Bondage,* p. 90

22. "The Rev. Peter Blagdon-Gamlen", *The Times,* 26 April 2004

23. 45 See his letter about "Protestant" removal of "idolatrous" items from St Wulframs in Friskney, where "Romanistic priests" had been accused of "Setting themselves up as 'little Hitlers'" ("Church 'Dictators'", *Lincolnshire Standard and Boston Guardian,* 11 December 1943, p. 8), in *Grantham Journal,* 23 December 1943, p. 2. Also his letter, "Corpus Christie", *Grantham Journal,* 26 June 1942, p. 6. For the one against the "Stab-in-the-back" exercised by the apparently anti-Catholic Church Union over this controversy, see "Confession to a Pillow'", *Skegness Standard,* 15 December 1943, p. 4

24. "Above All Else, He was Sincere", *Evesham Standard & West Midland Observer,* 22 January 1954, p. 3

25. "Move against MPs Who Oppose Death Penalty", *Birmingham Daily Post,* 21 October 1957, p. 25

26. "Vicar Urges Church to run Football Pools", *Birmingham Daily Post,* 14 September 1959, p. 3

27. "No Curate for 'High' Church", *Birmingham Daily Post,* 5 January 1961, p. 18

28. "Vicar Urges Trade Union for Clergy", *Birmingham Daily Post,* 16 May 1961, p. 5

29. "This Man of God Preaches a Dangerous Gospel", *The People,* 25 November 1962, p. 16

30. "Vicar: 'Stem Flow of Immigrants'", *Acton Gazette,* 16 May 1968, p. 1

31. "Vicar Agrees with Every Word", *Acton Gazette,* 30 May 1968, p. 4

32. "Prophet, Pastor, Pilgrim", *Birmingham Daily Post,* 11 April 1968, p. 25

33. "Provost on 'Lesson' of Dr King", *Coventry Evening Telegraph,* 29 April 1968, p. 8

34. "Sheppey Vicar in Propaganda Shock", *Sheerness Times Guardian,* 11 July 1975, p. 1

35. "Letter from R.E. Hargrave of Minster", *Sheerness Times Guardian,* 18 July 1975, p. 4

36. Max Frisch, *From the Berlin Journal*, tr. Wieland Hoban, London 2017, p. 115.
37. *Anniversaries*, II, pp. 831–2
38. "Ukip councillor's...", *BBC News,* 5 April 2019. https://www.bbc.co.uk/news/uk-england-kent-47824367. See also https://www.kentonline.co.uk/sheerness/news/kent-ukip-councillor-has-miracle-escape-from-sri-lanka-bombing-203692/

10. Coincidence on England's Baltic Shore

1. Pawel Starzac, "Unsettled Ground: Revisiting the Lost Sites of the Yugoslav Wars", *The Calvert Journal*, 24 March 2016. http://www.calvertjournal.com/features/show/5761/landscape-memory-yugoslav-war-camps. See also: https://www.lensculture.com/articles/pawel-starzec-makeshift

2. Bernd Neumann, "Neues über Uwe Johnson: Besichtigung der Stätten seiner Jugend in Mecklenburg — Begegnung mit Augenzeugen der Anfange eines Schriftstellers in der DDR: Landfahrt in ein mythisches Wasserreich", *Die Zeit*, 12 August 1988

3. *Anniversaries* IV, p. 1303

4. *A Saunter Through Kent, with Pen and Pencil*, "The Isle of Sheppey", p. 17

5. "Notice to Mariners. Buoyage of the East Swale", *Public Ledger and Daily Advertiser,* 15 February 1827, p. 1

6. "Model Motor Tours. Week-Ends in England. XVII — The Isle of Sheppey", *Pall Mall Gazette,* 12 July 1913, p. 5

7. Lorna Bradbury, "A Writer's Life: Nicola Barker", *Daily Telegraph*, 29 August 2004

8. "The £100,000 Prize", *Irish Independent,* 6 May 2000, p. 39

9. As Barker once told the *Scotsman*, "What's disastrous about me as a writer is that my work doesn't say I am like you ... I'm not writing books that reach out to people. My books make people feel like someone has thrown a porcupine fish at them, they've caught it, and gone arrrgggh! Then they go, "look at his funny little face". "Interview: Nicola Barker, Author", *Scotsman,* 9 May 2010

10. Jimmy Hobbs Jnr., "Kent Cobs", *The Stage*, 3 September 1964, p. 5

11. "Harris, Roderick Harry and Harris, Paul Jones: murder

of Eric Percival Nichols and aggravated burglary..." National Archives (NA), DPP 2/5617

12. Herman Melville, "The Encantadas" [1854], in *Billy Budd, Sailor and Other Stories*, London: Penguin, 1972, pp. 182–3

13. "Bomb Land Delay", *Sheerness Times Guardian*, 11 July 1975, p. 3

14. "The End of Stan's Dream Home", *Sheerness Times Guardian*, 20 January 1978, p. 10

15. *Anniversaries* IV, p. 1609

16. "Hitler in Motor Smash", *Derry Journal*, 16 August 1933, p. 5

17. "Girl in Boat Shot Dead by Midland Plane", *Birmingham Daily Gazette*, 16 August 1933, p. 1

18. *Anniversaries* I, p. 428

19. "Girls in Rowing Boat Fired on by Plane", *Belfast Telegraph*, 16 August 1933, p. 4

20. "Misadventure Verdict on Shot Girl", *Leeds Mercury*, 18 August, 1933, p. 1

21. "The Sheppey Aeroplane Shooting Fatality", *Dover Express*, 25 August 1933, p. 14

22. "Firing at Island Goes On: Protests from All over Country", *Daily Herald*, 17 August 1933, p. 9

23. *A Saunter Through Kent, with Pen and Pencil*, "The Isle of Sheppey", p. 96

11. Leysdown: The "On-Sea" Scenario

1. Michael McGillen, "Historical Passages and Scenes of Transport in Uwe Johnson's *Jahrestage*", *The Germanic Review: Literature, Culture, Theory*, Vol. 93, 2018, Issue 2, pp. 130–54.

2. *Colonel Stephens: A Celebration: A Brief Outline of the Life of Holman Fred Stephens and His Light Railways*, Tenterden: Kent & East Sussex Railway, nd., p. 1.

For a report of the opening see "Light Railway at Sheppey", *St James's Gazette,* 1 August 1901, p. 8. By October, the South Eastern and Chatham and Dover Railway Company would announce that they would not be running trains as far as Leysdown between 31 October and 1 April, explaining that there were "only a coastguard station and a few houses" in the village of Leysdown. It was anticipated however, that this would change: "it is thought that the new line will be the means of developing this part of Sheppey Isle". "Sheerness", *Canterbury Journal, Kentish Times and Farmers' Gazette,* 12 October 1901, p. 8

3. "This Morning's News", *London Daily News,* 16 January 1901, p. 5

4. "Sheerness", *Canterbury Journal,* 12 October 1901, p. 8

5. Arthur Mee, *The King's England: Kent: The Gateway of England and its Great Possessions,* London: Hodder & Stoughton, 1936. p. 7

6. Georgina M. Taylor, *"Ground for Common Action": Violet McNaughton's Agrarian Feminism and the Origins of the Farm Women's Movement in Canada,* doctoral dissertation, Carleton University (Ottawa), 1997

7. Michel Welton, "Violet McNaughton: The Mighty Mite Reformer from Saskatchewan", *Counterpunch,* 28 March 2018. https://www.counterpunch. org/2018/03/28/violet-mcnaughton-the-mighty-mite-reformer-from-saskatchewan/

8. "Leysdown Chalets Over-Rated", *East Kent Gazette,* 28 February 1958, p. 6

9. "Hell Broke Loose", *East Kent Gazette,* 22 July 1960, p. 1

10. "Pen and Hinks", *East Kent Gazette,* 27 April 1962, p. 4

11. *Sheerness Times Guardian,* 31 December 1971

12. "When Betting Office was like 'Black Hole of Calcutta'", *East Kent Gazette,* 22 October 1964, p. 5

13. Sinclair, *Downriver,* p. 398

14. Ibid., 397

15. Jonathan Meades, "Last Resort" [1991], *Museum Without Walls,* London: Unbound, 2012, pp. 264–5

16. Tim Moore, "Iceland's Wild Westfjords", *Financial Times,* 8 February 2020

17. Monstrous events do occasionally confirm Leysdown's reputation as a sink of human degradation — as in the case of the "body on the beach", discovered by a metal detectorist on the sands just north of Leysdown in August 2013. This victim was not killed by an aerial machine-gunner, nor by an accident at sea such as the nationally lamented "Leysdown tragedy" of 4 August 1912, when an accompanying adult and eight boy scouts from Southwark drowned after a squall overturned the sailing cutter bringing them round Warden

Point for their summer camp
at Leysdown. Gary Pocock,
who was thirty-four years old
and from Dagenham, had been
taken out drinking, lured to the
beach and then savagely beaten
with baseball bats by three men
who claimed that he had been
molesting a teenage girl. Pocock
was left on the beach north
of Leysdown with fatal head
injuries and, as the BBC chose
to put it, "Stripped from the
waist down".

18. *Anniversaries* I, p. 408.
19. Rosanna Greenstreet, "Q&A:
    Eddie Marsan", *Guardian*,
    2 August 2014. https://
    www.theguardian.com/
    lifeandstyle/2014/aug/02/
    eddie-marsan-interview
20. Andy Gray, "Leysdown Holiday
    inspired Isle of Sheppey's
    Place in Pop Music History",
    Kent Online, 22 February
    2015. www.kentonline.co.uk/
    sheerness/news/kent-beach-
    inspiration-for-holiday-32168/
21. See the comments on the
    Leysdown page of Trevor
    Edwards' Sheppey website:
    http://www.pbase.com/
    luckytrev/leysdown&page=all.
    See also R.E. Pahl, *Divisions
    of Labour*, London: Blackwell,
    1984, p. 179
22. "Variety Ousts Bingo on
    Kent Coast", *The Stage and*

Television Today, 17 July 1962,
p. 5
23. W. Somerset Maugham,
    Sheppey: A Play in Three Acts,
    London: Heinemann, 1933, p.
    17
24. Ibid., p. 22
25. Ibid., pp. 60 & 74
26. Ibid., p. 72
27. Ibid., p. 99
28. Ibid., p. 112
29. *Divisions of Labour*, p. 167
30. Ibid., footnote 4, p. 154
31. Dennis Hardy & Colin Ward,
    *Arcadia for All: The Legacy
    of a Makeshift Landscape*,
    London and New York:
    Mansell, 1984, p. vii
32. Ibid., pp. 116–20
33. *East London Observer*, 21
    September 1901, p. 2
34. *Daily Express*, 5 August 1903,
    quoted in *Arcadia for All*, 132
35. *London Evening Standard*, 5
    June 1903, p. 12
36. *Morning Leader*, 20 June, 1903.
    Cited in *Divisions of Labour*,
    p. 179
37. "The Success of Minster-on-
    Sea", *East London Observer*, 28
    May 1904, p. 6
38. "The Manor of Leysdown",
    London Daily News, 17 April
    1903, p. 4
39. "Shellness-on-Sea and
    Leysdown Estate, Isle of
    Sheppey, Kent", *Whitstable*

Times and Herne Bay Herald,
25 July 1903, p. 4

40. "A New Seaside Resort", *Surrey Comet*, 29 August 1903, p. 8
41. *Divisions of Labour*, p. 179
42. "Leysdown", *Sheerness Times*, 1 August 1903
43. "A New Seaside Resort: Important Land Sale", *Surrey Comet*, 29 August 1903, p. 8
44. "Land Sale — Shellness-on-Sea", *Hendon & Finchley Times*, 9 December 1904, p. 7
45. "Leysdown"
46. "Land Sale of Shellness-on-Sea and Leysdown Estate", *Sheerness Times*, 29 August 1903
47. "Land Sale on the Minster Cliffs Estate", *Sheerness Times and General Advertiser*, 18 July 1908
48. "The "Finding" of Whitstable", *Canterbury Journal, Kentish*

Times and Farmers" Gazette,
14 October 1911, p. 3

49. *The King's England*, p. 317
50. Post-war local guide book, quoted in *Arcadia for All*, p. 134
51. Sheila M. Judge, "The Manor of Borstal Hall", reproduced from a copy of *Scapeia* dated 2000, The Sheppey History Page (https://www.facebook.com/groups/26905273 6530087/permalink/ 1111947778907241/)
52. Adrian Waller, interview with George Ramuz, *Sheerness Times Guardian*, 16 June 1961
53. *Arcadia for All*, p. 136
54. "Flexible Planning" (editorial), *Sheerness Times Guardian*, 3 December 1971, p. 4
55. *Arcadia for All*, p. 134

12. Rolls Without Royce: Leysdown Aloft.

1. "A Ballooning Adventurer", *Western Daily Press*, 6 April 1909, p. 9
2. "Missing Balloonist", *Yorkshire Evening Post*, 14 April 1909, p. 4. See also "The Danger of Inexperience", *The Field*, 24 April 1909, p. 60
3. "Missing Balloon", *London Daily News*, 16 April 1909, p. 5
4. "Lost Aeronaut", *Leicester Daily Post*, 22April 1909, p. 2
5. "The Missing Balloonist", *Woolwich Gazette*, 30 April 1909, p. 3
6. "Hydroplane on the Thames", *Derby Daily Telegraph*, 6 April 1909, p. 2. Also "Trial of M. Bellamy's Hydroplane", *Belfast News-Letter*, 21 January 1907

7. "An Exciting Descent: French Balloonist's Adventure in Buckinghamshire", *Leominster News,* 9 April 1909, p. 3

8. "Trial of M. Bellamy's Hydroplane", *Manchester Courier and Lancashire General Advertiser,* 21 January 1907, p. 8

9. "Aero Club's New Ground", *Eastern Daily Press,* 23 April 1909, p. 5

10. "Art of Flying", *Daily Telegraph and Courier,* 8 April 1909, p. 5

11. "Early British Flights", *Flight,* 21 February 1929, pp 132–3

12. *The King's England*

13. "Art of Flying", *Daily Telegraph and Courier,* 8 April 1909, p. 5

14. "Flights from the Isle of Sheppey", *Daily Telegraph & Courier,* 8 April 1909, p. 5

15. *Divisions of Labour,* p. 179

16. "Muscular Aviatics", *Belfast Telegraph,* 4 May 1909, p. 4

17. H. Massac Buist, "Aeroplaning in England: suitability of Shellbeach", *Morning Post,* 18 May 1909, p. 4

18. David Edgerton, *England and the Aeroplane: An Essay on a Militant and Technological Nation,* Basingstoke: MacMillan, 1991, p. 3

19. "Flying at the Aero Club's Grounds, Shellbeach", *Flight,* 6 November 1909, p. 703

20. "Shellbeach Still Expanding", *Flight,* 14 August 1909, p. 493

21. "Getting Ready at Shellbeach", *Flight,* 15 May 1909, p. 275

22. "Britain and the Airship", *Nottingham Evening Post,* 11 March 1909, p. 5

23. "Women's National Health Association", *Irish Times,* 23 April 1909, p. 9

24. "Aero Club Flight Grounds at Shellbeach", *Flight,* 6 March 1909, p. 135. Towards the end of June that year, the Unionist MP for Yarmouth, Sir Arthur Fell, would ask the First Lord of the Admiralty for reassurance that he would not dispose of coastguard stations on government land around the east coast, without at first establishing that "they cannot possibly be required in the near future for the erection of garages for dirigibles or aeroplanes, and that the buildings would not be of advantage for the accommodation of men in charge of them"."Our London Letter", *Belfast News-Letter,* 26 June 1909, p. 5

25. Griffith Brewer, "Aeronautics: Aviation at Sheppey", *The Field,* 17 April 1909, p. 678. On Brewer and his work as a patent agent in the new field of aeronautics, see Jonathan

Hopwood-Lewis, "Griffith Brewer, 'The Wright brothers' Boswell': Patent Management and the British Aviation Industry, 1903–1914, *Studies in History and Philosophy of Science* Part A, Vol. 44, Issue 2, June 2013, pp. 256–268

26. "Aero Club of the United Kingdom: Official Notices to Members", *Flight*, 5 June 1909, p. 330

27. "Flying Grounds at Shellbeach", *Flight*, 11 September 1909, p. 558

28. "The Marquis De St Mars", *Tatler*, 26 January 1910, p.11

29. "The Costliest Kite on Earth", *Pearson's Weekly*, 30 September 1909, p. 11

30. "He won £1,000 for a Two-Minute Flight", *Lincolnshire Echo*, 12 May 1941, p. 2

31. *Manchester Courier and Lancashire General Advertiser*, 1 March 1909, p. 7

32. "Brothers Wright at Shellbeach", *Flight*, 8 May 1909, p. 267

33. "Aeronautics", *The Times*, 5 May 1909, p. 10

34. Vernon Lee, "French Roads", *The Tower of Mirrors and Other Essays on the Spirit of Places*, London: John Lane, 1914, p. 14

35. "Fifteen Miles Flight", *Manchester Courier and Lancashire General Advertiser*, 23 December 1909, p. 10

36. "The Brothers Wright", *Manchester Courier and Lancashire Advertiser*, 5 May 1909, p. 7

37. "The Disappearance of Mr Cecil Grace", *Illustrated Sporting and Dramatic News*, 31 December 1910, p. 36

38. "Cecil Grace does 67-Minute Flight", *Dundee Courier*, 3 September 1910, p. 6. See also "Mr Cecil Grace", *Dublin Daily Press*, 20 August 1910, p. 10

39. "Seen over North Sea", *Sunderland Daily Echo and Shipping Gazette*, 23 December 1910, p. 8

40. "Flying up the Thames", *Exeter and Plymouth Gazette*, 12 August 1912, p. 6

41. "Automatic Stability, Lieut. Dunne Flies with His Hand Off the Lever", *London Daily News*, 27 December 1910, p. 5

42. "Flying Machine Races", *Morning Post*, 17 August 1909, p. 3

43. "From the British Flying Grounds", *Flight*, 13 May 1911, p. 422

44. "Aviation News of the Week", *Flight*, 19 February, 1910, p. 128

45. "British Flyers at Sheppey", *Flight*, 30 April 1910, p. 331

46. "The Conquest of the Air", *Dundee Courier,* 14 August 1913, p. 8

47. Quoted in "The War in the Air", *Globe,* 13 August 1913, p. 7

48. "The New Aeroplane", *Leeds Mercury,* 19 August 1913, p. 5

49. "The Atholl Aeroplane", *Perthshire Advertiser,* 12 May 1909, p. 2

50. Ibid., 4

51. "Remarkable Experiments", *Leicester Daily Post,* 27 December 1910, p. 1. For the Aeronautical Society's "Official Report" on the flights, written by Orville Wright and Griffith Brewer, see "The Dunne Biplane: Report on Automatic Stability Trials", *The Aeronautical Journal,* 1 January 1911, p. 15

52. J.W. Dunne, *An Experiment with Time,* London: Faber, 1934, p. 95

53. "The Conquest of the Air", *Dundee Courier,* 14 August 1913, p. 8

54. E.T. Wooldridge, "Early Flying Wings (1870–1920)", http://www.century-of-flight.net/Aviation%20history/flying%20wings/Early%20Flying%20Wings.htm

55. "Lieut. Dunne's Aeroplane", *Flight,* 8 May 1909, p. 268

56. "Interesting Interview", *Dublin Daily Express,* 6 May 1909, p. 5

57. Edgerton, *England and the Aeroplane,* p. 4

58. "From the British Flying Grounds", *Flight,* 12 August, 1911, p. 696

59. "Interesting Interview", p. 5. See also "The Atholl Aeroplane", *Perthshire Advertiser,* 12 May 1909, p. 2

60. "The Command of the Air; Story of the Dunne Aeroplane", *Northern Whig,* 15 August 1913, p. 10.

61. Ibid.,, p. 10

62. "The Dunne-Huntington Machine", *Flight,* 1 March 1913, p. 254

63. "The New Aeroplane", *Leeds Mercury,* 19 August 1913, p. 5

64. *An Experiment with Time,* p. 60

65. "From the British Flying Grounds", *Flight,* 13 May 1911, p. 422

66. "Royal Navy Find 61 Bombs in Two-Day Sweep at Nudist Beach", *Daily Telegraph,* 12 October 2011 https://www.telegraph.co.uk/news/newstopics/howaboutthat/8823835/Royal-Navy-finds-61-bombs-in-two-day-sweep-at-nudist-beach.html

13. Two Ways Down to the Sea: The Trade Union Baron and the Suffragists

1. Quoted from Natural England's review of the Warden Point Site of Special Scientific Interest and Geological Conservation Review Site, "Sheppey Cliffs and Foreshore", at https://designatedsites. naturalengland.org.uk/ PDFsForWeb/Citation/ 1001313.pdf

2. Gerald Mayr, discussing the discovery of the skull of a Dasornis in "Dasornis Emuinus: Prehistoric Goose was the Size of a Small Plane and had Bony Teeth", *Science 2.0*, 26 September 2008, https://www.science20. com/news_releases/dasornis_ emuinus_prehistoric_goose_ was_the_size_of_a_small_ plane_and_had_bony_teeth. See also Gerald Mayr, "A Skull of the Giant Bony-Toothed Bird Dasornis (Aves: Pelagornithidae), from the Lower Eocene of the Isle of Sheppey", *Paleontology*, Vol. 51, Part 5, 2008, pp. 1107–1116

3. "Landslip near Minster, Isle of Sheppey, Kent", *Illustrated London News*, 16 July 1870, p. 65

4. "Landslip in Sheppey", *Buckingham Advertiser and Free Press*, 2 June 1883, p. 6

5. "Serious Landslip at Sheppey, *Western Daily Press*, 17 April 1890, p. 3

6. "General News", *Wrexham Advertiser*, 14 April 1894, p. 7

7. "Our Wasting Shores", *Gravesend Reporter, North Kent and South Essex Advertiser*, 16 May 1896, p. 8

8. "Circular Tours for Saturday Cyclists: Sheppey", *London Daily News*, 23 September 1899, p. 7

9. "Tours Round London — Sheerness", *Sheerness Times & General Advertiser*, 6 Seotember 1873, p. 5

10. John R. Broughton recalled his memories for "WW2 People's War: An Archive of World War Two Memories", *BBC*, 23 December 2003, https:// www.bbc.co.uk/history/ ww2peopleswar/stories/19/ a2155619.shtml

11. Ben Dakin, the Western London Area Padre, provided this summary of the principles members should try to follow while speaking to Toc H's group in Iver, South Buckinghamshire, in

November 1938. See "The Main Resolution", *Uxbridge & West Drayton Gazette,* 25 November 1938, p. 10

12. "To Introduce Toc H", *Northern Whig,* 16 February 1924, p. 6
13. "Toc H", *West Sussex Gazette,* 22 February 1934, p. 7
14. J. Vennari, "How were the Transalpine Redemptorists Founded?: An Interview with Father Michael Mary", www.archconfraternity. com>News"Int...
15. "Warden Residents Live in Fear after Cliff Slide", *Sheerness Times Guardian,* 26 November, 1971, p. 1
16. "Pay Increase", *Aberdeen Evening Express,* 8 May 1970, p. 7
17. "Scanlon is Rapped for Intervening in Ford Strike", *Daily Mirror,* 4 May 197, p. 11
18. "Confusion at TUC", *Birmingham Daily Post,* 8 September 1971, p. 1
19. "Golf goes Yugoslav", *Birmingham Daily Post,* 21 December 1971, p. 3
20. "Now the Queen Knows about the Crumbling Cliffs", *Sheerness Times Guardian,* 8 November 1974, p. 7

21. Hansard, House of Commons, Vol. 633 13 December 2017
22. "Eastchurch Cliff Fall", BBC News, 31 May 2020. https://www.bbc.co.uk/news/uk-england-kent-52868241 See also "Home falls after cliff edge collapse on Isle of Sheppey", *Guardian,* 2 June 2020.
23. Alys Russell, "Suffrage in the Isle of Sheppey", *Common Cause,* 19 August, 1909, p. 243
24. K. Raleigh, letter, *Women's Franchise,* 2 September, 1909, pp. 752–3
25. "By One of Those suffragettes", "Our Suffrage Campaign", *Sheerness Times and General Advertiser,* 20 August 1910, p. 6
26. K. Raleigh, "Holiday Campaign in the Isle of Sheppey", *The Vote,* 27 August 1910, pp. 206–7
27. C. Despard, "A Holiday Message", *The Vote,* 27 August, 1910, p. 207
28. The Rambler, "Notes & Comments", *Sheerness Times and General Advertiser,* 15 August 1910, p. 6

Part III. The Five Towns of Sheerness: Definitely Not Berlin, New York or Rome

14. Moving In

1. Conversation with Inge Weber-Newth, April 2018

2. Roman Bucheli, "Rückkehr eines Verfemten", *Neue Zürcher Zeitung,* 17 October 2013 https://www.nzz.ch/feuilleton/buecher/rueckkehr-eines-verfemten-1.18168677

3. Colin Riordan, "Ein Sicheres Versteck": Uwe Johnson and England", John L. Flood, *Common Currency? Aspects of Anglo-German Literary Relations since 1945: London Symposium,* Stuttgart: Verlag Hans-Dieter Heinz, 1991, p. 88

4. *Anniversaries IV,* p. 1557

5. *Anniversaries I,* p. 262

6. *Anniversaries II,* p. 571

7. Ibid., p. 602

8. *Anniversaries I,* p. 12. In her earlier abridged translation of *Anniversaries I,* Leila Vennewitz translates Johnson's "Institut zur Pflege Britischen Brauchtums" as the "Institute for the Preservation of British Customs" (see Uwe Johnson, *Anniversaries: From the Life of Gesine Cresspahl,* New York and London: Harcourt Brace Jovanovich, 1974, p. 103). Damion Searls opts for the less backward-sounding "Institute for the Promotion of British Culture". Given the imaginary Institute's sealed windows and eighteenth-century paintings, as well as the worn arm chairs and snobbish staff who can't bear the visitors, I have followed Vennewitz here.

9. Eberhard Fahlke (ed.), *"Ich überlege mir die Geschichte..." Uwe Johnson in Gespräch,* Frankfurt am Main: Suhrkamp, 1988, p. 329.

10. Uwe Johnson, letter to Max Frisch, 14 August 1974, *Inselgeschichten,* pp. 63–69

11. Ilse Aichinger, "Dover", in *Bad Words,* p. 100

12. *Inselgeschichten,* pp. 65–9. Here as in other extracts from Johnson, words and phrases printed in bold appear in English in the original German texts.

13. Ibid., p. 70

14. Ibid., p. 144

15. Uwe Johnson, *Begleitumstände: Frankfurter Vorlesungen,* Frankfurt am Main: Suhrkamp, 1980, p. 72

16. Uwe Johnson, letter to Siegfried Unseld, 21 October 1974, in Eberhard Fahlke & Raimund Fellinger (eds.), *Uwe Johnson — Siegfried Unseld; Der Briefwechsel,* Frankfurt am Main: Suhrkamp, 1999, p. 841

17. Ibid.

18. Uwe Johnson, letter to Michael Hamburger, 19 December, 1974. In Michael Hamburger's archive, at the British Library

19. "Uwe Johnson: A Friendship", p. 119.

20. Uwe Johnson, letter to Fritz J. Raddatz, 11 February 1975, *"Liebes Fritzchen" „Lieber Groß-Uwe". Uwe Johnson — Fritz J. Raddatz, Der Briefwechsel,* p.170

21. "Uwe Johnson: A Friendship", p. 119

22. Quoted in Norbert Gstrein "Das Sheerness des Erzählens Dankesrede", in Carsten Gansel & Nicola Reidel (eds.), *Internationale Uwe-Johnson Forum,* Vol. 10, 2006, p. 165

23. Günter Kunert, *Ein englisches Tagebuch,* München: DTV, 1980, p. 31

24. Uwe Johnson, "Baume, Baume", *Inselgeschichten,* p. 54

25. Eberhard Fahlke, "Auf der Suche nach 'Inselgeschichten'", *Inselgeschichten,* p. 170.

26. Uwe Johnson letter to Hannah Arendt, 18 December 1974, *Inselgeschichten,* p. 75

27. "Uwe Johnson: A Friendship", p. 113

28. ""An Unacknowledged Humorist", p. 407

29. Anne Beresford, interviewed by the author for "A Secret Life: Uwe Johnson in Sheerness", Sunday Feature, BBC Radio Three, 19 April 2015. https://www.bbc.co.uk/programmes/b05qyjsr

30. "Uwe Johnson: A Friendship", p. 119

31. G.K. Chesterton, "The Inhumanity of Insurance", *Daily Herald,* 22 March 1913, p. 7

32. From the new verse that Dr Leslie Haden Guest reckoned should be added to "The Red Flag". Quoted in Mrs Snowden, *Through Bolshevik Russia,* London: Cassell, 1920, p. 180

33. *Anniversaries* IV, p. 1785.

34. These extracts are from *Anniversaries* III, pp. 1060–2

35. *Anniversaries* IV, p. 1223

36. Rev. W.F.C. Hargreaves in "Points from Letters", *The Times,* 7 September 1925, p. 8

15. Blue-Faced and Shivering: A New Town on England's Fatal Shore

1. Kurt Fickert, *Neither Left Nor Right: The Politics of Individualism in Uwe Johnson's Work*, New York: Lang, 1987, p. 121

2. Uwe Johnson letter to Hannah Arendt, 18 December 1974, *Inselgeschichten, p. 76*

3. Robert Goodsall, *The Widening Thames*, London: Constable, 1965, p. 229. Goodsall may have borrowed his phrase from an early Victorian source, in which the land in question is described as a "watery swamp or morass". See Henry T.A. Turmine, *Rambles in the Isle of Sheppey*, London: Newman & Co., 1843, p. 26

4. Mary Dobson, *Contours of Death and Disease in Early Modern England*, Oxford University Press, 2003

5. This phrase is used in an handwritten account, written in French by an unknown hand, on the flypapers of a copy of Leclerc's *Histoire de la Médecine* (1702). See Rudolph E. Siegel and F.N.L. Poynter, "Robert Talbor, Charles II, and Cinchona: A Contemporary Document", *Medical History*, 1962 Jan; 6 (1), pp. 82–5. Talbor is discussed as a "quack physician" in *Contours of Death and Disease in Early Modern England*, p. 295 and elsewhere.

6. "Malaria Among Fighting Men in Kent", *Globe*, 21 September 1917, p. 2. See also "Malaria in England", *Yorkshire Evening Post*, 21 September 1917, p. 5

7. Angus Macdonald, Major RAMC, "Report on indigenous Malaria and on Malaria Work performed in connection with the troops in England during the year 1918", Ronald Ross (ed.), *Observations on Malaria by Medical Officers and Others*, London: HMSO, 1919, p. 224

8. Ibid., p. 235

9. "Malaria Could Spread in Kent: Doctor Warns of Mosquito Menace", *Thanet Advertiser*, 20 May 1949, p. 4

10. The Medical Officer of Health for Sheerness, Dr W.N. Crichton wrote to P.G. Chute at the Ministry of Health's Malaria Laboratory, at Horton Hospital in Epsom on 8 July 1949. Chute replies on 15 July and again on 23 July. Chute's recommendation that Crichton consider spraying DDT on the saltmarsh grass as well

as the water behind the Ship on Shore was made in a letter dated 5 July 1950. London Metropolitan Archives, H22/HT/MTU/L/01/063

11. Uwe Johnson, letter to Alice and Dorothy Hensan, 13 January 1976, *Inselgeschichten,* p. 73

12. Alvin D. Coox, "The Dutch Invasion of England: 1667", *Military Affairs,* Vol. 13 No. 4 (Winter, 1949), p. 223

13. M. Oppenheim, "The Royal Dockyards", in William Page (ed.), *The Victoria History of the County of Kent,* Vol. II, London: St Catherine Press, 1926, p. 353

14. Ibid., p. 354.

15. *A Characterisation of Sheerness, Kent: Project Report",* produced by Ramboll Environ for Historic England, February 2016, p. 6

16. "The Dutch Invasion of England: 1667", p. 228

17. H.B. Wheatley (ed.), *The Diary of Samuel Pepys* M.A. F.R.S.,London: George Bell & Son, 1893, 11 June 1667. All further quotations from Pepys diary are from Project Gutenberg's digital version of Wheatley's edition at https://www.gutenberg.org/files/4200/4200-h/4200-h.htm

18. "328. Dutch Account of the Attack on the Thames, 1667" (Calendar of State Papers Domestic, 1667, pp. xxi–xxiii), in Andrew Browning (ed.), *English Historical Documents, 1660–1714,* London: Eyre & Spottiswoode, 1953, p. 835

19. Samuel Pepys, diary entry for 10 June 1667, quoted in "The Dutch Invasion of England: 1667", p. 228

20. Sir Arthur Bryant, *Samuel Pepys, the Man in the Making,* Cambridge University Press, 1939, p. 330

21. "328. Dutch account of the attack on the Thames, 1667". Johnson mentions the Dutch assessment of Sheppey to Hannah Arendt in his previously quoted letter of 18 December 1974.

22. Samuel Pepys, "Of the Arsenals for the Royal Navy in KENT", in *Camden's Britannia newly translated into English, with large additions and improvements, published by Edmund Gibson, of Queens-College in Oxford,* London: Printed by F. Collins, for A. Swalle, a the Unicorn at the West-end of St Paul's Church-yard, and A. & J. Churchil, at the Black Swan in Pater-noster-Row, 1695

23. Sir Thomas Hyde Page, *An account of the commencement and progress in sinking wells, at Sheerness, Harwich and Landguard Fort, for supplying those Dock-Yards and Garrisons with fresh water. To which is annexed, the Correspondence between the Master General of the Ordnance and the Commanding Engineer of those places, (sir Thomas Hyde Page) upon the subject, in the Years 1778,1781, and 1783*, London: Printed for John Stockdale, Piccadilly, 1797, p. 17

24. Ibid.

25. *Derby Mercury*, 9 September 1784, p. 2

26. "Opening of Sheerness Docks", *Cambridge Chronicle and Journal*, 12 September 1823, p. 4

27. Sir John Rennie, *Autobiography*, London: Spon, 1875 p. 164

28. "Canterbury, April 25", *Kentish Gazette*, 25 April 1815, p. 4

29. "The Confirmation of the Surrender of Buonaparte...", *Hull Packet*, 25 July 1815, p. 3

30. "Opening of the New Basins at Sheerness", *Public Ledger and Daily Advertiser*, 8 September 1823.

31. *Cambridge Chronicle and Journal*, 12 September 1823, p. 4. On the Lord Melville, see "Rise and Progress of Steam Navigation", *The Gentleman's Magazine*, Vol. 132, 1822, p. 161

32. W.R., "Trip to Sheerness", *Morning Chronicle*, 10 September 1827, p. 3

33. *Third Report from the Committee on the Laws Relating to Penitentiary Houses*, House of Commons 27 June 1812, p. 136

34. Ibid., p. 139

35. Ibid., p. 150

36. *Hampshire Chronicle*, 15 January 1816, p. 3

37. The thirty-year-old Roman Catholic William Coleman, who was about to be hanged for the murder of Thomas Jones, on board the Retribution hulk at Woolwich, used this phrase while protesting his innocence and the unreliability of the "convict witnesses" whose testimony had condemned him in March 1810. See *Kentish Weekly Post or Canterbury Journal*, 20 March 1810, p. 4.

38. For a report of fifty-five convicts from Sheerness said to have been embarked on the *Guildford* for New South Wales, together with forty-five from the hulks at Woolwich and one hundred from those at Portsmouth, see *Kentish Weekly Post or Canterbury Journal*, 13 August 1811, p. 4

39. Instructions from the Secretary of State's Office, to the said Superintendent, 23 August 1815, published in in *Two Reports of John Henry Capper, Esquire, Superintendent of the Several Ships and Vessels for the Confinement of Offenders under Sentence of Transportation (16 October 1815 & 26 January 1816)*, London: House of Commons, 1816, p. 10

40. *Christian Herald and Seaman's Magazine,* Vol. 4, New York: Caldwell, 1817, pp. 362–3

41. Ibid., p. 363

42. *Hampshire Chronicle,* 7 April 1823, p. 2

43. *Hampshire Chronicle,* 3 March 1823, p. 3

44. *The Journal of John Wesley,* Chicago: Moody Press, 1951, See p. 187 of the online version at: http://www.ccel.org/ccel/wesley/journal.htm

45. "Alterations at Sheerness", *Morning Post,* 15 October 1821, p. 2

46. "The Royal Dockyards", p. 359

47. John Newman, *Kent: North-East and East,* Buildings of England, New Haven and London: Yale University Press, 2013, p. 543

48. "The Royal Dockyards", p. 358

49. Uwe Johnson, letter to Lore and Joachim Menzhausen, 29 October 1980, *Inselgeschichten,* p. 81.

50. Peter Gurney, *Co-Operative Culture and the Politics of Consumption in England, 1870–1930,* Manchester University Press, 1996, p. 12

51. William Shrubsole, *A Plea in Favour of the Shipwrights belonging to the Royal Dock Yards Humbly Offering Reasons to the PUBLIC for an Addition to their PAY: With a Method to Effect it,* Rochester, 1770, p. 10

52. Ibid., pp. 9–10

53. Ibid., p. 16

54. W. Shrubsole, *Christian Memoirs in the Form of a New Pilgrimage to the Heavenly Jerusalem,* London: E. Baynes, 1807, pp. 7 & 4

55. Records of the Sun Insurance Office, London Metropolitan Archives, CLC/B/192/F/001/MS11936/passim

56. "The Mutiny at the Nore", *Sheerness Guardian,* 12 June 1869

57. "Alterations at Sheerness, p. 2

58. "Postscript", *Hampshire Chronicle,* 1 October 1827, p. 4

59. "Sheerness New County Court", *Maidstone Journal and Kentish Advertiser,* 11 May 1847, p. 3.

60. "Sanitary State of Sheerness", letter to the editor by

"Sanitarius", *London Daily News*, 28 December 1858, p. 7

61. "Marriages, Births, and Deaths", *Morning Post*, 4 August 1857, p. 7

62. "Sanitary State of Sheerness"

16. Fritz J. Raddatz's Perambulation

1. Uwe Johnson, letter to Fritz Raddatz, 14 May 1977, *Inselgeschichten*, p. 72.

2. August A. Daly, *The History of the Isle of Sheppey from the Roman Occupation to the Reign of his Most Gracious Majesty King Edward VII*, London: Simpkin, Marshall, Hamilton, Kent & Co., 1904, p. 268

3. *Hampshire Chronicle*, 17 January 1825, p. 4

4. William Cobbett, *Rural Rides*, ed. Pitt Cobbett, London: Reeves and Turner, 1886, p. 52

5. John Newman, *The Buildings of England, Kent: North-East and East*, New Haven and London: Yale University Press, 2013, p. 544

6. John Newman, *The Buildings of England; Kent: North East and East*, Harmondsworth: Penguin, 1969, p. 439

7. "Opening of a Conservative Club", *Whitstable Times and Herne Bay Herald*, 19 March 1887, p. 5

8. Ray Pahl, *Divisions of Labour*, p.166

9. Newman, *Kent: North East and East Kent*, pp. 106 & 439.

10. "Sheerness", *Kentish Gazette*, 18 August 1835. Also *Kentish Gazette*, 6 September 1836, p. 4

11. Simon Bradley, email to the author, 9 March 1918

12. *Hampshire Chronicle*, 23 April 1827, p. 1

13. "Hotel, at Banks Town, Sheerness — To be let", *Morning Post*, 11 June 1827, p. 1

14. "Sheerness", *Morning Post*, 19 January 1831, p. 3

15. *South Eastern Gazette*, 30 January 1827, p. 3

16. "An inhabitant of Sheerness", letter to the editor, *Maidstone Gazette and Kentish Courier*, 13 August 1933, p. 4

17. "Sheerness", *Kentish Gazette*, 3 September 1833, p. 3

18. "A Citizen of the World", *Kentish Gazette*, 10 September 1833, p. 3

19. "Sheerness", *Morning Post*, 20 September 1833, p. 3

20. *Rambles in the Isle of Sheppy,* p. 28

21. "Royal Hotel", *Kentish Independent,* 21 February 1863, p. 4

22. Four boys fined for robbing the garden of Mr Smithson of the Royal Hotel in "Sheerness", *Kentish Independent,* 11 September 1852, p. 3. A decade later, some twenty boys were found pillaging the garden, and three fined for beating up the gardener who confronted them. "Assault by Boys", *South Eastern Gazette,* 28 January 1862, p. 5

23. "Gravesend Mechanics' Institute", *Kentish Mercury,* 19 January 1839, p. 2

24. On 23 September 1854, the *Illustrated London News* reported that 1140 Russian prisoners captured by the Baltic fleet at the vanquished Russian fortress at Bomarsund on the Åland Islands, were being held at Sheerness on the prison ships Devonshire and Benbow prior to being moved to inland jails. Drawing by Robert Thomas Landells, held at the Royal Army Museum, NAM. 1976-10-2-1

25. See, for example, "Sheerness Local Board of Health",

Sheerness Guardian, 18 September 1860, p. 2

26. "Isle of Sheppy, Kent, Long Leasehold Property Producing a Gross Rental of £301 15s. per Annum", *Kentish Independent,* 4 October 1856, p. 1

27. The Admiralty dockyard remained one of the expanding "establishments" promising growth. Within a few years, however, the army garrison would also be enlarged and rebuilt. When completed in 1861, it would provide accommodation for at least one thousand men, while the casemented fort overlooking the Medway would, so Commander Scott R.N. assured a military and naval audience gathered in the garrison schoolroom, house forty one-hundred-pounder Armstrong guns capable of firing every kind of projectile — "solid, case, and grape shot as well as common diaphragms and Martin's liquid iron shells" — at any enemy ship trying to enter the Medway, *Kentish Gazette,* 22 October 1861

28. "Long Leaseholds, Marine Town, Sheerness", *Morning Advertiser,* 26 March 1857, p. 8

29. "Contemplated Increase of the Town of Sheerness", *Kentish*

Chronicle, 22 October 1859, p. 4. The fact that Berridge fought the case with a partner named Henry Bateman Jenkins may follow from the fact that Sir Henry Meux had been declared insane a year previously in 1858

30. "Opening of the Sittingbourne and Sheerness Railway", *Kentish Gazette*, 24 July 1860, p. 3

31. "Sheerness", *Kentish Gazette*, 22 October 1861, p. 6

32. *Melville & Co.'s Directory and Gazetteer of Kent*, London: F. R. Melville & Co., 1858, p. 226

33. "Thursday — Nisi Prius Court", *South Eastern Gazette*, 29 July 1856, p. 3

34. "Commission of Lunacy on Sir Henry Meux", *John Bull*, 12 June 1858, p. 14

35. "Local Board of Health", *Sittingbourne, Faversham and Sheerness Gazette*, 17 December 1859, p. 4

36. As explained in the editorial of the *Sheerness Times and General Advertiser*, 21 March 1868

37. "Sheerness", *Kentish Mercury*, 15 December 1849, p. 3

38. "The Chancery Ditch", *Globe*, 26 February 1864, p. 4.

39. "Past, Present and Future" letter to the editor, "The Local Board of Health", *East Kent Gazette*, 14 January 1860, p. 4

40. *Sittingbourne, Faversham and Sheerness Gazette*, 7 Jan 1860, p. 4

41. "Sheerness", *South Eastern Gazette*, 6 November 1860, p. 5

42. "Sheerness", *Kentish Gazette*, 16 October 1860, p. 3

43. "Meeting of the Sheerness Local Board of Health", *Kentish Gazette*, 18 October 1860, p. 3

44. "Testimonial to Lieut-Colonel Montagu", *East Kent Gazette*, 17 November 1860, p. 4

45. "Sheerness", *South Eastern Gazette*, 4 August 1863, p. 5

46. "Sheerness — The Chancery Suit", *South Eastern Gazette*, 30 October, 1860, p. 5.

47. "Sheerness", *Kentish Mercury*, 20 March 1852, p. 7

48. *Sheerness Guardian*, 28 November 1863

49. "Equity Courts — Jan. 16", *Morning Post*, 18 January 1864, p. 7

50. "Sheerness", *South Eastern Gazette*, 24 November 1863, p. 5

51. "Sheerness", *Guardian and East Kent Advertiser*, 3 January 1863

52. "Sheerness", *South Eastern Gazette*, 15 March 1864, p. 5

53. Editorial in *Sheerness Times and General Advertiser,* 22 February 1868

54. "Remarkable Divorce Case — Five Thousand Pounds Damages", *Herts Guardian, Agricultural Journal, and General Advertiser*, 27 December 1862, p. 2

55. "Court for Divorce and Matrimonial Cases", *Southern Reporter and Cork Examiner,* 23 December 1862, p. 4.

56. Ibid.

57. See the papers concerning the property and estate of Richard Berridge, London Metropolitan Archives, ACC/1406

17. Becoming "Sheerness-on-Sea": The Scramble for a Second Horse

1. John Newman, *Kent: North East and East,* Harmondsworth: Penguin, 1969, p, 440. For a less dismissive article, which also informs us that Sheerness had six cinemas in 1937, see Paul Smith, "A Picture Palace in Miniature: Recreating Sheerness's Lost Art Deco Gem", Art Deco Society, 30 Jan 1920. https://artdecosociety. uk/2020/01/30/a-picture-palace-in-miniature-recreating-sheernesss-lost-art-deco-gem/. For the cinema as it was in the late Eighties, see https://player. bfi.org.uk/free/film/watch-an-art-deco-cinema-in-sheerness-1988-online

2. John Newman, *Kent: North East and East,* 1968, p. 439

3. Raddatz had edited Tucholsky's collected works and Johnson joked that it would be annoying to stumble unawares upon a Kentish mountain range named after Tucholsky without knowing more about his visit. See his letter to Raddatz, 2 March 1976, in Erdmut Wizisla (ed.), *"Liebes Fritzchen" Lieber Groß-Uwe". Uwe Johnson — Fritz J. Raddatz, Der Briefwechsel,* Frankfurt" Suhrkamp, 2006, p. 202 (see also pp. 204 & 208)

4. "Sheppey — St Henry and St Elizabeth", *Taking Stock: Catholic Churches of England & Wales*, www.taking-stock. org.uk

5. Quoted in "Tipperary at the Crystal Palace", *Cork Examiner,* 3 September 1860, p. 4

6. "Militia Riot at Sheerness", *Lloyd's Weekly Newspaper,* 17 October 1858, p. 2

7. "Irish Militia Riots", *Yorkshire Gazette,* 16 October 1858, p. 11

8. "The Constitutional Force at Sheerness", *Chester Chronicle,* 23 October 1858, p. 2

9. "The Late Disturbances at Sheerness", *Dublin Evening Mail,* 5 November 1858, p. 4

10. *Cork Examiner,* 18 October 1858, p. 2

11. *Cork Examiner,* 3 November, 1858, p. 2

12. "The North-Cork Rifles", letter to *The Times,* reprinted in *Freeman's Journal,* 10 November 1858, p. 3

13. "Sheerness-on-Sea", *Whitstable Times and Herne Bay Herald,* 15 July 1882, p. 3

14. Newman, *Kent North East and East,* 1969, p. 440.

15. "Opening of a New Working Men's Club at Sheerness", *East Kent Gazette,* 15 July 1882, p. 8

16. *Naval & Military Gazette and Weekly Chronicle of United Service,* 23 February 1881, p. 8

17. *Sheerness Guardian and East Kent Advertiser,* 23 January 1858

18. *Sheerness Guardian,* 3 January 1863

19. "The Royal Dockyards", p. 359

20. *Autobiography,* p. 163

21. "Sheerness", *South Eastern Gazette,* 12 July 1833, p. 4

22. Commander Adolphus Slade, *A Few Words on Naval Construction and Naval Promotion,* London: Saunders and Otley, 1846, p. 3

23. Captain Sir Adolphus Slade, *Maritime States and Military Navies,* London: Ridgeway, 1859

24. "Dockyard Economy", *Spectator,* 12 November 1859, p. 12

25. J.M. Haas, *A Management Odyssey: The Royal Dockyards, 1714–1914,* Lanham, New York & London: University Press of America, 1994, p.100

26. *Report of the Commissioners Appointed to Enquire into the Control and Management of Her Majesty's Naval Yards, together with the Minutes of Evidence and Appendix,* London: Eyre and Spottiswoode, 1861, p. vi

27. "Sheerness Dockyard — Question", HC Deb 19 June 1865 vol. 180 c 469

28. Rear-Admiral S. K. Hall, C.B., speaking to a committee of the "principal" inhabitants of Sheerness on his retirement, *Sheerness Times,* 10 April 1869, p. 5

29. *A Management Odyssey,* p. 104

30. A.W. Marks (of 14 Edward Street, Sheerness), "Letter to the Editor", *Evening Standard,* September 15, 1869, p. 3

31. "Shall Sheerness Dockyard be Abolished?" *Sheerness Times and General Advertiser,* 18 April 1868, p. 4

32. "Sheerness", *Whitstable Times and Herne Bay Herald,* 26 March 1870, p. 3. The ongoing dismissals had already lead the *Manchester Evening News* to declare "it is further deemed probable that that establishment will eventually be closed altogether", 17 February 1870

33. "Is the Sheerness Dockyard to be Maintained?", *Sheerness Times and General Advertiser,* 11 July 1868, p. 1

34. Rear-Admiral S. K. Hall, C.B., *Sheerness Times,* 10 April 1869, p. 5

35. "A Good Word for Sheerness", *Sheerness Times,* 16 August 1873, p. 4

36. Ibid.

37. *Whitstable Times & Herne Bay Herald,* 13 September 1873

38. "Sheerness-on-Sea", *Sheerness Times,* 25 October 1873, p. 5

39. "A Good Word for Sheerness"

40. *Whitstable Times & Herne Bay Herald,* 22 July 1876

41. *Whitstable Times & Herne Bay Herald,* 10 July 1876

42. "The Swimming Bath", *Sheerness Times and General Advertiser,* 7 November 1874

43. *Whitstable Times & Herne Bay Herald,* 11 December 1875

18. "Black Tuesday": The Day the World Ended

1. Defence: Outline of Future Policy, 3rd draft, Presented by the Minister of Defence to Parliament by Command of Her Majesty, March 1957, London: HMSO, 1957, p. 11

2. "Royal Dockyards, Naval Air Establishments and Home Commands", HC Deb 18 February 1958 vol 582 cc1043

3. "Changes in Royal Naval Establishments, HL Deb 18 February 1958, vol. 207 cc775

4. "Navy Leaving Medway Towns", *Birmingham Evening Post,* 19 February 1958, p. 25

5. The full record of Shinwell's question is given as follows: "Is the hon. Gentleman aware

HL Deb 18 February 1958, vol. 227 cc775

that while we shall always applaud any effort on the part of Her Majesty's Government to reduce expenditure — which, by the way, is consistent with the policy of the Labour Party — we do not believe the Government have gone far enough and we shall welcome further steps in this desirable direction? Will he say whether, in promoting this new scheme of reduction in personnel and the like, the Government have taken appropriate measures to ensure that the men being displaced in various parts of the United Kingdom will be absorbed in other occupations?" HC Deb 18 February 1958 vol 582 cc1047

6. "Nothing Done for New Workless Yet", *Sheerness Times Guardian,* 21 February 1958, p. 1

7. *Sheerness Times Guardian,* 28 Feb 1960, p. 7

8. "Kent Labour Agent Loses Vote", *Kent & Sussex Courier,* Friday 7 September 1923, p. 3

9. "The Strikers' March Yesterday", *Dover Express,* 7 May 1926, p. 4

10. "Farmworkers Meeting at East Langdon", *Dover Express,* 7 June 1935, p. 13

11. "The Habituals", *Hartlepool Mail,* 2 April 1947, p. 1

12. "Protest Meeting Demands Retention of Sheerness Yard", *Sheerness Times Guardian,* 28 February, 1958, p. 3

13. "Miss Pat does her own Food Snoop", *Daily Herald,* 10 March 1954, p. 3

14. "Dockland Jeers a Woman Tory", *Daily Herald,* 24 February 1958, p. 5

15. "Mrs Olsen Angers Island", *Sheerness Times Guardian,* 28 February 1958, p. 3

16. "18 Hats", *Birmingham Daily Post,* 16 June 1964, p. 17

17. HC Deb 24 February 1958, vol. 583 c. 104.

18. Uwe Johnson, letter to Siegfried Unseld, 7 August 1976, *Uwe Johnson — Siegfried Unseld Der Briefwechsel,* p. 894

19. First Moves on the Afterlife: The Modernist Chair Comes to Sheerness

1. Uwe Johnson, "Welcome Back", letter to Lore and Joachim Menzhausen, 2 September 1978, *Inselgeschichten,* pp. 104–5

2. "Blue Town is Not Dead", *Sheerness Times Guardian*, 29 April 29 1960, p. 2

3. "Town is Lifeless…", *Sheerness Times Guardian*, 8 January 1960, p. 5

4. "Engineering Firm to Buy Dockyard", *Belfast Telegraph*, 26 June 1959, p. 1

5. "Mr Jack Cotton on Year of Great activity", *Birmingham Daily Post*, 27 October 1960, p. 27

6. "Mr Cotton's Interest in Sheerness", *Birmingham Daily Post*, 5 August 1961, p. 27

7. "Industrial Gamble Pays Off", *East Kent Gazette*, 28 April 1961, p. 11

8. "Development Plan Change for Island", *Sheerness Times Guardian*, 12 February 1960, p. 1

9. "New Industrialists Say 'Town has everything we have been seeking", *Sheerness Times Guardian*, April 22, 1960, p. 5

10. "Hundreds Will Get Jobs in Pye's Big Dockyard Factory", *Sheerness Times Guardian*, 15 January 1960, p. 1

11. *Sheerness Times Gurdian*, 14 July 1961, p. 5.

12. "Angry Yard Industrialist Gets Reply from Premier", *Sheerness Times Guardian*, 20 January 1961, p. 3

13. John Nurden, "The Revolutionary Car that Never Was", *Kent Evening Post,* 9 February 1982, p. 6

14. http://www.lathes.co.uk/murad/page3.html

15. http://www.lathes.co.uk/murad/index.html

16. Bel Austin, "Dream Machine Lies Rusting While Inventor Battles in the Courts", *Sheerness Times Guardian*, 23 March 1984, p. 5

17. http://www.lathes.co.uk/murad/page5.html. Composed in 1889, "The Red Flag" was sung in the House of Commons on 1 August 1945, but it is possible that Murad was also remembering the performance of 27 May 1976, when Labour MPs repeated the song, causing Michael Heseltine, then widely known as "Tarzan", to swing the mace over his head.

18. "He Coined Island's Publicity Slogan", *Sheerness Times Guardian*, 13 January 1961, p. 3

19. Email Mark Beswick, Archive Infomation Officer, Met Office National Meteorological Archive, Exeter, 13 October 2015

20. "Cigarette Sales Dropped", *Sheerness Times Guardian*, 23 March, 1962, p. 2

21. "New Year Prospects Good for More Island Industry",

Sheerness Times Guardian, 5 Jan, 1962, p. 1

22. "Fruit Trees Turned into Modern Furniture", *Sheerness Times Guardian*, 9 February, 1963, p. 3

23. "Another Firm for Sheerness", STG, 23 June 1961, p. 5

24. Noel Jordan, Letter to Ernest Race, 14 August 1945. Quoted in Hazel Conway, *Ernest Race*, London: Design Council, 1982

25. Ibid., p. 26

26. Ibid., p. 45

27. "Race's Open New Factory", *Sheerness Times Guardian*, 5 April 1962, p. 2

28. "Navy Yard Workers Now Make Race Furniture at Sheerness", *Bedding, Upholstery & Furniture*, May 1962

29. "Fruit Trees for Furniture", *Furniture Record*, February 1962

30. Gustaaf Johannes Renier, *The English: Are They Human?*

London: Williams & Norgate, 1931

31. "Navy Yard Workers Now Make Race Furniture at Sheerness"

32. *Ernest Race*, p. 66.

33. Ibid., p. 67

34. Gemma Joanna Mansi, *Socio-Historical Perspectives on Young Fatherhood: Exploration of Social Change on the Isle of Sheppey*, PhD dissertation, University of Greenwich, September 2013, p. 144.

35. *Ernest Race*, p. 66

36. The *Guardian*, 7 February 1962

37. Richard Carr, "The Award Winners Speak Out", *Design Journal 1966*, pp. 72–3

38. Uwe Johnson, "You see, Charles?", Letter to Walter Kempowski, 27 October 1980, *Inselgeschichten*, pp. 123–4

39. "Furniture by Charles Eames at the Museum of Modern Art", press release 27, April 17 1973, p. 3

Part IV. Culture: Three Island Encounters

20. All Praise to the Sheerness Times Guardian

1. "'An Unacknowledged Humorist'", p. 401

2. Uwe Johnson, *A Trip to Klagenfurt: In the Footsteps of Ingeborg Bachmann*

[1974] (trans. Damion Searls) Evanston: Northwest University Press, 2004, p. 4

3. Ibid., p. 26.

4. *Anniversaries* I, p. 63.

5. Ibid., p. 62

6. *Anniversaries* II, p. 445

7. *Anniversaries* I, p. 143

8. *Anniversaries* II, p. 441

9. *Anniversaries* I, p. 62

10. *Anniversaries* II, p. 525

11. *Anniversaries* I, p. 61

12. Ibid., p. 63

13. *Anniversaries* II, p. 443

14. *Anniversaries* I, p. 63

15. Uwe Johnson, Letter to Max Frisch, 18 December 1974, *Inselgeschichten*, p. 64

16. Uwe Johnson, Letter to Helen Wolff, 6 March 1979, *Inselgeschichten*, p. 141

17. "Auf der Suche nach 'Inselgeschichten'", p. 178

18. *The Structural Transformation of the Public Sphere*

19. "Sheerness County Court", *Kentish Gazette*, 23 April, 1861, p. 6

20. "Vice Chancellor's Court", *East Kent Gazette*, 26 December 1863, p. 5

21. "Sheerness Police Court", *East Kent Gazette*, 6 March 1869, p. 5

22. "The Alleged Libel at Sheerness", *Maidstone Journal and Kentish Advertiser*, 29 July 1872, p. 8

23. Walter Cole, "Reminiscences of the 'Sheerness Times'", *Sheerness Times Guardian*, 2 Febuary 1962, p. 4

24. Uwe Johnson, Letter to Burgel Zeeh, *Inselgeschichten*, p. 153

25. Uwe Johnson, Letter to Christa Wolf, 11 February 1983, *Inselgeschichten*, p. 154

26. *Sheerness Times Guardian*, 27 February 1976, p. 14

27. "I Want to be Loved — Rape Charge Man", *Sheerness Times Guardian*, 16 January 1976, p. 1

28. "Island Gymslip Mother's Scandal", *Sheerness Times Guardian*, 8 August 1975, p. 1

29. "500 Lose Jobs at Steelworks", *Birmingham Evening Post*, 17 August 1974, p. 3

30. "The Siege of Sheerness Steel", *Sheerness Times Guardian*, 20 Febuary 1980, p. 3

31. See the advertisement placed in the *Central Somerset Gazette*, 6 March 1980, p. 10

32. "Nurses in Revolt over Working Conditions", *Sheerness Times Guardian*, 22 August 1975, p. 12

33. *Inselgeschichten*, p. 153

34. In fact, the Sheppey NUT association was nervous of this decision and eventually withdrew it on the grounds that

the goodwill of its members had been taken too much for granted. By that time, however, the school had already decided not to leave the children locked out during the lunch break (*Sheerness Times Guardian*, 10 March 1978).

35. Ibid.

36. "With Faith in Mind", *Sheerness Times Guardian*, 9 September 1983, p. 4

37. "With Faith in Mind", *Sheerness Times Guardian*, 7 October 1983, p. 4

38. Rev. R.J. Cockrell, "With Faith in Mind", *Sheerness Times Guardian,* 28 October 1983, p. 4

39. Uwe Johnson, Letter to Christa Wolf, 11 February 1983, *Insel-Geschichten,* p. 154

40. *Sheerness Times Guardian,* 15 August 1975, p. 40. *Sheerness Times Guardian,* 22 August 1975, p. 12

41. "Your Zulus are Wonderful", *Sheerness Times Guardian,* 1 July 1977, p. 4.

42. "Carnival Crowds invade Sheppey", *East Kent Gazette,* 26 August 1960, p. 1

43. "Zulus Fight for Territory", *Sheerness Times Guardian,* 29 July 1977, p. 2

44. Uwe Johnson to Helen Wolff/ Harcourt Brace Jovanovich, 6 August 1979, Uwe Johnson- Archiv, University of Rostock, UJA/H/15246.

45. The "Sheppey Zulus" would survive considerably longer than the blackface performances of the enormously popular *Black and White Minstrel Show,* dropped from British television in 1978, and longer even than the "golly", removed from Robertson's jam jars in 2001. By the second decade of the twenty-first century, however, numbers were dwindling, funds were short, and the embattled "Zulus" were up against it on two further fronts. Their performances were increasingly constrained by "Health and Safety" regulations, which are said to have made it impossible for the "Zulus" to brandish their spears with customary vigour, or even to walk in the road without wearing High Viz jackets. Objections were also raised by people, including some islanders, who argued that the time for such egregiously racist displays was long gone. This would please the Conservative press, which reported on the challenges that eventually brought about the disbandment of the Sheppey Zulus in 2015. On

14 November 2015, the *Daily Telegraph* blamed "political correctness" combined with a "ferocious social media backlash". Some would express lingering regrets, including "grandmother Maggie Bowry", who on 13 September 2017 told the *Sun* it was "a crying shame" to see the end of "part of the island's heritage". There is, at the time of writing, still a Facebook page dedicated to the revival of the "Zulus" but volunteers appear to remain in short supply and news of the promised relaunch has not, so far as I know, been forthcoming.

46. "Mailbag Found on Beach at Sheerness", *Sheerness Times Guardian,* 6 September 1963, p. 1

47. "Large Drugs Haul from Banana Boat", *Sheerness Times Guardian,* 12 August 1977, p. 1

48. Boaden was planning to launch a new business in Blue Town, making fibreglass boats, garages and doors, and doing repairs too. See "Maori Tribesman Starts New Sheppey Business", *Sheerness Times Guardian,* 22 January 1960, p. 2

49. "John's Lonely Blue Town House Gets a Close Shave",

Sheerness Times Guardian, 2 May 1975, p. 8

50. "Exile barber who fled from Reds", *Sheerness Times Guardian,* 12 Feb 1960, p. 4

51. "Italian Attacked Policeman, Court Told", *Sheerness Times Guardian,* 2 May 1975, p. 1

52. "Resistance Memories Flood Back for Exiled Yugoslav", *Sheerness Times Guardian,* 15 November 1974, p. 12

53. George Bilainkin, "Frayed Temper May Endanger the World", interview with Bertrand Russell, printed in the *Yorkshire Observer*, 11 October 1956 and republished in Bertrand Russell and Andrew Bone, *The Collected Papers of Bertrand Russell, Volume 29: Détente or Destruction, 1955–57,* London: Routledge 2005, p. 353

54. "Father Fails in Appeal Against 'No Access to Daughter' Order", *Harrow Observer,* 25 December 1958, p. 7

55. "500 Told: Clean Up Stations", *Birmingham Daily Gazette,* 18 May 1950, p. 5

56. "Author's Friendship with Makarios", *Sheerness Times Guardian,* 12 August 1977, p. 6

57. *Kingston Gleaner,* 21 July 1980, p. 16

58. Bel Norris, "Beating Different Drums", *Sheerness Times Guardian,* 19 September 1975, p. 51

59. Interview with Curtis Pierre, https://whensteeltalks.ning.com/forum/topics/meet-curtis-pierre

60. Joseph "Reds" Perreira, *Living My Dreams,* Bloomington: AuthorHouse, 2011, pp. 22–3

61. Carole Contant, telephone conversation with the author, 25 April 1919.

62. Allen Whitnell, *The Rise and Fall of the Beat Groups in Sittingbourne,* Faversham Society, 2015.

63. "Contant Family Make Rainbows", *Sheerness Times Guardian,* 22 August 1975, p. 6

64. "Rainbow Band Steals Show", *Sheerness Times Guardian,* 26 December 1975, p. 27

65. "*Upstairs Downstairs* Brings Isle Memories of the 'Great War'", *Sheerness Times Guardian,* 24 January 1975, p. 4

66. "Did You Ever Visit the Puddin' Shop?", *Sheerness Times Guardian,* 21 March 1975, p. 4

67. *Whitstable Times and Herne Bay Herald,* 19 October 1895, p. 4

68. "Sheerness Police Court, Monday, before Mr. Gibson, Deputy Stipendiary Magistrate, "Throwing stones", *Guardian and East Kent Advertiser,* 8 July 1905

69. "From Our Files", *Sheerness Times Guardian,* 14 July 2005, p. 11

70. "Mr. Losel and Pier Tolls", *Sheerness Times,* 15 July 1905

71. 'Important Prosecution', *Bath Chronicle and Weekly Gazette,* 10 August 1905

72. 'Charge of Photographing Fortifications', *Whitstable Times and Herne Bay Herald,* 12 August 1905

73. Uwe Johnson, "Oh! You're a German?", *Inselgeschichten,* pp. 9-15

21. A Painter of Our Time

1. Uwe Johnson, Letter to Hannah Arendt, 18 December 1974, *Inselgeschichten,* p. 75

2. Uwe Johnson, Letter to Hann Trier, 24 February 1979, in *Hann Trier: Gemälde, Zeichnungen, Graphiken Retrospektive,* Köln: Kölnischer Kunstverein, 1979, p. 52

3. Bruce McCall, *The Last Dream-O-Rama: The Cars Detroit Forgot to Build 1950–1960*, New York: Crown, 2001

4. "Artist's work on show", *Sheerness Times Guardian*, 7 February 1964

5. Billy Childish, *Childish: Paintings of a Backwater Visionary*, London: The Aquarium, 2005

6. Uwe Johnson, letter to Max Frisch, 18 December 1974, *Inselgeschichten*, p. 68

7. *Anniversaries* III, p. 927

8. *Anniversaries* IV, p. 1239

9. *Two Views*, p. 10.

10. UJ letter to Hannah Arendt, 18 December 1974. *Inselgeschichten*, p. 76

11. Tilman Jens, *Unterwegs an den Ort wo die Toten sind: Auf der Such nach Uwe Johnson in Sheerness*, Munich: Piper, 1984, p. 58

12. Uwe Johnson, letter to Burgel Zeeh, 26 August 1982, *Inselgeschichten*, p. 82.

13. *Anniversaries* I, p. 44

14. Uwe Johnson, Postcard to Leila Vennewitz, 25 January 1971",*Ich überlege mir die Gerschicht*" p. 323

22. A Job for the Town Photographer

1. Uwe Johnson, Letter to Hann Trier, 24 February 1979, *Hann Trier: Gemälde, Zeichnungen, Graphiken Retrospektive*, p. 49

2. Uwe Johnson, Letter to Hann Trier, 11 January 1979, Ibid., p. 45

3. Mr Fred Warner would later blame the decision to sell rather than redevelop the site on "Sheppey's fading attraction as a holiday resort" compared with "places like the Isle of Wight"."Warner's site for Sale", *Sheerness Times Guardian*, 24 June 1983, p. 3

4. Margaret Loxton, *The Job*, London: Longman, 1977

5. Margaret Loxton, *Inside and Out*, London: Hutchinson & Co. (Spirals), 1979

6. Margaret Loxton, *The Dark Shadow*, London: Hutchinson & Co. (Spirals), 1981

7. George Poule, email to the author, 25 November 2015

Part V. Society: "I Don't Want to Get Personal"

23. Becoming "Charlie"

1. Jeremy Thornton, *Praise and Applause: Meyrick Road Hall Sunday School and Theatre, A History*, Sheerness: Terrestial and Universal Publications UK, n.d. p. 15

2. Newman (1969), p. 439

3. "School to Come Down", *Sheerness Times Guardian*, 16 May 1975, p. 1

4. Bel Norris, "The Tech School Makes Way for Other Things", *Sheerness Times Guardian*, 15 August 1975, p. 35

5. In 1978, the building would be listed Grade II for conservation together with the Catholic Church of St Henry and St Elizabeth.

6. "Relief as Blight Notice is Removed", *Sheerness Times Guardian*, 10 January 1975, p. 1

7. "Marine Town is Well Worth Saving", *Sheerness Times Guardian*, 17 December 1976

8. "Council Offers Bath and Basin Grants", *Sheerness Times Guardian*, 30 April 1976, p. 12

9. *Inselgeschichten*, p. 142

10. Ian Lambeth, email to the author, 20 May 2015. Mr Lambeth got in touch after hearing my BBC Radio 3 documentary, *A Secret Life: Uwe Johnson in Sheerness*. Accessible at: https://www.bbc.co.uk/programmes/b05qyjsr

11. Uwe Johnson, Letter to Lore and Joachim Menzhausen, 2 September 1978, *Inselgeschichten*, p. 107

12. *Inselgeschichten*, p. 80

13. Uwe Johnson, Letter to Helen Wolff, 6 March 1979, *Inselgeschichten*, p. 142

14. Ibid., p. 141

15. UJ letter to Burgel Zeeh, 4 April 1979, *Inselgeschichten*, p. 111

16. Tilman Jens, *Unterwegs an den Ort wo die Toten sind: Auf der Suche nach Uwe Johnson in Sheerness,* München & Zürich: Piper, 1984, p. 29

17. Günter Kunert, "Ein Fremdling", in R. Berbig & E. Wizisla (eds.), *"Wo Ich Her Bin..."*, *Uwe Johnson in der DDR*, Berlin: Kontext, 1993, p. 129

18. *Inselgeschichten*, p. 129

19. "Uwe Johnson: A Friendship", p. 110

20. *Unterwegs an den Ort wo die Toten sind*, p. 27

21. She wasn't to know that Johnson understood quite a lot about the bombing of Coventry by 450 German planes on 14 November 1940, or that in *Anniversaries* II he had weighed that destruction ("there was a cathedral there too") against the firestorm that the RAF created over St Mary's Church in Lübeck on 28–9 March 1942 (*Anniversaries* II, p. 757)

22. *Unterwegs an den Ort wo die Toten sind*, pp. 109 & 113

23. Ibid., p. 8. See also photographic insert, pp. 32–3

24. Uwe Johnson, Letter to Walter Kempowski, 3 August 1981, *Inselgeschichten*, pp. 135–6

25. Uwe Johnson, "Unfreiwillige Reise", *Inselgeschichten*, p. 102

26. *The Rise and Fall of the Beat Groups in Sittingbourne*

27. Telephone conversation with Bel Austin (formerly Norris), 3 October 2019

28. "A Trip Down Memory Lane", *Sheerness Times Guardian*, 4 October 1974, p. 4

29. *Sheerness Times Guardian*, 28 February 1975, p. 2

30. *Sheerness Times Guardian*, 5 November 1976

31. Uwe Johnson, Letter to Helen Ritzenfeld, 20 December 19 75, *Inselgeschichten*, pp. 150–1

32. Uwe Johnson, Letter to Alice and Dorothy Hensan, 15 September 1978, *Inselgeschichten*, pp. 153–4

33. "Publican Nominated for a National Title", *Sheppey Gazette and North-East Kent Times*, 28 December 1978, p. 1

34. *Inselgeschichten*, pp. 129–131

35. *Inselgeschichten*, p. 102.

36. Uwe Johnson, Letter to Antonia and Felix Landgraf, 31 October 1982, *Inselgeschichten*, p. 132

37. Uwe Johnson, Letter to Burgel Zeeh, 4 April 1979, *Inselgeschichten*, p. 111

38. Ibid.

39. Letter to Antonia and Felix Landgraf, *Inselgeschichten*, p. 132

24. Sheerness as "Moral Utopia"

1. Uwe Johnson, "Ein Vorbild", first published in *Literaturmagazin* 10, February 1979. Reprinted in *Inselgeschichten*, pp. 12–15

2. *Inselgeschichten*, pp. 17–18

3. Johnson read about this initially in the *Sittingbourne, Sheppey and Faversham Evening Post* (11 December 1974, p. 1) and later in the *Sheerness Times Guardian,* which reported the Harris brothers were facing murder charges (21 Febuary 1975) and noted the sentence on 25 July 1975

4. Mia Dolan, *The Gift: The Story of an Ordinary Woman's Extraordinary Power,* London: Element, 2003

5. "The Psychic Keeping up Fergie's Spirit", *Daily Mail*, 11 August 2010

6. N. Tertulian, "Lukács' Ontology", in Tom Rockmore (ed.), *Lukács Today: Essays in Marxist Philosophy,* Dordrecht: Reidel, 2012, p. 265

7. *Bertolt Brecht's Me-ti: Book of Interventions in the Flow of Things,* edited and translated by Antony Tatlow, London: Bloomsbury, 2016,

8. Ibid. For a description of Johnson's edition see Tatlow's "Introduction", Ibid., p. 13

9. Ibid., pp. 125 & 127. See also Jost Hermand, "Brecht on Utopia", *Minnesota Review,* No. 6. Spring 1976, pp. 102–4

10. Theodore Roszak, *Where the Wasteland Ends: Politics and Transcendence in Post-Industrial Society,* London: Faber, 1973, p. 465

11. Martin Cockerham, "Old boot wine", Spirogyra, *Bells Boots and Shambles,* Polydor, 1974

12. Marshall Sahlins' *Stone Age Economics* (London: Tavistock, 1972) is acknowledged in R.E. Pahl, *Divisions of Labour,* p. 12. For the Unabomber's critique of Sahlins' idea of the "original affluent society" see Ted Kaczynski, "The Truth about Primitive Life: A Critique of Anarchoprimitivism", The Anarchist Library, 2008

13. *Divisions of Labour,* p. 334

14. J.I. Gershuny & R.E. Pahl, "Work Outside Employment: Some Preliminary Speculations", *New Universities Quarterly,* 34:1, Winter 1979/80, p. 122

15. *Divisions of Labour,* p. 334

16. "Work Outside Employment: Some Preliminary Speculations", p.120

17. *Divisions of Labour,* p. 2

18. Ibid., p. 9

19. Ibid.

20. *Inselgeschichten,* p. 163

21. *Divisions of Labour,* p. 9

22. Jonathan Gershuny, "Informal, but *not* 'an economy'", Graham Crow & Jaimie Ellis, *Revisiting Divisions of Labour: The*

Impacts and Legacies of a Modern Sociological Classic, Manchester University Press, 2017, p. 111

23. R.E. Pahl, "Employment, Work and the Domestic Division of Labour", *International Journal of Urban and Regional Research,* 4 (1), 1980, p. 1

24. *Divisions of Labour,* p. 200

25. Ibid., p. 3

26. E.P. Thompson, "The Poverty of Theory or An Orrery of Errors" in *The Poverty of Theory and Other Essays,* London: Merlin Press, 1978, pp. 193–397

27. Cyril Poster, *The School and the Community,* London: Macmillan Education, 1971, p. 13

28. Ibid., p. 77

29. Ibid., p. 81

30. "Getting it all Together at Sheppey School", *Sheerness Times Guardian,* 24 December 1974, p. 40

31. "Sheppey School Head is Named" *Sheerness Times Guardian,* 17 December 1976, p. 1

32. Ray Pahl, "Living Without a Job: How School Leavers See the Future", *New Society,* 2 November 1978, p. 259

33. Ibid., p. 262

34. Ibid., p. 261

35. Ibid., p. 262

36. Ibid., p. 261

37. Ibid., p. 262

38. See R. E. Pahl's review of Mike Savage, *Identities and Social Class Since 1940: the Politics of Method, Sociological Review,* 59/1 February 2011, pp. 176–181

39. *Inselgeschichten,* pp. 92–3.

40. Wallace, *For Richer For Poorer: Growing Up In and Out of Work,* p. 4

41. R.E. Pahl, "Patterns of Urban Life in the Next Fifteen Years", *New Universities Quarterly,* 30 (4), 1976, p. 416

42. "Living Without a Job: How School Leavers See the Future", p. 262. Pahl makes the same point in "Employment, Work and the Domestic Division of Labour", p 5

43. "Work Outside Employment: Some Preliminary Speculations", p. 127

44. *Inselgeschichten,* p. 104

45. "Employment, Work and the Domestic Division of Labour", p. 16

46. Ibid., p. 10

47. Ibid., p. 14

48. Ibid., pp. 16 & 17

49. "Work Outside Employment: Some Preliminary Speculations", 132

50. Ibid., p. 130

51. Ian Bradley, "Discussing the Culture of Unemployment: An Overview of the Conference", *New Universities Quarterly,* 34: 1, Winter 1979/80, p. 139
52. Ibid.
53. *Divisions of Labour*, p. 10
54. Ibid., p. 11
55. Ibid., p. 319
56. In the later stages of his research, Pahl would also come to be concerned about the consequences of his advice for people he got to know on Sheppey. See Jane Elliott and Jon Lawrence, "Narrative, Time and Intimacy in Social Research: Linda and Jim Revisited", in Graham Crow & Jamie Ellis (eds.), *Revisiting Divisions of Labour: The Impacts and Legacies of a Modern Sociological Classic,* Manchester University Press, 2017, pp. 189–204
57. *Divisions of Labour,* p. 198
58. Ibid. p. 213
59. Ibid., p. 201
60. On Sheppey as elsewhere, the new "Right to Buy" policy may have been deplored by some, including those who followed Tony Benn in warning that a newly-painted front door on a newly-purchased council house was no alternative to a working welfare state. However, it is also remembered as an unexpected opportunity by others. Andre Whelan, the proprietor of the garden ornaments factory in Blue Town, remembers the sudden boom in cement lions (rampant), which his father, who was then building the company, made from moulds he had acquired from a seller advertising in *Exchange and Mart,* and which he sold to proud new homeowners interested in placing them either side of the gates leading to the front doors they could now call their own.
61. *Divisions of Labour,* p. 183.
62. *Ibid.,* p. 241
63. Ibid., p. 313
64. Ibid., p. 319
65. Ibid., p. 253
66. Ibid., p. 320
67. Ibid., p. 324
68. Ibid., p. 195
69. "Employment, Work and the Domestic Division of Labour", p. 7
70. *Divisions of Labour,* pp. 196–7
71. Ibid., p. 154
72. Uwe Johnson, letter to Helen Wolff, 6 March, 1979, *Inselgeschichten,* p. 142.
73. Tilman Jens "Der Unbekannte von der Themse: Auf den Spuren des toten Dichters Uwe

Johnson", *Stern*, No. 22, 24 May 1984, pp. 132 & 133. For the howitzer, see Martin Walser, *Breakers*, London: Deutsch, 1987, p. 25.

74. *Divisions of Labour,* p. 175
75. Ibid, p. 322
76. Ibid., p. 193
77. Ibid., p. 153
78. Wilko Johnson, Speaking on "The River", episode 1, BBC 2 30 October 1999. See also Patrick Wright, *The River*, London: BBC Worldwide, 1999, pp. 68–76
79. *Divisions of Labour,* p. 186
80. Ibid., p. 188

81. Ibid., p. 323
82. Ibid., p. 191
83. Ibid., p. 189
84. Ibid., pp. 324 & 325
85. Ibid., p. 326
86. Uwe Johnson, letter to Helen Wolff, 6 March, 1979, *Inselgeschichten*, p. 142.
87. Robert Ford and Matthew Goodwin, *Revolt on the Right: Explaining Support for the "Radical" Right in Britain,* London: Routledge, 2014
88. Uwe Johnson, letter to Erika Klemm, 3 November 1975, *Inselgeschichten*, pp. 98–99

25. "It's Your Opinion": A Postcard for the Kent Evening Post

1. *Anniversaries* I, p. 502
2. Editorial, *Kent Evening Post,* 12 May 1975
3. "Benn Starts Oil Gushing", *Aberdeen Evening Express,* 18 June 1975, p. 1
4. "Britain on the Brink", *Birmingham Daily Post,* 18 June 1975, p. 33
5. Sidney Hooper, "Is it Against the Law to be British?", 22 January 1981
6. John Baker White, "Inshore Fishing Industry Bill", HC Deb 18 October 1945, vol. 414 cc1441–4

7. John Baker White, "A Welcome — But Concern from Europe", *Sheerness Times Guardian,* 19 November 1971, p. 3
8. Uwe Johnson, letter to Christa Wolf, 16 June 1981, *Inselgeschichten*, p. 155.
9. "Young Hippies Invade Commuter Trains, says County Councillor", *Sheerness Times Guardian,* 11 July 1975, p. 8

26. Implosion: Two Stories from the Site

1. The phrase "necklace of poverty" was used repeatedly by Derek Wyatt, when he was Labour MP for Sittingbourne and Sheppey arguing that Kent and the Medway towns would fall behind despite recent investment under the "Thames Gateway" scheme if the British government failed to emulate the nations of the North Baltic in prioritising investment in high quality broadband. (See his contribution to the Westminster Hall debate on the Structure Plan for Kent and Medway, HC Deb 2 February 2005 c267WH). Wyatt had first located this "necklace" in "the North and East Kent. Area" (HC Deb 23 June 1999 vol 333 c1145). He later enlarged it, claiming that it ran from Woolwich all the way to Southampton, including Sheerness, which had "lived with poverty for most of the twentieth century" (HC Deb 2 March 2004 vol 418 c819)

2. Uwe Johnson, Letter to Max Frisch, 21 March 1976, *Max Frisch − Der Briefwechsel 1964–1983*, p. 159

3. Bernd W. Seiler, "Johnsons Prager Geheimagent: Schluss-Strich unter eine Legende"

    ["Johnson's Prague Secret Agent: Final Stroke under a Legend"], first published in *Internationales Uwe-Johnson-Forum* 10/2006, pp. 25–54, and reprinted in another version at https://www.uni-bielefeld. de/lili/personen/seiler/drucke/ geheimagent/uebersicht.html

4. Uwe Johnson, "Statement to my Executors", 21 February 1983, quoted in Heinrich Lübbert, *Der Streit um das Erbe des Schriftstellers Uwe Johnson*, Frankfurt: Suhrkamp, 1998, p. 29

5. Uwe Johnson, Letter to Hannah Arendt, 3 August 1975, *Inselgeschichten*, p. 78

6. Uwe Johnson, Letter to Helen Wolff, 1 June 1977, *Inselgeschichten*, pp. 148–9

7. Bernd Seiler, email to the author, 7 January 2020

8. Jeffrey Schneider, "Masculinity, Male Friendship, and the Paranoid Logic of Honor in Theodore Fontane's *Effi Briest*", *German Quarterly*, vol. 75, No. 3 (Summer, 2002), pp. 265-281.

9. D. G. Bond, *German History and German Identity*, Amsterdam: Rodopi, 1993, pp. 189-90

10. "'Der vierte Band ist entweder ein Selbstmordversuch oder es ist der Versuch, eine Tür aufzustoßen.' Ein Gespräch mit Thomas Brasch über Uwe Johnson, geführt von Thomas Wild" in R. Berbig (ed.) *Uwe Johnson: Befreundungen: Gespräche, Dokumente, Essays*, Berlin: Kontext, 2002, pp. 518-19.

11. "Uwe Johnson: A Friendship", p. 120

12. Uwe Johnson, *Begleitumstände: Franfurter Vorlesungen*, Frankfurt am Main: Suhrkamp, 1980, p. 452

13. Seiler, quoting from Günter Grass, "Distanz, heftige Nähe, Fremdwerden und Fremdbleiben. Ein Gespräch mit Roland Berbig", in Günter Grass, *Die Deutschen und ihre Dichter*. München 1995, p. 299

14. "'Der vierte Band ist…'", p. 519

15. Heinz Ludwig Arnold, " Zu Thomas Braschs Gedicht 'Halb Schlaff'", *Planet Lyrik*, posted 27 September 2019, http://www.planetlyrik.de/heinz-ludwig-arnold-zu-thomas-braschs-gedicht-halb-schlaf/2019/09/

16. Gerhard Zwerenz, *Die Vertiedigung Sachsens und warum Karl May die Indianer liebte*, chapters 25 & 26. http://www.poetenladen.de/zwerenz-gerhard-sachsen.htm

17. Uwe Johnson, *Skizze eines Verunglückten*, Frankfurt am Main: Suhrkamp, 1982, pp. 7–9

18. Uwe Johnson, "'Mir bleibt nur, ihr zu danken': Zum Tod von Hannah Arendt" (first published in *Frankfurter Allgemeine Zeitung*, 8 December 1975), in Eberhard Fahlke (ed.), Uwe Johnson, *Porträts und Erinnerungen*, Frankfurt am Main: Suhrkamp, 1988, pp. 76–7

19. *Skizze eines Verunglückten*, pp. 22–3

20. Ibid., p. 35

21. Ibid., p. 48

22. *Skizze eines Verunglückten*, p. 49

23. Ibid., p. 66

24. Ibid., p. 62

25. Ibid., p. 63

26. Max Frisch's text was published as "Study of a Disaster" in an English translation by Jessica Wolff and Lore Segal, *New Yorker*, 22 July 1972, pp. 28–32

27. Kurt Fickert, "Three Witnesses: Narration in Johnson's *Skizze eines Verunglückten*", *Colloquia Germanica*, vol. 28, No. 2 (1995) p. 155. "Autobiography as Fiction: Uwe Johnson's Skizze eines Verunglückten",

International Fiction Review,
14, no.2, 1987, pp. 63–7

28. Ibid.

29. D.G. Bond, *German History
and German Identity:
Uwe Johnson's Jahrestage,*
Amsterdam: Rodopi, 1993, p.
188

30. *Skizze eines Verunglückten,* p.
48

31. Fritz J. Raddatz, "Das verratene
Herz: Uwe Johnson: *Skizze
eines Verunglückten", Zeit,* 12
November 1982

32. Heinrich Blücher, "III. Homer
(1954)", transcript available
online at the Blücher Archive,
Stevenson Library, Bard
College. http://www.bard.edu/
bluecher/lectures/homer_54/
homer_1954.php

Part VI. The Storm of Memory: A New Use for the Sash Windows of North Kent

27. Unsticking Marcel Duchamp's Large Glass

1. Brian Dillon, "In Herne Bay",
London Review of Books, Vol.
35 No. 16, 16–29 August 2013,
p. 10. See also Brian Dillon,
The Great Explosion, London:
Penguin, 2015, pp. 18-19.

2. Jeremy Millar, "Looking
through the Large Glass:
Marcel Duchamp in England",
Tate, Issue 7, Summer 2006

3. Jeremy Millar, "Marcel
Duchamp in England", note on
Marcel Duchamp's "The Large
Glass" or "The Bride Stripped
Bare by her Bachelors, Even",
Tate, Issue 7, Summer 2006

4. *Inselgeschichten,* p. 95.

5. Thomas Herold, "Through the
Window: City, Imagination,
and the Framed Gaze in Uwe
Johnson's *Jahrestage*", *The
German Review: Literature,
Culture, Theory,* Vol. 98, 2018,
Issue 2, pp. 96–108

6. *Anniversaries* I, p. 152

7. Uwe Johnson, "A Part of
New York", *Dimension:
Contemporary Arts and
Letters,* Vol. 1, No. 2, 1968, p.
335

8. Uwe Johnson, "How
Anniversaries Came to be
Written", a lecture given in
Munich on 18 July 1974 and
published in Uwe Johnson,
*Speculations about Jakob and
other Writings* (ed. Alexander
Stephan), New York & London:

Continuum, 2000, p. 231.
Johnson describes the view
from his apartment in some
detail in "A Part of New York",
pp. 333–337

9.   Henri Bergson, *Matter and
     Memory* [1896], New York:
     Zone Books, 1991, p. 33

10. "About Myself"

28. Sea Defences: From God's Will to "Puddicombe's Folly"

1.   *Inselgeschichten,* pp. 78–9
2.   *Contemporary German Arts
     and Letters,* Vol. 15/3, 1982, p.
     401
3.   *Anniversaries* I, p. 35, See
     also A Leslie Willson, "'An
     unacknowledged humorist':
     Interview with Uwe Johnson,
     Sheerness-in-Kent, 20
     April 1982", *Dimension:
     Contemporary German Arts
     and Letters,* Vol 15/3, 1982
4.   "Sheerness", *Whitstable Times
     and Herne Bay Herald,* 7
     November 1875, p. 3
5.   Joseph Conrad, *The Mirror
     of the Sea* [1906], reprinted
     in *A Personal Record and the
     Mirror of the Sea*, ed. Mara
     Kalnins, London: Penguin,
     1998, p. 221
6.   Daniel Defoe, "The Storm.
     An Essay", in *The Storm*, ed.
     Richard Hamblyn, London:
     Penguin, 2005, p. 208

7.   Daniel Defoe, "The Layman's
     Sermon upon the Late Storm",
     Ibid., p. 187
8.   Richard Hamblyn,
     "Introduction", Ibid., p. x
9.   "The Layman's Sermon upon
     the Late Storm", p. 186
10. William Shrubsole,
     *Sheshbazzar, and his sons.
     Being the substance of a
     discourse delivered at the
     Bethel Chapel, Sheerness, at the
     request of the Master and lodge
     of the ancient and honourable
     Society of Free and Accepted
     Masons on Sunday, the 24th
     of June 1787. And published at
     their request.* Rochester: Printed
     by W. Gillman, for J. Edmonds,
     Sheerness, 1787, pp. 31–2
11. "Dangerous Condition of
     Sheerness", *United Services
     Gazette,* reprinted in *West Kent
     Guardian,* 28 February 1852,
     p. 4
12. Roy Spencer, *D.H. Lawrence
     Country: A Portrait of his*

*Early Life and Background
with Illustrations, Maps and
Guides,* London: Cecil Woolf,
1979, pp. 64–81

13. Quoted from Lawrence's poem
"Red-Herring" (*Pansies,* 1929),
Spencer, p. 64

14. D.H. Lawrence, *Sons and
Lovers* [1913], Oxford World's
Classics, 1995, pp. 10–11

15. "The Council's £25,000
Scheme" *Sheerness Times,* 6
Feb 1930, p. 2

16. "Sheerness in the 'Sixties'",
Sheerness Times, 30 April 1931

17. "Sheerness", *Whitstable Times
and Herne Bay Herald,* 7
November 1875, p. 3

18. Mr John Taylor's visit to
Sheerness to conduct his
enquiry into the matter is
reported in "Sheerness. The
Marine Town Esplanade",
*Whitstable Times & Herne Bay
Herald,* 11 December 1875

19. "The Council's £25,000
Scheme"

20. "The Great Snowstorm",
*Whitstable Times and Herne
Bay Herald,* 22 January 1881,
p. 3

21. "Sheerness", *Whitstable Times
and Herne Bay Herald,* 27
November 1880, p. 3

22. "The Thaw in London",
*Yorkshire Post & Leeds
Intelligencer,* 28 January 1881,
p. 8

23. Ibid.

24. "Gales, Snowstorms, and
Floods", *Bury Evening Post,* 25
January 1881, p. 3

25. "Notes by the Way", *Sheerness
Times,* 5 February 1881

26. "Sheerness-on-Sea", *Whitstable
Times and Herne Bay
Guardian,* 26 February 1881,
p. 3.

27. "Sheerness", *Whitstable Times
and Herne Bay Herald,* 18
September 1881. See also "The
Sea Defences at Sheerness",
Tamworth Herald, 10
September 1881, p. 3, which
reports this work near the
garrison and dockyard, but
also that the Board of Health
was refusing other measures to
"prevent inundations" on the
grounds that the sea defences
were "Government property".

28. "The Floods", *London Daily
News,* 31 October 1882, p. 6

29. "The Prevention of Thames
Flooding", article from the
Builder, reprinted in *Jersey
Independent and Daily
Telegraph,* 5 February 1881,
p. 1

30. On this occasion, Mr Brice at
Elmley lost his sheep, cattle
and almost his own life; his
less fortunate neighbour, Mr
W. Sage, drowned when he
stepped into the water from a
flat-bottomed boat in order to

round up some cattle, and sank into a submerged ditch. "Great Disaster", *Sheerness Times and General Advertiser,* 4 December 1897. Also available on Kent History Forum.

31. "High Tide on the Thames", *Morning Post,* 30 November 1897, p. 3

32. "Great Disaster", *Sheerness Times and General Advertiser,* 4 December 1897

33. "Damage in the Coast Towns", *South Wales Daily News,* 30 November 1897, p. 5

34. "Great Disaster"

35. *Anniversaries* I, p. 12

36. Ibid., p. 81

37. Ibid, p. 87

38. Hilda Grieve, *The Great Tide: The story of the 1953 Flood Disaster in Essex,* Chelmsford: County Council of Essex, 1959, p. 52

39. Ibid., pp. 53–4

40. "Abnormal Tide", *Sheerness Guardian and East Kent Advertiser,* 6 November 1921

41. Grieve, p. 52. See also "London Floods", *Western Gazette,* 13 January 1928, p. 15

42. "Highest Tide since 1897", *Sheerness Times,* 12 January 1928, p. 5

43. "How Sheppey was Saved", *Sheerness Times,* 12 January 1928

44. "Urban District Council: The Sea Defences: Coun. Carpenter Complains of Lack of Money Spent", *Sheerness Guardian,* 9 March 1929

45. "Council and the Sea Defences", *Sheerness Times,* 18 April 1929

46. "The Sea Defences", *Sheerness Times,* 21 March 1929

47. "Council and the Sea Defences" *Sheerness Times,* 18 April 1929

48. "Urban District Council", *Sheerness Times,* 23 March 1929

49. "A Scandalous Scare Exploded", *Sheerness Guardian,* 1 October 1931

50. "Freedom is Ours", *Sheppey Guardian,* 6 July 1929

51. "Well-Known Artist in Sheppey", *Sheerness Guardian,* 21 September 1929

52. "Gardens Along Marine Parade", *Sheerness Times,* 20 February 1930

53. "Urban District Council" *Sheerness Guardian,* 17 May 1930

54. *Anniversaries* I, pp. 120 & 122

55. "The Promenade Scheme", *Sheerness Guardian,* 28 June 1930, p. 4

56. *Sheerness Guardian,* 2 January 1932

57. "Council Tenders. Sea-wall Expenditure", *Sheerness Times* 14 January 1932

58. "Marine Parade Improvements", *Sheerness Times*, 21 January 1932

59. "Around the Clock. A Ruling Passion", *Sheerness Times*, August 18 1932

60. "£25,000 Loan Expended", *Sheerness Times*, 17 November, 1932

61. "Marine Parade Improvement Scheme", *Sheerness Times*, 1 December 1932

62. "Around the Clock: The Parade Controversy", *Sheerness Times*, 8 December 1932

63. "Around the Clock", *Sheerness Times*, 4 December 1932

64. "Labour's New HQ", *Sheerness Times*, 8 December 1932, p. 1

65. Uwe Johnson, Letter to Hans Joachim Schädlich, 7 July 1978, *Inselgeschichten*, p. 85

29. Beach, Sea and "The View of a Memory"

1. Uwe Johnson, Letter to Antonia and Felix Landgraf, 7 June 1977, *Inselgeschichten*, p. 172

2. Uwe Johnson, Letter to Antonia and Felix Landgraf, *Inselgeschichten*, p. 160

3. *Anniversaries* I, p. 53

4. *Anniversaries* II, p. 446

5. *Anniversaries* I, p. 53

6. *Anniversaries* III, p. 874

7. *Anniversaries* II, p. 442

8. *Anniversaries* III, p. 881

9. Ibid., p. 883

10. *Anniversaries* II, p. 419

11. Uwe Johnson, Letter to Friedrich A. Denk, 22 February 1984. Michael Hamburger Archive, British Library

12. *Anniversaries* I, p. 40

13. *Anniversaries* III, p. 1177

14. *Speculations about Jakob,* pp. 169–70

15. *Anniversaries* I, p. 3.

16. *Anniversaries* III, p. 1060

17. Jean Paul Sartre, *Nausea* (trans. Robert Baldick) London: Penguin, 2001, p. 179

18. Uwe Johnson, untitled typescript numbered 211080 sh. I was sent a copy of this late and rather chaotic document by the Deutsches Literatur Archive at Marbach, where the Johnson papers where lodged before being moved to their present location at the Uwe Johnson Archive, University of Rostock.

19. *Von dem Fischer un syner Fru. Ein Märchen nach Philipp Otto Runge mit sieben Bildern von Marcus Behmer, einer*

Nacherzählung und mit einem Nachtwort von Uwe Johnson, Frankfurt am Main: Insel Verlag, 1976.

20. Uwe Johnson, "Nachwort", *Von Dem Fischer un Syner Fru*

21. Ibid., p. 60.

22. Ibid., p. 63.

23. Ibid., p. 57.

24. *Anniversaries* II, p. 499.

25. Ibid., pp. 533–4.

26. *Anniversaries* III, p 881.

27. Ibid., p. 883.

30. What Is That Thing?: The SS Richard Montgomery

1. Uwe *Johnson,* "Ein unergründliches Schiff", *Merkur,* 1979, H.6, pp. 537–550. Collected in Inselgeschichten, pp. 19–40.

2. *Ulrich Beck, Risk Society: Towards a new Modernity [1986], London*: Sage, 1992.

3. "Welcome to Sheerness? Fury over sulky 40 ft mermaid mural that greets visitors to seaside town", *Daily Mail,* 19 August 2015. www.dailymail.co.uk/news/article-3203381/She-looks-like-wants-blow-Locals-Sheerness-left-furious-bizarre-grumpy-mermaid-mural-painted-welcome-visitors-seaside-town.html

4. *Iain Sinclair, "Diary", London Review of Books,* Vol. 35 No. 9, *9 May 2013, pp. 38–9*

5. *David Cotgrove, cited in Jon Connell,* "The Thames Timebomb", *Sunday Times,* 27 August 1978

6. *Frederick J.* Lang & Terence Phelan, *Maritime: A Historical Sketch and a Workers' Program,* New York: Pioneer Publications, 1943. Quoted in John M. Williams, *S.S. Richard Montgomery: "Risk & Reality",* Volume 1, version 1.2., Benfleet: self-published, 2016

7. Connell, "The Thames Timebomb"

8. David A. Atkinson, Richard Anthony Baker & David F. Cotgrove, "The Explosive Cargo of the USS 'Richard Montgomery': A study into the developing hazard of a marine wreck in the Thames Estuary between Sheerness and Southend-on-Sea", duplicated typescript published by Southend -on-Sea & District Chamber of Trade & Industry Ltd, 1972, Section 4.6

9. Atkinson, Baker & Cotgrove, "The Explosive Cargo of the

USS "Richard Montgomery",
Section 4.7.

10. *Williams, p. 19*

11. *Atkin*son, Baker & Cotgrove,
Section 4.4

12. *Lloyds Register of Shipping,*
August 1944, photocopy in
John M. Williams, *S.S. Richard
Montgomery: Risk & Reality,*
Benfleet: self-published, p. 74.
This informative but unusually
arranged document contains
much that is drawn from David
Cotgrove's papers about the
Richard Montgomery, which
appear to remain uncatalogued
and not easily available at
the Essex Record Office in
Colchester.

13. Extracts from legal acts with
a bearing on the SS Richard
Montgomery, prepared to
inform Admiralty discussion
with the Port of London
Authority, 1952. Folder E 154
in NA. ADM 1/24082

14. J.W. Edwards, Assistant Mooring
& Wreck Raising Officer,
"Salvage Operations on "SS
Richard Montgomery" at East
Nore Sands", NA. ADM 331/64

15. Port of London Au*thority*
Memorandum on
responsibilities for the USS
Richard Montgomery, Folder E
154 in NA. ADM 1/24082

16. "War Wrecks Replacing Coastal
Mine Menace", *Lincolnshire
Echo,* 13 May 1946, p. 1

17. "S.S. Richard Montgomery",
a brief prepared by J.L. Bligh
of the Admiralty's Works and
Salvage Section, and submitted
on 16 July 1952, National
Archives, ADM 1/24082

18. James C. Scott, *Seeing Like a
State: How Certain Schemes to
Improve the Human Condition
have Failed,* New Haven and
London: Yale University Press,
1998

19. Nearly twenty years later, it
would be officially confirmed
that the US War Shipping
Administration had indeed
sold the wreck to a New
York salvage operator named
Phillips, Kraft and Fisher, Inc
on 24 April 1948. The deal,
however, was rescinded on
14 December 1951 and the
US Maritime Administration
had no records indicating
whether any work had been
done by the company, which
had by then disappeared
without trace (the US Navy
Supervisor of Salvage, who
made enquiries throughout
the US maritime community,
could find "no one who had
ever heard of this company".)

Typescript of USA report, NA. ADM 331/64

20. "Medway Wreck", HC Deb 23 April 1952, vol. 499 cc21-2W

21. Bennett is said to have been in discussion with Sir Stephen McAdden, MP for Southend East, in David Cotgrove et. al, "The Exolosive Cargo of the USS 'Richard Montgomery'"

22. Percy Wells M. P., letter to First Lord of the Admiralty, 18 June 1952, NA. ADM 1/24082

23. J.P.L. Thomas (Admiralty), "Private Memo Describing Meeting with Lord Waverley", dated 18 June 1952, National Archives, ADM 1/24082

24. "Note of a meeting held by the First Lord on Tuesday 22nd July [1952] with Lord Waverley to discuss the question of the 'RICHARD MONTGOMERY'", NA, ADM 1/24082.

25. Assistant Treasury Solicitor, note for Admiralty, 18 May 1949. NA, ADM 1/24082, file E 154

26. "Private Memo Describing Meeting with Lord Waverley", NA, ADM 1/24082

27. "Note of a Meeting held by the First Lord on Tuesday 22 July [1952] with Lord Waverley [PLA] to discuss the question of the "Richard Montgomery", NA, ADM 1/24082.

28. "Wreck of S.S. Richard Montgomery", briefing document for the First Lord of the Admiralty, 1952, NA, ADM 1/24082

29. Undated PLA "Memorandum on the subject of the wreck of the SS Richard Montgomery", NA, ADM 1/24082. File E.154

30. "Notes of points of substance argued or established at meeting between First Lord and Lord Waverley at 10 a.m. Monday 22 July 1952", NA, ADM 1/24082.

31. Ibid.

32. Note on JPL Thomas, private memo describing meeting with Lord Waverley, 18 June 1952, NA, ADM1/24082

33. This arduous process involved retrieving the original loading manifest, matching it's inventory against the record of the bombs that had been successfully salvaged, and then seeking American help with understanding the codes used for various types of bomb. That this was a complicated matter is demonstrated by a letter dated 29 July 1952 by Lt. Col. A.W. Stoddard, of Officer Group No. 1, United States Army, 7 North Audley St, London W.1. See also H.J. Hawkins, A Proposal for

Salvage of the S.S. "Richard Montgomery", Explosives Research and Development Centre, Waltham Abbey, National Archives SUPP 6/948

34. Statement for Percy Wells, prepared by J. P. L. Thomas to be sent by the First Lord of the Admiralty, NA ADM 1/24082

35. "Town That Could Have Been Blown Up Any Day in the Past Eight Years: 3,000 Tons of Bombs in Shipwreck", *Sunday Dispatch*, 11 May 1952, p. 5

36. "Anti-Spy Ring Round British Dockyard", *Sunday Dispatch*, 18 May 1952, p. 1. Having been developed under the direction of Sir William Penney, said to have discovered his interest in mathematics while attending Sheerness Technical High School for Boys in the mid-Twenties, the device would be brought over by barge from the Atomic Weapons Research Establishment at Shoeburyness and loaded aboard a redundant river class frigate HMS Plym, which was then moored at Stangate Creek, a few miles up the Medway from Sheerness. HMS Plym was later joined by the frigate Tracker and the aircraft carrier Campania, which had recently completed service as exhibition ship of the Festival of Britain, and set off on the eight-week voyage to the Montebello Islands, off the coast of North West Australia, where it w*ould serve as* the cradle of the 25 kiloton explosion produced on 3 October, 1952.

31. The Doomsday Shuffle

1. Desmond Wettern, "A Sunken Ghost Ship", *Daily Sketch,* 28 April 1962, p. 6

2. Desmond Wettern, "Her Cargo-Bombs: Could She Still Blow Up?", *Daily Sketch,* 8 May 1962, p. 13

3. David Lampe, "The Doomsday Ship", *Wide World,* October 1964, pp. 224–229 & 286–290

4. Major A.B. Hartley, MBE, RE, *Unexploded Bomb: A History of Bomb Disposal*, with a foreword by the Rt. Hon. Herbert Morrison CH, MP, London: Cassell, 1958.

5. "Sheerness Would Be Wiped Out", *East Kent Gazette,* 8 October 1964, p. 11

6. HC Deb 18 March 1965, vol. 708 cc321-2W

7. HC Deb 24 November 1965, vol. 721 cc489–60

8. *Jack Griffiths MBE, Solicitor and Clerk of Sheerness Urban District Council, letter to Terry Boston MP, 22 December 1965.*

9. "Bomb Ship: New Plea", *Sheerness Times Guardian,* 18 March 1966, p. 6

10. "Notes on Meeting on 22 April 1966 between the Navy Department and the Sheerness Urban District Council to discuss the Wreck of the SS Richard Montgomery", NA, ADM 331/64

11. NA, ADM 331/64

12. Maritime and Coastguard Agency, *Report on the Wreck of the SS Richard Montgomery,* Southampton: MCA, March 2000, p. 25

13. "'Act Now on Danger Ship" Plea,' *Evening News,* 20 November 1967

14. One of these questions was intended to establish unequivocally whether the cluster bombs were fitted with fuses that might have degenerated to produce highly dangerous and volatile azides, while another concerned the possibility of the "entire cargo" being detonated by the explosion of single fragmentation bomb. Letter from P.D. Jewitt, Shore Division (Naval), Ministry of Defence, to Lieut-Colonel R. H. Lee of the United States Army Standardisation Group UK, in London, 13 May 1966, National Archives, DEFE 69/525

15. "US Army and Navy Comments Regarding the S.S. Richard Montgomery", National Archives, DEFE 69/525

16. "Loose Minute. Wreck of the SS Richard Montgomery", National Archives, DEFE 69/525

17. Letters to DTI from Persad (26 November 1971) and H. N. Brunby (12 November 1971) National Archives, ADM 331 / 64

18. Sheppey Congregational Church, letter to the Minister of the Environment, 20 October 1971, National Archives, ADM 331/64

19. Norman Baldock, Chairman of governors at St George's Church of England Middle School, Sheerness, letter to Education Secretary Margaret Thatcher, 28 October 1971, National Archives, ADM 331/64

20. Hydraulics Research Station, Wallingford, "Wreck of the S.S. Richard Montgomery off Sheerness: An Investigation into

Proposed Schemes for Protecting the Wreck", January 1971, National Archives ADM 331/64

21. "Combined Effort to Avert Thameside Flooding", *Times*, 13 November 1971, p. 4

22. V. Marlow of the Board of Trade, letter to the Ministry of Defence, 10 March 1972. National Archives ADM 331/64

23. "Effects of Detonation on Wreck of SS Richard Montgomery", *National Archives* AVIA 37/916

32. Becoming Unfathomable: The Bomb Ship as "Murky Reality"

1. Uwe Johnson, Letter to Rudolf Augstein, 6 December 74, *Inselgeschichten,* p. 187

2. *Ein englisches Tagebuch,* pp. 31–2

3. Karl Jaspers, *Man in the Modern Age* (trans. Eden and Cedar Paul), London: Routledge & Kegan Paul, 1951

4. The letter is here quoted from the English edition of Jurgen Habermas (ed.), *Observations on "The Spiritual Situation of the Age"* [1979] (trans. Andrew Buchwalter) Cambridge Mass & London: MIT Press, 1985, pp. 1–4

5. "'Ein sicheres Versteck': Uwe Johnson and England", p. 96

6. Jurgen Habermas, Letter to the author, 6 January 2017

7. Uwe Johnson, Letter to Jürgen Habermas, 13 February 1979, *Inselgeschichten,* p. 188

8. Uwe Johnson, "Ein unergründliches Schiff", *Merkur* 1979, H.6, pp. 537–550. This is the version republished in *Inselgeschichten*, pp. 19-40

9. Uwe Johnson, "Ein unergründliches Schiff", *Inselgeschichten,* p. 20

10. Ibid., p. 26

11. Ibid., p. 21

12. Ibid., p. 21

13. Ibid., p. 21

14. Ibid., p. 22

15. Ibid., p. 22. Made by KPM (the Royal Porcelain Factory of Berlin) and inscribed, like the original Freedom Bell, with the promise "That This World Under God Shall Have a New Birth of Freedom" these 12cm-high porcelain bells are nowadays easily examined on eBay.

16. Ibid., p. 23.

17. Ibid., p. 24.

18. *Anniversaries* I, p. 19

19. "Ein unergründliches Schiff", *Inselgeschichten,* p. 25

20. Ibid., p. 26-7

21. Ibid., p. 29

22. Ibid., p. 30

23. "Survey on Bomb Ship is Started", *Sheppey Gazette and East-Kent Times*, 28 September 1978, p. 1

24. Ian Read, "Dive to Danger", *Kent Evening Post*, 27 September 1978, p. 11

25. "The Thames Timebomb", *The Sunday Times,* 27 August, 1978, pp. 4-5

26. John Cotgrove, telephone conversation with the author, 10 November 2016

27. Michael Thomas, text message, 11 November 2016

28. David A. Atkinson, Richard Anthony Baker & David F. Cotgrove, "The Explosive Cargo of the USS 'Richard Montgomery': A study into the Developing Hazard From A Marine Wreck in the Thames Estuary Between Sheerness and Southend-on-Sea", Westcliff-on-Sea: Southend-on-Sea & District Chamber of Trade & Industry Ltd, 1972

29. Press release enclosed with letter to the Secretary of State at the Ministry of Defence by V.T. Steward, General Secretary of Southend Chamber of Trade, 18 April 1972, National Archives, ADM 331/64

30. Stephen Barlay, "New Hearts for Old", *Wide World,* October 1964, pp. 278–231 & 294–295

31. Stephen Barlay, *Blockbuster,* London: Hamish Hamilton, 1976, p. 132

32. "Ein unergründliches Schiff", *Inselgeschichten,* p. 36.

33. Nick Barlay, *Scattered Ghosts: One Family's Survival through War, Holocaust and Revolution,* London: I.B. Tauris, 2013, p. 170

34. David Cotgrove, quoted in John M. Williams, *S.S. Richard Montgomery: Risk & Reality,* Benfleet: Williams, 2016, p. 7

35. John Cotgrove, telephone conversation with the author, 7 November 2016

36. Lampe, "The Doomsday Ship", p. 224

37. *Sheppey Gazette,* 21 August 1978, p. 1

38. Martin Collier, "Thames Timebomb, or Simply a Damp Squib?", *Sheppey Gazette and East-Kent Times*, 7 September 1978, p. 3

39. Ibid.

40. Ibid.

41. Ibid.

42. "Ein unergründliches Schiff", *Inselgeschichten,* p. 35

43. Ibid., p. 39.

44. Ibid., p. 36.

45. Ibid., p. 37.

46. Ibid., p. 38.

47. "New Fear for Bomb Ship", *Sheppey Gazette and North-* *East Kent Times,* 31 August 1978, p. 1

48. Ian Read, "May the Bomb Ship Rust in Peace", *Kent Evening Post,* September 28 1978, p. 16

49. Collier, "Thames Timebomb, or Simply a Damp Squib?"

33. Explosion: From the Richard Montgomery to the Cap Arcona

1. Renate Mayntz, email to the author, 1 November 2016

2. *Man in the Modern Age,* p. 21

3. Karl Jaspers, *Reason and Existenz: Five Lectures,* New York: Noonday Press, 1955, p. 104

4. Ibid., pp. 32 & 38

5. William James, *The Varieties of Religious Experience: A Study in Human Nature* (1902), London : Routyledge, 2003, p. 110

6. *The Great Explosion: Gunpowder, the Great War, and a Disaster on the Kent Marshes.* See also Arthur Percival, *The Great Explosion at Faversham 2 April 1916,* unattributed pamphlet distributed by the Faversham Society, reprinted from *Archaeologia Cantiana,* Vol. C, 1985

7. D.G. Bond, "Two Ships: Correspondences between Uwe Johnson and Johann Peter Hebel", *The German Quarterly,* Vol. 64, No. 3, Focus: Nineteenth Century (Kleist), Summer 1991, pp. 313–324

8. Frauke Meyer-Gosau, *Versuch, eine Heimat zu finden: Eine Reise zu Uwe Johnson,* Munich: C.H. Beck, 2014, p. 7

9. Rudi Goguel, *Cap Arcona. Report über den Untergang der Häftlingsflotte in der Lübecker Bucht am 3. Mai 1945,* Frankfurt am Main, 1972. Johnson describes his reliance on this book, which did not come out in time for him to include the episode in its proper place within the chronology of *Anniversaries,*

in an interview with Manfred
Durzak, quoted in D.G. Bond
and Julian Preece, "'Cap
Arcona' 3 May 1945: History
and Allegory in Novels by Uwe
Johnson and Günter Grass",
Oxford German Studies, 20,
1991, p. 150

10. *Anniversaries* III, p. 963. My
quotations from Johnson's
account of the sinking of the
Cap Arcona are from pp. 963–7

11. Benjamin Jacobs and Eugene
Pool, *The 100-Year Secret:
Britain's Hidden World War
II Massacre*, Guilford, Conn.:
Lyons Press, 2004, p. 40

12. "Winter Holidays", *Yorkshire
Post and Leeds Intelligencer*,
29 October 1935, p. 6

13. "Wandering Jews", *Sunderland
Daily Echo and Shipping
Gazette*, 27 March 1939, p. 1

14. Jacobs & Pool, p. 26

15. Robert P. Watson, *The Nazi
Titanic: The Incredible Untold
Story of a Doomed Ship in
World War II*, Philadelphia: Da
Capo Press, 2016, pp. 69-74

16. Ibid., p. 254

17. Daniel Long, "A Controversial
History? An Analysis of British
Attitudes and Responsibility
in the Bombing of the Cap
Arcona, 3 May 1945", Available
online at: www. southampton.
ac.uk

18. Ibid., p. 967

19. D.G. Bond and Julian Preece
tell us that the work mentioned
by Goguel is Charles Webster's
*The Strategic Air Offensive
Against Germany*, published
in 1961, not 1956 as Johnson
has it.

20. Terence McQullin, Royal Army
Medical Corps (Oral History)
15540, recorded on 28 June
1995, Imperial War Museum,
London

21. Jacobs and Pool, p. 172

22. Ibid., p. 102

23. Piet Ketelaar, 'Oral History
Interview' 9725 recorded by
Conrad Wood on 9/3/1987,
Imperial War Museum, London

24. For my attempt to describe this
"revivalist fable" as it unfolded
in the late eighties, see my A
*Journey Through Ruins: The
Last Days of London* [1991],
enlarged edition, Oxford
University Press, 2009, pp.
307-319

25. John Nurden, "Sheppey
'bombship' Richard
Montgomery to have masts
chopped off", *KentOnline*, 28
May 2020

26. I take this phrase from
Heathcote Williams, *Boris
Johnson: The Beast of Brexit
A Study in Depravity*, London
Review of Books, 2016. As
Williams also announced,
"There's a German word

for people like Johnson: *Backpfeifengesicht*. It means 'a face that needs to be punched'." Heathcote Ruthven, "Back with a Vengeance", *Independent,* 29 May 2016

27. John Nurden, email to the author, 3 June 2020

34. Triumph of the Sheerness Wall

1. *Inselgeschichten,* p. 82

2. Siegfried Unseld, Letter to Uwe Johnson, 8 September *1982, Uwe Johnson-Siegfried Unseld Der Briefwechsel,* p. 1024

3. "Tidal Wave Brings Disaster to Sheppey: Stricken Island Counts its Losses", *Sheerness Times and Guardian* (Emergency Edition), 2 February 1953

4. Hilda Grieve, *The Great Flood: The Story of the 1953 Flood Disaster in Essex,* Chelmsford: County of Essex, 1959, p. 178

5. "Royal Visitor Saw Town Rally", *Sheerness Times and Guardian,* February 6 1953, p. 1

6. Roland Berkeley Thorn, *The Design of Sea Defence Works,* London: Butterworths Scientific Publications, 1960. p. ix

7. Ibid., pp. 48–9

8. "Terror Struck for Disabled Pensioner", *Sheerness Times Guardian,* 13 January 1977, p. 2

9. Letter to Helen Wolff, 16 March 1978, quoted in Eberhard Fahlke, "Auf der Suche nach "Inselgeschichten", *Inselgeschichten,* p. 174

10. *Inselgeschichten,* p. 38.

11. Ewan Forster, email to the author, 7 November 2014

12. "Chamber Checks All Sea Defence Work", *Sheerness Times Guardian,* 22 December 1978, p. 4

13. Roger Moate, MP, House of Commons Debate, 25 January 1979, Hansard vol. 961 cc 878–90

14. See Fig. 40, Roland Berkeley Thorn and Andrew G. Roberts, *Sea Defence and Coast Protection Works,* London: Telford, 1981, p. 131

15. Alberto Montanari, Professor of Hydraulic Works and Hydrology at the University of Bologna. https:// distart119.ing.unibo.it/ albertonew/?q=node/104

16. Cement and Concrete Association, "Light Relief: Sea Defence Wall, Marine Parade, Sheerness-on-Sea, Kent", *Concrete Quarterly* 143,

October–December 1984,
p. 16–19

17. Barbara Jones, *The Unsophisticated Arts,* London: Architectural Press, 1951. Also Paul Nash, "Swanage or Seaside Surrealism", *Architectural Review,* 79, July 1936, pp. 150-4

18. "Titan Sees the End of Sea Defence Work for the Island", *Sheerness Times Guardian,* 11 May 1984, p. 3

19. Leon Krier (ed.), *Albert Speer: Architecture 1932-42,* Paris & Brussels: Archives d'Architecture Moderne, 1985.

Afterword

1. Siegfried Unseld, *Uwe Johnson "Für wenn ich tot bin"* [1991], mit einer Nachbemerkung 1997, Frankfurt am Main: Suhrkamp, 1997, p. 38

2. Ibid., p. 46

3. Ibid., p. 47

4. Siegfried Unseld, letter to Uwe Johnson 7 December 1982, in E. Fahlke & R. Fellinger, (eds) *Uwe Johnson – Siegfried Unseld: Der Briefwechsel,* Suhrkamp, 1999, p. 1032-3

5. Uwe Johnson, letter to Siegfried Unseld, 23 December 1983, Ibid., pp. 1033-5

6. For Johnson's will of 16 October 1975, see Heinrich Lübbert, *Der Streit um das Erbe des Schriftstellers Uwe Johnson,* Frankfurt am Main: Suhrkamp, 1998, pp. 17-20

7. For Johnson's revised will of 22 March 1983, see Ibid., pp. 36-9

8. Uwe Johnson, "Statement to my Executors", 21 February 1983, in ibid.

9. Ibid., p. 30

10. Siegfried Unseld, *Uwe Johnson "Für wenn ich tot bin",* p. 64

11. Siegfried Unseld, note of 23 March 1984, in E. Fahlke & R. Fellinger, (eds) *Uwe Johnson – Siegfried Unseld: Der Briefwechsel,* Suhrkamp, 1999, p. 1083

12. Tilman Jens, "Der Unbekannte von der Themse: Auf den Spuren des Toten Dichters Uwe Johnson", reportage mit Fotos von Nomi Baumgartl, *Stern,* 24 May 1984, pp. 126-136.

13. "Sheerness house hits the headlines in Germany", *Sheppey Gazette and North-East Kent Times,* 5 July 1984, p. 1.

14. See, for example, "'stern' ohne Scham", *Die Zeit,* 1 June 1984.

15. Unseld, *Uwe Johnson "Für wenn ich tot bin"*, p. 56.

16. Siegfried Unseld, "Nachbemerkung 1997", ibid., pp. 85-6.

17. Elisabeth Johnson, "Nachtwort", in Werner Gotzmann, *Uwe Johnsons Testament oder Wie der Suhrkamp Verlag Erbe wird*, Berlin: Edition Lit. Europe, 1996, p. 147.

18. *Anniversaries* II, p. 1635

19. Ibid., p. 1227

20. Uwe Jonson, letter to Burgel Zeeh, 17 April 1983, E. Fahlke & R. Fellinger, *Uwe Johnson — Siegfried Unseld Der Briefwechsel*, Frankfurt: Suhrkamp, p. 1070

21. "Conversation on the Novel..."

22. *Anniversaries* IV, p. 1481.

23. Ibid., p. 1224

24. Ibid., p. 1543

25. Ibid., p. 1247

26. Ibid., p. 1564

27. *Anniversaries* I, p. 35.

28. *Anniversaries* IV, p. 1531

29. "Berlin Wall", BBC Radio 4, 13 August 1981

30. Nicholas Dames, "Departures and Returns", *N+1*, 5 June 2020

31. Edwina Currie, Norman Tebbitt, and Currie again.

32. Brian Jenkins, interviewed in "Three ex-Chatham dockyard workers...", *KentOnline*, 31 March 2014

33. "Chatham Dockyard closure 'very positive for the area'", BBC News, 31 March 2014

34. "Obituary: Uwe Johnson East German novelist", *The Times*, 15 March 1984, p. 16

35. *Anniversaries* IV, pp. 1250-57

36. Ibid., p. 1601

37. Ibid., p. 1475

38. Ibid., pp. 1481-1484

39. Ibid., p. 1640

40. Ibid., p. 1619

41. Ibid., p. 1406

42. Ibid., p. 1404

43. Ibid., p. 1620

44. Ibid., p. 1620

45. Ibid., p. 1292

46. Ibid., p. 1265

47. Stephen Marche, "David Shield's "Reality Hunger" in the Age of Trump; or, How to Write Now", *Los Angeles Review of Books*, 5 August 2017

GAZETTEER

1. UWE JOHNSON

WORKS

THEMES AND INVENTIONS

FRIENDS, CORRESPONDENTS, INSPIRATIONS, WITNESSES

INVENTED PERSONS

2. THE ISLE OF SHEPPEY

AVIATORS, FLYING GROUNDS AND AIRPORTS (REAL AND IMAGINED)

ISLANDERS

PREACHERS, HERMITS AND A POET

SHEERNESS: AREAS, STREETS, INSTITUTIONS

OTHER SHEPPEY PLACES

3. PRIMARY NEWSPAPERS, MAGAZINES AND PUBLISHERS

4. ENVIRONMENT (DENATIONALISED HERITAGE)

RIVERS AND ESTUARIES

5. SHIPS – WRECKED AND LOST

HULKS

SS RICHARD MONTGOMERY

6. POLITICS

7. PLACES ELSEWHERE — ACTUAL, REMEMBERED AND IMAGINED

8. THEMES, MOTIFS AND PREFIGURATIONS

9. GENERAL

ACKNOWLEDGEMENTS

I was first alerted to the existence of Johnson's *Island Stories* by Heinrich von Berenberg, whom I had got to know in the Nineties, when he translated some articles of mine for publication in Wagenbach's journal *Freibeuter*. It was, however, not until 2011 that I contacted Suhrkamp Editions to explore the possibility of producing an English translation. They put me in touch with Damion Searls, who was already preparing to embark on his translation of *Anniversaries*, published by New York Review Books in 2018. Damion has been vital to this project, providing beautifully articulate translations of a widening array of texts, and helping in so many other ways with information, questions, enthusiasm and patience.

The translations were made possible by a grant from the Patsy Wood Trust, the trustees of which generously overlooked the fact that the proposed investigation was not strictly an "environmental" initiative. The pace quickened in 2015-16 when I received a Leverhulme Research Fellowship for the project, by then entitled "Learning from Sheppey: Place, Culture and Identity at England's Periphery". This gave me a full year in which to concentrate on my investigations both on Sheppey and in Germany, where I have been greatly assisted by the Uwe Johnson-Gesellschaft and the associated Johnson Archive at the University of Rostock. I would have got nowhere without the assistance of Holger Helbig, Antje Pauke, Katja Leuchtenberger, Martin Fietze and their colleagues, and also of the Society's friends and affiliated scholars in Britain, Irmgard Müller and Astrid Köhler. My thanks are also due to Miriam Häfele at the Deutsches Literaturarchiv at Marbach. More formally, I am grateful both to the Johannes and Annitta Fries Stiftung and to the Peter Suhrkamp Stiftung for permission to quote from Johnson's "Conversation on the Novel...", his letter to Helen Wolff (6 August 1978) and the CV he prepared for Friedrich Denk on 22 February 1984, a copy of which is among Michael Hamburger's papers at the British Library.

I was much encouraged in my research by colleagues at the Department of English at King's College London. I remain indebted for various hints and suggestions to Jon Day, Clare Lees, Jo McDonagh, Josh Davies, Clare Pettitt, Richard Kirkland, Alan Read and also to Neil Vickers, who was always encouraging about an investigation that wasn't conceived with the Research Excellence Framework in mind. I have also benefitted greatly from conversations with the historians I encountered at meetings and events associated with KCL's Institute of Contemporary British History.

The project's first "output" was a BBC Radio 3 "Sunday Feature" broadcast as *A Secret Life: Uwe Johnson in Sheerness* on 19 April 2015 (available online at BBC Sounds). My thanks to the producer, John Goudie, to Helen Whittle, whose research was more incisive and helpful than we had any right to expect, and also to former island inhabitants Jackie Cassell and Ian Lambert, who heard the programme and got in touch with helpful reprimands and comments. Towards the end of 2015, I started planning with Chris Reed of the Sheerness arts organisation, Big Fish, to organise a community reading of selections from the translated articles and letters in which Uwe Johnson describes his impressions of Sheerness. The final outcome was a combined talk, performance and reading at Sheerness's Little Theatre on 5 March 2016 (see photograph on p. 393). Having learned a great deal from these conversations, I am especially grateful to Chris Reed of Big Fish Arts for initiating it, and to Cliff Tester, Shirley West, Jim Enright, Sue Percival, Jo Eden, Janys & Jeremy Thornton and everyone else who squeezed into the Rose Street Cottage of Curiosities for our preliminary rehearsals, and who participated both in the main event at the Little Theatre and in a later performance on the Goodwin Sands light ship LV21, now converted into a floating arts venue and moored at Gravesend during Metal's Estuary festival later that same year. Thanks also to Daniel Nash, who had us on his review programme for BRFM Sheppey (BRFM stands for "Best Radio For Miles"), the island's independent answer to the BBC, which transmits from a container perched above the advancing cliff not far from the place where the now ethereal Royal Oak pub once stood.

I am very grateful to Will and Heloise Palin both for providing me with somewhere to stay and also for introducing me to diverse people and aspects of Sheppey life. Others who have helped me understand the island and its modern history include Tim Kermode, Tim Oxley, Simeon Haselton, Jane Washford, George Poule, Carol Contant, Jeanette Contant-Gallitello, Mavis Caver, and Dot Cruikshank. I owe a huge amount to the island's journalists, especially Bel Austin (neé Norris) & John Nurden of the *Sheerness Times Guardian*, without whose accumulated work and present generosity this book would have been a lesser thing. My thanks to Emma and Louise Harris, who kindly provided a photograph of their father, Martin Aynscomb-Harris. A salute, too, for the "wandering shade" and Medway poet Barry Fentiman Hall, not least for his rendering of "the Poet" in his island miscellany, *the unbearable sheerness of being* (wordsmithery: 2016)

The project is all the better for my conversations with two filmmakers: Patrick Keiller, with whom I collaborated from 2007 on a project entitled "The Future Landscape and the Moving Image", and Shona Illingworth, who joined me in this later exploration a few years ago, and with whom I continue to work towards a film based on the same researches. The visual perspective, which is, I hope, also embedded in this book, has been enormously helpful. I would like to thank Bevis Bowden for the cinematographic skill he brought to the day we spent — with additional thanks to the then owners Dave and Lorraine Beechinor — filming inside 26 Marine Parade, Sheerness.

I have long been indebted to Iain Sinclair, who first reminded me of Sheppey when he was at work on *Downriver* in the late Eighties and later hinted that north Kent was surely worth revisiting. Thanks also to Rachel Lichtenstein, author of *Estuary: From London Out to the Sea*, who put me in touch with John Cotgrove in Southend on-Sea, and invited me to participate in Metal's estuary festival in 2016, and — also on the Essex shore — to my late friend Michael Thomas who gave me the benefit of his memories of growing up in Southend in the Sixties.

My thanks to Renate Mayntz and Wolfgang Streeck for their help in Germany; to David Spiegelhalter (light railways) and Jeremy Purseglove (floods); to Brian Dillon (Duchamp in Herne Bay and *The Great Explosion*); and to Humphrey Ocean, Stephen Bann, Peter Rhodes, Ed Dickinson, Germaine Dolan, Barbara Gaskin and Pete Ball, for memories of life at the University of Kent and at Canterbury College of Art in the early Seventies. I am grateful to Anne Beresford, Richard Hamburger and Claire Hamburger, who have each gone out of their way to be helpful, and also to Christian Wolff and Johnny Homer (definitely not just any "Communications Executive" at Shepherd Neame). My understanding of Ray Pahl's work is all the better thanks to Tim Strangleman, Dawn Lyon, Graham Crow and Claire Wallace. I am grateful to Tim Meacham for various now distant memories of the island; Penny Pole of Garnham Wright Associates for being so helpful about the design and construction of the present sea wall along Marine Parade; Edmund de Waal for his recollection of growing up in the Deanery at Canterbury; Gareth Evans, for maintaining his interest in the project since February 2013, when he curated a conference on PLACE at Aldeburgh; and Ewan Forster for his memories of Sheerness. Rachel Calder gave me some very helpful advice and my publishers at Repeater have been remarkable in their contrary fearlessness, enthusiasm and attention to detail (which has extended to the choice of fonts — a version of Exelsior for the main text, and the GDR-associated Drescher Grotesk for headings and Johnson's Sheerness writings). Special thanks, then, to Tariq Goddard, Alex Niven, Josh Turner, James Hunt, Michael Watson and everyone else involved — including Johnny Bull, whose brilliant cover stands as a tribute to the glory days of the Canterbury College of Art, where he studied too. For the paperback edition I am also indebted to Katy Jackson, Jonathan Meades and Ian Stewart, who contributed corrections and further information now incorporated into the text.

More obliquely, I must acknowledge the late African

732

American baritone Aubrey Pankey, in whose memory I have identified Sheppey's flamingo as a "firebird" (see the children's story Pankey published during his McCarthy-induced exile in the GDR — *Der Feuervogel,* illustrationen von Bert Heller, Berlin: Alfred Holz Verlag, 1964). Finally, I would like to thank Dr Claire Lawton, who has accompanied me throughout this adventure as so many others, and managed to avoid following our three sons out of the front door.

ILLUSTRATIONS

By page number:

Shona Illingworth, 3, 63, 132, 492 (I & ii). Michael Thomas, 322. National Maritime Museum, 221. Royal Army Medical Corps, 206 (I & ii). J. Styles for R.E. Pahl, 431, 434; R.E. Pahl, 438 (reproduced by kind permission of Graham Crow and Dawn Lyon). Hulton Archives, 147. Race Furniture Ltd, 303, 307, 308, 312. Wymer, F. J., 14. Richard Hamburger, 53. Brigitte Friedrich/ *Süddeutsche Zeitung* (Alamy), 74. Alamy (Historical Images), 103. YRM archives, RIBA/Victoria and Albert Museum, 85, 88. Luftgeographische Einzelheft Großbritannien, 182. Acme NewsPictures, 123. Flight, 152, 155, 161. *Tatler*, 153. Martin, R. S. (Camera Press), 284. Harris, Emma and Louise, 353. Renate Mayntz, 39. Shutterstock, 286. Getty images: Jochen Blume/ullstein bild, 98; Hulton Archives, 135. Alamy, 118. Cambridge University Collection of Aerial Photography, 171. Poule, George, 192, 196, 373. Royal Army Medical Corps, 225 (i & ii). Garnham Wright Associates, 617. National Archives: Register of Proprietors of Copyright in Paintings, Drawings and Photographs, Stationers' Hall, 341. Michael Blackwood Productions, 54, 59. Simeon Haselton, 620. Patrick Wright, 5, 21, 27, 28, 30, 31 (i), 87, 99, 104, 116, 117 (i & ii), 142, 202, 203, 223, 228, 231, 236, 238, 244, 266, 268, 315, 331, 342, 347, 386, 393, 474, 482, 490, 527, 559, 571, 588, 603, 619. Postcards and some other historical images are beyond meaningful acknowledgement, although eBay has played its part.

COMING SOON FROM REPEATER BOOKS

"I DON'T THINK I HAVE READ A BETTER BOOK ABOUT THIS COUNTRY."
MICHAEL HOFMANN

"WRIGHT IS A FINDER, A NOTICER, A POWERFUL SUSTAINER OF ARGUMENT."
IAIN SINCLAIR

A reissue of Patrick Wright's 1995 classic The Village that Died for England, with a new introduction taking in Brexit and a new wave of British nationalism.

Shortly before Christmas in 1943, the British military announced they were taking over a remote valley on the Dorset coast and turning it into a firing range for tanks in preparation for D-Day. The residents of the village of Tyneham loyally packed up their things and filed out of their homes into temporary accommodation, yet Tyneham refused to die.

Back in print and with a brand new introduction, this book explores how Tyneham came to be converted into a symbol of posthumous England, a patriotic community betrayed by the alleged humiliations of post-war national history. Both celebrated and reviled at the time of its first publication, *The Village that Died for England* is indispensable reading for anyone trying to understand where Brexit came from — and where it might be leading us.

14TH SEPTEMBER 2021

WWW.REPEATERBOOKS.COM

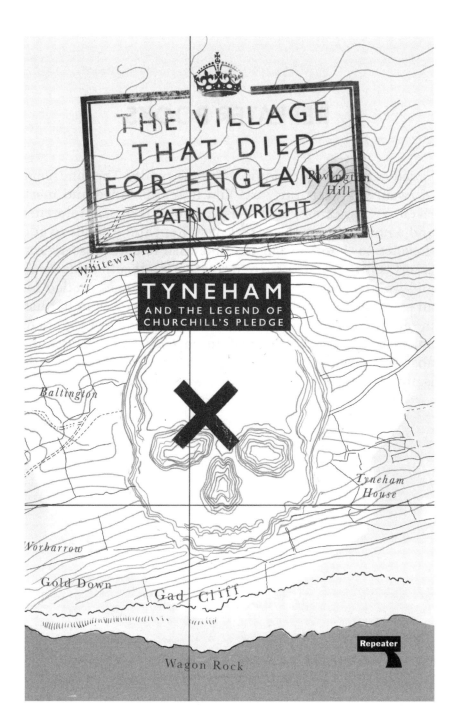

REPEATER BOOKS

is dedicated to the creation of a new reality. The landscape of twenty-first-century arts and letters is faded and inert, riven by fashionable cynicism, egotistical self-reference and a nostalgia for the recent past. Repeater intends to add its voice to those movements that wish to enter history and assert control over its currents, gathering together scattered and isolated voices with those who have already called for an escape from Capitalist Realism. Our desire is to publish in every sphere and genre, combining vigorous dissent and a pragmatic willingness to succeed where messianic abstraction and quiescent co-option have stalled: abstention is not an option: we are alive and we don't agree.